The "Dematerialized" Insurance

Pierpaolo Marano • Ioannis Rokas •
Peter Kochenburger
Editors

The "Dematerialized" Insurance

Distance Selling and Cyber Risks from an International Perspective

Springer

Editors
Pierpaolo Marano
Faculty of Banking
Finance and Insurance Sciences
Catholic University of the Sacred Heart
Milan, Italy

Counsel PWC Legal
Milan – Rome, Milan, Italy

Ioannis Rokas
Department of Business Administration
Athens University of Economics and Business
Athens, Greece

Peter Kochenburger
School of Law
University of Connecticut
Hartford, CT
USA

ISBN 978-3-319-28408-8 ISBN 978-3-319-28410-1 (eBook)
DOI 10.1007/978-3-319-28410-1

Library of Congress Control Number: 2016941939

Printed on acid-free paper

This Springer imprint is published by Springer Nature
The registered company is Springer International Publishing AG Switzerland

Preface

Why "dematerialized" insurance? This is not a term traditionally used to define insurance, nor does it refer to a proposed grouping of existing risks or seek to further describe insurance operations. In short, it is external to the nature of insurance.

We chose this term to describe new, rapidly developing types of insurance relationships, where the point of sale and distribution methods, along with many of the risks themselves, lack the physicality that have characterized traditional insurance undertakings. Therefore, dematerialized insurance is essentially a terminology that examines the movement to online sales of insurance, the benefits and risks that accompany the vast collecting and use of data—big data and cyber risks—and the development and use of cyber insurance as a tool to address these risks.

This dematerialized world is made possible by information technology. Transactions and risks are increasingly characterized by the transition from individuals to data bits. Therefore, "dematerialized" appeared to be a term able to bring together and better describe a common feature to this "bits generation."

Dematerialized markets are naturally intolerant to territorial limitations, whether of geography or political or jurisdictional boundaries. Therefore, as far as possible, this research has aimed to consider the transnational dimension of the risks and relationships that are defined as dematerialized.

"Dematerialization" examines relations between insurance undertakings and policyholders, both when realized through insurance intermediaries and directly between the insurance undertakings and the customer. Accordingly, the first two parts of the book are devoted to on-line distribution and distance selling, where the relationship between the parties involved is entrusted, in whole or in a large part, to technology rather than face-to-face interaction.

The original version of this book was revised. An erratum to the book can be found at (DOI: 10.1007/978-3-319-28410-1_15).

The third part examines cyber risks, i.e. a range of specific risks that relate to online connectivity and information technology, including where computers and information systems are involved either as a primary tool or as a primary target.

Unfortunately, the dematerialized character assumed by these relationships and risks has not reduced insurance disputes, which are taking on even greater complexity. These disputes are increasingly transnational in nature because of the ease of access to information technologies, regardless of the location of the client and the insurance service provider. The legal issues that arise are treated in the last part.

Milan, Italy — Pierpaolo Marano
Athens, Greece — Ioannis Rokas
Hartford, CT, USA — Peter Kochenburger

Contents

List of Contributors

Aviva Abramovsky Syracuse University College of Law, Syracuse, NY, USA

Fabio Ancarani Department of Management, Alma Mater Studiorum, University of Bologna, Bologne, Italy

SDA Bocconi – School of Management, Milan, Italy

Theodore P. Augustinos Locke Lord LLP, Hartford, CT, USA

Christos S. Chrissanthis Faculty of Law, University of Athens, Athens, Greece

Alkistis Christofilou Rokas Law Firm, Athens, Greece

Andrada Comanac Inspiration Services – Digital strategy, BTO, Milan, Italy

Maria Kazamia South Zone EMEA, AIG, Athens, Greece

Peter Kochenburger School of Law, University of Connecticut, Hartford, CT, USA

Tadao Koezuka Faculty of Law, National University Corporation, Kagawa University, Takamatsu, Kagawa, Japan

Sano Shigeru Yoshida Law Firm, Takamatsu, Kagawa, Japan

Katarzyna Malinowska BMSP Legal Advisors, Warsaw, Poland

Pierpaolo Marano Faculty of Banking, Finance and Insurance Sciences, Catholic University of the Sacred Heart, Milan, Italy

Counsel PWC Legal, Milan, Italy

Carlo Eligio Mezzetti Ughi & Nunziante Law firm, Milan, Italy

Kirsty Middleton AIG, Paris, France

Ioannis Rokas Department of Business Administration, Athens University of Economics and Business, Athens, Greece

Paola Musile Tanzi Department of Economics, University of Perugia, Perugia, Italy

SDA Bocconi – School of Management, Milan, Italy

Anna Tarasiuk Counsel Hogan Lovells, Warsaw, Poland

Efi Tziva Faculty of Law, Aristotle University of Thessaloniki, Thessaloniki, Greece

Hsin-Chun Wang National Taiwan University, College of Law, Taipei, Taiwan

Abbreviations

CIRC	China Insurance Regulatory Commission
COBS	Conduct of business sourcebook
CRL	Communications Research Laboratory
DFD	Distance selling of financial services directive
DIP	Distribution of insurance products
DMD	Directive 2002/65 concerning the distance marketing of consumer financial services
DPA	Data Protection Authority
EC	European Commission
ECD	Directive 2000/31 of June 2000 on certain legal aspects of information society services, in particular electronic commerce, in the internal market
EIOPA	European Insurance and Occupational Pensions Authority
ENISA	European Network and Information Security Agency
EU	European Union
FCA	Financial Conduct Authority
FoE	Freedom of establishment
FoS	Freedom of services
FSA	Financial Services Authority
HDPA	Hellenic Data Protection Authority
IAIS	International Association of Insurance Supervisors
IC	Integrated circuit
ICO	Information Commissioner's Office
ICOBS	Insurance conduct of business
ICSA	Institute of Chartered Secretaries and Administrators
ICT	Information and communications technology
IIM(s)	Internet insurance intermediary(ies)
IMD 1	Directive 2002/92 on insurance mediation
IMD 2	Proposal for a revision of IMD 1
JASRAC	Japanese Society for Rights of Authors, Composers and Publishers

JAXA	Japan Aerospace Exploration Agency
JNSA	Japan Network Security Association
MS(s)	Member State(s) of the EU
NICT	National Institute of Information and Communications
NSRI	Network Security Research Institute
PIL	Private international law
PRA	Prudential Regulation Authority
Rome I	Regulation No 593/2008 of the European Parliament and of the Council of 17 June 2008 on the law applicable to contractual obligations
SAL	Security Architecture Laboratory
SEC	Securities and Exchange Commission
SFL	Security Fundamentals Laboratory
SHPAITNS	Strategic Headquarters for the Promotion of an Advanced Information and Telecommunications Society
SMEs	Small and medium-size enterprises
Solvency II	Directive 2009/138 on the taking-up and pursuit of business of the business of Insurance and Reinsurance (recast)
TAO	Telecommunications advancement organization technology
UECA	Uniform Electronic Commerce Act in Canada
UETA	Uniform Electronic Transactions Act in the US
UNCITRAL	United Nations Commission on International Trade Law

Part I
On-Line Distribution

European and International Online Distribution of Insurance Products

Ioannis Rokas

Contents

Abstract This article does not aim to focus on the differences between the traditional and the relatively new concept of the online distribution of insurance products (**DIP**). It is rather an overview of the online DIP from a legal point of view, which -to a large extent- does not differ from the traditional (offline) one. It focuses, further, on the main EU law and principles which affect DIP and the balance between them which the EU secondary legislation has achieved so far. The new era which e-commerce has opened to the DIP within the EU and worldwide; the new complex

I. Rokas (✉)
em. Professor, Department of Business Administration, Athens University of Economics and Business, Athens, Greece

Senior Partner, Rokas International Law Firm, Athens, Greece
e-mail: i.rokas@rokas.com

P. Marano et al. (eds.), *The "Dematerialized" Insurance*,
DOI 10.1007/978-3-319-28410-1_1

insurance products, in particular those which include an investment element; and the increasing importance and priority which is given to the consumer protection in combination with the progress towards EU integration, have led to the emergence, in the EU, of a new legal environment for the DIP, as briefly analysed in this article.

1 Professional Insurance Intermediaries, the Distribution of Insurance Products and the Internet

1.1 General European Issues

1.1.1 Overview

a) The European **regulatory framework** on insuranceintermediation activities has undergone through **three stages** of development during the last decades, which coincided with the transitional period from traditional to online business transactions. The **first stage** commenced with the first insurance mediation Directive dated 1977,[1] for the purpose of facilitating the effective exercise of the freedom of establishment (**FoE**) and the freedom to provide services (**FoS**) in respect of the activities of the **profession of the insurance intermediaries (IIMs)**. The core of the Directive was to set the **minimum requirements** for the exercise of the activities of **insurance agents**, **subagents** and the **insurance brokers**, and it further provided rules to secure that certain professional requirements were satisfied. A certain issue was the recognition of certificates attesting the adequacy of professional requirements throughout the European Member States (**MSs**). At the time, when said legislation was introduced, **e-commerce** was not yet of consumer acceptance and use, something that happened for the first time during the following years.
b) The **second stage** commenced in 2005 with the Insurance Mediation Directive 1 (**IMD 1**), which replaced the 1977 Directive.[2] Not only do the provisions of IMD 1 consider the issue of **online intermediation activities**[3], but also the

[1] Directive 1977/92/EEC of December 1976.

[2] IMD 1 has been implemented by the MSs in different ways since the implementation way was left to the national legislators' extended discretion.

[3] IMD 1 (recital no. 19) provides that a MS may introduce more stringent rules which may be imposed on IIMs, including the obligation of providing the set of information to the customer imposed by the Directive, independently of their place of residence where they are pursuing intermediation activities in its territory, provided that such provision complies with the e-commerce Directives and that the above set of information can be communicated in any durable medium available and accessible to the customer (art. 13 para. 1 a), whereas a durable medium is any instrument which enables the customer to store information addressed to him in a way accessible for future reference for a period of time adequate to the purposes of the information and which allows for the unchanged reproduction of the information stored (art. 2 para. 12).

special secondary legislation on e-commerce (E-Commerce Directive—**ECD**) that was implemented in the meantime,[4] as well as the very comprehensive financial services **Distance Marketing Directive (DMD)**.[5]

c) Lastly, the **third stage** commenced with **IMD 2, now named as "IDD"**,[6] which replaced IMD 1[7] and provides for further regulation of IIMs in order to promote e-commerce and guarantee a higher level of protection for the insured.[8]

d) E-commerce in the modern society facilitated to an unprecedented extent the distance selling of goods and services. Distance marketing of financial services (including insurance products) has been promoted extensively within the framework of the internal market, so that recipients of such services can have access to the widest possible range of financial services.[9] To achieve that goal, the EU has reacted with regulations, in particular, on the level of consumer protection, e-commerce and freedom of services, including DIP.

1.2 *IMD 2, ECD and the EU Law on Information Duties to Customers in the Online Business*

(a) IMD 2 focused[10] on enhancing the protection of any customer by imposing an obligation on (re)insurance intermediaries to provide customers with a set of

[4] Directive 2000/31 of June 2000 on certain legal aspects of information society services, in particular electronic commerce, in the Internal Market, see Commission Communication on bringing e-commerce benefits to consumers, Com (2011) 942 final, SEC (2011) 1641 final.

[5] Directive 2002/65/EC concerning the distance marketing of consumer financial services and amending Council Directive 90/619/EEC and Directives 97/7/EC and 98/27/EC.

[6] Com (2012) 360 final. The recast of the Directive, under the name "IDD", has to be transposed into the national legislation of MSs by 22.2.2018.

[7] At the time this article was prepared, IMD 2 was still a recast pending approval of the Parliament's position on 1st reading by the European Council.

[8] The IMD 2 introduced an online registration system consisting of one single registration form available on an Internet website, which shall allow the form to be completed directly online. The new European Insurance and Occupational Pensions Authority (**EIOPA**) will keep a single electronic register with records on (re)insurance intermediaries which have notified their intention to carry cross-border business (in the EU). This register shall have a hyperlink to each relevant competent authority in each MS, as well as links to be accessible from each MS's competent authority website (art. 3 paras. 2 and 4). In addition, IMD 2 provides that if the information that is to be provided under this Directive to policy holders is realised **by means of a website on the Internet**, special conditions should apply (art. 20 paras. 5–6).

[9] See Recital 3 of the DMD.

[10] For the rules which govern insurance intermediation, EU secondary legislation and related Regulations mentioned in this article equally apply to the remaining three countries of the European Economic Area (Norway, Iceland and Lichtenstein).

information[11], which was previously not required, to such extent, by EU secondary legislation and, also, by the imposition of stricter professional requirements for the IIM and further aimed at facilitating cross-border business within the EU, including the provision of **online services**.

(b) The IMD 2 protects even more[12] the insured by statutory rules, unless the insurance contract covers one or more "**large risks**" within the meaning of EU law[13], as regards its rules which provide the obligation of granting information.

[11] Art. 16 IMD 2 provides that prior to the conclusion of an insurance contract, the insurance intermediary (which according to IMD 2 includes not only the traditional work of them but also the tied intermediaries and the insurers when they proceed with direct sales, but not the claims managers and the loss adjusters, although their work is included within the insurance mediation activities covered by the Directive) shall make the following **disclosures** (**information**) to customers: (**a**) his **identity**; **address**, if he is **qualified** as an IIM; whether he provides any **advice on the product**; the procedure to register **complaints** against him and the **out-of-court complaint redress procedure**; the **register** in which he has been included and the means for verifying that he indeed is registered; and the very important information of whether the IIM is **representing the customer or acting on behalf of an insurance undertaking**. It is to be noted that **EU legislation does not find sufficient in this regard if the IIM is titled insurance agent or insurance broker, since agents do not always represent insurers and brokers often are dependent on insurers and partially represent them and not the insured**; (**b**) whether the IIM has a **holding of more than 10 % in the capital** of given insurance undertakings or a given insurance undertaking holds more than 10 % of the insurance intermediary's capital (rules which aim to protect the insured from **conflict of interest** issues and enhance **transparency**), whether he gives **advice on the basis of a fair analysis**, whether he has a contractual obligation to conduct insurance **mediation exclusively with one or more insurance undertakings** and to provide the names of such undertakings and, in addition, to provide the names of the insurance undertakings with which he may or does conduct business for the cases where he is not contractually obliged to conduct mediation business exclusively with one or more insurers and does not give advice on the basis of fair analysis; (**c**) the nature of each **remuneration** (if it is based on a fee or commission or a combination thereof, the basis of calculations of all the fees or commissions, the amount of the commission based on the achievements of agreed targets, etc.). Correctly the opinion of Committee on Legal Affairs of the European Parliament, rapporteur K.H. Lehne, points out that the consumer should additionally be aware if any of the employees will receive a fee or a commission of any kind—21.3.2013, 2012/0175 COD).

[12] Insured's level of protection under IMD 1 was due to upgrade since right after its implementation.

[13] According to the definition provided in Directive 2009/138 on the taking-up and pursuit of the business of Insurance and Reinsurance (**Solvency II**), the term **large risks** means (a) risks classified under classes 4, 5, 6, 7, 11 and 12 in Part A of Annex I (see directly below); (b) risks classified under classes 14 and 15 in Part A of Annex I, where the policy holder is engaged professionally in an industrial or commercial activity or in one of the liberal professions and the risks relate to such activity; (c) risks classified under classes 3, 8, 9, 10, 13 and 16 in Part A of Annex I in so far as the policy holder exceeds the limits of at least two of the following criteria: (i) a balance-sheet total of EUR 6.2 million; (ii) a net turnover, within the meaning of Fourth Directive 78/660 on the annual accounts of certain types of companies of EUR 12.8 million; (iii) an average number of 250 employees during the financial year. The first generation non-life Directives classifies in its Annex I the non-life insurance, among others, as follows: **3.** land vehicles (other than railway rolling stock), **4.** railway rolling stock, **5.** aircraft, **6.** ships, **7.** goods in transit, **8.** fire and natural forces, **9.** other damage to property, **10.** motor vehicle liability, **11.** aircraft liability, **12.** liability for ships, **13.** general liability, **14.** credit, **15.** suretyship, **16.** miscellaneous financial loss.

However, the MS can provide that said protection must also include large risks since it is a **minimum harmonisation Directive**. In addition, IMD 2 introduces **information** obligations on insurance undertakings as well.[14] It provides, further[15], that insurers and/or IIMs have to inform customers, in case they declare to provide advice on the basis of a **fair analysis**, if that analysis is based on a sufficiently large number of insurance contracts available on the market to enable it to make a recommendation, in line with the professional criteria regarding the adequacy of an insurance contract in view of the customer's needs.[16] The question, though, remains: on which market? The EU internal market, the home MS market or the host MS market of the customer where the IIM provides its services on the basis of FoS? It rather seems that the market should be that of the host MS taking into consideration the required notification to the supervisory Authority before conducting business in another MS on a FoS basis. Furthermore, it provides the conditions under which the package of the **information** can be provided using a durable medium[17] other than paper or by means of a website. The customer must have been given a choice between information on paper or using a durable medium or by means of a website and, in addition, the customer must have chosen that other medium.

IMD 2 provides that all **information** to the customer may be provided by means of a **website,**[18] but only when it is personally addressed to the customer or the provision of the information is **appropriate** in the context of business conduct, and as long as the **customer has consented to receiving information** by means of a website, he has been notified electronically of the address of the website and the section of the website where the information can be accessed and, further, the local law secures that said **information remains accessible on the website for such period of time as the customers might reasonably need** to consult it. The appropriate provision of the information by the IIM and the insurer presupposes that **the customer has regular access to**

[14] The information provided for in IMD 2 (arts. 16–18) must be given by IIM (IMD 2, art. 16 para. a, art. 17 and art. 18), including insurance undertakings (IMD 2, art. 16 sec. b—but not reinsurance undertakings—art. 17 paras. 3–5 and art. 18), to all customers except those who are falling under **large risks** (IMD 2, art. 19 para. 1), including reinsurance mediation and insured which are credit institutions, insurance and reinsurance intermediaries and investment firms, other authorised or regulated financial institutions, insurance and reinsurance undertakings, collective investment schemes and management companies of such schemes, pension companies and management companies of such funds, commodity and commodity derivatives dealers, locals and other institutional investors (IMD 2, Annex I). The information includes the identity and the address of the insurance undertaking, whether or not they provide any type of advice about the insurance product, as well as the procedure to register complaints about insurance undertakings and about the out-of-court redress procedure (arts. 12 and 13).

[15] IMD 2, art. 18 para 3.

[16] The insurer and/or the IIM must also specify to the customer the underlying reasons for the advice they give to the customer on a specified insurance product (art. 18 para. 1 (b)).

[17] IMD 2, art. 20, para. 2 (a).

[18] IMD 2, art. 20, para. 2 (b), 5.

the Internet. In spite of the question of the burden of proof (which is to be governed by applicable procedural law), the provision by the customer of an e-mail address for the purpose of that business shall be regarded as such evidence.[19] It is a matter of interpretation what the term 'appropriate' indicates and what are its prerequisites.

(c) **Information** duties are also introduced by statutory rules (a) under DMD, but only towards consumers and not customers who do not qualify as consumers,[20]

[19] IMD 2 art. 20 para 6.

[20] Pursuant to DMD, art. 3, the service provider must ensure that in good time before the consumer is bound by any distance contract or offer, he shall be provided with information concerning (1) the **supplier** (it includes the identity and the main business, the geographical address at which it is established and any other geographical address relevant for the customer's relations with it; the identity of its representative established in the consumer's MS of residence and the geographical address relevant for the customer's relations with the representative, if such representative exists; when the consumer's dealings are with any professional other than the supplier, the identity of this professional, the capacity in which he is acting vis-à-vis the consumer and the geographical address relevant for the customer's relations with this professional; where the supplier is registered in a trade or similar public register, the trade register in which the supplier is entered and his registration number), (2) the **financial service** (it includes description of the main characteristics of the financial service; the total price to be paid by the consumer to the supplier for the financial service, including all related fees, charges and expenses, and all taxes paid via the supplier, or, when an exact price cannot be indicated, the basis for the calculation of the price enabling the consumer to verify it; where relevant notice indicating that the financial service is related to instruments involving special risks related to their specific features or the operations to be executed or whose price depends on fluctuations in the financial markets outside the supplier's control and that historical performances are no indicators for future performances; notice of the possibility that other taxes and/or costs may exist that are not paid via the supplier or imposed by him; any limitations of the period for which the information provided is valid; the arrangements for payment and for performance; any specific additional cost for the consumer of using the means of distance communication, if such additional cost is charged), (3) the **distance contract** (it includes the existence or absence of a right of withdrawal and, where the right of withdrawal exists, its duration and the conditions for exercising it, including information on the amount which the consumer may be required to pay, as well as the consequences of non-exercise of that right; the minimum duration of the distance contract in the case of financial services to be performed permanently or recurrently; information on any rights the parties may have to terminate the contract early or unilaterally by virtue of the terms of the distance contract, including any penalties imposed by the contract in such cases; practical instructions for exercising the right of withdrawal indicating, inter alia, the address to which the notification of a withdrawal should be sent; the MS or States whose laws are taken by the supplier as a basis for the establishment of relations with the consumer prior to the conclusion of the distance contract; any contractual clause on law applicable to the distance contract and/or on competent court; in which language, or languages, the contractual terms and conditions, and the prior information referred to herein are supplied, and furthermore in which language, or languages, the supplier, with the agreement of the consumer, undertakes to communicate during the duration of this distance contract), (4) **redress** (i.e., whether or not there is an out-of-court complaint and redress mechanism for the consumer that is party to the distance contract and, if so, the methods for having access to it; the existence of guarantee funds or other compensation arrangements, not covered by Directive 94/19 on deposit guarantee schemes and Directive 97/9 on investor compensation schemes). Lastly, where there are provisions in the EU legislation governing financial services which contain prior information requirements additional to those listed above, these requirements shall continue to apply.

as well as (b) under ECD for all customers[21] affecting the service provider, i.e. the IIM. Pursuant to a regularly referred ECJ judgment (Bundesverband der Verbraucherzentralen),[22] an online **insurer** has to provide additional information, which will facilitate rapid communication in a direct and effective manner (not necessarily a telephone number). This finding applies to IIMs as well. The obligation to disclose, especially, the **telephone** number only upon a request by a customer may become of reduced significance when the IIM provides advice to the applicant for the insurance. According to the ECJ, the ECD, by giving access to electronic communication, does not mean that it

---

[21] According to ECD, the service provider shall inform the recipients of the **service** and **competent authorities**, at least on **its name**, the **geographic address** at which he is established, details, including his **electronic mail address, where he is registered** in a trade or similar public register, the trade register in which he is entered and his registration number, or equivalent means of identification in that register, where the activity is subject to an **authorisation scheme**, the particulars of the **relevant supervisory Authority**, and as concerns the regulated professions, any **professional body** or similar institution with which the service provider is **registered**, the **professional title** and the MS where it has been granted, a reference to the applicable professional rules in the MS of establishment and the means to access them, where the service provider undertakes an activity that is subject to VAT, the identification number referred to in art. 22 (1) of the sixth Directive 1977/388 on the harmonisation of the laws of the MS relating to turnover taxes, a common system of value added tax. In addition, commercial communications which are part of, or constitute, an information society service must comply at least with the following conditions: the commercial communication shall be clearly identifiable as such**; the natural or legal person on whose behalf the commercial communication is made shall be clearly identifiable**; promotional offers, such as **discounts, premiums and gifts**, shall be clearly identifiable as such, and the conditions which are to be met to qualify for them shall be easily accessible and be presented clearly and unambiguously; promotional competitions or games, as established, shall be clearly identifiable as such, and the conditions for participation shall be easily accessible and be presented clearly and unambiguously. With regard to the provision of information, ECD provides that (1) in addition to other information requirements established by EU law, the service provider must ensure, except when otherwise agreed by parties who are not consumers, that at least the following information is given by the service provider clearly, comprehensibly and unambiguously and prior to the order being placed by the recipient of the service: the different technical steps to follow to conclude the contract, **whether or not the concluded contract will be filed by the service provider and whether it will be accessible; the technical means for identifying and correcting input errors prior to the placing of the order; the languages offered for the conclusion of the contract**; (2) except when otherwise agreed by parties who are not consumers, the service provider must indicate any relevant **codes of conduct** to which he subscribes and information on how those codes can be consulted electronically; (3) **contract terms and general conditions** provided to the recipient must be made available in a way that allows him to store and reproduce them. Points (1) and (2) above are inapplicable to contracts concluded exclusively by exchange of **electronic mail** or by equivalent individual communications.

[22] C-298/07 *Bundesverband der Verbraucherzentralen und Verbraucherverbände—Verbraucherzentrale Bundesverband e.V. v. deutsche Internet Versicherungs AG* (see ECD, art. 5 (1) (c)). See also art. 6 (1) (c) of Directive 2011/83 ('Consumer Rights Directive'), which obliges any trader to provide the consumer with its geographical address, telephone number, fax number and e-mail address, where available, to enable the consumer to contact the trader quickly and communicate with him efficiently and, where applicable, the geographical address and identity of the trader on whose behalf he is acting.

intended to abolish other forms of non-electronic communication. Furthermore, the ECJ has ruled that the durable medium must ensure that the consumer receives the information in a way similar to paper so that he will be able to exercise his rights where necessary.[23]

Under IMD 2,[24] the information to be provided by the insurance intermediary to the customer shall be communicated on paper. It can also be communicated by using a **durable medium** other than paper or by means of a **website**. In the latter case, **a paper copy shall be offered to be provided to the customer upon request and free of charge**.

(d) Transactions with the IIM can **affect information (disclosure) obligations of the applicant** during the pre-contractual period. The lack of personal contact should lead to a limited application of sanctions for breaches of such disclosure obligation. Online customers may be treated more leniently in this regard. Applicants' pre-contractual obligation to disclose circumstances of the risk should be restricted (by regulations)[25] to the obligation of answering to clear and unambiguous questions of the insurer, taking into consideration that they are being addressed online. In case the breach derives from unclear and ambiguous questions, soft or no sanctions should be imposed, as the case may be.

(e) An important issue which emerges is whether insurers and IIMs alike must be obliged to provide **information** about **the insurance product**. IMD 2 provides that the IIM **or** the insurer must provide such information,[26] while Solvency II rules that the insurer must provide policyholders with a list of information, which partially is "information about the insurance products".[27] Thus, information which must be provided to customers by insurance undertakings are partially the same when the product is sold by an IIM, regardless of whether the sale is conducted by distance or not, while limited additional information is required when distribution is made online. The aim is the proper information of the insured regarding the status of the insurance undertaking and of the distributor, the necessary characteristics of the product in order to better understand it and to make a correct decision and the special rights of the consumer. Therefore, to the extent that the same information duties are imposed on both the insurer and the IIM, it is adequate if the customer is informed once. It is self-evident, however, that when such information is not provided either by the insurer or by the IIM, then neither of them may claim to be absolved of liability on the ground of the other's failure to fulfil the obligation to provide this information respectively.

---

[23] Case C-49/2011, *Content Services Ltd v Bundesarbeitskammer* [2012] WLR (D), 195, 42.

[24] IMD 2, art. 20.

[25] It is a separate issue which piece of regulation could host such proposal.

[26] IMD 2, art. 18 para 4.

[27] Solvency II art. 183 para. 1 for non-life insurance, which, however, **applies only to cases where the policy holder is a natural person,** and art. 185 for life insurance.

(f) Among the characteristics of IMD 2, as well as IMD 1, is that it focuses not on differentiations between the different types of intermediaries, but on the actual essence of intermediation, while the scope of intermediation activities is expanded by IMD 2 to include all persons involved with the sale of insurance contracts, with certain exceptions, and that it is structured in order to protect insurance customers dealing via the Internet. IMD 2 (and IMD 1) agree with DMD and also ECD, but, contrary to the IMDs, the ECD is a **maximum harmonisation** Directive, aiming to remove unnecessary obstacles to transactions over the Internet.

ECD is not an instrument to enhance the position of the consumer, but it nevertheless does not conflict with the highly prioritised consumer protection under EU law. Its goal is the promotion of e-commerce, including cross-border e-commerce. By strengthening IIM's professional requirements by MS legislation, which would result to the augmentation of impediments set to online cross-border transactions, the ECD has itself inserted such borders by setting the exceptions to the restrictions of the freedom to provide information society services from one MS to another (art. 3(4)), which include the reservations provided for in art. 52 of the Treaty for the Functioning of the EU (TFEU) regarding FoE and, in addition, consumer and investment protection measures.[28]

1.3 From a Law on Intermediation to a Law on Sales of Insurance Products

1.3.1 Intermediaries Under EU Secondary Legislation

(a) Insurance intermediation as such has additional characteristics to those of mere direct sales, as is the case in particular of the intermediation activities of an independent broker. IMD 2 scope does not include the function of the intermediaries, unless it directly affects consumer protection. The European legislation which we examine here regulates professions only to the extent that their activity affects the interests of the insured during the distribution proceedings.[29] This, however, does not prevent national legislation from further categorizing traditional professions, e.g. whether a broker is totally independent or not independent at all in a case where an insurance undertaking participates in the broker's share capital, even with a 100 % share ownership, or whether a broker is contractually bound with insurance undertakings. This essentially means that if a MS does not allow an intermediary to present oneself as a broker while not being independent, this is contrary to EU law

[28] See below Sect. 3.3.

[29] However, it recognises the categories of intermediaries who work in the EU; see IMD2, art. 6 para. 1(c).

as this issue is already exclusively regulated by the secondary EU law imposing an obligation to declare whether one is independent or not; it is contrary to FoE and FoS principles. It may be justified as a right deriving neither from the MS **general good provisions**[30] nor from the fact that IMD 2 enables MS to impose stricter rules since a potential prohibition of a dependent broker from working as a broker is not a matter of implementation of stricter rules. MSs can introduce stricter rules, particularly on professional requirements for the distributor of the insurance product; nevertheless, this is not possible for distributors that conduct business online, as far as the stricter rules go further than the four exceptions to the freedom to provide online services included in ECD. However, IMD 2 does not provide for an obligation on intermediaries to provide updated information to the customers throughout the duration of the contract. This is an obligation on insurers arising from Solvency II and on intermediaries arising from national laws of the MS. IMD 2, which aims to protect the insured during the distribution proceedings and not to regulate the overall obligations of insurance brokers and agents, does not include rules on this important issue.

(b) The **contractual rights of IIMs** are not within the objectives of IMD 2 since its primary goal is to ensure the **qualitative requirements** for intermediaries and their obligations towards the insured. IMD 1 and IMD 2 regulation is introduced from the point of view of the **protection of the insured**. The rights of intermediaries towards the insurers and the insured do not fall within the scope of IMD 2.

(c) IMD 2 includes within its framework the **tied intermediation**, i.e. the activity of any person who carries on intermediation for and on behalf of one or more insurance undertakings or intermediaries as far as insurance products are concerned.[31] Large business units, in particular credit institutions, commonly become tied intermediaries, among others, in order to take advantage of **the trust of their large clientele** that they enjoy at the existing level, for other financial products they sell. It is obvious that the reputation that big commercial brand names, especially **banks**, have and the trust they enjoy in the market place (as people rely on them for their savings!), as to the products they sell, is much higher than an average insurance intermediary enjoys. At the same

[30] IMD 2, art. 9 requires MSs to **publish the general good rules** and requires EIOPA to **collect and publish information about such rules** (for an indicative exposition of the principles of general good in relation to the third generation insurance Directives, see the Commission's Interpretative Communication on FoS and the general good 2000/C43/03). See relevant national legal provisions at www.eiopa.europa.eu. For ECJ' s interpretation of "general good", see Case C-577/11, *DKV Belgium SA v Association belge des consommateurs Test-Achats ASBL* [2013], not yet published, paragraph 28 and Case C-59/01, *Commission v Italy* [2003] ECR I-759, paragraph 38.

[31] Tied insurance intermediary must act under the full responsibility of insurance undertakings or insurance intermediaries, provided that the insurance intermediaries under whose responsibility the person acts do not themselves act under the responsibility of another insurance undertaking or intermediary (IMD 2, art. 2 para. 8).

time, the bank enjoys the privilege of dealing with its already existing large clientele.

(d) A bank as a tied intermediary must provide customers with **information** in both offline and online transactions, while in the latter case the information is not deemed given if the consumer, in order to reach the information[32], must make an effort at his own initiative pressing the button ("click"). Further, the intermediary must give information not only for the main financial (investment) product they sell[33], but also for the ancillary insurance product.[34] In addition, in case that the ancillary product is an "**insurance investment product**",[35] the tied intermediary must give the information which is provided for every insurance product and the additional information required by IMD 2 for the insurance investment products,[36] such as appropriate guidance and warnings of the risks associated with them. Lastly, as a tied intermediary, a bank which has created the main investment product must, according to PRIIPs Regulation,[37] provide a **key information document (KID)**, which is possible to be provided by means of a website, including at least 16 kinds of information (such as the type of investment; the term of investment, if known; any guarantee or capital protection provided; etc.).[38] The obligation to provide

---

[32] According to the ECJ in *Content Services Ltd v Bundesarbeitskammer*, Case C-49/2011 [2012] WLR (D), 195, the Court defined the ways in which consumers that enter into distance contracts must receive the information required under EU law and specifically under Directive 97/97 (which was amended by DMD). Consumers must "receive" the necessary information, which means that they should be given the information **without any effort** on their part; therefore, according to ECJ, the fact that the customer is given the information on a web page only, which he can access by clicking on a link shown when the contract is concluded (hyperlink), means both that the customer has not "received" the information as well as that the latter has not been provided in a "durable medium" (for the definition of "durable medium", see and art. 2(f) of DMD).

[33] See arts. 24–25 of Markets in Financial Instruments Directive (**MiFID 2**).

[34] See IMD 2, arts. 15–21. It is to be noted that the seller must also fulfil both the requirements provided for the sale of the main financial product as well as insurance product.

[35] As to the definition of insurance investment products, see art. 2 (a) of the Regulation on Packaged Retail Investment Products (**PRIIPs**), which provides that this Regulation does not apply to insurance products which do not offer a surrender value or where the surrender value is not wholly or partially exposed, directly or indirectly, to market fluctuations. This definition will clarify an open-until-now question: it was not clarified if the IIM should fulfil the requirements for all insurance products containing investment elements, for both simple and complicated products. Furthermore, it was disputed whether there exists a precise and adequate mechanism to trace the existence of the investment element.

[36] IMD 2, arts. 22–25.

[37] See below under Sect. 1.2.2.

[38] See PRIIPs, art. 8. The tied intermediary in his capacity as agent of the insurer must provide to the customer the information referring to any insurance product (IMD 2, arts. 15–20) and the additional information referring to the insurance investment products (IMD 2, arts. 23–25), and in addition, because the insurance investment product is an investment product according to PRIIPs, he must as a person selling investment products provide to the customer (PRIIPs art. 12) the key information document which must be prepared by the manufacturer of this product (PRIIPs, art. 5), who, in our case, is the insurer.

information varies. According to **ECD**, information has to be given to any category of customers; according to **IMD 2** and **PRIIPs**, information is not necessary to be given to insureds against large risks; according to **Solvency II,**[39] information must be given only to natural persons; and according to **DMD**, it must be given only to consumers (i.e., policyholders who purchase insurance products for private use). Furthermore, no requirements are provided as to the information that has to be given to the insured in case the latter is not the policyholder. In other words, numerous cases of asymmetric information arise.

(e) Furthermore, intermediation activities are carried by **employees of an insurance undertaking**, which may receive payment on a commission basis. IMD 2 includes in its scope such employees, regardless of whether they are taking a commission out of policies concluded or not, since their involvement to the policy sale suffices in order for their work to be characterised as intermediation.[40]

IMD 2 includes the work of the employees of an insurance undertaking who are involved in sales which fall within the meaning of insurance mediation activities in order, among others, to introduce the obligation on the MS to provide in its national legislation that such employees have adequate knowledge and ability, professional experience, etc. Higher requirements than those of IMD 2, which can be introduced by a MS for the employees of the insurer that provides intermediation services, can constrain the offline intermediation, while not the online, unless they are falling within the four exceptions provided by ECD (public policy, health, security, consumers and investor protection).[41]

(f) The so-called **placement of risk between insurance undertakings** is an intermediation activity, without IMD 2 mentioning it expressly. The Directive should, however, apply since the first insurer to whom the customer has applied for covering its risks proceeds with further placement to the other insurer and in doing so provides (regulated) insurance intermediation itself[42] being responsible towards the insured for granting the provided information. The placement should be provided under the responsibility of the seller, i.e. the insurer which the client has contacted.

---

[39] Solvency II, art. 183.

[40] Sales which fall under the meaning of intermediation shall, however, include advising on carrying out other work **preparatory to the conclusion of insurance contracts** or concluding such contracts or assisting in the administration or performance of them (IMD 2, art. 2 para. 3).

[41] See below under Sect. 2.3.

[42] According to art. 2 paras. 3, 5, an insurance undertaking can provide insurance intermediation and in so far as this activity is considered to be insurance intermediation. We are of the opinion that this should be the case not only if they proceed with direct sales but also if they proceed with "placement".

1.3.2 Marketing of Insurance Products with Investment Elements

For a long time, it has been a common practice for insurance undertakings to sell insurance products that combine investment elements, often with marginal or without transfer of risk (such as unit linked or management of group pension funds), or products which include few risk elements (assistance). Since the protection of all buyers of products sold by insurance undertakings became of high priority, it was important for the law to focus, in this respect, on products which affect consumers greatly, these primarily being insurance products with an investment element. Thus, as far as an insurance product can be classified as an investment product,[43] an extra set of **information** has to be given to the customers of online as well as of offline transactions according to PRIIPs.[44] PRIIPs lay down uniform rules on the format and content of the key information document to be drawn up by investment product undertakings (including insurance investment products) and uniform rules on the provision of this document to retail investors.[45] IMD 2 also introduces a set of rules regarding additional protection requirements in relation to insurance investment products, not exclusively of informative and consulting character,[46] or on suitability and appropriateness of the reporting to

[43] See above footnote 35.

[44] Arts. 6–12 of Regulation 1286/2014 on key information documents for packaged retail and insurance-based investment products (PRIIPs).

[45] The PRIIPs Regulation does not apply to UCITS (collective investment in transferable securities) until 31 December 2019. Directive 2009/65 on the coordination of laws, regulations and administrative provisions relating to undertakings for collective investment in transferable securities (UCITS) as amended provides for specific key investor information which must be given to investors.

[46] According to IMD 2 art. 24, insurance intermediaries/undertakings have the obligation to act **honestly**, **fairly** and **professionally** in accordance with the **best interests of their clients** when carrying out insurance mediation acts with/for customers and all **information** addressed by them shall be **fair**, **clear** and **not misleading**. Moreover, appropriate information shall be provided to (potential) customers about **(a) the insurance intermediary/undertaking** and its **services**, **(b)** the **insurance products** and **proposed investment strategies** and **(c) costs** and **associated charges**. This set of information shall enable the (potential) customers **to understand the nature and risks of the specific insurance product that is offered and take investment decisions on an informed basis**. When the insurance intermediaries/undertakings inform the customer that advice is provided on an independent basis, they **(a)** shall assess a sufficiently large number of insurance products available on the market and shall not be limited to insurance products issued/provided by entities with close links with the insurance intermediary/undertaking and **(b)** shall not accept/receive fees, commissions or any monetary benefits paid or provided by any third party in relation to the provision of the service to customers.

the customers,[47] but also on conflict of interests[48] of the distributors (insurers and intermediaries). A detailed reference is made to the online sales of insurance investment products. PRIIPs allow for publication of the KID by the investment product manufacturer by means of a **website of its choice**. All sets of additional information oblige equally both online and offline sellers.

Lastly, MiFID 2 introduced, among others, specific requirements for the sale of investment products.[49] Some MSs have introduced equal requirements for the distributors of insurance products with investment elements, however without achieving uniformity as to the definitions of this kind of insurance (such as whether they include only unit linked and not other kinds of insurance). This situation leads to a serious distortion of competition, in particular if distribution is conducted online. The EU law aims to resolve this issue with MiFID 2[50] in combination with PRIIPs and IMD 2.[51]

---

[47] Pursuant to IMD 2, art. 25, the insurance intermediary/undertaking shall obtain the necessary information regarding the (potential) customer's **knowledge and experience** in the field relevant to the specific type of product or service, **financial situation**, **investment objectives** and provide the **suitable** products for the (potential) customer according to this information. Also, as far as sales where no advice is given is concerned, the insurance intermediary/undertaking shall obtain information concerning the (potential) customer's **knowledge and experience** in the investment field relevant to the specific type of product/service in order to enable the insurance intermediary/undertaking to assess whether the insurance service/product envisaged is **appropriate** for the customer. The (potential) customer should be **warned** when the product/service is considered as inappropriate. When the (potential) customer does not provide the above-mentioned information or provides insufficient information, the insurance intermediary/undertaking shall warn that it is not able to determine whether the service/product is appropriate. Moreover, the insurance intermediary/undertaking shall establish a **record** which includes document(s) that set out the rights and obligations of the parties and must send **adequate reports** to its customers and clarify how its advice meets their personal characteristics.

[48] IMD 2 art. 23 provides that insurance intermediaries/undertakings should take all appropriate steps to identify **conflicts of interest** between themselves, including their managers, employees, etc., and any other person directly or indirectly linked to them by control and their customers or between one customer and another that arises in the course of carrying on insurance mediation. If information duties according to art. 15, 16 and 17 are insufficient to prevent risks of damage to the interests of customers, the insurance intermediary/undertaking shall **clearly disclose the general nature or sources of conflicts of interest** to the customer before undertaking business on the customer's behalf.

[49] MiFID 1, arts. 24–26, 28 and 29.

[50] According to the explanatory memorandum of IMD 2, point 1, p. 2, the European Parliament requested this Directive to meet the **same consumer protection standards** as MiFID 2, as far as the insurance mediator sales insurance investment products are concerned. However, IMD 2 does not include all the content of the provisions of arts. 24–26 and 28 MiFID 2, which introduce protection standards for consumers. It is to be mentioned that the protected persons are the retailers, i.e. all customers, which are all those who are not insured against large risks (PRIIPs, art. 4 c) and not only the consumers.

[51] MiFID 2 does not apply to insurance intermediaries unless they are at the same time investment firms, e.g. the receipt and transfer order in relation to financial instruments (Annex I, section A (1)), but in this case it applies only to this activity. IMD 2 introduces extra consumer protection requirements for the insurance products which are according to PRIIPs insurance investment products.

1.3.3 Conclusion

In an attempt to ensure better protection for policyholders, the scope constantly becomes wider with every reformation attempt, which might allow us to say that it is apparently about to become wide enough to include non-intermediation activities, practically applying to insurance and insurance investment product sales in general.

2 The Impact of Electronic Commerce on the Distribution of Insurance Products

2.1 E-Commerce and Insurance Intermediaries

2.1.1 E-Commerce Does Not Aim to Replace Insurance Intermediaries

The aim of e-commerce and its regulation by the ECD is to **replace** legal rules, which are possible to be replaced as not being set in order to safeguard superior principles such as consumer protection and as far as it presents satisfactory alternative proceedings without reducing the protection granted by the replaced rules. It aims to strengthen the proper functioning of the internal market of the EU by removing unnecessary **legal obstacles**. Its target is **not to replace the IIMs profession.** It merely constitutes a very useful tool for the business of both insurance undertakings and professional IIMs, as well as any other person engaged in the distribution of insurance products.

Particularly for some **simple insurance products**, such as motor third party liability (MTPL) insurance or other non-life and non-liability insurance products which do not require particular knowledge of the insurance coverage, there is very little need for the physical presence of an intermediary. Such products can be very effectively sold via the Internet.[52]

2.1.2 E-Commerce Favours the Distribution of Simple Insurance Products

It is obvious that insurance undertakings are able to sell directly and, in particular, over the Internet some simple insurance products with low premium more easily than other, less simple products.[53] Thus, these products fall partially out of the

[52] In the US in 2011, there was an increase of 6 % in MTPL policies being purchased online.

[53] IMD 2 does not apply to very simple insurance products which do not require knowledge of the cover, if the principal professional activity of the person who sells the product is not insurance mediation. This happens if the annual amount of premiums does not exceed €600, in which case the insurance is complementary to goods supplied by any provider and cover the risk of damage of these goods supplied by the provider.

regulated business of insurance mediation, and the seller does not need to fulfil the regulatory requirements.[54] E-commerce of very simple insurance products does not necessarily involve professional intermediaries since providers of these mediation services may become non-regulated providers as well.

In some countries, insurance undertakings increase direct sales via e-commerce more than insurance intermediaries, probably because insurance undertakings are more eager to adopt and promote online sales since, in that way, they not only facilitate their business, as is the case with IIMs as well, but also may cover the intermediation business more easily.

2.1.3 Comparison Websites

Aggregator websites and, in general, the different kinds of comparison websites, [55] i.e. companies that work with a large number of insurers and/or intermediaries for the purpose of bringing via their websites 'aggregated' sources in one single place, do not replace intermediaries. They rather help intermediaries bring online persons who look for 'comparative shopping'. However, depending on the work carried out by the comparison websites, they can act as IIMs and consequently must satisfy the requirements set by the applicable law, in particular regarding the general information IIMs have to provide to customers, including proper **information** on issues of **conflict of interests** and **warnings** if they sell **insurance investment products,** and to protect the insured at the same level as required by all other distributors of insurance products.

The criteria which distinguish simple comparison websites from those which include the core of the work of an insurance intermediary and/or seller of insurance products have not yet been completely formed. If the visitor of the comparison website has the possibility to select insurance products based on price or features and to **conclude** the insurance contract or if he is diverted via a link to the insurer's website and then buys the insurer's products, the comparison website owner might qualify as providing intermediation,[56] in spite of the possible objection that a certain comparison website cannot be liable for the information transmitted, in case it falls within the restrictions of ECD. According to ECD restrictions, the online service provider is not liable for information transmitted on conditions that the provider (a) does not initiate the transmission, (b) does not select the receiver of the transmission and (c) does not select or modify the information contained in the transmission. There appears to be a contradiction in this regard since in case a

[54] However in EU level, since IMDs 1 and 2 are Directives of minimum harmonisation, national MS law may regulate simple insurance products as well.

[55] See EIOPA (2014).

[56] See above Consultation Paper on Draft Report on Good Practices on Comparison Websites of EIOPA, and IMD 2, explanatory memorandum, point 14, p. 8.

comparison website cannot be deemed as bearing liability, it can further not be deemed to be an insurance intermediary within the meaning of IMD 2, which obviously presupposes that the intermediary does not provide its services without liability![57] The possibility given to customers to compare different products should not be regarded as 'mere conduit' within the meaning of art. 12 ECD since the **customer is driven to a result** which includes a characteristic of advising, i.e. the possibility given to customers to find out the cheapest products. Focusing on the price without proper explanation on the differentiations of the several structures of the coverage which can partially explain some price differences without disclosure as to whether price comparison covers all the market where customers can have access to and without disclosure of potential economic relations between aggregators and insurance undertakings can mislead customers who should be protected by the competent supervisory Authority and the applicable national law.

What counts the most is the protection of the insured which cannot vary depending on whether all rules that govern online distribution of insurance products apply or not in each particular case. The particularities of aggregators require diversified application of the legal rules.[58]

In any case, transactions via comparison websites as any other online transaction of any kind based on FoS must not circumvent applicable national law and must follow applicable legislation which regulates distance selling, intermediation of investment or non-investment insurance products, data protection even without any special rules which oblige them to abide by them if according to the applicable law their work can be judged as falling partially or wholly under such regulation.

2.1.4 Conclusions

Insurance contracts that are concluded via the Internet are not restricted to direct sales. **The Internet provides the means of communication, while the intermediary provides the means of intermediation which includes all that is deemed and regulated as intermediation (e.g., consultancy services, etc.). Therefore, the Internet is the means of communication, equally for insurance intermediaries and insurance undertakings**. In addition, online distribution is an issue not for consumers only but also for any customer, even for large risks.

---

[57] Art. 2 para. 3 IMD 2.

[58] According to the UK FSA "guidance on the selling of insurance policies through price comparison websites", a website can treat consumers unfairly and mislead them about the services they are receiving from price comparison, among others; in particular, they can assist unauthorised firms in arranging or advising on policies without the consumer to be able to make a complaint against them. Those regulations led the UK supervisory Authority to regulate the major online comparison websites before the implementation of IMD 2.

2.2 E-Insurance Intermediation and Cross-Border Transactions

2.2.1 Freedom of IIM Services

(a) IIMs based in an MS that wish to proceed with cross-border business via FoS or FoE must **communicate** their intention, including a set of information, to the competent Authority of their home MS, which in turn communicates[59] to the competent Authority of the host MS/MSs. Online transactions do not differ in this respect from offline transactions. The fact that the insurance undertaking has itself proceeded with the communication to its competent Authority does not absolve the IIM from proceeding with its own communication when it sells insurance products of this undertaking (notification procedure).

It is obvious that the facility which enables to provide online services in the IIMs home MS enables it, depending on the kind of the insurance, equally without any important additional preparation, to provide services in other MSs as well. Therefore, it cannot be easy to find out in which cases a prior notification is necessary or not, since the extension of IIMs business in a MS other than its own can be dependent **exclusively on the mere decision of the intermediary without any other preparatory work, especially in online transactions.**

Some indications have been judged to be **signs** of the intention of an IIM to work under FoS and lead to the notification obligation. Such indications include cases that the intermediary **asks for** or **organises, on its own initiative, meetings with clients established in another MS**, **gives** or **sends** information on **specific** products/conditions, etc. to **selected groups of clients established in a given country** or in specific languages of some MSs, and therefore the advertisement has an **active character**. Same applies to electronic distance or distance marketing activities.[60] If the IIM's advertisements/ marketing of its services are accessible not only to consumers of its MS but also to consumers situated in other MSs, this is not yet a sign of its **intention** to work under FoS. On the contrary, there may be evidence of the IIM's intention if its **commercial behaviour** can be assessed to be addressed to customers situated in other MSs[61] when the IIM is **marketing** or **providing** insurance mediation **services** or when the IIM is **actively seeking business** from a client resident or established in that MS.

[59] See art. 5 IMD 2 regarding information which is required for FoS and art. 6 regarding information which is required for FoE.

[60] See 'The IMD and other intermediaries' related issues—practical solutions and examples', CEIOPS-DOC-19/09, June 2009, p. 13.

[61] See below under Sect. 2.2.3.

If the IIM does not fulfil its notification obligation, the transaction remains to be valid. The aim of the obligation for communication/notification to the competent Authority is not consumer protection.

(b) Within the EU, online insurance intermediation is the best way to simplify cross-border transactions and to facilitate the EU principle of FoS. Online intermediation is equally useful for transactions both within the same country as well as for transactions within the EU.

From the EU point of view, the directness that is provided by the Internet in cross-border transactions is a factor substantially widening the concept of online cross-border transactions and gives rise to the question whether the criteria developed by the ECJ as to when services should be provided by establishment and not any more by FoS lead to the necessity for the **IIM to work under the condition provided for the FoE appropriately adjusted, regardless of whether it is in possession or not of a subsidiary, a branch, a simple office or a representative in the host MS**. These criteria are **lasting duration** and/or **regularity** and/or **periodicity** and/or **continuity.**[62] It is to be mentioned that according to art. 57 TFEU, without prejudice to the provisions of its chapter relating to the right of establishment, the person providing a service may, in order to do so, **temporarily** pursue his activity in the MS where the service is provided, under the same conditions as are imposed by that MS on its own nation.

2.2.2 When Is a FoS Notification Necessary? Should Notification Cover All MSs Where the Site of the Intermediary Is Accessible?

The Committee of European Insurance and Occupational Pensions Supervisors (CEIOPS),[63] which is "replaced" by EIOPA,[64] has provided a non-exhaustive list of examples to test whether the IIM is required to proceed with a **FoS notification.**[65] These mainly focus on whether the IIM provides **information on specific products, conditions of cover**, etc. to selected groups of clients; whether the IIM's **website is general** and only in the **language** of its MS; and whether it is addressed to **specific groups of clients** or clients from a specific MS. The list provides

---

[62] Commission interpretative Communication on FoS and the general good in the insurance sector 2000/C273/03. The Commission in the above Communication, p. 13, correctly indicates that the place where the **server** is located is not important since that device can be moved according to the wishes of the provider and in any way does not influence the place where the activity, organisation and the acceptance of the services took place.

[63] CEIOPS was transformed into EIOPA with effect from 01.01.11 pursuant to art. 80 of Regulation 1094/10.

[64] See footnote 6.

[65] See CEIOPS Proposals for a Definition of Cross-Border Provision of Service under the IMD, CEIOPS-DOC-15/07, p. 4. See also Protocol relating to the Cooperation of the Competent Authorities of the MSs of the EU in particular concerning the application of Directive 2002/92 on insurance mediation, CEIOPS-DOC-02/06 Rev 1 Oct 2008, point 2.2.3, p. 9.

examples of **behaviour** capable of evidencing the direction by a merchant of his activities to the MS/MSs of the consumer/s, thus establishing jurisdiction in that MS.[66] In this case, **irrespective of the actual and active sale of insurance products**, an IIM must proceed with the required notification to each national supervisory Authority.

Moreover, the IIM is not considered to direct the activity to another MS only by **mere accessibility** of its website from the consumer's MS of domicile, mention of an email address and other contact details and use of a language or currency that is generally used within the MS where it is established.[67]

The above mentioned correspond to the criteria distinguishing non-solicited from solicited businesses in online transactions. **However, if the IIM actively begins working on a FoS basis, its national supervisory Authority will have to be informed that its work does not fall within the examples of the EIOPA list. It is important whether the IIM provides in another MS marketing or sales insurances or is seeking to do business in order to be obliged to proceed with FoS notification to its national supervisory Authority. It is self-evident that if the IIM fails to dully notify, in spite of selling insurance products, etc., in another MS, it still provides legal binding insurance intermediation business to the other MSs.**

It is possible for the host MS national law to provide stronger protection in favour of insureds than the EU secondary law and the home MS national law to provide the minimum protective rules of the EU law. This results in national IIMs being treated in a way that is stricter than the IIMs from less protective MSs. This situation may be avoided **by applying the existing national law on competition and equal treatment.** However, national measures may not result to a distortion of the EU internal market. Thus, more strict national measures must always be assessed within the scope of the EU principle of **proportionality**.

2.2.3 Cross-Border Online Business and the FoE of the Intermediary

(a) With regard to the obligation to proceed with an **establishment** rather than to work under FoS anymore, the ECJ has developed several criteria as mentioned below.[68] The complexity of this issue and the fact that distinction between FoS

---

[66] These examples include **intent** to direct, which is apparent from the merchant's website and overall activity, **international nature of the activity**, use of **foreign language** or **currency** with the possibility to conclude a contract in that language or currency, **mention of itineraries from other MS** for going to the place where the merchant is established, mention of **telephone numbers with an international code**, outlay of expenditure on an Internet referencing service to facilitate access to the merchant's site of consumers domiciled in other MSs, use of a **top-level domain name other than that of the merchant's home** MS and mention of international clientele from various MS. See also below footnote 105.

[67] See footnote 66.

[68] See below under 2.2.1 and 2.2.3.

and FoE differs when one deals with an IIM, rather than with an insurance company, could be simplified if IMD 2 included rules on this matter.

(b) Nowadays, at EU level, the exercise of business exclusively online cannot be regarded as business which should be done by establishment, notwithstanding if the criteria applicable for the business to be provided by establishment are met. This is due to the fact that establishment, according to the common business conduct, refers to a physical presence at the place of the establishment.[69] Indeed, one may say that online business **cannot really cover all activities/relationships** of insurance intermediaries to customers, the State and other stakeholders, when such IIMs permanently work in a MS, but rather cover or principally cover **merely sales** of insurance products. Obligations of IIMs towards host MS's tax authorities, supervisory authorities, consumer protection authorities cannot easily be replaced through Internet communication. This had been long stated by the European Commission, according to which FoE cannot be achieved over the Internet because the crucial factors are, for the establishment, the **location of the operations** and the **host of the provider** of the services.[70]

It is true that many customers are keen on having the alternative of a parallel, physical communication with the IIM, and they still trust the established IIM. However, the ever-rising use of e-commerce has led especially younger people to become accustomed to the use of electronic means and computers to communicate and obtain information and input from the Internet, instead of expecting to be approached by an IIM. This development, in combination with the advancement of IT, might have created a new European regulatory framework for the conditions of online establishment. In the future, we can face the situation where an online direct sales practice of insurance product without the physical presence in the host MS can be judged to be obliged to follow by analogy the rules of FoE, although not an "establishment" exists if duration and/or regularity and/or periodicity and/or continuity exist. Within the EU, establishment is necessary because the local supervisor is close to such establishment and can more easily find potential irregularities.[71] Thus, if an IIM fulfils the criteria for establishment, one should either oblige it to turn its online provision of services to offline in order to enable it to be established or introduce special rules for the cases of online transactions which fulfil the characteristics of business conducted under establishment. The second solution is in line with ECD purposes.

---

[69] See below footnote 115. See Case C-347/09, *Staatsanwaltschaft Linz v Jochen Dickinger and Franz Ömer* [2011], ECR I-0000, paragraphs 61–66 and Case C-196/04, *Cadbury Schweppes and Cadbury Schweppes Overseas*, [2006] ECR I-7995, paragraphs 111–112.

[70] See, *Sprindler* 2002, p. 1049 ff. stating that the Internet can only cover the freedom of services within the EU. However, from the tax point of view, OECD MTC commentary of art. 5, para. 42.4, computer equipment at a given location may constitute a permanent establishment if it is being fixed, "even though no personnel of that enterprise is required".

[71] See similar position for the investment companies (MiFID 2, recital 57).

2.2.4 Cross-Border Transactions via a Representative in the Country Where the Service Is Rendered

The EU Commission sees a grey area[72] as to the application of art. 57 TFEU and, based on ECJ case law, defines **additionally** the borderline between FoS and FoE of an insurance undertaking as to the way the latter's **representative** in the host MS conducts its work. The Commission's view is that an IIM that provides its services via an independent representative in another MS is conducting business under establishment if such representative works under its control and direction. This is because in doing so, it **accumulates the characteristics of a branch or agency** under the condition that the person is managed by the parent intermediary and equipped in the host MS in a way that customers do not have to deal directly with it, possesses a permanent brief and is able to commit the parent intermediary.[73]

There is no obligation of establishment if a representative of the parent IIM merely transmits orders without being involved in their terms or their execution and without being entitled to enter into contracts with third parties, regardless of whether the parent IIM possesses establishment facilities in the host MS.[74] To sum up, the **obligation of establishment** exists when the IIM works in the host MS with a representative who cumulatively satisfies the above-said three criteria (being subject to the direction and control of the parent IIM, having received a permanent brief and being able to commit the IIM[75]) regardless of its services' lasting duration and/or the regularity and/or the periodicity and/or the continuity or if this representative is an independent person.

In order to judge if insurance services should be provided under establishment (FoE), it is important to examine whether their core activity, such as the underwriting decisions, remains with their home office or not. The core business criterion is not easily applicable to IIMs services; we could say that it corresponds up to an extent to the existence of a representative that meets the above-mentioned three

[72] See Commission Interpretative Communication 2000/C43/03, p. 9.

[73] ECJ Case C-89/91 *Shearson Lehman Hutton v TVB Treuhandgesellschaft für Vermögensverwaltung und Beteiligungen mbH* [1993] ECR I-139.

[74] It is to be noted that the information society service provider is **not liable** for information merely transmitted to customers if it has not initiated the transmission, has not selected the receiver of the transmission and does not select or modify any information contained in the transmission ECD, art. 12 para. 1. As mentioned, ECD is a maximum harmonisation Directive; thus, **MSs cannot introduce liability of distributors of insurance products by the Internet** that do not initiate transmission, etc., but merely conduct the transmission. In addition, ECD excludes the possibility of the MSs to introduce liability for transient storage under the conditions provided in art. 12 paras. 2, 13 and 14 of ECD. These restrictions refer only to the liability for the transmission of **information** included in the ECD and any other information to be provided by the applicable law, as well as for typical IT works (storage of information, etc.).

[75] See Commission Interpretative Communication 2000/C43/03 and the ECJ case law which is referred in it. Also, see Opinion in Case C-154/11, *Ahmed Mahamdia v People's Democratic Republic of Algeria*, [2012] WLR (D) 218, paragraphs 39–41.

requirements. The Commission in its interpretative communication[76] mentions seven activities which an intermediary can conduct without being obliged to be established (e.g., to appoint a local expert; to assess risks, damages, medical and actuarial services; to manage claim files, permanent structure for collecting premiums). However, additional necessary activities, necessary for FoS, can enrich the above list depending on the development of insurance products. But as far as the structure of such activities is a sign of the IIM's intention to work in a continuous basis, the supervisory Authorities should check if FoE requirement applies and intervene respectively. As mentioned, it is advisable that secondary law sets the rules in order to draw a clear line between FoS and FoE within the meaning of 57 TFEU, instead of an ad hoc intervention of a Supervisor.

We can assume that according to the ECJ,[77] an insurance undertaking (in our case IIM) which carries its business online via a fixed, ATM-type machine[78] in another MS is not a "person" and therefore cannot be treated as establishment,[79] even more if the sales are conducted directly via a commercial website using the server of an IIM located in its home MS.[80]

The principal criterion[81] to assess whether an IIM has to work in another MS under establishment and not under FoS is its intention to provide professional services non occasionally. The ECJ criteria of lasting duration and/or regularity and/or periodicity and/or continuity are evidence that such intention occurs and is identified. For this reason, if it is not clear that the above criteria are fulfilled, we can check if the aforementioned three cumulative requirements developed by ECJ case law occur. If they occur, we can assume that the provider

[76] 2000/C43/03, p. 11.

[77] See above footnote 65.

[78] An ATM-type machine is also not equalised with a person according to Commission Interpretative Communication 2000/C43/03 p. 12.

[79] According to the above (footnote 78) Communication, for an ATM-type electronic machine to be capable of being treated as an establishment, it would have to have a **management,** which is by definition impossible, unless the Court acknowledges that the concept can encompass not only **human management** but also electronic management. However, such a machine is unlikely to be the only place of business of an insurance undertaking in an MS. It is likely to be attached, in the same country, to a branch or an agency. In that event, the machine is not an entity in its own right as it is covered by the rules governing the establishment to which it is attached. The above applies also to intermediaries. Thus, the ATM-type electronic machines or the **servers** alone which are not attached to a branch or establishment cannot be regarded as establishment, according to this view, and the same can be said as regards simple websites.

[80] OECD Model Tax Convention (MTC) on Income and on Capital, 2010, Commentary on art. 5, paras. 42.1–42.10, according to the Interpretation and application of article 5 (permanent establishment) of the OECD Model Tax Convention (12 October 2011 to 10 February 2012), p. 8, "art. 5, par. 1, MTC has always properly been interpreted to require some degree of physical presence, some type of fixed place of business at its disposal".

[81] "Criterion" derives from the Greek word «κριτήριο» (kritērion), which means a rule or principle for evaluating or testing something.

works in the host MS non occasionally.[82] We cannot exclude the possibility of the providers' intention to be further evidenced by other means in the future, in our case due to the technological advancement of IT transactions.

2.2.5 Procedural Matters

IMDs 1 and 2 apply to all **customers (not only to consumers)**. Customers who may not be characterised as "consumers" under EU legislation cannot bring proceedings against the broker of an insurance contract before the courts of their domicile if the insurance policy covers a risk located in another MS because Regulation 44/01[83] on jurisdiction provides consumers only with a right to bring proceedings before their domestic courts. Establishment defines jurisdiction according to local law and fills this gap in favour of the non-consumer customer.[84] Establishment is necessary once more, while this gap has not been adequately covered by e-commerce.[85]

2.2.6 Priorities of the EU Which Affected E-Insurance Intermediation

(a) The IIM activities vary from simple sale of insurance to demanding and sophisticated intermediation activities regarding complex products. The latter case mainly applies to multifaceted and commercial risks and is usually carried by brokers.

The recent major issues which are involved with the distribution of insurance products are the achievement of a **high level of protection of the insured**, and in particular of the **consumer**; the protection of **competition**; the principle of the **FoS** and the **FoE** within the EU. Other priorities exist as well, such as **public confidence towards the insurance industry**, **data protection** and the avoidance of unnecessary impediments in **e-commerce**. Certain of these main principles are affected amidst the special attention if the transaction is conducted online.

[82] In our opinion, the fulfilment of the Commission's criteria is only a prima facie evidence of the provider being able to provide counter-evidence that in fact it works only occasionally.

[83] Regulation No 44/2001 on jurisdiction and the recognition and enforcement of judgments in civil and commercial matters.

[84] A consumer, according to Regulation 44/01, is only the customer who purchases insurance intermediation services for reasons irrelevant to their trade and profession and not only the customer of non-large risks within the meaning of Solvency II Directive, art. 13 para. 27.

[85] In order for an IIM to be established in another MS, it must notify the competent Authority of its home MS regarding (a) its name, address and registration number; (b) a programme of its operations indicating the identity of agents where the IIM intends to use; (c) the persons responsible for the management; (d) its name and address in the host MS; (e) the relevant classes of insurances; (f) the MS where he plans to be established and the address in this MS where documents can be obtained (IMD 2, art. 6 para 1).

(b) **Consumer protection** comes first by means of the following:

a. The obligation of the insurance undertakings/insurance IIMs to provide them with transparent and clear **information**[86] and with additional information obligation for distance and online sales – the consumer must have a clear picture of the product he intends to buy in order to understand it. The information must bring him in the position to select and make a decision among the different products that exist in the market, notwithstanding whether this option is used by the consumer or not.[87] Online transactions do not obstruct information dissemination.b. The avoidance of **conflict of interests** not only in the distribution of insurance products but also in all insurance and investment industries, including the disclosure of the **remuneration of the IIM**–e-intermediation, does not impede the conflict of interests check imposed on IIMs currently, or in the future. The same applies to the disclosure of the commission as well.c. The obligation of insurance mediators as well as, in some national jurisdictions, of the insurance undertakings to inform customers if they provide **advice** to the applicants of insurance and to the policyholders – IMD 2 provides that intermediation activities can include, among others, advising customers. Advising activities refer to sales conducted by insurance undertakings as well. The content of advice given on the one hand by IIM and on the other hand by insurance undertakings is not necessarily identical to its full extent.

The **advice** gives rise not only to questions as to its scope, but also in terms of its online execution. It is doubted whether the advice should cover all insurance products. Insurance investment product intermediation should be executed by intermediaries qualified to sell such investment products[88] and to provide additional information according to IMD 2. IIMs must be able to describe the profile of the investor since according to this, the advice and the information can vary. The lack of personal contact and the **difficulties to correct mistakes** have led to the opinion that the Internet cannot reach same quality of advice and information required by MiFID 2. However, it is doubted if the lower quality on the transmission of information and advice actually harm in an unacceptable way the consumer even as to simple insurance products, while the IT evolution may provide possibilities of online formation of a customer's profile in a quite satisfactory degree and even an oral supplementation of the information via the Internet. This evolution can probably fill adequately the gap.

---

[86] See footnote 14 above.

[87] The content of "transparency" does not exceed the information that the average consumer is able to understand; it is not necessary to include knowledge of complicated financial instruments and/or knowledge of an IT expert.

[88] According to the Greek Supervisory Authorities, insurance intermediaries who mediate for insurance investment products must pass the exams provided for the staff of investment companies who are involved in selling investment products.

2.3 *Online Freedom of Services vs "Traditional" (Offline) Freedom of Services*

1. IMD 2 specifically submits national restrictions on online passporting IIMs to the provisions and restrictions of the ECD. The ECD allows for limited exemptions from the freedom to provide information society services, which include (a) public safety, (b) public security, (c) public health[89] and (d) consumer protection, including investors.[90] As a result, the FoS by an offline IIM is subject to home MS rules which are based on the **general good** of this country[91] and can be stricter than the requirements of IMD 2. The Directive provides that every MS shall proceed with the **proper publication of such national legal provisions.**[92] In other words, an IIM conducting FoS **via traditional means** is subject to more restrictions than an IIM that pursues the same business on the Internet. There are numerous substantial reasons based on the general good concept[93] that could justify obstacles to the traditional passporting of EU-established IIMs. Moreover, under the ECD, national restrictive measures falling under the nature of the four categories mentioned above (safety, security, health and consumer/investor protection) must be taken on a case-by-case basis against a specific service provided by a given operator, in our case the IIM.
2. To be mentioned, online sales by insurance undertakings, unlike online sales by IIMs, are not restricted to the above limited exceptions[94] included in the ECD.[95] We face again an asymmetry.

2.4 *Communications via E-Mail with Insurance Intermediaries and Online Selling of Insurance Products*

Customers commonly communicate with IIMs and insurers via the Internet and receive a policy via e-mail in order to print it and subsequently conclude it in a physical form. This is not e-commerce.

[89] See Sect. 1.1.2, f.

[90] Art. 3 para. 4 ECD. Thus, all existing EU legislations on consumer protection apply, including data protection legislation.

[91] See IMD 2, art. 9; see also above Sect. 1.2.1 and footnote 30.

[92] See Commission Interpretative Communication 2000/C 43/03, p. 15 ff.

[93] According to ECJ case law, the following areas fall within the scope of general good: (a) professional conduct rules designed to protect the recipient of services, (b) consumer protection (e.g., language of the contract terms), (c) preservation of the good reputation of the national financial sector, (d) prevention of fraud, (e) social order, (f) protection of intellectual property, (g) cohesion of the tax system, (h) road safety, (i) protection of creditors, (j) fairness of commercial transactions, (k) protection of the proper administration of justice.

[94] See Annex concerning derogations from ECD, art. 3.

[95] Provided in the Annex of ECD.

The following are some differentiations, which are important in terms of the application of the ECD.

Electronic conclusion of contracts with IIMs presupposes that the IIM must acknowledge the receipt for the placement of the recipient's order without any undue delay and by electronic means. Moreover, the placement of the order and the acknowledgement of receipt are deemed to have been received when the parties to whom they are addressed have the ability to access them. In addition, the IIM must provide the contracting party (who according to EU law is the customer) with appropriate, effective and accessible technical means allowing for the identification and the correction of errors, prior to the placement of the order. The IIMs have to maintain the information and insurance documents in a durable medium, which will enable customers to store the information addressed personally to the customer in any form that may be accessible for future reference, for a period of time sufficient for the purposes of the given information, and which will allow for the unaltered reproduction of the information stored.

3 Worldwide Aspect

3.1 The Borders of the Online Market: Geographical, Technological and Regulatory Means

The **registration** of IIMs in their home MS, as well as the related **notification** to the competent Authority of their home MS, constitutes the "**passport**" for providing services and for the establishment in one or more other MSs. The passport is limited to cross-border transactions within EU, but the registration is also necessary for the entitlement of the intermediary to provide its services in its own country, as well as in non-EU countries (such as members of OECD or GATS[96]).

IMD 2 does not **apply** to insurance and reinsurance mediation **services** provided in relation to **(a) risks** and **commitments located outside the EU**. Furthermore, it does not **regulate (b)** mediation **activities carried out in non-EU countries.**[97] Therefore, in both of the aforementioned cases, only **technology** and **geography** set borders in the conduct of business. In the above two cases, the limits, if any, are set by IT, while EU law does not set any geographical limits to the EU IIMs, unless it refers to countries which EU has included in a "black" list which prohibits traders and/or service providers from engaging in commercial business with them. Nevertheless, in the first case, EU regulation applies to the **qualification** of the insurance

[96] The General Agreement on Trade Services (http://www.wto.org/english/docs_e/legal_e/48-dsfin.pdf) also provides regulations on rendering of insurance mediation services.

[97] See art. 1 para. 3 of IMD 2.

intermediary as far as risks and commitments located outside the EU concern citizens or legal entities of an MS.[98]

3.2 *Third Country Online v EU Online Insurance Intermediaries*

1. Online insurance activities, which cover **risks and commitments located in an MS** other than the MS in which the insurer that covers the risks is established, are subject, among others, to the TFEU principle of FoS, the relative secondary regulation[99] and the related ECJ case law. Insurance intermediation activities **should not be treated differently**.[100] But online IIMs of **third countries** not established in the EU that provide **solicited services** in the EU cannot of course follow EU FoS proceedings! In order to level the competitive advantage towards EU IIMs, IMD 2 provides that when the host MS law accepts services of third countries' IIMs, then the same law must guarantee that all persons pursuing mediation activities in the market shall be **equally treated by the law**. However, this provision is quite vague and leads to different interpretation by the national law as to what extent a rule is in breach of equal treatment. In addition, this rule does not affect the unsolicited services by third country IIMs.
2. From the operation and implementation point of view, there are **only slight differences** between solicited and unsolicited insurance intermediation when conducted via the Internet, while this is not the case when solicited and unsolicited mediation is conducted via traditional means. The same applies to insurance undertakings.[101] Differences in the pre-Internet era resulted in different treatment between solicited and unsolicited services. In the pre-Internet era and nowadays, **active consumers** who wish to purchase insurance intermediation services **by correspondence**, from IIMs situated in a third country (and not established in the country where the service is provided), do not need to be protected by law that governs intermediation. According to the general principles, the special local regulation does not apply if the service is received by the

[98] As mentioned above MSs can insert rules which extend the application of the IMD 2 rules over the above two limits.

[99] Second and third generation Directives (non-life Directives 1988/357 and 1992/49, as well as the consolidated life Directive 2002/83 now included in Solvency II Directive).

[100] As mentioned above under Sect. 1.1.2, a, in order for EU IIMs to conduct business in accordance with the law, in a MS other than their home MS, they have to meet notification requirements and also to appoint tax representatives when national law of MSs so requires.

[101] It is worth to mention that the notification of an insurer working under FoS does not release its agent from the obligation to proceed with the notification for his own FoS activity.

exclusive initiative of the consumer.[102] Crucial is, however, what should be judged as "own initiative". Nevertheless, nowadays **passive consumers** can be easily misled by third countries' IIMs that have the **intent** to conduct business in an MS and practically fulfil ECJ's criteria evidencing the intention to direct their activity to the MS of the customer.[103] This situation derives from the facilities that the Internet provides and from the numerous commercial websites existing in the market, as well as the numerous choices for the customer which enable online sales. Legislation reacts in order to protect customers from dealing with non-regulated providers without always releasing if a sale is unsolicited or in fact solicited. As mentioned, CEIOPS[104] developed criteria evidencing the intention of the commercial website to conduct business in another MS,[105] which in turn is obliged to proceed to a notification. These criteria are not, however, sufficient for online services provided by a third country IIM because they are developed in order to check whether the EU IIM has fulfilled its notification obligation for the cross-border transaction within the EU and aims at the protection of the insured. The experienced online consumer is always him who navigates the websites. Electronic solicited activities provided by third country IIMs should be dealt differently, e.g. with an electronic ban which allows to be removed only following procedure by a customer who is sufficiently warned that he buys on his own responsibility the services and/or to limit the ban to the special category of small risks.

3. An example of a situation indicative of potential complications in online insurance intermediation is the following. A person in a MS is insured on his own exclusive initiative via an online IIM of a third country, and the legislation of this third country does not provide any requirements for conducting insurance mediation. Eventually, the third country insurance broker fails to renew the insurance policy. If the insurance event occurs after the lapse of the insurance period, the insured will remain uncovered. This could become a common issue due to the expansion of online insurance intermediation.

---

[102] See recital 111 of MiFID 2: Where a third-country firm solicits clients or potential clients in the Union or promotes or advertises investment services or activities together with ancillary services in the Union, it should not be deemed as a service provided at the own exclusive initiative of the client.

[103] See above under Sect. 2.2.

[104] See under Sect. 2.2.

[105] See also the Luxembourg Protocol (02/06 Revision 1 Oct. 2008) according to which signs which are capable of evidencing the **intention** of the IIM to passport services are, among others, its actively **seeking of business in other MS**; **marketing**; asking for or **organising meetings with clients established in another MS; sending information on specific products**; conditions of cover to selected groups of clients; using the **language of other MSs**; providing **marketing accessible to other MSs**, as well as the **international nature of its activity**; **mentioning a telephone number with an international code**; mention of **international clientele from various MSs**, use of a **top level domain name other than of the merchant's home MS**. See above under Sect. 2.2.1.

In the light of the above, in case the law and practice of the third country do not include special provisions for the broker's liability, while according to the legislation of the MS, the rendering of services according to these particulars constitutes liability in tort, the following shall apply. Based on Rome II Regulation,[106] the law of the MS where the service is rendered will apply to rule on the broker's behaviour and whether it substantiates liability in tort. Under Rome II, the applicable law is not *lex loci delicti commissi* but the *lex loci damni*, in our case the law of the MS where the service is rendered.[107] The broker will be submitted to a jurisdiction which is stricter and more rigorous than its own. From the broker's point of view, the brokerage agreement should provide for the applicability of the law of his own country. The same will occur if the third country broker deals with the insurance of a risk located outside the MS country.

3.3 E-Commerce Within Non-EU Countries

1. According to **OECD Liberalisation Code,**[108]cross-border provision of insurance and private pension services covers transactions and transfers concluded both on the initiative of the insurer and the proposer ("correspondence insurance"). Same Code provides that transactions and transfers, including provision of services of insurance intermediation between a proposer in a Member State and a foreign provider, **shall be free.**[109] The scope of the relevant provision of the Code covers both the activities of entities providing other insurance services under the **establishment** regime and the **freedom to provide cross-border services** and all activities under the freedom to provide services **whether service provision is on the initiative of the provider or the beneficiary of the service**. This freedom to provide services is, however, not understood within the EU concept of FoS. EU MSs, according to IMD 2, have to introduce rules which guarantee equal treatment between all IIMs carrying out or being authorised to carry out intermediation activities in that market.[110] Thus, IIMs based in OECD third Countries not only have to fulfil the requirements provided for the IIMs in IMD 2 and conduct their business according to the obligations introduced in it, but also if the EU MS law has stricter provisions than this Directive, they have to fulfil these stricter obligations, if they work in this MS. The same applies regardless of whether the business is conducted online or not. In order to

[106] Regulation No 864/2007 on the law applicable to non-contractual obligations (Rome II).

[107] See art. 4 para. 1 of the Regulation.

[108] Code of Liberalisation of current invisible operations, 2013, Annex 1 to Annex A: Insurance and Private Pensions, art. D/2–D/8, p. 35.

[109] Part IV, art. D7.

[110] See above under Sect. 3.2 and art. 1 para. 3 IMD 2.

check if OECD MS intermediaries fulfil the obligations provided in the MS and hinder the entry for those that do not fulfil them, we could use the above-mentioned ECJ criteria.[111]

2. **OECD Guidelines for consumer protection** in the context of electronic commerce, which apply to business-to-consumer electronic transactions, set general principles for conducting such transactions, such as transparency, fair business, advertising and marketing practices, and provide for a set of "online disclosures"[112] concerning information about the business, the goods or services, the transaction and the security of payment mechanisms. OECD invites both Member and non-Member States of this Organisation to take into account OECD's consumer policies, recommendations and initiatives.
3. As regards **OECD Model Tax Convention,**[113] it is important to have a quick look at the income tax issues of those IIMs and meet the requirements of lasting duration and/or regularity and/or continuity. Online cross-border transactions presenting one or more of these characteristics could be treated as to establish, among others, their obligation to pay in the host country the relative income tax.[114] Income tax is always the most important issue as regards the differences between FoS and establishment.[115] It is to be mentioned that regarding transactions within the EU, MSs can set their rules freely, since taxation does not fall within the competence of the EU.[116] As mentioned, the general view is that via the Internet it is not possible for the business to be regarded as falling within the obligation of establishment.

---

[111] See above under Sect. 3.2.2.

[112] See OECD (2000), p. 15–17. OECD (2002). Also see OECD (2013).

[113] See above footnote 76.

[114] See above under Sect. 3.2. According to the UN Model Double Taxation Convention between Developed and Developing Countries (http://www.un.org/esa/ffd/tax/unmodel.htm) art. 5 para. 6, "notwithstanding the preceding provisions of this article, an insurance enterprise of a Contracting State shall, except in regard to (re)insurance, be deemed to have a permanent establishment in the other Contracting State if it collects premiums in the territory of that other State or insures risks situated therein through a person other than an agent of an independent status to whom paragraph 7 applies".

[115] A basic principle of OECD is that income tax is not charged on cross-border transactions unless a certain volume is exceeded.

[116] As mentioned, the general view is that via the Internet it is not possible for the business to be regarded as falling within the obligation of establishment; see above under Sect. 1.1.2, b, and footnote 80. See further recital 19 of ECD, according to which the place of establishment of a company providing services via an Internet website is not the place at which the technology supporting its website is located or the place at which its website is accessible but the place where it pursues its economic activity. The lack of physical presence always defined the business as service provided without the obligation of establishment. A basic principle of OECD is that income tax is not charged on cross-border transactions unless a certain volume is exceeded.

4. Similar principles are included in GATS as regards cross-border activities, among others, of IIMs within Countries/Members of this Agreement[117] (principles of the most-favoured-nation treatment[118]).
5. It is a different case if the non-EU IIM, whether originating from an OECD/GATS Country or not, provides services clearly on the exclusive initiative of the customer. In this case, the restriction of IMD 2 with regard to equal treatment does not apply.[119] But it should apply if the unsolicited services are of lasting duration and/or present a regularity and/or continuity with a big number of clients or if they have a representative[120] in the MS and if that representative possesses a permanent brief and is able to commit the parent intermediary. The non-EU IIM must be established according to the provisions of its national law.[121]

4 Final Remarks

I. The **legal environment** of the insurance intermediation, mainly if it is conducted via the Internet, aims at **strengthening the policyholder's position, in particular in retail insurances**, which, however, cover all the non-large risks according to the secondary legislation, regardless of whether this would result to the detriment of the professional interests of the traditional IIMs, which have to adapt their profession accordingly. In addition, said legal environment does not touch upon the differences which exist between the professional interests of IIMs and insurers even if it leads to changing the existing balance between those interests. In addition, the national supervisory Authority has to follow potential pathologies of the online sales, inherent with

[117] See footnote 118.

[118] As mentioned, the general view is that via the Internet it is not possible for the business to be regarded as falling within the obligation of establishment. According to art. II, para. 1 of GATS, with respect to any measure covered by this Agreement, each Member shall accord immediately and unconditionally to services and service suppliers of any other Member treatment no less favourable than that it accords to like services and service suppliers of any other country. Further, according to art. XVII, para. 1 of GATS, each Member shall accord to services and service suppliers of any other Member, in respect of all measures affecting the supply of services, treatment no less favourable than that it accords to its own like services and service suppliers.

[119] See above Sect. 3.2.1.

[120] According to art. 5, para. 7 of OECD Tax Convention, the mere collaboration of an independent agent or broker with an insurer in another OECD MS cannot be regarded as a permanent establishment.

[121] If the non-EU intermediary originates from a Country other than OECD/GATS, MS legislation can introduce even stricter requirements than that existing in its Country or even prohibiting the work of this intermediary if, for instance, no reciprocity exists in the Country of origin of the intermediary.

the IT technologies which can harm the interest of the insured in order to intervene with the appropriate measures.[122]

II. Online DIP is the utmost efficient means of promoting distance marketing of these important financial services and allows customers to have access without discrimination to the widest possible range of financial services available in the EU. This promotes competition within the single market and enhances customers' interests, which are able quickly and simply to choose from a wide market the products that are best suited for their needs.

 Online insurance affects the marketing of insurance products; thus, it is important not only for insurance undertakings, in particular, when they proceed with direct sales, but also for intermediaries, which ex definition are occupied with sales.

III. E-commerce **reduces the cost of intermediation**. The limits of its spread are to be found in the interests of the insured, especially in the retail business. The achievement of the optimal limit goes beyond the applicable legal rules. It is rather determined on the one hand by the dynamic evolution of the level of consumer protection, which is driven by the contemporary social and political perceptions, and on the other hand by the evolution of IT. With the spread of e-commerce, cross-border selling of insurance products encounters another obstacle which has nothing to do with the insurance sales as such, but is inherent in the nature of the insurance product. The legal environment of the Internet insurance intermediation covers one side of the consumer rights, i.e. the information as regards the personal status of the intermediary and the insurer; information about the product, typical consumer rights provided to all retail financial products, such as out-of-court resolution proceedings, the right to rescind, but not the insurance terms and conditions. But the insurance product is a legal product, which is based on a set of national mandatory rules of the applicable Insurance Contract Acts (ICAs), which differ from one country to another. Consumer protection not only contains information duties, warnings and the right to rescind but also refers to **the nature of the insurance product** which must be adapted to national law. So far, no harmonisation of national mandatory laws exists on OECD/EU level,[123] so that the product to be sold cross-border has to be adapted to the statutory law of the country which will govern the law of the policy. But even if we would face harmonised ICAs, this would not include all sales of retail insurance products without the

---

[122] According to the "Principles on the Supervision of Insurance Activities on the Internet", Oct. 2004, of the International Association of Insurance Supervision, national Supervisors should be focused on solving IT immanent risks such as transaction, data security, legal and reputational risks or other risks arising out of failure or default of IT infrastructure and to secure that same principles of transparency and disclosure should apply to the Internet as to other media.

[123] At the European level, a group of academics (Restatement project) has established Principles of European Insurance Contract Law (please see for the general part www.restatement.info), which could be a future optional EU Regulation and which is available at http://www.uibk.ac.at/zivilrecht/restatement/sprachfassungen/peicl-en.pdf.

necessity to be designed especially for the market of the country where it is sold, because parameters further to statutory laws oblige the insurers to design the insurance products in compliance also with local habits and customs of the country where they are sold.[124]

IV. E-commerce for IIM faces a big volume of strict and soft laws which have immediate effect on their business and are only a part of the whole legal environment of this industry. These are, in particular, IMD 2, ECD, DMD, PRIIPs, Regulation on jurisdiction, Rome I and Rome II and MiFID 2 (in the latter case, as far as insurance products are sold by institutions governed by this Directive), general good concept of MS, ECJ case law on criteria to demand establishment, European Commission's communications, EIOPA/CEIOPS instructions, OECD/GATS rules, as well as local law. It is of no wonder that a part of such law overlaps with others due to their different objectives[125] and makes the implementation for the stakeholders difficult, even for the consumers who are overloaded and confused by the excessively detailed information. We could consider that in the near future, all important priorities of the EU (such as consumer protection, competition, FoS, FoE) will be able to be safeguarded within a simpler specialised legal framework, e.g., by replacement of several information duties regarding simple products with a notification to the customer that he has the right to ask for more information with simple instructions on how to reach it.

V. IT is not only developing with remarkable results, but is also used by larger and larger parts of the population. Online insurance intermediation is at the same time partially **e-commerce for insurers** that are assisted by the IIMs or **e-commerce for IIMs** when they work independently from the insurers. The EU legislator has been slow in adjusting its high level of consumer protection to the technological advancement and therefore acts defensively by introducing pieces of fragmented legislation attempting to bridge the gap. The same happens on an even greater scale with the national Legislator and/or Regulator. It does not seem realistic to create the perfect regulation by inserting more and more rules, because the more details of the transaction those rules cover, the more new issues requesting regulations arise, since at the end of the day every individual sale presents a different case, unless we deal with very typical, simple, mass products. In order to overcome this situation, there may be a need to replace some part of the very extended volume of legislation, which is overlapping, in particular as regards the information duties, with clear, complete and fair principles that will ensure mainly consumer protection, and will secure, in particular, fair dealing and competition, as well as data protection. In other words, it is not that more regulation is needed but rather the strengthening of the said principles and the quality of their implementation.

---

[124] See *I. Rokas* (2010), p. 977.

[125] See Discussion Paper for the working group meeting on 2 December 2003, 26 (http://ec.europa.eu/internal_market/insurance/docs/markt-2541-03/markt-2541-03_en.pdf).

VI. Consumers must be provided with a volume of crucial information which reasonably can be expected that they will read and understand. It should be clearly indicated that they can have further information if they so wish with a simple click.

VII. Lastly, it is important to mention that in our days, online insurance intermediation is governed by a law which includes little insurance law. Much more is governed by the law on cross-border transactions within the EU and worldwide, the consumer protection and e-commerce law, because these areas of law equally cover all other financial products and services.

References

CEIOPS (2009) The IMD and other intermediaries' related issues – practical solutions and examples, DOC-19/09

CEIOPS (2008) Protocol relating to the cooperation of the competent authorities of the MSs of the EU in particular concerning the application of Directive 2002/92 on insurance mediation, DOC-02/06

CEIOPS (2007) Proposals for a definition of cross-border provision of service under the IMD, DOC-15/07

CEIOPS (2006) Protocol relating to the cooperation of the competent authorities of the MSs of the EU in particular concerning the application of Directive 2002/92 on insurance mediation, DOC-02/06

EIOPA (2014) Report on good practices on comparison websites, CCPFI-13/100

EU Discussion Paper for the working group meeting (2003) 26 (http://ec.europa.eu/internal_market/insurance/docs/markt-2541-03/markt-2541-03_en.pdf)

OECD (2013) Empowering and protecting consumers in the internet economy, OECD Digital Economy Papers, No. 216, OECD Publishing (http://dx.doi.org/10.1787/5k4c6tbcvvq2-en)

OECD (2002) Best practice examples under the OECD guidelines on consumer protection in the context of electronic commerce, OECD Digital Economy Papers, No. 61, OECD Publishing (http://dx.doi.org/10.1787/233574467655)

OECD (2000) OECD guidelines for consumer protection in the context of electronic commerce, p 15–17 (http://www.oecd.org/sti/consumer/34023811.pdf)

Rokas I (2010) Droit européen du contrat d' assurance. De la creation d' un cadre communautaire pour l' industrie de l' assurance à la creation d' un cadre communautaire pour les produits de l' assurance, in Revue General du Droit des Assurances

Sprindler (2002) Versicherungsaufsicht über Internetangebote ausländischer Versicherer, VersR 1049

E-commerce and Distribution of Insurance Products: A Few Suggestions for an Appropriate Regulatory Infrastructure

Hsin-Chun Wang

Contents

Abstract After the global financial crisis caused by sub-prime mortgage market, electronic commerce in insurance becomes one of the essential components for insurers to improve their competitiveness and performance. In terms of cost-efficiencies in operation and acquisition, it is evident that electronic commerce has already and constantly changed the traditional distribution channels in several no-life insurance markets. Among these markets, the Internet provides a new channel for distributions for insurers particularly in auto insurance products. While a new distributional channel seems to reduce transaction costs between consumers and insurers, risks consequently will cause new challenges to global

H.-C. Wang, Ph.D. (✉)
College of Law, National Taiwan University, Taipei, Taiwan

Queen Mary College, University of London, London, UK
e-mail: hcwang@ntu.edu.tw

P. Marano et al. (eds.), *The "Dematerialized" Insurance*,
DOI 10.1007/978-3-319-28410-1_2

insurance market. How to develop an appropriate level of regulation is essential to promote this transaction method and to ensure the interests of consumers.

This Article addresses insurance regulation governing electronic commerce and analyses various developed regulatory models and their frameworks. In terms of prudential regulation, it is suggested that operational risk arising from E-commerce should be incorporated into solvency regulation. In encountering with risks caused by electronic transactions, an insurer should be required to hold adequacy of capital and maintain a certain level of risk management. In relation to market conduct regulation, this Article intends to apply behavioural theory to re-examine the current information-based insurance regulation.

1 Introduction

After the global financial crisis caused by sub-prime mortgage market, electronic commerce in insurance becomes one of the essential components for insurers to improve their competitiveness and performance.[1] It was also witnessed that investment incomes remain lower than in the pre-crisis years in most non-life markets.[2] In addition, more stringent solvency regulations have restricted their investment strategies, which may lead to more conservative investment options.[3] Under this circumstance, it is suggested that "insurers have been forced to concentrate on improving the building blocks of underwriting performance: claims, and operational and acquisition ratios[4]". In terms of cost-efficiencies in operation and acquisition, it is evident that electronic commerce has already and constantly changed the traditional distribution channels in several no-life insurance markets.[5] Among these markets, the Internet provides a new channel for distributions for insurers particularly in auto insurance products.

While a new distributional channel seems to reduce transaction costs between consumers and insurers, risks consequently will cause new challenges to global insurance market. How to develop an appropriate level of regulation is essential to promote this transaction method and to ensure the interests of consumers. Part II describes possible risks caused by electronic commerce. Based on the twin-peak regulatory approach, relevant risks will be categorised into market conduct regulation and prudential regulation. Part III begins with three developed regulatory

[1] *See* CAPGEMINI (2012), p. 7.

[2] *Ibid.*, p. 10.

[3] *Ibid.*

[4] *Ibid.*, p. 11.

[5] When E-commerce has improved the transaction costs, the Internet and mobile devices have become important tools for insurers to acquire new businesses in several countries, such as Canada, France, India, the Netherlands, Spain, and the US. *Ibid.*, pp. 11–19.

models to discuss the regulatory framework. Part IV begins with our critique on disclosure regulation and argues that more attention should be drawn on human limitation and behavioural biases.

2 Risks and Insurance Regulation Concerning E-commerce

With the fast-growing E-commerce via the Internet, several risks which may impede not only the consumers' interests but also insurers' operation have been caused. Taking into account the recent regulatory reform, the risks arising from E-commerce will be categorised as follows.

In 2002, the risks relating to E-commerce identified by IAIS[6] are strategic risk, operational risk, transaction risk, data security risk, connectivity risk and conduct of business risk. In this work, the author will choose a different approach to analyse these risks by taking into account the recent regulatory framework reform. After the financial crisis in 2008, there are significant financial market regulatory reforms in many countries. Among these markets, the introduction of a twin-peak model[7] to the UK is a symbolic model for the new generation of financial regulatory structure. In terms of twin-peak regulatory model in the UK, the Financial Service Authority (FSA) ceased to exist and has been restructured into the Financial Conduct Authority (FCA) and the Prudential Regulation Authority (PRA) on 1 April 2013.[8] Before that, the FSA was responsible for both prudential regulation and conduct regulation of financial services. Under the new regulatory structure, the FCA will be responsible for the business conduct of all financial service firms and also be responsible for the prudential regulation of those financial service firms not regulated under the PRA.

The main task of the PRA is to promote the safety and soundness of the major financial institutions (banks, building societies, credit unions, insurers and major investment firms) through prudential regulation.[9] With regard to insurance regulation under this new regulatory framework, two main objectives of the PRA are to "promote insurers' safety and soundness thereby supporting the stability of the UK financial system and to contribute to securing an appropriate degree of protection for those who are or may become policyholders".[10] In evaluating the soundness of insurers, the PRA takes risk assessment framework to judge whether it is necessary to allow the PRA to intervene insurers. This risk framework captures three main

[6] *See* International Association of Insurance Supervisors (2002), pp. 4–10.

[7] The debate concerning the choice between a single regulator and a twin-peak structure has existed in the UK prior to the 1997 reform. *See* Taylor (2009–2010), p. 78.

[8] *See* Financial Services Authority (2012), p. 11.

[9] *See* Bailey (2012), p. 1.

[10] *See* Prudential Regulation Authority, Bank of England (2013), p. 9.

elements: the potential impact,[11] the external context[12] and mitigating factors (business risks).[13]

When the financial soundness of insurers is the core task of the PRA, conduct of business of insurers is regulated by the FCA. The FCA's operational objectives contained in the Financial Services Act 2012 are to deliver consumer protection, enhance market integrity and build competitive market.[14] The FCA also has identified several conduct risks which may affect its supervision to achieve these objectives.[15]

Following this regulatory structure, it is reasonable to assume that risks arising from E-commerce will be regulated by these two sets of regulations or different agencies (e.g., PRA and FCA in the UK) if the financial market regulation has been restructured into a twin-peak model. In this regard, it is worth categorising these risks into business conduct regulation and prudential regulation.

2.1 Risks of E-commerce and Business Conduct Regulation

Among E-commerce risks identified by the IAIS issues paper in 2002, electronic commerce gives rise to many new legal issues concerning conduct of insurance business.[16] It is suggested that the business conduct regulation of E-commerce should be consistent with that applied to other conducts through different distribution channels[17] particular in person basis with paper documents. As E-commerce

[11] This assessment is to identify and analyse "an insurer's potential to affect adversely the PRA's objectives by failing, coming under stress, or by the way it carries on its business". As a result, the PRA divides financial deposit takers, designated investment firms and insurers into five categories of impact based on the capacity to affect the UK financial system. *Ibid.*, pp. 19–20.

[12] This element mainly focuses on the assessment of the macro-prudential environment and system-wide risks, such as interest rates and longevity risk. *Ibid.*, p. 20.

[13] The PRA examines the sustainability and vulnerability of an insurer's business model. Under this assessment, the PRA analyses an insurer's "profitability, risk appetite, performance targets and underlying assumptions, and an insurer's own forecasts and their plausibility". In doing so, the PRA can determine the capacity of the insurer to mitigate risks. *Ibid.*, p. 20.

[14] These objectives were also the main task of the FSA before the establishment of the FCR. *See* Financial Conduct Authority (2013), pp. 15–32.

[15] These conduct risks described in the FCA business plan in 2013 are as follows: "Firms do not design products or services that respond to real consumer needs or are in consumers' long-terms interests; distribution channels do not promote transparency for consumers on financial products and services; Over-reliance on, and inadequate oversight of, payment and product technologies; Poor understanding of risk and return, combined with the search for yield or income, lead consumers to take on more risks than is appropriate". *See above footnote 14*, pp. 15–22.

[16] *See above footnote 6*, pp. 9–10.

[17] From this issues paper, it proposed that many new issues should be dealt with, such as the identification of the consumer, security of electronic documents and signatures, notification of contract-related information, the format and style of presentation to meet the requirements, proof of coverage for the policyholder, electronic payment acceptability and record retention. *See* International Association of Insurance Supervisors (2004), pp. 5–6.

business is conducted virtually via the Internet, insurers should assure the adequacy of consumer protection not only for the conclusion of insurance contract but also for the potential contractual relationship (such as quotes and information of insurance products via the Internet). Besides, data security risks, connectivity risks and transaction risks arising from insurance business via the Internet should be regulated and categorised into the business conduct regulation. In general, data security risks could be caused by the internal system of an insurance company, as well as external data breaks such as hacking.[18] In addition to data security risks, connectivity risk is when failure of the certain part of an insurer's operational system may consequently cause critical effect on the entire insurer's system.[19] Transaction risks usually arise from faulty information or flaws in the insurer's operational system.[20] To prevent with activities which may endanger the consumer's interests, insurance regulators should evaluate the online security level and operational system of an insurance company. The risk assessment of insurer's ability and risk management would also pose a new challenge for regulators due to lack of expertise and competence.

2.2 *Risks of E-commerce and Prudential Regulation*

While the issues regarding E-commerce in insurance generally have been focused on the consumer protection and market conduct regulation, operational risks caused by E-commerce should also be emphasised in the regime of prudential regulation. As more insurers seek for low-cost distributional channels to replace the traditional business acquisition approach, strategic risks[21] caused by the E-commerce would impede the solvency of insurers if they fail to develop adequacy of risk management. Before engaging into E-commerce business, possible threats[22] on the solvency and reputation of the insurance company should be considered. For example, the fast-growing online business may also become price predatory competition among insurers. The cost of the Internet may not be less as we expected due to other costs arising from legal disputes and online security. When carrying out insurance business via the Internet, operational risks[23] from E-commerce should be properly managed. As the failure of the Internet technology infrastructure could possibly endanger the solvency of an insurer, it is necessary to maintain an insurer's capacity to tackle the

[18] *See above footnote 6*, p. 8.

[19] *See above footnote 6*, p. 9.

[20] Due to fault in the process of information flows, both parties may have disputes over the insurance products. For example, the insurance provisions and conditions are ambiguous on the website. *See above footnote 6*, p. 7.

[21] *See above footnote 6*, p. 5.

[22] For others concerning strategic risks, *see above footnote 6*, pp. 5–6.

[23] *See above footnote 6*, p. 6.

possible impact and establish risk management. Therefore, operational risks relating to E-commerce should been emphasised in the solvency regulation of an insurer.[24]

3 Current Developed Insurance Regulatory Infrastructure

After analysing risks caused by E-commerce, we turn to introduce and analyse the current developed regulatory infrastructure for insurance business via the Internet. With the information technology innovation, online transaction has become part of our daily life. Based on the protection of consumer, these developed insurance regulations tend to focus on the business conduct regulation. Among them, the regulatory infrastructure in the European Union seems to be the most comprehensive model. In this regard, the author would use this model as a case study to propose a sound insurance regulatory infrastructure concerning E-commerce.

3.1 European Union

With regard to the regulatory infrastructure concerning E-commerce in the EU, the main directives which are developed to harmonise the diversified regulations among different member states are E-commerce Directive (ECD)[25] and Electronic Signature Directive.[26] Following these main directives applied to general E-Commerce activities, the Distance Marketing of Consumer Financial Services Directive (DMD)[27] specifically deals with financial services, including insurance.

The ECD was adopted to harmonise the legal framework of electronic commerce and to ensure that "Information Society services benefit from the Internal Market..."[28] in 2000. This directive therefore establishes specific rules concerning the transparency requirement of information, commercial communication and obligation of the online service providers. In addition, it also deals with the issues,

---

[24] For example, operational risks are treated as one of three main elements of the Solvency Capital Requirement in the Solvency II. However, the standard formula calculation is roughly based on an insurer's business volume rather than an insurer's risk profile. For life insurance contracts, "the calculation of the capital requirement for operational risk should take account of the amount of annual expenses incurred in respect of those insurance obligations". For other insurance contracts, it should "take account of the volume of those operations, in terms of earned premiums and technical provisions...." article 107 of Solvency II Level 1 Text, available at http://eur-lex.europa.eu/LexUriServ/LexUriServ.do?uri=OJ:L:2009:335:0001:0155:en:PDF.

[25] Directive 2000/31/EC on certain legal aspects of information society services, in particular electronic commerce, in the Internal Market (Directive on electronic commerce) [2000] OJ L178/1.

[26] Directive 1999/93/EC on a Community framework for electronic signatures [1999] OJ L 13/12.

[27] Directive 2002/65/EC concerning the distance marketing of consumer financial services and amending Council Directive 90/619/EEC and Directives 97/7/EC and 98/27/EC, [2002] OJ L 271/16.

[28] *See* European Commission (2000).

including conclusion and validity, of electronic contracts; liability of internet intermediaries; online dispute settlement and the role of national authorities; as well as mutual recognition and derogation.[29] As the ECD applies to all the financial services, the insurance activities over the Internet should not be restricted by member states.[30] It should be noted that written form requirements for insurance contracts in some member states may challenge the validity of electronic insurance contracts. In Dutch, certain provisions of the Dutch Code of Civil Procedure (DCCP) and the Dutch Civil Code (DCC) were recently amended to enable parties to conclude and send insurance policies by electronic transmission of information instead of written transmission of information in 2010.[31] Although the ECD provides the fundamental principles to apply almost all contracts concluded by electronic means, the particular rules governing e-commerce in financial services, DMD, furthermore is developed in 2002.

As the transparency requirements of information have been emphasised in the ECD, the DMD lays down the details of the obligation of the retail financial service providers.[32] In this directive, the financial service suppliers are required to provide with the four essential parts of information prior to the conclusion of the contract.[33] These essential parts of information include the supplier,[34] the financial service,[35] the distant contract[36] and redress.[37]

In addition, the DMD also gives the consumers several rights for the financial services negotiated at a distance (e.g., telephone, fax or over the Internet). These rights include the following:

---

[29] *Ibid.*

[30] Art. 8 (1)(2) of Directive 2000/31/EC on certain legal aspects of information society services, in particular electronic commerce, in the Internal Market ('Directive on electronic commerce') [2000] OJ L178/11-12. *See also* European Commission (Internal Market DG) (2002), p. 2.

[31] Lennartz (2010), p. 1; s*ee also* Flanagan (2012), p. 11.

[32] While the ECD governed all the financial services, the DMD only governs the retail financial sector. Flanagan (2012), p. 25.

[33] Art. 3, para. 1 of Directive 2002/65/EC concerning the distance marketing of consumer financial services and amending Council Directive 90/619/EEC and Directives 97/7/EC and 98/27/EC, [2002] OJ L 271/16.

[34] E.g., the identity and the main business, the representative of the supplier, any professional other than the supplier, the trade register and the relevant supervisory authority. *Ibid.*, art. 3 para. 1(1).

[35] E.g., the main characteristics of the financial service, the total price to be paid by the consumer, relevant notice concerning special risks, notice of possibility relating to taxes or costs, limitations of period for which the information provided is valid, the arrangements for payment and performance and any costs of using the means of distance communication. *Ibid.*, art. 3 para. 1(2).

[36] E.g., the existence or absence of a right of withdrawal, and where the right of withdrawal exists, its duration, and the condition for exercising, the minimum duration of the distant contract, information on any rights the parties may have to terminate the contract, practical instructions for exercising the right of withdrawal, the Member State or States whose laws are taken by the supplier as a basis, any contractual clause on law or compete court and languages used in the contract. *Ibid.*, art. 3 para. 1(3).

[37] E.g., out-of-court complaint and redress mechanism, the existence of guarantee funds or other compensation arrangements. *Ibid.*, art. 3 para. 1(4).

1. the right to reflect: the supplier is required to transmit the relevant information mentioned above in writing or on a durable medium (e.g., floppy disk, CD-ROM or e-mail); all the terms and conditions will remain valid for 14 days;[38]
2. the right to withdraw: the consumers can exercise the right of withdrawal within at least 14 days (30 days in the case of life assurance and personal pension operations);[39]
3. the right to cancellation of a payment in the event of fraudulent use of payment card.[40]

As the purpose of the Directives is to harmonise the varied regulations among member states, it is also worth analysing the substantial regulations implemented in these member states, e.g., the United Kingdom. In the UK, the business conducts of financial service providers are regulated by the Financial Conduct Authority. In connection with electronic commerce in financial services, the general requirements are set out in Conduct of Business Sourcebook 5.2 E-Commerce (COBS 5.2).[41] For insurance business carrying on an electronic commerce activities, they are required to comply with the Insurance Conduct of Business 3.2 E-Commerce (ICOBS 3.2).[42] As it has been addressed by article 5 (1) of E-Commerce Directive mentioned above, the firm must make the relevant information about the firm and its products or services "easily, directly and permanently accessible to the recipients of the information society services it provides" (ICOBS 3.2.2). When referring to price, it must be declared clearly and unambiguously with the information concerning tax and delivery costs (ICOBS 3.2.3). In addition, requirements relating to the placing and receipt of orders are set out in ICOBS 3.2.6 and ICOBS 3.2.7. A firm is required to give the consumers (ECA, electronic commerce activity, recipients) the following information prior to the order being placed: (a) technical steps to follow to conclude the contract, (b) whether or not the concluded contract will be filed by the firm, (c) the technical means for identifying and correcting input errors, (d) the languages offered for the conclusion of the contract (ICOBS 3.2.6), as well as contractual terms and conditions (ICOBS 3.2.7).

3.2 United States

With regard to E-commerce in insurance regulation, it is found in the US that the selling of insurance via the Internet is treated equally to the conventional insurance

[38] *Ibid.*, art. 5.

[39] *Ibid.*, art. 6.

[40] *Ibid.*, art. 7.

[41] Financial Consumer Authority, Conduct of Business Sourcebook (COBS), http://fshandbook.info/FS/html/handbook/COBS/5/2.

[42] Financial Consumer Authority, ICOBS Insurance: Conduct of Business Sourcebook (ICOBS), http://fshandbook.info/FS/html/handbook/ICOBS/3/2.

transactions by the insurance regulators.[43] As a result, the insurance regulatory authorities in the US have not established a particular regulatory framework for the E-commerce in insurance. However, some issues that have been addressed only focused on the use of an electronic record when the law required information in writing such as the US Uniform Electronic Transactions Act (UETA) in 1999. Based on the United Nations Commission on International Trade Law (UNCITRAL) Model Laws on Electronic Commerce 1996 and Electronic Signatures 2001, the purpose of the UETA is to ensure the permit of use of electronic record is the equivalent of a paper record and remove the barriers to electronic commerce.[44] As the notices of cancellation, nonrenewal or renewal of insurance contract are required non-electronic delivery methods by state insurance laws, this would raise significant barriers to promote the electronic E-commerce. As a result, many state laws have been working to dismantle the current restrictions in certain conditions.[45] In addition, the formatting of insurance forms and notices has also been an issue affecting E-commerce in insurance. Many state insurance regulators require that the specific information in paper documents should also be accentuated in an electronic version, e.g., South Carolina Department of Insurance.[46] Other issues include the admissibility of electronic records and the use of electronic transmissions to provide information to the policyholder.[47] Although the distribution channels sprang up in the US (e.g., telephone, mail and the Internet),[48] it is still unclear whether there will be any particular regulation developed by the state regulators.

3.3 Canada

In 2012, a discussion paper published by the Canadian Council of Insurance Regulators (CCIR) has analysed the issues regarding E-commerce in insurance sector and consumer protection.[49] According to this paper, there is no particular insurance regulation governing the online distribution of insurance products. However, there are a number of laws and regulations that apply to electronic commerce generally, e.g., Uniform Electronic Commerce Act in 1999, Canadian Code of Practice for Consumer Protection in Electronic Commerce in 2004 and Personal

---

[43] New York State Insurance Department (2000) cited from Canadian Council of Insurance Regulators (2012), p. 12.

[44] *See* Uniform Law Commission (1999).

[45] E.g., Tennessee, Maryland, and Alaska. *See* Insurance Advocate (2013).

[46] *Ibid.*

[47] *Ibid.*

[48] For example, it is estimated that nearly 3.1 million auto insurance policies were purchased through the Internet in 2012. *See* Insurance Information Institute (2014).

[49] *See* Canadian Council of Insurance Regulators (2012).

Information Protection and Electronic Documents Act (PEPEDA) for electronic signatures in 2000.[50] In connection with consumer protection and E-commerce, the Uniform Electronic Commerce Act and Canadian Code of Practice for Consumer Protection in Electronic Commerce are worth noting. Based on the 1996 United Nations Commission on International Trade Law (UNCITRAL) Model Law on Electronic Commerce,[51] the Uniform Electronic Commerce Act[52] (UECA) was developed by the Uniform Law Conference of Canada to build up a set of standards to facilitate electronic commerce. The UECA has three parts. In the first part, there are the basic rules concerning the functional equivalence when the contracting parties agreed to use electronic documents, as well as some special rules to government. The second part of the UECA sets out general guidance and applies to common law rules of contracts. The third part focuses on the carriage of goods because of necessity of harmonisation of the relevant laws across borders.[53] In general, the UECA provides the fundamental rules of the legal recognition and validity of the form of electronic documents. With regard to consumer protection, the original guidelines published by the Organisation for Economic Co-Operation and Development (OECD) in 1999 have consequently been adopted and developed as the Canadian Code of Practice for Consumer Protection in Electronic Commerce (the Code) by the Working Group on Electronic Commerce and Consumers in 2003. After being reviewed and finalised from the E-Commerce Leaders Code Review Committee, the Code was endorsed by federal, provincial and territorial ministers responsible for consumers' affairs in 2004.[54] The Code sets out several eight essential principles of good practice in E-commerce, including information provision, language, contract of formation and fulfillment, online privacy, security of payment and personal information, redress, unsolicited mail and communications with children.[55]

To date, there is no specific regulation governing the E-commerce in insurance sector in Canada.[56]

---

[50] *Ibid.*, pp. 12–14.

[51] UNCITRAL, Model Law on Electronic Commerce (1996).

[52] Uniform Law Conference of Canada (1999).

[53] *Ibid.*

[54] Canadian Consumer Measures Committee (2004), p. 1.

[55] *Ibid.*, pp. 5–13.

[56] However, Canada Electronic Commerce Committee (ECC) in Canada Council of Insurance Regulators (CCIR) released several research papers addressing the issues concerning E-commerce in the insurance sector. The final position paper which intends to communicate with stakeholders has been published in November 2013. This paper indicates that it is possible to have more specific regulations governing insurance business in E-commerce in the future. *See* Canada Electronic Commerce Committee (ECC) in Canada Council of Insurance Regulators (CCIR) (2013).

3.4 China

In November 2013, China's first online insurance firm, Zhong'an Online Property Insurance, has been established in Shanghai. Most significantly, Zong'an's major shareholders include E-commerce company Alibaba Group Holding Ltd., Ping An Insurance (Group) Co. and the Internet firm Tencent Holdings Ltd. This company was assigned by the China Insurance Regulatory Commission (CIRC) as a Pilot for online insurance in February 2013 and then approved by the CIRC to get the first licence in October 2013.[57]

In April 2014, the CIRC requested further advice from the public and issued a "Call for Advice for Insurance Regulation of Life Insurers concerning Online Insurance".[58] The aim of this initiative is to improve the development of online insurance and the protection of consumers. This CfA sets out several fundamental issues regarding regulation of life online insurance.

Firstly, it provides with several entry requirements for carrying out online business for life insurers. These requirements may include the financial solvency of insurers, operative system in handling online activities, the licence of online business, the competence of management and the licensing requirements for selling employees.[59]

Secondly, life insurers who intend to conduct online business are required to choose their insurance intermediaries and Internet companies in a prudent way. In addition, life insurers would be held liable for any misconduct of these insurance intermediaries and Internet companies.[60]

Thirdly, life insurers should disclose the geographic scope of their service and should notify the consumer the availability of their service if the consumer's address of residence is out of scope. Life insurers also are required to disclose the essential information regarding the insurance products, including characteristics and material information. As for insurance products, this CfA addresses that life insurers can sell accident insurance, term life insurance and normal life insurance to the area where there is no branch through the online channel if insurers can maintain their internal control and to provide adequate services for consumers. With regard to participating policy, investment-linked insurance and universal insurance, insurers should clearly indicate the uncertainty of profit and possible losses.[61]

Fourthly, life insurers in online selling should disclose the business information on their websites. The information regarding activities in online selling includes the websites of online selling, co-operative institutions and their methods, as well as the period, product information, consumer service and complaints.[62]

---

[57] Xinhuanet News (2013).

[58] China Insurance Regulatory Commission (2014).

[59] China Insurance Regulatory Commission (2014), *para* 2(1)–(5).

[60] *Ibid., para* 3.

[61] *Ibid., para* 4–5.

[62] *Ibid., para* 6.

Fifthly, the Commission intends to lay down the requirements to enhance the security and safety of insurance documents, payment system, privacy of consumers and record keeping.[63]

Although the relative regulations concerning life insurance have not been officially announced after this CfA, three life online companies are required to halt online selling activities by the CIRC in August 2014.[64] As the current regulatory regime has not addressed the problems arising from the online selling, these online insurers intend to mislead consumers in the short-term policies with high expected yield. These policies often offer an annualised yield between 5 and 7 %, which is higher than term-deposit rate offered by the banks. With fast-growing development and vicious competition among life online insurers in China, a sound and comprehensive regulatory regime is urgent to be implemented.

3.5 Issues Relating to the Regulatory Structure

While specific insurance regulations have been developed in the European Union, the US, Canada and China still lack relevant regulations in the insurance sector. Although the fundamental structure and concepts in consumer protections have been set out in general rules governing electronic commerce and validity of electronic documents, how to apply these principles to the insurance business still remains an uncertainty to the stakeholders, including consumers, regulators, insurers and even other potential cross-sector financial institutions such as Bancassurance and financial conglomerate.

The broad advantages based on the general laws of E-commerce and relevant privacy data protection regimes are that they can be applied across different sectors and less enforcement burden on insurance regulatory agencies. In essence, the consistency principles can be developed across sectors and the need of specific regulation is avoided.

However, some drawbacks arising from the broad principals should also be addressed. Although the need of specific regulation might be less at first, the general principals may not provide with appropriate solutions to technical and operational problems in a particular sector. As a result, it may need more guidelines developed by the particular regulatory agencies. In the end, the burden of insurance regulatory agencies still remains. Insurance regulatory agencies will be expected to develop more specific regulations to deal with these issues, and more guidelines are needed to reduce the legal uncertainty. Therefore, the general principals developed by these rules[65] can only be deemed as the basic purposes which the relevant insurance regulations intend to achieve. It is suggested that more specific insurance regulation

[63] *Ibid., para* 9–11.

[64] CaixinOnline (2014).

[65] E.g., Canadian Code of Practice for Consumer Protection in Electronic Commerce.

should be set out to reduce the uncertainty of legal compliance and consumer protection.

4 Consumer Protection and Disclosure Regulation

With regard to current developed specific insurance regulation concerning E-commerce, the European Union Model is mainly based on disclosure regulation, in particular the Distance Marketing of Consumer Financial Services Directive (DMD).[66] The financial suppliers (insurers) are required to provide four essential parts of information, including the supplier, the financial service, the distant contract and legal redress. In addition, the suppliers are required to ensure that all the contractual terms and conditions and information mentioned above should be available and accessible to the consumers. This directive also requires that the consumer should have a period of 14 days to withdraw from the contract without penalty. With appropriate level of disclosure regulation, consumers can reduce a substantial amount of transaction costs in searching financial product and reduce the information asymmetries with financial institutions. Although the financial suppliers, including insurers, are required to provide with the essential information of their financial services, the main question concerning the protection of consumers still remains. As a result, this work will identify the possible obstacles regarding the disclosure regulation of E-commerce in insurance.

Structuring the disclosure of information into regulations can be found in many areas such as financial market, food and drinks sectors. Disclosure rules will allow consumers of financial services to make decisions based on the information which is accurate, accessible and affordable.[67] As information asymmetries in financial markets become one of essential issues of consumer protection, using disclosure as regulation is deemed to enhance the ability of consumers and improve market efficiency. Due to the characteristics of financial products as incomplete contracts in that the value of financial product can only be determined after the point of purchase,[68] the consumers may be unable to ascertain quality when purchasing, to argue the definitions of terms of financial contracts and to assess the safety and soundness of financial institutions.[69] As a result, the transaction costs in searching the products, monitoring the behaviours of financial institutions, verifying the value of contacts[70] and securing redress in the event of contract failure are enormous.[71] In

[66] *See* above *footnote 31*.

[67] *See* Baldwin and Cave (1999), p. 12.

[68] *See* Llewellyn (1999), p. 35.

[69] *Ibid.*, p. 22.

[70] It is observed that the characteristics of financial products are different from other goods and services. For instance, "it may be a long time before the consumer is aware of the value and faults of a financial product". This can usually be found in the disputes arising from insurance contracts in the event of accident of insured or damage of insured properties. *Ibid.*, pp. 37–38.

[71] *Ibid.*, p. 35.

terms of regulation of E-commerce in insurance, it seems that the purpose of these regulations intend to require an insurer to provide the relevant information via the Internet equally to the information through the conventional distributional channels. However, even with the same level of disclosed information, would the consumer be capable to choose the insurance product to suit his needs? In this regard, it is suggested to address that disclosure-based regulation may have some drawbacks and fundamental limitations.[72] This may not only lead to increase the transaction costs with unnecessary information but also fail to accomplish the regulatory goal.

4.1 Fundamental Limitations of Disclosure Regulation

To ensure the adequacy of information for consumers, it is suggested that consumers may encounter several problems such as cost of information and incentive to falsify information.[73] Even with high level of information, consumers may lack the expertise to analyse the information in an accurate manner and fail to assess risks.[74] How people process information and make appropriate decision becomes the key issue to examine and evaluate the disclosure regime. Developed from psychology and economics, it has been identified that heuristic biases and bounded rationality may impede the information-based regulatory regime.[75] Especially with more complex insurance products such as investment-linked insurance, there are several biases which may affect and distort the consumer's decision.

First, it is evident that people may tend to be more easily persuaded by face-to-face communication than by written documents.[76] Furthermore, some biases are observed that people often accept information from unreliable sources which are more influential during the process of decision-making.[77] As people tend to receive information from different means, in particular the Internet, it is foreseeable that there may be more falsified information to induce decision-makers. These "anchoring" biases[78] may affect decision-makers (consumers) to properly analyse the

[72] *See* Dalley (2006–2007), p. 1113.

[73] *See* above *footnote 67*, p. 12.

[74] *Ibid.*, p. 49.

[75] For heuristic biases, *see generally* Tversky and Kahneman (1974), pp. 1124–1131; with regard to information regime in the financial market regulation, *see* Packin (2013), pp. 449–452; for the behavioral approach to securities regulation, *see* Choi and Pritchard (2003–2004), pp. 7–20; for financial market regulation, see *Avgouleas* (2009), pp. 31–34; Juurikkala (2012–2013), pp. 38–50.

[76] *See* above *footnote* 72, p. 1114.

[77] *Ibid.*

[78] "In many situations, people make estimates by starting from an initial value that is adjusted to yield the answer. The initial value, or starting point, may be suggested by the formulation of the problem, or it may be the result of a particular computation. In either case, adjustments are typically insufficient. That is, different staring points yield different estimates, which are biased toward the initial values." See above *footnote* 72, p. 1128, quoted by George et al. (2000), pp. 195–196.

disclosed information. Anchoring, which may lead consumers to start with some initial reference point and then adjust in the direction they believe, will cause consumers to stick on the initial decision and being remarkably resistant to further information.[79]

Second, information-based regulation tends to provide more information which people may lack expertise to process, namely "information overload".[80] As the costs of processing the information increase, it will consequently lead people to misjudge risks or misuse information. Even an increase in the quality of information available can also lead to the same phenomenon.[81] In this regard, it is suggested that the regulatory framework of disclosure regulation should address this potential drawback and should be designed to provide standardised information which is easier for comparison and analysis for decision-makers.[82] In case of lack of standards of information set out by an independent agency or regulator with expertise and accountability,[83] consumers with limited ability would tend to accept the partial information and fail to understand possible risks, particularly in some complex insurance products (complex pensions arrangements or life insurance with varied options). Furthermore, even with sophisticated and experienced advisors, potential problems arising out of principal–agent relationship[84] and conflicts of interests may still cause adverse effect on the process of decision-making.

Third, the main function of disclosure regulation is to let consumers make decisions with the information available. However, people may "not respond in anticipated ways to the follow of information".[85] Consumers may choose cheaper insurance products without responding to information concerning the quality of service or the financial condition of insurers. They would make decisions according to price rather than other considerations with the disclosed information.

Therefore, the design of regulatory framework for online insurance based on information should consider these possible behavioural biases[86] created by people's limited ability to process information.

4.2 Some Suggestions for Current Information-Based Regulation Based on the Behavioural Biases

Although insurers are required to provide the information by the regulators, these disclosure regulations would be positively influential only if the behavioural biases

[79] Lin (2010–2011), p. 345. *See generally* Rabin (1998), pp. 26–29.

[80] *See* above footnote 72, p. 1115.

[81] *Ibid.*

[82] *See* above footnote 72, p. 1116.

[83] *See* above footnote 68, p. 33.

[84] *See* Erta et al. (2013), p. 24.

[85] *See above footnote* 67, p. 49.

[86] *See above footnote 84*, pp. 13–24.

mentioned above are taken into account. As a result, the main purpose of disclosure regulation is to efficiently influence consumer behaviour rather than to reveal all the information. In terms of applying behavioural insights in the design of insurance regulation, it has been suggested[87] that there are four main ways which a financial regulator could intervene to reduce the risk of harm caused by these biases.

First, information provided by financial suppliers should be in a way that would not lead to exacerbate consumer weakness or target behavioural biases or misunderstanding. Second, regulation should adjust the choice environment of financial services to prevent any inappropriate distortion of consumer decision-making process. Third, the distributional channel should be intervened and controlled by regulators particularly in complex products with high level of expertise. Fourth, some products that appear to cause consumer detriment should be restricted or subject to a certain level of product controls. If some products cause severe problems, regulators may consider prohibiting or limiting the availability of these products.

By applying to E-commerce in insurance sector, this work proposes two suggestions which can be integrated and applied into the insurance regulation concerning E-commerce as follows. It should also be worth noting that the use of E-commerce may reduce substantial transaction costs in communication. However, more stringent requirements may hamper these distributional channels and consequently increase unnecessary transaction costs for consumers through the Internet.

4.2.1 Information Asymmetric and Complexity of Insurance Products

To compare with conventional distributional channel for insurance products, the gap arising from E-commerce still remains due to lack of suitable advice or guidelines to interpret these products. Unlike conventional distributional channel involving face-to-face communication, the consumers may not be able to gather suitable and accurate information when making decisions.

As a result, it is suggested that "the level of advice needed may vary depending on the complexity of the product…".[88] In addition, the level of advice needed may also depend on the ability of consumers. Even with the same complexity of insurance products, some sophisticated consumers may need less advice to make an appropriate decision without any other advice or independent intermediaries. In this regard, an online insurer should ensure to offer the appropriate level of interpretation and advice for different levels of consumers when making decisions on the Internet. As a result, an insurer is required to provide with the appropriate level of advice when needed through the website such as online interaction or online assessment. As any communication or interaction in the Internet can be

[87] These four ways include "1. Provide Information; 2. Change Choice Environment; 3. Control Product Distribution; 4. Control Products". *Ibid.*, pp. 42–43.

[88] *See above footnote 56*, p. 5.

recorded and traceable, this method of communication may bring advantages for consumers if any misleading information is provided by insurers.

Another drawback caused by behavioural biases should also be noted particularly in less complex insurance products such as auto insurance. Even with the information available, people may tend to choose cheaper insurance products without considering the quality of service that the insurer will offer. As the quality of auto insurance may be revealed only after the event of accident, e.g. claim and settlement, price becomes the main consideration for consumers and fierce competition among insurers may lead to unreasonable pricing or even predatory pricing. Therefore, information-based regulation should not only require insurers to reveal the terms and condition of the insurance contracts but also establish the disclosure system which provides information regarding the quality of insurance product for consumers in making decision.

4.2.2 Information Overload and E-Commerce

Even with more information which could be easily gathered from the Internet, information users would definitely encounter the above phenomenon "information overload". As the information of the insurance product is mainly provided by the insurer offering that product, it is necessary for regulatory agencies to ensure that the relevant information provided is clear, accurate and accessible.[89] However, this information may not entirely affect the process of decision-making in choosing insurance products. Consumers may receive other information from different resource and websites. When comparing with other insurance products, the relevant information regarding analysis on the various insurance suppliers would become an essential element for consumers to purchase an insurance product even through the conventional distributional channel. If these websites would have involved conflict of interests and have not provided the information independently, this consequently might distort the process of consumers' decision-making. In essence, these activities regarding promotion of the insurance products should be subject to relevant regulations. It has been suggested that "the line between simple comparisons only versus transacting insurance must be clear" to these websites. These websites should be properly licensed to be supervised by the same regulatory framework as other insurance undertakings if they provide information and advice regarding insurance products.[90] However, it may cause enormous enforcement costs for regulators. How to identify, monitor and even analyse these websites for their ownership, independence and accuracy would be a challenge for regulators. To

[89] E.g., the main characteristics of the product; terms, exclusions and conditions of that product; the total premium and other charges that the consumer may have to pay; options and coverage. *Ibid.*, p. 7.

[90] Unlicensed entities must not "provide advice; hold themselves out as licensed insurers or firms; or post insurance publications, which could mislead a consumer into thinking they are an insurance provider", *ibid.*, p. 12.

ensure the fair competition and interests of consumers, insurance regulators may consider developing relevant approval procedure to ensure transparency and accountability of information provided in the websites. By doing so, it would reduce substantial costs for consumers to search and identify the trustworthiness of these websites.

5 Concluding Observation

This Article addresses insurance regulation governing electronic commerce and analyses various developed regulatory models and their frameworks. Although there are other important issues such as privacy and data protection, which are beyond the scope of this Article, the risks caused by relevant tort liability and sanctions should be brought to mind. In examining the adequacy of insurance regulation in E-commerce, this Article proposes a twin-peak regulatory approach to analyse relevant issues. In terms of prudential regulation, it is suggested that operational risk arising from E-commerce should be incorporated into solvency regulation. In encountering with risks caused by electronic transactions, an insurer should be required to held adequacy of capital and maintain a certain level of risk management. In relation to market conduct regulation, this Article intends to apply behavioural theory to re-examine the current information-based insurance regulation. The purpose of this Article is not to deny all the advantages which disclosure regulation has brought. However, it is essential to take into account these possible human limitations when designing the relevant regulatory regime. It would be more beneficial to test the workability of behavioural-related regulation with more empirical studies on behavioural biases. This article has suggested that an online insurer should offer the appropriate level of interpretation and advice for difference levels of complexity of insurance products, as well as different levels of consumers through the website such as online interaction or online assessment. Even with less complex insurance products, consumers can easily obtain information regarding the quality of insurance product such as claim and settlement when making decisions on the Internet. To encounter information overload, insurance regulators should develop relevant approval procedure and supervise the websites which provide information and advice regarding insurance products.

References

Journal Articles

Choi SJ, Pritchard AC (2003–2004) Behavioral economics and the SEC. Stan Law Rev 56(1):7–20

Dalley PJ (2006–2007) The use and misuse of disclosure as a regulation system. Florida State Univ Law Rev 34(1089):1113

George GF, Duffy K, Ahuja M (2000) Countering the anchoring and adjustment bias with decision support systems. Decis Support Syst 29:195–196. http://citeseerx.ist.psu.edu/viewdoc/download?doi=10.1.1.21.3329&rep=rep1&type=pdf

Juurikkala O (2012–2013) The behavioral paradox: why investor irrationality calls for lighter and simpler financial regulation. Fordham J Corp Financ Law 18(33):38–50

Lin Tom CW (1998) A behavioral framework for securities risk. Seattle Univ Law Rev 34:325, 345

Packin NG (2012–2013) It's (not) all about the money: using behavioral economics to improve regulation of risk management in financial institutions. Univ Pan J Bus Law 15:419, 449–452

Rabin M (1998) Psychology and economics. J Econ Lit 36:11–46

Taylor MW (2009–2010) The road from twin peaks and the way back. Conn Ins Law J 16:61, 78

Tversky A, Kahneman D (1974) Judgment under uncertainty: heuristics and biases. Science (New Series) 185(4157):1124–1131. http://www.jstor.org/sici?sici=0036-8075%2819740927%293%3A185%3A4157%3C1124%3AJUUHAB%3E2.0.CO%3B2-M

Book & Book Chapter

Avgouleas E (2009) The global financial crisis, behavioural finance and financial regulation: in search of a new orthodoxy. J Corp Law Stud 9(23):31–34

Baldwin R, Cave M (1999) Understanding regulation-theory, strategy and practice. Oxford University Press, Oxford, p 12

Online Documents & Articles

Bailey A (2012) The prudential regulatory authority, quarterly bulletin 2012 Q4. http://www.bankofengland.co.uk/publications/Documents/quarterlybulletin/qb120405 pre.pdf

CaixinOnline (2014) Insurance firms stop online sales, as regulator takes long look, (Wang Shenlu). http://english.caixin.com/2014-08-29/100723029.html. Accessed 29 Aug 2014

Canadian Consumer Measures Committee (2004) Canadian Code of Practice for Consumer Protection in Electronic Commerce. http://cmcweb.ca/eic/site/cmc-cmc.nsf/vwapj/EcommPrinciples2003_e.pdf/$FILE/EcommPrinciples2003_e.pdf

Canadian Council of Insurance Regulators (CCIR) (2012) Electronic Commerce in Insurance Products. http://www.ccir-ccrra.org/en/init/Elec_Commerce/ECC%20issues%20paper%20EN.pdf

Canadian Council of Insurance Regulators (CCIR) (2013) Final Position Paper-Electronic Commerce in Insurance Products. http://www.ccir-ccrra.org/en/init/Elec_Commerce/ECC_finalized_position_paper_EN.pdf

CAPGEMINI (2012) 2012 World insurance report. http://www.capgemini.com/resource-file-access/resource/pdf/World_Insurance_Report_2012.pdf

China Insurance Regulatory Commission (2014) Call for advice for insurance regulation of life insurers concerning life online insurance. http://www.circ.gov.cn/web/site0/tab5208/info3913089.htm

Erta K, Hunt S, Iscenko Z, Brambley W (2013) Applying behavioural economics at the financial conduct authority, p. 24, Occasional Paper No. 1, Financial Conduct Authority, http://www.fca.org.uk/static/documents/occasional-papers/occasional-paper-1.pdf

European Commission (2000) Electronic Commerce: commission welcomes final adoption of legal framework directive, IP/00/442, 04/05/2000, http://europa.eu/rapid/press-release_IP-00-442_en.htm?locale=zh

European Commission (Internal Market DG) (2002) Electronic-commerce and Insurance (Discussion paper for the working group), MARKT/2522/02-EN Rev.1 Orig. http://ec.europa.eu/internal_market/insurance/docs/markt-2522/markt-2522-02-rev1_en.pdf

Financial Conduct Authority (2013) FCA Business Plan 2013/14. http://www.fca.org.uk/static/documents/business-plan/bp-2013-14.pdf

Financial Services Authority (2012) FSA Annual Report 2012/13. http://www.fca.org.uk/static/documents/annual-report/fsa-annual-report-12-13.pdf

Flanagan A (2012) E-Commerce: the Regulation of Insurance in the Age of the Internet, https://qmro.qmul.ac.uk/jspui/bitstream/123456789/3207/2/FLANAGANE-Commerce2012POST.doc (Note: This is the author's version of a chapter subsequently published as Flanagan, A. (2012). E-Commerce: The Regulation of Insurance in the Age of the Internet. In Edward Elgar Publishing, Inc., Research Handbook on International Insurance Law and Regulation)

Insurance Advocate (2013) E-Commerce: Is the Insurance Industry Really Ready for Electronic Transactions? Issue: 2013:08–19, http://www.insurance-advocate.com/E-Commerce-Is-the-Insurance-Industry-Really-Ready-for-Electronic-Transactions-c1546.html

Insurance Information Institute (2014) Buying Insurance: Evolving Distribution Channels, http://www.iii.org/issues_updates/buying-insurance -evolving-distribution-channels.html

International Association of Insurance Supervisors (2004) Principles on the Supervision of Insurance Activities on the Internet. http://www.dgsfp.mineco.es/sector/documentos/IAIS/PRINCIPIOS%20INGLES/PRINCIPIO%204%20EN%20Principles_on_the_supervision_of_insurance_activities_on_the_internet.pdf

International Association of Insurance Supervisors, (2002) Risk to Insurers Posed by Electronic Commerce, Issues Paper, http://www.mirkin.ru/_docs/articles02-057.pdf

Lennartz Y(2010) Developments in the field of electronic communications, Norton Rose Fulbright, http://www.nortonrosefulbright.com/knowledge/publications/31536/developments-in-the-field-of-electronic-communications#pg hdr

Llewellyn D (1999) The Economic Rationale for Financial Regulation, Financial Services Authority Occasional Paper Series 01. http://www.fsa.gov.uk/pubs/occpapers/OP01.pdf

New York State Insurance Department (2000) Insurance Transactions Over the Internet. http://www.dfs.ny.gov/insurance/ogco2000/rg000362.htm

Prudential Regulation Authority, Bank of England (2013) The Prudential Regulation Authority' Approach to insurance supervision. http://www.bankofengland.co.uk/publications/Documents/praapproach/insuranceappr1304.pdf

UNCITRAL, Model Law on Electronic Commerce (1996), http://www.uncitral.org/uncitral/en/uncitral_texts/electronic_commerce/1996Model.html

Uniform Law Commission, Electronic Act Summary, http://www.uniformlaws.org/ActSummary.aspx?title=Electronic%20Transactions%20Act

Uniform Law Conference of Canada, (1999) Uniform Electronic Commerce Act Annotated 1999. http://www.ulcc.ca/en/1999-winnipeg-mb/359-civil-section-documents/1138-1999-electronic-commerce-act-annotated

Xinhuanet News (2013) China Gets First Online Insurance Firm, 2013/11/07, http://news.xinhuanet.com/english/china/2013-11/07/c_132867133.htm

The EU Regulation on Comparison Websites of Insurance Products

Pierpaolo Marano

Contents

Abstract Comparison websites have proliferated in recent years as online technologies have developed and consumers have sought fast, easy access to comparative information about various products, including insurance. Comparison websites have stimulated competition between insurers and intermediaries and helped enhance the transparency and comparability of information available to consumers. However, the subsequent chapter points out the possible bias caused to customers by the lack of an appropriate regulation of the comparison websites of insurance products.

Associate Professor of Insurance Law at the Catholic University of the Sacred Heart in Milan.

P. Marano (✉)
Faculty of Banking, Finance and Insurance Sciences, Catholic University of the Sacred Heart, Milan, Italy

Counsel PWC Legal, Milan – Rome, Milan, Italy
e-mail: pierpaolo.marano@unicatt.it; pierpaolo.marano@it.pwc.com

P. Marano et al. (eds.), *The "Dematerialized" Insurance*,
DOI 10.1007/978-3-319-28410-1_3

1 Introduction

According to Eurostat, the official statistics board of the European Union, nearly 60 % of EU Internet users shopped online in 2012.[1] A survey of consumers' e-commerce habits in 12 European countries reveals that 240 million consumers in these European countries bought goods online during the past year[2] and that more than half of e-commerce consumers have bought online from abroad at some point in time.[3] A source reports that 191.1 million U.S. citizens were online shoppers and had browsed products, compared prices, or bought merchandise online at least once in 2013, while their number would surpass 200 million in 2015.[4] Another source notices that e-commerce sales were over $ 433 billion in Asia-Pacific, i.e. more than one-third of all global e-commerce sales in 2013, and such a region should surpass North America becoming the world's first market for business to consumer e-commerce sales.[5]

These data support the importance of e-commerce for consumers and, obviously, businesses that cater to them.[6] Complying with this trend, companies from the insurance industry are introducing websites that sell or promote a range of insurance products of retail nature (including automobiles, homeowners, and other small, simple/standardized commercial policies[7]). The insurance companies thus intend to have a direct relationship with potential customers skipping the intermediation activities traditionally carried out by insurance intermediaries (agents and brokers), but facing strategic risks.[8]

The online offering of insurance products/policies posted by an insurer on its website, however, refers only to its own insurance products/policies. Therefore, the

---

[1] See http://www.ecommerce-europe.eu/news/2013/10/eurostat-releases-figures-on-online-shopping-in-europe.

[2] The European Countries were Germany, the UK, France, Spain, Poland, Belgium, the Netherlands, Italy, Norway, Denmark, Finland and Sweden.

[3] See Postnord, *E-Commerce in Europe*, 2014, http://www.postnord.com/globalassets/global/english/document/publications/2014/e-commerce-in-europe-2014.pdf.

[4] See http://www.statista.com/statistics/183755/number-of-us-internet-shoppers-since-2009/.

[5] See http://www.emarketer.com/Article/Ecommerce-Sales-Topped-1-Trillion-First-Time-2012/1009649.

[6] About the awareness of price comparison websites by consumers, see Consumer Futures, *Price comparison websites: consumer perceptions and experiences*, 2013, 13 ff. http://www.consumerfutures.org.uk/reports/price-comparison-websites-consumer-perceptions-and-experiences.

[7] According to the Insurance Information Institute, *Buying Insurance: Evolving Distribution Channels*, October 2014, a 2013 study by comScore estimates that 3.1 million auto insurance policies were sold online in 2012 in the US, about the same as in 2011 but up about 6 percent from 2010, while 83 percent of consumers would use the Internet to research life insurance before purchasing a policy if they had the option, according to the 2014 Insurance Barometer survey by the Life and Health Insurance Foundation for Education (LIFE) Foundation and LIMRA.

[8] The IAIS' s Issue Paper, *Insurance Risks in E-Commerce*, 2013, 4 s, provides a list of the points to be taken into account by the board of directors of an insurance company and executive management when they make the decision to engage in e-commerce.

comparison websites could constitute a more effective tool for customers interested in the purchase of insurance products online because they offer a quick access to a wide range of insurance products for each class of insurance, making the insurers compete against each other.

There is no generally agreed definition of comparison websites. The European Insurance and Occupational Pension Authority (EIOPA) provided the following for the purpose of its report on such a tool: *<<interfaces, the objective of which is to display to Internetusers a number of insurance offers, and compare their prices and/or what is covered>>*.[9]

Comparison websites have proliferated in recent years as online technologies have developed and consumers have sought fast, easy access to comparative information about various products.

According to a 2013 report, for a great portion of consumers, price comparison websites are part of the usual decision-making process for insurance products (especially motor vehicle insurance, home insurance, and travel insurance), while the next most frequently mentioned category/sector is gas and electricity.[10]

Consumers use comparison websites primarily as a source of information in order to compare prices and go bargain-hunting to get the best deal. Some also make use of the possibility to buy contracts online or to switch providers,[11] and it is a considered fact that consumers more frequently switch insurance providers, rather than other providers, because they believe there is little to gain from being loyal to their current insurance provider.[12]

Comparison websites can be differentiated in different categories. The possible distinctive features of comparison websites are (*i*) their purpose, (*ii*) their activities, (*iii*) their business model (remuneration), (*iv*) the status of the website operator, and (*v*) the comparison method.[13]

The purpose of the comparison websites can be either commercial or non-commercial (i.e., without having a profit-making purpose).

If the purpose is commercial, the comparison websites have a link on the Web page with one or more insurance undertaking(s), and thus they are remunerated to

---

[9] EIOPA, Report on Good Practices on Comparison Websites, 2014, p. 6.

[10] Consumer Futures, *Price comparison websites: consumer perceptions and experiences*, cit., p. 21.

[11] Atticus, *Price comparison websites: Consumer market research*, April 2014, p. 7, https://www.fca.org.uk/static/documents/research/price-comparison-website-consumer-research.pdf, highlights that the price comparison websites were perceived to allow consumers to achieve in minutes what would otherwise take hours and make a potentially boring and difficult job relatively painless by presenting complex information in a simple and accessible way. See also Consumer Futures, *Price comparison websites: consumer perceptions and experiences*, cit., p. 34 ff.

[12] Consumer Futures, *Price comparison websites: consumer perceptions and experiences*, cit., p. 40 ff.

[13] EIOPA, *Consultation Paper on Draft Report on Good Practices on Comparison Websites*, 2013, p. 11 f.; Comparison Tools, *Report from the Multi-Stakeholder Dialogue*, March 2013, p. 20, http://ec.europa.eu/consumers/documents/consumer-summit-2013-msdct-report_en.pdf.

include information on the insurance products marketed by the latter. Therefore, the business model (remuneration) of these comparison websites can be one or a combination of the following: pay per sale,[14] pay per click,[15] advertisement.[16] However, other business models exist (insurance undertakings pay for positions in comparison results, they pay to list products, etc.).[17]

If the purpose is not commercial, the comparison websites aim to collect and provide Internet users with aggregate and concise information on insurance products. Non-commercial websites can be run by public authorities (notably, the national supervisory authorities), by private organizations (such as consumer and/or industry associations), or jointly. The fees are paid by the consumer directly rather than by the insurance undertakings, and the fees are addressed to cover the costs of running the comparison website and ensure the impartiality of the comparisons. This is mainly the case of comparison websites run by consumer associations. The consumer will pay every time he asks for a comparison, or he will pay a subscription to become a member of the consumer association (pay per view or through a subscription approach). In the last case, he will have unlimited access to the comparison website.[18]

The activities of the comparison websites can go from providing links to insurance undertakings and/or intermediaries and/or providing quotes/rankings to the consumer (based on price and/or guarantees or other criteria) to giving quotes and proposing a specific contract to the consumer that matches his/her demands and needs. They can also present the details of insurance companies/intermediaries who offer the most appropriate contracts and/or offer the consumer the possibility to close a contract at the end of the process.[19]

Finally, with regard to the status of the comparison's website owner, the owner operates the comparison tool which redirects the customer to an insurer or intermediary or the owner outsources the operation of the comparison tool to a third-party provider (white label websites).[20]

[14] This is the case where an insurance undertaking pays to a comparison website each time a consumer concludes an insurance contract by following an offer listed by the comparison website.

[15] In this case, an insurance undertaking pays to the comparison website each time a consumer clicks on the link to its website listed on the comparison website.

[16] An insurance undertaking pays each time the brand name is mentioned on the comparison website.

[17] EIOPA, *Consultation Paper on Draft Report on Good Practices on Comparison Websites*, 2013, p. 10 f.; EIOPA, Report on Good Practices on Comparison Websites, 2014, p. 9.

[18] EIOPA, *Consultation Paper on Draft Report on Good Practices on Comparison Websites*, 2013, p. 12. EIOPA, Report on Good Practices on Comparison Websites, 2014, p. 11.

[19] EIOPA, *Consultation Paper on Draft Report on Good Practices on Comparison Websites*, 2013, p. 11. EIOPA, Report on Good Practices on Comparison Websites, 2014, p. 10.

[20] EIOPA, Report on Good Practices on Comparison Websites, 2014, p. 10.

2 The Consumers' Associations' perception of Comparison Websites

Several consumers' associations have conducted surveys on comparison websites in recent years. These surveys acknowledge that comparison websites have stimulated competition between insurers and intermediaries and helped enhance the transparency and comparability of information available to consumers.[21]

The surveys, however, highlight the possible bias caused to customers by the lack of appropriate regulation of the comparison websites.[22]

Consumers place a high degree of confidence in comparison websites,[23] but different requirements are expected to improve the reliability of this tool.[24]

Several position papers issued by the consumers' associations highlight that transparency in the business model would allow consumers to assess the impartiality of the advice.[25]

Comparison websites should at least indicate to the consumer, in a prominent and easily understandable way, their ownership or shareholders,[26] the financing model (who pays for which service),[27] the frequency of updating, the geographic coverage, the methodology applicable for the purpose of extraction of the relevant findings (upon reference to ranking criteria/factors, source of information), and the scope of the sector at issue covered through the use of website operators (i.e. all providers, only a percentage of sector concerned, only those who participate in the scheme, why some providers do not participate in the scheme).[28]

---

[21] EIOPA, *Consultation Paper on Draft Report on Good Practices on Comparison Websites*, 2013, p. 7; Comparison Tools, *Report from the Multi-Stakeholder Dialogue*, cit., p. 5; Consumer Futures, *Price comparison websites: consumer perceptions and experiences*, cit., p. 54 ff.; Atticus, *Price comparison websites: Consumer market research, cit.*, p. 7.

[22] EIOPA, *Report on Good Practices on Comparison Websites*, 2014.

[23] Consumer Futures, *Price comparison websites: consumer perceptions and experiences*, cit., p. 48 ff.

[24] Comparison Tools, *Report from the Multi-Stakeholder Dialogue, cit.*, 18 ff.

[25] BEUC, *Position Paper on Comparison Websites,* p. 3 f. available at http://www.beuc.org/publications/2012-00536-01-e.pdf; Consumer Futures, *Price comparison websites: consumer perceptions and experiences*, cit., p. 48 ff.

[26] In order to better clarify the ownership of the comparison websites to the customers, a specification on the business activity of its shareholders would be useful.

[27] These surveys do not specify the independence requirement claimed by consumer associations. A first meaning of this requirement may be in the sense that independence is legal, that is, the absence of equity or voting rights in the property of the comparison website. The independence, however, could also be required as financial. If a comparison website receives a fee, for example for passing on leads or requests for an offer or in the event of the purchase of a product or a service via the website or for including products in the comparison, such remuneration may constitute a financial interest in recommending these products.

Comparison Tools, *Report from the Multi-Stakeholder Dialogue, cit.*, 19.

[28] BEUC, *Position Paper on Comparison Websites, cit.*, p. 4.

In addition, the consumers' associations claim that the provider of the comparison website should be independent of the individual companies that are surveyed on the website,[29] in order to safeguard a non-discriminatory overview of the market at issue and the findings produced in this context.[30]

Other expected requirements refer to coverage. The more exhaustive the website is, in terms of providers/products of the category searched by the consumer, the more extensive the consumer's choice is. However, it is important not to overly focus on the quantity of information but to concentrate on the information that meets the consumer's real needs and expectations, and its suitability should be gauged in line with specific purpose, content, presentation, and context.[31]

For what concerns information, the consumer should be prominently informed about the frequency of updating, as well as the last update; the rapidity of Internet implies that the consumer expects all the information online to be updated. Furthermore, the information provided by the comparison websites must be precise, relevant, understandable, and readable. Difficult legal and technical concepts must be avoided wherever possible. Such information must be easily verifiable by the consumer, i.e., via a link to the concerned provider, every time it is possible. Ultimately, consumers must be able to trust the information that is provided. Accordingly, the comparison websites must in no way mislead the consumer as to the accuracy of the information displayed.[32]

With reference to accuracy, the position papers highlight that a major ranking factor is the price, so it is essential to include as much as possible the final price (charges, fees, delivery costs, taxes). Partitioned pricing should be allowed only in cases where it is not possible to provide a general global price for all searches. The key concept in this respect is comparability, which must be compatible with the comprehensiveness of the information provided. Therefore, comparison websites should clearly state for each offer the main terms of subscription, fees, and special clauses and clearly indicate if they are unusual or burdensome. This information should be presented in a comparable format for all offers, to make it easy for consumers to have an overview. This is a key element because if too much emphasis is laid on prices, companies could be tempted to lower prices in order to look more attractive on the website, by worsening the other terms of subscription, which the consumer will become aware of only afterwards.[33] In addition, price

[29] BEUC, *Position Paper on Comparison Websites, cit.*, p. 5.

[30] BEUC, *Position Paper on Comparison Websites, cit.*, p. 5.

[31] BEUC, *Position Paper on Comparison Websites, cit.*, p. 4.

[32] BEUC, *Position Paper on Comparison Websites, cit.*, p. 4 f.

[33] According to eDigitalResearch, *Price Comparison Website Mystery Shopping*, March 2012, a research report prepared for Consumer Focus, available at http://www.consumerfocus.org.uk/files/2013/01/Comparing-comparison-sites.pdf, charges which cannot be removed are slightly more prevalent within the car insurance market with windscreen cover (12 percent) and personal injury insurance (11 percent) as examples. These costs only occur in a small proportion of cases, but the inability to remove these costs means that consumers may be purchasing additional cover that they neither wanted nor needed. In 37 percent of home insurance shops, emergency home cover was

information should include discounts, as well as information on the termination date and conditions for the discount.[34]

The consumers' associations, however, are concerned that the benefits that arise from the additional use of comparison websites could be not understandable or accessible to all consumers. Therefore, they claim that the comparison websites should be user friendly, i.e. user interfaces should be built in a user-friendly way and in ways that actually seem appealing to users and facilitate the interaction of non-experienced users with the website. Futhermore, the comparison websites should use technical features that enable visually impaired or other disabled consumers to use the device. It is also important to make comparative information available for consumers that do not have access to the Internet for free or at a minimal cost (regular printed reports, printed version sent on request, by telephone, etc.).[35]

Finally, the position papers highlight that supervisory authorities should proactively monitor the observance of these conditions in order to enhance the consumer's trust in the information provided by comparison websites.[36] Therefore, they suggest that regular reports should be made available, at least on a monthly basis, on methodology and market coverage, when a comparison is unlimited in time. Otherwise, a report should be made available to the different providers and to market authorities in order to check methodology and market coverage, when a comparison has taken place and is limited in time because it relates a particular advantage to a specific moment in time (e.g., "best product of the month").[37]

3 The Supervisory Authorities' perception of Comparison Websites

In the matter of insurance products comparison websites, some insurance supervisory authorities have surveyed this tool reporting criticalities in terms of consumer protection and fair competition.[38]

---

added onto policy costs, and while consumers had the option to remove it, this relies heavily on them noticing the additional charge and understanding how to take it off (see p. 122).

[34] BEUC, *Position Paper on Comparison Websites*, *cit*., p. 5.

[35] BEUC, *Position Paper on Comparison Websites*, *cit*., p. 5.

[36] BEUC, Position Paper on Comparison Websites, *cit*., p. 5.

[37] BEUC, Position Paper on Comparison Websites, *cit*., p. 5.

[38] IVASS, Investigation into comparison websites in the Italian insurance market, November 2014, http://www.ivass.it/ivass_cms/docs/F4449/INVESTIGATION_INTO_COMPARISON_WEBSITES_IN_THE_ITALIAN_INSURANCE_MARKET.pdf; FCA, Price comparison websites in the general insurance sector, July 2014, https://www.fca.org.uk/static/documents/research/price-comparison-website-consumer-research.pdf.

Outside of Europe, however, authorities call for a regulatory framework that does not hinder, or even incentives, the introduction of this tool in their jurisdictions: see, e.g., Monetary Authority of

A lack of transparency can be found in the information on the comparison websites. The commercial purpose of their activities is not immediately noticeable,[39] as well as how to submit complaints is not clearly indicated.[40]

A lack of transparency can also be reported in respect of the information provided by the comparison websites. There is no clear information on conflicts of interest.[41] Websites compare only (or mainly) insurers with which they have signed partnership agreements and from which they receive commissions.[42] The commissions that are received whenever a single contract is concluded are not included in the quotations published in the comparison output but are only mentioned later on the undertaking's website.[43] Hence, the user is not immediately aware that the comparison websites get a fee connected to the possible conclusion of the contract.[44]

Market coverage, i.e. the percentage of insurers compared to the total, is absent or misleading as the advertised number of insurers is greater than the one they actually compare.[45]

The comparison is based solely on price, and the characteristic features of the coverage (e.g. deductibles, exclusions, limits) are not compared. The more the products being compared are structured, however, the more numerous the criteria for comparison should be. Therefore, the coverage offered is likely to be not

Singapore, Consultations on Recommendations of the Financial Advisory Industry Review, March 2013, p. 31 ff.

[39] FCA, Price comparison websites in the general insurance sector, cit, p. 12, highlights that comparison websites often did not make clear what role they were performing when providing quotes for insurance products or the nature of their service. This was because this information was rarely provided at an appropriate time or formed part of the quote journey but was instead found in other locations on their website (such as within terms and conditions or other generic firm information).

[40] IVASS, Investigation into comparison websites in the Italian insurance market, *cit.*, p. 19; FCA, Price comparison websites in the general insurance sector, cit., p. 16.

[41] FCA, Price comparison websites in the general insurance sector, cit., p. 13, reported that such an authority sought participants' reactions to the statement 'the price comparison website may be owned by or is part of the same company as the insurance provider.' The statement was a cause for concern among many respondents. Few were sure if the statement was true, but many expressed concern that it may potentially bias results and undermine the assumed and expected impartiality of the PCWs and the search results they provide.

[42] IVASS, Investigation into comparison websites in the Italian insurance market, *cit.*, p. 13.

[43] IVASS Investigation into comparison websites in the Italian insurance market, *cit.*, p. 13, also reported that information on the extent of the commissions paid by each undertaking is sometimes provided in tabular and aggregate form and is, however, difficult to find on the website.

[44] IVASS, Investigation into comparison websites in the Italian insurance market, *cit.*, p. 13.

[45] IVASS, Investigation into comparison websites in the Italian insurance market, *cit.*, p. 14. In addition, the investigation also reported that the compared insurers are mainly online insurers because of their sales methods, which are not affected by the presence of a distribution network established on the territory, and by the characteristics of their technological infrastructure that fits in well with the typical propensities of web consumers, whose commercial choices are generally based on the criteria of speed in the acquisition of information and decision-making autonomy (see p. 7 ff.).

adequate for the clients' insurance needs because the insurance premium reflects the content of the insurance guarantee. A comparison carried out solely on price ends up comparing not homogeneous products, undermining the goodness of the comparison.[46]

The focus on price exacerbates the insurers' practice of stripping out features from the core product to be price competitive and to appear at the top of the quote rankings.[47] The compared products are often combined with other insurance products that offer insurance guarantees, ancillary to the compared products (add-ons), e.g. legal expenses cover, key cover, and courtesy car cover, which are included within the price quoted by other insurers. This combination is often automatic, and it takes place after the comparison carried out by the comparison website or, more often, by the insurer, and the comparison website is getting further commissions from this combination. Such an automatic combination is an element of opacity of the output, with potentially distorting effects in relation to the will expressed by the customer, the homogeneity and comparability of products, and the neutrality of comparison.[48] In addition, comparison websites do not always take reasonable steps to provide appropriate information about add-on policies, including the main features of the product, the price of the cover, the level of cover, and the main exclusions and limitations.[49]

Although based on the price, the comparison criteria are not clearly explained. The comparison websites usually have neither the tariff bases for the quoting of risks nor the power to grant discounts on premiums set by insurers. They need access to information to be made available by insurers, but they do not specify how often such information is updated.[50] Moreover, the variation of certain risk profiles, e.g. age or residence, sometimes prevents the listing by some insurers, without the comparison website justifying the failure to include these insurers in the panel compared to that specific risk profile.

The lack of information on the comparison criteria is a potential risk for the customer that could also ignore the existence of possible agreements between insurers and comparison websites. The comparison website may enter into an agreement with some insurers placing them among the top three on the list. This position, in fact, is likely to influence the customer's decision-making process, because of the brand strength of the insurer despite the possibility of it being in second or third place on the list.[51]

---

[46] IVASS, Investigation into comparison websites in the Italian insurance market, *cit.*, p. 15; FCA, Price comparison websites in the general insurance sector, cit., p. 13.

[47] FCA, Price comparison websites in the general insurance sector, cit., p.8.

[48] IVASS, Investigation into comparison websites in the Italian insurance market, *cit.*, p. 17 f.

[49] FCA, Price comparison websites in the general insurance sector, cit., p.10.

[50] IVASS, Investigation into comparison websites in the Italian insurance market, *cit.*, p. 16.

[51] IVASS, Investigation into comparison websites in the Italian insurance market, *cit.*, p. 16.

On the other hand, the absence of the insurer in the listing, which has been made with reference to certain risk profiles, may be not random. Conversely, it could reflect the choice of the insurer to evade the obligation to accept those risks, which is instead placed in some countries for car liability insurance.[52]

The lack of information on the comparison criteria does not allow to evaluate even the advertising aspect.[53] Messages such as "Best buy," "Products of the week," "Compare the best insures," "Save up to ..." are frequently advertised by comparison websites, but they are not verifiable because of missing information on the evaluation criteria adopted to support these claims. Their undue influence on the consumer's decision is not clear, as well as that deriving from statements such as 'it costs you nothing to use our service.' Statements of this sort could be misleading. While all of the above is true from a direct cost perspective, there is an indirect cost for the consumer, as insurers may include the fee they paid the comparison websites in determining the ultimate price of their product.[54]

A "dual capacity" of some comparison websites has also been reported.

The comparison covers only products of a class of insurance, usually car liability insurance, while the website is limited to providing estimates of the other classes, often in products offered by just one insurer.[55] Therefore, consumers find themselves in front of a tied agent instead of a broker. Many Member States, however, do not allow them to act in such a double *status*. In any case, the EU law requests intermediary to inform the customers on their contractual relationship with the insurer, concerning the contract that is provided (see Article 12 Directive 2002/92/EC), and the customer may not be informed by the comparison website on its dual contractual obligation.

On the other hand, some 'white labelled' comparison websites—firms which host and prominently brand under their own name a comparison tool provided by a third-party comparison website—did not have appropriate permissions because the host firm had introducer appointed representative permissions only, as they considered that they were doing no more than introducing the consumer to the third-party comparison website. However, the entire journey quote was prominently branded with the host firm's logo, so the consumers may be led to believe they were arranging their insurance policy with the host firm using the third-party comparison tool.[56]

[52] IVASS, Investigation into comparison websites in the Italian insurance market, cit., p. 15 f.

[53] IVASS, Investigation into comparison websites in the Italian insurance market, cit., p. 17 f.

[54] FCA, Price comparison websites in the general insurance sector, cit., p. 13; Atticus, Price comparison websites: Consumer market research, cit., p. 8.

[55] IVASS, Investigation into comparison websites in the Italian insurance market, cit., p.19.

[56] FCA, Price comparison websites in the general insurance sector, cit., p. 17. If the host firm was only introducing then, by prominently branding the entire quote journey with its own name, the host firm could be considered to be in breach of Principle 7 and ICOBS 2.2.2R.

With reference to data, consent to the processing of personal data is collected in ways that weaken the level of customer awareness on the consent made,[57] and the use of customer's data is often not clearly explained.[58]

During the data entry stage, comparison websites may require consumers to choose the amount of the excess, but the quote results did not always reflect the amount selected and the PCW often did not explain the difference between the two.[59] Moreover, preexisting medical conditions for travel insurance are not always clearly processed since no medical questions are asked or the questions are too vague.[60] This exposes consumers to a risk that they may buy a product under which they would be ineligible to make a claim.[61]

The process carried out to ensure the accuracy of data being transferred between comparison websites and the insurers must be performed regularly on an ongoing basis in order to avoid the consumers ending up with a policy that is unsuitable for their needs.[62]

Finally, an empirical research whose key aim was to provide insights into the consumer's journey when using comparison websites reports that consumers suggest improving this tool with reference to filter options and policy information.[63]

A series of filter options at the data entry stage of the comparison process would ensure that the search results delivered a smaller number of product options based on these preferences, allowing consumers to compare 'like with like' products. This would make consumers interact with product options more effectively and before the headline price in the search results dominates their attention.[64]

---

[57] IVASS, Investigation into comparison websites in the Italian insurance market, *cit.*, p. 18 f.; FCA, Price comparison websites in the general insurance sector, cit., p. 14.

[58] FCA, Price comparison websites in the general insurance sector, cit., p. 15 f. Comparison tools, Report from the Multi-Stakeholder Dialogue, cit., p.32 highlights, that the data submitted can be used for purposes that go beyond the simple operation of the comparison website, often without the consumer's explicit and informed consent. Selling "market data" is a source of revenue for some of the privately run comparison websites. From a regulatory point of view, this report recommended that, even though most of them claim that these data are aggregated and anonymised, attention must be paid to safeguarding consumer privacy, in accordance with the established legal framework on data protection.

[59] FCA, Price comparison websites in the general insurance sector, cit., p. 9.

[60] FCA, Price comparison websites in the general insurance sector, cit., p. 10, where reported as an example of vague question the following: 'do you have any pre-existing medical conditions?' without any explanation of what constituted a preexisting medical condition.

[61] FCA, Price comparison websites in the general insurance sector, cit., p. 11.

[62] FCA, Price comparison websites in the general insurance sector, cit., p. 16, reported instances where the data entered on the comparison website was not correctly transferred from the website to the insurer. For travel insurance, instances were found where the information on date of birth of additional insured persons and the date of travel did not transfer across accurately to the provider's website. A question for household insurance asked whether the property was located within 400 m from a river and was answered 'Yes.' When transferred over to the provider's website, the question changed to within 200 m of a river and the answer defaulted to 'No.'

[63] Atticus, Price comparison websites: Consumer market research, cit., p. 69 f.

[64] Atticus, Price comparison websites: Consumer market research, cit., p. 69.

Moreover, such empirical research shows that consumers identified a need for a more consistent approach to the information on the insurance policy. This should comprise a clear explanation of what is included, the level of cover, and excess amounts, allowing users to have an immediate and interactive feedback on the questions concerning the quote without feeling they are committed to buy.[65]

4 The EU Rules Applicable to the Comparison Websites

4.1 The Insurance Mediation Directive

After having explained the pros and cons of comparison websites, the analysis will now address the rules applicable to these tools, as well as their owners.[66]

The qualification of the comparison websites of insurance products as insurance intermediaries, under the EU law, depends on the concrete activities carried out.

Recalling the activities of the comparison websites, they range from activities such as providing links to insurance undertakings and/or intermediaries and providing quotes/rankings to the consumer to activities like giving quotes and

[65] Atticus, Price comparison websites: Consumer market research, cit., p. 70, where it is reported that consumers were looking for three levels of information:

1. search results: a basic summary of level of cover and add-ons included;
2. policy summary: accessible from the search results but labeled 'more detail' vs. 'buy now.' Key Facts would be the ideal at this stage being recognised, accessible and a consistent look, feel and content. Some spontaneously mentioned Key Facts as the optimal format, while others were prompted with a sample version during this stage in the research sessions;
3. policy schedule: available at the purchase stage on the insurer website and with full detail about the policy.

[66] A census of the applicable European legislation to comparison websites is made by EIOPA, Report on Good Practices on Comparison Websites, cit., p. 8, while a further analysis on the impact of this legislation on comparison tools is provided by comparison tools, Report from the Multi-Stakeholder Dialogue, cit., p. 9 ff. as well as the report produced under the Consumer Programme (2007–2013) called EAHC/FWC/2013 80 07, Study on the coverage, functioning and consumer use of comparison tools and third-party verification schemes for such tools, available at http://ec.europa.eu/consumers/consumer_evidence/market_studies/docs/final_report_study_on_comparison_tools.pdf, pp. 273 ff.

Depending on their business model, such websites must comply with several rules. This may include but may not be limited to the Insurance Mediation Directive (IMD—currently being repealed by IDD), the Financial Services Distance Marketing Directive (DMD), the Unfair Commercial Practices Directive, the E-commerce Directive, as well as the Data Protection Directive, Misleading and Comparative Advertising Directive, Consumer Rights Directive, Price Indication Directive, and Online Dispute Resolution (ODR) Regulation.

Nevertheless, EIOPA has deemed to issue good practices on comparison websites, as we are reporting in the text, while the abovementioned report "Comparison tools" recommended that work should have been undertaken at EU level to establish guidelines on horizontal principles for the transparency, impartiality, and reliability of comparison tools and to address issues specific to the functioning of these tools in key sectors of the EU Single Market (see p. 46 f.).

proposing a contract to the consumer. They can also present the details of insurance companies/intermediaries who offer the contracts and offer the consumer the possibility to close a contract at the end of the process.

Until the implementation in the EU Member States of Directive 2016/97 on insurance distribution, which must take place in early 2018, Directive 2002/92/EC on insurance mediation (IMD) provides a definition of insurance mediation as *the activities of introducing, proposing or carrying out other work preparatory to the conclusion of contracts of insurance, or of concluding such contracts, or of assisting in the administration and performance of such contracts, in particular in the event of a claim* (see Article 2, n.3), while the insurance intermediary is *any natural or legal person who, for remuneration, takes up or pursues insurance mediation* (see Article 2, n. 5).

The link to the insurer, which is often provided by the comparison websites, allows the customer to conclude the contract directly with the insurer. Therefore, comparison websites may argue that they are not under the obligation to provide the information listed in the IMD because they are not mediating the insurance contract. However, the link to the insurer falls into the *other work preparatory to the conclusion of contracts of insurance* because it allows customers to conclude directly an insurance contract at the end of the comparison process. Accordingly, these comparison websites should be regarded as insurance intermediaries and therefore be subject to the requirements of IMD, as opposed to websites that simply enable consumers to compare information from various providers.

However, IMD is a minimum harmonization Directive. This allows Member States to implement such a Directive into national legislation in a way that may be "not convergent" to its definitions. Accordingly, the comparison websites, which allow customers to buy the presented products, could be considered as insurance intermediaries in some of the Member States but not all. In any event, the business conduct rules set forth by IMD do not cover many of the reported criticalities arising from the comparison websites because the latter did not exist when the IMD was drawn up.

In addition, the website owner is often a legal person other than the person charged to carry out the comparison, this at least if the compared products fall among the financial services as in the case of insurance products. Such a splitting allows the site owner to carry out the comparison of a plurality of financial products through subsidiaries that are eligible to carry out the insurance mediation and also banking or financial brokerage as in the case of mortgages or loans. The site owner, therefore, could be neither regulated nor supervised by the insurance authorities because the current regulation and supervision is addressed to the intermediaries and the insurers. As a result, a possible joint liability of the site owner, together with the insurance intermediary, is certainly questionable, at least in relation to the acts adopted by the supervisory authority.

4.2 The Unfair Commercial Practices Directive

If the current version of the IMD does not seem effective to protect prospective policyholders through comparison websites, Directive 2005/29/EC on Unfair Commercial Practices could be rather useful for this purpose.

Such a Directive applies to business-to-consumer commercial practices,[67] setting forth a general ban on commercial unfair practices.[68] It covers all sectors of the economic life with no exception, while Member States may impose requirements, which are more restrictive or prescriptive than the Directive, in relation to financial services (see Article 3, para. 9).

The commercial practice is referred to the 'trader,' who is either *any natural or legal person who, in commercial practices covered by this Directive, is acting for purposes relating to his trade, business, craft or profession* or *anyone acting in the name of or on behalf of a trader*. This definition includes both insurance undertakings and insurance intermediaries, but the website owner should also fall within the definition regardless of whether he is an insurance intermediary.

A 2011 study on the application of Directive 2005/29/EC in the EU, which had been commissioned by the EU Commission, reported that the most common unfair commercial practices in financial services fall into these three categories: (*i*) essential information not included in advertising, (*ii*) misdescribed product, (*iii*) risks about the product or service not being made clear.[69]

Recalling the findings of the surveys on comparison websites of insurance products, which have been promoted by consumer's associations and insurance supervisory authorities, the provisions of Directive 2005/29/EC could be a useful deterrent to the issues raised by these surveys, at least in principle. This could be the case of several issues, such as the advertised market coverage/number of insurers compared, the savings indeed achieved by virtue of comparison provided by the website, the suitability of the insurance products, which are tailored according to their price rather than their characteristics, to the needs of the customers.

The above mentioned study, however, highlights that a very important factor of unfair commercial practices law is its enforceability and enforcement. To this purpose, the study reveals a clear connection between the sector-specific rules (if going beyond the standards of Directive 2005/29/EC) and enforcement issues.[70]

---

[67] According to Article 2, let. d), of the Directive 2005/29/EC, business-to-consumer commercial practices means *any act, omission, course of conduct or representation, commercial communication including advertising and marketing, by a trader, directly connected with the promotion, sale or supply of a product to consumers.*

[68] Article 5 states that a commercial practice shall be unfair if (*i*) it is contrary to the requirements of professional diligence and (*ii*) it materially distorts or is likely to materially distort the economic behavior with regard to the product of the average consumer whom it reaches or to whom it is addressed or of the average member of the group when a commercial practice is directed to a particular group of consumers.

[69] Civic Consulting, *Study on the application of Directive 2005/29/EC on Unfair Commercial Practices in the EU*, 2011, p. 82.

[70] Civic Consulting, *Study on the application of Directive 2005/29/EC on Unfair Commercial Practices in the EU*, 2011, p. 160.

Many Member States have reported difficulties in enforcing unfair commercial practices law as derived from Directive 2005/29/EC,[71] with its open-textured provisions that wait to be concretized by case law.[72] The situation is aggravated in Member States where the designated enforcement body risks having to bear the litigation costs.[73]

4.3 The Enforcement of the Unfair Commercial Practices Directive. A 2015 Case on Comparison Websites of Insurance Product Assessed by the Italian Competition Authority

Despite these limits, the application of Directive 2005/29/EC to comparison websites of insurance products was the subject of two decisions in 2015 of the Italian Competition Authority in charge of protecting customers from unfair commercial practices under the Italian law.[74]

The proceedings opened on October 2014 investigated possible unfair commercial practices. These practices concerned (*i*) the lack of transparency of information included in comparison tool websites with respect to their business model, this with specific reference to their source of income since they act as brokers for insurance companies and, as a consequence, the potential impartiality of the comparison mechanism; (*ii*) the lack of information about the coverage of the comparison (name and/or total market share of the insurance firms included in the comparison) and the ranking criteria; (*iii*) possible misleading claims concerning savings advertised by the comparison tool, this because it was not clear whether those savings could be obtained simply through the use of the comparison websites or whether they were in fact already offered by the insurance companies, sometimes under specific conditions; (*iv*) the "opt-out" mechanism for optional covers. The comparison results—sometimes and for some insurance companies only—included covers such as third-party liability, fire, and car theft insurance, even when the consumer asked for car insurance only

[71] Civic Consulting, *Study on the application of Directive 2005/29/EC on Unfair Commercial Practices in the EU*, 2011, p. 160.

[72] To this purpose, see Collins H., A Private Right of Redress for Unfair Commercial Practices. A Report for Consumer Focus, April 2009, http://www.consumerfocus.org.uk/assets/1/files/2009/08/A-Private-Right-of-Redress-for-Unfair-Commercial-Practices-Hugh-Collins.pdf.

[73] In order to overcome this limits, the abovementioned Study highlights that *two elements of national rules have often been mentioned to mediate that risk: a greater level of detail, and the avoidance of the Directive's 'transactional decision making' test that is felt to make the success of litigation less calculable. At the same time, this type of regulation increases legal certainty, as the assessment of what is allowed and what is not is easier for all sides.*

[74] Autorità Garante della Concorrenza e del Mercato, Cases PS9212 and PS9518, *Bollettino n. 14* del 27 aprile 2015, pp. 64 ff., available on www.agcm.it.

(mandatory by law). Sometimes, the results even included optional covers different from those asked by the consumer.

The Italian Competition Authority opened these proceedings because the described conducts could qualify as misleading information and omission and allegedly infringe Articles 6 and 7 of Directive 2005/29/EC, as transposed into Articles 21 and 22 of the Italian Consumer Code.

The lack of transparency on the characteristics of the service, the real source of the savings advertised on comparison tools, and the lack of information on the actual insurance firms included in the comparison could deceive the average consumer and cause him to take a transactional decision that he would not have taken otherwise.

Moreover, the conflict of interest of the intermediary is not properly managed. The lack of transparency concerning the economic incentives that the intermediary receives for each policy sold, which is a fee differing among companies and depending on the additional covers sold, likely deceives consumers about the impartiality of the comparison tool.

Finally, the "opt out" provisions on additional covers and the inclusion in the comparison results of policies which have not been requested by the consumer might alter the ranking, thus inducing consumers to choose those companies and policies that ensure more profits for the comparison tool itself, distorting consumers' economic choices.

To address the concerns stated by the Authority in starting the proceedings, parties offered commitments that include the following proposals:

(*i*) to provide detailed information on the website about the business model of the comparison tool, also disclosing the names of the insurance companies that have commercial agreements with the website, the companies included in the comparison and their total market share, and the fees gained from each insurance company;

(*ii*) to provide on the website more transparent information on how savings are calculated (either when they derive from a mere comparison between competitors or when they stem from specific tariffs applied by the comparison website);

(*iii*) to offer additional and optional covers only through an opt-in mechanism.

The Italian Competition Authority accepted the commitments proposed by the parties and, as set by the procedural rules, made them mandatory and did not assess whether the conducts infringed the Consumer Code.

The Decisions above, however, raise some concerns at least on the compliance of the commitments assumed by the parties on the transparency of the business model and how the advertised savings are calculated, which does not seem to protect effectively customers as Directive 2005/29/EC would aspire to do.

As regards the business model, the websites claim that the insurance intermediary, which is carrying out the comparison, belongs entirely to the website owner. However, the websites do not reveal who their owner is. This makes it easy to keep information that is essential to allow the customer to understand the reliability of the comparison hidden.

Both websites are still advertising that customers can, respectively, "Save up to 500€*" and "Save up to 800€*." The asterisk on the symbol of the euro should lead the customer to read a link below that states, in a much smaller font than that used for advertising, "Find out how we calculate the savings." The Calculation of savings is based on the average of the differences between the more expensive and the cheapest gross premium compared to estimates calculated periodically on the website.

One of the websites fails to declare the frequency of the update, while the other states that it is monthly. In neither of the cases, however, the data used for this purpose were shown. Above all, the mathematical or statistical rule under which the difference, at a given time, between the more expensive and the cheapest premium should always be equal to the sum advertised before that particular time is unknown: the savings possibly obtained in the past are not a guarantee of similar savings when comparing. Likewise, it is difficult to exclude the persistence of a deceptive message by reading that calculation of savings advertised on 13 February 2016 is based on data collected in September 2014. How long can a statistical survey be advertised before ceasing to be trusted?

5 The Upcoming EU Rules Applicable to Comparison Websites

5.1 The Insurance Distribution Directive

Current gaps in the EU rules applicable to comparison websites, especially with regard to the prevention of their misconducts, are inconsistent with the demand for clarity in order to protect the millions of consumers who are accessing services offered by the comparison websites.

The new Directive 2016/97 on insurance distribution (IDD) shall be implemented by February 2018. It repeals the current IMD on insurance mediation, but it is not decisive on these aspects.

IDD sets forth a definition of "insurance distribution" instead of "insurance mediation." This new definition states, *inter alia*, that "The provision of information concerning one or more insurance contracts in accordance with criteria selected by customers through a website or other media and the compilation of an insurance ranking list, including price and products comparison, or a discount on the price of an insurance contract, when the customer is able to directly or indirectly conclude an insurance contract using a website or other media shall be considered to be insurance distribution" (see Article 2, para. 2, let. a).[75]

[75] Conversely, Recital n. 13 states that IDD *should not apply to mere introducing activities consisting of the provision of data and information on potential policyholders to insurance or reinsurance intermediaries or undertakings or of information about insurance or reinsurance products or an insurance or reinsurance intermediary or undertaking to potential policyholders.*

According to such a definition, the website owner should fall within the scope of the Directive as an insurance intermediary,[76] but IDD will apply only to the entity that is providing intermediation in case of splitting between ownership of the website and intermediation through the comparison website.

Conversely, IDD does not apply to websites managed by public authorities or consumers' associations, which do not aim at the conclusion of any contract and merely compare insurance products available on the market (see Recital 12). The final text of IDD no longer includes the phrase *without being remunerated*, unlike the previous one. Therefore, IDD allows consumers' associations to charge customers for the access to their comparison website, but the derogation in favor of such associations should require that providers of insurance products do not remunerate them, directly or indirectly.

The upcoming Directive, however, is still based on principles, which need to be implemented into domestic legislations by the Member States. There are a few detailed rules concerning the information on the intermediary, its contractual relationship with customers and insurers, the nature of its remuneration, but no specific rule is addressed to comparison websites.

IDD does not replicate the contents of Directive 2014/92/EU of 23 July 2014 on payment accounts, which acknowledges that <<*independent comparison websites are an effective means for consumers to assess the merits of different payment account offers in one place*>> (Recital n.22), and accordingly it includes a list of provisions to which the comparison websites must comply (see Article 7).[77]

IDD pursues the harmonization by requiring Member States to implement into national legislation the following principles: (*i*) an insurance distributor acts

---

[76] Article 2 of the IDD sets forth the definition of "insurance distributor," i.e. any insurance intermediary, ancillary insurance intermediary, or insurance undertaking, while 'insurance intermediary' means any natural or legal person, other than an insurance or reinsurance undertaking or their employees and other than an ancillary insurance intermediary, who, for remuneration, takes up or pursues the activity of insurance distribution.

[77] According to article 7, comparison websites, which can be operated either by a private operator or by a public authority, shall

(a)	be operationally independent by ensuring that payment service providers are given equal treatment in search results;
(b)	clearly disclose their owners;
(c)	set out clear, objective criteria on which the comparison will be based;
(d)	use plain and unambiguous language and, where applicable, the standardised terms set out in the final list referred to in Article 3(5);
(e)	provide accurate and up-to-date information and state the time of the last update;
(f)	include a broad range of payment account offers covering a significant part of the market and, where the information presented is not a complete overview of the market, a clear statement to that effect, before displaying results; and
(g)	provide an effective procedure to report incorrect information on published fees.

honestly, fairly, and professionally in accordance with its customers' best interests; (*ii*) all information related to the subject of the IDD, including marketing communications, addressed by insurance distributors to customers or potential customers shall be fair, clear, and not misleading, as well as marketing communications shall be clearly identifiable as such; (*iii*) insurance distributors are not remunerated in a way that conflicts with their duty to act in their customers' best interest.[78]

As regards conflict of interests, IDD now requests insurance intermediaries to inform customers whether, in relation to the insurance contract, they work, *inter alia*, on the basis of other types of remuneration, including an economic benefit of any kind offered or given in connection with the insurance contract.

Both principles and detailed rules refer to all insurance intermediaries, but Member States should not overlook the distinctive features of each of them. Specific rules would be desirable for the comparison websites, when the critical issues are referring only, or mainly, to these intermediaries.

Member States might consider the rules addressed to comparison websites as rules protecting the "general good" in order to avoid regulatory arbitrage to the detriment of their respective residents.[79] Comparison websites that are based in a Member State without specific regulations on this tool/intermediary could take an advantage of this lack of regulation by carrying out their activities under the freedom of services to the customers who are located in the host Member States that have set forth rules on comparison websites.[80]

In conclusion, the lack of harmonized rules on comparison websites could lead to different rules in the Member States. These rules would probably be considered of general good hindering the cross-border operations of the comparison websites.[81]

[78] In particular, an insurance distributor shall not make any arrangement by way of remuneration, sales targets, or otherwise that could provide an incentive to itself or its employees to recommend a particular insurance product to a customer when the insurance distributor could offer a different insurance product that would better meet the customer's needs (see Article 17, para 3).

[79] To this purpose, Article 9 of IDD does not affect the power of the host Member State to take the measures set forth in such an Article, where the relevant activity is entirely or principally directed towards the territory of the host Member State with the sole purpose of avoiding the legal provisions, which would be applicable if that insurance distributors had its residence or registered office in that host Member State and, in addition, where its activity seriously endangers the proper functioning of insurance and reinsurance markets in the host Member State as regards the protection of consumers.

[80] With reference to general good, the IDD sets forth that Member States shall establish a single point of contact responsible for providing information on general good rules in their respective Member State. Therefore, EIOPA shall include on its website the hyperlinks to the websites of competent authorities where information on general good rules is published. In addition, EIOPA shall examine in a report and inform the Commission about the general good rules published by Member States in the context of the proper functioning of the IDD and the Internal Market before 23 February 2019 (see Article 11).

[81] In general terms, the importance of improving cross-border operation of the price comparison websites is highlighted by consumer representatives; see Comparison tools, *Report from the Multi-Stakeholder Dialogue*, cit., p.28 f.

On the other hand, national regulators could fail to introduce appropriate rules to neutralize the reported criticalities raised by the comparison websites, and this lack or inadequacy of the rules might be detrimental to the customer's protection.

5.2 *The Product Oversight and the System of Governance: The Monitoring Role of the Insurance Undertakings*

The activity of the comparison website should also be monitored by the insurance undertakings. This statement comes from some rules of the IDD and Solvency II.

The IDD requires insurance undertakings—and, in those jurisdictions where this is the case, even insurance intermediaries manufacturing insurance products for sale to costumers—to have a product oversight (see Article 25). The aim of this oversight is to include the customers' protection within the strategies of the insurance undertakings starting from the process of designing a new insurance product. Insurance undertakings have to identify a target market of customers for each product, the distribution strategy shall be consistent with the identified target market, and insurers shall take reasonable steps to ensure that the insurance product is distributed to the identified target market. All appropriate information on the insurance product and the product approval process, including the identified target market, shall be made available to any distributor.

Therefore, comparison websites should acknowledge this information and make the comparison accordingly, while the insurance undertakings shall assess at least whether the product remains consistent with the needs of the identified target market and whether the intended distribution strategy remains appropriate (see Article 25).

The more the target is specific, the less comparison websites will be able to compare it with other targets. However, insurance undertakings cannot ignore how the products are compared because they are responsible for monitoring the appropriateness of the distribution strategy under the product oversight, while, in case the identified target is too broad and "fits all," insurance undertakings run the risk of noncompliance with Article 25 in front of the supervisory authority.

The noncompliance risk should be included in the risk-management system requested by Solvency II for insurance and reinsurance undertakings (see Article 44). This system must be effective, and it comprises strategies, processes, and reporting procedures necessary to identify, measure, monitor, manage, and report, on a continuous basis, the risks, at an individual and at an aggregated level, to which (re)insurance undertakings are or could be exposed, and their interdependencies.

The risk-management system is a key function of the system of governance of (re)insurance undertakings, which provides for sound and prudent management of the business (see Article 41 of Solvency II). Therefore, the risk-management system shall cover the risks to be included in the calculation of the Solvency Capital Requirement, as well as the risks that are not or not fully included in the calculation thereof because they can also affect the business of the (re)insurance undertakings (see Article 44).

An insurance undertaking, whose product is listed as the most expensive or one of the most expensive by the comparison websites, should not ignore such a result.

If the comparison websites show that the premium charged for the insurance product issued by an insurer is higher than that of the other insurers, the system of governance of such an insurer should assess whether its underwriting process works properly.[82]

Although not explicitly mentioned in Article 44 of Solvency II, the materialization of strategic and reputational risks could have a potential impact on the business of the undertaking. Therefore, they are included within the Guidelines on the system of governance issued by EIOPA to implement Solvency II.[83]

An insurance undertaking should ascertain how the comparison is made, i.e. the parameters taken into consideration by the comparison websites, and ultimately whether the products being compared are homogeneous in terms of risks, conditions, and so on, this in order to assess whether the comparison is affecting its reputation and considering the expectations of stakeholders and the sensitivity of the market, as well as the impact on its business strategies.

It is difficult to predict whether and how such a monitoring of insurance undertakings on comparison websites affects actual techniques of comparison. However, this "induced-supervision" of the insurance undertakings could help increase the transparency of the comparison websites, even though it might not be the only decisive factor.

5.3 *The Good Practices on Comparison Websites Issued by EIOPA*

EIOPA takes a leading role in promoting transparency, simplicity, and fairness in the market for consumer financial products or services across the internal market,

[82] To this purpose, see EIOPA, *Guidelines on system of governance*, January 2015, available at https://eiopa.europa.eu/Publications/Consultations/EIOPA_EIOPA-BoS-14-253-Final%20report_Governance.pdf, in particular Guideline n. 20—Underwriting and reserving risk management policy.

[83] See EIOPA, *Guidelines on system of governance*, cit., in particular Guideline n. 23—Strategic and reputational risk.

including, *inter alia*, (*i*) collecting, analyzing, and reporting on consumer trends[84] and (*ii*) contributing to the development of common disclosure rules.[85]

EIOPA identified comparison websites as an emerging consumer trend in the EU in 2012. After a consultation paper in 2013, EIOPA issued good practices on Comparison Websites in 2014. These good practices are not legally binding on national competent authorities or financial institutions and are not subject to the "comply or explain" mechanism provided by the Article 16 of Regulation 1094/2010 establishing EIOPA. Nevertheless, EIOPA expects these good practices to be adopted by the relevant market players on a voluntary basis and may serve as reference for further work by national competent authorities.

The good practices issued by EIOPA concern primarily the activities of commercial comparison websites, but non-commercial websites' operators are equally encouraged to check whether their practices are in line with the good practices and to adapt them accordingly, if needed.

Good practices are related to many of the critical issues that have been outlined above.

The information provided on the comparison websites about the website itself, its operation, and the contact details must appear on the website, and they shall be given in a clear and easy-to-find way.

The market coverage shall be communicated transparently and in a way that makes it easy for Internet users to locate and understand it. To this purpose, disclosure is requested on how many products the website compares per type of policy, as well as the number of insurers whose products are compared and their names, while the comparison website shall clearly go into details on how the implemented criteria has selected the insurers.

Internet users need to be aware of the different factors that may influence the comparison website's results. Therefore, EIOPA considers it good practice for a comparison website to disclose those providers with whom a comparison website has a commercial, contractual, or ownership relationship and explain the meaning of "Editor's choice," "product of the week," "most popular," "best buy" features and the information on which they are based. Recalling the criticism towards the decisions of the Italian Antitrust Authority, such good practice should be implemented avoiding loopholes in the information addressed to the customer. Therefore, disclosure must be provided either to the insurance intermediary which is carrying out the comparison or the owner of the website.

---

[84] EIOPA Regulation does not provide a definition of the term "consumer trend." EIOPA therefore devised the following working definition: *Evolutions in consumer behavior in the insurance and pensions markets related to the relationship between consumers and undertakings (including intermediaries) that are significant in their impact or novelty.* The term "Trends" must be understood in a broad sense; it means, for example, evolutions in volume, evolution in the way the relationship between customers and undertakings/intermediaries is determined, and also evolutions on certain practices or types of plans or products that are only emerging in the market and which can play a significant role in the future.

[85] See Article 9, para. 1, Regulation n.1094/2010 establishing EIOPA.

Good practices are also related to the criteria used to make the ranking. To this purpose, comparison websites shall ensure a consistent listing of product features, i.e. present clearly and in detail main features and characteristics of products, insurance cover, and limitations (e.g., deductibles, threshold, limits, exclusions, etc.). On a given comparison website, a standardized form should be used for all selected products to allow easy comparison, so as not to use price as the sole criterion for comparison, and allow Internet users to select a balanced listing of product features, other than price (such as the type of guarantee, exclusions, or limitation clauses), enhancing the list of criteria, when necessary. The more complex a product, the more criteria (other than price) may need to be taken into consideration when comparing products. If the comparison website chooses not to disclose all the quotes, then the criteria used to select the products should be explained.

The presented comparable information shall include the main features and characteristics of products, insurance cover, and limitations such as deductibles, thresholds, limits, exclusions, etc., as well as the length of the validity of the quote. Information shall be presented in a manner that is uniform and appropriate for the complexity of the products and shall be communicated in a clear and simple language avoiding jargon and unnecessary technical terms as much as possible. Information on price will show either the final premium or details of all fees and charges to be paid by the customer.

Finally, the comparison websites must publish accurate and up-to-date information disclosing the date of the latest update before the search for products is initiated. Recalling the criticism towards the decisions of the Italian Competition Authority, this good practice should be interpreted as the prohibition of the advertising of data that are outdated. In addition, Member States should request to report periodically to the supervisory authorities on the statistical evidence that has been used, as well as advertised, by comparison websites.

In conclusion, good practices issued by EIOPA can be appreciated as a very useful tool for Member States, that are requested to introduce national rules to both implement IDD and neutralize the criticalities arising from the comparison websites. The national regulations should be as harmonized as possible to EIOPA's suggestions in order to ensure a level playing field across the EU for comparison websites and customers.

6 Possible Developments in the Comparison of Insurance Products and New Challenges for Regulators

Good practices, overseen by insurers, and the expected national regulations on comparison websites aim to achieve a Single Market in the EU for what concern the protection of customers and the freedom of the intermediaries.

Marketing strategies, however, have been evolving as quickly as technology and they are now threatening to make regulations that are laboriously close to being adopted in the Member States of the EU obsolete.

A survey highlights that it is important to distinguish comparison websites from "reviews," where "consumers" indicate their assessment of products or services.[86] These Web pages, which are often trusted by consumers, cause many problems of credibility because their validation process is not guaranteed, many fake consumers participate in the process, and the uploading of negative comments is sometimes prevented.[87] These types of shortcomings lead to consumer detriment and put into question the credibility of the more respectable websites. Therefore, it is essential to also regulate and monitor the observance of the rules of consumer information, the absence of misleading messages, and unfair marketing practices for those Web pages.[88] The challenge is to find a balance between an efficient system for the gathering of user reviews and an effective control mechanism to avoid abuses.[89]

Another survey highlights the interest of consumers in alternative comparison models and services.[90]

Collective switching websites are used to approach electricity and gas providers. These websites allow consumers to act as a group, registering their household, along with others, to build a group in order to negotiate a better deal with their gas and electricity suppliers. There is no set model for how individual schemes will operate; however, a third party who works on behalf of the members of the group will usually facilitate this kind of activity.[91]

It can be speculated that a third party may aggregate consumers through the website in the near future in order to facilitate their purchase of insurance products, such as car liability insurance or householder insurance. If so, the regulation should at least clarify (*i*) if the process of initially registering an interest via the website—or of actually signing a deal it generates—is binding, i.e. if registered consumers are under obligation to accept the offer once it is acknowledged, and (*ii*) if the insurer is entitled to raise premium further down the line, e.g. in order to offset the loss of one or more households who may drop off the scheme later on or in the case of increased claims rate.

Another possible evolution of the current model of the comparison websites may be the data analyzer service. This tool can help consumers analyze detailed data on their consumption patterns to come up with the most suitable deal compared to the consumer's lifestyle and usage,[92] and it is currently used for mobile phones.

---

[86] Comparison Tools, *Report from the Multi-Stakeholder Dialogue*, cit., p. 22; BEUC *Position Paper on Comparison Websites, cit.*, p. 3.

[87] Comparison Tools, *Report from the Multi-Stakeholder Dialogue*, cit., p. 22. BEUC *Position Paper on Comparison Websites, cit.*, p. 3.

[88] BEUC *Position Paper on Comparison Websites, cit.*, p. 3.

[89] Comparison Tools, *Report from the Multi-Stakeholder Dialogue*, cit., p. 22.

[90] Consumer Futures, 73 ff. reports that 64 percent of consumers in the qualitative study say that they are interested in an alternative price comparison service for insurance.

[91] See Department of Energy & Climate Change, *Collective Purchasing and Switching: What consumers need to know*, available at https://www.gov.uk/government/uploads/system/uploads/attachment_data/file/36699/5368-collective-purchasing--guidance-for-consumers.pdf.

[92] On the advisability of regulating RECAP (Record, Evaluate and Compare Alternative Prices), see Thaler R., Sunstein C., Nudge. Improving Decision About Health, Wealth and Happiness, Yale

When applied to insurance products, data shall be referred to the consumer's risk profile and the service should replace or supplement the current comparison based solely or mainly on the price. Data compared will be not related to information on actual consumption as for the mobile phones, but they should be the result of targeted questions that are proposed to the customer in order to reconstruct his preferences and needs. Therefore, the insurance proposal that results from the analysis would be considered as a personal recommendation to the customer because it is based on data that refer to his/her risk profile.

Such a characterization of the proposal is likely to be relevant under the IDD.

The IDD shall introduce the definition of 'advice', as *the provision of a personal recommendation to a customer, either upon their request or at the initiative of the insurance distributor in respect of one or more insurance contracts* (see Article 2, n. 15). In addition, IDD requests Member States to ensure that in good time before the conclusion of an insurance contract, an insurance intermediary provides the customers with, *inter alia*, the information on the intermediary's obligation in relation to the contract proposed or advised upon (see Article 19, para. 1(c)).

Therefore, proposals resulting from data analyzer service, together with, or without, the comparison of prices, can be characterized as a piece of advice based on a fair and personal analysis. Accordingly, such a proposal would fall into the provisions set forth by IDD under which (*i*) where advice is provided prior to the conclusion of any specific contract, the insurance intermediary shall provide the customer with a personalized recommendation explaining why a particular product would best meet the customer's demands and needs (see Article 20, para. 3); (*ii*) when the insurance intermediary informs the customer that the advice it provides is based on a fair and personal analysis, it is obliged to give that advice on the basis of an analysis of a sufficiently large number of insurance contracts available on the market, to enable it to make a recommendation, in accordance with professional criteria, regarding which insurance contract would be adequate to meet the customer's needs (Article 20, para 5).

The suggested characterization should also be able to attenuate the concern about the fact that new technologies give companies unprecedented power in profiling consumers, resulting in social sorting and segmentation and ultimately price discrimination, i.e. by offering the same products at different prices based on individual users' online profiles.[93]

The third possible evolution of the comparison websites could be a dedicated price comparison app for smartphones. These apps give consumers the opportunity to undertake price comparisons "anytime, anywhere." Therefore, they can help

University Press, 2008, pp. 95 f.; Kamenica E. et all, Helping Consumers Known Themselves, in American Economic Review, vol. 101, 3, 2011, 417 ff.

[93] See Comparison Tools, *Report from the Multi-Stakeholder Dialogue*, cit., p. 24, where the concern that personalized pricing may in certain cases lead to higher prices and therefore be detrimental for consumers—as businesses are likely to propose the maximum price that a consumer is willing to pay. Prices offered to an impulsive buyer could be higher than those offered to buyers whose profile shows that they usually visit different sites before purchasing.

consumers find the best deal online and in-store because they range across barcode scanners, deal aggregators and online shopping.

The considerations made for the other tools are to be proposed for this, depending on their concrete mode of operation when applied to insurance products. Such tools could allow a greater reaction of the consumers in front of "emotional" insurance offers, namely bids that the insurer or intermediary submits to the purchaser when the latter begins to face certain risks, e.g., buying a sky pass or travel tickets. In a nutshell, the app could help consumers face new forms of door-to-door sale, whether or not the app complies with the rules that should apply to comparison websites.

Insurance Companies and E-Marketing Activities: An Empirical Analysis in the Italian Market

Andrada Comanac, Paola Musile Tanzi, and Fabio Ancarani

Contents

Abstract The relationship between insurance companies and digital technologies has been studied less than the one of the banking industry. The first step in this process was to review some relevant literature about e-marketing and e-service quality (e-SQ) in service industries—with particular focus on the insurance and banking industries. On this basis, we develop a framework for assessing e-SQ and

A. Comanac (✉)
Inspiration Services – Digital strategy, BTO, Milan, Italy
e-mail: andrada.comanac@btoresearch.com

P.M. Tanzi
Department of Economics, University of Perugia, Perugia, Italy

SDA Bocconi – School of Management, Milan, Italy
e-mail: Paola.musiletanzi@unipg.it; paola.musiletanzi@sdabocconi.it

F. Ancarani
SDA Bocconi – School of Management, Milan, Italy

Department of Management, Alma Mater Studiorum, University of Bologna, Bologne, Italy
e-mail: fabioguido.ancarani@unibo.it

P. Marano et al. (eds.), *The "Dematerialized" Insurance*,
DOI 10.1007/978-3-319-28410-1_4

e-marketing activities for insurance companies, both traditional and native digital, and we tested our research hypotheses in an empirical setting for the Italian market.

This study identified six dimensions of e-service, drawn from items previously tested by Kaynama and Black (A proposal to assess the service quality of online travel agencies: an exploratory study. J Prof Serv Mark 21(1): 63–88, 2000), Sohn and Tadisina (Development of e-service quality measure for Internet-based financial institutions. Total Qual Manag 19(9): 903–918, 2008), Van Riel et al. (E-service quality expectations: a case study. Total Qual Manag 14(4): 437–450, 2003), and Zeithaml et al. (Service quality delivery through web sites: a critical review of extant knowledge. J Acad Mark Sci 30(4): 362–375, 2002), that explain a high proportion of the variance of e-SQ. As expected, the six factors have a positive impact on both willingness to use the website and Net Promoter Score (NPS). Ease of use becomes fundamental on first impact with the consumer, especially for an e-commerce activity, differently than in previous work in which trust and reliability were considered to be of supreme value (Parasuraman and Grewal 2000; Service quality delivery through web sites: a critical review of extant knowledge. J Acad Mark Sci 30(4): 362–375, 2002). Moreover, trust was found to positively and directly influence consumers' decisions to promote their experience on a website. This dimension is highly correlated with the level of safety and reassurance the insurance company gives to consumers. Web aesthetics play a significant role when consumers evaluate website quality, as suggested in Zeithaml et al.'s (E-service quality: definition, dimensions and conceptual model. Marketing Science Institute, Cambridge, 2000) work but lacking in the majority of prior research. Reliability, in the Italian market, is the one factor that, contrary to similar research, was found to be less important when judging e-commerce; Wolfinbarger and Gilly (eTailQ: dimensionalizing, measuring and predicting eTail quality. J Retail 79(3): 183–198, 2003) and Zeithaml (Service excellent in electronic channels. Manag Serv Qual 12(3): 135–138, 2002) found reliability to be the most important factor in financial services, whereas in the Italian market it was proven otherwise.

Following Parasuraman et al. (2005) definition that reliability means the accuracy of the promised service, we find it to be relevant even upon first encounter with a website. Content, not surprisingly, has been found to be significant and important in this analysis. Consumers are demanding and have high expectations online (Valarie and Bitner 2000); thus, it is no wonder that consumers do not tolerate low content-adequateness. The last significant dimension in our study is responsiveness. This feature deals with courtesy, communication, and problem handling by customer service. Even if for a possible new consumer this might not be a critical issue, investing in responsiveness variable might offer additional comfort about client's security and on how his data is treated. Past researchers (Measuring the service quality of internet banking: scale development and validation. Eur Bus Rev 22.1: 5–24, 2010; Measurement of service quality in Internet banking: the development of an instrument. J Mark Manag 20(1–2): 185–207, 2004; Measuring service quality in Internet banking: the case of Hong Kong. J Int Consum Mark 17(4): 99–116, 2005) maintain this variable's importance as well. Last but not least, it was seen that customization is not to be a relevant and significant factor in the hypothesis testing.

Based on the research findings, we would recommend to companies to always work on improving their service quality online and understand ex ante what consumers are looking for when they are online. Ease of use and trust must receive proper attention if consumers should be satisfied with a company standard service. However, different opportunities lie in dealing with aesthetics and content of the online proposal in order to differentiate the service from the competitors.

1 Introduction

The integration within nations of information technology, in terms of developments in telecommunications and Internet technologies, has considerably changed how financial services conduct business. Many predicted that the existence of information technology would transform all businesses, especially services (Harridge-March and Quinton 2009). Because almost everyone now has access to the World Wide Web, many institutions, including financial organizations, have launched websites: for some initially just to save money, then for some because it created competitive advantages or because they thought customers would benefit from a superior service value (Yakhlef 1998). The invention of the Internet and creation of electronic devices have simplified the relationship between institutions and their customers, at a reduced cost. The traditional human-to-human interaction is being challenged and often replaced by human-to-machine interface, to the convenience of consumers (Odoyo and Nyangosi 2011).

The relationship between insurance companies and digital technologies has been studied less than that of banking companies; thus, in this paper we seek to contribute and to interpret the conceptualized framework accepted by the literature in the insurance industry. Insurance has been considered less appealing because consumers describe it as "a necessary evil" (Gidhagen and Persson 2011). Banking services are becoming an everyday routine if we think about conducting financial transactions, checking credit accounts, and making online payments. Basically, insurance consumers interact with the insurance companies when requesting an estimate or paying a premium or filing a report or a claim, activities that appear to be conducted less frequently than those associated with banking (Järvinen et al. 2001; Gidhagen 2002).

This need raises two important issues that an insurance company must consider with respect to banks: how useful do consumers perceive the company website to be, and how comfortable do consumers feel using the online service, hence interacting virtually with the company itself?

While the pattern of consumer behavior is changing in concomitance with the evolution of the technology in the delivery of financial services, there is also a need to build customer confidence and trust in such systems. Mainly, this happens because consumers are not yet prepared to avail themselves of this technological service delivery, and there is proof of human frustration while interacting with the digital interface (Parasuraman et al. 2000).

This chapter is structured as follows. We first review some relevant literature about e-marketing and e-service quality (e-SQ) in service industries—mainly in the insurance and banking industries. On the basis of this literature review, we then develop a framework for assessing e-SQ and e-marketing activities for insurance companies. We develop our research hypotheses, test them in an empirical setting in the Italian market, and present and discuss the results. We derive implications for companies and discuss limitations and further directions for future research.

2 Marketing, Technology, and Insurance Framework

Most of the research related to e-marketing and e-service quality addresses the banking rather than the insurance sector. As a result of continuous environmental and technological changes, the insurance industry has developed multiple distribution channels. These institutions do not rely solely on traditional channels and human interaction (agents and brokers), but they entered also in the online world. Recent economic events have intensified the competition between the players, and consumers have become less and less loyal. As consumers integrate the Internet more and more into their daily routines and actively participate in the Web, even insurance companies are becoming prepared to interact online with their clients (Gidhagen and Persson 2011).

Insurance is divided into two main categories—life insurance and nonlife insurance—mainly due to the different variables that companies and individuals evaluate while estimating the premiums for the two products. Non-life insurance is a contract according to which the insurer compensates the insured if loss of or damage to the latter's property or assets occurs because of a particular event, such as destruction, theft, damage, or inability to produce profits. Life insurance, on the other hand, is a contract between the insurer and the policyholder according to which the insurer is obligated to pay a sum of money or benefits to a designed beneficiary upon the death of the insured or upon events such as terminal illness or predetermined age of the policyholder.

Traditionally, the most frequently used insurance distribution channels are the nondirect channels: agents, brokers, financial promoters, and the so-called bank-insurance entities.[1] Direct distribution is especially limited in Germany and Italy, largely because consumers prefer to keep a relationship with the company through agents and not because there is a lack of technical know-how. The mature markets in the U.K. and the U.S. have multiple distribution channels, increasing the overall

[1] Bank-insurance entities are considered to be companies with a hybrid system, offering both banking and insurance services.

cost of acquisition (World Insurance Report 2011). Even if Italy is considered one of the largest nonlife insurance markets in Europe, the market penetration is low, with policyholders typically resorting to minimal and compulsory coverage only.

The Italian market favors the relationship between the agent and the client instead of pushing for a fair choice of possible less costly solutions. If we think about life insurance distribution, the most frequently used channel is the bank branch, which is identified by the presence of an internal consultant who takes care of the client's needs and demands (Table 1) (ANIA 2014–2015).

If we think about the distribution of nonlife insurance, the agent is the most important point of contact between the company and the consumer.

Nonlife insurers rarely have propriety networks and have only limited exposure to direct channels (Table 2) (ANIA 2014–2015). As a result, even their financials are not positive. The operational ratio is slightly lower than the European average, and acquisition costs are slightly higher. The inflated acquisition investment is a direct consequence of the low penetration of the direct distribution channels in the Italian market, given that the arrival of the Internet decreased on average the acquisition ratio, along with the high bargaining power of agents.

This study investigates proper digital marketing for nonlife insurance, in order to comprehend how insurance companies communicate with consumers in the Italian market and whether, as a result, they must learn from a two-way interaction channel.

3 Studies Related to E-Marketing and E-Service

The existence and prevalence of e-service in financial industries is highly related to its adoption by users and likewise to the trust consumers assigned to it. Because of the nature of the online service delivery, some consumers may fear possible risks (Yap et al. 2010). The difference between the online and offline worlds lies in a temporal and spatial separation; thus, transactions that are carried out online often do not entail simultaneous transactions of money and services or goods (Grabner-Kraeuter 2002). As such, a trust[2] gap can occur between the e-service provider and the client (Hoffman et al. 1999).

[2] Trust in literature has been defined as a belief or expectation about the other party, or as a behavioral intention or willingness to rely on another party, coupled with a sense of vulnerability or risk when trust is violated (Mayer et al. 1995; Rousseau et al. 1998).

Online trust is a belief or expectation about a website, the website vendor as the trusted party, or behavioral intention or willingness to depend on the trusted party (McKnight et al. 1998; 2002).

Trust in e-commerce has been divided (McKnight and Chervany 2001–2002) into three typologies, depending on the context the consumer is put in: dispositional trust, institutional trust, and interpersonal trust. Most empirical studies focus on interpersonal trust (Gefen 2002; Gefen et al. 2003; Suh and Han 2003). For the purposes of this research, we limit ourselves to the use and definition of institutional trust or "an individual's belief that favorable conditions are in place which are conducive to situational success" (McKnight and Chervany 2001–2002, p. 45).

Table 1 Life insurance business by distribution channel: 2010–2014

	Gross premium (millions of euros)					Market share (%)						Annual variation (%)					Average variation (%)
Channels	2010	2011	2012	2013	2014	2010	2011	2012			2010–2014	2010	2011	2012	2013	2014	
Bank counter	54,310	40,419	33,807	50,469	68,995	60.3	54.7	48.5	59.3	62.4	57.0	15.0	−25.6	−16.4	49.3	36.7	4.9
Financial promoters	14,367	13,582	16,272	14,008	18,065	15.9	18.4	23.3	16.5	16.3	18.1	9.3	−5.5	19.8	−13.9	28.9	4.7
Agents	13,811	12,103	11,385	12,274	14,120	15.3	16.4	16.3	14.4	12.8	15.0	7.1	−12.4	−5.9	7.8	15.0	0.4
Direct selling	6689	6994	7458	7552	8708	7.4	9.5	10.7	8.9	7.9	8.9	−5.2	4.6	6.6	1.3	15.3	5.4
Brokers	936	771	791	797	626	1.0	1.0	1.1	0.9	0.6	0.9	15.4	−17.6	16.4	0.8	−21.3	−7.7
Total	90,114	73,869	69,713	85,100	110,515	100.0	100.0	100.0	100.0	100.0	100.0	11.1	−18.0	−5.5	22.1	29.9	4.2

Source: ANIA, Annual report, 2014–2015

Table 2 Nonlife insurance business by distribution channel: 2010–2014

Channels	Gross premium (millions of euros)					Market share (%)					Average	Annual variation (%)					Average variation
	2010	2011	2012	2013	2014	2010	2011	2012	2013	2014	2010–2014	2010	2011	2012	2013	2014	(%)
Agents	29,329	29,748	28,687	27,120	26,004	82.4	81.8	81.0	80.5	79.3	81.0	1.3	1.4	−3.0	−5.4	−4.2	−2.4
Brokers	2730	2768	2691	2648	2867	7.7	7.6	7.6	7.9	8.7	7.9	−1.4	1.4	−1.8	−1.6	8.2	1.0
Direct selling	2357	2549	2858	2663	2596	6.6	7.0	8.1	7.9	7.9	7.4	7.9	8.1	12.3	−3.3	−2.6	2.0
Of which Internet and phonecalls	1273	1491	1669	1603	1586	3.6	4.1	4.7	4.8	4.8	4.3	18.9	16.9	12.1	2.3	−1.1	4.5
Bank counter	1142	1247	1123	1202	1269	3.2	3.4	3.2	3.6	3.9	3.5	17.3	9.2	−5.5	7.1	5.5	2.1
Financial promoters	48	47	49	53	64	0.1	0.1	0.1	0.2	0.2	0.2	−5.7	−0.4	2.7	8.5	21.5	6.0
Total	35,606	36,358	35,407	33,687	32,800	100	100	100	100	100	100	2.2	2.1	−1.9	−4.6	−2.7	−1.6

Source: ANIA, Annual report, 2014–2015

Many researchers, such as Suh and Han (2002), Rexha et al. (2003), and Lichtenstein and Williamson (2006), find that trust plays a crucial role in determining a consumer's initial and continued use of any e-commerce service, especially those services related to the banking industry. Balasubramanian et al. (2003) echoed that the virtual attributes of e-banking can create trust in an online environment. For the evaluation of e-SQ, this is highly important. Past research (Koufaris and Hampton-Sosa 2004, 2005; Vatanasombut et al. 2008) has identified the following online attributes of e-banking: perceived privacy, perceived usefulness and ease of use, and perceived security.

Trust is important because of its relevance to the consumer's communication with the website. When interacting with a website, consumers need to sense security and reliability (Suh and Han 2003). What counts most for consumers when trusting in e-banking services is the level of service the bank legitimates. According to Patricio et al. (2003) and Yap et al. (2010), consumers' faith in online service is related to the quality of offline service, but this is not a *de facto* relationship.

Grabner-Kräuter and Faullant (2008) contradict Yap et al. (2010) with respect to the importance of the traditional bank position; even more, their results support the theory that the adoption process of Internet banking is a question of adequate Web design.

The adoption of financial e-services was not as fast as predicted, and trust is one reason for this. The consumer's dispositional trust is extremely relevant during the initial stages of developing a relationship (Chau et al. 2006; McKnight et al. 1998). According to Grabner-Kräuter and Faullant (2008), e-banking trust is relevant for conceptualizing the *operationalization* of Internet trust itself. Basically, previous research has shown that trust works both ways; it represents *the centrum* of both Internet acceptance and e-service acceptance. Another determining factor in terms of adoption is the level of risk a consumer is willing to assume (Cunningham et al. 2005; Pavlou 2003).

The relationship between insurance and consumers is much harder to build than that between banks and consumers, mostly because the client's interaction with insurance institutions is infrequent and does not involve daily financial transactions (Gidhagen 2002). However, a consumer's understanding of technology, the Internet as a communication channel, and website design and familiarity with working online can affect his or her relationship with an e-insurance provider.

In Academia there exists a widely accepted model that confirms the relationship between a consumer and the services based on its commitment to technology: the Technology Acceptance Model (TAM) (Davis et al. 1989; Venkatesh and Davis 2000). According to its principles, individuals will adopt an IT system if they perceive that the system benefits them and that it will improve their performance (Davis et al. 1989, Benamati et al. 2010). Conceptually, the scholars argue that a consumer's intentions to use an online provider's website are affected by both technology belief (present in TAM) and principles of trust.

Gidhagen and Persson (2011) completed the work of Benemati et al. (2010) and added trustworthiness as an important element of TAM. They argue that first we must understand how the consumer perceives a firm itself, and then we can comprehend the consumer's perceptions of and intentions to use the Internet as a channel for communicating with that firm. A consumer's negative or positive beliefs are in strong relation to organizational trustworthiness (Bramall et al. 2004; Gidhagen and Persson 2011).

4 Service and E-Service Quality Dimensions and Management

IT has increased the effectiveness and efficiency of service delivery. Today, financial institutions must differentiate their value proposition from those of their competitors. Technology adoption, from the perspective of service companies, provides an opportunity to design better service and deliver better results to clients. Consumer perceptions of service quality in the banking system are becoming increasingly important, as service quality has proved to be a predictor of satisfaction and loyalty (Andreassen and Lindestad 1998; Dabholkar et al. 2000; Zeithaml et al. 1996).

Many studies related customer satisfaction to purchasing behavior (e.g., Bolton 1998; Jones and Earl 1995; LaBarbera and Mazursky 1983; Newman and Werbel 1973; Loveman 1998) and have also established a relation between customer satisfaction and behavioral intentions (Levesque and McDougall 1996; McDougall and Levesque 2000; Oliver 1980) and customer satisfaction and technology security (Ganguli and Roy 2011). East (1997) found that consumers, if satisfied, are willing to use a product or service again and that they are likely to use a product line extension as well.

Although customer satisfaction in relation to service quality is the subject of many studies, customer loyalty has encountered more difficulties, mainly due to its complex construct, especially in the service industry (Mittal and Lassar 1998). According to Lewis and Soureli (2006), no uniform definition of the concept of customer loyalty exists, but many studies assume that loyalty has two important dimensions: behavioral and attitudinal (e.g. Day 1976). Lee and Zeiss (1980) added to these two dimensions a third: cognitive. Berry (1983) found that loyalty in the service sector depends on the development of interpersonal relationships.

Most recently, Schloffer, Maloles, and Chia (2009) found that customer satisfaction variables vary according to age. They claimed that especially within the youth market,[3] satisfaction decreases as age increases. They found that whereas customer satisfaction is related to customer loyalty, customer loyalty and behavioral intensions vary between age groups and are less solid over the age of 20. The same study outlined that young consumers are more willing to adopt online banking services over traditional banks than are older people.

[3] The study considered youths from 10 to 30 years old, the members of so-called Generation Y.

Chang et al. (2009) developed a model that puts in the same equation customer satisfaction, customer loyalty, and e-SQ. They found that a positive e-SQ improves customer satisfaction, which can lead to customer loyalty.

Possible approaches to evaluating SQ can be separated into those based on search properties, experience properties, and credence properties. For example, Zeithaml (1981) argued that most services contain few search properties but many experience and credence properties.

Parasuraman et al. (1985) echoed that service involves three characteristics: intangibility, heterogeneity, and inseparability. Intangibility refers to service performance, and it implies that it is tricky to understand consumer perceptions and evaluations of service quality. Heterogeneity addresses variations of service performance among firms, employees, and clients, as well as variation over time, which entails the difficulty of ensuring consistent service. On the other hand, inseparability is related to service delivery storage; hence, service performance cannot be evaluated before the service is delivered to customers, and it can only occur during interaction between service providers and receivers.

Lewis and Booms (1983) argued that SQ measures the gap between the level of service delivery and customer expectations. Supporting their affirmation, Grönroos (1982, 1984) found that customer perceptions are innate to the comparison between service expectation *ex ante* and service experience *ex post*.

Yang and Fang (2004) conceptualized the development of e-SQ measurements as a necessary condition for controlling and improving an institution's performance online. E-SQ measurement has seen different conceptualization models throughout past research (Bauer et al. 2006; Loiacono et al. 2000; Wolfinbarger and Gilly 2003; Yoo and Donthu 2001; Zeithaml et al. 2002).

The traditional measurement of SQ, even before the advent of the electronic environment, was the SERVQUAL model (Parasuraman et al. 1985). The original version of SERVQUAL was a 97-item instrument for measuring 10 SQ dimensions. Following a two-stage data analysis, Parasuraman et al. (1988) decreased their number to five dimensions that can be measured using a 22-item instrument: (1) tangibles, (2) reliability, (3) responsiveness, (4) assurance, and (5) empathy.

The problem that arises when considering SERVQUAL for an electronic environment is that the model was created taking into consideration variables related to human interaction and physical identity, which are no longer present. The same problem arose with the SERVPERF model (Cronin and Taylor 1992). The fundamental difference between the two models is that SERVQUAL evaluates SQ in terms of the difference between perceived and expected service (Parasuraman et al. 1988), whereas SERVPERF considers only perceived service as relevant to the analysis (Cronin and Taylor 1992, 1994). Dabholkar (1996) claimed that e-SQ measure should focus on website design, reliability, ease of use, delivery, enjoyment, and control.

A well-known e-service measurement was developed on the basis of extensive research by Zeithaml et al. (2002). According to them, e-SQ should be analyzed, along with five dimensions that are the fruit of consumers' perceptions: (1) information availability, (2) ease of use or usability, (3) privacy and security, (4) graphic style, and (5) reliability. In a subsequent study, Parasuraman et al. (2005)

reexamined the e-SQ measurement model and came up with four dimensions adequate to evaluating any shopping website: (1) efficiency, (2) fulfillment, (3) availability, and (4) privacy.

In line with the first scale proposed by Parasuraman et al. (2005), Santos (2003) added new dimensions to the analysis such as website appearance, linkage, structure and layout, content, support, communication, and incentive.

Loiacono et al. (2002) developed a different e-SQ quality measurement scale, the so-called WEBQUAL, composed of 12 dimensions, and Kaynama and Black (2000) adopted the traditional SERVQUAL, adding the dimensions design, personalization, access, navigation, content, response, and background. Yang and Jun (2002) measured the quality of e-service by dividing a sample into two groups: Internet purchasers and non-Internet purchasers. They found that Internet purchasers are interested in the reliability, security, credibility, access, ease of use, and personalization that an e-service can offer, whereas nonpurchasers are mainly influenced by security, reliability, availability, responsiveness, ease of use, access, and personalization.

Cox and Dale (2001), in a study of online retailing, found six dimensions needed to evaluate SQ: website layout, communication, accessibility, credibility, availability, and understanding. Yoo and Donthu (2001) created the so-called SITEQUAL, an adaptation of the WEBQUAL model proposed by Loiacono et al. (2000), a four-dimension scale that measures a website's SQ. The underlying dimensions are aesthetics design, ease of use, and interactive responsiveness (Yoo and Donthu 2001). Parasuraman et al. (2005) observed that neither WEBQUAL nor SITEQUAL captures all aspects of purchasing online procedures; thus, according to their critique, these two scales cannot plainly evaluate e-SQ.

5 Previous Research Hypotheses Related to Current Study

E-service quality has become an object of extensive study for many scholars, with large applications in the e-commerce and banking industries and much less in the insurance sector. We therefore remind readers of some of the well-established scholars (Bauer et al. 2006; Collier and Bienstock 2006; Kim et al. 2006; Parasuraman et al. 2005; Wolfinbarger and Gilly 2003; Zeithaml et al. 2002) and continue with a short presentation of some previous hypothesis testing.

Sahadev and Purani (2008) identified privacy, service availability, system delivery, and functionality as significant variables for measuring e-SQ. They also argued that these four dimensions that affect e-SQ have a positive impact on customer satisfaction and customer loyalty. Yen and Lu (2008) also identified efficiency, privacy, fulfillment, and system availability as important dimensions that link e-SQ to satisfaction. Zeithaml et al. (2002) found ease of navigation, flexibility, efficiency, site design, and security to influence customer satisfaction, perceived value, and e-loyalty.

Siu and Mou (2005) proposed a study adapted to the dimensions of e-SERVQUAL (Zeithaml et al. 2000, 2002) to examine customers' SQ perceptions of Internet banking, as well as the impact of these perceptions on customer satisfaction. Their research generated four dimensions: credibility, efficiency, security, and problem handling. Only one dimension, efficiency, remained the same as the original construct (Zeithaml et al. 2000, 2002). New factors labeled credibility, security, and problem handling were formed (Siu and Mou 2005).

Sohn and Tadisina (2008) conceptualized a measurement framework for Internet-based financial institutions by adapting their scale to the SERVQUAL (Parasuraman et al. 1985, 1988) and SERVPERF (Cronin and Taylor 1992, 1994) models. They formed their hypotheses to explore how consumers evaluate e-services, considering that "service rather than price is the key to long-term competitive advantage in a digital era" (Sohn and Tadisina 2008). The validated measurement contained five final dimensions: trust, customized communications, ease of use, website content, and functionality (Sohn and Tadisina 2008).

The research of Vrechopoulos and Atherinos (2009), even if not concentrated on SQ measurement overall, emphasized that website layout in the banking sector significantly influences consumer behavior. The attitude towards e-banking is strongly affected by website structure, whereas clients' intention to use Web-based banking services bears little relationship to the Web store layout. In essence, Web layout has an effect on user acceptance of e-banking in terms of perceived usefulness, ease of use, and attitude towards technology acceptance.

Ho and Lin (2010) validated a new scale instrument that measures e-SQ in the banking sector. The five resulting dimensions—Web design, customer service, assurance, preferential treatment, and information provision—are in accordance with Cristobal et al.'s (2007) proposal. Khaled Atallah Al-Tarawneh (2012) conceptualized a study in which reliability, website design, security level, responsiveness, personalization, and ease of use were positively related to customers' perceptions of e-SQ in e-banking services (Table 3).

Table 3 Summary of key dimensions of online service quality

Study	Key dimensions
Cox and Dale (2001)	Accessibility, communication, credibility, understanding, appearance, availability
Zeithaml et al. (2002)	Access, ease of use, trust, efficiency, flexibility, reliability, personalization, responsiveness, security, site aesthetics, and price knowledge
Wolfinbarger and Gilly (2003)	Privacy, reliability, accessibility, and customer service
van Riel et al. (2003)	Accessibility, design, personalization, navigation, and responsiveness
Sohn and Tadisina (2008)	Trust, customized communications, ease of use, website content, and functionality
Vrechopoulos and Atherinos (2009)	Website layout
Ho and Lin (2010)	Web design, customer service, assurance, preferential treatment, and information provision
Al-Tarawneh (2012)	Reliability, website design, security level, responsiveness, personalization, and ease of use

6 Research Gap and Study Objectives

We have seen a great many work study and research proposals in the e-service environment that sometimes can create confusion. There is still no "right" instrument for companies to use to evaluate, measure, and improve their e-SQ, and great discrepancies between different cultures persist (Kettinger et al. 1995).

Two aspects motivate our research:

- First, there is a large gap in the prior literature with respect to the insurance industry in general and in particular with respect to the linkage between the industry's service proposal and consumer perceptions;
- Second, there has been no investigation of what influences the Italian market's predisposition to e-insurance services.

A main concern in the insurance world is the role of human interaction and how far this can be limited *de facto*. Durkin et al. (2008) investigated this relationship in the U.K. market, evaluating the relationship between customer needs for product complexity[4] and their choice of channels: face-to-face or Internet-based service. Their findings provide a strong foundation for our research, namely that consumers who need simple products prefer Internet to face-to-face interaction, that if the perceived suitability of the Internet is increasing then even the willingness to use a website for medium-complex products increases, and that the most demanding consumers are mainly motivated by improved Internet service when purchasing a simple product (Durkin et al. 2008). Durkin et al. further analyzed factors that push consumers to use e-services in financial sectors, highlighting issues such as convenience, reassurance about security, and improved technology.

The objective of this research is to use a suitable number of dimensions validated in the literature to explore how consumers judge an insurance e-service, the most important attributes that an insurance company should care about, what dimensions would pull consumers to repeated usage and future purchase, and, last, whether there is any benchmark to follow, comparing ten of the largest European insurance companies present in Italy.

Building on previous studies and suggestions, and without a specific focus on a single model, we posit that an e-SQ construct of the following six dimensions, in the Italian insurance market, has a positive and significant impact on customers'

[4] Product complexity in insurance:

- simple products (auto, building insurance)—applied in instances where certainty of outcome was high, process stages were relatively few; and product was deemed easy to understand;
- medium products (life insurance)—derived mainly from feedback from the qualitative interviews and indicative of products that were deemed to fall between purely complex and purely simple products;
- complex products (pension insurance, mortgage)—applied in instances where certainty of outcome was low and outcome needed to be monitored, process stages were varied, and product was difficult to understand (Durkin et al. 2008, p. 350).

willingness to use an online site and that a positive e-SQ increases Net Promoter Score (NPS).

Our hypothesis testing model is as follows:

1. Reliability has a positive impact on willingness to use.
2. Ease of use has a positive impact on willingness to use.
3. Trust has a positive impact on willingness to use.
4. Customization has a positive impact on willingness to use.
5. Content and efficiency have positive impact on willingness to use.
6. Web interface has a positive impact on willingness to use.
7. E-quality has a significant impact on NPS.

The major difference between the current research studies and past studies is the sample selection. If the vast majority of the studies investigated current users of the financial services, and thus the respondents had knowledge of how the system works, the present study investigates how the above-mentioned dimensions influence decisions yet to be made by new and potential consumers, not experts or mandatory current customers of companies.

7 Research Design and Methodology

To test our hypotheses, we received after a Web survey 184 valid questionnaires to predominantly college students or recent graduate students and focused on a new task: at the primary level, taking out a car insurance policy online and, at the secondary level, navigating quickly on the company's Web page. A purposive sampling model was used in order to select consumers who interact with the new technologies (computer, smartphone, Internet) in their daily routine.

The study has two main focuses: first, the study's objective is to validate a new e-quality model for the insurance companies present in the Italian market.

Second, the study draws a comparison map between the top five traditional insurance services which are present online too and the top five Web-based insurance services from the consumers' perspective.

8 Model Design

The model design, as previously mentioned, was developed following the literature review, especially of models applied to the financial sectors, and personal adaptation of the "traditional" dimensions for the current study's purpose.

1. RELIABILITY: This refers to the correct technical functionality of the website and emphasizes how accurate the service provided is (Zeithaml et al. 2000) or, put more simply, the level of the accuracy of product information (Kaynama and

Black 2000). The items were tested by Lee and Lin (2005) and by Van Riel et al. (2003), with a Cronbach's $\alpha = 0.72$.

1. Insurance website is available 24/24.
2. Information on the website is up to date.
3. The company online system is working well.
4. Links are problem free, and pages download quickly.

2. EASE OF USE: This means that website functions are designed to help consumers easily navigate the site, there is a good search engine, and customers can easily maneuver through the Web pages (Zeithaml et al. 2000). These items were entirely adopted from the work of Zeithaml et al. (2000), Yang and Fang (2004), and Fassnacht and Koese (2006), where a Cronbach's $\alpha = 0.81$.

   1. Website text/labels/menu are easy to understand.
   2. Learning to operate the site does not require a lot of effort.
   3. I find this website easy to use.
   4. The website is well organized.

3. TRUST: This refers to the site's trustworthiness; most importantly, the dimension is built upon two important constructs: consumer confidence and the company's reputation (Zeithaml et al. 2000). The items were adopted taking into consideration Sohn and Tadisina's (2008) research, with a Cronbach's $\alpha = 0.88$.

   1. When I access my account I feel secure, the insurance website instills confidence.
   2. I trust the company.
   3. I am comfortable engaging in financial transactions with the company.

4. CUSTOMIZATION: This refers to how much the website can be tailored to individual preferences and wants (Zeithaml et al. 2000). Items were reformulated and adapted to the context based on Kaynama and Black (2000) and Van Riel et al. (2003), with a Cronbach's $\alpha = 0.77$.

   1. The service is able to customize your use of the website.
   2. The website adapts to your personal needs.
   3. Personal assistance is available if needed.

5. CONTENT AND EFFICIENCY: This refers to the amount of information the consumer is provided with and how efficiently it is endowed on the consumer (Ribbink et al. 2004; Sohn and Tadisina 2008), with a Cronbach's $\alpha = 0.74$.

   1. The Web pages have content that meets customers' needs.
   2. The website offers multimedia functions that match the provided content.
   3. I can easily find the information I need from the insurance company website.
   4. Using the service online is time consuming.
   5. The insurance online offers abundant service-related information.
   6. I can easily file a complaint.

6. WEB INTERFACE: This covers the overall design of the Web page, the visual design, and the information structure (Cox and Dale 2001; Yoo and Donthu 2001), with a Cronbach's $\alpha = 0.70$, in terms of the following:

    1. Website incorporates a good color scheme (easy on the eye, visually attractive, effective layout).
    2. Website includes interactive features (e.g., demos) which are very useful.
    3. Hyperlinks have a logical structure and are easily connected.

9 Sample and Questionnaire Design

The population of interest of our study—a panel of 600 respondents—were located in Milano and Bologna. In total, 184 responses were returned (30.6 % response rate), but only 105 were complete and thus valid for the research (data were manually screened, and missing cases were eliminated because of the large number of missing values). The sample included 61 % male and 39 % female respondents; 94 % of the sample was less than 30 years old. In terms of education, almost 50.0 % of the sample had at least a bachelor's certificate, whereas only 9.5 % had only a high school diploma; thus, the respondents are considered to have a high degree of education. Of the interviewees, 73.3 % were still students, and 23.8 % were employed. Almost 82.0 % of the sample had a monthly income less than 1000 euros. The summary of all sample characteristics is shown in Table 4.

The justification for the use of a university-student-based sample is mainly its proven value in previous studies (Haistead et al.1994; Sinha and Desarbo 1998).

Moreover, we designed the study to identify openness to technology, as well as level of interaction with technology, and assumed prior to the analysis that it would find a great openness to digital environments. The results are presented in Table 5.

As we expected, the sample used for the research has a high openness to technology, and they are well familiar with digital instruments and online commerce.

10 The Model: Hypotheses Testing

In order to perform a confirmatory factor analysis, researchers test the two-level relationship between the SQ dimensions (Jayawardhena 2004; Bauer et al. 2005; Ho and Lin 2010; Wu, Tao, and Yang 2012) or apply regression analysis (Jayawardhena 2004; Siu and Mou 2005; Khan and Mahapatra 2009). For the current study, the most appropriate approach is regression analysis, as all the items used were already validated in prior literature.

Table 4 Sample characteristics

Variable	Frequency	Percentage
Gender		
Male	64	61.0
Female	41	39.0
Age (number of years)		
20–25	81	82.0
26–30	12	12.0
31–35	2	2.0
>35	4	4.0
Education		
High school diploma	10	9.5
Bachelor diploma	52	49.5
Master/M.Sc.	40	38.1
PhD/MBA	3	2.9
Occupation		
Student	77	73.3
Employee	25	23.8
Apprentice/Internship	1	1.0
Manager	2	1.9
Monthly income		
<500 euros	62	59.0
500–1000 euros	24	22.9
1001–2000 euros	13	12.4
>2000 euros	6	5.7

Table 5 Sample characteristics: technology openness

Item and response	Frequency	Percentage
Do you own a smartphone?		
Yes	91	86.7
No	14	13.3
Do you own pay TV?		
Yes	50	47.6
No	55	52.4
How much time do you spend online?		
1–5 h	12	11.4
6–10 h	19	18.1
11–20 h	18	17.1
21–40 h	41	39.0
>40 h	15	14.3
Have you ever bought a product/service online?		
Yes	92	88.5
No	12	11.5

Table 6 Multiple regression analysis results: H_1–H_6

Model	Coefficients						
	Unstandardized coefficients		Standardized coefficients			Collinearity statistics	
	B	Std. error	Beta	*t*	Sig.	Tolerance	VIF
(Constant)	6.384	0.071		89.742	0.000		
Trust	0.836	0.071	0.393	11.779	0.000	1.000	1.000
Website aesthetics	0.819	0.072	0.379	11.354	0.000	0.998	1.002
Ease of use	0.568	0.072	0.264	7.924	0.000	0.999	1.001
Reliability	0.373	0.072	0.173	5.202	0.000	0.999	1.001
Content	0.297	0.071	0.139	4.161	0.000	0.999	1.001
Responsiveness	0.190	0.071	0.089	2.664	0.008	0.999	1.001

The previously developed model was further analyzed to assess the criterion validity of the new dimensions measured in terms of willingness to use and subsequently to NPS. The statistical significance is targeted to alpha = 0.05, which is typical of most of the prior literature (Cooper and Schindler 2006). All seven factors were used in the analysis ($R^2 = 0.431$; adjusted $R^2 = 0.425$; sig. $F = 0.000$).

The results of the first regression analysis, conceptualizing the first six-hypothesis stepwise method, are reported in Table 6. The value of the variance explained by the model is 0.431, which is significant with $F = 64.7$ and *p*-value = 0.000. As expected from the previous analysis, the last factor, personalization, was not found to be significant to the first hypothesis analysis. All items except responsiveness have a *p*-value = 0.000, the latter having a *p*-value = 0.008. All items have a positive relation with willingness to use the company's website. The most relevant in terms of loading (beta = β) are trust, Web aesthetics, and ease of use ($\beta = 0.393$, $\beta = 0.379$, and $\beta = 0.264$, respectively). The least important item, nevertheless, is responsiveness, which in this case has a low beta level (0.089).

The results of the second regression analysis are shown in Table 7.

The second regression analysis was used to test the last hypothesis of the model, which assumed that e-quality has a significant impact on NPQ. Even in this case, it has been used Linear Regression, Stepwise, in order to get the best-fitted model. All seven initial factors were included, but the last one, personalization, was not found to be significant, in accordance with previous exploratory analysis ($R^2 = 0.498$; adjusted $R^2 = 0.492$; sig. $F = 0.000$).

All six dimensions positively influence the NPS measure, with a *p*-value = 0.000. In this scenario, the most important items are ease of use, trust, and Web aesthetics with $\beta = 0.437$, $\beta = 0.385$, and $\beta = 0.272$, respectively. Responsiveness has a weaker relation with NPS, but its beta is superior to 0.1 ($\beta = 0.120$). According to the final results, consumers are prone to promote an insurance website if they find it, first, easy to use and, second, trustworthy. Nevertheless, if the website aesthetics are considered adequate, this could create another advantage that consumers are willing to talk about.

Table 7 Multiple regression analysis results: H_7

Model	Coefficients						
	Unstandardized coefficients		Standardized coefficients			Collinearity Statistics	
	B	Std. error	Beta	*t*	Sig.	Tolerance	VIF
(Constant)	6.478	0.078		83.204	0.000		
Ease of use	1.092	0.078	0.437	14.014	0.000	1.000	1.000
Trust	0.961	0.078	0.385	12.337	0.000	1.000	1.000
Website aesthetics	0.680	0.078	0.272	8.726	0.000	1.000	1.000
Reliability	0.474	0.078	0.190	6.079	0.000	1.000	1.000
Content	0.467	0.078	0.187	5.988	0.000	1.000	1.000
Responsiveness	0.301	0.078	0.120	3.861	0.000	1.000	1.000

Dependent variable: would you recommend to a friend/family/acquaintance to visit the following website?

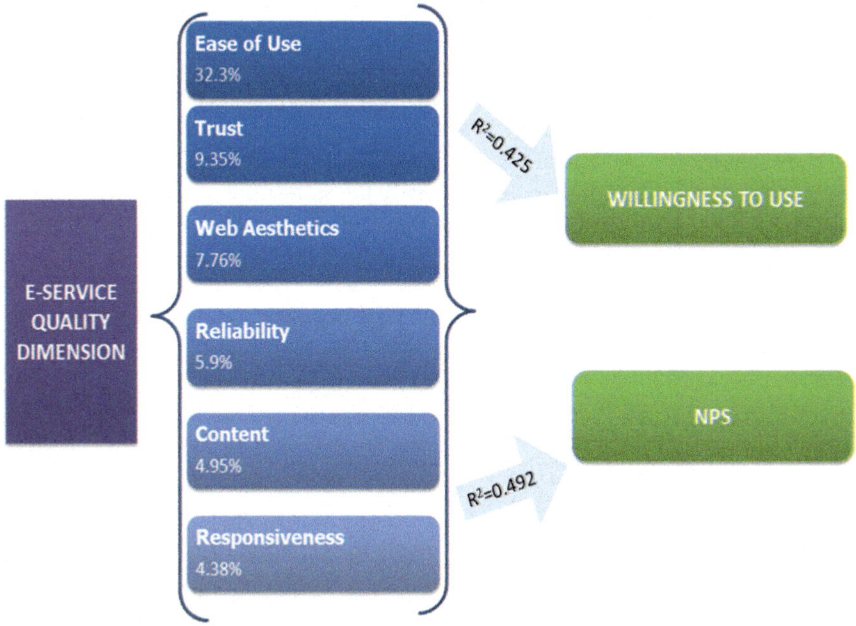

Fig. 1 Variables which measure the E-quality of the Italian market insurance companies

In order to validate the proposed model, correlation measures have been identified between the two inferred variables, willingness to use the company's website and NPS. The correlation factor exceeds 0.6, but it is still at an acceptable value ($r = 0.73$).

The final validated model is represented in Fig. 1.

11 Comparison Model: Benchmarking

After testing the proposed model, we initiated the comparison analysis of the ten insurance websites. The choice of companies is directly linked to data elaborated by ANIA (2011), in terms of market share for each of them. Therefore, in the analysis we used the top five traditional companies and the top five direct insurance companies. A collateral result to the analysis is the difference between the online service proposal between the two categories of companies—traditional versus online.

Before mapping consumers' perceptions of the quality of these companies' services, we asked respondents about their interaction with the insurance companies in their daily lives. In essence, 46 % of our sample had previously acquired an insurance policy, and a quarter of them had bought it online.

In order to better assess the evaluation results, we used discriminant analysis. The discriminant functions explain the differences in the evaluations of the different "objects" or the differences in the explanatory variables, which determine membership in the different "groups." The dependent variable was the company, and the factors analyzed were the previous seven dimensions resulting from the EFA.

The most significant variables (F-test) are ease of use, trust, content, and website aesthetics. The variables that are statistically not relevant, circled in red, are therefore potentially less discriminant (Table 8).

A second Wilks's Lambda, the test to verify the significance of the difference in the means of the discriminant scores, calculated for the several groups of observation, resulted in two significant functions for the analysis (significance of 0.000 for two functions).

The data elaborated statically are shown in Table 9. Subsequently, the perceptual mapping is present in Figs. 2 and 3, with both highlights on the x-axis and the y-axis.

Table 8 Tests of equality of group means

Model	Wilks's Lambda	F	df1	df2	Sig.
EASE OF USE	0.899	6.395	9	513	.000
TRUST	0.796	14.634	9	513	.000
WEBSITE AESTHETICS	0.970	1.772	9	513	.071
RELIABILITY	0.983	0.965	9	513	.468
CONTENT	0.951	2.909	9	513	.002
RESPONSIVENESS	0.994	0.349	9	513	.958
CUSTOMIZATION	0.974	1.498	9	513	.145

The red box highlights the least significant variables that discriminate the quality of the online service

Table 9 Rotated matrix: discriminant analysis

Dimensions	1	2
Trust	0.969[a]	0.045
Website aesthetics	0.018[a]	0.003
Ease of use	−0.037	−0.809[a]
Content	−0.094	0.417[a]
Reliability	−0.159	0.234[a]
Customization	0.059	0.229[a]
Responsiveness	0.006	−0.096[a]

[a]largest absolut correlation between each variable and any discriminant function

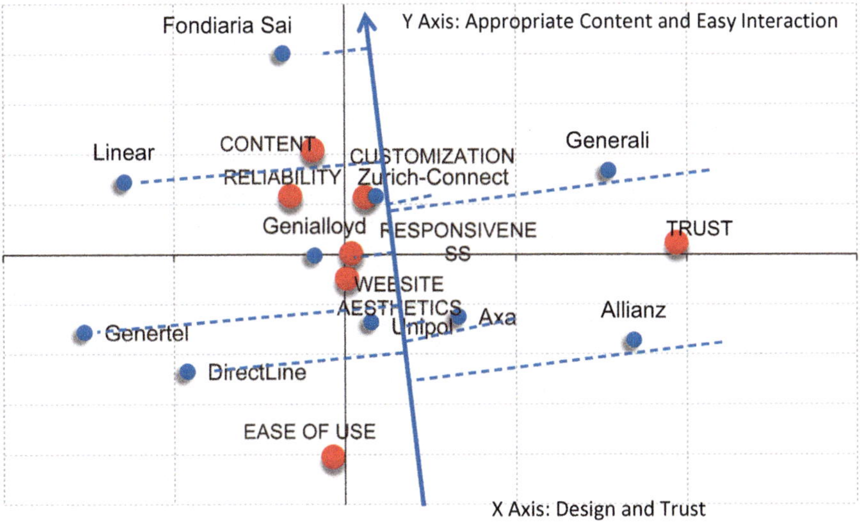

Fig. 2 Perceptual mapping: focus on the *y*-axis

Recalling the most discriminant functions, trust (F-value = 14.6), ease of use (F-value = 6.4), and content (F-value = 2.9), we will see where in the consumer's mind the 10 websites analyzed are located.

Figure 2 takes into consideration the "physical" proximity of the companies in terms of appropriate content and easy interaction. DirectLine is the best in terms of easy interaction, which is one of the most discriminant factors in our analysis. Genertel is the second best in terms of ease of use, but it is "located" far away from the rest. Genialloyd has the best positioning in terms of ease of use and content appropriateness. Zurich-Connect is the best in terms of customization and content but is far away from ease of use. Unipol and Axa are somehow close to ease of use but far away from the appropriateness of content. Linear, Generali, and Allianz are far away from both categories of analysis. The worst positioning on the map, though, is the one crowned by Fondiaria Sai. On top of the positioning map, it seems that the service this website offers does not have any competitive advantage.

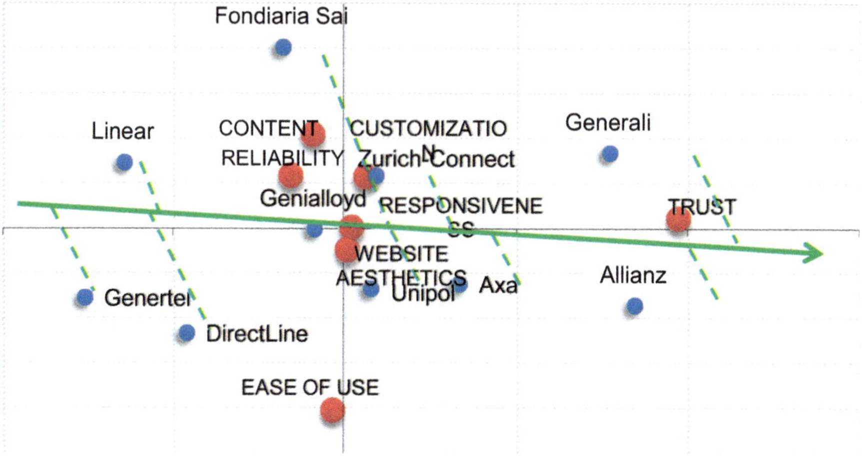

Fig. 3 Perceptual mapping: focus on the *x*-axis

In Figure 3, we can see the relative distance of the companies in terms of trust and Web design. In terms of trust, the most relevant and discriminant term of the entire analysis, Allianz, and the second best, Generali, are seen as most trustworthy. Axa is in third place in terms of trust. Zurich-Connect is the only online-based insurance company that earns a good trust vote. The worst two companies in terms of trust are Linear and Genertel. In terms of design, the best positioned is Genialloyd, followed by Zurich-Connect. DirectLine has a neutral position. Fondiaria Sai takes the worst place even in this scenario.

Basically, the mapping identifies two important trends: first is that the traditional insurance companies' e-service entails more trust, whereas the online-based insurers create an easy-navigation experience. Second, the mapping shows that there are companies that are kept in the middle but always separated by one key element: whether they are online based (Zurich-Connect and Genialloyd) or traditional based (Axa and Unipol).

Moreover, consumers were asked to rate their overall satisfaction with the company's e-service and to choose the best one, excluding the price tag of a possible car insurance policy. For the purpose of this study, the key element to focus on is online quality. The results are present in Table 10.

Looking at the results, we see a concrete confirmation of the discriminant analysis, previously presented. Consumers seem to be more satisfied with a traditional company's website, and most importantly there is a net preference for well-established companies at the cost of the online-based ones. There is much room for improvement, especially for the new-generation insurance companies, and even if these companies' websites have been evaluated as easy to use and as well designed, they have to work on gaining consumers' trust. Overall, the best in class, from the consumer's point of view, are Generali, from the traditional part, and Genialloyd, from the online part. The more surprising result overall is Genertel, part of the Generali Group, which is considered as not trustworthy and not satisfying. These

Table 10 Consumers' evaluation: comparison analysis

	Company				
Question	Generalli	Zurich-Connect	Fondiaria Sai	Genialloyd	Linear
How do you rate the overall quality of the website?	7.90	7.33	6.12	7.71	6.96
How much did the service satisfy you?	7.73	7.22	6.24	7.35	6.59
Are you willing to use this company's website?	7.17	6.67	6.10	7.21	6.06
Considering the insurance fee is the same, which company would you choose?	7.53	5.84	5.43	5.48	5.26
	Allianz	Unipol	Axa	Genertel	DirectLine
How do you rate the overall quality of the website?	7.04	6.49	6.94	6.21	6.32
How much did the service satisfy you?	7.06	6.02	6.94	5.86	6.00
Are you willing to use this company's website?	6.87	6.08	6.40	5.48	5.90
Considering the insurance fee is the same, which company would you choose?	7.52	6.38	6.42	5.66	5.60

The colors highlight the average evaluation of each variable under examination where green = highest values, orange = normal values, red: lowest values

findings leave room for debate, as Genertel is the largest online-based insurance company in terms of market share in Italy.

12 Conclusion and Management Implications

The new measure found in this study has both similarities to and differences from the previous "well-established" models. First, the purpose of this research was to understand what variables actually make consumers return to a website and use one e-service rather than a competitor's. *De facto*, satisfaction and loyalty come after a relationship has been built between the company and the consumer. The first step, though, is the initial impact when choosing the best solution and is what, at least until today, has been taken for granted and thus neglected. This study tries to understand exactly the incipit of a possible relationship, what makes consumers talk about that e-service, and what they actually expect to get.

This study identified six dimensions of e-service, drawn from items previously tested by Kaynama and Black (2000), Sohn and Tadisina (2008), Van Riel et al. (2003), and Zeithaml et al. (2002), that explain a high proportion of the variance of e-SQ. As expected, the six factors have a positive impact on both willingness to use the website and NPS. Ease of use becomes fundamental on first impact with the consumer, especially for an e-commerce activity, differently than in previous work in which trust and reliability were considered to be of supreme value (Parasuraman and Grewal 2000; Zeithaml et al. 2002). Moreover, trust positively and directly influences consumers' decisions to promote their experience on a website. This dimension is highly correlated with the level of safety and reassurance the insurance company gives to consumers. Web aesthetics plays a significant role when consumers evaluate website quality, as suggested in Zeithaml et al.'s (2000) work but lacking in the majority of prior research. Reliability is the one factor that, contrary to similar research, was found to be less important when judging e-commerce, contrary to Wolfinbarger and Gilly (2003) and Zeithaml (2002), who found reliability to be the most important factor in financial services. Following Parasuraman et al. (2005) definition that reliability means the accuracy of the promised service, we find it to be relevant even upon first encounter with a website. Content, not surprisingly, has been found to be significant and important in this analysis. Consumers are demanding and have high expectations online (Zeithaml and Bitner 2000); thus, it is no wonder that consumers do not tolerate low content-adequateness. The last significant dimension in our study is responsiveness. This feature deals with courtesy, communication, and problem handling by customer service. Even if for a possible new consumer this might not be a critical issue, investing in responsiveness variable might offer additional comfort about his security and how his data is treated. Past researchers (Ho and Lin 2010; Jayawardhena 2004; Siu and Mou 2005) maintain its importance as well. This study, though, does not find customization to be a relevant and significant factor in the hypothesis testing. This finding is consistent with Gwynne et al.'s (2000) and Van Riel et al.'s (2003) findings and contrary to the findings of Zeithaml et al. (1993) and Parasuraman and Grewal (2000).

Based on these findings, we recommend that companies always improve their service quality and understand what consumers are looking for when they are online. Ease of use and trust must receive proper attention if consumers are to be satisfied with a company's service. Opportunities lie in dealing with aesthetics and content in order to differentiate the online proposition. Competition in insurance markets is intensifying, and nowadays, cost savings and customer retention have become critical. Profitability and cost savings were the first two factors driving insurance companies to seek alternative distribution channels. Nowadays, changes in customer behaviors, buying habits, and preferences are driving the development of alternative distribution. As seen before, insurance companies look for new partnerships in banks (bank assurance) in order to take advantage of banks' network and positioning in the consumer's mind.

The evolution of technology has revealed new ways for insurance companies to distribute their services in the online hub. The Internet has become a daily routine, a perfect medium for companies to "be there" when consumers want them. Technology seems to be useful for insurance companies as well; they can better understand and integrate consumers' desires with their sales policies.

The study poses several limitations in terms of the sample and the design. First, the sample was biased in terms of age distribution. As a result of this situation, generalization to a larger population is limited (Parasuraman and Grewal 2000). We recommend repeating the analysis with a larger number of respondents randomly selected that reflect a wider age range.

Second, the respondents had to perform a task before answering the survey. In this case, the questionnaire was administered online; we recommend repeating the test in an experiential environment in order to better control the external stimuli and to ensure accuracy of the responses. Respondents in the current research had to compare five websites; future analysis could randomly assign just one or two in order to avoid the effect of boredom or repeated untrue answers due to time-consuming task involvement. Most probably, a limited exercise will increase the response rate and the default rate, which in this case was pretty high (44 %).

The model should be tested and integrated when dealing with consumer satisfaction and loyalty as well in the Italian market. The sample should be similar to prior studies (Zeithaml et al. 2000); thus, the respondents must be familiar with online insurance.

There is also a lack of studies of cultural effects on the choice of insurance companies. Because many of the characteristics used by consumers to evaluate their experience on a website are behavioral dimensions (Jarvenpaa et al. 1999; Parasuraman et al. 2005), differences in the role played by each of them would be interesting to see.

Acknowledgment The Authors are grateful to SDA Bocconi School of Management, which generously funded some research projects related to Marketing in the Insurance& Banking Industry. This research benefited from this funding.

References

Andreassen TW, Lindestad B (1998) Customer loyalty and complex services: the impact of corporate image on quality, customer satisfaction and loyalty for customers with varying degrees of service expertise. Int J Serv Ind Manag 9(1):7–23

ANIA (2011) Edizione 2012, Premi del lavoro diretto italiano 2011, http://www.ania.it

ANIA, L'Assicurazione italiana, 2014–2015, 208–201, http://www.ania.it

Al-Tarawneh AK (2012) Measuring e-service quality rom the customers' perspective: an empirical study on banking services. Int Res J Finance Econ 19:123–137

Balasubramanian S, Konana P, Menon NM (2003) Customer satisfaction in virtual environments: a study of online investing. Manag Sci 49(7):871–889

Bauer HH, Hammerschmidt M, Falk T (2005) Measuring the quality of e-banking portals. Int J Bank Mark 23(2):153–175

Bauer HH, Falk T, Hammerschmidt M (2006) eTransQual: a transaction process-based approach for capturing service quality in online shopping. J Bus Res 59(7):866–875

Benamati J, Fuller MA, Serva MA, Baroudi J (2010) Clarifying the integration of trust and TAM in ecommerce environments: implications for systems design and management. IEEE Trans Eng Manag 57(3):380–393

Berry LL (1983) Relationship marketing. American Marketing Association, Chicago

Bolton RN (1998) A dynamic model of the duration of the customer's relationship with a continuous service provider: the role of satisfaction. Mark Sci 17(1):45–65

Bramall C, Schoefer K, McKechnie S (2004) The determinants and consequences of consumer trust in e-retailing: a conceptual framework. Ir Mark Rev 17(1/2):13

Capgemini World Insurance Report (2011) http://www.it.capgemini.com/pubblicazioni/world-insurance-report-2011

Chang HH, Wang YH, Yang WY (2009) The impact of e-service quality, customer satisfaction and loyalty on e-marketing: Moderating effect of perceived value. Total Qual Manag Bus Excell 20(4):423–443

Chau PYK, Hu PJ-H, Lee BLP, Au AKK (2006) Examining customers' trust in online vendors and dropouts: an empirical study. Electron Commer Res Appl 6(2):172–183

Collier JE, Bienstock CC (2006) Measuring service quality in e-retailing. J Serv Res 8(3):260–275

Cooper DR, Schindler PS (2006) Marketing research. McGraw-Hill/Irwin, New York

Cox J, Dale BG (2001) Service quality and e-commerce: an exploratory analysis. Manag Serv Qual 11(2):121–131

Cristobal E, Flavián C, Guinaliu M (2007) Perceived e-service quality: measurement validity and effects on consumer satisfaction and web site loyalty. Manag Serv Qual 17(3):317–340

Cronin J, Taylor S (1992) Measuring service quality: a re-examination and extension. J Mark 56 (3):55–69

Cronin JJ, Taylor SA (1994) SERVPERF versus SERVQUAL: reconciling performance-based and perceptions-minus-expectations measurement of service quality. J Mark 58:125–131

Cunningham LF, Gerlach J, Harper MD (2005) Perceived risk and e-banking services: an analysis from the perspective of the consumer. J Financ Serv Mark 10(2):165–178

Dabholkar PA (1996) Consumer evaluations of new technology-based self-service options: an investigation of alternative models of service quality. Int J Res Mark 13(1):29–52

Dabholkar PA, Shepherd CD, Thorpe DI (2000) A comprehensive framework for service quality: an investigation of critical conceptual and measurement issues through a longitudinal study. J Retail 76(2):139–173

Davis FD, Bagozzi RP, Warshaw PR (1989) User acceptance of computer technology: a comparison of two theoretical models. Manag Sci 35(8):982–1003

Day GS (1976) A two-dimensional concept of brand loyalty. In: Mathematical models in marketing. Springer, Berlin/Heidelberg, p. 89

Durkin M, Jennings D, Mulholland G, Worthington S (2008) Key influencers and inhibitors on adoption of the Internet for banking. J Retail Consum Serv 15:348–357

East R (1997) Consumer behaviour: advances and applications in marketing. Prentice Hall, London

Fassnacht M, Koese I (2006) Quality of electronic services conceptualizing and testing a hierarchical model. J Serv Res 9(1):19–37

Ganguli S, Roy SK (2011) Generic technology-based service quality dimensions in banking: impact on customer satisfaction and loyalty. Int J Bank Mark 29(2):168–189

Gefen D (2002) Customer loyalty in e-commerce. J Assoc Inf Syst 3:27–51

Gefen D, Karahanna E, Straub DW (2003) Trust TAM in online shopping: an integrated model. MIS Q 27(1):51–90

Gidhagen M (2002) Critical business episodes—the criticality of damage adjustment processes in insurance relationships. Department of Business Studies, Uppsala University, Uppsala

Gidhagen M, Persson SG (2011) Determinants of digitally instigated insurance relationships. Int J Bank Mark 29(7):517–534

Gonzalez ME, Dentiste MR, Rhonda MW (2008) An alternative approach in service quality: an e-banking case study. Qual Manag J 15(1):41

Grabner-Kräuter S (2002) The role of consumers' trust in online-shopping. J Bus Ethics 39 (1):43–50

Grabner-Krauter S, Faullant R (2008) Consumer acceptance of Internet banking: the influence of Internet trust. Int J Bank Mark 26(7):483–504

Grönroos C (1982) Strategic management and marketing in the service sector. Research Reports No. 8, Swedish School of Economics and Business Administration, Helsinki

Grönroos C (1984) A service quality model and its marketing implications. Eur J Mark 18(4):36–44

Gwynne AL, Devlin JF, Ennew CT (2000) The zone of tolerance: insights and influences. J Mark Manag 16:545–564

Haistead D, Hartman D, Schmidt SL (1994) Multisource effects on the satisfaction formation process. J Acad Mark Sci 22(2):114–129

Hampton-Sosa W, Koufaris M (2005) The effect of web site perceptions on initial trust in the owner company. Int J Electron Commer 10(1):55–81

Harridge-March S, Quinton S (2009) Virtual snakes and ladders: social networks and the relationship marketing loyalty ladder. Mark Rev 9(2):171–181

Ho CTB, Lin WC (2010) Measuring the service quality of internet banking: scale development and validation. Eur Bus Rev 22(1):5–24

Hoffman DL, Novak TP, Peralta M (1999) Building consumer trust online. Commun ACM 42 (4):80–85

Jarvenpaa SL, Tractinsky N, Saarinen L (1999) Consumer trust in an internet store: a cross-cultural validation. J Comput Mediat Commun 5(2): 0–0

Järvinen R, Eriksson P, Saastamoinen M, Lystimäki M (2001) Vakuutusket verkossa Vakuutusyhtiöiden tarjonta ja kuluttajien odotukset (Insurance on the internet – insurance companies' offerings and consumer expectations). National Consumer Research Centre, Helsinki. Publications 7/2001

Jayawardhena C (2004) Measurement of service quality in Internet banking: the development of an instrument. J Mark Manag 20(1–2):185–207

Jones TO, Earl SW (1995) Why satisfied customers defect. Harv Bus Rev 73(6):88

Kaynama S, Black C (2000) A proposal to assess the service quality of online travel agencies: an exploratory study. J Prof Serv Mark 21(1):63–88

Kettinger WJ, Lee CC, Lee S (1995) Global measures of information service quality: a cross-national study*. Decis Sci 26(5):569–588

Khan MS, Mahapatra SS (2009) Service quality evaluation in Internet banking: an empirical study in India. Int J Indian Cult Bus Manag 2(1):30–46

Kim M, Kim J-H, Lennon SJ (2006) Online service attributes available on apparel retail web sites: an E-S-QUAL approach. Manag Serv Qual 16(1):51–77

Koufaris M, Hampton-Sosa W (2004) The development of initial trust in an online company by new customers. Inform Manage 41(3):377–397

LaBarbera PA, Mazursky D (1983) A longitudinal assessment of consumer satisfaction/dissatisfaction: the dynamic aspect of the cognitive process. J Mark Res 20:393–404

Lee GG, Lin HF (2005) Customer perceptions of e-service quality in online shopping. Int J Retail Distrib Manag 33(2):161–176

Lee BA, Zeiss CA (1980) Behavioral commitment to the role of sport consumer-an exploratory analysis. Sociol Soc Res 64(3):405–419

Levesque T, McDougall GH (1996) Determinants of customer satisfaction in retail banking. Int J Bank Mark 14(7):12–20

Lewis RC, Booms BH (1983) The marketing aspects of service quality. Emerg Perspect Serv Mark 65(4):99–107

Lewis BR, Soureli M (2006) The antecedents of consumer loyalty in retail banking. J Consum Behav 5(1):15–31

Lichtenstein S, Williamson K (2006) Understanding consumer adoption of internet banking: an interpretive study in the Australian banking context. J Electron Commer Res 7(2):50–66

Loiacono E, Chen D, Goodhue D (2002) WebQual™ revisited: predicting the intent to reuse a Web site. In: Eighth Americas Conference on Information Systems, pp. 301–309

Loiacono E, Watson RT, Goodhue D (2000) WebQual™: A web site quality instrument. Working Paper. Worcester Polytechnic Institute

Loveman GW (1998) Employee satisfaction, customer loyalty, and financial performance an empirical examination of the service profit chain in retail banking. J Serv Res 1(1):18–31

Mayer RC, Davis JH, Schoorman FD (1995) An integrative model of organizational trust. Acad Manag Rev 20(3):709–734
McDougall GH, Levesque T (2000) Customer satisfaction with services: putting perceived value into the equation. J Serv Mark 14(5):392–410
McKnight HD, Cummings LL, Chervany NL (1998) Initial trust formation in new organizational relationships. Acad Manage Rev 23(3):473–490
McKnight DH, Chervany NL (2001–2002) What trust means in e-commerce customer relationships: an interdisciplinary conceptual typology. Int J Electron Commer 6(2):35–59
Mittal B, Lassar WM (1998) Why do customers switch? The dynamics of satisfaction versus loyalty. J Serv Mark 12(3):177–194
Newman JW, Werbel RA (1973) Multivariate analysis of brand loyalty for major household appliances. J Mark Res 10:404–409
Odoyo FS, Nyangosi R (2011) E-insurance: an empirical study of perceived benefits. Int J Bus Soc Sci 2(21):166–171
Oliver RL (1980) A cognitive model of the antecedents and consequences of satisfaction decisions. J Mark Res 17:460–469
Parasuraman A, Berry LL, Zeithaml VA (1988) Communication and control processes in the delivery of SQ. J Mark 52:35–48
Parasuraman A, Grewal D (2000) The impact of technology on the quality-value-loyalty chain: a research agenda. J Acad Mark Sci 28(1):168–174
Parasuraman A, Zeithaml VA, Berry LL (1985) A conceptual model of service quality and its implications for future research. J Mark 49:41–50
Parasuraman A, Zeithaml V, Malhotra A (2005) E-S- QUAL. A multiple item scale for assessing electronic service quality. J Serv Res 7(3):213–233
Parasuraman R, Sheridan TB, Fellow, IEEE, Wickens, CD (2000) A model for types and levels of human interaction with automation
Patricio L, Fisk RP, Falcão E Cunha J (2003) Improving satisfaction with bank service offerings: measuring the contribution of each delivery channel. Manag Serv Qual 13:471–482
Pavlou PA (2003) Consumer acceptance of electronic commerce: integrating trust and risk with the technology acceptance model. Int J Electron Commer 7(3):101–134
Rexha N, Kingshott RPJ, Aw ASS (2003) The impact of the relational plan on adoption of electronic banking. J Serv Mark 17(1):53–65
Ribbink D, Van Riel AC, Liljander V, Streukens S (2004) Comfort your online customer: quality, trust and loyalty on the internet. Manag Serv Qual 14(6):446–456
Rousseau DM, Sitkin SB, Burt RS, Camerer C (1998) Not so different after all: a cross-discipline view of trust. Acad Manag Rev 23(3):393–404
Sahadev S, Purani K (2008) Modelling the consequences of e-service quality. Mark Intell Plan 26 (6):605–620
Santos J (2003) E-service quality: a model of virtual service quality dimensions. Manag Serv Qual 13(3):233–246
Sinha I, DeSarbo WS (1998) An integrated approach toward the spatial modeling of perceived customer value. J Mark Res 35:236–249
Siu NYM, Mou CWJ (2005) Measuring service quality in Internet banking: the case of Hong Kong. J Int Consum Mark 17(4):99–116
Sohn C, Tadisina SK (2008) Development of e-service quality measure for Internet-based financial institutions. Total Qual Manag 19(9):903–918
Suh B, Han I (2002) Effect of trust on customer acceptance of internet banking. Electron Commer Res Appl 1:247–263
Suh B, Han I (2003) The impact of customer trust and perception of security control on the acceptance of electronic commerce. Int J Electron Commer 7(3):135–161
Valarie AZ, Bitner M (2000) Services marketing: integrating customer focus across the firm. Copyright by the McGraw-Hill Education

van Riel ACR, Semeijn J, Janssen W (2003) E-service quality expectations: a case study. Total Qual Manag 14(4):437–450
Vatanasombut B, Lgbaria M, Stylianou A, Rodgers W (2008) Information system continuance intention of web based applications customers: the case of online banking. Inf Manag 45 (7):419–428
Venkatesh V, Davis FD (2000) A theoretical extension of the technology acceptance model: four longitudinal field studies. Manag Sci 46(2):186–204
Vrechopoulos A, Atherinos E (2009) Web banking layout effects on consumer behavioural intentions. Int J Bank Mark 27(7):524–546
Wolfinbarger M, Gilly MC (2003) eTailQ: dimensionalizing, measuring and predicting eTail quality. J Retail 79(3):183–198
Wu YL, Tao YH, Yang PC (2012) Learning from the past and present: measuring Internet banking service quality. Serv Ind J 32(2):1–31
Yakhlef A (1998) The internet as a new locus for value creation. Manag Decis 36(9):610–614
Yang Z, Fang X (2004) Online service quality dimensions and their relationships with satisfaction: a content analysis of customer reviews of securities brokerage services. Int J Serv Ind Manag 15(3):302–326
Yang Z, Jun M (2002) Consumer perception of e-service quality: from Internet purchaser and non-purchaser perspectives. J Bus Strateg 19(1):19–41
Yap KB, Wong DH, Loh C, Bak R (2010) Offline and online banking—where to draw the line when building trust in e-banking? Int J Bank Mark 28(1):27–46
Yen CH, Lu HP (2008) Effects of e-service quality on loyalty intention: an empirical study in online auction. Manag Serv Qual 18(2):127–146
Yoo B, Donthu N (2001) Developing a scale to measure perceived quality of an Internet shopping site (SITEQUAL). Q J Electron Commerce 2(1):31–46
Zeithaml VA (1981) How consumer evaluation processes differ between goods and services
Zeithaml VA (2002) Service excellent in electronic channels. Manag Serv Qual 12(3):135–138
Zeithaml VA, Berry LL, Parasuraman A (1993) The nature and determinants of customer expectations of service. J Acad Mark Sci 21(1):1–12
Zeithaml VA, Leonard LB, Parasuraman A (1996) The behavioral consequences of service quality. J Mark 60:31–46
Zeithaml VA, Parasuraman A, Malhotra A (2000) E-service quality: definition, dimensions and conceptual model. Marketing Science Institute, Cambridge
Zeithaml VA, Parasuraman A, Malhotra A (2002) Service quality delivery through web sites: a critical review of extant knowledge. J Acad Mark Sci 30(4):362–375

Part II
Distance Selling

Insurance Online: Regulation and Consumer Protection in a Cyber World

Aviva Abramovsky and Peter Kochenburger

Contents

Abstract Insurers and insurance intermediaries sell and market insurance online and utilize social media to promote their products and evaluate consumer behavior. Historically, insurance companies have been significant collectors and users of customer-related information; the age of "Big Data" has greatly accelerated both the types of information collected and how it is used, creating new opportunities for developing, underwriting, and marketing insurance products. However, the online or cyber world similarly creates new challenges for regulators and risks to consumers, including the complexity of underwriting and risk classifications, multiple distribution channels that cross regulatory boundaries and are increasingly global in reach, and consumer privacy and ownership of data. These new realities in turn

A. Abramovsky (✉)
Syracuse University College of Law, Syracuse, NY, USA
e-mail: aabramov@law.syr.edu

P. Kochenburger
School of Law, University of Connecticut, Hartford, CT, USA
e-mail: peter.kochenburger@uconn.edu

P. Marano et al. (eds.), *The "Dematerialized" Insurance*,
DOI 10.1007/978-3-319-28410-1_5

implicate the growing risk of cyber or data breaches and the ability of third parties to illegally access and utilize the immense amounts of confidential information insurers and other institutions now routinely collect.

This chapter examines these issues in the United States. The online world is fluid almost by definition, and perhaps one of its few certainties is that any quantitative summary will be out of date shortly after publication. Therefore, while we have attempted to provide the most current information available, our focus is on industry and regulatory trends and the structure and sources of insurance and consumer protection regulation in the U.S., which provide the framework for evaluating the future of insurance online and the relationships among insurers, insurance intermediaries, regulators (state, federal, and international), and insurance consumers. While there are relatively few laws that specifically address the online sale of insurance, existing consumer protection and insurance laws and regulations are often sufficiently flexible to encompass the online world, particularly in areas of deceptive advertising, unfair trade practices, and email spam. In other areas, such as cybersecurity, regulatory responses are rapidly emerging.

After the introduction in Sect. 1, our chapter reviews the online sale of life and property casualty insurance, summarizes insurance regulation in the United States (itself in a state of flux), and then discusses insurance regulation and consumer protection laws applicable to the online sale and marketing of insurance, concluding with the security of data held by insurers and other financial service companies. Insurers are both sources of cyber risk and, by underwriting cyber insurance, providers of an important tool to address and mitigate this risk. In this area, the interests of government, insurers, intermediaries, policyholders, and other consumers potentially merge, with the acknowledgement that a strong cyber insurance market can contribute significantly to the nation's economy and security.

1 Introduction

The economic, political, and social transformations brought about by our online world have altered insurance no less than other areas of commerce. Along with the related phenomena of "Big Data"—the explosive growth in both the amount and type of information collected and the ability to utilize it—insurers, insurance producers, consumers, and regulators have both opportunities and challenges not imagined 30 years ago. The future potential is unknown, and the world of insurance may look as different in 2045 as 1985 does to 2015. However, regulation and consumer protection, whether in insurance or other markets, have not evolved with similar speed. That regulators are a step behind the industries they are regulating is the norm,[1] but the speed of industry change brought about by the Internet exacerbates the challenges regulators face.

[1] *See*, e.g., Latimer and Maume (2014), p. 142.

However, the insurance regulatory system in the United States also has the flexibility, or at least ability, to apply many of the existing laws and regulations to the sale of insurance online, as well as to marketing, underwriting, and handling of claims. For example, the National Association of Insurance Commissioners (NAIC) Model Unfair Trade Practices Law prohibits "untrue, deceptive or misleading" advertising related to the "business of insurance,"[2] and while the Law was originally drafted in 1947, this section is equally applicable to insurance marketing online, including social media such as Facebook, Twitter, and YouTube. Similarly, consumer protection laws not specifically directed towards insurance may also apply, such as State Unfair and Deceptive Acts and Practices statutes[3] and federal statutes regulating the sale and use of personally identifiable consumer information.[4]

This chapter discusses the intersections of insurance regulation, consumer protection, and the online marketplace in the United States. Section 2 reviews the growth of online sales of insurance by insurers and insurance producers. Section 3 summarizes the U.S. insurance regulatory system, necessary as it is both distinctive and decentralized, with important consequences for supervising the online insurance sector, while Sect. 4 examines the relatively modest body of law specific to online marketing and other activities. Finally, Sect. 5 explores the issues of cyber risk, security, and insurance from several perspectives, including regulatory initiatives by the states and the federal government to establish cybersecurity standards for financial institutions that access and utilize consumer financial and health information, consumer rights when a data breach occurs, and the early stages of regulating cyber insurance.

[2] NAIC Model Law 880-1 § 4.B. "False Information and Advertising Generally. Making, publishing, disseminating, circulating or placing before the public, or causing, directly or indirectly to be made, published, disseminated, circulated, or placed before the public, in a newspaper, magazine or other publication, or in the form of a notice, circular, pamphlet, letter or poster, or over any radio or television station, or in any other way, an advertisement, announcement or statement containing any assertion, representation or statement with respect to the business of insurance or with respect to any insurer in the conduct of its insurance business, which is untrue, deceptive or misleading."

[3] Every state in the U.S. has an Unfair and Deceptive Acts and Practices statute applicable to a range of consumer (and sometimes business) transactions and enforceable by state officials, as well as providing a private cause of action; virtually, all states have adopted similar laws for insurance (though typically without a private right to enforce). The National Consumer Law Center publishes excellent summaries of state consumer protection laws http://www.nclc.org/issues/unfair-a-deceptive-acts-a-practices.html. NAIC model laws include appendixes that enumerate state adoption with specific references to each state's statutory or regulatory section. http://www.naic.org/prod_serv_model_laws.htm.

[4] Gramm-Leach-Bliley Act, codified in part at 15 U.S.C.A. 6801, et seq.; Federal Trade Commission's Guidance on complying with federal laws protecting consumer information, available at: https://www.ftc.gov/tips-advice/business-center/privacy-and-security/gramm-leach-bliley-act.

2 The Growth of Online Sale and Distribution of Insurance in the United States

Consumers[5] generally purchase property casualty and life insurance products through independent insurance producers,[6] through captive agents,[7] or directly from the insurer. "Direct writers" sell through these last two categories, captives and direct purchase from an insurance company, either online or through another medium.[8] Increasingly, insurers utilize multiple distribution channels, such as offering insurance products both through independent agents and directly from the company online.[9] These transactions, starting from the initial query through sale, can be conducted largely or entirely online, as well as through traditional face-to-face interaction or telephone sales. The plethora of communication touch points and increased complexity in the web of sales and underwriting contacts can lead to an array of hybrid situations, a far cry from the traditional insurance "agent" at his desk. In addition, consumers may obtain life insurance, insurance-related investment products, and occasionally property casualty insurance (e.g., personal automobile) through their workplace, from financial institutions and from investment advisors. This chapter limits itself to examining the interaction between consumers, insurance intermediaries, and insurers themselves.

While purchasing insurance through independent agents continues to be a common method of sale, direct sales from insurers is increasing, dominating, for example, the personal lines property casualty market. While the actual purchase of insurance online still represents a small percentage of the distribution channel each year, it is growing and contributing to the decreasing use of independent pro-

[5] As used in this article, "consumer" refers to individuals purchasing personal lines insurance products and small businesses obtaining liability, property, and workers' compensation insurance.

[6] Insurance producers—intermediaries—are often classified as "agents" (representing the insurer) or "brokers" (representing the policyholder). However clear this distinction is in theory, in practice it is thoroughly muddled and the determination heavily fact dependent. This chapter will adopt the increasingly common practice of designating them as "producers" and distinguish between agent and broker only when necessary to the discussion. Insurance producers for consumers and small businesses would typically be considered agents for the insurers, with the potential to bind the insurer to various representations and actions.

[7] "Captive agents" are either independent contractors or employees of a single insurer and sell only that company's products (with some variation by company).

[8] The online sale and purchase of insurance is not synonymous with "direct writing," which also includes sales through telephone communication, through mail service, and through captive agents.

[9] "As the number of companies opting to use multiple channels grows, categorizing a company as a direct writer or agency writer is becoming less helpful." Insurance Information Institute, "Buying Insurance: Evolving Distribution Channels," available at http://www.iii.org/issue-update/buying-insurance-evolving-distribution-channels.

ducers.[10] Soon, it may be appropriate to refer to online sales of insurance as the "common" method of sale, while purchases largely transacted face to face or by telephone communication the "alternative" channel.

The term "sale" also needs to be clarified. As noted below, many consumers will utilize online resources to learn more about insurance products and to comparison shop. The actual insurance purchase may then take place online, via the telephone, or through insurance producers (via face to face, telephone, and online). Insurers and insurance producers utilize a growing number of online resources to promote their products, including company websites and social media, such as Facebook and Twitter. Consumer protection concerns exist throughout this continuum, and the multiplicity of potential insurer to consumer online communication methods generates both greater complexities and opportunities for insurance regulators and consumer (policyholder) advocates.

2.1 *Life Insurance*

In 2014, written premium for life insurance and annuities products exceeded $603 billion.[11] Of this amount, $166 billion were for life products.[12] Ninety percent of new life insurance sales were through producers—50 % by independent agents and 40 % by captive agents—and only 5 % through direct marketing by insurers, which include both telephone and online sales.[13] However, a far larger percentage of consumers who purchase life insurance first research various products online before contacting a producer or the insurer directly.[14] While consumers aged 25–44 are more likely than other age categories to prefer purchasing life insurance online, the number is still low—27 %. However, 83 % of all respondents (regardless of age)

---

[10] Independent producers are well aware of this trend—or threat. *See* IIAB Feb 2013 report available at: http://www.independentagent.com/Resources/Research/MarketShareReport/default.aspx.

[11] National Association of Insurance Commissioners 2014 Industry Analysis Reports, available at http://www.naic.org, Center for Insurance Policy and Research. Accident and Health insurance premiums are often included within life insurance reports but are excluded from data provided in this chapter.

[12] Annuities are sold as investment vehicles through many different intermediaries and institutions, and this brief discussion of distribution channels is limited to life insurance products.

[13] Insurance Information Institute, "Buying Insurance: Evolving Distribution Channels," note 9, above.

[14] The Life Insurance Marketing and Research Association (LIMRA) 2014 Insurance Barometer Study reports that 44 % of survey respondents said they would research life insurance questions online but buy from an independent agent or financial adviser, 25 % would both research and purchase online, and 14 % preferred researching online but then purchasing directly from the company (17 % would not utilize the Internet). Available at https://www.limra.com/Login/?returnURL=%2fResearch%2fAbstracts%2f2015%2f2015_Insurance_Barometer_Study.aspx%3fLangType%3d1033.

would utilize the Internet to research life insurance products and then purchase through an agent, directly with the insurer or online. While the percentage of consumers 65 and over who would utilize the Internet to research or purchase life insurance is the lowest for the four age categories; three-quarters of them (74 %) still indicated they would research online.[15]

2.2 *Property Casualty Insurance*

The property casualty industry wrote almost $570 billion in direct written premium in 2013.[16] Private automobile insurance generates more premium income than any other property/casualty industry product. Homeowners insurance ranks second in size among property casualty products. Together, these two personal lines account for about half of all property casualty premiums.[17] Direct writers accounted for 51.2 % of the net written property casualty premiums, which as noted includes sales through captive agents, online purchases, and insurance acquired via telephone or mail.[18] Direct writers dominated personal lines market at 71 %, with auto and homeowner markets at 72.1 % and 68.4 % respectively.[19] Consumers were more likely to both shop for and purchase property casualty insurance online than for life insurance products, particularly in the personal auto line. As reported by the Insurance Information Institute, in 2012 67 % of personal auto shoppers obtained an online quote and 3.1 million policies were sold online.[20]

Independent producers have suffered declining market share in personal lines for years, where direct channel writers (e.g., GEICO) and insurers utilizing captive agencies (e.g., State Farm and Allstate) are better able to capitalize on increasing

---

[15] *Id.*

[16] National Association of Insurance Commissioners 2013 Industry Analysis Reports, available at http://www.naic.org, Center for Insurance Policy and Research.

[17] *See* Insurance Information Institute, Fact Book 2016 p. 59; American Council of Life Insurers, Life Insurers Fact Book 2012 35 (2012).

[18] Insurance Information Institute, note 9, *supra*, citing a A.M. Best study. This has been a growth of almost 350 % since 2004, when 700,000 policies were purchased online. "A.M. Best Eyes Auto Insurance Distribution Methods in Ratings," September 17, 2013, available at http://www.propertycasualty360.com/2013/09/17/am-best-eyes-auto-insurance-distribution-methods-i.

[19] *Id.* In contrast, 70.2 % of commercial lines premiums were written by independent insurance producers and 30.6 % written by direct writers, citing the A.M. Best Special Report, *supra. See also* Federal Insurance Office, Annual Report on the Insurance Industry, June 2013, pp. 36–37 (Distribution Channels).

[20] *Id.*, citing comScore 2013 study, "The results are based on data from a research panel of one million U.S. consumers and a survey of more than 4000 Internet users."

consumer confidence in utilizing the Internet to research and purchase personal lines insurance products.[21] The importance of online distribution methods is noted by rating agencies, for example, A.M. Best 2013 statement: "Companies that can demonstrate defensible and sustainable competitive advantages—such as control over distribution, multiple distribution channels, low cost structure, and the effective utilization of technology—are likely to be viewed favorably from a rating perspective."[22] Independent producers are not sitting still and are also utilizing the Internet to capture consumer customers.[23] The relevance of this competition is that regardless of how independently producers fair in the future, the sale of insurance online will continue to grow, and therefore consumer protection concerns related to online sales are increasingly important.

3 Insurance Regulation in the United States

While the United States remains the world's largest national insurance market,[24]it still employs a highly decentralized regulatory model. With the exception of health insurance,[25] individual states rather than the federal government exercise virtually exclusive regulatory control over the insurance industry within their jurisdiction.

---

[21] *See* Property Casualty Insurance Market Opportunities & Competitive Challenges for Independent Agents & Brokers (2012), available at, http://www.independentagent.com/Resources/Research/SiteAssets/MarketShareReport/IIABA-2014-Marketshare-Report-2012-Data-FINAL.pdf.

[22] A.M. Best Eyes Auto Insurance Distribution Methods in Ratings," September 17, 2013, *supra* note [13]. "The direct channel's rise has been driven by aggressive marketing, competitive pricing, user-friendly online tools and innovative technologies, all of which can be funded with money once earmarked for agent commissions."

[23] "Today, more agents and brokers are realizing that online auto insurance shoppers are willing to establish a relationship with someone who can act as a trusted advisor to help them understand risk and protection in today's economy. The advantages that direct response carriers may enjoy during marketing and customer acquisition can become disadvantages during the remainder of the customer life cycle." Independent Insurance Agents & Brokers of America, Inc. "2012 Property-Casualty Insurance Market: Opportunities & Competitive Challenges for Independent Agents and Brokers," p. 3, February 27, 2014, available at http://www.independentagent.com/Resources/Research/MarketShareReport/default.aspx.

[24] As of 2014, the U.S. accounted for 35.81 % of the world's premium volume, four times more than Japan, the second largest market. National Association of Insurance Commissioners, Financial Data Repository, available at http://www.naic.org/cipr_statistics.htm. This amount includes health insurance premiums.

[25] Though the federal government has played a major role in funding health insurance and health care since the 1960s with the creation of the Medicare and Medicaid programs, states have still been largely responsible for regulating health insurance, though with significant limitations over employer-provided health care insurance. The advent of the Affordable Care Act (Public Law 111–148 (2010) puts the federal government into direct regulation of healthcare insurance and creates an even more complex interplay between federal and state regulatory authority. *See*, e.g., Keith and Lucia (2014).

This means there are 56 regional insurance regulators in the U.S.—the 50 states, the District of Columbia, and 5 territories. In most states, the insurance commissioner is selected by the state governor and serves at her pleasure; in ten states and one territory insurance commissioners are elected directly by the voters. Turnover is frequent with either system.[26] With the exception of several national insurance programs such as the National Flood Insurance Plan and the Terrorism Risk Insurance Act, the federal government has not asserted supervisory or regulatory authority over life and property-casualty insurance, and until July 2010 there was not even a federal agency charged with assessing the insurance industry in the United States. Subtitle A of Title V of Dodd-Frank created the Federal Insurance Office, which is authorized to 'monitor' the insurance industry, negotiate international treaties, and in very limited circumstances preempt state laws that are inconsistent with international prudential treaties.[27]

The reasons for this structure are historical and political.[28] Insurance regulation became prevalent in the second half of the nineteenth century when the federal government had yet to assume a major role in regulating financial institutions. By default, the states became the insurance regulators. Spurred by the industry's growth and several significant insurance scandals, the states enlarged their role and in 1871 established the National Association of Insurance Commissioners (NAIC).[29] State insurance regulation was set firmly in place by an 1868 US Supreme Court decision holding that insurance was not considered 'interstate commerce' and was therefore outside the federal government's authority.[30] In 1944, the Supreme Court came to a different conclusion and held that insurance was interstate commerce and within the federal government's regulatory authority.[31]

Congress responded quickly, upon the urging of the NAIC, state regulators, agents, and insurers, and in 1945 passed the McCarran-Ferguson Act,

[26] For example, in 2015, approximately 44 % of the state insurance commissioners were new; this turnover was largely due to the results of the fall 2014 elections. State insurance department personnel, including senior staff, are often civil servants and may serve for many years.

[27] The legislation authorizing the Federal Insurance Office is codified at 31 U.S.C. § 313(f).

[28] *See* Schwarcz and Schwarcz (2014); Thomas (2010).

[29] The NAIC is a nongovernmental body that attempts to harmonize state insurance regulation. *See* Susan Randall (1999). The NAIC has become the de facto representative of state insurance commissioners at the international level and has representatives on multiple committees of the International Association of Insurance Regulators (IAIS). *See* http://naic.org/committees_g.htm. State regulators also participate and sometimes lead Supervisory Colleges evaluating internationally active insurance companies. http://www.naic.org/cipr_topics/topic_supervisory_college.htm. Connecticut, for example, is the lead regulator for eight supervisory colleges. http://www.ct.gov/cid/cwp/view.asp?a=1260&Q=562980.

[30] *Paul* v *Virginia*, 75 U.S. 168 (1868). In the United States, the federal government's authority is not plenary but determined by the Constitution. The source of federal regulatory authority over commercial practices is typically located in the Interstate Commerce Clause, U.S.C.A. Const. art. I § 8, cl. 3.

[31] *U.S.* v *South-Eastern Underwriters Association*, 322 U.S. 533 (1944).

15 U.S.C. 1011, which grants insurers limited immunity to federal antitrust laws, and more significantly reconfirmed an explicit preference for state insurance regulation.[32] Though sometimes inaccurately referred to as "preempting" federal law, McCarran-Ferguson essentially establishes a rule of statutory construction that seeks to preserve state regulation over the "business of insurance" unless Congress has clearly indicated its intent to include insurance within the scope of the federal law at issue.[33] Congress can legislate so that the federal government will supervise insurance in specific areas or substitute an entire federal regulatory structure preempting much or all of state insurance regulation, and the states maintain regulatory control over their insurance markets for only as long as Congress does not alter the system.

The greatest threat—or promise, depending upon one's perspective—of federal encroachment into state regulatory preeminence likely comes from international pressure rather than domestic politics. The rapid development of international insurance markets (e.g., the European Union, China), increasing desire by insurers to increase their international presence, and regulatory pressure for internationally accepted capital standards for insurers are forcing U.S. regulators to consider and likely accommodate in some manner international demands for consistency in supervising insurer solvency across borders.[34] While states largely have achieved regulatory consistency in this area, thanks in part to the NAIC and domestic influences,[35] states lack the power to formally regulate or enforce consistency outside their state borders or to bind the United States to international treaties, functions that only the federal government can accomplish.[36]

The Dodd-Frank Act created several mechanisms to augment the federal government's ability to monitor and address systemic risk in the financial services

[32] "No Act of Congress shall be construed to invalidate, impair, or supersede any law enacted by any State for the purpose of regulating the business of insurance, or which imposes a fee or tax upon such business, unless such Act specifically relates to the business of insurance." 15 U.S.C. § 1012(b). The industry remains subject to state antitrust laws, many of which mimic their federal counterparts.

[33] Congress can remove all doubts as to its intent in specific legislation to regulate insurance simply by so indicating, as for example in the Terrorism Risk Insurance Act, codified as a note to 28 U.S.C. § 1610.

[34] *See Insurance Sector 2014 Year End Review and Forecast for 2015 (2014)*, available at https://www.dlapiper.com/en/hongkong/insights/publications/2015/02/insurance-2014-year-end-review-2015-forecast/.

[35] *See* Risk-Based Capital (RBC) for Insurers Model Act (2012), which has been adopted in 27 states, http://naic.org/committees_index_model_description_r_z.htm#rbc_act (MDL 312). From the NAIC's mission statement: "Through the NAIC, state insurance regulators establish standards and best practices, conduct peer review, and coordinate their regulatory oversight." http://naic.org/index_about.htm.

[36] The Federal Insurance Office is authorized to negotiate foreign treaties in coordination with the U.S. Trade Representative and has the ability to preempt state laws inconsistent with international treaty obligations related to solvency regulation—though only after completing a daunting administrative process. See 31 U.S.C. § 313. FIO has yet to utilize this authority.

sector, including the Financial Stability Oversight Council, which reviews financial institutions—banks and "nonbank financial companies" (which includes insurers)—to determine if their failure could threaten national financial stability.[37] As of fall 2015, the Council has designated three U.S. insurers as potentially posing "systematic risk," subjecting them to regulatory oversight by the Federal Reserve Board.[38] Thus, the Board has now entered the crowded U.S. insurance regulatory sector and could become the dominant U.S. insurance regulator on international issues; it has already obtained Member status at the IAIS.[39] The Board is responsible for group or consolidated supervision of specific insurance group holding companies, which as of fall 2015 amounted to one-third of U.S. insurance industry assets.[40] However, there are also political counterweights to an increased federal regulatory role, perhaps most significant being Republican control of both houses of Congress (as of 2015), which are unlikely to support significant expansion of federal regulatory powers, particularly in a field long regulated by the states. The NAIC, the states individually, and large segments of the insurance industry (at least for now) also oppose a larger federal role.

In addition to dispersing regulatory authority throughout the country, the state-based regulatory system has another important consequence. Insurers must comply with the laws of every state they do business in and not simply the laws of their domiciliary or home state. Coupling this requirement with the prevalence of rate and form regulation in the majority of states (particularly for personal lines products), this means that insurers cannot utilize the same policy forms or rate structure throughout their market and must seek regulatory approval from each state they do business in.[41] Fortunately, state regulators generally utilize the same solvency and prudential regulatory standards, and there are formal coordinating bodies in specific areas or lines of insurance, such as the Interstate Insurance Product Regulation Commission, which provides a "central point of electronic filings" for life insurance and disability products.[42] The NAIC provides a forum and methodology for

[37] Dodd-Frank Wall Street Reform and Consumer Protection Act. 12 USC 5301 § 113 (2010), Authority to Require Supervision and Regulation of Certain Nonbank Financial Companies.

[38] American International Group, MetLife and Prudential Financial. *See*http://www.treasury.gov/initiatives/fsoc/designations/Pages/default.aspx.

[39] http://www.iaisweb.org/index.cfm?event=getPage&nodeId=25189. The Federal Insurance Office is also an IAIS member.

[40] The 3 FSOC-designated companies and 12 other insurance holding companies that own a bank or thrift. http://www.federalreserve.gov/newsevents/testimony/sullivan20150929a.htm.

[41] In contrast, in the European Union, an insurer operating in multiple jurisdictions generally need only conform to its home Member State's insurance laws, particularly in the areas of solvency and prudential regulation. Directive 2009/138/EC (November 25, 2009), title I, Chapter VIII, Right of establishment and freedom to provide services. Regulation of insurance rates is not allowed and regulation of insurance policy forms discouraged. Title I, Articles 154, 181–182.

[42] Approximately 44 states belong, though 2 states responsible for supervising the largest concentration of life insurers, Connecticut and New York, are not members. http://www.insurancecompact.org/about.htm.

cooperation and potential consistency in other areas, even when there is less formal statutory uniformity.[43]

Whether the federal government will supplant state-based solvency regulation is an issue well beyond this brief introduction to the U.S. insurance regulatory system. Our point is that the current balance between state and federal regulatory oversight of insurance is in flux, which *may* (not will) significantly affect how insurance is regulated, including the online sale of insurance products. What is certain, though, is that after deliberation the NAIC will develop new model laws and standards and revise existing ones in response to online innovation and marketing, which some states will adopt in whole, others in part, and some not at all. Insurers and insurance producers operating across state boundaries in the United States will continue to maintain state-specific compliance programs and keep a careful eye out for developments by the states, the NAIC, and the federal government in the online realm.

Finally, litigation involving insurers and policyholders has an indirect, though powerful, regulatory effect on insurer's conduct. The development and modification of insurance policy language is closely associated with not only the development of particular risks, market competition, and regulatory requirements, but also how courts have interpreted policy language. Insurance coverage litigation is common in the United States, and each year thousands of lawsuits are filed contesting insurer interpretation of policy language and conduct, often seeking damages beyond the policy benefits ("bad faith" lawsuits). Since contract interpretation, including insurance contracts, is largely governed by state common law, courts are frequently examining similar or identical policy language and sometimes arriving at inconsistent interpretations. Insurers are bound by common law and statutory and regulatory requirements in each state they write in, adding to the complexity of crafting and interpreting policy language. As discussed in the next section, the online sale of insurance exists within this multijurisdictional framework.

4 Regulation of Insurance Sales and the Internet

In the United States, the regulation of insurance sales and most operational enforcement has reacted very minimally to the advent of the Internet, with a few notable exceptions. In most instances, online activities have simply been folded into the existing regulatory structure. The Internet is generally seen simply as another platform for the delivery and acquisition of information, not particularly distinct from other existing mediums. Insurance sales and advertising are subject to the same web of regulation as all other commercial industries and will encounter both

[43] *See* note 29 above. In the market conduct area, for example, the NAIC developed a common set of investigative and reporting standards for exams. http://www.naic.org/prod_serv_marketreg.htm.

state and federal regulators tasked with consumer protection. Certain unique challenges do exist and are slowly being identified as they emerge—such as social media's particularly muddled blending of the commercial testimonial and the genuinely organic opinion. Likewise, the inherent anonymity of email or online Internet communication does present some problems distinct from older terrestrial forms of advertising or solicitation. This section will focus on those areas which US law has identified as areas of particular regulatory activity.

4.1 Applicability of Regulatory Scheme to Online Marketing

For a variety of historic and cultural reasons, the United States has been and remains slow in adopting rules restricting or regulating activity on the Internet. A historic and formalized legalized protection of speech, very broadly applied, combined with a laissez-faire attitude toward emerging Internet industries, has made the US a laggard among other industrialized countries in formal protections for online consumers. The Unites States generally has some of the weakest defamation and libel laws of any comparable developed nation and an overall relaxed attitude towards privacy and private information. Increasing cyber attacks and hacking combined with a growing recognition of the value of such data have created a countervailing pressure on legislators to expand specific consumer protection availability.

In general, however, the online marketing of insurance is regulated by the same laws which regulate marketing in any other context, with no particular enhancement or distinction for that marketing being "virtual" or "online." Some states, such as New York, do explicitly include in the definition of advertising Internet postings in particular lines of insurance, such as life insurance policies pursuant to life settlement contracts. Likewise, New York has clarified that the use of social media platforms such as Facebook or LinkedIn or similar such websites when used for the promotion of insurance, insurers, or insurance agents would constitute advertisements under New York law. Thus, while the majority of states have not seen the need to specifically amend existing definitions to include online activities, others have chosen to simply expand those definitions explicitly or through regulatory interpretation to govern Internet communications as subsets or extensions of existing regulatory schemes.

In most contexts, the extension of existing marketing regulations to the online sphere—including social media—are relatively intuitive, with advertisements generally self-evident in the medium. A pop-up advertisement or static banner ad is not sufficiently dissimilar in kind to either television or newsprint to have provided the regulator's need for much-detailed explication. Some aspects of online marketing, particularly in the social media context, such as testimonials, have come under additional regulatory scrutiny.

Testimonials are a long-cherished marketing tool employed by insurance carriers and producers. At least 37 states regulate the use of testimonials by insurance carriers and producers in certain lines of business,[44] with five states (Minnesota, Oklahoma, Pennsylvania, Texas, and Utah) regulating the use of testimonials for advertising and marketing in all lines of business.[45]

A testimonial, by its nature, can be unduly influential to a potential purchaser of a product if not regulated to ensure its appropriateness in context. Generally, the regulation of testimonials requires the statement to be (1) genuine, (2) the actual opinion of the person making the statement, (3) applicable to the product being promoted, and (4) accurately reproduced.

Social media platforms, like Facebook, Twitter, and LinkedIn, have made the task of collecting and distributing testimonials more conveniently than ever. These platforms, however, could easily conceal or confuse a user of the media platform as to whether the testimonial was organically produced by a user or actually part of a media and advertising campaign. The use of the now nearly ubiquitous "like buttons" or other aggregators of user endorsements such as "star ratings" could be construed as creating testimonials. The Securities and Exchange Commission has warned that features such as "like buttons" on social media platforms could lead to testimonials, which are regulated communications for investment advisors, a group often similarly regulated to insurance producers. It warned that even a third party's use of the "like button" on an investment adviser's Facebook page could be deemed a testimonial if it is an explicit or implicit statement of clients' experiences with the investment advisor.[46] Such regulatory attention would be even more likely to arise should the insurance company or producer have deliberately arranged the testimonial or "likes."

As such, the general US regulatory preoccupation with primarily concerning itself with ensuring transparency rather than content is continued. The issues concerning regulators are not so much with the online medium itself. Rather, it is to the extent that the general principles preventing misrepresentation or fraudulent inducement could be aggravated by the Internet which the regulators have so far primarily concerned themselves.

4.2 The Can-Spam Act and Regulation of Commercial Email

Even in the United Sates, certain limitations on commercial emails have been promulgated as a result of irritating marketing practices such as mass or "spam" email blasts and will apply to insurance companies and producers. The colorfully named Controlling the Assault of Non-solicited Pornography and Marketing (Can-SPAM) Act of 2003 applies not only to such blast or "Spam" email marketers

[44] **AL**—Ala. Admin. Code r. 482-1-013-.08.

[45] **MN**—Minn. R. 2790.0900.

[46] Securities and Exchange Commission, *Investment Adviser Use of* ***Social Media***, National Examination Risk Alert Vol. II, Issue 1 (Jan. 4, 2012).

but also to all commercial emails, regardless of numbers, and requires the Federal Trade Commission (FTC) to enforce its provisions.

Thus, though the business of insurance, as explained above, is still primarily and exclusively the domain of the various state regulators, aspects of online marketing do come within certain federal regulatory schemes, particularly the Can-Spam Act. This law does not just apply to bulk emails, rather it applies to all commercial messages, which the law defines as "any electronic mail message the primary purpose of which is the commercial advertisement or promotion of a commercial product or service," including email that promotes content on commercial websites. The law makes no exception for business-to-business email. That means all email—for example, a message to former customers announcing a new product line—must comply with the law.[47]

According to the Federal Trade Commission, the Can-SPAM Act was designed not to be particularly repressive and offers seven clear elements for compliance:

1. **Don't use false or misleading header information.** Your "From," "To," "Reply-To," and routing information—including the originating domain name and email address—must be accurate and identify the person or business who initiated the message.
2. **Don't use deceptive subject lines.** The subject line must accurately reflect the content of the message.
3. **Identify the message as an ad.** The law gives you a lot of leeway in how to do this, but you must disclose clearly and conspicuously that your message is an advertisement.
4. **Tell recipients where you're located.** Your message must include your valid physical postal address. This can be your current street address, a post office box you've registered with the U.S. Postal Service, or a private mailbox you've registered with a commercial mail receiving agency established under Postal Service regulations.
5. **Tell recipients how to opt out of receiving future email from you.** Your message must include a clear and conspicuous explanation of how the recipient can opt out of getting email from you in the future. Craft the notice in a way that's easy for an ordinary person to recognize, read, and understand. Creative use of type size, color, and location can improve clarity. Give a return email address or another easy Internet-based way to allow people to communicate their choice to you. You may create a menu to allow a recipient to opt out of certain types of messages, but you must include the option to stop all commercial messages from you. Make sure your spam filter doesn't block these opt-out requests.
6. **Honor opt-out requests promptly.** Any opt-out mechanism you offer must be able to process opt-out requests for at least 30 days after you send your message. You must honor a recipient's opt-out request within 10 business days. You can't

[47] https://www.ftc.gov/tips-advice/business-center/guidance/can-spam-act-compliance-guide-business.

charge a fee, require the recipient to give you any personally identifying information beyond an email address, or make the recipient take any step other than sending a reply email or visiting a single page on an Internet website as a condition for honoring an opt-out request. Once people have told you they don't want to receive more messages from you, you can't sell or transfer their email addresses, even in the form of a mailing list. The only exception is that you may transfer the addresses to a company you've hired to help you comply with the CAN-SPAM Act.

7. **Monitor what others are doing on your behalf.** The law makes clear that even if you hire another company to handle your email marketing, you can't contract away your legal responsibility to comply with the law. Both the company whose product is promoted in the message and the company that actually sends the message may be held legally responsible.

Violations of the Can-Spam Act could result in fines of up to $16,000 per email, making compliance a financially prudent decision for any insurance producer. Thus, direct email marketing in the insurance industry is relatively straightforward and limited in the variations of technique available to the marketer.

4.3 Insurer Data Security and Consumer Protection

A related regulatory concern is how companies that collect private health and financial information from consumers secure this information and how they respond when data breaches occur.[48] As with other areas of financial service regulation, cybersecurity and data breach notification requirements must also be considered within the framework of existing (and future) state and federal laws regulating data security, the majority of which were not drafted specifically for the insurance industry. For example, in 2015 the State of Connecticut amended its data security laws to require all businesses to provide notice to affected consumers not later than 90 days after discovery of a data breach and to provide a minimum of 1 year of free identify theft protection to these consumers.[49] The same legislation also requires health insures to develop enhanced data security programs and mandatory encryption of personal health information.[50] An open question is how

[48] "There are two types of companies: those who have been hacked and those who don't yet know they have been hacked." This oft-quoted declaration is attributed to John Chambers, Chief Executive Officer of Cisco, among others.

[49] Connecticut Public Act No. 15-142, Sect. 6 (2015).

[50] *Id.*, Sect. 5. Enforcement of the Act's provisions is divided among a number of state agencies, including the state Attorney General and the Insurance Department.

future federal statutory and regulatory requirements will affect the ability of states to establish and enforce different (more strict) data security standards for insurers and consumer/policyholder rights upon a data breach.[51] Section 5 below focuses on cyber issues.

The NAIC is also addressing these issues when insurance consumers' information has been hacked or otherwise misappropriated by a third party.[52] At the end of 2015, the NAIC Cybersecurity Task Force finalized its "NAIC Roadmap for Cybersecurity Consumer Protection" (the industry objected to its initial title "Cybersecurity Bill of Rights"). This document sets out a list of rights for consumers, including requiring insurers and insurance producers to inform insurance consumers about the type of "personally identifiable information" they collect and the approximate length of time they maintain it, to adequately protect such information from unauthorized disclosure to other parties, to notify affected consumers no late than 60 days after a data breach is discovered, describe its mitigation plan to remedy the breach, and to offer a minimum of one year of identity theft protection.[53] While these standards are an important acknowledgement that cybersecurity is essential to maintaining consumer confidence in online commerce and the privacy of their sensitive data, they are aspirational, as it is up to each state legislature to determine whether to codify the this Roadmap, to modify it, or to do nothing.

Further, as discussed in the previous paragraph, legal rights and obligations related to data breaches of consumer health and financial information implicate numerous federal and state laws enforced by many different regulatory or law enforcement agencies, with the interplay among them intricate and not always discernable. The understandable rush by Congress, state legislatures, and federal and state regulators to address cybersecurity and protection of the nation's economy and national security will almost certainly result in new legislative and regulatory initiatives which may simplify compliance and enforcement issues, add even more regulatory uncertainty, or do both.[54]

---

[51] For example, in 2015 a number of bills were introduced in the U.S. Congress that would establish national standards for data security and data breach notification standards; states responded quickly, urging Congress not to preempt state laws providing additional or different standards or the ability of states to enforce them. http://www.naag.org/naag/media/naag-news/federal-data-breach-legislation-should-not-preempt-states1.php (July 7, 2015 letter from 47 state attorneys general to Congress). These issues are not limited to insurance or financial services legislation and are often fiercely debated whenever Congress considers consumer-related legislation in areas where the states also regulate.

[52] Cyber regulatory issues are reviewed in Sect. 5.3, below, including the industry's obligations to adopt and enforce reasonable cybersecurity protocols.

[53] http://www.naic.org/committees_ex_cybersecurity_tf.htm. A data breach is defined as "[W]hen an unauthorized individual or organization sees, steals or uses sensitive, protected or confidential information—usually personal, financial and/or health information."

[54] While simplicity typically eases the industry's compliance concerns (or at least its costs), it does not always lead to better public policy, at least in consumer protection. For example, a federal law that preempts all state-law-related consumer rights and remedies in the event of a data breach could just as easily lead to less rather than more consumer protections (e.g., see note 51 above).

5 Cybersecurity, Cyber Risk, and Cyber Insurance

The growth of online options for marketing, insurance, and the industry's ability to gather and utilize an ever-increasing amount of consumer data is mirrored by the substantial risks of unauthorized access to this information. Cybersecurity has quickly emerged as a primary concern for large businesses, particularly financial service entities.[55] However, with these risks come opportunities, as the market for cyber insurance is projected to grow substantially.[56] State insurance regulators have responded relatively quickly to both cyber risks and cyber insurance, and the U.S. government is examining how to encourage a strong cyber insurance market as one tool to defend the private sector against organized cyber attacks.[57] These issues are briefly reviewed below.

5.1 *Data Management and Cyber Breaches*

Insurers and other financial institutions have long acquired, stored and utilized detailed financial, medical, legal, and other valuable information on individuals and businesses, including policyholders, claimants, vendors, and medical providers. Electronic, Internet-based usage creates tremendous benefits—many still developing—but also new vulnerabilities to data loss from inadequate network security and negligence of employees or vendors, as well as from ideologically motivated individuals or groups, business competitors, organized crime, foreign governments, and other parties who illegally access, utilize, or destroy electronically stored data.

This information makes them a rich target for cyber attacks, and the effects of data breaches from whatever source can have serious consequences for individuals and companies whose data have been impermissibly accessed and undermine consumer confidence in the security of financial institutions and the economy in

[55] *Cyber liability insurance market trends,* October 24, 2014, PartnerRe, available at http://www.partnerre.com/risk-solutions/treaty/specialty-casualty/cyber-risk?location=north-america; *Cyber Risks: The Growing Threat,* The Insurance Information Institute, June 2014, pp. 4–11, http://www.iii.org/white-paper/cyber-risks-the-growing-threat-040813.

[56] See Sect. 5.2, below.

[57] The European Union is also considering new data breach notification requirements. "On 15 June 2015, the European Council reached a general approach on the general data protection regulation that establishes rules adapted to the digital era. The twin aims of this regulation are to enhance the level of personal data protection for individuals and to increase business opportunities in the Digital Single Market." http://www.consilium.europa.eu/en/press/press-releases/2015/06/15-jha-data-protection/. The European Parliament will review this proposal.

general.[58] Damages caused by cyber breaches and attacks include loss and illegal use of customer and proprietary information; damage to information systems; loss of operating capacity and business income until the systems are rendered safe and operational; reputation risk and loss of consumer confidence; costs of responding to regulatory actions, including fines and penalties; and liability to third parties potentially harmed by the cyber breach or attack.

In early 2015 alone, the U.S. insurance sector had two significant data breaches. In January 2015, Anthem Inc., one of the nation's largest health insurers, reported a cybersecurity breach affecting more than 80 million consumers,[59] and in March 2015 Premera Blue Cross, another health insurer based in Washington state, reported a breach where data involving approximately 11 million consumers may have been illegally accessed.[60] State insurance regulators, coordinating through the NAIC, immediately announced multistate investigations of both breaches.[61] In addition, private parties filed lawsuits with equal dispatch.[62]

The likelihood, extent, and cost of third-party liability are dependent upon the nature of a jurisdiction's tort and legal liability regime, including when a party is legally responsible for harm to another (e.g., statutory and common law actions for

---

[58] Cyber attacks are increasing against the commercial sector and government agencies. See, e.g., *Cyber Attacks on U.S. Companies Since November 2014,* The Heritage Foundation Issue Brief No. 4487 (November 18, 2015); *Cyber attacks a growing concern around the world,* Property Casualty 360, March 1, 2016, http://www.propertycasualty360.com/2016/03/01/cyber-attacks-a-growing-concern-around-the-world. In April 2015, the federal Office of Personnel Management announced a data breach involving the theft of personal and financial information of 4.2 million current and former federal employees; while investigating this incident, OPM determined that similar information on an additional 21 million individuals had also been stolen. https://www.opm.gov/cybersecurity/.

[59] See, e.g., http://www.nytimes.com/2015/02/07/business/data-breach-at-anthem-may-lead-to-others.html. Anthem reported that while medical records may not have been compromised, individual Social Security numbers and related personally identifiable information was likely stolen, which would make consumers particularly vulnerable to identity theft and other cyber crimes.

[60] http://www.nytimes.com/2015/03/18/business/premera-blue-cross-says-data-breach-exposed-medical-data.html. Data stolen included both policyholder medical and financial information and Social Security numbers.

[61] http://naic.org/Releases/2015_docs/state_regulators_call_for_multi-state_exam_of_anthem.htm; http://naic.org/Releases/2015_docs/naic_responds_to_premera_breach.htm.

[62] http://www.modernhealthcare.com/article/20150206/NEWS/302069967 (Anthem); http://www.seattletimes.com/seattle-news/premera-negligent-in-data-breach-5-lawsuits-claim/ (Premera). Typically in the United States, lawsuits filed on behalf of potentially harmed individuals and companies will follow immediately upon the announcement of a government investigation of practices or actions involving financial institutions and other large corporate entities that market to consumers. These are often filed as class actions—the plaintiff or complaint is a class of individuals alleging similar damages from a specific event or practice—and for defendants the cost of defense alone may exceed government fines and penalties. In some instances, corporate defendants may simultaneously confront government civil investigations and litigation from both federal and state authorities, criminal investigations by law enforcement agencies, and lawsuits filed by consumers and other affected persons or groups.

negligent breach of a duty that is the proximate cause of verifiable damages) and the remedies available, such as actual and compensatory damages, recoupment of attorneys' fees, and punitive damage. The scope of liability and available remedies varies among the states, sometimes considerably, and federal law can provide additional causes of action. Data breach notification requirements and required assistance to consumers are a major risk for insurers, as there are specific federal and often state requirements for data breaches involving personally identifiable health and financial information.[63] The cost of notification and providing credit monitoring and identify theft detection varies depending upon the scope of the data breach, type of information accessed, cause of the breach, and organizational preloss planning, with one study estimating the cost at $217 per record accessed.[64]

5.2 Cyber Insurance

5.2.1 Market Growth

Stating that the cyber insurance market is dynamic is an understatement. Though still described as a market in its "infancy,"[65] cyber insurance premium volume has doubled every 2 years since 2009[66] Industry estimates put cyber insurance premiums at $750 million in 2011, $1 billion in 2012, and between $2 and $2.5 billion

---

[63] The federal Health Insurance Portability and Accountability Act (HIPPA) requires customer notification within 60 days of a data breach involving personally identifiable health or financial information. HIPPA Breach Notification Rule, 45 CFR §§ 164.400-414. Title V of the Gramm-Leach-Bliley Act of 1999 (GLBA) 15 U.S.C. §6801–6809 requires financial institutions to provide customers with notice of their privacy policies and requires financial institutions to safeguard "the security and confidentiality of customer information, to protect against any anticipated threats or hazards to the security or integrity of such records, and to protect against unauthorized access to or use of such records or information which could result in substantial harm or inconvenience to any customer." 15 U.S.C.A. § 6801(b).

[64] Ponemon Institute Research Report, *2015 Cost of Data Breach Study: United States*, available at http://www-03.ibm.com/security/data-breach/. The average cost per record for the Financial sector was higher ($259 per record). *Id.* at p. 7.

[65] "Infancy" is an ubiquitous description for this market. The search phrase "cyber insurance infancy" in Google pulls up over a hundred sources. *See*, e.g., *Cyber Insurance: Just One Component of Risk Management*, Wall Street Journal, March 27, 2014, http://blogs.wsj.com/cio/2014/03/27/cyber-insurance-just-one-component-of-risk-management/.

[66] "Cyber insurance has been the fastest-growing property-casualty insurance line in recent history ... Cyber insurance premium ... has grown at an average annual rate of 36 % since the market took off in 2009, approximately doubling every 2 years." Conning, Inc., "Cyber insurance, the new model for new insurance products?" The Conning Commentary, p. 1, July 2015—used with permission.

in 2014.[67] While the take-up rate for cyber insurance varies significantly by business sector and size, the percentage of companies buying cyber insurance is increasing, with financial institutions among the major purchasers.[68]

5.2.2 Types of Cyber Insurance

Insurance coverage for data-related loss is not a new product and has been available in the United States for several decades.[69] Similarly, the harm or damages that can arise from cyber-related losses are also familiar. These damages can be intangible, such as disruption/lost profit and reputational harm, as well as lost or damaged data and software systems, liability to third parties, data breach notification requirements, and regulatory investigations and fines. As well as insuring for damage to tangible property, first-party property coverages have long covered business interruption losses, as well as other damages related to business disruption.

What is new is the magnitude of cyber breaches and how cyber risks are viewed in the eyes of the public, government agencies, insurers and brokers, and (potential) commercial policyholders. The nature of cyber risks, its causes and consequences, and the cost of claims change quickly, as do the perceptions and new understandings of these risks among insurers, insurance intermediaries, policyholders, commercial entities, independent rating agencies, and regulators. Legal and regulatory responses are evolving rapidly, and sometimes hastily, affecting both the legal responsibilities of potential insured and the availability of insurance to protect them. Cyber insurance is a diverse as well as a growing market, with an estimated 35–40 insurers writing stand-alone policies in 2014 and dozens more providing some form of coverage coupled with existing policies.[70] Market competition and the demands of brokers and large commercial policyholders also influence product development, as they do in other areas. Cyber insurance itself is a regulated product, subject to the vicissitudes of 56 regulatory jurisdictions and the possibility of federal intervention in the market.

---

[67] *Insurance Against Cyber Attacks Expected to Bloom*, New York Times, December 23, 2011; *The Betterley Report*, Cyber/Privacy Insurance Market Survey, June 2014; *Benchmarking Trends: As Cyber Concerns Broaden, Insurance Purchases Rise*, Marsh Risk Management Research, March 2015. Lloyds of London estimates approximately 90 % of the cyber insurance market is placed in the United States. The Conning Commentary, pp. 1, 3.

[68] *Cyber Risks: The Growing Threat*, The Insurance Information Institute, June 2014, pp. 20–24; http://www.iii.org/white-paper/cyber-risks-the-growing-threat-040813.

[69] "Cyber isn't so new, at least in terms of its availability (we started writing about Cyber in 2000). But it is 'new' in terms of its recognition as a key component of most commercial insurance portfolios and in terms of its evolution of coverage wordings ... [and] exposures being underwritten." *The Betterley Report*, Cyber/Privacy Insurance Market Survey, p. 4, June 2014.

[70] *The Betterley Report*, Cyber/Privacy Insurance Market Survey, pp. 5–7, June 2014; PartnerRe study, note 55, *supra*.

Conceptually, we can classify cyber insurance within several matrixes, including (1) first party and third party coverage, (2) cyber-specific coverage endorsements within existing standard commercial policies versus stand-alone specialty policies, and (3) the potential for cyber coverage within existing policy language such as Business Interruption coverage within commercial property policies and Personal and Advertising Injury coverages in ISO's Commercial General Liability (CGL) policy forms.[71] These orderings are not mutually exclusive but illustrate several ways to evaluate the cyber insurance market.

Considering the third matrix, a common pattern with emerging risks and insurance is as follows: (1) policyholders attempt to find coverage for these risks or claims in existing policy language, (2) insurers initially rely on existing exclusions to limit or deny coverage for these new risks, (3) move to redrafting forms or creating specific exclusions, and then (4) gradually providing risk-specific coverage with carefully tailored limits through new stand-alone policies or endorsements to standard policies. Much of this dynamic takes place within and is shaped by insurance coverage litigation in multiple jurisdictions, as discussed in Sect. 3.[72]

Cyber insurance is following a similar path.[73] For example, "Personal and Advertising Injury" coverage has been part of standard CGL forms for decades and, as defined, offers potential coverage for liability claims arising from cyber breaches.[74] Insurers amended these provisions to more clearly exclude certain risks, litigation has resulted in inconsistencies on a state-by-state basis,[75] and ISO has

[71] ISO, formerly known as Insurance Services Office, serves as a statistical agent for many property casualty insurers. It drafts many of the standard forms utilized in personal and commercial lines and also seeks state regulatory approval for its forms. http://www.verisk.com/iso.html. ISO is now part of Verisk Analytics.

[72] This scenario is exemplified by decades of litigation surrounding coverage for environmental damage, the use of increasingly explicit exclusions (leading to the "absolute pollution exclusion," which is not absolute either by its own terms or as judicially interpreted), and the growth of environmental insurance products in both the liability and property sectors. Professor Jeffrey Stempel describes this process well: STEMPEL ON INSURANCE CONTRACTS, chapter 14:11, 3rd ed. (Wolters Kluwer, 2014). Other examples include coverages for mold damage and trademark claims.

[73] Podolak (2015), pp. 369, 377–379. This article provides an excellent summary of the cyber insurance market in the United States, along with litigation shaping and defining the products.

[74] Particularly, "Oral or written publication, in any manner, of material that violates a person's right of privacy." This language is standard in ISO's CGL policies and remains current through the most recent version, CG 00 01 04 13 (Section V, 14(e)). *See also Cyber Risks: The Growing Threat,* The Insurance Information Institute, June 2014, pp. 17–18, note [55], above.

[75] For example, in 2015, the Connecticut Supreme Court ruled that loss of data tapes containing personal information and subsequent claims against the insured did not constitute "Personal Injury" as the information had not been "published." *Recall Total Information Management v. Federal Insurance Co.*, 115 A3d 458, 460 (Conn. 2015). In contrast, a California appellate court ruled that the publication requirement in the coverage grant did not necessarily require disclosure to third parties. *Zurich Am. Ins. Co. v. Fieldstone Mortg. Co.*, 2007 WL 3268460 at *5 (D. Md. Oct. 26, 2007).

recently created a CGL endorsement to eliminate coverage.[76] Property casualty insurers now provide cyber risk coverage, including data protection, through separate policies, as well as new coverage endorsements.

Liability insurance constitutes the majority of cyber insurance premium written in the United States,[77] though major insurers may write both third and first party coverages within the same policy. For example, CNA and Chubb cyber policies include liability coverage for third-party claims such as data breaches resulting in the unauthorized disclosure of individual health and financial information and reputational damage ("crisis management expenses"), as well as direct (first-party) losses or damage, including business interruption, damage to the insured's own data and network system, and coverage for "cyber extortion."[78] While ISO policies do not dominate the specialty coverage market as they do in personal lines and standard commercial liability and property coverages, it has its own form for "damage to electronic data liability."[79]

The major cost driver in liability policies is not defending policyholder lawsuits, as was anticipated, but post-breach response costs which are either required by federal or state law (see Sect. 5.3, below) or as part of a settlement agreement between third-party claimants and the policyholder.[80] Data breaches cost financial service organizations an average of $257 per record hacked,[81] and some industry analysts believe that tailoring insurance products to addressing data breach response requirements and costs will be the most significant—and beneficial—protection cyber insurers may offer.[82]

---

[76] Podolak, 33 Quinnipiac Law Rev. at pp. 380–395. ISO Endorsement CG 21 07 05 14 excludes bodily injury, property damage, and personal and advertising injury liability "arising out of any or disclosure of any person's or organization's confidential or personal information, including patents, trade secrets, processing methods, customer lists, financial information, credit card information, health information or any other type of nonpublic information."

[77] Standard & Poor's Ratings Direct, *Looking before They Leap: U.S. Insurers Dip Their Toes In The Cyber-Risk Pool*, June 9, 2015.

[78] Chubb ForeFront Portfolio 3.0, CyberSecurity Coverage Part, available at http://www.chubb.com/businesses/csi/chubb822.html. CNA NetProtect Essential, available at www.cna.com (select "Look for Products and Services").

[79] Electronic Data Liability Coverage Form, form number CG 00 65 04 13.

[80] The Conning Commentary, p. 4, note [66] above.

[81] Ponemon Institute Research Report, p. [7] note [64] above.

[82] "The service-led response by insurers to cyber risks may point the way to insurers' future product development strategies." The Conning Commentary, p. 4, note [66] above; "Remediation is an area that is no longer new for Cyber Risk insurance (in fact, we believe that it is the primary reason why many insureds buy Cyber Risk insurance)." *The Betterley Report,* Cyber/Privacy Insurance Market Survey, p. 9, note [64] above.

5.3 Regulation of Cyber Risks and Cyber Insurance

Federal and state interests in cyber risk and cyber insurance include enhancing cybersecurity in the private sector to minimize cyber-related losses, to create and enforce minimum standards for insurers (and other regulated entities) on data protection and duties after a breach, and to regulate cyber insurance consistent with each state's insurance regulatory regime. Any discussion of legislative and regulatory responses to cyber risk will be outdated soon after it is written; this brief review provides a snapshot of federal and state initiatives in this area, identifying key government agencies and their views and actions related to cyber insurance. However, their work in this area will likely continue indefinitely.

The federal government's national security concerns include maintaining confidentiality of sensitive government information, protection of infrastructure, and preventing cyber attacks or breakdowns that could paralyze or cripple the U.S. economy.[83] In February 2013, President Obama signed Executive Order 13636, "Improving Critical Infrastructure Cybersecurity," directing federal agencies to create a "Cybersecurity Framework" which would develop standards to improve the cyber resilience of the "Nation's critical infrastructure," working in partnership with the private sector.[84] Cyber insurance's potential to enhance cybersecurity is recognized by the federal government. The Treasury Department, in an August 2013 report to the President on progress implementing Executive Order 13636, noted that "insurers could require policyholders to comply with minimum security standards, ... [offer] premium discounts to [policyholders] to make additional security investments that reduce risks ... [and] lead to a better understanding of cyber threat patterns ... because insurers need credible data to appropriately

[83] For example, a July 2015 Lloyds/University of Cambridge report estimated that a cyber attack on the power grid for the Northeastern United States could cost the U.S. economy between $243 Billion and $1 Trillion. "Business Blackout," https://www.lloyds.com/lloyds/press-centre/press-releases/2015/07/business-blackout.

[84] https://www.whitehouse.gov/the-press-office/2013/02/12/executive-order-improving-critical-infrastructure-cybersecurity. In August 2013, the President's Cybersecurity Coordinator noted the importance of cyber insurance to the Cybersecurity Framework project, stating that the goal of collaboration with the insurance industry "would be to build underwriting practices that promote the adoption of cyber risk-reducing measures and risk-based pricing and foster a competitive cyber insurance market." https://www.whitehouse.gov/blog/2013/08/06/incentives-support-adoption-cybersecurity-framework.

underwrite and price policies."[85] The U.S. Department of Homeland Security is engaged in similar evaluations.[86]

The federal government's purpose is a familiar one: to utilize the traditional risk-mitigation functions of the private insurance market to research and evaluate risks, develop standards and practices to minimize them, enforce these standards through risk-based pricing, and serve as a source of compensation when losses occur. Insurers have strong economic incentives to reduce policyholder losses, and their ability to serve as private regulators and "gatekeepers" for activity important to public as well as private interests (e.g., driving a car, online commercial activity) is well recognized.[87] The industry has the same expectations. "Cyber insurers can help insureds do this, [reduce and mitigate cyber risk] just as insurers have done for property and boiler and machinery insurance for a century—invest more in minimizing claims and spend less on claims payments."[88]

Within the states, New York has taken a lead role in evaluating cyber risks and financial institutions. In 2013 and 2014, the Department of Financial Services, New York's dual banking and insurance regulator, surveyed regulated institutions on the nature and scope of their cybersecurity programs, funding allocated, and placement of information technology and security departments within the institution's organizational and reporting structure. DFS issued a report on cyber risk and banking institutions in May 2014 and a similar report on insurance companies in February 2015.[89] In addition to describing the survey results, the Department stated it expected financial institutions to address cyber

[85] Available from the U.S. Treasury Department website: www.treasury.gov (search terms "cyber insurance"). In a frequently quoted December 3, 2014, speech to the Texas Bankers Association, Deputy Treasury Secretary Sarah Raskin stated: "Cyber insurance cannot protect your institutions from a cyber incident any more than flood insurance can save your house from a storm surge or D&O insurance can prevent a lawsuit. But what cyber risk insurance can do is provide some measure of financial support in case of a data breach or cyber incident. And, significantly, cyber risk insurance and the associated underwriting processes can also help bolster your other cybersecurity controls. Qualifying for cyber risk insurance can provide useful information for assessing your bank's risk level and identifying cybersecurity tools and best practices that you may be lacking." http://www.treasury.gov/press-center/press-releases/Pages/jl9711.aspx.

[86] http://www.dhs.gov/publication/cybersecurity-insurance-reports.

[87] For example, in 1959 the insurance industry created the Insurance Institute for Highway Safety, which funds research on automobile design and safety, as well as sponsoring public advocacy campaigns on safe driving. http://www.iihs.org/iihs/about-us. There is substantial academic work on this subject. *See*, e.g., Ben-Shahar and Logue (2012) (providing examples of homeowners insurers funding research facilities to study effective construction techniques, insurers collecting "information concerning the circumstances that gave rise to [a workplace] injury," insurers educating insureds about how to reduce risk, and the insurance industry lobbying for air bags); Ericson et al. (2003), pp. 43–65; Kochenburger (2014), pp. 1267, 1270–1272.

[88] *The Betterley Report*, Cyber/Privacy Insurance Market Survey, pp. 16–17, note [67] above.

[89] These reports can be accessed from the DFS website: http://www.dfs.ny.gov.

risks and cybersecurity within their corporate governance structure.[90] In March 2015, DFS followed up on these general expectations with new regulatory examination procedures focusing on cybersecurity, requiring regulated financial institutions to provide detailed quantitative and qualitative information on cybersecurity protocols, budget, personnel qualifications, incident response plans, and similar issues.[91]

The National Association of Insurance Commissioners (NAIC) created a Cybersecurity Task Force in late 2014, which will likely serve (as the NAIC intended) as a focal point for state regulatory initiatives in this area. After notice and comment, the NAIC approved the Task Force's "Principles for Effective Cybersecurity: Insurance Regulatory Guidance" in June 2015. These Principles are necessarily general and by themselves do not institute specific measurable standards. In addition to establishing a consistent regulatory approach among the states—at least in theory—they also provide a regulatory framework for state insurance departments who would not have the resources to independently develop best practices in this area.

In addition to establishing cyber-related standard insurance entities, state insurance supervisors also regulate the cyber insurance market, with authority to review solvency, rates and forms, and market conduct (conduct of business).[92] While solvency risks often come from investment risk, unsuccessful business strategies such as mergers and acquisitions, and inadequate capitalization, they can also come from faulty products, particularly if that insurance product dominates the insurer's product portfolio.[93] The cyber insurance market is small compared to the overall property-casualty market, but it is also a relatively new product where the source, nature, and extent of risks are constantly changing, scope of damages uncertain (and potentially enormous) and with limited historical underwriting and claim information on the various products or on data breaches generally.[94] In July 2015, the NAIC

[90] "As awareness surrounding cyber security increases, it is expected that future ERM [Enterprise Risk Management] filings will include more frequent explicit references to cyber security." DFS Report on Cyber Security in the Insurance Sector, February 2015, p. 13.

[91] Letter dated March 26, 2015 from DFS Superintendent Benjamin M. Lawsky to regulated entities. http://www.dfs.ny.gov/about/news.htm.

[92] As described in Sect. 3, State insurance regulators typically have discretionary authority to review and regulate insurance policy forms and often proposed rates, though the precise regulatory authority, and willingness of regulators to utilize it, varies significantly. Either by regulatory inclination or specific statutory standards, form and (especially) rate regulation is often minimal for insurance products purchased by large commercial policyholders.

[93] For example, in the 1990s and early 2000s, Lloyds' existence was threatened by the long-term tail exposures to U.S. asbestos and environmental claims that its syndicates had insured or reinsured, typically decades previously. More recent is the role played by credit default swaps in AIG's collapse in fall 2008; that insurance regulators (and others) did not consider this product within their supervisory purview is perhaps the point most relevant here.

[94] Insurers also have well-recognized underwriting tools to address and limit the amount of risk transferred, including aggregate and per occurrence limits, sublimits on specific damages, well-crafted coverage and exclusion sections, and conducting and funding research on cybersecurity and risks. Congress and federal regulatory agencies are also exploring ways to encourage information sharing within and across various industry sectors (e.g., financial services) without violating antitrust laws and similar restrictions.

approved a "cybersecurity and identity theft insurance coverage supplement" requiring insurers writing cyber insurance (first or third party coverage) to regularly report on premium volume, types of policies, claim frequency, and loss expenses. The NAIC's actions related to cybersecurity and cyber insurance are good examples of both the strengths and weaknesses of the insurance regulatory structure in the United States. The NAIC responded quickly to this emerging threat and developed several important documents specifying insurer responsibilities and consumer rights, and did so in a transparent manner with multiple opportunities for public comment. It also played an important role in coordinating and supporting state regulatory actions related to the Anthem and Premera data breaches which affected over 90 million policyholders (Sect. 5.1, above). However, the NAIC is not a regulator and cannot compel state compliance or agreement, nor can the states and the NAIC ensure a consistent approach nationwide to protect against a growing global threat.

Acknowledgement The authors thank research assistants Adrian Burgos-Padilla and Amanda Coriddi; Yan Hong, Director of Insurance Law Research at UConn Law School; and former Insurance Law Center Directors Patricia McCoy and Peter Siegelman.

References

Ben-Shahar O, Logue KD (2012) Outsourcing regulation: how insurance reduces moral hazard. Michigan L Rev 111:197, 210, 212, 219, 224

Ericson R, Doyle A, Barry D (2003) Insurance as governance. University of Toronto Press, Toronto, pp. 43–65

Kochenburger P (2014) Liability insurance and gun violence. Connecticut L Rev 46:1267, 1270–1272

Keith K, Lucia KW (2014) Implementing the affordable care act: The State of the States, The Commonwealth Fund. Available at http://www.commonwealthfund.org

Latimer P, Maume P (2014) Promoting Information in the Marketplace for Financial Services. Springer, p 142 (commenting on regulation of the securities markets)

Podolak G (2015) Insurance for cyber risks: a comprehensive analysis of the evolving exposure, today's litigation and tomorrow's challenges. Quinnipiac L Rev 33:369, 377–379

Randall S (1999) Insurance regulation in the United States: regulatory federalism and the National Association of Insurance Commissioners. Florida St U L Rev 26:625

Schwarcz D, Schwarcz SL (2014) Regulating Systemic Risk in Insurance. U Chi L Rev 81:1569, 1578–1580

Thomas JE (2010) Insurance perspectives on federal financial regulatory reform: addressing misunderstandings and providing a view from a different paradigm. Villanova L Rev 55:773, 781–86

Online Sales of Insurance Products in the EU

Christos S. Chrissanthis

Contents

Abstract The chapter is an attempt to describe the marketing techniques behind online sales, the concerns raised for consumer protection therefrom, and how the EU legislation has responded to such techniques and concerns. Electronic commerce, including online sales, is of particular importance nowadays, and a strong EU policy has been developed in this respect. At the same time, online sales raise particular concerns regarding contract conclusion and consumer protection. From the legal point of view, there are insurance sales, particularly those relating to investment and life insurance, where the insurer is required to properly advise the insured; in online sales, it is difficult to efficiently provide such advice on a

C.S. Chrissanthis, Ph.D, LL.M. (✉)
Assistant Professor, Faculty of Laws, University of Athens, Attorney at Law at Athens, 12 Solonos street, Athens 10673, Greece
e-mail: chrissan@otenet.gr

P. Marano et al. (eds.), *The "Dematerialized" Insurance*,
DOI 10.1007/978-3-319-28410-1_6

precontractual stage. The purpose of this essay is to identify how the EU legislation tries to strike a balance between the policy of facilitating electronic commerce and the policy of consumer protection, whether this attempt is successful, and what the possible further improvements are.

1 Online Sales from a Marketing Point of View

Online sales are by far the most important recent development in the retail business. They have increased dramatically since the '90s, when emails and the Internet were introduced into consumers' life. The development of telecommunications made distance sales (online sales in particular) much more easy, efficient, and profitable. The diffusion of the Internet, particularly through mobile telephony, during the past 5 years has resulted to the rewriting of most marketing books and the redesigning of marketing policies and techniques to meet the new trends in advertising and sales promotion. The Internet has proved to be an advanced telecommunications means, which combines both oral and visual communication, and can support both advertising and sales at the same time. So it is self-explanatory why distance sales are nowadays mostly Internet (online) sales.[1]

1.1 The Impact of Online Sales

There are three characteristics that make online sales so important: (a) the reduction of distribution costs achieved through Internet sales, (b) the creation of a new marketing and purchasing experience for consumers, and (c) the development of niche markets into profitable and viable business.[2] Evidently, points (a) and (c) are of particular interest to insurance.

1.1.1 Reduction of Distribution Costs

Online sales are primarily direct sales without intermediaries. This makes it possible to reduce dramatically distribution costs. Such direct sales are usually employed as a supplementary distribution channel, which is ancillary to traditional distribution channels consisting of intermediaries, branch offices, and traditional outlets. However, recently more and more enterprises rely on direct online sales

[1] On recent technological and marketing developments on online sales, see Heinemann and Schwarzl (2010), p. 19 seqq.

[2] Heinemann and Schwarzl (2010), p. 210 seqq.

exclusively, hence increasing the benefits from doing away with intermediaries and expensive branch offices.[3] Insurance sales are traditionally commission driven and, hence, involve relatively high distribution costs, as well as a vast number of intermediaries (i.e., sales force). The use of the Internet can potentially transform consumer insurance sales from an intermediary-based market into a direct sales market. The potential benefit for both consumers and insurers is obvious, at least in terms of reduction of transaction (i.e., intermediaries) costs.

1.1.2 Purchasing Experience

Successful online sales are achieved through creating a satisfying online customer experience.[4] The Internet is more than a means of telecommunication; the Internet has to be used to offer consumers more satisfaction and convenience in their attempt to meet their consumer needs. This would involve offering a series of financial services, i.e. not only insurance products but other supplementary products as well, together with adequate advice and guidance and follow-up, after sales, services.[5] From the point of view of insurance sales, this would mean an active, convenient, and continuous support to clients with respect to all their financial service needs. Ideally, a website would be convenient and satisfactory to consumers if it could assist them in connection to online payments for their day-to-day transactions (i.e., standing payment orders for utility bills, etc.), transferring funds in general, obtaining a personal loan, arranging for a pension scheme participation, investing in mutual funds or other collective investments, as well as obtaining motor insurance coverage or arranging for a payments protection policy (PPI), a mortgage payment policy (MPI), a health policy, a unit-linked policy, or any other life or nonlife policy. So it would require combining together all or most of the financial services (banking, credit, investment, and in insurance) to achieve a level of convenience and satisfaction to consumers and to make such a website appealing to them, but it would be far more difficult to attract consumers' interest and make a consumer revisit a website that would offer insurance policies alone. Hence, it would be more successful from the point of view of online sales to combine all financial services in a single website. This is much more easy and possible for financial conglomerates and financial intermediaries, who are able to represent banking institutions, insurance companies, and investment firms at the same time. Evidently, the development of successful and profitable online sales would very much depend on bank-assurance cooperation and on banking, insurance, and investment firms joining forces together and offering consolidated services. From the legal point of view, however, this raises certain regulatory issues and complexities, as insurance companies are regulated as single-purpose companies (i.e.,

[3] Kotler and Armstrong (2011), p. 497.

[4] Heinemann and Schwarzl (2010), p. 45 seqq.

[5] Kotler and Armstrong (2011), p. 494.

companies allowed to offer insurance policies alone and prohibited from carrying on any other type of trade or transactions). The same applies to banking institutions, investment firms, and all other financial service enterprises. Intermediaries, however, are usually allowed in most jurisdictions to represent banking, insurance, and investment firms, under special regulatory regimes that provide at least a limited level of regulatory flexibility. Websites operated jointly by banking, insurance, and investment firms are another option, not involving intermediaries. One would need, though, to consider whether it is worth making any necessary amendments to financial service regulation and supervision, to accommodate better the business necessity to offer online combined financial services.

1.1.3 Niche Market

Traditionally, the bulk of sales are generated by few products, while the majority of products generate few sales; from a statistics point of view, 80 % of a company's sales are generated by 20 % of its products. So in the context of traditional marketing, "hit" products are far more important for business success. This trend has changed due to the progressively increasing use of the Internet by consumers. The Internet made it possible to emphasize more on niche markets and niche products and, hence, demand now shifts from "hits" to "niches." It is submitted that now the percentage among hits and niches in a company's revenue is about 50/50. Investing in niches is now possible due to lower costs (particularly lower distribution costs) achieved through the use of Internet sales.[6] Insurance involves many different types of coverage and respective policies, in both life and nonlife sectors, and most of such types are regarded as rather sophisticated, addressed to few insured only, and being "niche market" products. The creation of a "critical mass" of insured (premium payers) is material for the financial viability of a policy portfolio for each insurer. One of the major reasons why insurance relies so much in intermediaries is because intermediaries are more able and efficient to create such a critical mass than insurers themselves. The use of the Internet, though, can potentially change this trend as well. The Internet is a medium that can greatly assist an insurer to communicate at limited costs with a vast number of potential insured and to develop a substantial number of policy holders (premium payers) even with respect to types of coverage and policies that are traditionally regarded to be "niche market" products. In this way, the Internet can potentially turn "niche market" insurance products into a viable and profitable business.

[6] Kotler and Keller (2012), p. 235.

1.2 Benefits of Online Sales

Internet sales result to substantial profits to both sellers and purchasers.[7] To give some characteristic examples: (a) there are no time limits, as web pages are open 24 h per day 7 days per week; (b) there are no geographical limits, as web pages are accessible from anywhere in the world, thus resulting to markets' globalization; (c) online marketing makes it possible to offer a vast variety of products and services and to satisfy even exceptional (niche) consumer needs; (d) it also makes it possible to provide customers with easy and readily available access to detailed market information, advice, and guidance; (e) it makes comparison of products easier and more efficient; (f) it reduces distribution costs; (f) it facilitates access to small groups of consumers and niche markets.[8]

1.3 Maximizing Online Sales Effects

Most people may believe that online sales is all about having a web page. However, a web page alone could hardly generate sales by itself, as it is quite difficult to be even noticed by consumers. Internet sales are active on the part of sellers, rather than passive. The most efficient techniques to maximize profits from Internet sales are aiming to personalize marketing (one-to-one marketing process).[9] Such techniques are indicatively listed below.[10]

1.3.1 Search Engines

Using Internet search engines and making websites more easily traced by search engines lead to increased online sales. This usually involves use of comparative advertising techniques, as well as use of third parties' trademarks and brand names as metatags and adwords, provided that there is no intellectual property right infringement.

1.3.2 Constant Direct Communication with Prospective Clients

This involves emailing current and prospective clients on a regular basis with information about either recent market developments or new products, thus creating a continuous communication with clientele. In addition to emailing, using RSS

[7] Heinemann and Schwarzl (2010), pp. 210 seqq., 215 seqq.

[8] Kotler and Armstrong (2011), pp. 497–498.

[9] Heinemann and Schwarzl (2010), p. 134 seqq.

[10] Kotler and Keller (2012), pp. 204–205.

communications and podcasts or vodcasts is an alternative communication technique. Consent on the part of consumers is required, as unauthorized solicitation of documents and unauthorized commercial communication usually qualify as a privacy and data protection infringement.

1.3.3 Clientele Analysis

Analyzing clients' personal data to identify their consumer profile and their consumer needs is of vital importance to Internet sales. Most of the success of Internet sales depends on the sellers' ability to predict clients' needs on an individual basis and to submit specific purchase proposals meeting each person's needs and preferences.

1.3.4 Diffusion of General Market Information

Using web blogs to diffuse information about the products offered and market developments in general and organizing webinars on contemporary issues are methods that are particularly efficient to increase brand awareness and to make consumers more familiar and more educated on what is available for them in the market.

1.3.5 Exchange of Information

Another efficient method supporting Internet sales is sharing and diffusion of market information and customers' data among companies that are not directly competing with one another, i.e. banks or investment firms on the one hand and insurance companies on the other.[11] Such exchange of information makes it possible to design products and services that match better customers' needs and to trace such customers' needs on an individual basis. From a legal point of view, exchange of information and personal data of clients requires prior consent on the part of consumers.

1.3.6 Retaining a Level of Communication and Reaching Mass Audiences

Internet sales depend very much on retaining a level of communication with prospective clients and reaching mass audiences. The enterprises that are more successful in Internet sales usually create an online buzz, through sponsoring and

[11] Kotler and Keller (2012), p. 197.

indirect marketing, i.e., by promoting cultural events, music, movies, and other activities with a broad resonance to mass audiences.[12] This makes consumers more familiar with the enterprise brand and increases product and service awareness.

1.3.7 Use of Databases

Databases are essential for efficient direct marketing. In business to consumer marketing, a database may contain customers' geographic, demographic, psychographic (i.e., activities, interests, etc.) data; data on education, income; data from past purchases and past transactions. In business-to-business marketing, databases contain data about contact persons, past transactions, purchasing needs and purchasing behavior, competing suppliers, etc. A database can assist the company to contact prospective clients and generate sales; to design its future products and services, so that they match customers' needs; to develop its advertising and marketing strategy; to build a strong and long-term customer relationship with its clientele; to carry on market searches; etc.[13]

1.4 Insurance Online Sales in Particular

Considering the above in connection to insurance sales in particular,[14] one concludes that Internet sales possibly require marketing techniques that may be more "aggressive" than usually permitted by current EU law on consumer and data protection and usually employed by insurers. Most of the success of online sales relies on the ability of the seller to trace specific Internet users visiting specific websites, thus identifying their consumer interests and needs at a particular point in time and taking the advantage to submit by email and timely a specific offer that meets the client's current needs. To give an example, if a seller of watches is able, through technical means, to trace that a particular Internet user is currently visiting specific websites that promote and sell watches, he is then in an advantageous position to submit by email an offer to this particular web user and to introduce himself and his website at a time when the consumer is really interested in his products or services. This is currently a major online sales technique applied broadly, but it does raise legal complications from the point of view of consumer and data protection. Such techniques are also supplemented by the use of data basis with clientele information, as well as by exchanging information about clients with other enterprises operating in similar, but not directly competitive, markets. The ultimate purpose is to identify potential clients at a time that they are really

[12] Kotler and Keller (2012), p. 220.

[13] Kotler and Armstrong (2011), p. 499.

[14] See also Hiwarker and Khot (2013), pp. 1–6; Meshkat et al. (2012), p. 640.

interested in a specific product or service, to predict the client's needs and preferences, and to submit a client convenient and satisfactory offer at this point in time. With respect to insurance business, this would possibly mean exchanging information with banking institutions and investment firms, or even car dealers, leisure yacht sellers and similar traders. To give an example again, a consumer who is discussing with a bank to obtain a loan is a potential insured for a payments protection policy (PPI), or a consumer who is about to purchase a private leisure yacht is a potential insured for a marine policy.

2 The EU Policy for E-Commerce

E-commerce has proved to be a source of progressively increasing turnover for businesses. Hence, many governments and international organizations, including the EU, have developed specific policies destined to facilitate e-commerce.

In the EU, during 1994–1997, many enterprises set up a web page, although no transactions were carried out electronically. Since 1997, electronic transactions over the Internet have become progressively popular, and since 2000 e-commerce has become a substantial source of income for European enterprises. The total volume of e-commerce turnover is estimated to have increased from 10 m. € in 2001 to 70 m. € in 2008. In 2008, 33 % of European consumers used the Internet to effect local transactions, while only 7 % cross-border transactions were concluded online.[15] On the basis of these findings, the EU policy to reinforce consumer confidence over e-commerce is justified as a means to promote further the single market integration.

Many international organizations such as the UN, the Council of Europe, OECD, WTO, and ICC have produced legal texts on e-commerce, like guidelines, model law rules, and soft law in general.[16] The most significant work has been carried out by UNCITRAL. UNCITRAL has created a Model Law on Electronic Commerce (1996). This has been signed by 48 countries, including the US, China, Australia, and Canada. However, among the signatories, only few EU member states are included, such as France, Ireland, and the UK. The UNCITRAL Model Law provides that electronic texts and electronic signatures can be legally equivalent to traditional written texts and traditional handwritten signatures. It also sets certain rules for electronic transactions dealing with issues such as transfer of risk, wrongful and fraudulent transmissions and communications, electronic offer and acceptance, etc. UNCITRAL has also produced a Model Law on Electronic Signatures (2001). This was signed by 22 countries, not including any EU member state. The model law provides that electronic signatures should be legally binding and enforceable, if their credibility is secured. It further provides certain criteria and

[15] Anagnostopoulou (2013).
[16] Geist (2010).

methods to secure such credibility. Credibility depends on the ability to identify in a secure manner the person from which a communication originates. The model law is based on the neutrality principle, meaning that all technical methods of identification should be treated equally by the law and that legislation should not favor one particular type of electronic signature over others. Finally, in 2005, UNCITRAL proposed an international convention on the "Use of Electronic Communications in International Contracts," which emphasizes on business-to-business commerce only. This did not attract great attention; it was signed by only 19 states and ratified by only 3. An overall inspection of UNCITRAL's work on e-commerce leads to the conclusion that UNCITRAL's attempt to promote electronic trade is based on three basic principles, i.e., nondiscrimination among traditional and electronic signatures and texts, technological neutrality as to the methods of electronic communication and identification, and, finally, functional equivalence.[17] Functional equivalence means that electronic signatures and electronic documents are legally equivalent to their traditional equivalents, so long as they serve the same transaction necessities (i.e., the purpose of authentication and verification) with the same or equivalent level of security and trust.

In 2004, the ICC published its E-Terms, which are model contract terms for electronic cross-border transactions. It has also set a Commission for Digital Economy, which acts as an advisory body to several other international organizations dealing with e-commerce. Other international organizations, like the Council of Europe and OECD, have emphasized on issues affecting e-commerce, like privacy, data protection, and consumer protection.[18]

The EU has developed a strong policy in favor of e-commerce and information society, which, however, coexists with a traditionally strong legal protection for privacy, personal data, and consumers. These coexisting policies (i.e., information society and e-commerce, data protection, consumer protection) are backed by a complex legislative system, consisting mainly of Directives on several aspects of the information society, consumer protection, and privacy.[19] It can be easily derived that the EU is anxiously trying to strike a fair balance among e-commerce on the one hand and data and consumer protection on the other. These targets are not always easy to reconcile. As evidenced from the marketing analysis in the previous chapter, contemporary Internet sales are heavily backed by efficient customers' data analysis, which cannot always be easily accommodated with the current legal framework on privacy and data protection.

---

[17] Boss and Kilian (2008), Faria (ICLQ 2006), p. 689.

[18] See OECD Guidelines on the protection of privacy and trans-border flows of personal data (1980), OECD Guidelines on e-consumer protection (1999). With respect to Council of Europe, see The Council's Convention on the protection of individuals with regard to automatic processing of personal data (1981).

[19] See the following Directives: 1995/46 as amended, and 2002/58 on personal data, 1998/34 as amended on the information society, 1999/93 on e-signatures, 2000/31 on e-commerce, 2002/65 on e-financial services, 2006/123 on e-services, 2006/112 on e-billing and vat, etc.

The E-Commerce Directive 2000/31 is influenced by this endeavor to reconcile the promotion of the information society with the protection of privacy. One can identify the main targets of the Directive as follows: to create a secure legal framework for e-commerce, where e-transactions will be equal to ordinary and traditional ones; to protect the e-consumer by obliging enterprises to provide adequate precontractual information; to set common requirements for certification providers. The Directive applies a "home passport" or "country of origin" system for e-service providers. E-service providers need to comply with the legal provisions of their home country where they have their establishment, irrespective of the country where a server is situated. Prior, authorization of e-service providers from host countries is not allowed. Finally, it is established that intermediaries are in principle not liable for checking and controlling the information transmitted through their systems and networks, nor are they obliged to actively seek for precautions against illegal information and illegal activities.

The E-Signatures Directive 1999/93 EC is destined to create a legal regime for electronic signatures. An electronic signature is considered to be a method of digital identification and authentication. An e-signature needs to perform two functions: (a) to identify the sender of a transmission (this is usually called the confirmation function) and (b) to secure that only the receiver of a transmission can read it, i.e. to prevent intruders (this is usually called the confidential function). Unlike UNCITRAL that follows the principle of technological neutrality as to e-signatures, the EU Directive favors one particular technological method, i.e. the one based on the use of a trusted third party (a certification service provider) who issues an electronic certificate. This electronic certificate is based on a private and a public key. The volume of use of e-signature remains relatively low, which has caused concern to the EU administration. This is due to technical difficulties as well, including poor interoperability of the various systems used by certification service providers.

EU Directives on consumer distance sales (Dir. 2011/83 EU and 2002/65 EC) mainly provide for precontractual information to be submitted to consumers before concluding a distance sale transaction, as well as for a right to withdraw from a distance sale contract within a certain period of time, for a right of consumers to be invoiced only after they have obtained delivery of the goods, for protection against unauthorized solicitation (spamming), etc.

The EU has not signed the UNCITRAL Model Laws on e-commerce, e-signatures, and e-communications. Obviously, the EU wished to have its own policy as to e-commerce and the information society. The EU legislation on the matter is certainly more detailed and more legally binding. The main difference, though, is that the EU legislation accommodates issues of privacy and consumer protection as well, i.e. issues that are not really touched upon by the UNCITRAL Model Laws. As a result, it is true that the legal framework in the EU as to e-commerce is more burdensome than in other countries, the US for example. Evidently, e-commerce has flourished in the US and other countries more than in Europe.

The lag encountered by the EU in the development of e-commerce has motivated the Commission to increase its efforts to promote digital economy. So, recently, the EU has set an updated policy for e-commerce. In 2003, the Commission produced a report on the application of Directive 2000/31 EC on e-commerce.[20] One of the sections of this report refers to the application of the Directive on regulated businesses and professions. The report concludes that the Directive made it possible to regulate businesses and professions to provide information to clients via websites, which was not previously possible in all member states. It also emphasizes that the Directive caused many professional associations to develop codes of conduct regarding use of commercial information over the Internet. In 2007, the Commission released an expert study on the economic impact of the E-Commerce Directive.[21] The study concludes that the Directive contributed very much to legal certainty, particularly through the "country of origin" principle, as well as through provisions on obligatory precontractual information. Moreover, the Directive reduced transaction costs through provisions on electronic contract conclusion. On 9.6.2010, the Commission issued its paper titled "A new strategy for the Single Market," which emphasizes on the importance of innovation and e-commerce. In this context, the EU adopted the same year "A Digital Agenda for Europe," which sets the target to increase the volume of e-commerce and Internet users by 2015 and to remove the barriers preventing cross-border digital transactions.[22] Revised legislation has also been prepared to assist a more lively growth of e-commerce in Europe. In 2012, the EU Commission produced two staff working documents on "Bringing e-commerce benefits to consumers"[23] and "Online services, including e-commerce, in the Single Market."[24] The first document emphasizes the importance of precontractual information and efficient redress and enforcement procedures, while the second provides a detailed evaluation of the efficiency of the Directive provisions and identifies the legal difficulties associated with it. In December 2012, the Commission presented a Code for EU online rights, codifying the rights that users of the Internet and other digital media should enjoy. The EU legislation on off-premises and distance sales transactions (dating back to 1997 and 1985) has been updated by way of a new Directive on these matters, i.e. Directive 2011/83 EU,[25] which repeals the older Directive 1985/577 EC and 1997/7 EC. The basic protective principles still apply. So before an order is placed, the consumer should be submitted with adequate precontractual information regarding his counterparty and the subject matter of the proposed transaction. After an order is placed, the consumer enjoys the right to withdraw and the seller should facilitate the

[20] COM (2003) 702 final, 21.11.2003.

[21] Kastberg Nielsen C. et al. (Ramboll Management).

[22] On this new EU policy, see more details in Anagnostopoulou (2013), p. 10.

[23] SEC (2011) 1640 final, 11.1.2012.

[24] SEC (2011) 1641 final, 11.1.2012.

[25] On the new consumer protection Directive, see also the DG Justice Guidance Document concerning Dir. 2011/83, dated June 2014.

exercise of this right by providing online in its website a model withdrawal statement. There are also uniform rules on transfer of risk in sales transactions and time limits for the delivery of the goods. In addition, there are detailed provisions preventing consumers from contingent charges or surcharges that are not reasonably justified. The new legal regime will be applicable to contracts regarding digital content, as well as public utility services.

Data protection law is also under reform, as it is a common conclusion that until now it has proved inefficient to both citizens and enterprises. The data protection Directive, whose implementation into national laws proved complex, will be replaced by a Regulation on this matter which will be directly enforceable into national laws. A Regulation will achieve a greater level of uniformity among member states and will be also applicable to non-EU enterprises transacting with European consumers.[26]

There are a couple of EU documents which address specifically issues of e-commerce and insurance. The first is a discussion paper issued within the DG Internal Market dated 2002.[27] The second is a discussion document on the same subject matter dated 1 year later, in 2003.[28] Both discuss the application of the "country of origin principle" (art. 3 §§ 1, 2 of the E-Commerce Directive), as well as the legislative derogation from this principle (art. 3 § 4). They also discuss legal difficulties that arise in case of obtaining compulsory insurance; in particular, it would be extremely difficult to secure that compulsory insurance obtained online on a cross-border basis from another member state complies with the specific compulsory insurance requirements in the host country. The conclusion of both discussion papers is that it would be inefficient and possibly detrimental to the protection of the insured to repeal the derogation of art. 3(4) from the "country of origin principle" in connection to insurances. Moreover, it is worth mentioning that the Annex of the E-Commerce Directive expressly excludes from its scope of application the rules on freedom to provide services and freedom of establishment in the insurance sector. In addition, the Annex expressly excludes compulsory insurance, as well as the rules on the law applicable to insurance contracts.

So the position as to the application of the E-Commerce Directive on insurances seems to be that the Directive does not make it unnecessary to comply with the freedom of services and freedom of establishment provisions of the Insurance Directives. Moreover, it does not cover compulsory insurance. It does not change the conflict of law rules regarding insurance contracts. It does, however, benefit insurances from the point of view that electronic contracting is acknowledged and is legally maintained. One could possibly argue that legal certainty suffers as to the

---

[26] EU Commission, A comprehensive approach to data protection in the EU, COM (2010) p. 609, 4.11.2010.

[27] EU Commission, DG Internal Market, Financial Services—Insurance, MARKT/2522/02-EN Rev. 1 Orig. This is followed by another EU document on E-Commerce and Financial Services, MARKT/2094/01-EN Orig.

[28] MARKT 2541/03—EN Orig., 24.10.2003.

interrelation of the E-Commerce Directive and other legislative instruments on insurance.

3 Online Sales of Insurances in EU Law

A distinction has to be raised among online sales of consumer and commercial insurances. Online sales of consumer insurances fall within the scope of the Distance Sales of Financial Services Directive 2002/65 EC. This Directive applies only to consumer financial services. This does not mean that commercial insurances cannot be offered online.

On the contrary, the Electronic Commerce Directive 2000/31 EC is destined to make it possible to provide any type of goods or services over the Internet and to establish a general legal framework to this effect. Hence, commercial insurances can be offered over the Internet according to the E-Commerce Directive provisions and principles, subject, of course, to compliance with the other insurance EU Directives, particularly with respect to freedom to provide services, freedom of establishment, compulsory insurance, and choice of law rules.

The analysis below emphasizes on consumer insurances which are dealt with by the Distance Sales of Financial Services Directive 2002/65 EC.

3.1 The Philosophy Behind Distance Sales Regulation

Distance sales are sales where the parties are not physically present negotiating at the same place but, instead, communicate, negotiate, and reach an agreement through some technical telecommunication means, i.e. over the telephone, on the Internet, etc. A more elaborate definition of distance sales contracts is found in art. 2 (7) of Directive 2011/83 EU on consumer rights (which includes regulation of distance sales in general) and in art. 2(a) of Directive 2002/65 EC on distance sales of financial services. In these articles, a distance contract is basically defined as one where the supplier uses one or more means of distance communication up to and including the time at which the contract is concluded. The legislative definition in these articles may be a little bit more sophisticated and detailed than the one proposed above, i.e. that distance sales are sales negotiated without physical presence of both parties at the same place. For example, the legislative definition refers to consumers only, so the respective Directives 2011/83 EU and 2002/65 EC would not apply to business entities, businessmen, and professionals. In addition, the legislative definition refers to "an organized distance sales or services provision scheme run by the supplier," so the Directives would not cover contracts that are only occasionally concluded through distance sales means.[29]

[29] This exception is confirmed by par. 18 of the preamble of Dir. 2002/65 EC.

However, what is important from the point of view of the legislator is the absence of physical presence and physical negotiation among the parties. Such absence of physical presence means that the consumer is not able to physically inspect the subject matter of the contract. To overcome this handicap, distance sales legislation obliges the supplier to provide certain information to the consumer prior to contract conclusion. To some extent, this information is destined to provide a substitute for the inability of the consumer to physically inspect what he is paying for. The obligation of the supplier to provide precontractual information seems to stand for an obligation to provide advice and guidance, which he might not be obliged to provide should the consumer have the chance of physical inspection. However, it is not only the absence of physical inspection which is a concern. Distance communication means are not regarded appropriate types of communication for the purpose of negotiation and evaluation of contractual risks. At least, they make communication, negotiation, and evaluation of risks more difficult, and distance communication certainly requires a greater level of responsiveness, vigilance, and circumspection on the part of the consumer. Because of such absence of physical presence, the legislator is rather suspicious about the efficiency, clarity, and quality of the negotiation that took place and is concerned that consumers' rights may be depleted under such circumstances.

The same justification applies to both distance sales in general and distance sales of financial services (including insurance policies) in particular. What makes a special Directive on distance sales of financial services necessary (i.e., Directive 2002/65 EC) is that financial services are abstract in nature, so it is easier to trade them on the Internet or over the phone. Furthermore, they are more complex, more important, and of a higher financial value than an average consumer transaction in tangible goods. Moreover, consumer protection is of particular importance in financial services since it is necessary to achieve a level of market confidence. Another aspect is that protection of financial service consumers (i.e., depositors, the insured, and investors) as such is one of the main targets of financial service supervision. It is such protection that creates confidence in the financial markets, and should such confidence fail, there will be no financial markets at all. One could argue that the whole regime of financial service regulation and supervision focuses on market confidence and protection of financial service consumers. A final point is that, from a civil law point of view, financial service transactions are usually regarded as contracts where the supplier usually has an obligation to provide some form of advice and guidance to its contractual counterparty. From this point of view, contracts for financial services differ substantially from other civil law contracts (i.e., the contract of sale of tangible consumer goods in particular) since in the latter case the obligation of the supplier to provide advice and guidance is rather limited. So there are ample reasons justifying a particular concern about distance sales of financial services.

It is worth mentioning that similar conditions of transacting, i.e. absence of physical presence through the process of negotiation, occur in ordinary insurance contracts as well. The usual process for concluding an insurance contract is that the prospective insured submits an application of insurance to the insurer, usually through an intermediary, and then, at a later stage in time, on the basis of such application, the insurer issues an insurance policy. The prospective insured, though, and the insurer are not acting by being both present on the same place and at the same time. The insurer issues the policy at a time when the prospective insured cannot reach and discuss with him. So there is a time interval between the submission of the offer (an insurance application) and the acceptance (the policy issued).

It is for the reasons mentioned above that the legislator intervenes. The intervention is achieved by establishing a different process of contract conclusion, which is described below. In distance sales, basically the supplier is obliged to provide certain information to the consumer and the consumer is granted the right to withdraw from the contract, within a certain period of time. In insurance law, the insurer is obliged to inform the insured about any deviations from the coverage applied for and the insured is granted a certain period of time to raise objections to any such deviations. Moreover, the insurer is obliged to provide to the insured certain information about the policy, the coverage, and the insured's legal rights, and if he has failed to do so, then the insured is again granted the right to avoid the insurance contract.

So there is a similar philosophy and justification behind the regulation of distance sales, distance sales of financial services (including insurances), and the process for contract conclusion of insurance contracts.

3.2 *The EU Legislation*

Online sales of insurance products in EU law is dealt with by Directive 2002/65 EC.[30] This Directive deals with distance sales of financial services (i.e., any service of a banking, credit, insurance, personal pension, investment, or payment nature, as per art. 2 b of the Directive). It should be recalled that off-premises and distance sales of products and services, other than financial products and services, are dealt with by Directive 2011/83 EU, which deals with consumer rights in general (including rights and remedies with respect to distance and off-premises sales in general) and amends and replaces Directives 93/13, 94/44, 85/577, 97/7 EC.

3.3 *Directive 2006/123 EC Not to Apply*

With respect to nonfinancial services covered by Directive 2011/83 EU, two other Directives should also be given consideration, namely the Services Directive 2006/123 EC and the E-Commerce Directive 2000/31 EC. In case of distance sales of goods or nonfinancial services, the above two Directives apply in addition to the

[30] This Directive amends prior Directives 90/619, 97/7, and 98/27 EC. Directive 2002/65 has been amended by Directives 2005/29 and 2007/64 EC.

Consumer Rights Directive 2011/83 EU. These two Directives impose additional obligations, particularly with respect to precontractual information.

The position is different with respect to financial services covered by Directive 2002/65 EC. The Services Directive expressly provides that it does not apply to financial services, including insurance services. However, it provides that service providers, whose services present a risk to the health or safety of the recipient or a third person or to the financial security of the recipient, should have appropriate professional liability insurance coverage and that providers of such services should make available to the recipient of the services information about such insurance coverage and in particular the contact details of the insurer and the territorial coverage (art. 22(1)k).

3.4 Directive 2000/31 EC on E-Commerce

As discussed above, the position seems to be rather complex as to the impact of the E-Commerce Directive 2000/31 on insurances.

According to a strict literal interpretation, the E-Commerce Directive provides that it applies to providers of information society services. These are defined in art. 1(2) of Directive 98/34 EC, as amended by Directive 98/48 EC and Regulation 2006/96 EC. This later Directive 98/48 EC expressly provides in art. 1 (5) subparagraph 3 that information society services do not include financial services, although they include any service normally provided for remuneration at a distance by electronic means and at the individual request of the recipient. Annex VI attached to this Directive confirms that insurance and reinsurance services are among those financial services to which the Directive does not apply.

On the other hand, there are some past EU documents that discuss the impact of the E-Commerce Directive on insurances and assume that insurance contracts are not altogether excluded from the scope of the Directive. The Annex attached to the Directive expressly provides that the "country of origin" principle established by art. 3(1) and (2) does not render inapplicable other provisions of the insurance Directives dealing with freedom to provide services, freedom of establishment, compulsory insurance, and the law applicable to insurance contracts. Although the situation seems to lack legal clarity, it would seem that insurance contracts are not altogether excluded from the scope of the E-Commerce Directive. It is more appropriate to consider that both commercial and consumer insurances benefit from legal maintenance of electronic contracting (art. 9). However, the "country of origin" principle of art. 3(1) and (2) would not make it unnecessary for an insurer who provides services online to comply with the operating license requirements or the requirements in connection to freedom of services and freedom of establishment.

It is submitted that the position is not the same for insurance intermediaries, i.e. that insurance intermediaries could benefit from the "country of origin" principle of the E-Commerce Directive, since they are not covered by the derogation of art. 3(3) or (4).[31] However, this does not seem to be a realistic legal interpretation. Insurance intermediaries is also a regulated profession as insurance business and the purpose of the E-Commerce Directive was not to relax any regulatory requirements, as this would render consumer protection inefficient.

Finally, with respect to consumer insurances, they fall within the scope of the Distance Sales of Consumer Financial Services Directive 2002/65 EC. So, in effect, although the Consumers Rights Directive 2011/83 EU should be read together with the Services and the E-Commerce Directives,[32] this is not the case as far as the Distance Marketing of Consumer Financial Services Directive 2002/65 is concerned.

3.5 *When Does Directive 2011/83 EU Apply?*

There are, though, certain exceptional cases where Directive 2011/83 shall apply to distance (online) sales of financial services (including insurance services), although in principle financial services (including insurance) are excluded from the scope of application of Directive 2011/83, according to its art. 3(3)d. Such an exceptional case is described in art. 15 of Directive 2011/83 EU. According to this article, if the consumer exercises his right of withdrawal from a distance or off-premises sale, any ancillary contracts shall be automatically terminated also. "Ancillary contracts" are defined in art. 2(15), and proper interpretation leads to the conclusion that they include insurance contracts as well. Hence, in case of insurance contracts that are ancillary to the purchase of goods or the provision of other services on a distance or off-premises sales basis governed by Directive 2011/83 EU, the exercise of the right of withdrawal on the part of the consumer as to the main contract will lead to automatic termination of the insurance contract as well. This is a case where insurance contracts concluded online which are ancillary to another main contract are, in effect, dealt with by Directive 2011/83 EU, instead of Directive 2002/65 EC, as far as automatic termination is concerned. Any other consequences of termination, however, are dealt with by sector-specific insurance rules, or general contract law, applicable in each member state.

Another exceptional case where an insurance contract concluded online may be caught by Directive 2011/83 EU, instead of Directive 2002/65 EC, is provided in arts. 3(3)k and 22 of Directive 2011/83 EU. According to art. 22, the consumer is entitled to reimbursement of any additional payment he made for any extra services for which he has not provided his express consent; default options that consumers need to reject (i.e., preticked boxes) are not considered a proper expression of consumer's consent. Such additional services and extra payments may relate to

[31] See the EU discussion papers on E-Commerce and insurance mentioned above: MARKT/2522/02 and MARKT 2541/03—EN Orig., 24.10.2003.

[32] DG Justice Guidance document on Dir. 2011/83 (June 2014), par. 4.2, p. 18.

insurance services and payment of premiums. Although financial services are expressly excluded from the scope of Directive 2011/83 EU according to art. 3(3) d, however, art. 3(3)k provides that the Directive does not apply to passenger transport services, with the exception of articles 8(2), 19, and 22. As a result, art. 22 of Directive 2011/83 EU would apply to an insurance contract concluded when buying transport services, such as an air ticket.

3.6 Scope of Directive 2002/65 EC

The scope of application of Directive 2002/65 EC is broad. It applies in connection to both life and nonlife policies, as well as in connection to unit-linked[33] and similar investment or pension policies. The Directive applies to both insurers and intermediaries, i.e. brokers or agents.[34] It applies to insurers and intermediaries residing within the EU, as well as outside it, so long as they provide insurance services through distance sales means within the EU, provided that the law of one of the EU member states is the law applicable to the insurance contract; this is likely to be so when the insured riskis situated within an EU member state or when the policyholder or the insured is residing within an EU member state. It is recalled that the Directive applies to consumers[35] and consumer services only. It is worth mentioning that par. 29 of the Directive's preamble submits that nonprofit organizations and persons making use of financial services in order to become entrepreneurs are also covered by the Directive. It is reasonably expected that in consumer insurances, either the insured risk or the policyholder or the insured will be situated within the EU. From the conflicts of law point of view, the provisions of the Directive, when implemented into the national law of the member states, are of a mandatory nature and cannot be derogated by contract, in the sense that consumers cannot validly waive the rights granted, as per art. 12(1). According to Sect. 2 of art. 12, consumers should not lose their rights granted by the Directive due to a choice of law of a nonmember state if the contract in question has a close link with the territory of one member state. The Directive also applies to insurers and brokers residing within the EU, when they provide insurance services through distance sales means outside the EU. Finally, it should be recalled that providing insurance services within the EU from an establishment outside it requires an insurance license granted by the insurance superintendent of one member state. So EU law on distance sales of

[33] In case C-166/11, 1.3.12, A.L. Gonzalez Alonso v. NN, the Court reasoned that a unit-linked policy falls outside the scope of Dir. 85/577, which is the predecessor of Dir. 2011/83 and deals with distance sales of goods and services other than financial services. Obviously, although unit-linked policies do not fall within Dir. 85/577, they do fall within the scope of Dir. 2002/65.

[34] An express reference to intermediaries is to be found in par. 19 of the preamble of Dir. 2002/65 EC.

[35] The legislative definition of a "distance contract" in art. 2 (a) of Dir. 2002/65 EC expressly refers to consumers only, thus excluding business entities, businessmen, and professionals.

financial services, including insurance, shall apply to foreign insurers and intermediaries who address themselves to consumers in the EU.

The Directive applies to consumer insurances only. Art. 2(d) provides that "consumer" means any natural person who is acting outside his business, trade, or profession. So the Directive shall not apply to legal entities at all, save that par. 29 of the Directive's preamble submits that nonprofit organizations are covered. Furthermore, it shall not apply to natural persons acting in the context of their trade or profession, save that par. 29 of the Directive's preamble submits that persons making use of financial services in order to become entrepreneurs are covered. Hence, an architect obtaining motor insurance for a vehicle used for his professional needs would not be covered by the Directive. It is true that in practice it may not be easily predictable when one is acting in the context of his trade or profession or not; from this point of view, the Directive may lack clarity in practice, although this is a problem that is likely to be more serious in other financial services (i.e., credit services) rather in insurance contracts where the policy will usually reveal the actual situation. Finally, art. 2(a) refers to an organized distance sales scheme; hence, distance sales which are only on an occasional basis are not covered by the Directive.

3.7 *Full Harmonization*

The Directive is a full harmonization one. This is expressly provided for in par. 13 of its preamble, which reads: "...Member states should not be able to adopt provisions other than those laid down in this Directive in the fields it harmonizes, unless otherwise specifically indicated in it." It is art. 4(2) that provides otherwise; according to it, member states may introduce stringent provisions on prior information. Art. 6(3) also allows member states to provide that there is no withdrawal right in certain cases.

Consumer protection is not the only target of the Directive. Uniformity of competition among all the member states and throughout the EU is also a legislative target. Such uniformity of competition conditions is imperative for market integration and free movement of goods and services. If each member state could introduce a different level of consumer protection, or different regulation of distance sales, such uniformity could not be achieved. It is to be recalled that distance sales and electronic commerce in general are considered to be material to achieve efficiency of free movement of goods and services and market integration.[36]

---

[36] See paras. 1 and 2 of the preamble of Dir. 2000/31 on electronic commerce.

3.8 *Consumer Rights*

As discussed, the purpose of the distance sales of financial services legislation is to compensate consumers for the absence of negotiating and agreeing by way of physical presence, or to put it in other words to provide some comfort and confidence to consumers willing to use telecommunication means, so as to negotiate and agree a financial service transaction. This aim is achieved by designing and granting some special rights to consumers.

3.8.1 Information Right

As per art. 3(1), the supplier is obliged to provide prior to the conclusion of the contract information about himself; its representatives; the intermediaries used; the respective professional registries for himself and the intermediaries; the supervising authorities; the main characteristics of the insurance coverage offered; the premium and any taxes, commissions, or other costs; any special risks related to the policy offered; details regarding payments and performance; legal rights granted to the consumer, such as the right to withdraw; the contract's duration; any out-of-court complaint procedures; etc. Additional information is required in case of voice telephony communication. Member states are allowed to provide for stringent provisions on prior information requirements (art. 4.2).

Where other Directives or national laws provide for prior information requirements, these are considered to be additional to those provided for in Directive 2002/65 EC (art. 4.1). Indeed, there are additional prior information requirements arising from Directives on life policies (Directive 2009/138 EU, arts. 183–185), as well as on insurance intermediation (Directive 2002/92 EC as amended by Directive 2014/65 EU). There are several EU jurisdictions where national law provides for additional precontractual information for nonlife policies as well.

The Directive leaves it to the member states and national laws to provide for sanctions where the supplier has failed to provide precontractual information (art. 11).

An important point to be made about precontractual information is that the provisions of the Directive address similarly all financial services. This means that article 3 of the Directive on precontractual information does not take into account the peculiarities of each financial service but assess them altogether. This raises certain issues of interpretation when applying art. 3 to each particular financial service. It may prove particularly difficult to apply art. 3 in insurance contracts and determine what information an insurer has to provide on a precontractual basis under art. 3. From this point of view, it might be prudent for national legislators or national supervision authorities to elaborate further on precontractual information and either introduce specific rules designed for insurance policies or at least provide detailed guidelines. This would increase legal certainty very much.

A final point to be made about precontractual information is about its efficiency in terms of consumer protection. It has been suggested that a lot of information may prove misleading and destructing instead of helpful to consumers.[37] It is not the volume of information but its quality and relevance to the contractual risks that is material from the point of view of consumer protection. A lot of information will either go unnoticed at all, or it will only distract attention from substantial and material aspects.

3.8.2 Right to Receive Contract Terms and Precontractual Information in Durable Form

According to art. 5, the insurer has to provide the policy terms and conditions, as well as all precontractual information in durable form, before the insured is bound by the policy. So the contract cannot become binding on the consumer before he has so received the terms and conditions and precontractual information. So there is something like a "cooling off" period, during which the contract does not come into force. However, the consumer may wish to waive this cooling off period and request that the contract come into force immediately. Moreover, the consumer may wish to proceed with contract conclusion through telecommunication means that do not make it possible to forward terms and conditions and prior information in durable form. In such cases, however, the consumer retains the withdrawal right discussed below.

3.8.3 Withdrawal (Cancelation) Right

The consumer enjoys a withdrawal (cancelation) right, which has to be exercised with 14 days in nonlife policies and 30 days in life insurances covered by Directive 90/619 EC, as well as in personal pension operations. The cancelation period does not commence before the consumer received the contract terms and precontractual information in durable form. In life insurances, the cancelation period does not commence before the consumer is informed about contract conclusion.

It is to be recalled that in individual life policies the insured enjoys a 14–30 days cancelation right under insurance contract law also (art. 186 of Directive 2009/138).

The Directive provides that this cancelation right does not apply in certain cases, while member states are granted the option not to grant cancelation rights in some other cases.

Finally the Directive contains provisions against unauthorized communication and efficient out of court complaint and redress procedures.

[37] de Meza et al. (2007).

3.9 *Directive 2011/83 EU and 2002/65 EC Compared*

It has been pointed out above that the legislation on distance sales in general (Directive 2011/83 EU) and distance sales of financial services (Directive 2002/65 EC) are supported by the same justifying philosophy, i.e. the absence of physical presence of both parties during negotiation and contracting and the impact that such absence has on consumer's protection. It has been pointed out, however, that there are also material differences among financial services and other ordinary consumer contracts. Financial services are more material than an average consumer contract, and the level of vigilance required by the consumer is higher. Moreover, the provider of financial services is usually expected to provide reasonable assistance, advice, and guidance to consumers. So one would reasonably expect the regulation of distance sale of financial services in Directive 2002/65 EC to be more restrictive for providers and more protective for consumers than the regulation of ordinary consumer distance sales in Directive 2011/83 EU. There are differences indeed, and most of such differences are due to the very nature of financial services. Most of the differences relate to the type of precontractual information. Under Directive 2002/65 EC, more information is required regarding the provider of the financial services; for example, information is required about the provider's representatives in the member state where the consumer is established, about any professional intermediaries, about the trade registry of the provider, and about the supervising authority. Financial service is a heavily regulated business, and the provider of the service and its intermediaries are licensed and regulated by some national supervisor. So this information is material to consumers to confirm that a proper professional license is in place, that the provider of the service complies with the current regulation, and possibly to allow consumers to exercise any legal rights they may have by addressing to the supervising authority. Another aspect is that the provider has to make available precontractual information regarding any special risks that financial services involve, as well as to advise that historical performances are no indicators for future performances. Information as to any guarantee funds or special compensation schemes is also required; such information relates to the creditworthiness surrounding the provider and the market in general, and creditworthiness is usually of essence in financial transactions. There are differences relating to the right of withdrawal as well. Under Directive 2011/83 EU, the time period for withdrawal is 14 days. The period is the same under Directive 2002/65 EC, save that in case of life insurances and personal pension operations it is extended to 30 days. It is worth reminding that under EU insurance contract law, as well as under national laws of several member states, there is also a right of withdrawal within, either 14 days, in case certain information which has to be provided precontractually has not been so provided, or 30 days (i.e., Directive 2009/138 EU, art. 186), in case the policy delivered deviates from the coverage requested in the application for insurance submitted by the insured. Another difference between Directives 2011/83 EU and 2002/65 EC with respect to the right of withdrawal is that in the later distance sales of financial service Directive, the right of withdrawal is expressly excluded in certain cases listed in art. 6(2). These are cases where practical difficulties and objective factors render withdrawal inefficient, complex, and disproportionate, such as where the price fluctuates during the withdrawal period due to reasons outside the supplier's control or where at consumer's request performance has been fully completed by both parties before the exercise of the withdrawal right or in travel and baggage insurance policies or in similar short-term insurance policies of less than one-month duration. Par. 3 of art. 6 provides for further cases where member states may provide that the right of withdrawal does not apply.

4 Conclusion

The development of the Internet has made online sales a valuable channel of distribution for insurance companies. At the same time, the use of the Internet in sales has made it necessary to adopt new techniques of marketing and promotion, which are more personalized. From the legal point of view, applying modern online sales marketing techniques may raise issues relating to privacy and data protection. Reconciling conflicts among privacy and data protection objectives on the one hand and business needs to facilitate online marketing and sales on the other seems to be a major challenge for legislators and policy makers.

Although in other fields of the economy (consumer goods in particular) online sales represent already a substantive part of total sales at both local and cross-border levels, the position seems to be different with respect to insurances. Online sales of insurances seem to be of local interest only and cross-border sales are not that developed yet.

From the legal point of view:

The E-Commerce Directive 2000/31 EC does not remove any regulatory requirements for insurers or intermediaries, particularly with respect to compliance with the freedom to provide services and freedom of establishment legal regime.

EU legislation on distance sales (i.e., Directives 2011/83 EU and 2002/65 EC) establishes a different type of contract conclusion process for online contracts. This process comprises a series of consumer rights, such as the right to receive precontractual information, the right to receive contract terms in durable form, and the right to withdraw within a certain period of time. These requirements are in line with similar provisions in the 2009/138 EU Insurance Directive, at least as far as individual life policies are concerned. In any case, any legal requirements specifically provided for in the insurance directives are additional to the requirements imposed by Directive 2002/65 EC and are not replaced by the later one.

Although Directive 2002/65 EC is in principle a full harmonization Directive, this is not without exceptions. Member states are expressly allowed to apply stringent requirements with respect to precontractual information and to provide exceptions from the cancelation right. Moreover, legal consequences resulting from cancelation very much depend on national law. From this point of view, further harmonization of national insurance contract laws seems to be a major necessity to facilitate further cross-border online sales of insurances.

Overall, the legal regime of online sales of consumer insurances seems to be quite complex. Much of the complexity may be due to the desire to secure privacy, data protection, and other consumers' interests in general. However, achieving a greater level of simplicity and legal certainty, without sacrificing consumer protection, would be desirable.

References

Books

Boss AH, Kilian W (eds) (2008) The UN convention on the use of electronic communications in international trade, Kluwer Law International, The Netherlands

Faria JAE (2006) The UN convention on the use of electronic communications in international trade. Int Comp Law Q, 689

Heinemann G, Schwarzl Ch (2010) New online retailing, innovation and transformation, Springer Gabler, Wiesbaden, p 19 seqq

Kotler Ph, Armstrong G (2011) Principles of marketing, 14th edn., Pearson Education, New Jersey, p 497

Kotler Ph, Keller KL (2012) Marketing management, Pearson Education, New Jersey, 14th edn., p 235

Journals

Hiwarker T, Khot PG (2013), E-insurance: analysis of the collision and allegation of e-commerce on the insurance and banking. J Bus Manag Soc Sci Res 2(6):1–5

Meshkat L et al. (2012), Electronic insurance and its application in e-commerce. Int J Contemp Res Bus 4(8):640

Studies

de Meza D, Irlenbusch B, Reyniers D (2007) Information versus persuasion, experimental evidence on salesmanship, mandatory disclosure and the purchase of income and loan payment protection insurance. Lond School Econ (November)

Kastberg Nielsen C. et al. (Ramboll Management), Study on the economic impact of the Electronic Commerce Directive, 7.9.2007, commissioned by the EU Commission DG Internal Market and Services Unit E2

Online Documents

Anagnostopoulou D (2013) E-commerce in international and European Union law. http://afroditi.uom.gr/jmc/wp-content/uploads/2013/06/Research-Essay-No-11.pdf
Geist M (2010) A guide to global e-commerce law. http://www.itu.int/ITU-T/special-projects/ip-policy/final/Attach04.doc
OECD Guidelines on the protection of privacy and trans-border flows of personal data (1980)
OECD Guidelines on e-consumer protection (1999)
The Council's Convention on the protection of individuals with regard to automatic processing of personal data (1981)

Insurance Contracts Online and Consumer Protection Under the European and Greek Laws

Efi Tziva

Contents

Abstract The chapter refers to the comparatively "new," in the Greek market, product of online insurance and especially to the protection of the policy holder, who acts as a consumer. After making some empirical observations on the sale of insurance products online the article examines the following issues the specific legal nature and content of the insurance contracts, as well as the legislative framework, are examined. The author deals also with the term of the consumer, especially in the field of insurance law and generally in the Greek special consumer protection law (L. 2251/1994). This law (art. 4a, renumbered as 4i), which refers to the distance marketing of financial services) has incorporated in the Greek law all the relevant articles of Directive 2002/65/EC ("Distance marketing of consumer financial services"), without any change, although according to art. 3 § 9 of the Directive, the Member States could impose requirements that are more restrictive or prescriptive in the field of financial services. In the following chapter, legal issues related to the conclusion of insurance contracts online are analyzed and particularly the rights and duties of the parties, such as the precontractual obligations of the insurance company, the information duties and rights, etc. An important place in the article is devoted to unfair commercial practices and the relative

---

E. Tziva (✉)
Faculty of Law, Department of Economic and Commercial Law, Aristotle University of Thessaloniki, University Campus, 54124 Thessaloniki, Greece
e-mail: efmtziva@law.auth.gr; tzivaefi@otenet.gr

P. Marano et al. (eds.), *The "Dematerialized" Insurance*,
DOI 10.1007/978-3-319-28410-1_7

protection of the consumer of insurance products online according to the Greek law that also in this case has fully incorporated the provisions in Directive 2005/29/EC ("Unfair B2C commercial practices"). The article is concluded by some final remarks according to the legal "safety" of the insurance online and especially to the relative consumer protection.

1 Empirical Observations on the Sale of Insurance Products Online

The Internet has a dual significance for the insurance sector. It can be used, firstly, as a means of communication (Kommunikationsmedium), mainly to provide information, concerning the insurance enterprises and the services they offer (their products) and, secondly, as a means for drawing up insurance contracts from a distance.[1] Although the appearance of the so-called insurance products on websites was accomplished relatively late in Greece, compared to other countries, it is currently presenting an increasing frequency, mainly due to the fact that the insurance enterprises operating in the Greek area strive, using the advantages provided by the online activity, to encounter the serious economic problems created by the general economic recession and to increase their profits, compressing their operating expenses and the intermediaries' commissions.[2]

The most significant online "presences" of insurance enterprises in Greece relate to "Greek" insurance enterprises, while the presence of foreign insurance enterprises in the Greek online insurance market appears limited. Given of course the universality of the Internet, and also the implementation of freedom of establishment and providing services within the EU, no one is able to prevent a user from seeking insurance coverage from an insurance enterprise, headquartered in another Member State, as respectively a "European" insurance enterprise[3] can enlarge the

[1] See **Lubinski**, in Rechtshandbuch Electronic Business (Hrsg. **Prof. Gounalakis**,), edn. 2003, § 40, Versicherungsgeschäfte, Rn. 1, **J. T. Eichhorn**, Online-Versicherungen aus aufsichts- sowie zivilrechtlicher Perspektive, p. 9.

[2] See in detail the importance of electronic trading activity for the insurance economy in **B. Wirtz/ P. Vogt/K. Denger**, Electronic Business in der Versicherungswirtschaft, ZVersWiss 2001, Vol. 90, p. 161–190.

[3] The fact is that the European legislator with a series of primary and secondary legislation of EU law has introduced a unitary for insurance companies headquartered in Member States. Mainly in view of the fundamental Community freedoms of establishment and provision of services and also the principle of single authorization, Community enterprises can, with or without establishment, carry out insurance operations, subject to control of the state of origin. In contrast, non-Community enterprises wishing to operate in Greece should have an establishment in the form of an agency or branch and be subject to the prescribed administrative control; see more, **I. Rokas**, Private insurance (11th edn). p. 737 ff. no. c. 1103 et seq.

circle of customers with online transactions in the Greek area,[4] particularly with users who are established in Greece. However, such an action appears not to be endearing to users who hesitate to transact with an insurance enterprise that is not domestic and also to insurance enterprises facing a difficult situation, when the insured risk is located in a country other than that in which they have received establishment and operation license. At the same time in the context of private international law, governing the insurance policy, the insurance enterprises may be faced with law, considered to be competent and applicable to resolve potential future disputes with the insured, that is not the law of their domicile.[5] This may occur when the clause of affiliation in the law of the insurance enterprise's establishment place, contained in the relevant GTCT (General Terms and Conditions of Trade), is not acceptable, particularly in view of the beneficial provisions of Directive 93/13 for the consumer, and thus provisions of Regulation 593/2008 (Rome I), provisions of Directives of 2nd and 3rd generation (88/357/EEC, 90/619/EEC, and 92/49/EEC), as well as provisions of Regulation 44/2001, are implemented, which are in turn characterized by a climate of consumer protection in cross-border transactions.[6]

The empirical observations concerning websites that enable the conclusion of insurance contracts online and irrespective of the insurance enterprise's "nationality" can be briefly summarized as follows: in most sites, providing primarily the

[4] In accordance with article 3 § 2 of Directive 2000/31 (L 178, p. 1–16), on electronic commerce, Member States may not, for reasons falling within the coordinated field, restrict the freedom to provide information society services from another Member State. This means, in principle, that any institution, in this case an insurance company established in a Member State, shall have free access to the single European market; see **El. Alexandridou**, The law of electronic commerce, Greek and community (2nd edn. 2010), p. 35. However, the Annex of this directive, among the excluded from the application of rules on free movement of information society services, defines the field of direct insurance other than life insurance, which has been subject of same preceding Community regulation, by means of Directives 92/49/EEC (article 30 and title IV thereof), 92/96/EEC (title IV), 88/357/EEC (articles 7 and 8), 90/619/EEC (article 4). This exception does not mean that the field of insurance services is excluded from the possibility of free electronic conduct but that especially for this field special regulations and even the provisions of Directive 2000/31 are applied, which made the field of insurance market a harmonized field based, however, on the peculiarities and mainly the need to protect policy holders, however, rightly emphasizing that a company providing financial services on the Internet is a service provider of the information society (information society service provider (ISSPs)), resulting in a parallel implementation of the provisions of the relevant Community provisions; see Stibbe, Distance marketing of consumer financial services, available on the Internet, ICT Law Newsletter, Special Edition, October 2003, **L. Tocca**, La direttiva 2002/65/CE sulla vendita di servizi finanziari, in http://www.consumerlaw.it. Basis for the legislative framework of Directive 2002/65 is considered the Directive on electronic commerce by **H.-W. Micklitz/M. Ebers**, Verbraucherschutz durch und im Internet bei Abschluss von privaten Versicherungsverträgen, in Verbraucherschutz durch und im Internet bei Abschluss von privaten Versicherungsverträgen (Hrsg. **von J. Basedow, Ul. Meyer, D. Rückle, H.-P. Schwintowski**), p. 43 (49).

[5] See. **T. Hoeren/J. Oberscheidt**, Verbraucherschutz im Internet, VuR 11/99, p. 371 (383).

[6] See details on private international law of insurance contract in **R. Chatzinikolaou—Angelidou**, Private Insurance Law (3th edn. 2012), p. 53 ff.

possibility of a motor vehicle liability insurance, the insurance is presented as a simple product, which someone can buy at a low price and has many advantages, such as free medical and legal advice, roadside assistance, without of course mentioning that in most cases it will be supplementary insurance, for which, apart from the agreement, the payment of an additional premium is required. It is not even clarified that the product one buys online is nothing more than the conclusion of an insurance contract, which generates mutual rights and obligations, whose fulfillment is regulated by the provisions of law and also by relevant contractual regulations, usually in the form of "standard policy terms" under the principle of the doctrine of "semi-compulsoriness," which distinguishes the insurance legislation. The impression created is that the crucial point is the insurance premium's collection by the potential insured, without mentioning his/her basic obligation, that is, the payment of premium, which in fact should be made in advance to start the insurance coverage. No information is provided in relation to the rights and obligations burdening the contracting party of the insurance enterprise, the breach of which can lead to the exclusion of coverage, in case of ascertained culpability on behalf of the policy holder or of the insurance beneficiary, if he is another person.

Given the impression of self-determination of the insurance contract's content using messages like "create your insurance, as you wish," this is a possibility that does not actually apply to the specific contracts, which are all accession contracts with preformulated standard contractual causes (GTCT) and special insurance terms,[7] without explaining that in this respect it concerns either different insurance products or programs forming the insurance coverage based on the declared insurance value, the insured risk, the personalization data of insurance interest, etc.

The anonymity existing on the Internet and the access need of insurance enterprises to the largest possible number of recipients result in the formation of offered products in a general and depersonalized way, a fact, however, regarding particularly life insurance, that does not allow rationalistic function. Life insurances that can be either insurances against damages or insurances of fixed sums not exempting mixed character contracts, despite the undeniable joining nature of contracts, are always given the possibility of content configuration so as to cover the needs of the particular insured. In the Internet world, at least so far, no possibility of sufficient information for the interested party to draw up an insurance contract is provided, nor is a "dialogue" accomplished in order to give a factual content to the personal qualities and needs so as to choose the proper insurance program. It is easily perceived that in this way, personal risk insurances are depersonalized and moving away from their typological elements.

[7] The intense accession nature of insurance contracts has led to the identification, in the public consciousness, of GTCT with Gen. Insurance Terms;· see **G. Triantafillakis**, Private insurance and consumer protection, Exemption clauses from insurance coverage liability in motor vehicle accidents and consumer protection, Business and Consumer Law (DEE), 2006, p. 142.

In case of drawing up an insurance policy, the contracting party does not desire to buy a product but claims insurance coverage. This must be identified or even identifiable, a real obligation, which the policy holder can claim resorting to the relevant provisions of law, a fact not highlighted on the relevant websites.

Furthermore, the potential "insured" is not informed of the release rights from the contract, the right to object, and also the right of withdrawal, the latter provided not only by the provisions of the insurance legislation but also by Article 4a and recently renumbered as 4i of Law 2251/1994 (par.6), which has incorporated into Greek law the provisions of Directive 2002/65/EC. The "insured" is not also granted a model declaration of objection and withdrawal respectively, in the manner, of course, that it is feasible in distance contracts. This means that it is not necessary to grant a model in printed form, as it is sufficient to administer the practical instructions or easy access to a model included on the website, which will help the insured exercise rights of withdrawal.[8]

Generally it is observed that precontractual information does not have the content, quality, extent specified by both the relevant provisions of insurance law and the respective consumer protection legislation, especially since the recent legislation cited and applied to contracts concluded online bring about serious consequences in cases of incomplete information, as will be in detail determined below, being the grant of the withdrawal right and also the relevant nullity of the contract in favor of the consumer-insured.[9]

The observations reported can easily be opposed by anyone with the argument that it is not possible for a website to have detailed reference of the legal framework and the content of insurance contracts due to space and time and because such a website would be tedious and therefore rejected by the non "special" users. We believe, however, that with the cooperation of insurance enterprises on the one hand and website designers on the other hand, it is possible to create websites that are friendly and attractive to use but at the same time complying with the law and safeguarding the interests of the parties.

2 Legislative Framework for the Insurance Contracts Online

The majority of insurance contracts that can be concluded online are contracts that cover personal risks, differently formulated consumer insurance contracts (B2C). This fact consequently defines their classification in a grid of legal regulations, derived from both the insurance law and the law of consumer protection.

---

[8] It is article 3 par. 3 c. d of Directive 2002/65/EC.

[9] See detailed **A. Despotidou**, in Consumer Protection Law (ed. **El. Alexandridou**), 2008, article 4a no. 27 et seq.

The fact is that, in recent years, principles derived from consumer protection law[10] have ventured the insurance law at EU and national levels, but at the same time specific conditions arising from the nature of insurance are maintained, resulting in the specific formation of protection for the insured-consumer framework. Against consumer rights, in a bidirectional relation, the insurer's obligations are developed, concerning the insured person's information, even during the precontractual stage,[11] when this quality has not even been acquired, a fact gaining importance in the insurance contracts from distance, with common ground in the majority of cases, the consumer's information deficit. The insurer's obligations to provide information are set out by both the insurance legislation and relevant Codes of Conduct of Insurance Enterprises, and also from the consumer protection law, the law of electronic commerce, as well as the domestic contract law of Member States, in case competence thereon exists to establish or maintain differing national regulations or relevant inadequacy, requiring completion, despite the multifarious specific legislation. The objective, however, should be the extensive information of potential insured and not the uncontrolled information, which essentially coincides with lack of information.

3 The Term of the Insured Consumer, According to the Provisions of European and Greek Laws

The concept of the consumer-insured in Greek law does not arise from an express provision of the relevant insurance legislation, but science has moved on a "ratione materie" approach. The view that prevailed characterizes as policy holder or insured consumer—when not the same person—a natural or legal person that carries out insurance to cover private or personal risks.[12] Since the policy holder's consumer identity is affirmed in an insurance contract, a specific cluster of insurance legislation protection then operates, in combination with the customary legal protection framework for all consumers. This cluster includes already known and applied to all consumer contract principles, such as epigrammatically the protection against unfair standard insurance terms, the duty of information, the right of withdrawal, the possibility of individual and collective protection.

[10] See **I. Rokas**, Insurance terms, consumer protection, civil penalties and reinsurance, in memory of M. Minoudi (2004), p. 593 ff. and esp. p. 599.

[11] See detailed **I. Rokas**, Private Insurance...aa. p. 244 ff., no. c. 385 et seq.

[12] See **R. Chatzinikolaou—Angelidou**, The Insurance Contract...aa. p. 32 ff., **I. Rokas**, Private Insurance, Insurance contract and insurance company law (11th edn. 2006), p. 239 ff. no.c. 377 et seq.

4 Information Duties of the Policy Holder

The institutionalized, by virtue of the insurance law, providing of information regarding the "status" of the insurance enterprise, the financial standing, i.e. the applicable law,[13] should take place before the person interested to enter into a policy of insurance submits the request to the insurance enterprise and before of course being given the insurance policy with the built-in terms, which constitutes the proof of drafting document. This ensures the updating so as the consciously decision to transact with this insurance enterprise.[14] Although this obligation of precontractual information is collateral as to the insurer's main obligation, that is, the providing of insurance coverage, however, it is of great importance in the formation of the legal will of the person interested to be an insured party, so justifiably characterized by science as a peculiar insurance burden of the insurer,[15] as a specialization of the principle of good faith, noncompliance or inadequate compliance of which has serious consequences, including the release ability of the insured, with the exercise of objection and withdrawal rights, as well as administrative sanctions by the supervisory authority, and even action for damages against the insurer and other parties responsible for informing persons, i.e. insurance intermediaries.[16]

The provision of information in the manner and to the extent specified is certainly difficult to place in the context of electronic insurance transaction, where for substantive, technical, temporal reasons thorough information of the user is impossible and not just at the negotiating stage but also subsequently during the function of the contractual relationship, as well as at the critical stage of the occurrence of insured risk, in the event that such thing takes place. However, the EU legislator spares no consumer protection measures in the context of information, as defined in paragraph 21 of the Preamble of Directive 2002/65/EC that the use of means of distance communication should not lead to an unacceptable restriction of the information provided to the customer. The necessary information should be provided to the consumer prior to the conclusion of the contract in order to correctly assess the financial service offered and make an informed choice.

Furthermore, the special nature of the insurance contract imposes an increased sensitivity in the field of information as the insured is not a simple consumer of

[13] See article 4 par. 2(H) και par. 3(D) of Decree-Law 400/1970 more in **R. Chatzinikolaou—Angelidou**, Insurance Contract...aa. p. 114.

[14] "Undoubtedly the provision of information is one of the key tools available to enhance consumer protection," emphasizes **G. Howells**, The Potential and Limits of Consumer Empowerment by Information, Journal of law and Society, Vol, 32/Sep. 2005, p. 349 (352).

[15] Cf. **R. Chatzinikolaou—Angelidou**, Insurance Contract...aa. p. 126.

[16] The abolition of ex ante control of insurance terms by the competent authorities has rendered important the role of insurance intermediaries in collecting, processing, and providing information to policy holders about different insurance products available, as provided for in Directive 2002/92/EC on insurance mediation See **S. Grundmann**, EC Financial Services-Development 2002–2005, ERCL 4/2005, p. 482 (492).

products or services, being not only economically the weaker and the negotiating party in an insurance contract but also a partaker of a society of similar risks formed to relieve those who suffer consequences from the occurrence of insured risks.[17] Thus, and given the nature of distance conclusion of insurance contracts, information should be provided, as in other similar contracts, in a clear and understandable manner, in compliance with the principle of good faith and the business usages, and at the same time adequate time should be granted to the consumer to weigh the data in order to move into a conscious transaction decision.[18]

A related issue with the obligation to inform the insured consumer is the protection against standard policy terms or special terms regarding the insurance relationship, as through these terms not only the purpose of information is served, but also the existence and extent of insurance coverage, while a large number of equivalent terms include legal exceptions to coverage, terms anyway valid based on the corresponding provisions of the law, but mainly contractual exclusions from insurance coverage, in other words, forms of pathogenesis of relationships that lead to frustration of purpose, i.e. in justified exemption of the insurer to provide insurance coverage.

Under Greek insurance law, when the contract is governed by general or special policy terms, the insurer is obliged to mention the section of the policy, citing the personalized elements of the contract, and deliver them with the policy. These terms include important information regarding the insurance coverage and also the exceptions. Information on the existence of General Insurance Terms, including both GTCT and Special Insurance Terms, should be provided no later than the conclusion of the contract, i.e. before the insurer accepts the submitted, by the interested, insurance application and before the issuance of the policy, which either way is not a constituent document. This means that the requirements to enclose general insurance terms (G.I.T.) in contract are (a) potentiality of knowledge by the interested to be insured and (b) delivery along with the policy.[19]

It is easily perceived that in online conclusion of insurance contracts, both the first and second conditions are not satisfied in the manner and extent defined in the Greek Insurance Law, a fact that finds its explanation in simplifying and shortening the time and generally in the specific nature of the whole process. As accepted in all similar cases of conclusion of contracts in electronic environment, the requirements of valid conclusion of the respective contracts applicable in the real, natural world should be proportionately respected. The knowledge of the intended to transact and then be insured should be ensured in insurance contracts drawn up online, after the conclusion of the contract, as to the existence and content of G.I.T., and most importantly, the insured should be informed about the release right of the drawn-up contract, with the exercise of the peculiar objection right, in cases of lack of information or incomplete information on the existence of G.I.T. Finally, and

[17] Cf. R. **Chatzinikolaou—Angelidou**, Insurance Contract. . .aa. p.9.

[18] Cf. **A. Despotidou**, in Consumer Protection Law. . .aa. article 4a no. 12–15.

[19] Cf. **R. Chatzinikolaou—Angelidou**, Insurance Contract. . .aa. p.171.

concerning G.I.T., we should note that even if they are included into a contract, it does not mean that they escape control, in terms of their validity. Regarding this topic, general provisions of Law 2251/1994 are implemented, and in particular article 2 thereof, which generally governs the protection of consumers, but always under the condition that specificities of the particular type of contract, purpose of contract, content of contract, reciprocal rights, and obligations differing from other contracts[20] are taken into account. The specificity of insurance contract certainly imposes supervisory control over the used, by insurance enterprises, G.I.T. in a limited extent today, in view of the adopted EU level deregulation, but actually existing control, particularly in compulsory insurance and health insurance.[21]

5 Withdrawal Right of the Policy Holder

Except the objection right, adopted by provisions of the insurance legislation, the policy holder is provided with another contractual release right, the right of insurance withdrawal, established in combination with both the provisions of the insurance law and the provision of Article 4a Law 2251/1994 and more specifically of §§ 6 and 7 applied—among others—in insurance contracts from distance, regulations that brought directly into Greek law the relevant provisions of articles 6 and 7 of Directive 2002/65/EC.[22]

The consumer, in this case, however, and in the strict "European" sense, i.e. the natural person, who performs transactions to cover personal risks has the right to withdraw within 14 days from distance contracts of financial services, without any penalty and reason. Especially, however, for insurance contracts from distance that an insurance enterprise can draw up, as well as for pension funds, the deadline is greater, specifically 30 calendar days, a deadline starting either from the day of conclusion of the contract or, if it comes from life insurance, from the day the consumer is informed of the conclusion of the contract or from the day the consumer received the contractual terms and information, if this date is later than the date indicated in the first indent.[23] The above deadline to exercise the withdrawal right is suspended for as long as the policy holder has the right to object, according to the provision of par. 6 article 2 Insurance Law. Finally, no right of withdrawal is provided in travel and luggage insurance policies, as well as in other

[20] See in detail **R. Chatzinikolaou—Angelidou**, Insurance Contract...aa. p. 180 ff.

[21] In detail, **R. Chatzinikolaou—Angelidou**, Insurance Contract...aa. p. 188 ff.

[22] See **A. Despotidou**, in Consumer Protection Law...aa. article 4a no. 39.

[23] So the relevant provision of article 6 of the Directive. Cf. even in the Italian law (d.lgs. n. 190/ 19.8.2005) bringing into that law the provisions of Directive 2002/65 in **C. Iurilli/L. Galli**, La vendita a distanza dei servizi finanziari, available on the website of Centro Europeo Consumatori Italia, p. 18.

policies with a duration of less than 1 month, as stated in b ii of par. 6 article 4a (now 4i) Law 2251/1994, mainly due to their short duration and low cost.[24]

It is perceived that the possibility of unjustified withdrawal is provided with favorable, for the consumer, terms and deadlines in conclusion of distance financial services, due to the conclusion conditions, to the content of these services and mainly due to the serious economic consequences induced to the contracting from distance consumer.[25] In particular, we should note that the specific regulations of Insurance Law have a clear lead over the corresponding consumer protection law, a fact confirming the defined above opinion that because of their peculiar content, insurance contracts are in principle subject to specific legislative status and only to complete identified loopholes in complementary application of more general nature regulations and especially provisions on consumer protection, provided of course that the counterparty of the insurance enterprise has, in this case, the consumer capacity.

Finally, we should not forget to mention yet another special right recognized by law on life insurance, concerning the release, on a broad basis, of the insured and for the existence of which no reference is made in life insurance contracts, drawn up online. This is the redemption right, as provided by article 29, paras 3 and 4 Insurance Law and granted to all relevant insurances with the same conditions[26] and regardless of the way these insurances were drawn up.

6 Consumer Protection in the Sector of the Insurance Online. Information and Unfair B2C Commercial Practices According to Late Decisions of the European Court of Justice

The importance of information, as well as advertising[27] and other commercial practices,[28] and in particular the possibility of Member States to introduce or maintain stricter requirements of the respective community in these areas, for the

[24] See, however, the right indication of **A. Despotidou**, in Consumer Protection Law (ed. **El. Alexandridou**), 2008, article 4a no. 47; this provision should be interpreted restrictively so that it would not be detrimental to the consumer, and while in the specific insurances the exercise of withdrawal would be a great burden for the supplier, due to the short duration and limited economic object, they are insurances usually drawn up sometime before departure and usually ancillary to the main travel or transport contract.

[25] See **A. Despotidou**, in Consumer Protection Law (ed. **El. Alexandridou**), 2008, article 4a no. 39.

[26] See R. **Chatzinikolaou—Angelidou**, Insurance Contract. . .aa. p. 322.

[27] See details in **K. Delouka—Inglessi**, Web advertising: consumer protection within the European Community, NOMOS, Liber Amicorum, Prof. L. Kotsiris, p. 279 (284).

[28] Among the commercial practices widely used are also the provision of financial services without prior request of the consumer and the unsolicited commercial communication (spamming), for

services offered online in Europe, are demonstrated by two important decisions of EU Court. It is the judgment of 5 July 2012, C-49/11, Content Services Ltd/Bundesarbeitskammer, and the judgment of 18 July 2013, C-265/12, Citroën Belux NV/Federatie voor Verzekerings-en Financiële Tussenpersonen (FvF). The first of the decisions concerns distance service contracts that do not belong to the category of financial services, and the second relates to unfair commercial practices for insurance benefits, concluded offline. Despite the different subject, the nondirect reference to information, and the use of unfair commercial practices in the provision of insurance services online, these two decisions allow through their study the generating of certain conclusions.

These conclusions are that Directive 97/7/EC and Directives 2002/65/EC and 2005/29/EC can be characterized as Directives of "partly" minimum harmonization, allowing Member States the possibility to regulate certain issues differently, sometimes even stricter, including the issue of information and commercial practices, in order to protect the financial interests of consumers. Furthermore, this view, despite the advanced coordination occurring at EU level, is confirmed both in distance contracts and in the specific field of distance financial services, with the objective of achieving a single European financial market, leaving Member States a scope for regulatory actions in order to serve another goal, which is to protect consumers. So, while these Directives are of full harmonization in the framework of the provision of services, they leave Member States scope for different regulation in consumer-related issues and are aimed to protect consumer's interests, including the issue of information and commercial promotion practices, becoming thus issues of crucial importance for the unhindered and consistent, with European standards, function of distance contracts.

In the first case, the Court faced the reference for a preliminary ruling from the Oberlandesgericht of Vienna, concerning the interpretation of article 5, par. 1 of Directive 97/7/EC on the protection of consumers in respect of distance contracts (OJ L 144, p. 19). This Directive has been replaced by Directive 2011/83 (OJ L 304, p. 64) in 13.6.2014; however, in this particular issue faced by the Court, subsequent changes do not alter the legal status. This is specifically the content and way of information from supplier to consumer, before the conclusion of the contract ("pre-contractual information duty"). In both the previous and latter Directive, the EU legislator emphasizes the need for prior information to be extensive, covering not only the data of the supplier and product but also the rights of the consumer, provided simultaneously in a clear and comprehensive manner to the potential consumer. As to the mode of providing information, while the first

which measures are taken from both the provisions of Directive 2002/65/EC and Directive 2002/29/EC, in combination with Directive 2002/58/EC on the protection of privacy in electronic communications. Greece has adopted the opt-in system in the sense that, to be acceptable to send advertising messages by any means of electronic communication and for any promotional purpose, there is explicit consent required of the recipient, before sending the messages **K. Delouka—Inglessi**, in Consumer Protection Law (ed. **El. Alexandridou**), 2008, articles 9,9a-9i, no. 50.

Directive quotes "in any way appropriate to the means of distance communication used...," the Directive 2011/83 refers to means of distance communication, used in plain and intelligible language. If such information is provided on a durable medium, it should be legible. In addition, in article 2 par. 10, the latter Directive of 2011 quotes that "'durable medium' means any instrument which enables the consumer or the trader to store information addressed personally to him in a way accessible for future reference for a period of time adequate for the purposes of the information and which allows the unchanged reproduction of the information stored."[29]

The Court invokes the corresponding regulation of article 2 (f) of Directive 2002/65/EC concerning the distance marketing of consumer financial services, which in the specific issue of clear and articulate prior information of the consumer refers to any instrument which enables the consumer to store information addressed personally to him in a way accessible for future reference, for a period of time adequate for the purposes of the information and which allows the unchanged reproduction of the information stored.

Thereafter, the Court citing provisions of relevant EU legislation, such as Directive 2002/92/EC (OJL 9/2003, p. 3), on insurance mediation, and Directive 2008/48/EC (OJL 133/2008, p. 66), which governs credit agreements for consumers, concluded that commercial practice, which enables access to information that should be provided by the supplier, only through a hyperlink, located on the enterprise's website, does not comply with the requirements of EU legislation and, in particular, Article 5, par. 1 of Directive 97/7/EC, which refers to durable medium available and accessible for obtaining information, mentioned in detail in the relevant Directive. According to the Court, providing information through hyperlink is equivalent to nonproviding of information by the enterprise and, consequently, nondownloading of information by the consumer, as a website with a disputed content is not a "durable medium," substitute of printed format, but has ephemeral nature, since it may at any time be altered unilaterally by the supplier, and also does not meet the conditions laid down in the Directive, as these are demonstrated in recitals No. 9, 11, 13, 14, and 22, where the purpose of the EU legislator appears. The objective is that the means of communication used, whatever they may be and even those for future use, should not lead to reduction of information provided to the consumer.

---

[29] The dispute in the main proceedings, which gave rise to the submission of the question referred for a preliminary ruling, arose from commercial practice, followed by a limited liability company, under English law, with a branch in Germany and which proposed various electronic services online on the website, accessible also in Austria. Consumers had the possibility, before the conclusion of the contract, to be informed about the right of withdrawal, just by clicking on a link that referred to a section of the company's website. After the conclusion of the contract, an invoice was issued, in which there was a reference that the consumer waives the right of withdrawal. Main proceedings initiated by an organization responsible for the protection of consumers, on the ground that this commercial practice violates the relevant provisions of European Union legislation (in particular of Directive 97/7) and also the corresponding Austrian law, which incorporated these provisions into domestic law.

This decision of EU Court and the following referred to help to draw certain conclusions, decisive of the information of the potential consumer generally in distance contracts, not only as to the nature and admittedly broad scope of information but also as to the way it should be done so that conditions of clear, distinct, and appropriate information is satisfied based on an average consumer, encountered in this type of transaction. Particularly in the case of distance marketing of financial services, the complexity and high risks, inherent in economic interests of consumers, have led the EU legislator to allow Member States to regulate more strictly the obligations of suppliers. Indeed, the tightening regulation is consistent with the fact that the relevant Directives, including Directive 2005/29/EC on unfair commercial practices,[30] although of full harmonization, allow Member States to impose more restrictive and detailed rules in this area, in other words explaining why these Directives do not introduce full harmonization on this issue, but allow Member States to maintain or introduce special regulation, which in order to be compatible with EU law should aim at consumer protection while respecting the principle of proportionality.

The EU Court therefore ruled in its judgment of 18 July 2013, Citroën Belux NV/Federatie voor Verzekerings-en Financiële Tussenpersonen (FvF), that the Belgian regulations applicable to commercial practices and prohibiting any combined offer to the consumer, of which at least one of the elements is a financial service carried out by an enterprise or several enterprises acting with a common purpose, does not conflict with article 3 par. 9 of Directive 2005/29 defining the scope of this Directive, as it is limited to the sector, which is not subject to full harmonization but allows Member States to adopt stricter national rules regarding financial services, without any clarification, such as the position limits as to the degree of restriction or criteria on the complexity and inherent serious risks, which financial services should have in order to be subject to stricter regulation.[31] At the same time, the specific national provision does not constitute a restriction on the free movement of services, which infringes the fundamental Community freedom of article 56 TFEU, and although a restriction, which according to established EU jurisprudence is admitted, if it has a legitimate aim compatible with the Treaty and

[30] This directive, which protects consumer economic interests from unfair commercial practices, due to the horizontal nature concerns also consumer financial transactions, carried out online, since no specific regulations of Directive 2002/65/EC are adopted, in relation to specified aspects of unfair commercial practices See more **A. Despotidou**, Provision of financial services by distance (2009), p. 43 ff., with further references.

[31] Cause for submission of the question referred for a preliminary ruling was given by a promotional offer of Citroën company that provided along with the purchase of every new vehicle 6-month free mixed insurance for the first year, for every new mixed insurance conclusion of full agreement. The federation of insurance intermediaries felt that the particular advertising contradicts the corresponding prohibitive provision of Belgian law and therefore claimed its cessation, bringing action before the competent Belgian courts. The submitted question then referred to was: whether article 3 par. 9 of Directive 2005/29 opposes a provision of a Member State, such as the disputed Belgian regulation, imposing a general prohibition of combined offers, when at least one of the elements is a financial service.

is justified by overriding reasons of public interest, it is appropriate to ensure that the objective pursued is achieved and does not go beyond what is necessary in order to attain it.

Consumer protection is recognized by EU jurisprudence as an overriding reason of public interest, capable of justifying restrictions on the freedom to provide services, and as regards the appropriateness of the restriction, the Court, in this case, invokes the financial service risk and complexity, resulting in a combined offer, considered sufficient to create to consumer the impression that there is a price advantage. An offer attached to a financial service can lead—as the Court explicitly states—in error as to the actual content and features of the offered combination and simultaneously deprives the possibility to compare the price and quality of the offer with similar benefits from other entrepreneurs. In this way, therefore, the Court accepts that the specific national regulation does not violate EU law (primary and secondary), contributes to consumer protection, and further respects the principle of proportionality.

7 Final Remarks

The continuous evolution of newly developed electronic commercial sectors, including electronic provision of insurance services, impedes a stable, dogmatic legal approach, consistent in fact with the universality of the phenomenon. The legal science follows, not as passive onlooker of events but as guardian of law and order, which does not distinguish within or outside the Internet. Quite the opposite is happening. Due to the risks inherent in electronic transaction, especially for the casual consumer, vigilance and readiness for immediate action of jurists are imposed. Specifically in insurance contracts, where confidence and relief of the insured from the created society of risks and the provided insurance coverage is crucial, transparency, information in all phases of the insurance relationship, the ability to release, and the protection against unfair trading practices should be promoted, even with stricter provisions of national legislation, mainly for policy holders who are consumers and therefore in need of increased protection.

Part III
Cyber Risks

Cyber Insurance: Underwriting, Scope of Cover, Benefits and Concerns

Kirsty Middleton and Maria Kazamia

Contents

Abstract This chapter examines how some indicative triggers from both the demand and the supply sides are contributing to the development of a specialised cyber insurance market and also how this development is held back, especially in Europe. Finally, some of the most characteristic features of the new specialised product offering are examined in the context of demonstrating the differentiating qualities of the new product which render it more of a risk management tool than a conventional insurance policy.

K. Middleton (✉)
AIG, Deputy General Counsel, Head of Zones, EMEA, London, UK
e-mail: kirsty.middleton@aig.com

M. Kazamia
AIG, Associate General Counsel, Head of South Zone EMEA, Athens, Greece
e-mail: maria.kazamia@aig.com

P. Marano et al. (eds.), *The "Dematerialized" Insurance*,
DOI 10.1007/978-3-319-28410-1_8

1 The Context

> In the place of guns and masks, this cybercrime organisation used laptops and the Internet. Moving as swiftly as data over the Internet, the organisation worked its way from the computer systems of international corporations to the streets of New York City.

This is how Loretta Lynch, United States Attorney for the Eastern District of New York, commented on the charging of seven hackers who used hacked data to make 40,500 transactions in just 10 h stealing $45 m from 27 countries worldwide.[1]

The digital economy is accompanied by new risks arising from the widespread use of new technologies like cloud computing, big data, the social media and mobile devices and their fast integration in the way of doing business. Despite the lack of widely used definitions of "cyber related' terminology (cyber risk, cybercrime, cybersecurity, etc), the European Commission (EC) understands cybercrime to encompass a broad range of criminal activities "where computers and information systems are involved either as a primary tool or as a primary target".[2] Cyber risk can also include a range of specific risks that relate to the use of computers, information technology and virtual reality.[3]

When big market players with advanced network security arrangements become victims of cyber attacks, the thought that criminals are close to surpassing the legitimate IT market in technological sophistication does occur. According to the UK government, 93 % of large corporations and 87 % of small businesses reported a cyber breach in the past year, with the cost for a cybersecurity breach estimated between £450,000 and £850,000 for large businesses and £35,000–£65,000 for smaller ones.[4]

The 2012 Verizon data breach investigation report indicates that 98 % of attacks were perpetrated by external agents and 4 % involved an employee of the organisation. In terms of how these breaches occurred, the report attributes 81 % to some form of hacking, 69 % to incorporated malware, 10 % to physical attacks, 7 % to social tactics and 5 % to the misuse of privilege.[5] The reasons behind the attacks vary from the pure activist motivations to industrial espionage, personal data theft and extortion. The consequences for the organisation also cover a wide range from liability and fines due to the loss of personal data to business interruption and reputational risk.

---

[1] Kirchgaessner (2013).

[2] European Commission (2013) Security Strategy of the European Union p. 3: "Cybercrime comprises traditional offences (e.g. fraud, forgery, and identity theft), content-related offences (e.g. on-line distribution of child pornography or incitement to racial hatred) and offences unique to computers and information systems (e.g. attacks against information systems, denial of service and malware)."

[3] Marsh (2013), p. 3.

[4] UK Government (2013) Keeping the UK safe in cyberspace.

[5] Verizon (2012), p. 23.

In this context, insurance market participants face the issue of whether and to what extent conventional insurance policies are flexible enough to adapt to the needs of the digital economy and address cyber risks adequately. Risk management controls do not always manage to meet the development pace of "the way of doing business". Cyber insurance seeks to contribute to the bridging of this gap.

According to the European Network and Information Security Agency (ENISA), "cyber insurance refers to insurance contracts having the purpose of covering a broad range of issues relating to risks in cyberspace. Researchers have identified contracts as covering things like: liability issues, property loss and theft, data damage, loss of income from network outage and computer failures or web site defacement". Asset protection, cyber extortion and privacy liability may also be covered.[6]

2 Demand Side Triggers

2.1 High Publicity, Reputational Risk and Remediation Costs

The accentuation of risks such as theft of personal data and other valuable information, denial of service and network outage, which accompany the growth of the digital economy, points to the integration of such considerations into firms' risk assessment and quantification exercises, addressing their reputational, their regulatory and the cost of business implications. According to Aon, about 80 % of reported breaches involve less than $1 m defence and indemnity costs, about 15 % are between 1 m and 20 m and about 5 % caused total costs exceeding 20 m.[7] The UK government data places the cost of cybercrime in the UK to 27 billion a year, 21 of which is incurred by businesses[8] in the form of theft of intellectual property, cyber extortion and industrial espionage.

Board of Directors can no longer ignore such exposures neither be comfortable in the perception that they are issues that their IT department should deal with without them needing to appear on the board's agenda. Network security failures are linked not only to legal and regulatory risks but also to reputational risk following the increasing publicity of cybercrime incidents, and eventual potential reduction in corporate value. A recent guidance note by the Institute of Chartered Secretaries and Administrators (ICSA) in the UK affirms the importance of cyber risks and encourages boards to challenge management on its understanding of the impact of cyber risks on the business, together with the proactive steps it has taken to address them.[9] Directors must have a firm grasp of such exposures to be able to

[6] ENISA (2013), p. 8.

[7] Kalinich (Aon) (2012), p. 10.

[8] Marsh (2013), p. 3.

[9] ICSA (2013), p. 7.

decide on the level of risk tolerance of the organisation and guide management towards appropriate and proportional risk management planning. These risks are largely managed through the strengthening of systems security and relevant internal governance arrangements, but risk managers are assessing to what extent a portion of such risks is transferrable to a third party and are looking at insurance products to that effect.

Although firms still tend to ask for business interruption endorsements which include reasons of cyber espionage, there is a tendency for the demand side to focus more on third party risk as opposed to first party one, most likely in light of the recent regulatory activity and increasing consumer prioritisation of data privacy.[10] Indicatively, 70 % of Europeans share the concern that their personal data maintained by companies may be used for purposes other than the ones for which it was collected. Phone companies, mobile phone companies and Internet service providers are trusted by less than 32 % of European Union (EU) citizens for the protection of their personal data, with just over 22 % stating that they trust Internet companies such as search engines, social networking sites and email services.[11]

2.2 Cyber Threats Targets and In-House Expertise

The areas most impacted by cybercrime threats appear to be energy, transport, financial services, public sector bodies and Internet services.[12] AIG believes that sectors like health, education, entertainment and real estate are also significantly affected. Both multinational conglomerates and small and medium-size enterprises (SMEs) are at risk and experience attacks on a daily basis. In a recent report, the Federation of Small Businesses ("FSB") in the UK found that cybercrime costs for its members reach around £785 m per year, with 41 % of FSB members having suffered an attack in the last year.[13] The UK government also issued cybercrime protection guidance to SMEs in April 2013 demonstrating strongly that criminals not only are interested in big corporations but also want to exploit potential loopholes in the systems of smaller companies. Insurance policies custom made for the needs of SMEs are a characteristic example with insurers like AIG that already see their cyber coverage premiums rise admit that they are keen for their product to reach the smaller companies which represent a bigger universe than the more sophisticated market players.[14]

Despite the growing awareness of cyber threats and the potential costs incurred after an incident, hiring resource with the experience and expertise to address a

[10] ENISA (2013), p. 16.

[11] European Commission (2011), Special Eurobarometer 359 p. 7.

[12] European Commission (2013), Security Strategy of the European Union p. 6.

[13] Federation of Small Businesses (2013).

[14] Buhayar and Bunn (2013) Bloomberg.

breach if and when it occurs may prove an even more costly and often disproportionate response to the specific risk. This is especially true for SMEs that are not expected to retain expertise of this nature but are no less targets of cyber attacks. However, stakeholders, including customers, shareholders, regulators and business partners, do expect firms to take every reasonable measure to protect their networks and be able to identify an incident and address its consequences without undue delay.[15] Providing access to expert resource that the company would require in the case of an incident while covering such costs can develop into one of the differentiating factors of cyber insurance products and a central proposition for an actual risk management support kit.

2.3 *Data Privacy Regulatory Developments*

A critical risk related to cybercrime is the misuse or loss of personal data which can trigger liability for the firm under an obligation to maintain the integrity and privacy of the data entrusted to it. The development of data privacy legislation, together with the manner of its enforcement by national data protection authorities is a crucial factor of the data privacy risk assessment for firms.

In the US, regulations imposing obligations on entities to provide timely notice to individuals and authorities in cases of data privacy breaches are more widespread than in Europe. Despite the absence of a relevant federal law, 46 states have enacted relevant legislation applicable to controllers and processors of personal data, raising compliance costs across the US where entities need to comply with state laws that are different in terms of scope and even the definition of personal information.

The current EU data protection framework is based mainly on the national implementation of Directives 95/46/EC and 2009/140/EC. Although article 13a of EU Directive 2009/140/EC imposes an obligation on providers of public communication networks to report significant security breaches and losses of integrity to their national competent authority, this notification requirement is much narrower in scope than the respective US requirements and has not proved a significant driver of the cyber insurance market.

However, the proposed revised EU data protection framework which aims at increased harmonisation towards minimising national divergences in interpretation and enforcement, as well as more effective responses to new technological challenges, appears to be changing the regulatory landscape.

According to the proposed EU General Data Protection Regulation:

> a personal data breach may, if not addressed in an adequate and timely manner, result in substantial economic loss and social harm, including identity fraud, to the individual concerned. Therefore, as soon as the controller becomes aware that such a breach has occurred, the controller should notify the breach to the supervisory authority without undue delay and, where feasible, within 24 h. Where this cannot be achieved within 24 h, an explanation of the reasons for the delay should accompany the notification. The individuals whose personal data could be adversely affected by the breach should be notified without

[15] HDPA 98/2013 (2013).

> undue delay in order to allow them to take the necessary precautions. A breach should be considered as adversely affecting the personal data or privacy of a data subject where it could result in, for example, identity theft or fraud, physical harm, significant humiliation or damage to reputation.[16]

Since the time of writing, progress has been made towards the adoption of the EU General Data Protection Regulation with an agreement on the Council confrming it reached an agreement with the Europen Parliament on the compromise text in December 2015. Aside from the apparent high compliance costs entailed, especially in relation to notices to large numbers of individuals affected, notification requirements also raise the possibility of legal action by the data subjects whose increased awareness of the breach is coupled by the increased importance consumers place on the protection of their personal information.

In terms of enforcement in the context of the current EU regime, a couple of cases handled by data protection authorities of member states are indicative.

A recent decision of the Greek Data Protection Authority (DPA) is indicative of a shift in the stance of the enforcement authorities towards a strict and more explicit view of the obligations of organisations controlling personal data. In this case, a wide range of data (including sensitive data) appearing to have been extracted from tax returns was discovered in the course of a DPA's audit of two companies engaged in trading of personal data. The DPA observed that despite some difference attributed to unlawful processing already having occurred by the audited companies, the range of data matched the database maintained by the General Secretariat of Information Services (a government department). The investigation into the Secretariat's security arrangements revealed a range of procedures and security controls, as well as incident response measures deemed inadequate in light of the nature of the data maintained (including sensitive data like disabilities) by the specific government department. The DPA did not limit its assessment to the content of the data controller's policies but extended it to the degree of their implementation which was also found unsatisfactory.

The DPA noted that the obligations of the data controller relate to both prevention—in the sense of the appropriate measures in place aimed at preventing an incident—and enforcement in the sense of enabling the incident to be identified and investigated. It deemed the unlawful processing of such data, through which a data subject's detailed financial profile can be constructed, to be a particularly strong violation of the data privacy right of individuals. The position was exacerbated by this unlawful processing indicating a series of incidents of security breaches which the department's control framework proved inadequate to identify and investigate. The measures taken after these events were still not deemed robust enough to prevent such incidents in the future. Therefore, the DPA called upon the data controller to strengthen its network security arrangements, detailing a project plan with specific timelines and progress reporting obligations and imposed a fine of €150,000.[17]

---

[16] EC Proposal for General Data Protection Regulation (2012) recital 67.

[17] HDPA Decision 98/2013 (2013).

In January 2013, the UK Information Commissioners Office (ICO) reached a decision imposing a fine of £250,000 on the entertainment company Sony Computer Entertainment Europe for a serious breach of the data protection legislation following the hacking of the Sony PlayStation Platform in 2011, which compromised personal data of millions of users, including names, addresses, dates of birth, emails and passwords. The ICO perceived the violation as serious on the ground that the controls in place did not ensure a level of security proportional to the nature and volume of the data, as well as the damage that could be caused by its unlawful processing. It noted the obligation of the data controller to have taken more appropriate preventative measures as it should have been aware of the possibility of a cyber attack and sited as a further accentuating factor the psychological distress that data subjects could experience on the basis of even the knowledge of the potential fraudulent use of their data. The ICO also noted a range of extenuating parameters, including the defence measures already in place, the level of sophistication of the attack, the notification of users and their efforts for their restitution, as well as the full co-operation of the firm with the Commission and the remedial action taken.[18]

It is interesting to note that the ICO also considered its voluntary notification of the incident by the data controller as an extenuating factor. In a very similar context,[19] the Greek DPA had cited the failure to proactively notify the authority of the incident as one of the accentuating factors of the data controller's crisis handling, indicating that the rationale of the enforcement authorities is already in the direction of demonstrating the increasing importance of timely breach notification.

2.4 Other Regulatory Action and Initiatives

The activity at the level of the European Commission specifically targeting cyber risks and security does bring the message home to companies that the cyber threat is real and action needs to be taken to prevent costs (both financial and social) from getting out of hand. The European Commission is demonstrating its strong commitment to address cybercrime, and following its March 2012 Communication on the establishment of a European Cybercrime Centre, it published in February 2013, together with the High Representative of the Union for Foreign Affairs and Security Policy, a cybersecurity strategy accompanied by a proposed directive on network and information security. As part of its strategy, the Commission encourages all stakeholders to work with the insurance sector in order to develop harmonised metrics for calculating risk premiums with a view to rewarding with lower premiums market players with good security infrastructure.[20] The Commission strategy also stresses as part of its objectives the facilitation of sharing of information on

[18] ICO Monetary Penalty Notice (2013).

[19] HDPA Decision 59/2012 (2012).

[20] European Commission (2013), Security Strategy of the European Union strategy p. 14.

identified breaches among authorities—particularly data protection authorities of member states in an effort to bring the EU legal framework in line with the new cross-border digital challenges. Since the time of writing, significant progress has been made in the development of the EU cyber framework, with the European Commission announcing in December 2015 that political agreement has been reached for the first EU wide legislation on cyber security along the lines of the proposal for a Directive put forward in 2013.

Activity has also been taking place at the level of regulated companies with regulators recognising the need for addressing cyber risks as part of regulated firms' obligations to maintain robust systems and controls supporting the organisation's governance arrangements. As an example, as far back as 2007, Nationwide Building Society was fined by the UK Financial Services Authority (FSA) following the theft of an employee's laptop which contained confidential customer data for failing to have effective systems and controls to manage its information security risks. According to the FSA Annual Report 2012/12, the regulator continues to work towards improving the understanding of the potential impact of large-scale cyber attacks while planning for "a follow up cyber-exercise later in 2013 to validate improvements to response structure and processes".[21]

In the US, the Securities and Exchange Commission (SEC) issued guidance for public companies specifically addressing cybersecurity in 2011. The guidance focused on disclosure obligations on the identification and management of cyber risks and specifically on the reporting of prior incidents and their consequences. Interestingly, insurance coverage for cyber risks was mentioned in the guidance with entities being asked to provide description of their relevant covers.

Looking at a more recent US example, the New York Governor Andrew M. Cuomo announced in May 2013 the launch of an inquiry into the measures taken by insurance companies to protect themselves and their customers from cyber threats. The focus on the insurance industry was justified on the basis of the amount and nature of sensitive personal data processed by them.[22]

3 Supply Side Response

3.1 The Challenges to the Development of the Cyber Insurance Market

The US insurance market is more mature than the European one in terms of its response to cyber risks with 30–40 insurance carriers offering such products as opposed to only a handful in the UK. The UK market is estimated at £3–4 m of gross written premiums in contrast to the faster evolving US market, ranging from $500 to 700 m.[23]

[21] FSA Annual Report (2012/13), p. 27.

[22] Governor of New York press release (2013).

[23] ENISA (2013), pp. 1 and 4.

According to ENISA, a number of obstacles to the development of a cyber insurance market in Europe have been identified, including the difficulty of estimating the extent of the risk and potential losses due to limited robust actuarial data, rendering in turn pricing more difficult as insurers are always aware of the moral hazard of a firm's disincentive to invest in network security post the purchase of the insurance product. A perception by brokers and firms that the insurance products already in the market include these coverages, however fragmented they may be, together with the lack of clarity as to the definition of insurable cyber risks, given that such risks do not necessarily exhibit common characteristics, are additional factors behind the slower development of the cyber insurance market in Europe.[24]

From the exchanges recently surveyed, only 22 % (42 % of which are located in the Americas) reported having cyber insurance or similar policies in place, citing a number of reasons, including that such insurance is not available, insufficient coverage is offered by the types of available products or it is cost prohibitive.[25] This evidence of insurance not being widespread is especially frustrating given the sensitivity of data handled in the securities markets.

Despite attempts from a variety of sources for a clearer definition of cyber-related terms ("cyber resilience", "cybersecurity", "cybercrime", etc), there seems to be some lack of clarity on the exact meaning of these notions.[26] As a result, it is difficult to reach consensus within the insurance market as to the risks that a specialised cyber insurance policy is expected to be addressing, especially taking into account that the legislation addressing that cybercrime is often fragmented. The action currently being proposed at the EU level is a characteristic example of relevant legislative proposals—the revamp of the data protection regime and the new cybersecurity strategy—being developed independently with the interaction among them, as well as with other instruments like the ePrivacy Directive failing to be fully addressed.[27]

Being less developed than the US cyber insurance market, the European market lacks the actuarial data that would lead to firms enjoying more flexible premium adjustment while not compromising the cost-effectiveness of insurers offering such covers. However, the gradual expansion of this market and the experience accumulated by insurers with a relatively longer presence in it already show signs of pricing becoming more rationalised. The proposed introduction at the EU level of mandatory breach disclosure requirement (see 3.3 below) is expected to improve

[24] ENISA (2013), p. 1.

[25] Tendulcar (IOSCO) (2013), pp. 4 and 37.

[26] European Data Protection Supervisor Opinion (2013), p. 7. As an example, the SEC accepts cybersecurity as the body of technologies, processes and practices designed to protect networks, systems, computers, programs and data from attack, damage and unauthorised access (SEC 2011 footnote 1), whereas the EC Strategy paper (footnote pg 3) and the European Commission as the safeguards and actions that can be used to protect the cyber domain, both in the civilian and military fields, from those threats that are associated with or that may harm its interdependent networks and information infrastructure.

[27] European Data Protection Supervisor Opinion (2013), p. 12.

the volume and quality of data that underwriters can use for the adjustment of their pricing models. Risk pricing already tends to respond to the risk assessment of the industry in which the prospective insured does business. For example, it is no surprise that the financial service sector is deemed riskier than the education sector. However, the target should be for an individual firm to see its premium adjusted in line with the strength of its network security policies (wide use of encryption, updated security software, regular security audits, employee training, due diligence of contractors, etc.).

3.2 Traditional Insurance Policies Against New Risks and Client Needs

Once the risk of a cyber attack has been assessed in the context of an organisation's governance arrangements, it might be expected that the organisation seeks an insurance solution to mitigate this risk in the same manner as other risks to which both risk managers and the insurance industry are more accustomed to addressing. Conventional policies cover traditional risks, but the rapid change of the business operating environment, especially in relation to integration of new technologies, alter the nature of the risks faster than the insurance products designed to cover them.

When assessing whether an insurance policy covers cyber risks, its coverage should be looked at mainly from two angles: scope and trigger. For example, although a general liability policy may be extended to cover the loss of data, it may transpire after a hacking attack that such intentional acts are not acceptable triggers of the policy.

The scope of a general liability or property policy may not include data as such, with the policy excluding anything intangible and limiting its scope to damage or loss of physical assets—with data not classified as such. Traditional Commercial General Liability policies tend to provide coverage on condition of the loss being tangible, making it doubtful whether intangible assets such as information stored in the systems is covered in view of the difficulty of the damage quantification.[28] The possibility also exists that a traditional policy may provide cover for loss of data but not when this is related to hardware loss or damage and not when it results from an accidental or intentional software damage. On the other hand, insurers may explicitly exclude cyber risks altogether from traditional policies given the potential for losses to rise to amounts not easily identifiable.[29]

Potential misconceptions regarding overlaps with Directors & Officers Liability policies may also exist, especially regarding the indemnification of investigations costs. Although this would most likely be the case for costs related to individual

[28] ENISA (2013), p. 15.
[29] ENISA (2013), p. 16.

directors and officers under investigation, the liability and related investigation costs for the entity itself are often not included in the scope of the policy, and in the cases where it is, it tends to be limited to defence and settlement costs related to shareholders' claims.

Traditional professional indemnity (errors & omissions policies) may include third party liability cover for data privacy violations, but some issues for the insured to review would include, first, whether cybercrime incidents qualify as triggers of the policy (as opposed to only a negligent act on the part of the insured) and, second, whether the limits are sufficient to cover larger scale cybercrime attacks or whether they are mostly tailored to respond to individual incidents more common in the past to regular professional activity.

Crime policies which are the ones most likely to include incidents caused by insiders tend to exclude loss of data from the scope and are designed to provide cover for more measurable losses like theft of money or securities.

The demand side may often adopt the position that even if cyber-related risks are not covered by their existing policies, it is more efficient for them to purchase endorsements to their current policies (e.g., for business interruption due to loss of data) rather than purchase a new policy specifically targeting cyber risks. Even if that could be arranged to overcome the indicative issues mentioned above, this approach is unlikely to respond to the wider emerging risk management needs like event management support.

3.3 Towards a More Comprehensive Risk Management Tool

Despite the continuous development of defence methodologies and the increasing recognition by organisations of the need to put in place adequate cyber risk management systems and controls, the realisation transpires at the level of both the government authorities and the firms themselves, that a number of sophisticated attacks may not be prevented or even preventable. Cyber insurance therefore aims to become a valuable second line of defence risk management tool, containing a big part of the damage in case of a successful attack.

At the same time, insurers also begin to recognise that reinforcing the insured company's first line of defence, its network security policies and controls, is a prerequisite for a successful cyber insurance market. In this context, insurers work with brokers to provide support to their clients in the form of advice, access to knowledge feeds and relevant expertise. In 2013, AIG, aiming to put "cyber information at user's fingertips", launched the CyberEdge Mobile application, which provides real time updates on data breaches across the US, together with opinions, an extensive cyber resources database and cyber risk analysis tools that assist in the estimate of liability costs. AIG complements the application with the provision to its clients of the "Cyber Edge risk tool", which is a single, web-based and highly customisable to the user's needs platform supporting the risk management process.[30] Among other modules, the platform provides an interface where an IT department can manage a company's shunning technology, blocking known cyber criminals from communicating with a company network. This hardware device utilises the latest intelligence of a constantly updated list of "bad" actors, thus isolating and keeping out of the company's network damaging Internet source areas.

The objective of such tools is to provide comprehensive support to the insured both from the prevention and response sides, emphasising the modern perception of cyber insurance as a service transcending the traditional notion of the insurance policy towards a more holistic risk management solution. Insurers have an interest to invest in this kind of loss prevention services as they are keen to see their clients stay ahead of the curve and therefore work towards leveraging their expertise for mutually beneficial arrangements.

4 The Specialist Product

A variety of specialist cyber insurance products are available and continuously evolving as underwriters become more responsive to the demand side requirements and the changing technological and regulatory landscape. Policies are claims made as a rule, and global cover is available. The majority of the insured purchased limits of $5 to $20 m, but there are corporations that prefer limits exceeding $100 or even $200 m.[31] The insurance product offerings vary among insurers and jurisdictions, and as products can be tailored to the needs of the specific clients it is not easy to distinguish their common features. The absence of agreement as to the definition and scope of cyber-related terms makes it even harder to categorise and compare the relevant specialised insurance products. However, some of the features encountered in a number of products can be distinguished as indicative of the emerging product development trends and are examined below.

4.1 Data Protection Breaches and Third Party Liability

One of the main reasons firms seek to purchase a specialised cyber insurance product is to ensure that they have appropriate scope and limit of coverage for both first party losses and third party claims arising from a failure to protect data

[30] AIG (CyberEdge). Indicative examples of the modules include the Compliance Module, which comes preloaded with security policy templates which can be adapted to meet the organisation's requirements, as well as the Employee Training module. The security policies in place can be uploaded, and employees and third parties can be asked to confirm acceptance.

[31] Kalinich (Aon) (2012), p. 19.

held in their systems as a result of network security being compromised or data being lost or in any way unlawfully accessed due to a failure of the firm's controls. Such claims may arise from the data subjects who suffered damage from unauthorised access to their personal data, with the insurance covering defence and indemnity costs. Subject to the restrictions applicable in each jurisdiction, the insurance policy may cover first party claims such as regulatory fines and related regulatory investigation costs.

Firms may also find themselves liable to business partners as well, especially in the context of outsourcing arrangements under which they may act as vendors with the contractual obligation to meet a certain level of security standards. As awareness of cyber risks increases, it is not uncommon for the purchase of privacy liability insurance to be a prerequisite for a vendor contract award as part of the due diligence exercise companies perform for the assessment of their prospective contractors. Alternatively, insured firms may want to ensure that their policies cover them for liability incurred by them due to a breach by one of their contractors.

In the current interdependent business environment, however, such third party claims may extend beyond privacy-related incidents, with firms that experienced system failures finding themselves in need to defend legal action potentially brought against them by business counterparties for damages incurred due to the systems' interoperability.

4.2 *Network Damage*

A cyber attack would most likely result in damages incurred by the organisation's network. Some specialised policies may cover the remediation cost of damages relating to the theft of hardware which included relevant information, data contamination due to a virus or a data leak resulting from the intentional or unintentional actions of an employee. Data restitution can also be included.

4.3 *Business Interruption from Network Failure/Shut Down*

Business interruption is one of the more common coverages also encountered in other insurance products like property insurance. In the case of cyber insurance, the insured is reimbursed for lost income and operating expenses when these are the result of a material interruption of an insured's business operations caused by a network security failure. The insured firm may also choose or be instructed by regulators to shut down its systems following an attack in the context of crisis management and damage limitation.

4.4 Cyber Extortion

One of the reasons behind cyber attacks is the use of the unlawfully obtained information for the extortion of money, securities and other valuables. This coverage includes the cost of investigation into the cause of the threat, as well as ransom (extortion loss) paid to end the threat.

4.5 Reputational Risk and Event Management

Potentially the most critical element of a cyber insurance product is the support it provides to the insured organisation to enable it to respond to an incident in a faster, more effective and more organised fashion. A competitive cyber insurance policy would include fast access to a range of specialists, including forensics and legal and communication professionals, together with the reimbursement of the relevant fees and expenses. If the insured firm is a larger one which already has access to such specialist teams who can support management in its handling of the crisis, the insurance policy would cover the fees and expenses of these independent advisors.

Information system forensic experts would determine the cause of the incident, legal and compliance professionals would advise management of the applicable notification requirements which vary among the various jurisdictions in which a company may do business and public relation strategists would work with management on containing the reputational risk that may be triggered by the publicity a data privacy breach incident may generate.

Some policies would also include services for the mitigation of potential reputational damage at the level of the individual manager of the firm (e.g., the Chief Information Officer). This is one of the examples of coverages not included as a rule in a conventional Directors & Officers or Errors & Omissions policy.

Finally, the insurance policy would cover the cost of meeting any applicable client breach notification requirements as these can be significant in the instances and jurisdictions where individual notifications are required. Taking this service a step further, more sophisticated cyber policies may also cover costs for proactive support of the data subjects affected through the provision to them of identity theft education and credit file monitoring services.

It is interesting to note that the policy may also cover investigation costs to determine the extent of the damage suffered under the assumption that although the insured firm may have the indications that an attack has taken place, it may not have the resources required to identify whether data has been compromised or whether it is still at risk.

5 Conclusion

As national and international bodies take steps to reiterate the significance of cyber risks and attempt to build the architecture to address them, while regulators want to know more about how the members of regulated industries like financial services manage such risks, cyber insurance has the potential to develop into an integral part of an effective risk management strategy. The insurance industry should continue to develop products that meet the fast-evolving risks, client needs and technological sophistication of the business-operating environment, while organisations of all sizes must hinder the warnings and take steps to mitigate cyber risks in the same manner that they have grown used to deal with operational, regulatory and other risks inherent in their way of doing business in a local or international environment.

After all, "the best defence for organisations is to have processes and measures in place to prevent attacks getting through, but we also have to recognise that there will be times when attacks do penetrate our systems and organisations want to know who they can reliably turn to for help".[32]

References

AIG (product presentation) CyberEdge: adding our expertise to yours. http://www.aig.com/Chartis/internet/US/en/CERTAutoShunApp_Brochure_FINAL_tcm3171-471157.pdf

Buhayar N, Bunn E (2013) Sock maker hack shows small-business risk chased by AIG, Bloomberg. http://www.bloomberg.com/news/2013-03-20/aig-among-insurers-seeking-more-sales-as-small-firms-get-hacked.html?cmpid=yhoo

European Commission, Joint Communication to the European Parliament, the Council, the European Economic and Social Committee and the Committee of the Regions. Security Strategy of the European Union: an Open, Safe and Secure Cyberspace (2013) http://eeas.europa.eu/top_stories/2013/070213_cybersecurity_en.htm

European Commission (2012) Proposal for a Regulation of the European Parliament and of the Council on the protection of individuals with regard to the processing of personal data and on the free movement of such data (General Data Protection Regulation) http://www.europarl.europa.eu/document/activities/cont/201305/20130508ATT65776/20130508ATT65776EN.pdf

European Commission Special Eurobarometer 359 (2011) Attitudes on data protection and Electronic Identity in the European Union. Publication June 2011. http://ec.europa.eu/public_opinion/archives/ebs/ebs_359_en.pdf

European Data Protection Supervisor, Opinion on the Joint Communication and of the High Representative of the European Union for Foreign Affairs and Security Policy on a "Cyber Security Strategy of the European Union: an Open, Safe, and Secure Cyberspace", and on the Commission Proposal for a Directive concerning measures to ensure a high common level of network and information security across the Union (2013) https://secure.edps.europa.eu/EDPSWEB/webdav/shared/Documents/Consultation/Opinions/2013/13-06-14_Cyber_security_EN.pdf

---

[32] Chloe Smith, UK Minister for cyber security (Warrell and Mance 2013).

European Network and Information Security Agency (ENISA) (2013) Incentives and barriers of the cyber insurance market in Europe. http://www.enisa.europa.eu/activities/Resilience-and-CIIP/national-cyber-security-strategies-ncsss/incentives-and-barriers-of-the-cyber-insurance-market-in-europe
Federation of Small Businesses (2013) Cyber security and fraud: the impact on small businesses. http://www.fsb.org.uk/News.aspx?loc=pressroom&rec=8083
Financial Services Authority (FSA) Annual Report 2012/13. http://www.fca.org.uk/static/documents/annual-report/fsa-annual-report-12-13.pdf
Governor of New York Press Release (2013) Governor Cuomo launches inquiry into cyber threats at Largest Insurance Companies. http://www.dfs.ny.gov/about/press2013/pr1305281.htm
Hellenic Data Protection Authority Decision (HDPA) 59/2012 (2012) http://www.dpa.gr/portal/page?_pageid=33%2C15453&_dad=portal&_schema=PORTAL&_piref33_15473_33_15453_15453.etos=2012&_piref33_15473_33_15453_15453.arithmosApofasis=59&_piref33_15473_33_15453_15453.thematikiEnotita=-1&_piref33_15473_33_15453_15453.ananeosi=%CE%91%CE%BD%CE%B1%CE%BD%CE%AD%CF%89%CF%83%CE%B7
Hellenic Data Protection Authority Decision (HDPA) 98/2013 (2013) http://www.dpa.gr/APDPXPortlets/htdocs/documentSDisplay.jsp?docid=108,1,36,73,199,229,114,178\
HM Government (2013) EU directive on network and information security; a call for views and evidence. https://www.gov.uk/government/uploads/system/uploads/attachment_data/file/200708/bis-13-880-eu-directive-on-network-and-information-security-call.pdf
Information Commissioner's Office (ICO) Monetary Penalty Notice Dated 14 January 2013 http://www.ico.org.uk/news/latest_news/2013/~/media/documents/library/Data_Protection/Notices/sony_monetary_penalty_notice.ashx
The Institute of Chartered Secretaries and Administrators (ICSA) (2013) Guidance note: cyber risks
Kalinich KP (2012) Aon plc. Network Security & Privacy Risk Insurance 2012 Update
Kirchgaessner S (2013) Cyber security: robbers with laptops are serious threat to world banking system. The Financial Times
Marsh (2013) Cyber risk explained: what they are, what they could cost, and how to protect against them. http://www.marsh.com.tr/documents/CyberRisks.pdf
McCarthy B (2013) Cost of cyber attacks triples in a year. The Financial Times
Proposal for a DIRECTIVE OF THE EUROPEAN PARLIAMENT AND OF THE COUNCIL concerning measures to ensure a high common level of network and information security across the Union (2013) http://europa.eu/rapid/press-release_IP-13-94_en.htm
Tendulcar R (2013) Joint staff working paper of the IOSCO Research Department and World Federation of Exchanges Staff Working Paper [SWP1 – 2013]. http://www.iosco.org/research/pdf/swp/Cyber-Crime-Securities-Markets-and-Systemic-Risk.pdf
Tett G (2013) Break a wall of silence on cyber attacks. The Financial Times
U.S. Securities and Exchange Commission (2011). Division of Corporation Finance. CF Disclosure Guidance: Topic No 2. Cybersecurity. http://www.sec.gov/divisions/corpfin/guidance/cfguidance-topic2.htm
UK Government. Office of Cyber Security and Information Assurance. Policy: Keeping the UK safe in Cyber Space. Published 20 February 2013 (Updated 22 August 2013) https://www.gov.uk/government/policies/keeping-the-uk-safe-in-cyberspace
Verizon (2012) Data Breach Investigations Report. http://www.verizonenterprise.com/resources/reports/rp_data-breach-investigations-report-2012_en_xg.pdf
Warrell H, Mance H (2013) Companies "critical" to UK to receive support against cybercrime. The Financial Times

The Cyber Insurance in Japan

Tadao Koezuka

Contents

Abstract The lives of people depend heavily on the computer system and its networks. Anonymous attackers and hackers terrify enterprises, organizations and governments into setting up the safety-nets by providing budgets and enacting some acts for protecting state secrets, trade secrets and personal information. Japan is no exception. When cyber attacks steal secrets, leak personal information, they cause lots of damage to countries, governments and enterprises. Thus, there is the need for the cyber insurance for covering damages and expenses arising from cyber attacks. There are two kinds of the cyber insurances: the first one is the first-party insurance, which is similar to property insurance, and the second one is the third-party insurance, which is similar to liability insurance. At least the original Japanese non-life insurance company has no insurance for specializing cyber attacks.

T. Koezuka (✉)
Faculty of Law, National University Corporation, Kagawa University, Takamatsu, Kagawa, Japan

Sano Shigeru Yoshida Law Firm, Takamatsu, Kagawa, Japan
e-mail: koezuka@jl.kagawa-u.ac.jp; koezukat@gmail.com

P. Marano et al. (eds.), *The "Dematerialized" Insurance*,
DOI 10.1007/978-3-319-28410-1_9

Namely, the cyber insurance in Japan has the same nature as traditional property insurance and traditional liability insurance. As anonymous attackers and hackers target enterprises, organizations and governments, it is seemed proper that its government takes these countermeasures for its attacks and hacks. According to the traditional understanding of the first-party insurance, in the case an insurer pays insurance money to insured, the insurer has the subrogation right to a tort-feasor and subrogates an insured's right of making a claim from a tort-feasor. But in the cyber insurance, the subrogation right is meaningless because the insurer cannot identify a tort-feasor. This phenomenon causes a question of whether the subrogation right is an essential of property insurance or not.

1 Introduction

Many countries address the urgent task of protecting their data and networks from cyber attacks. If the Data system and networks break down, the function of each nation and enterprise will not work and majority of the people will not live comfortably their everyday life in advanced countries.

On October 7th and 8th, 2014, the Japanese Government held a meeting for information security politic council among ASEAN countries to confirm the drafting of the core principle of protecting the basic infrastructure such as electricity and gas.[1] Further, the Japanese Government strengthens an international connection with foreign countries with a view to cope well with borderless frequent cyber attacks.[2]

In December 2014, several news media made a headline around the world that Sony Pictures Entertainment Company, which was located in USA, was attacked and hacked on the cyber to prevent it from showing the movie "THE INTERVIEW" on the screen. The hacker gave notice of the happening terror at the movie theater playing the movie.[3] Recently, the importance of protecting personal information is growing up with the rapid development of Information Technology all over the world. Japan is doing the same. For instance, some companies issued several **Integrated Circuit** (**IC**) cards that record the activities, such as payment for goods or foods in the stores, public transportation or cellular phone uses, among

---

[1] The NIKKEI (Evening Ed.), at p. 3 on Sep. 18th, 2014 [Nihon Keizai Sinbun, Choukan Ed., 3Men, 2014Nen 9Gatsu 18Nichi].

[2] The NIKKEI (Morning Ed.), at p. 2 on Dec. 22th, 2014 [Nihon Keizai Sinbun, Choukan Ed., 2Men, 2014Nen 12Gatsu 22Nichi].

[3] The NIKKEI (Morning Ed.), at p. 6 on Dec. 20th, 2014 [Nihon Keizai Sinbun, Choukan Ed., 6Men, 2014Nen 12Gatsu Hatsuka]. Japan is third in the world in terms of number of cyber attacks stealing a secret. The NIKKEI (Morning Ed.), at p. 11 on Dec. 31st, 2014 [Nihon Keizai Sinbun, Choukan Ed., 11Men, 2014Nen 12Gatsu 31Nichi].

others, of each people; or each hospital has sensitive personal information of diseases. The release of this information leads to invasions of privacy of the people. The information released in the digital world cannot be deleted and is recorded for ever. The corporations are collecting personal and other information to use them in developing the efficiency of their business to increase big business chances.

But the personal information might be released by negligence of an employee or when someone attacks the cyber of the corporation, breaks the cyber and leaks the personal information.

When these accidents happen, the damages arising from the release of privacy cannot be correctly estimated and the economic value of privacy itself cannot be assessed. Further, a person whose information was leaked necessarily suffers loss and institutes an action against the corporation where the personal information came from.

In Japan, the Act on the Protection of Personal Information[4] was enacted in 2003 and went into effect in April 2005. Thereafter, the insurance companies begin to sell insurance policy for protecting personal information coming from corporations in case of leakage through cyber attacks, among others.

This chapter aims to present the cyber Insurance in Japan. Firstly, I will account the recent occurrences of cyber attacks in Japan. Secondly, we will overlook what is cyber Insurance in Japan. Thirdly, I will think of the Legal Issues on the cyber Insurance. Lastly, I will make a conclusion of this chapter from this study.

Besides, there is no leading case in which any court can make a decision on the Cyber Insurance Contract in Japan.

[4] The Act on the Protection of Personal Information will be partially amended in near feature. The Cabinet Secretariat/The **Strategic Headquarters for the Promotion of an Advanced Information and Telecommunications Network Society** (**SHPAITNS**),"*The Policy Outline of the Institutional Revision for Utilization of Personal Data*", p. 12 (June 24th, 2014) [Naikakuhu/ Koudo Jouhoutsuushin Nettowaku Shakai Suishin Senryaku Honbu, "Personal Data no Rikatsuyou nikansuru Seidokaiseitaikou" p. 12 (Heisei 26 Nen 6 Gatsu 24 Nichi)]. This aim of the amendment is to make the statements consistent among other countries (SHPAUTNS, *Id* at p. 7, p. 9 and p. 7 note. 2–4). OECD, The Recommendation of the OECD Council concerning Guidelines governing the Protection of Privacy and Trans-border Flows of Personal Data (2013), White House, "Consumer Data Privacy in a Networked World: A Framework for Protecting Privacy and Promoting Innovation in the Global Digital Economy" (2012) and European Parliament, European Parliament legislative resolution of 12 March 2014 on the proposal for a regulation of the European Parliament and of the Council on the protection of individuals with regard to the processing of personal data and on the free movement of such data (General Data Protection Regulation) (2014). http://japan.kantei.go.jp/policy/it/20140715_2.pdf).

2 The Recent Occurrences in Japan

In Japan, the cyber attack to the computer systems and servers[5] of big companies, the **Japan Aerospace Exploration Agency** (**JAXA**), the Ministry of Finance, the Liberal Democratic Party and **Japanese Society for Rights of Authors, Composers and Publishers** (**JASRAC**) from foreign countries in 2011, 2012 and 2013 in Japan, and cyber threat has been increasing. When the Website and the servers are attacked, sensitive personal information[6] usually leaks out from some companies, government agencies and local governments. For example, the server of Yahoo Japan was hacked and personal information (22,000,000 IDs) was leaked out. The Sony Play Station Network was hacked by an anonymous person and great amount of personal information leaked in 2011. Consequently, a class action was brought and reached reconciliation in 2014. If the classified information of a big company is revealed, the damages cannot be assessed. In the case of National Defense Confidential Data, the damages cannot be absolutely assessed. How much is information assessed?

The more that the Internet Technology develop, the more cyber attacks threat will increase all over the world. In Japan, the **National Institute of Information and Communications Technology** (**NICT**), an incorporated administrative agency, has been established in 2004. The NICT was created by merging the **Communications Research Laboratory** (**CRL**), an incorporated administrative agency, and the **Telecommunications Advancement Organization** (**TAO**).[7] The purpose of NICT[8] is to promote **Information and Communications Technology** (**ICT**) and the full spectrum of research and development in ICT from basic to applied research with an integrated perspective, and thus promotes the advancement of Japan as an intellectual nation that leads the international community. Moreover, the NICT forms close ties with the academic and business communities in Japan together with research institutes overseas and returns its R&D findings to society in a broad range of fields. Thereafter, the NICT set up its **Network Security Research Institute** (**NSRI**). The NSRI, which aims to protect Japanese network infrastructures against cyber attacks, is seeking to establish a global center of excellence in network security research and development from a sophisticated

[5] The illegal access to the computer systems and servers makes the companies and organizations suffer in leaking information. The NPO **Japan Network Security Association** (**JNSA**), "Research Report on Information Security Incidents—A Part of Leaking Information—" p. 7, p. 20, p. 21, p. 22 (1.2ed, Aug., 14th 2014 Rev.) [NPO Joho Nettowaaku Sekyurithy Kyoukai, "2011Nen Jouhou Sekyurityi Inshident nikansuru Chosa Houkokusyo—Kojin Joho Rouei Hen—" p. 7, p. 20, p. 21, p. 22 (1.2 Han, 8 Gatsu 14 Ka 2012 Nen Kaitei)].

[6] Recently, a system engineer (a non-regular employee) in a company leaks personal information an education company keeps and manages in 2014. But in this article, the cases where sensitive personal information is leaked by taking out of company are not written off because these cases have no relevance to cyber attacks which leak information from companies or organizations.

[7] http://www.nict.go.jp/en/about/about/history.html.

[8] http://www.nict.go.jp/en/about/charter.html.

combination of theory and practice, taking full advantage of the NICT stance of neutrality.[9] The NSRI includes the two laboratories, the **Security Architecture Laboratory** (**SAL**) and the **Security Fundamentals Laboratory** (**SFL**).[10]

It is important to not leak out sensitive personal information. Companies and organizations have some means to protect corporate secrets, and punish employees who leak them.

But individuals have no means to do so when their sensitive personal information are leaked. The Japanese Diet enacted the Act on the Protection of Personal Information to protect personal information in 2003.[11] This means that personal information is sensitive, persons, organizations and companies let others in on personal information.

After enacting this law, the numbers of companies and municipalities which bought private information leak insurance are increasing. Further, insurance companies, which enter into insurance contracts with them, asked them to establish effective internal controls for keeping personal information. But it is a matter of course that cyber attacks to their Website and servers are going on.

On May 24th, 2013, the so-called "My Number" bill has been passed, "law for using number identifying specific individuals in administrative proceeding" has been enacted and all Japanese people will have a number that Government gives to identify individual.[12] This number in Japan is likened to the Social Security number in USA. The numbers given to specific individuals make individual privacies open to public. If individual privacy is opened on Internet world, nobody can delete their information at all.

---

[9] http://www.nict.go.jp/en/nsri/.

[10] http://www.nict.go.jp/en/nsri/arch/index.html; http://www.nict.go.jp/en/nsri/fund/index.html.

[11] The Act on the Protection of Personal Information (2003) has been decided to be revised, namely, (1) to"[s]ubmit the relevant bills to the Diet as early as possible in or after January 2015", (2) to"[s]et up a third-party authority and commence business as early as possible, as well as enforce the amended law early after enactment, except the part that requires notification and preparations", (3) to "[s]ubsequently enforce the remaining part as soon as possible". The Cabinet Secretariat/SHPAITNS, *supra* note (4) at p. 12.

Japanese Government has the outline of a proposition for the Protection of Personal Information into shape: (1) to stipulate the penal provision, called "a charge of providing database of personal information", for persons who provide the third party personal information with an illegal aim and (2) to create a Committee to protect Personal Information which has power to supervise manage of personal information in Japanese Cabinet and to conduct an on-site inspection to business operator. The NIKKEI (Morning Ed.), at p. 38, on Dec. 20th, 2014 [Nihon Keizai Sinbun, Choukan, 38Men, 2014Nen 12Gatsu Hatsuka].

[12] The aims of the law are to (1) effective management, use and speedy transfer of information, (2) reduced burden by simplifying procedures, (3) ensure appropriate handling of personal information (§1). http://www.cas.go.jp/jp/seisaku/jouhouwg/hyoka/dai5/siryou1-1.pdf.

As Japan's Large Package of Tax Revisions, "My Number" has been decided to be applied to each account in the banks to avoid evasion of tax and fraudulently obtain livelihood protection subsidy in January 2016. The NIKKEI (Morning Ed.), at p. 4, on Dec. 31st, 2014 [Nihon Keizai Sinbun, Choukan, 4Men, 2014Nen 12Gatsu 31nichi].

As stated above, in the nation and in private company, the protection of private information is of utmost importance and cyber Insurance is increasing in demand.

On November 6th, 2014, the bill of the "Basic Act on Cyber Security" has been passed to protect the important infrastructures, such as governmental organizations, electric companies and financial institutions, from cyber attacks. The Japanese Cabinet will set up the strategy head office for Cyber Security next year.

3 The Cyber Insurance in Japan

3.1 The Definition: What Is Cyber Insurance in Japan?

We, Japanese, have no academic accepted definition of "Cyber Insurance" in the justice field. There is no fixed definition of it even in the field of insurance law. Also, no legal scholar discusses or has discussed on it even though Japan is one of the most highly-developed scientific and technological nations.

On a side note, corporations are collecting to build and maintain database of customer's information, such as ages, sexes, occupations, annual incomes, civil status, child or not, and owned house or not, to open up business opportunities. Data Base makes it possible to record and analyze customer information and explore business opportunities.

But according to the law, corporations must keep personal information, as not to leak it; in the off-chance that corporations negligently leak personal information. Non-Life Insurance Companies does not sell the "Cyber Insurance targeted for cyber attack from anonymous[13]" itself at all in Japan. The insurance for leaking personal information is not specified for cyber attack and cyber Terror, but is one similar to traditional fire insurance.

Therefore, in this article, Cyber Insurance[14] means an insurance for the damage caused by personal information leakage and the running of business which costs the

[13] "Cyber Insurance for Cyber Attacks" is a necessary product to sell in Japan. But usually Cyber Attacks and Cyber Terrors target State Governments, Local Governments or Enterprises in the level of a nation. This means the scale of Cyber Attacks and Cyber Terrors are not in the level of a person. Cyber Attacks and Cyber Terrors are a way of the NEW WAR, which is not different from a real traditional war using missiles, tanks and fighter planes. Therefore, "Cyber Insurance for Cyber Attacks" that insurance companies market as product and sell in Japan does not satisfy the real needs of Governments or Enterprises.

[14] In this article the Cyber Insurance Policies are ones that Tokio Marine & Nichido Fire Insurance Co., Ltd sells. The first is the insurance for leaking personal information, as third party insurance, that is, as a special agreement, included in General Liability Insurance Policy. And the Second is the Computer Comprehensive Insurance Policy, as first party insurance (applied from June 1st, 2012). And Sompo Japan Nipponkoa Insurance Inc, Japanese arm of American Insurance Underwriters (hereinafter cited as AIU) and other companies sell the Cyber Insurance, too. But on February 9th, 2015, Tokio Marine & Nichido Fire Insurance Co., Ltd put, a full-scale comprehensive "Cyber Risk Insurance" for Business Enterprises, which covers the costs for

insured.[15] The cyber insurance mainly defines to cover damages that a corporation, as a manager or administrator of personal information, is legally required to be paid, caused by leaking of personal information, including costs for accident response, such as apology advertisement costs and by running the business as if nothing had happened, including damages which the server, computer or the media for recording where the data is obtained, suffered. When the server, computer or the media for recording the data is broken by something, including hacking activities, as personal information has proprietary nature, their destruction will cause damages in corporations. The corporations need to run the business for customers and connections, and they have to incur expenses for running the business, even if the server or the computer has been broken. Nowadays, majority of corporations rely on benefits of the computer systems. Hence, the corporations need the insurance for the breakage of the server or computer; and the Insurers in Japan sell them. Therefore, the Cyber Insurance in this article includes two kinds: (a) insurance for damages caused by negligently leaking personal information by manager or administrator of personal information ("Coverage for leaking Personal Information"); and (b) insurance for damages caused by the breakage of the server or computer ("the Computer Comprehensive Coverage"). Meaning, the first kind is third-party insurance, as one of liability insurances; on the other hand, the latter insurance is the first-party insurance, as one of property insurances. The insurance (a) and the insurance (b) are

crisis-management by the enterprises, the indemnities in filing a damage overseas suit caused by leaking information and the expenses for disputes. Insurance (Non-Life ed.) No. 4604, February 26th, 2015 at 2 [Inshuaransu, Sonpo Ban, 2604go, February 26th, 2015 at 2]. I could not write the "Cyber Risk Insurance" in this article.

[15] AIU, that does not the origin of Japan but USA, has sold a kind of Cyber Insurance, which name is the "Cyber Edge", to the Global Enterprises on December in 2012. The "Cyber Edge" is provided in the form of a special agreement attached the "Professional Liability Specified Professions Liability Policy". AIU provide three protections to insured through the "Cyber Edge": Article 2. Coverage A—Data Liability; (1) Cover under this Article is solely with respect to Claim first made against an Insured by a Third Party during the Policy Period (···) and reported to the Insurer as required by this policy, (a) Personal Data, (b) Corporate Data Liability, (c) Outsourcing Liability, (d) Data Security Liability and (e) Defense Costs, (2) The Insurer shall be under no obligation to pay Loss, unless the alleged or actual Breach of Personal Information, Breach of Corporate Information or act, error or omission first takes place on or after the Retroactive Data and at or prior to the expiration of the Policy Period; Article 3. Coverage B—Data Administrative Procedures; (1) Cover under this Article is afforded solely with respect to an Investigation which first occurs during the Policy Period (···) and is reported to the Insurer as required by this policy (a) Data Administrative Investigation, (b) Data Administrative Fines,(2) The Insurer shall be under no obligation to pay Loss, unless the Breach of Data Security or Breach of Personal Information first takes place on or after the Retroactive Data and at or prior to the expiration of the Policy Period.; Article 4. Coverage C—Repair of Reputation; Cover under this Article is afforded solely with respect to (a) a Claim which this policy may respond to under Article 2 (Coverage A—Data Liability) in this Endorsement, or (b) a Breach of Personal Information, a Breach of Corporate Information or a Breach of Data Security (···) which first occurs during the Policy Period; and reported to the Insurer as required by this policy. (a) Repair of Company's Reputation, (b) Repair of Individual's Reputation, (c) Notification & Monitoring, (4) Electronic Data, (5) Pro-active Forensic Services, (6) Crisis Loss.

separate insurance products and they are separately sold. The insurance (a) is called "Kojin Joho Rouei Hoken" and the insurance (b) is called "Konpyuta Sougou Hoken" in Japanese.

3.2 *Liability Insurance and General Property Insurance in Japan*

3.2.1 Liability Insurance for Business Enterprises

1. Liability Insurance for Business Enterprises[16] is valid under the Japanese "Insurance Act", which was enacted on May 30th, 2008. Liability Insurance for Business Enterprises is generally defined as one that the insurer provides the coverage for damages the insured sustains when he or she causes damage to the victim by negligence.[17] Sec. 17 (2) of the Japanese "Insurance Act" defines the liability insurance as, among the kinds of non-life insurances,[18] one that the insured shall be covered against damage the insured is liable to the victim. A part of coverage, in the Cyber Insurance for Business Enterprises, for liability that the company damages data or business of the victim; liability falls into liability insurance classes.

   Generally, the liability insurance is said to have the following features[19] in Japan: namely, the risk which the liability insurance covers is not stable, as compared with fire insurance for residence and automobile insurance. For instance, the liability insurance is one that the insured shall be covered against damage the insured is liable to the victim, if the legal system and case law has been changed as the Act on the Protection of Personal Information (2005) has come into force in 2005, and as a consequence, there is a growing need for the insurance for the Act on the Protection of Personal Information, the new risk is arising or the risk is changing. Secondly, the liability insurance is controlled to a large degree by social trends, as patient's right consciousness is rising, coupled with media coverage of malpractice, as a consequence the events of the liability insurance are increasing. Thirdly, the liability insurances make it difficult for the insurers to run the companies, to the point that it is difficult to accept the balance

---

[16] Sec.36 of the Japanese "Insurance Act"(2008), where a kind of enterprise insurance is stipulated, is not applicable to the unilateral compulsory provisions (Sec.7, 12, 23 and 33) for protecting the consumers (the policyholders or the insured), as the purpose of Japanese "Insurance Act" is to protect them by promoting proper insurance contracts. Ochiai (2009), pp. 113–114; Koezuka (2014).

[17] Tokio Marine & Nichido Fire Insurance Co., Ltd (2010), p 149.

[18] Sec. 2(6) of the Japanese "Insurance Act" defines the non-life insurance as, among the kind of insurances, the insurance that the insurer promises to indemnify for damage arising from a fixed accident event.

[19] Tokio Marine & Nichido Fire Insurance Co., Ltd (2010).

of payments and validity of insurance rate for a long time as it takes a fair amount of time to accept liability for damages as final.

2. A part of the Cyber Insurance, which covers damages caused by negligently leaking personal information by manager or administrator of personal information, has the nature of a kind of liability insurance. The insurers prescribe the subjects common to various types of liability insurance in the liability Insurance Clauses and the Liability Insurance for Business Enterprises has the following basic structure:[20] (a) an insurer prescribes in general insurance policy "this company shall pay insurance money for damage by the events which the insured takes legal responsibility for indemnifying damages arising from others body injuries and property destruction."[21]
3. The Liability Insurance Clause. The "insured" means a person who has an insurable interest, but liability insurance contract is protection for a tort-feasor, who causes the damage to the victim or a person, who becomes liable for the damage by breaching a contract. The "insured" is the tort-feasor or the person in the liability insurance contract. Concerning the Cyber Insurance Contract, the "insured" is typically the company or corporation which is liable for managing or administrating the personal data.

It follows that the Cyber Insurance includes the two questions; first, is the "insured" in the Cyber Insurance Contract liable for the damage arising from the Cyber attacks by an anonymous person? Because hackers are always acquiring skills for breaking the Network Security of the companies or corporations, the technicians or engineers are having a hard time catching up on their skills. Second, does the "insured" need to have an insurable interest in, as a part of the liability insurance, the Cyber Insurance? Lastly, how much does the insurer cover?

First, the company or corporation is liable for legally managing or administrating personal information so as not to leak it even if an anonymous person hacks its server or computer by breaking the security and succeeded, because it can take strategize a plan to double or triple its security measures. The company or corporation can also hire some security specialist or technicians with required standard care.

Secondly, the Cyber Insurance Contract is silent whether the "insured" needs to have an insurable interest.

Insurable interest is in relation to economic loss arising from damage by occurrence of events.[22] This definition of "insured" in the liability insurance clause is said to be those who have no relation in accelerating loss by occurrence

---

[20] Tokio Marine & Nichido Fire Insurance Co., Ltd (2010), p. 151.

[21] This provision is the one of which Tokio Marine & Nichido Fire Insurance Co., Ltd., sell the insurance product.

[22] Omori (1952); Nishijima (1998); Kurasawa (1997); Kanazawa (2001); Yamashita (2005). This definition of "insurable interests" (Sec.3) under the Japanese "Insurance Act" is the same concept as the one in Sec.630 under Commercial Law (Koezuka 2014, p. 60).

of events.[23] But does the "insured" in the Cyber Insurance Contract have insurable interest? In Japan, as far as the case of liability insurance contract is concern, there are arguments for and against. Generally, negative property is considered to be included in insurable interest. Meaning, if a person has responsibility for indemnifying damages to others, he or she gets more negative property. When there is a possibility that he or she will bear responsibility for indemnifying damages by his or her negligence, we can regard this possibility as "insurable interest".[24] I agree with this view.[25]

Further, the "insured" should be the company or corporation which manages and keeps personal information. When it does not appropriately manage and keep it, the company or corporation negligently leak the personal information through cyber attackers. Furthermore, as anonymous attackers are persons who are liable for the damage, it becomes controversial in the insurer's subrogation of the liability insurance. Conversely, the insurer cannot subrogate the victim's claim to the anonymous attacker.

Truthfully, the insurer's right of subrogation is meaningless in the Cyber Insurance, as a part of liability insurance. It is difficult for the investigating authorities in the majority of countries to identify the cyber attackers overseas. I think that this phenomenon leads the review of the question, "is there a subrogation nature in non life insurance?" if its phenomenon is not regarded as an expectation of the liability insurance. Also, cyber attackers who intend to destroy the server or computer system do not make the contract for damage they will be liable for.[26] If there is any chance of them making the contract, the insurance companies could claim for exclusion from liability as the cause of intent.

Thirdly, the liability insurance covers damages, additionally dispute cost, sue and labor expense, emergency measure expense and cooperation cost.[27] Regarding the amount limit, generally, the policyholder set it up with the insurer.[28] Legal damages are likewise available, but it does not included dispute cost and cooperation cost.

---

[23] Nishijima (1998), p. 269.

[24] Yamashita (2005), p. 257.

[25] But I believe that there is no insurable interest in an accident and health insurance of indemnification type.

[26] The insurer is exempted from obligation of insurance money due to insured's intention. Saiko Saibansho [Sup. Ct.] Mar. 30, 1993, Heisei5, Saiko saibansho Minji Hanreishu [Minshu] Vol. 47, No. 4, 3262 (Japan).

[27] Tokio Marine & Nichido Fire Insurance Co., Ltd (2010), p. 154. In the liability insurance contract, after the accident happens, an insurance company generally has the right of resolving the disputes to the victim, in the place of the insured, the insured have an obligation to cooperate with the insurance company under liability insurance policy. This obligation is called as "cooperation for resolving disputes". In this case, the insured bears the expenses for cooperation, namely, traveling or living expenses, the insurance company must pay them as "cooperation cost". Tokio Marine & Nichido Fire Insurance Co., Ltd (2010), p. 157.

[28] Tokio Marine & Nichido Fire Insurance Co., Ltd (2010), p. 157.

4. The Relation to the Japanese "Insurance Act"[29]—The Japanese "Insurance Act" was enacted on May 30th, 2008, promulgated on Jun 6th, 2008, and come into force in April 2010. Before this reform, the legal regulation for insurance contract was included in the Commercial Code that has no accident insurance provision, but this insurance contract regulation was inconsistent with the modern insurance business practice. For the first time in almost 100 years, the insurance contract regulation has been amended and the new insurance law has been enacted, separating it from the Commercial Code.[30]

   As regards the liability insurance, the important provision has been prescribed in the new act. Sec. 22(1) of the liability insurance provides that the insurance money has to be paid to the insured when the amount of the liability is settled by a final judgment, conciliation or other agreement with the victim.[31] But the victim cannot be paid the full insurance money and be relieved when the insured is insolvent after the insurer has paid insurance money to the insured. This situation is not rational. To protect the victim, the Japanese "Insurance Act" has introduced a new provision that entitles the victim to a lien over the claim for insurance money.[32] Moreover, to prevent the insurance money from being paid to the insured without the victim knowing it, it is also provided in Sec. 22(2) of the liability insurance that the indemnification shall be made only to the extent that the insured has performed its liability to the victim or when the victim has given consent.[33]

   But it is to be noted that Sec. 22 (1), (2) is not available to the liability insurance for Business Enterprises because the purpose of the New Act is to protect the insurance consumers. It does not include business enterprises. In fact, business enterprises can take some measures for covering this risk. Therefore, Sec. 22(1), (2) is not available to the Cyber Insurance for Business Enterprises.

3.2.2 General Property Insurance for Business Enterprises

The General Property Insurance for Business Enterprises is a kind of enterprise insurance and this Insurance for Business Enterprises is valid under the Japanese "Insurance Act". But this insurance is not applicable to the unilateral compulsory provisions in this Act.[34] The typical insurance of the General Property Insurance is the Fire Insurance. The kind of the Cyber Insurance is the first-party insurance for damages caused by breaking the server. This insurance is similar to the fire

[29] Many books and papers on the "Insurance Act" written in Japanese are published. For example, Yamashita and Yoneyama (2010); Hagimoto (2009); Yamashita (2008a, b); Junko and Kenkyukai (2008); Uematsu and Hokenho (2008), etc.

[30] *See,* Ochiai et al. (2011), p. 747, p. 748.

[31] Kozuka and Lee (2008), p. 79. Art. 22 (2) Insurance Act. Yashima (2009); Kitamura (2012).

[32] *Ibid.*

[33] *Ibid.*

[34] See note (16).

insurance. The purpose of the fire insurance for business enterprises, like the Cyber Insurance, the Computer Comprehensive Insurance, is to cover the promised risk, such as fire, explosion, wind disaster, water disaster, which arises from business activity. The purpose of Cyber Insurance, the Computer Comprehensive Insurance, is to cover the promised risk which arises from almost all damages caused by destroyed computer and its related material. Further, this insurance covers loss arising from suspension of business and obstruction of business, too, when the enterprise sustains damage from destroyed computer and its related material. This shows that the Computer Comprehensive Insurance has the following two functions: first, the insurance protects the enterprise of the insured object from direct damage; second, the insurance protects it from indirect damage of losing interests by suspension of business and obstruction of business.[35]

3.3 The Nature of the Cyber Insurance

The Cyber Insurance has two kinds of the insurances, namely, the third-party insurance and the first-party insurance.

According to a research report on the cause of leaking information from corporations, the leakage by hacking had a 4 %.[36] The leakage cases of personal information are almost attributable to negligence of employees, companies or corporations as to information management. The employees, companies or corporations negligently leak personal information arising from the cyber attacks, human error in operation or intentionally stealing the data. Therefore, one kind of the Cyber Insurance is made up as third-party insurance and aims to cover the damages which the employees, companies or corporations are liable for leaking personal information and treatment expenses.

In the case that the servers in companies or corporations are broken by cyber attacks, provided the companies or corporations have no legal responsibilities in the leakage of personal information, the insurer will cover damages caused by the breakage of the server and theft of the media for recording the data under the movable comprehensive insurance contract. The treatment expenses of the broken server are likewise covered by the Cyber Insurance. Concretely, the insurance company pays the claim paid or payable in the case of any damages arising out of an unexpected and sudden accident on the computer and its peripheral devices or information media. Moreover, the company pays expenses for residue removal, such as demolition cost, cleaning cost and carrying-out cost, among others.

[35] Tokio Marine & Nichido Fire Insurance Co., Ltd (2010), p. 116.

[36] A Beam Consulting Ltd., "A Research Report on Counter Measure Situations by enterprises regarding the Private Information Protection Law", p.14 (2005). http://jp.abeam.com/collaterals/pdf/RR062.pdf.

Therefore, this insurance is set up as the first-party insurance. This insurance does not have an element of liability of the insured and generally movable insurance.

3.4 The Structure and Contents

3.4.1 The Cyber Insurance as Liability Insurance

This insurance has a fundamental structure as follows; (1) The Insured: entrepreneurs that manage personal information (except one-man business) and the officers and the employees (who manage their affairs); (2) The Named Insured: the insured who written the name as the insured on this policy; (3) Personal Information: protected personal information is one that identifies a specified person, such as the name, the birthday, and other descriptions. But recording media are required to be in Japan; (4) Leaking: personal information is required to be leaked by the following circumstances; (a) event occurred on the Network, (b) loss or theft of paper or magnetic disk and (c) taking out by employees of the named insured, excepting, from the term, "leaking", the case that policyholder, the named insured or its officers, intentionally obtained personal information to the third party personal; (5) The Limited Amounts: in this policy the payable amounts are set up in the limitation; (6) Deductible Amount: the amounts that the insured will pay which are deducted from damages; (7) The Accidental Response Term: this term is one from the next date when either of policyholder, the insured or this company first finds to 180 days; (8) The Treatment Expenses for leaking personal information: the expenses are required to be absolutely essential for treating accident response, such as (a) expenses for apology and interview, (b) expenses for treatment accident and solution, (c) consolation payments and condolence gift costs and (d) attorney's fees and consulting fees.

3.4.2 The Cyber Insurance as Property Insurance

This insurance has a fundamental structure as follows; this insurance policy is composed of four clauses and special agreements; the 4 clauses, which are: (1) the information equipment clause, (2) the information media clause, (3) the business continuation clause and (4) the passive damages clause, are fundamental. Meaning, this insurance is property insurance for dealing with the risk that the server, the computer and media are broken and stolen, or passive damages arising from business suspension. Therefore, if a cyber attack breaks the server and computer, this insurance will cover damages by it, whether the insured is negligent or not.

(1) The Insured: the enterprise who has or manages the information equipment and the information media. (2) The obligation to disclose: the policyholder or insured has an obligation to correctly disclose the important facts that this company asks regarding risk in making an insurance contract. (3) The obligation to manage:

the policyholder, the insured or its representative has an obligation to appropriately manage the information devise, the information media and so on. (4) Assignment of covered items: when the insured assigns the covered items, such as the information devise or the information media, after making this insurance contract, the policyholder or the insured must inform this insurance company assignment of the covered item. (5) Investigation of covered items: this insurance company has authorization to investigate, any time, covered items, place to keep them, premise on its policy and items, files or documents identified information (program or data). (6) The claim for insurance money: the insured has claim to this company for insurance money after (a) payment term in the passive damages clause, (b) the 30 days including the day when carrying instruments equipped with covered objects are lost in the case of presuming damages in the information equipment clause and the information media clause, (c) time when damages happened in clauses other than the passive damages clause, the information equipment clause and the information media clause.

4 The Legal Issues on Cyber Insurance

4.1 The Cyber Insurance as Liability Insurance: General Liability Insurance and Special Policy for Leaking Personal Information

4.1.1 Who Is the Policyholder?

As the Cyber Insurance of this kind is commercial lines, the policyholder is the enterprises that collect, analyze and manage personal information from customers. Meaning, the enterprises take risk of leaking personal information when they have business activities. Thus, the policyholders would all be enterprises, excepting from it personal enterprises, which deal with personal information.

But the following enterprises are excluded from the scope of the policyholders: (1) professionals, such as attorneys, enrolled agent, certified public accountants, judicial scriveners, (2) local public entities, (3) carriers, transporters and warehouse owners. Regarding the third group, when the main risk is leaking personal information caused by theft or loss in transportation, and transporters will have or had cargo insurance contracts, then this risk is covered.

4.1.2 Who Is Covered by Cyber Insurance?

The Cyber Insurance of this kind is liability insurance in third party insurance. Hence, this insurance is commercial lines. Therefore, the insured is the enterprise that is liable to damages arising from leaking personal insurance. The scope of the insured is (1) enterprises (the named insured) who deal with personal information and (2) officers or employees (who treat with personal information) of the enterprises.

4.1.3 What Is Covered Information?

Covered personal information is defined as follows: personal information, including name, birthday and other descriptions, is one for distinguishing specific individuals, is verified other personal information with difficulties and, by which, is made a sharp distinction among individuals, provided there must be recording media in Japan.

4.1.4 What Is "The Accident"?

According to this policy, the accident is to suffer damage arising from treating with leakage of personal information. Additionally, the accident are required to be revealed by the following: (1) notification or report by the insured through his/her writing to a public institution, (2) announcement or report by newspaper, magazine, television, radio, internet or comparable to media or (3) the time when anybody, the policyholder, the insured or this company, first find the accident is held to be the time when the accident happens, in the case that nobody can rationally presume when the accident happens.

This insurance is liability insurance, but as stated above, it is difficult to recognize when the accident happens, this policy requires that it becomes evident when personal information is leaked through the media.

4.1.5 The Limited Compensation

This insurance covers damages caused by personal information leakage, including compensation and apology advertisement costs.

But this policy has the sublimit amounts within liability for damage in the case that third party claim for indemnity of expenses. To illustrate, A collects personal information and A delegates analysis to B. C makes insurance contract with B. According to this policy, the part of liability for damage is limited up to the same amount of the expenses. When B leaks the information, A publishes an apology in a newspaper and expresses its regret and sends consolation payment to individuals. Thereafter, A claims these costs from B.

In this case, if the part of expenses is set up to $30 million, the sublimit amount of liability for damage is the same amount ($30 million). This sublimit is applicable to the part that the third party claim indemnity of costs. C cannot pay more than the sublimit amount regarding indemnity of costs by third party. Meaning, even if the third party claims indemnity of costs by apology advertisements, among others, the insurance company is not allowed to pay more than the setup insurance amount as the limited expenses that are the same as the sublimit amount in the part of liability for damage. Of course, it stands to reason that the limit amount in the part of liability for damage are set up as more than the sublimit amount.

This company likewise pays the dispute expenses. But in the case that the ad damnum amount is more than the limit amounts, this company should pay insurance money calculated by the following computation expression: insurance money = the dispute expenses × the limit amounts/the ad damnum amount.

Moreover, this company should pay all expenses for suits and labor expenses, emergency measure expenses and cooperation expenses.

4.1.6 The Exclusion Clauses

This policy consists of two main parts: one part is liability insurance as a basic contract, the other part is coverage for leaking personal information as a special contract.

How are the exclusion clauses different from the former to the latter.

This company does not pay insurance money for damages, under coverage for leaking personal information, directly or indirectly arising from the following causations: (1) intent of policyholder or the insured, (2) war (whether declaration of war or not), social disturbance, riot, civil disorder or industrial dispute, (3) earthquake, eruption, flood or tidal wave, (4) law violation, deed that damages to others by the policyholder, the insured or officer, (5) physical difficult of others, (6) destruction, loss, thrift, cheat of things of others or out of commission, obstruction of things of others. Regarding (1), this company should not pay treatment expenses for leaking personal information in the case that the named insured or the officer indemnifies against loss arising from employee's act of bringing out of information.

The exclusion clause of the liability insurance is from (1) to (3). On the other hand, the one covering the leakage of personal information is from (4) to (6). Conversely, it differs from the former to the latter in whether the immunity reasons are objective or subjective. In the former, the immunity reason is outside the scope of the parties of the policyholder, or natural disaster. But in the latter, or the coverage for leaking personal information, the immunity reason is from the deed of the parties of the policyholder.

4.2 *The Cyber Insurance as Property Insurance: The Computer Comprehensive Insurance*

4.2.1 Who Is the Policyholder?

Generally, anyone could make the comprehensive computer insurance contract with the insurance company as the policyholder under the policy. Thus, the policy is not written to be restricted in qualification as the policyholder who is required to be enterprises or individuals. As anyone has some digital media or personal computers containing economic valuable information, he or she needs to have this insurance contract to deal with the risk of losing or breaking down the media or computers.

4.2.2 What Risk Is Covered by the Cyber Insurance?

Information is not a tangible entity, like a building, but intangible. Information is managed and controlled on media. Meaning, nobody cannot directly manage and control information itself that when information is lost or stolen by someone, it is difficult to recognize the person who lost or who stole it, unlike in the case of fire.

What risk is covered by this insurance? This insurance covers the risk of the insured. Concretely speaking, the risks are the kinds of (1) damage arising from information equipment, information media, and (2) lost earnings by accident. It is to be noted that the risk this insurance covers are not the information itself but equipment and media where information is recorded, and lost earnings which the insured suffered because of the accident. Information is extremely important in business and corporations, they can efficiently do business on information, but information itself cannot be directly managed and controlled. It can be managed and controlled only through equipment and media.

4.2.3 What Is "The Accident"?

As personal information is not tangible, what is "the accident" becomes controversial. In other words, could intangible information be an object of the accident? This answer is "no". Information could not be an object of the accident. What then is "the accident"?

In the information equipment and information media clauses regarding damages, the accident means the unexpected and sudden event by which the information equipments suffered damages. Regarding expenses, the accident means fire, thunderbolt, burst and explosion by which the information equipments suffered damages and the insured must pay specific expenses.

In the lost earning and business continuity expense clause, the accident means the one defined in the information equipment and information media clauses.

4.2.4 Can "Damages" Be Calculated?

It seems difficult for damages arising from cyber attack which breaks information equipment and digital media to be calculated. In fact, can anyone calculate the damages caused by the leaking of personal information or breaking information equipment, digital media and business profit losses? Because information itself is not economically valued, it then follows that damages by the leaking of personal information cannot be economically valued.

Nobody assesses the damages by cyber attack in the big information companies and nobody finds the measure for calculating the damages when data base for collecting information is broken by cyber attacks.

According to the information equipment and digital media clauses, the insurance company does not pay the damages of information itself but pays the damages of repair costs for the broken information equipment and digital media and, in the case of having the insured's information equipment and digital media stolen, the damages of the expenses for taking them back to the insured. In the lost earning and business continuity expense clause, the insurance company pays the lost earning and business continuity expenses as the payable losses.

The point we should notice is that the limits the insurance company pay the insurance money is the amount covered the insurance party and the insurance company agree, in the aforesaid two cases.

4.2.5 The Exclusion Clauses

What cause the insurance company to refuse insurance payment? Stated otherwise, what absolves the insurance company from its obligation to pay the insurance?

According to the information equipment and the digital media clauses, the insurance company is not held responsible in any of the following cases; (1) intent, culpa lata and law violation by the insurance party, the insured and the legal representative, whom the insurance company pay insurance money to, (2) intent by the employee of the insurance party and the insured, (3) Exercise of public authority, such as attachment, expropriation and destruction, by a nation or public bodies, (4) natural wear and tear or natural deterioration on subject of insurance, (5) defect in subject of insurance, (6) negligence or primitive on work while repair of subject of insurance, (7) misplacing, losing and negligent destruction of subjects of insurance, (8) flood by typhoon, rainstorm and heavy rain, snow flood, high tide and water disaster by mudslide, (9) air dry, change in humidity and temperature, (10) war, use of force by a foreign countries, revolution, assumption of power, civil war, rebellion with armaments and incident or riot similar to them, (11) Earthquake, eruption or tsunami by them and (12) accident rising from nuclear fuel material or the radioactivity, the explosion or the rest caused by nuclear contaminated material. These immunity reasons do not seem to be unique to non-life insurance which includes the Computer Comprehensive Insurance.

And it is stipulated on the immunity in Sec. 17 of the Japanese "Insurance Act", "the Insurer does not have liability for indemnifying loss arising from willfulness or negligence of the policyholder or the insured".

4.2.6 The Subrogation Clauses

As this coverage is a kind of property insurance, as the first-party insurance, this policy has the subrogation clause. Meaning, an injured party has a right to claim compensation for leaking personal information and then the insurance company is assigned the right of the injured party after the insurance company pays insurance money to the injured party.

In Japan the purpose of the subrogation clause is generally and traditionally three follows[37]:

(1) Profits Prohibition Principle—insured is prohibited from executing the rights to the torts-feasor and to the insurer, (2) Impediment of immunity—insurer's payment to insured does not immunize the tort-feasor and (3) Rational intention between the contract parties—they have an intention of transferring to the insurer the insured's right against the tort-feasor.

The three purposes of the subrogation are not changed after the Japanese "Insurance Act" has been enacted.

But the subrogation clause in the Japanese "Insurance Act" protects consumers to the point that the insurance company cannot subrogate the injured party's ("insured's") right of indemnity for tort-feasor as long as the insurance company compensates the loss when the insurance company pays a part of the loss,[38,39]

---

[37] Nishijima (1998), p. 181, p. 185; Okada (2007), pp. 42–102; Yamashita (2005), pp. 545–555. *See,* Suzaki (1991), p. 1, p. 1; Nakaide (1996), p. 449; Yamamoto (1996), p. 471, p. 839.

[38] Sec. 25 on the subrogation of the Japanese "Insurance Act" revised the scope of subrogation in the case of a part insurance to protect the insured. But generally, Sec. 26, which stipulates Sec. 25, a compulsory provision for the insurance company and makes an insurance clause against a policyholder or insured invalid, is not applicable to the enterprise insurance contracts under its Sec. 36.

[39] Saiko Saibansho [Sup. Ct.] made a decision, on Feb. 20, 2012, on the scope of the subrogation as regards Sec. 25 of the Japanese "Insurance Act". After an automobile insurer, who sells the Voluntary Automobile Coverage for Personal Injuries like an accidental coverage for damages, paid insurance money to the insured who was injured in a traffic accident, based on the evaluation standard of personal injury in policy, the insured filed a suit in court challenging for scarce insurance money. Sec. 25 of the Japanese "Insurance Act", which is one of the compulsory provisions for the insured and policyholders, stipulates that the insured shall receive complete compensation for the full loss from the insurer when the insurer pays a part of insurance money to the insured. Certainly the scare money causes the conflict of interests between the insured and the insurer as regards the scope of the insured's subrogation right. The Supreme Court made a decision as follows: in the case that the insured received first not indemnities from the tort-feasor but insurance money from the insurance company, as long as the amount that is added on the limit of indemnity to ad damnum amount is above the damages that the insured suffers, in the scope of the excess amount, the insurance company gets a subrogation right to a tort-feasor from a person who

But could the insurance company subrogates the injured party ("insured"), the company or corporation, and exercise the right of indemnifying the injured party for damages to a tort-feasor who attacks the server or computer when the insurance company pay insured money to the injured party? Does this subrogation clause in this policy have the special meaning that the insurance company has the subrogated right to the tort-feasor? Traditionally, the tort-feasor lives in same country as the insured and the insurer; at least in Japan this condition seemed to be the precondition on the subrogation. But the cyber attackers, who the insurance company has the subrogated right to, are or might be the outside of the countries where the loss by cyber attacks arise. In this case, the insurance company would not be able to exercise the subrogated right which was transferred from the insured to the insurance company. Moreover, the insurance company could not find the cyber-attackers in foreign countries.

In the case of the cyber attacks from foreign countries, actually, the insured, whose server or the computer in the corporate was attacked, could not exercise the right to be reimbursed of the damages. Therefore, the insurance company could not exercise the right to be reimbursed of the loss of the insured against the cyber attackers. Therefore, in this case, the subrogation, which is the insured's right to the tort-feasor that is transferred to the insurance company, is abstract and conceptual. The cyber attacks from foreign countries have been able to damage the server or the computer system in a corporation with the development of information technology. This phenomenon means "the borderless", beyond the border among the countries. The "borderless" would gradually exercise influence over the mechanism of insurance contract.[40]

Increasing globalization makes border low, allowing more anonymous attackers to make a rush from foreign countries on servers or computer systems in companies. It would be difficult for the insurer to execute the right of subrogation as the insurer could not find and identify the real attacker in foreign countries.

---

has a right to claim insurance money. I understand that the insured, as a consumer, gets more protection than the insurer just as long as the insured receive the complete compensation. Therefore, in my opinion, the case that the insured is not a consumer but an enterprise or corporation is not applicable to this case. Saiko Saibansho [Sup. Ct.] Feb. 20, 2012, Heisei 24, Saiko saibansho Minji Hanreishu [Minshu] Vol. 66, No. 2, 742, Hanreijiho [Hanji] No. 2145, 103 (Japan).

On the other hand, the above decision seemed to be not applicable to this case in that the insured received first not insurance money from the insurance company but indemnities from the tort-feasor. Japan's Supreme Court has decided nothing to this case, but Osaka High Court made the decision that the insurance company shall pay the insurance money, worked out on the basis of the standard for calculating the damages, which sets off indemnities the insured has received from the tort-feasor or liability insurer. Osaka Kouto Saibansho [Osaka High Ct.] Jun. 7, 2012, Heisei 24, Hanreijiho [Hanji] No. 2156, 123 (Japan).

[40] Of course, in accordance with this influence, the sound way of the insurance regulation in each country would change gradually and in the far future, each insurance regulation would be unified by the activities of IAIS (International Association of Insurance Supervisor).

In the future, globalization would deprive the insurer of a chance to execute the right of subrogation to the tort-feasor who attacked them from foreign countries. This would force the non-life insurer to reconsider whether the subrogation is essential in the non-life insurance or not.

5 The Conclusion

As state above, the Cyber Insurance is not a special kind of insurance, but a general kind of non-life insurance. Personal information itself is not a tangible entity with assessed economic value. Therefore, Cyber Insurance provides protection when the information media on the personal information is stolen or broken. In a way, Cyber Insurance makes Personal Information tangible by the way of information media.

Further, Personal Information itself is not assessed with economic value. So the protection scope of loss, which the Cyber Insurance provides, is limited to the calculable expenses.

Secondly, regarding subrogation, in the case of the cyber attacks from foreign countries, really the insurance company could not execute the right to claim damage, but the insurance company should have the subrogation to the insured when the insurance company reimburses to the insured.

Thirdly, the cyber attack from foreign countries makes it difficult for the insurance company to execute the right of the subrogation to the foreign cyber attackers. If the insurance company finds and identifies the foreign cyber attackers, the costs of subrogation would go up and the insurance company would burden itself with unreasonable expenses. The more globalization in economics spreads, the more that this phenomenon happens. The Cyber Insurance questions whether the subrogation is an essential of non-life insurance. Because, from the point view of the economy, the insurance company does not make a choice of executing the rights of subrogation to the foreign cyber attackers, even if the losses by cyber attack are usually heavy and the victim cannot neglect them.

Finally, recently Tokio Marine & Nichido Fire Insurance Co., Ltd put the "Cyber Risk Insurance"[41] for Business Enterprises which is a full-scale comprehensive coverage for cyber-risk arising from business activities on February 9th, 2015.

[41] See note (14). The "Cyber Risk Insurance" covers the several damages caused by the cyber risk events; its insurance covers (1) damages caused by information leakage, arising from defects in possession, use and manage of the network (The IT User Clauses (The Basic Coverage)), (2) expenses for crisis management and legal costs caused by information leakages and illegal accesses (The Clauses of Coverage for the Cyber Security Accident Costs), (3) lost earnings, or operating losses, and costs for continuing business caused by computer system crashes arising from accidental, unexpected and sudden events (The Clauses of Coverage for Network Interruption Cost. This coverage is optional). This insurance has been revised on 1st October in 2015 as stated below; (a) this insurance provides the comprehensive support services for checking risk and introducing special technician; (b) this insurance covers the costs of checking whether anyone accesses illegally the server or computer system in the insured when a public organization or a

The other non-life insurance companies are strengthening the dealing of a kind of cyber insurance and Japanese Government will support its dissemination.[42]

References

Hagimoto O (ed) (2009) Questions and answers on the insurance act (ICHIMON ITTOU HOKEN-HO). Shojihomu

Junko O, Kenkyukai NS (Ed) (2008) Commentary on the insurance act (KAISETSU HOKEN-HO). Kobundo

Kanazawa O (2001) Insurance law (HOKENHOU JOUKAN), vol 1. SEIBUNDO, p 107, Revised

Kitamura S (2012) Liability insurance contract and the victim in legal position when the offender go to bankrupt (Kagaisha Hasan no saino Sekininhokenkeiyaku to Higaisha no Chii) Kinyu/ Shoji Hanrei, No.1386. In: Ochiai S, Yamashita N (ed) The analysis and development (HOKEN HANREI NO BUNSEKI TO TENKAI).Keizaihorei Kenkyukai, pp 44–49

Koezuka T (2014) In: Yamashita T, Nagasawa T (eds) The systematic dispute points insurance law (RONTENTAIKEI HOKENHOU), vol 1. DAIICHI HOKI, pp 434–435

Kozuka S, Lee J (2008) The New Japanese Insurance Act: comparisons with Europe and Korea. Zeitschrift für japanisches Recht 14(28):79

Kurasawa Y (1997) An introduction of insurance law (HOKENHOU TSUURON). Sanreisha, p 58

Nakaide S (1996) Hokendaii nitsuite (A study on the insurable subrogation). J Political Econ (Kyusyudaigaku keizaigaku kenkyu) 62(1–6):449

Nishijima U (1998) Insurance law (HOKENHOU), 3rd edn. Yuyusya, p 131

Ochiai S (ed) (2009) Annotation on insurance act (HOKENHO KONMENTARU). The General Insurance Institute of Japan, pp 113–114

Ochiai S, Takahashi S, Takeda R (2011) Japan: the insurance concept in the Insurance Act and the Insurance Business Act. In: Burling J, Lazarus K (eds) Research handbook on international insurance law and regulation. Edward Elgar p. 747, 748

Okada T (2007) The legal theory of the subrogation (SEIKYUKENDAII NO HOURI). Nihonhyoronsha, pp 42–102

Omori T (1952) The legal structure on insurance contract (HOKENKEIYAKU NO HOUTEKIKOUZOU). Yuhikaku, pp 83–84

Suzaki H (1991) Hoken Daii to Ritoku Kinshi Gensoku (1)(2) (The insurance subrogation and the principle of a ban on insurable profit(1)(2)). Hougaku Ronsovol 129(1/3): 1

Tokio Marine & Nichido Fire Insurance Co., Ltd. (ed) (2010) No-Life Insurance Business Law and Practice (SONGAIHOKEN NO HOUMU TO JITSUMU). KINZAI, p 149

Uematsu K, Hokenho S (2008) The point commentary article by article on the amendment of the new insurance act (Non-life insurance accident and health insurance) ((SONHAIHOKEN SYOUGAISIPPEIHOKEN) CHIKUJO KAISEI POINTO KAISETSU). Hoken Mainich Shinbunsha

Yamamoto T (1996) A study on insurable subrogation (Hokendaii nikansuru Ichikousatsu). Hokkaido Law Rev (Hokudai Hougaku Ronso) 47(2/3): 471, 839

Yamashita T (2005) Insurance law (HOKEN HO). Yuhikaku, p 247

Yamashita T (2008a) The new insurance act: general provisions and some common issues (Atarashii Hoken-Ho: Soronteki Jikô oyobi Jakkan no Kyotsu Jiko), Jurisuto No. 1364, p 10

specified company informs the insured of illegal access to the insured; (c) this amounts or limits of this coverage is modified. I could not refer to this insurance in this article.

[42] Shikoku News Paper, March 25, 2015 at 8 [Shikoku Shinbun, March 25, 2015 at 8].

Yamashita T (2008b) The significance of the modernisation of the insurance law (Hoken-Ho Gendai-Ka No Igi), Jurisuto No. 1368, p 60

Yamashita T, Yoneyama T (ed) (2010) A commentary on the insurance act of Japan (HOKENHO KAISETSU-SEIMEIHOKEN SYOUGAISIPPEITEIGAKUHOKEN). Yuhikaku

Yashima K (2009) The bankrupt insured and victims' compensation in the liability insurance contract (Sekininhoken ni okeru Hihokendya no Hasan to Higaisya kyuusai). In: Otsuka H, Kodama Y (eds) The new insurance law and the new development of the leagal theory on the insurance contract (SHIN HOKENHO TO HOKENKEIYAKUHOURI NO ARATANA TENKAI). Gyosei Pub., pp. 149–154, Compiled under the supervision of Osamu Kanazawa

Data Protection in the Insurance Sector Under EU Law

Carlo Eligio Mezzetti

Contents

Abstract The connection between data protection and insurance practice is significant: virtually all Europeans population have taken out one or more insurance policies; the automated processing of personal data for insurance purposes is widespread to ease management; the mobility of individuals and the globalization of commercial activities need a trans-border exchange of information in the insurance sector. Accordingly, insurers are among the largest data controllers, and the cross border flow of data is an unavoidable consequence of globalization.

This chapter aims to give a presentation of the rules currently in force on data protection in the EU and contained in Directive 95/46. The rules, described and presented with their application issues with reference to claims management, are compared with the new rules which will be adopted following the approval of an

C.E. Mezzetti (✉)
Ughi e Nunziante Studio Legale, Milan, Italy
e-mail: CMezzetti@unlaw.it

P. Marano et al. (eds.), *The "Dematerialized" Insurance*,
DOI 10.1007/978-3-319-28410-1_10

envisaged new EU Regulation. What emerges is that the new Regulation, clearly conceived keeping in mind other specific sectors (such as the internet and social networks), could be the source of new obligations and higher costs for insurance companies.

1 An Overview of EU Law on Data Protection

Over the last 20 years data protection has become increasingly important in the European Union legal system: from the harmonization of Member States' laws with Directive 95/46,[1] and the "proclamation" of data protection as a fundamental right (Art. 8 of the Charter of Fundamental Rights of the European Union), to its "constitutionalisation" by the Lisbon Treaty (Art. 16 of the Treaty on the Functioning of the EU) and the consequent envisaged adoption of a regulation directly applicable in all Member States which would put an end to the cumulative and simultaneous application of 28 (harmonized, but still) different national data protection laws.

Directive 95/46—which the European Commission quite emphatically describes as "a milestone in the history of data protection"[2]—for the time being remains the central legislative instrument for the protection of personal data in Europe. Its main purpose is to reconcile the free circulation of data in the Single Market and the protection of the freedoms of individuals, namely what is called the right to *informational self-determination*. In this respect it is worth underlining that data protection is something different and broader than privacy protection because it applies also to information pertaining to the public sphere of individuals, such as information on political opinions and trade-union membership.

It is, first of all, worth recalling some key-features of the Directive:

- The notion of *personal data* refers to any information relating to an identified or identifiable natural person (the *data subject*); information regarding legal entities thus falls outside the scope of the Directive (Art. 2.a).
- The kind of medium carrying the information is neutral as to the legal definition of data: in so far as they convey information on an identifiable individual, the Directive applies also to audio or video recordings, photographs, etc.

[1] Directive 95/46/EC of the European Parliament and of the Council of 24 October 1995 on the protection of individuals with regard to the processing of personal data and on the free movement of such data (OJ L 281, 23.11.1995, p. 31).

[2] Communication from the Commission to the European Parliament, the Council, the European Economic and Social Committee and the Committee of the Regions of 25 January 2012, *Safeguarding Privacy in a Connected World A European Data Protection Framework for the 21st Century* (COM/2012/09 final).

- The Directive applies to all digital or otherwise automatic data processing, and also to the "processing otherwise than by automatic means" provided that the data form part (or are intended to form part) of a filing system. The notion of *processing* is broad, encompassing any operation performed on personal information, "such as collection, recording, organization, storage, adaptation or alteration, retrieval, consultation, use, disclosure by transmission, dissemination or otherwise, making available, alignment or combination, blocking, erasure or destruction".
- In so far as natural or legal entity "determines the purposes and means of the processing of personal data" it shall be regarded as the *controller* of the same data (Art. 2.d); therefore, the *data controller* status is not triggered by a formal appointment, but arises by operation of law at the time a natural or legal entity autonomously starts to process personal data.
- Different from the data controller is the *data processor*; this optional position may come into play where the data controller gives a different natural or a legal entity the task of processing the data; the appointment shall be made in writing "by a contract or a legal act binding the processor to the controller", stipulating in particular that the processor shall act only on instructions from the controller and that security duties set forth in Art. 17.1 are incumbent also on the same data processor. It can be inferred from such mandatory responsibility, and from the wording of Art. 16, that, when appointed, the processor/s (if necessary, several entities may be designated as data processors) has a supervision authority on data processing.
- The data controller is responsible for the compliance of processing to data protection law, notably to the *data quality* principles laid down by Art. 6: he shall ensure that personal data are (a) processed fairly and lawfully; (b) collected for specified, explicit and legitimate purposes and not further processed in a way that is incompatible with those purposes; (c) adequate, relevant and not excessive in relation to the purposes for which they are collected and/or processed further; (d) accurate and, where necessary, kept up to date; (e) kept in a form which permits identification of data subjects for no longer than it is necessary for the purposes for which the data were initially collected or for which they are further processed.
- Fair collection and processing presuppose (i) information to be provided by the controller to the data subject, listed at Arts. 10–11 (e.g. information on the identity of the controller and of his representative, if any, on the purposes of the processing, etc.), and (ii) that the same data subject has unambiguously given his consent to the processing of personal data. The directive, however, provides for a specific list of cases where the data subject's consent is not needed.
- The data subject enjoys a "right of access" to the data, consisting in the right to obtain from the controller, at reasonable intervals and without excessive delay or expense:—confirmation as to whether data relating to him are being processed, and information at least as to the purposes of the processing, the categories of data concerned, and the recipients or categories of recipients to whom the data are disclosed;—communication to the subject in an intelligible form of the data

undergoing processing and of any available information as to their source;— knowledge of the logic involved in any automatic processing of data concerning him at least in the case of automated decisions. Moreover, in cases where data processing does not comply with the provisions of the Directive, in particular because of the incomplete or inaccurate nature of such data, the data subject has the right to obtain, as appropriate, the rectification, erasure or blocking of data, and the notification to third parties to whom the data have been disclosed of any such rectification, erasure or blocking.

- As mentioned, the data controller and—when appointed—the data processor shall be responsible for security requirements; in this regard, the general principle is that personal data undergoing processing shall be kept and controlled (also in consideration of technological innovations, of their nature and of the specific features of the processing) in such a way as to minimise, by means of suitable technical and organizational measures, the risk of their destruction or loss, of unauthorized disclosure or access, or of processing operations that are either unlawful or inconsistent with the purposes for which the data have been collected.

1.1 The European Commission's Proposal for a Data Protection Reform

A proposal for a new legislative instrument—a *General Data Protection Regulation*—was adopted in January 2012 by the European Commission[3] with the aim of "modernizing" the EU's data protection rules, keeping abreast of the development of information technologies and evolving social behavior.

In its Communication "Safeguarding Privacy in a Connected World—A European Data Protection Framework for the 21st Century"[4] the Commission points mainly to the sharing of information through social networks and the remote storage of large amounts of data, as well as to the fact that personal data has become an asset for many businesses, as the main factors exerting pressure on the present data protection legal framework. In the Commission's view, this not only turns into a threat for individuals' liberties, but it also curbs economic growth and the competitiveness of EU industries: "lack of confidence makes consumers hesitant to buy online and accept new services".[5]

[3] Proposal for a regulation of the European Parliament and of the Council on the protection of individuals with regard to the processing of personal data and on the free movement of such data (General Data Protection Regulation) of 25 January 2012 Brussels, 25.1.2012 (COM 2012 11 final).

[4] Quoted above, at 2.

[5] *Ivi.*

The envisaged reform mainly aims at strengthening consistency and effectiveness in the application and enforcement (both public and private) of data protection, but the general principles remain almost the same as those laid down by the Directive. In particular, it is the degree of harmonization reached with the Directive on the side of the means of recourse granted to individuals and of the powers of the data protection national authorities which is to be considered insufficient, rather than the catalogue of rights that can be asserted by a *data subject*. While the proposal does directly touch on the area of individuals' rights, it is more in the sense of reshaping already existing rights rather than introducing brand-new ones. This also applies to the (apparently) new "right to be forgotten" included in the proposal, a point which has been subject to criticism in the US[6]: for the most part, under that label there is a more detailed regulation of the "old" right to erasure, already provided for by the Directive[7]; in addition to this, the new right to data portability seems to be a refined and updated version of the already existing right to obtain a copy of the stored data in an intelligible form from the data controller, even if the interoperable format would ease for the data subject working on his own data, and lower his *switching costs*.

The "procedural" features of the proposal focus on the strengthening of national data protection authorities' independence and powers (including carrying out investigations, taking binding decisions and imposing "effective and dissuasive sanctions", i.e. fines determined as a percentage of the annual worldwide turnover of companies), the coordination between the national authorities in question, and the enhancing of administrative and judicial remedies for the violation of data protection rights (including the grant to "qualified associations" of the standing to bring actions to court on behalf of individuals).

Besides, a higher level of data protection effectiveness is pursued by increasing the burden on data controllers. An example is the new duty to notify data breaches without undue delay to both the competent data protection authority (within 24 hours of the breach being discovered, when feasible) and the concerned data subjects. A further example is the requirement for data controllers to designate a Data Protection Officer in companies with more than 250 employees and in organizations which are involved in "risky processing", also introducing the obligation to carry out a "data protection impact assessments". In the Commission's perspective, this would turn in an advantage for EU companies in global competition, because "they will be able to assure their customers that valuable personal information will be treated with the necessary care and diligence".

Reinforcement of data security is also pursued on the technical side, with the introduction of a "Privacy by Design" principle to have data protection safeguards considered at the planning stage of procedures and systems, and by encouraging the

[6] See Benet (2012), p. 161.

[7] A partially different line of reasoning was recently followed by the Court of Justice in the ruling of May 13th, 2014—case C-131/13, *Google v AEPD and Gonzales*, however considering the "right to be forgotten" as already existing under the Directive.

use of privacy-enhancing technologies minimizing the storage of personal data and encompassing privacy-friendly default settings ("Privacy by Default").

2 "Local" Policies, "Master/Euro" Policies, "Global/Multinational" Policies: The Initial Collection of Data Referring to the Policyholder and to the Insured Persons; Issues Related to Data Flows Across the Borders

The collection of personal data by an insurance company is likely to involve three kinds of "data subjects": i.e. (i). the policyholder, (which may be a different entity from) (ii). the insured, and/or (iii). (as to civil liability policies) the damaged persons.

It can be assumed that when data subjects identify with the insurer's contracting parties only minor issues of personal data protection may arise because the insurer usually provides the information and—if necessary—acquires the consent for processing data (including for their communication to third parties) at the moment of the policy execution. Thus, in the forthcoming pages we will focus on aspects related to processing of personal information of the insured and/or to the damaged party when these persons are not the policyholder.

Still, a preliminary data protection issue may arise also in connection with the policyholder's data: is the collection and processing ruled by the EU law? Which national data protection law is applicable thereof?

At the present stage of European harmonization the answer to the two questions above is the same, and can be found in Art. 4 of the Directive, according to which each Member State shall apply the national implementing provisions where: (i) the processing of data is carried out in the context of the activities of an establishment of the controller on the territory of such Member State; (ii) the controller is not established on EU territory but, for data processing purposes, makes use of equipment located in the territory of the Member State (that being the case, the controller must designate a representative established in the territory of the relevant Member State). Clearly, this is a conflict rule favoring the cumulative application of multiple domestic laws: when the same controller is established in the territory of several Member States, he must comply with the obligations laid down by the laws of each single State where his branches are establishment.

While this would probably be a merely organizational issue for an insurer dealing with "local" policies (i.e. insurance policies issued by its local branch in a given Member State, where data are collected and processed), the picture becomes far more complicated for policies covering more than one European country and involving more than one local branch, or for so called "master policies" operating for specific losses not covered by the "local" policy, or triggered when the loss exceeds the maximum coverage provided by the same policy, and often administered by the insurer's European headquarter. In the latter situations, two or more offices of the same insurer, located in different Member States, would process the same personal data, but each of them shall comply with different national laws and face a different national data protection authority.

The scenario would change with the adoption of the proposed Regulation as a single legislative instrument directly applicable in all Member States would supersede the present 28 national laws implementing the Directive. Moreover, the proposal designs a "one-stop-shop" system, where the data protection authority of the Member State where the company has its "main establishment" will be competent also for the processing carried out by the same company in other Member States.

In this respect, the envisaged reform would lead to an higher degree of consistency and legal certainty for companies, but such benefit for non-EU companies might be counterweighted by the expansion of the scope of application of the EU law: according to Art. 3 of the proposed Regulation, EU data protection law would apply to the processing of personal data of subjects residing in the Union even if it is carried out by controllers which are neither established in the Union, nor using any processing equipment located in the EU, if the processing activities are related to: (a) the offering of goods or services to such data subjects in the Union; or (b) the monitoring of their behavior. The express intent of the Commission, in this respect, is that "EU data protection standards have to apply regardless of the geographical location of a company or its processing facility".

Actually, the same philosophy already applies to the transfer of data from the EU to third countries, even if the receiver of the data is a foreign subsidiary of the same data controller or a service provider (e.g. an outsourcer processing the data on behalf of the controller or a company offering cloud computing services). Under the Directive (Arts. 25–26) transfers of personal data from the EU to third countries may only take place if the third country in question ensures "an adequate level of protection", to be *certified* by a Commission's decision.

In the absence of an adequacy decision, a data transfer may still take place if one of the derogations listed in Art. 26.1 (Art. 44.1 of the proposed regulation) applies. In the framework of multinational or worldwide insurance programmes such derogations may play an important role because they encompass not only cases where the data subject has given his consent unambiguously to the proposed transfer, or the transfer is necessary for the performance of a contract between the data subject and the controller, or the implementation of pre-contractual measures taken in response to the data subject's request, but also the case where the transfer is necessary for the conclusion or performance of a contract concluded *in the interest* of the data subject between the controller and a third party. The latter may well be the case of a policy where the insured and the policyholder are not the same person.

If none of the derogations set forth in Art. 26.1 apply, and without an "adequacy finding" by the Commission, the controller may nevertheless transfer data to non EU countries if he is authorized to do so by a national data protection authority according to Art. 26.2. To have such authorization granted, the controller shall show that, once the data has been exported outside the EU, adequate safeguards will be in place with the receiver, namely through the use of contractual clauses binding the same receiver to European data protection standards. In this latter respect, in the year 2001 the Commission adopted two decisions setting up *standard contractual clauses* for the transfer of personal data to third countries (decision 2001/497/EC applies to transfers from data controllers in the EU to data controllers in third countries, while decision 2002/16/EC6 applies to transfers from data controllers in the EU to data processors in third countries[8]).

Moreover, the common practice of national data protection authorities, in the framework of the coordination body "Article 29 Working Party", has developed so called *Binding Corporate Rules*, aimed at limiting the administrative requirements for each individual transfer of data within the same corporate group. In practice, instead of having single contracts among EU and non-EU affiliates of the same group incorporating the above mentioned clauses on data protection, a corporate group may issue a single set of rules or codes of practices based on European data protection standards, and submit such rules to an adequacy review by three national data protection authorities. It is worth mentioning that the data protection reform provides for a simpler clearance process.

3 The Claims Handling Process

As mentioned, major data protection issues may arise when the insurer is processing information not pertaining to the contracting party, but to a different person such as an insured party that is not the policyholder, or a damaged/injured party in civil liability insurance. As a matter of experience, such issues mainly arise in the claims handling and adjusting process. Preliminarily, it might be useful to outline the steps composing such process:

1. The broker (or, less often, the client itself) sends a report, containing preliminary information: loss date, description of the occurrence, individuation of the damaged/injured party, if any; in case of bodily injuries a medical documentation may be attached to the report.
2. Once received, the report is recorded and the insurer registers the loss in a database by inputting the information transmitted by the broker or by the client.
3. A loss adjuster is appointed, and he will acquire further information and documentation from the policyholder, the insured, the injured party and/or his lawyers, or from third parties, to evaluate if a loss actually exists, its root causes and its extent.
4. In case of bodily injury, a medical examination of the injured party will occur, and the insurer will collect the notes and evaluation of the appointed physician.
5. In case of coinsurance, the collected information is shared with co-insurers.

[8] Then amended by Decisions on 27.12.2004 and 5.2.2010.

6. After a comprehensive evaluation of the policy coverage and the loss adjuster's and/or medical examiner's findings, the insurer assess if an indemnity is due and the subsequent amount.

3.1 Dispatching the Loss Report: Is the Broker a Data Controller or a Data Processor?

Data collection and transmission are encompassed in the definition of *processing* set forth in Art. 2 of the Directive, thus triggering the obligations of the data controller under the same Directive, which include information to be provided as detailed in Arts. 10–11 and consent by the data subject acquired.

This leads to two different options: either to consider data collection and transmission by the broker as an autonomous processing of data, different from the one the insurer will carry out once the loss report is received; or, alternatively, to consider the broker's activity as the initial stage of the processing undertaken by the insurer. In the first case, both the broker and the insurer shall be regarded as data controllers, each of them responsible for the respective processing that is carried out; in the second case, the formal appointment of the broker as data processor pursuant to Art. 17.3 would be required.

As seen above, the data controller status arises by operation of law at the time a natural or legal entity starts to process personal data determining the purposes and means of such processing. It is, therefore, the degree of autonomy of the broker in the processing operations, and whether he is processing data for his own purposes, that must be focused on to determine if he is a data controller and thus subject to the main obligations set forth by the Directive, or a mere data processor needing a formal appointment by the insurer.

3.2 Receiving the Loss Report: Data Protection Issues Concerning Third Parties

According to the definition set forth in Art. 2.b of the Directive even mere data collecting shall be regarded as "data processing". Assuming that the issue raised immediately above is solved in the sense of the autonomy of the broker's data processing, the insurer's data processing starts at the moment of receiving the loss report and the relevant documentation.

Right at the time the loss report is received—and not subsequently during the registering process—the Directive requires the insurer to perform two different obligations to lawfully process data pertaining to subjects that are not the policyholder[9]: (i) to give the information; and (ii) if needed, to acquire the data subject's consent. Preliminarily, the insurer ought to identify any *sensitive data*[10] which may be included among the information received.

3.2.1 The Information

According to Arts. 10–11 the data subject shall be preliminary informed on various information listed in the Directive: the identity of the controller, the purposes and modality of the processing, the obligatory or voluntary nature of providing the requested data, the consequences of failure to reply, the entities or categories of entity to whom or which the data may be disclosed, the scope of dissemination (if any) of said data, the existence of the right to access to and the right to rectify the data.

Furthermore, as specified in Art. 11, whenever the personal data are not collected from the data subject, the information shall include the categories of processed data and the same information has to be provided to the data subject at the time of data recording or, if their disclosure to third parties is envisaged, no later than the moment the data are first disclosed.

3.2.2 The Consent of the Data Subject

As a general principle, the processing of personal data shall be regarded as legitimate only if the data subject has "unambiguously" given consent. As such consent is qualified at Art. 2.h as "specific and informed", it should be inferred from the same definition of *consent* that the receipt of the information provided by the data controller pursuant to Arts. 10–11 is a *prius*; hence, if the consent of the data subject is needed, a prompt supply of the information is required, with it not being lawful to postpone the information to the time the data are recorded or at the time of their disclosure to third parties.

According to Art. 7 in specific cases processing might be carried out without the express consent of the data subject; however, none of these cases seem to occur in the claims handling and adjusting process, as it is not necessary:

(a) to comply with a legal obligation imposed by the law, having its source in the insurance contract;
(b) to perform obligations resulting from a contract to *which the data subject is a party*, or else to take steps at the request of the data subject *prior to entering into a contract*: clearly the damaged/injured party (unless identical with the

---

[9] As anticipated above, as far as the policyholder is concerned, it is assumed that such obligations have already been fulfilled at the moment of execution of the policy.

[10] Defined below at 3.2.3.

policyholder) is not party to the insurance contract nor does the case of pre-contract negotiations arise;
(c) to safeguard the life or health of the data subject or third parties;
(d) to establish or defend a legal claim in Court (at least in principle, at the beginning of the adjustment procedure).

The adjusting process may surely be regarded as "necessary to pursue a legitimate interest of the data controller" (i.e. the insurer), but the Directive requires a balancing of such interests with the data subject's fundamental rights and freedoms, which leads to a certain degree of uncertainty regarding the fairness of a processing carried out without consent in the frame of insurance loss adjusting.

3.2.3 "Sensitive" Data

As a general principle, Art. 8 prohibits the processing of data revealing racial or ethnic origin, political opinions, religious or philosophical beliefs, trade unions membership, or information concerning health or sexual orientation.

Considering their nature, the Directive provides particular regulations according to which such sensitive data may be processed with the data subject's consent, but only if, and to the extent to, national implementing laws vest the data subjected with the power to lift the prohibition.

As an example, information related to health may be required when adjusting bodily injuries claims: in this case, the ample discretionary power left to national laws (which is maintained by the proposed Regulation—see Art. 9.2.a) may prove to be a hindrance to the adjusting process, even if the express and explicit consent of the injured person has been acquired.

3.3 Disclosing Data to Other Offices of the Insurance Company and/or to Co-Insurers

The data subject shall be made acquainted with the information mentioned above and of the possible disclosure or transmission of data, and in principle his consent shall be acquired also in this respect. However, such consent would not be required if the transfer of data is necessary for the performance "of a contract concluded *in the interest* of the data subject", as in the case of insurance or co-insurance contracts providing for the adjusting and subsequent compensation of the loss suffered by the insured or by damaged/injured third parties. This is actually one of the derogations set forth by Art. 26 for the transfer of personal data to third countries, but it can be inferred that the same derogation *a fortiori* implicitly applies for intra-EU disclosure or transmission of data.

Moreover, the different branch of the insurer or the co-insurer receiving the relevant data may be regarded as a new data controller, meaning that a second data processing thus begins, subject to the laws of the country where it is carried out.

3.4 Data Inputting in the Insurance Company's Information System

At this stage no particular formality is necessary, but it is worth mentioning that among the principles laid down by the Directive there exists a *data minimisation principle* (see Art. 6.1.c). Under this, only data that are strictly necessary for the achievement of the specific purposes of the data controller (as disclosed to the data subject via the abovementioned information) can be lawfully processed. It would, therefore, be unlawful to process data that are unnecessary or being used for superfluous operations.

3.4.1 Accessible to All Branches of the Insurer in the World?

A procedure whereby—either through proprietary servers, or "in the cloud"—the insurer permits free access to the data stored in its information system to all of its branches in the world, would be improper. Such data would probably be irrelevant or redundant information for the branches not involved in the claim management and adjusting process, thus conflicting with the above mentioned data minimisation principle (which, incidentally, is further strengthened in the proposed Regulation—see Art. 5.c).

3.5 Appointing of Adjuster(s) or Medical Experts

According to Art. 17, data processing operations shall only be performed either by the data controller directly, or by a data processor carrying out the processing on behalf of the controller and on his instructions. In this respect, loss adjusters, medical examiners and technical experts may be better regarded as data processors, than as autonomous data controllers: the opposite solution may lead to a useless duplication of administrative burdens, in terms of information to be given, consents to be acquired, etc.

The appointment by the insurer shall be made either by contract or by a different kind of binding legal act; some issues may arise as to the organizational and technical qualification of the loss adjuster or medical examiner, because they must, *inter-alia,* provide "sufficient guarantees in respect of the technical security measures" (Art. 17.3).

3.6 The Assessment of the Loss and the Right of the Data Subject to Access Documents and Evaluations of the Claims Handling Process

At this stage, the most delicate issue that could come into consideration is the data subject's right to access the claims handling documents and the outcomes of the medical or technical examinations.

Article 12 of the Directive gives the data subject the right to obtain the confirmation whether personal data relevant to him exists, even if such data is not yet registered. In this case, the communication of the same data and of any available information as to their source must be provided.

The problem in this case is to ascertain if this right encompasses also opinions, analysis and evaluations by the claims manager or by the appointed loss adjuster or medical examiner. In other words, if the notion of *data* refers here only to informative content or is extended to evaluative content. Generally, this is an issue that will have to be solved with a case by case approach, taking in to consideration that the right of access of the data subject should be balanced with the right to privacy of the natural or legal persons that expressed such evaluations assuming they would have been kept confidential.[11]

4 Final Remarks

The connection between data protection and insurance practice is relevant, for three main reasons, which are also outlined in the Preamble of the Council of Europe Recommendation on the Protection of Personal Data Collected and Processed for Insurance Purposes:

1. "virtually the entire population of the Member States is affected by one or more insurance contracts and [. . .], for this reason, insurance professionals are in possession of a large volume of personal data, some of which are sensitive";
2. "automated processing of personal data for insurance purposes is increasingly widespread, not only for the preparation, conclusion, implementation and

[11] E.g. according to the Italian Data Protection Authority's decisional practice, the data subject is granted the right to access not only the objective outcomes, but also the evaluation criteria (cf. decisions of June 9th, 1999; September 21st, 1999; May 8th 2002; May 16th, 2002 available in Italian at the Authority's website www.garanteprivacy.it). In the Authority's opinion, "the notion of *personal data* must be referred to any report, information or element with an information content such to import the disclosure of a 'knowledge input' concerning an identified or identifiable subject. This must be referred to both information objectively characterized (capable of verification and objective evaluation) and to opinions, analysis, evaluations, though only referred, in this case, to the present or future disability of a subject" (decision September the 21st, 1999, pp. 6–7).

termination of insurance, but also to facilitate rational and economic management of insurance and to fight against fraud";

3. "the mobility of individuals and the globalisation of markets and commercial activities necessitate a trans-border exchange of information in the insurance sector".[12]

Accordingly, insurers are among the largest data controllers, processing data is a necessity that is present in all areas of the insurance practice, and cross border flows of data is an unavoidable consequence of globalisation.

After more than a decade there has been a prevailing aspect that has changed the scenario: in the age of social networks, big data and "dominant positions" over information, the significance of the insurance sector as "data controller" has considerably diminished. Of course, this does not mean that the amount of personal information collected daily and processed by insurers has become negligible, but it is clear that the European Commission had in mind Facebook and Google, rather than insurance companies, while drafting the proposed regulation.

This is also reflected in the economic costs and benefits assessment of the proposed Regulation, which can be summarized as follows: it is true that the implementation of new and detailed prescriptions will increase operating costs and limit business opportunities, and the introduction of significant fines calculated as percentage of annual worldwide turnover is worrisome, but this is overweighed by the competitive advantage to attract confident users, willing to share personal information.[13]

The reasoning is most likely correct when applied to large internet companies, whose business model is based on extracting value from a constant (and possibly trusted) flow of data, but could be considered at least questionable when applied to certain sector—such as insurance—not based on the direct economic exploitation of personal information.

Reference

Benet SC (2012) The *Right to be Forgotten*: reconciling EU and US perspectives. Berkley J Int L 30:161

[12] Recommendation No. R (2002) 9 on the protection of personal data collected and processed for insurance purposes, Adopted by the Committee of Ministers on 18 September 2002, respectively recitals 6, 3 and 8.

[13] See Commission's Communication, quoted at 2, *passim* and Mantelero, "Competitive Value of Data Protection: the Impact of Data Protection Regulation on Online Behavior", *Int. Data Privacy Law*, 2013.

Requirements for Privacy and Protection of Consumer Information in the U.S.: *Implications for the Insurance Industry*

Theodore P. Augustinos

Contents

Abstract The legal and regulatory landscape for maintaining the privacy and protection of consumer information in the United States is complicated, adding costs and risks that impose a challenge for any company, with particular implications for the insurance industry. The complications result from various factors. First, in the U.S. legal and regulatory requirements related to the privacy and protection of consumer information are imposed, often differently, at both the federal and state level, with the states often differing among themselves. Second, some of these laws and regulations apply to information based on its nature, such as

T.P. Augustinos (✉)
Locke Lord LLP, Hartford, CT, USA
e-mail: Ted.Augustinos@lockelord.com

P. Marano et al. (eds.), *The "Dematerialized" Insurance*,
DOI 10.1007/978-3-319-28410-1_11

Social Security numbers or health and medical information. In contract, other laws and regulations create obligations based on the nature of the activity that gave rise to the data, such as online behavior or video viewing practices. In addition, some of the laws and regulations are industry specific, imposing different standards and requirements based on the industry of the entity collecting the data. All of this has implications for the insurance industry, as insurers, producers and others seek to address their own obligations, devise insurance products to meet the growing need for coverage of the related risks of their insureds, and address claims that may be made under policies that may never have been intended to cover the risks related to the privacy and protection of consumer information.

This chapter will provide an overview of the U.S. legal and regulatory regime for protecting consumer information, and consider the particular implications for the insurance industry.

1 Introduction to the U.S. Legal and Regulatory Regime for Protecting Consumer Information and Privacy and Its Implications for the Insurance Industry

The implications of the requirements and trends related to the protection of consumer information and privacy in the U.S. have had a significant effect on the insurance industry, both as an industry comprised of insurers, agents, brokers, adjustors and others that are subject to these same requirements and trends, and as an industry that assumes the privacy and data security risks of others. As described below, sometimes this assumption of risk is intentional, and the industry is challenged to underwrite and price these risks in a changing legal, regulatory, and litigation environment. In other cases, however, the insurance industry may be assuming unintended risks, which were not priced into policies that were not originally intended to cover losses from evolving privacy and data security exposures. These exposures are often, and often inaccurately, referred to as "cyber" risks, and the term will be used sparingly in this chapter for reasons described below.

In the United States, protection of the confidentiality, privacy, and security of certain types of consumer information is required by various statutory and regulatory regimes, and developing case law, at both federal and state levels. Some of the requirements and restrictions are industry-specific, applying to companies in the healthcare or financial services industries, for example; others apply more generally to particular types of information regardless of the industry of the company collecting it. Today, there is a myriad of federal and state requirements, with nearly all U.S. jurisdictions having adopted laws generally focused on protecting the privacy and security of the personal information of consumers.[1] Overlap, and sometimes inconsistency, among these laws and regulations between federal and state, and among the various states, adds cost and complexity to compliance with the U.S. regulatory scheme.

The U.S. approach to protecting consumer information and privacy, at both the federal and state level, focuses on (1) restrictions on collection; (2) restrictions on use and disclosure; (3) requirements to protect against loss, unauthorized access or misuse; (4) requirements to disclose practices for data collection, use and sharing; and (5) requirements for notification in the event of exposure of certain consumer information. Unlike the EU and other jurisdictions, the U.S. approach does not restrict or inhibit the transfer of data, provided that these restrictions and requirements are satisfied.

The healthcare industry is an example of an industry with relatively robust requirements for the privacy and protection of certain health and medical information in the U.S. Financial institutions (broadly defined to include banks, credit unions, mortgage brokers, insurance companies, securities firms, pawn brokers, and some auto dealers, among others) are also subject to specific industry-focused privacy and data security requirements. Even among financial institutions, banks, insurance companies and producers and others have their own, specific requirements.

In addition, under federal law, disclosure of information concerning an individual's credit or credit-worthiness, when collected by a creditor or credit reporting agency is subject to restrictions against unauthorized disclosure. U.S. federal law also provides student inspection rights and protects the privacy and security of educational records collected by schools or other educational institutions that receive funds under a U.S. Department of Education program.[2] Information collected on-line concerning minors, geographical location, online behavior, records or rentals and viewing of videographic information such as movies and videos are also afforded federal legal protections.

At the state level, there are various industry-specific requirements as well, affecting typically the financial services and healthcare industries. These requirements are different from, and in addition to, the general statutory requirements in each state for protection of certain types of personal information, such as Social Security numbers.

In comparing, and attempting to comply with, various privacy and data security requirements in the United States and other countries, it is important to note that many other countries are more restrictive than the U.S. in defining the permissible

[1] For convenience, these laws are referred to in this chapter as "privacy laws" or "data protection laws." They may restrict the collection, use, or disclosure of certain information, or set forth affirmative security requirements for its protection against loss, or unauthorized access, or acquisition.

[2] Citations are provided where these laws are discussed below.

uses and disclosures of consumer data. For example, in some other countries, the range of protected consumer data includes even simple name, email address and other basic identifiers. The ability to use, sell or even transfer such information across borders can be tightly restricted in many countries including the European Union, and may require explicit consumer consent.

In the United States, however, most federal and state privacy and data security laws typically apply to a more narrowly defined set of data, such as name together with Social Security number, driver's license number or financial account number, and in some cases medical or health information, commonly referred to as personal information or personally identifiable information, and abbreviated PI or PII (herein referred to as "PI"). Companies that collect such data from consumers, including their customers, in the U.S. typically have considerable flexibility in using or disclosing such data, depending on their privacy policies and terms of use.

On the other hand, if the privacy or security of PI is compromised, the U.S. (at both the federal and state levels) imposes a highly onerous and expensive set of notification requirements. Most other countries do not have comparable requirements, but some have been moving toward breach notification requirements that are more similar to those in the U.S., requiring that each affected individual, as well as governmental agencies in many cases, receive notification of an event compromising the confidentiality or security of personal information.

Another important source of protection of consumer information is found in the contractual requirements of the payment card industry, which are also discussed below.

The format of consumer information is also relevant to compliance obligations. While most U.S. laws and regulations apply to data in electronic format, some also cover paper records. For example, most data breach notification laws in the U.S. apply only to electronic records, but the federal requirements protecting healthcare data apply to certain health and medical information in any medium.

A recent trend in the U.S. is to extend privacy and security protections to consumer data that is not specifically afforded such protection under the U.S. legal and regulatory regime, based on the activity that generated the data. For example, the collection and use of information concerning certain consumer behaviors and activities, such as online activity, video rental, and other information, may be subjected to various requirements and restrictions even though the underlying information itself may not generally be considered particularly sensitive. This trend, which may extend to consumer name, income level, shopping and purchasing patterns and other information, is further discussed below.

Finally, it should be noted that federal and state regulatory agencies, and class action lawyers, have been increasingly active in pursuing companies that have experienced a breach of privacy or data security. The numbers of enforcement actions, and the amounts of settlements, have increased in recent years, as the Federal Trade Commission, the Department of Health and Human Services, the Financial Industry Regulatory Authority, state attorneys general and various other state agencies have all pursued enforcement actions against companies (including insurance companies), charging inadequate protections and safeguards. Class action lawsuits have also been brought under a variety of theories. A discussion of these actions is outside the scope of this chapter, but must be considered in weighing the costs and risks of compliance with U.S. requirements.[3]

As noted above, similar to companies in any industry, insurance companies are exposed to costs and risks related to their collection of data from and about individuals, including an insurance company's policyholders, claimants, employees, producers and others. Unlike companies in most other industries, however, insurers may also have indirect exposure to these costs and risks. Indirect exposure of insurance companies occurs where an insured makes a claim under a policy that may be implicated in privacy and data security incidents, whether or not the policy was intended to cover such incidents, as discussed in Sect. 8 below.

This chapter reviews the various sources of privacy and data security exposures under U.S. law, and considers developments in the insurance markets as they attempt to address them.

2 Types of Consumer Information Subject to Protection in the U.S.

2.1 *Financial Information*

Most privacy and data security requirements in the U.S. apply to financial information. The Gramm-Leach-Bliley Act of 1999 (the "GLBA") provides federal protection for "nonpublic personal information," defined to mean personally identifiable financial information (1) provided by a consumer to financial institutions; (2) resulting from any transaction with the customer or any service performed for the consumer; or (3) otherwise obtained by the financial institution, with exceptions for publicly available information.[4] For this purpose, "financial institution" is defined by the GLBA to include insurance companies.[5] The GLBA requirements and restrictions are the subject of regulations promulgated by the Consumer

[3] Information on regulatory enforcement actions related to privacy and data security incidents may be obtained directly from government websites such as www.ftc.gov/enforcement (for actions by the Federal Trade Commission), and www.hhs.gov/ocr/privacy/hipaa/enforcement (for actions by the Department of Health and Human Services). While readily available papers and studies consider and discuss litigation risks and related costs, "the first comprehensive empirical study of data breach litigation" was recently published. Romanosky et al. (2014), p. 74–104.

[4] 15 U.S.C. § 6801 *et seq.*

[5] 15 U.S.C. § 6809(3). All insurance companies that collect nonpublic personal information from consumers as insureds must comply with the requirements of state regulations adopted pursuant to the GLBA. In addition, to the extent that insureds are financial institutions, such as banks, securities firms and others, insurance companies issuing the various coverages described in Sec. 8 below may also be exposed to their privacy and data security risks with respect to nonpublic personal information as well.

Financial Protection Bureau, the Securities and Exchange Commission, the Federal Trade Commission, and state insurance departments, each with authority over institutions subject to its jurisdiction. Other industries also have specific requirements.

When a financial institution establishes a relationship with a consumer (including as an applicant for services or products, such as an insurance policy, where the consumer never becomes a customer), the institution must provide the consumer with written notice of its policy governing the collection and use of nonpublic personal information, and must provide customers (*i.e.*, consumers that do enter into a customer relationship with the institution, such as a policyholder) with privacy notices thereafter.[6] If the financial institution intends to disclose such information to an unaffiliated third party other than to perform functions on behalf of the financial institution, then the financial institution must provide the consumer with the right to opt out of such disclosure.[7] In addition, in furtherance of the GLBA privacy requirements, the GLBA requires financial institutions to establish appropriate security safeguards.[8] As a result, the value to insurance companies and producers of the vast array of data they collect is impinged; it cannot be used for other purposes or disclosed to other parties without providing the applicant with the opportunity to opt out of the sharing of information.

Specific to the insurance industry, the National Association of Insurance Commissioners ("NAIC") promulgated and model privacy statute, and model privacy and security regulations to guide the adoption of state insurance laws and regulations pursuant to federal law designed to protect the privacy and security of nonpublic personal information collected from or about individuals by both life and health and property-casualty insurers.[9] Pursuant to the NAIC model regulations, or similar regulations, which have been adopted by the various states, insurance companies must, among other requirements, provide privacy notices disclosing their collection and use of personally identifiable financial, health, and medical information.[10] To avoid duplication and additional cost, licensees such as insurance agents can generally rely on the privacy notices of the insurance companies, if their only use of the information is restricted to their actions on behalf of the insurance companies.[11] If a producer uses the individual's information for any other purpose, or offers other products and services, then the producer would be required

[6] 15 U.S.C. § 6803; *See* NAIC Privacy of Consumer Financial and Health Information Regulation 672 §4.I (Jan. 2003).

[7] 15 U.S.C. § 6802.

[8] 15 U.S.C. § 6801.

[9] NAIC Insurance Information and Privacy Protection Model Act 670 (October 1992); NAIC Standards for Safeguarding Customer Information Model Regulation 673 (April 2002); NAIC Privacy of Consumer Financial and Health Information Regulation 672 (Jan. 2003).

[10] NAIC Privacy of Consumer Financial and Health Information Regulation 672, Sections 5 and 6 (Jan. 2003).

[11] *Id.* at Section 4a.

to comply with the privacy requirements, including the requirement to prepare and distribute privacy notices to individuals. Id.

Licensees such as claims adjusters, third party administrators and others acting on behalf of the insurer would not be independently considered to be subject to these requirements if the disclosure by the insurance company to these licensees is for the limited purposes provided in the exceptions from the notice requirement, including servicing a claim.[12] Insurance companies must contractually require such third parties to comply with the same restrictions that apply to the insurance company. Therefore, claims information should be made available as needed by the adjuster, third party administrator or other third party, only to the extent necessary to fulfill a function on behalf of the insurer, and only where contractual provisions and other safeguards are in place to maintain the protection of the data when in the possession of the third party.[13]

The Fair Credit Reporting Act protects the privacy of consumer credit reports, as discussed in Sect. 3.5 below, and provides consumers certain controls over the content and dissemination of such reports.

At the state level as well, most privacy and data security laws, regulations and other formal and informal regulatory issuances are focused on the protection of individuals' financial information, such as Social Security numbers, financial account numbers, and government issued identification numbers.[14] Unlike the GLBA, however, most of these state privacy and data protection requirements address data security, but not privacy. Also unlike the GLBA, these requirements apply to any company in any industry, thereby including insurance companies and other financial institutions, as well as companies in any other industry.

For example, states generally do not restrict the ability of a company to use, sell or transfer data collected from consumers, with some exceptions for particularly sensitive data, such as Social Security numbers and health information, so long as the consumer receives adequate notice of the data collector's practices.[15] Some states such as Massachusetts require a variety of data security protections, and all but three states[16] require notifications to affected individuals in the event of a compromise of security of state residents' personal information. In addition to

[12] Id at Sec. 16.

[13] Workers' compensation is an area that presents particular challenges, as some laws provide that the employer, as policyholder, has access to certain data about claims by their employees that can seem to conflict with other laws generally protecting medical and health information (as discussed below). These laws vary from state to state, and must be considered carefully by workers' compensation insurers when responding to a request for disclosure of personally identifiable claims information. *See, e.g.*, Cal. Lab. Code § 3762.

[14] Credit card information is also subject to PCI-DSS, as further discussed below.

[15] Pursuant to the GLBA, states may afford persons greater protection, but cannot adopt otherwise inconsistent requirements for privacy and security of nonpublic personal information. 15 U.S.C. § 6807.

[16] As of May 2015, the states that do not yet have such notification laws are Alabama, New Mexico and South Dakota.

individual notifications, approximately one-third of U.S. states also require notification to one or more state agencies, most commonly the Attorney General's office, in the event of a breach exposing personal information of state residents.

Some states also impose industry-specific requirements. In Connecticut, for example, the Insurance Department issued a bulletin dated August 18, 2010 requiring licensees to report to the Department any information security incident within five calendar days.[17] Similarly, the California Department of Public Health requires its licensees to notify the Department and affected patients regarding unlawful or unauthorized access, use, or disclosure of patient medical information within five business days of discovery.[18]

Individual and agency notices required by both general and industry-specific add significant, usually insurable, costs to the U.S. privacy and data security regime, as further discussed in Sect. 8 below.

New York law requires safeguards necessary or appropriate to preclude unauthorized access to, and protect confidentiality of, Social Security numbers,[19] and the Massachusetts data security regulation has a fully developed set of requirements, including, among other requirements, encryption of mobile devices containing PI, and of wireless transmission of PI.[20] Massachusetts and certain other states also require, for example, that companies transferring and/or disclosing PI of state residents to third party service providers: (1) take reasonable steps to select and retain third-party service providers that are capable of maintaining appropriate security measures to protect PI; and/or (2) require by contract that third party service providers to whom the Company transfers the PI of state residents implement and maintain security measures to protect such information.[21]

In addition, Connecticut, Michigan, New Mexico and Texas require companies collecting Social Security numbers to develop policies satisfying specific content requirements regarding their collection, retention, storage and disclosure of Social Security numbers. Specific content and publication requirements vary. For example, Michigan requires that such privacy policies be "published in an employee handbook, procedures manual, or similar document," while Connecticut requires that they be "published or publicly displayed."[22] Many states also have laws restricting the following: disclosing another's Social Security number to the general public; printing another person's Social Security number on a card required for employee to access work related information; requiring an employee to use his or

[17] Connecticut Insurance Department Bulletin IC-25, August 18, 2010.

[18] Cal. Health Safety Code § 1280.15.

[19] N.Y. Gen. Bus. Law § 399-ddd.

[20] 201 Mass. Code Regs. 17.00 *et seq.*

[21] Cal. Civ. Code § 1798.81.5; Md. Comm. Code § 14-3503; Mass. Gen. Laws Ch. 93H, § 2(a); 201 Mass. Code Regs. 17.00 et seq.; Nev. Rev. Stat. 603A.210; Or. Rev. Stat. § 646A.622; R.I. Gen. Laws § 11-49.2-2(3).

[22] Mich. Comp. Laws § 445.84; N.M. Stat. § 57-12B-3; Conn. Gen. Stat. § 42-471.

her Social Security number to access the employer's website; and printing an individual's Social Security number on material to be mailed to the individual.

An important subset of financial information is credit card data, including credit card number, with or without cardholder name, expiration date and security code. Payment card data is typically subject to the U.S. federal and state data protection and breach notification laws that apply to financial information generally, and also to the Payment Card Industry Data Security Standard ("PCI-DSS"), which are contractually imposed by the payment card industry on merchants that accept credit card transactions. PCI-DSS has also been incorporated into state law in Minnesota, Nevada and Washington.[23] PCI-DSS imposes an onerous set of restrictions and obligations on merchants, credit card processors and merchant banks that collect, use and store data from customer payment cards.

In the U.S., several large retailers disclosed that hackers stole credit card, debit card and other personal data during a critical three week period of the 2013 holiday shopping season, potentially affecting more than 100 million customers. The breach, which may not have indicated any failure to comply with PCI-DSS or applicable legal requirements, appears to have involved a breach of security at point of sale, in real time, as transactions were processed. By December 30, 2013, two U.S. Senators had called for hearings to consider whether current standards for protecting customer payment card data are adequate.

2.2 *Identification and Credentials*

In the U.S., a consumer's name alone is generally not subject to privacy and data security protections at either the federal or state level. There are nuances, however, where the name is linked to certain healthcare providers that may indicate a medical condition or treatment, and pursuant to CalOPPA and FERPA, as further discussed below.

In addition, credentials are generally not the subject of federal and state laws, unless they may be used to provide access to a financial account. One notable exception to this rule is a recent amendment to California's breach notification statutes effective January 1, 2014, which extends notification requirements to the breach of California residents' online account credentials.[24] Florida followed suit, enacting a similar amendment effective July 1, 2014,[25] and other states may soon

[23] Minn. Stat. § 325E.64 (Prohibiting retention of certain card data); Nev. Rev. Stat. § 603A.215; Wash. Rev. Code § 19.255.020.

[24] Effective January 1, 2014, SB 46 expands the definition of "personal information" in California's breach notification statutes applicable to businesses (Cal. Civ. Code § 1798.82) and government agencies (Cal. Civ. Code § 1798.29) to include "user name or email address, in combination with a password or security question and answer that would permit access to an online account."

[25] Fla. Stat. § 817.5681.

follow as well, as they did after California enacted the first U.S. breach notification statute in 2003.[26]

Against this backdrop, the events involving Epsilon in 2011 were particularly interesting.[27] As the world's largest email vendor providing email marketing and communications services to some of the largest financial institutions, securities firms, retailers, and other firms, Epsilon maintained a large database of customer names and email addresses. Epsilon discovered that its database had been hacked by attackers who stole email addresses of tens of millions of customers of approximately 75 companies. Although no U.S. laws would have required notifications to affected individuals or governmental agencies in the event of a compromise of name and email addresses, Epsilon and its financial institution clients notified affected individuals of the event. Undoubtedly, the notifications were provided as a risk mitigation measure, to enable customers to protect themselves against potential phishing attacks. This case is an important illustration of the fact that compliance with minimum legal requirements may not always be the only objective in making decisions concerning privacy and data security of customer information.

In a similar case, in 2012, Twitter account details were stolen by hackers and posted online. Unlike Epsilon, in the Twitter incident, customer usernames and passwords to Twitter accounts were also exposed. While these passwords were not passwords to customer financial accounts, many individuals use the same username and password for multiple different accounts, making credentials, even for Twitter or other seemingly harmless applications, sensitive from a risk mitigation standpoint.

Several states including California, Delaware, Illinois, Maryland, Michigan and New Jersey have recently enacted legislation regulating access by employers and/or educational institutions to individuals' social media accounts. For example, effective January 1, 2013, California law restricts companies from requesting or requiring that current or potential employees provide their social media account login credentials, access personal social media in the presence of the employer, or divulge any personal social media.[28] California law also imposes similar restrictions on public and private colleges and universities located in the state with regard to social media of current or potential students,[29] and requires that private colleges and universities post their social media privacy policies on the college or university's website.[30] Such restrictions are subject to limited exceptions, such as where social media is reasonably believed to be relevant to an investigation of allegations of employee misconduct, so long as the social media is used solely for purposes of that investigation or related proceedings.[31]

---

[26] Within a few years, 45 other states adopted breach notice requirements modeled in varying degrees on California's.

[27] *See*, http://krebsonsecurity.com/2011/04/epsilon-breach-raises-specter-of-spear-phishing.

[28] Cal. Lab. Code § 980.

[29] Cal. Educ. Code § 99120.

[30] Cal. Educ. Code § 99122.

[31] *See, e.g.*, Cal. Lab. Code § 980(c).

2.3 Health and Medical Information

Health and medical information is considered highly sensitive, due to its private nature. In addition, the ramifications of thefts of health insurance account information can be life-threatening if a person obtains medical treatment using stolen insurance and the medical records of the actual patient are changed to reflect the medical condition of the thief. Consequently, U.S. federal and state laws have been enacted to address these concerns.

The Health Insurance Portability and Accountability Act of 1996 ("HIPAA")[32] and standards and regulations issued thereunder by the U.S. Department of Health and Human Services ("HHS") impose privacy, data security, and breach notification requirements on health plans, healthcare clearinghouses, and any healthcare provider engaged in electronic data interchange using one or more of the "standard transactions" as defined by HIPAA (collectively referred to as "covered entities"). These requirements also apply to business associates of covered entities. Therefore, health insurers, health care clearinghouses, and most healthcare providers (*e.g.* hospitals, nursing homes, home care providers, clinics and doctor's offices) in the U.S. that transmit protected health information ("PHI")[33] in electronic form in connection with the standard transactions are subject to these requirements as covered entities. Persons and entities that perform certain functions or activities that involve the use of or disclosure of protected health information on behalf of, or provide services to, such covered entities may be deemed "business associates" and thus also subject to such requirements in their own right. Common examples of business associates include medical billing companies and medical transcription companies, but even law firms and other service providers can be business associates.

It is important to note that while life, liability, and workers' compensation insurers also collect health and medical information from insureds, claimants and others (including their own employees), they are not covered entities under HIPAA. Health and medical information they collect from insureds and claimants is, however, subject to protections under the NAIC model privacy regulation and model security regulation discussed above.

Pursuant to HIPAA, HHS adopted Standards for Privacy of Individually Identifiable Health Information (the "Privacy Rule"), which govern the use and disclosure of an individual's PHI by covered entities and their business associates.[34] The

[32] 42 U.S.C. § 201 *et seq.*

[33] "Protected Health Information" is defined to by HIPAA to include information created or received by a health care provider, health plan, employer or health care clearinghouse that relates to the past, present or future health of an individual, the provision of health care to the individual, or payment for the provision of health care to the individual, and which could be used to identify the individual. It does not include information protected by the Federal Educational Rights and Privacy Act, or health information held by an employer in its capacity as an employer.

[34] Business associates are subject to the Privacy Rule pursuant to the HITECH Act.

Privacy Rule applies to PHI in all forms, *i.e.*, electronic form, on paper, and orally disclosed. The Privacy Rule also establishes and requires disclosure of an individual's right to understand and control the use of his or her PHI. Federal and state requirements for privacy of financial information discussed above do not require mitigation in the event of a compromise of privacy or data security, other than notification to affected individuals under certain circumstances. In contrast, the Privacy Rule requires that covered entities and business associates mitigate, to the extent practicable, any harmful effect that is caused by an improper disclosure of PHI of which it becomes aware.

HHS also adopted a Security Rule,[35] which is designed to protect the confidentiality and security of PHI in electronic form ("ePHI"). The Security Rule sets forth standards for securing the storage and transmission of ePHI, including administrative safeguards (*i.e.*, written policies and procedures, and business associate agreements), physical safeguards (*i.e.*, limitations on physical access to systems containing ePHI), and technical safeguards (*i.e.*, protective controls for information systems and networks).

In addition, state laws may also apply to health and medical information, and there are specific statutes that protect the privacy and confidentiality of particular types of health information, such as HIV/AIDS test results and mental health records,[36] as well as state statutes requiring notification to affected individuals, and in some cases state governmental agencies, in the event of exposure of medical information.[37] These state laws may apply to any business, and are not limited to covered entities as defined by HIPAA. Therefore, all insurance companies and their commercial insureds are typically subject to these statutes.

2.4 Employment Information

Employers, including insurance companies as well as their commercial insureds, collect and maintain a myriad of data of their employees, and of applicants for employment. Typically, prospective employers collect identifying information of new employees, such as driver's license and Social Security numbers, for identity verification, background checks, and payroll. Employees often also provide employers with bank account information for purposes of direct deposit, and potentially health related information when an employee takes a sick day, period of disability, or maternity leave. All of these types of information in the

[35] 45 C.F.R. Part 160 and Part 164, Subparts A and C.

[36] *See, e.g.*, Cal. Civ. Code §§ 56,101 and 56.36 (Confidentiality of Medical Information Act); Cal. Health Safety Code § 120980 (providing for civil penalties in the event of negligent disclosure of HIV test results); Cal. Welfare & Inst. Code §§ 5238; 5330 (The Lanterman-Petris-Short Act, which mandates that information about and records of recipients of mental health services shall be kept confidential and may only be disclosed in certain enumerated circumstances).

[37] *See, e.g.*, Cal. Health Safety Code § 1280.15.

employment context are covered by protections focused on the information itself, and not on the employment relationship. The Fair Credit Reporting Act ("FCRA") can, however, be a source of particular concern in the employment context, as further described below in Sect. 3.5.

Companies that provide health insurance to employees through a self-insured health plan are regulated as covered entities under HIPAA with respect to PHI collected or maintained in connection with the self-insured health plan. It is important to distinguish between health related information maintained by the employer in connection with its self-insured health plan, which is subject to HIPAA, and health information otherwise maintained the employer, such as in its human resources department or function, which is not subject to HIPAA.

Certain states impose notice or consent requirements relating to disclosure of employee records.[38] In addition, certain states require that a private employer maintain the confidentiality of all information relating to an employee's leave of absence relating to domestic violence, and prohibit disclosure of such information except under specified circumstances.[39]

2.5 Educational Records

Another sector-focused set of privacy protections applies to most U.S. educational institutions. The Family Educational Rights and Privacy Act ("FERPA") applies to any institution that provides educational services or instruction and receives funds under any program administered by the U.S. Department of Education (the "DOE").[40] Subject to certain limited exceptions, FERPA gives students (or in some cases their parents) the right to inspect and challenge the accuracy of a student's own education records, while prohibiting schools from disclosing those records, or any personally identifiable information about a student contained in those records, without the consent of the student or, in the case of a minor, the student's parent. FERPA, and the DOE rules promulgated thereunder, define "Personally Identifiable Information" ("PII") to include the name of the student

[38] *See, e.g.*, Conn. Gen. Stat. § 31-128f (Restricts employer disclosure of individually identifiable information contained in the personnel file or medical records of any employee to any person or entity not employed by or affiliated with the employer without the employee's written authorization, subject to certain exceptions, *e.g.*, disclosure of records to a "third party that maintains or prepares employment records or performs other employment-related services for the employer"); 820 Ill. Comp. Stat. 40/7 (Providing that "an employer or former employer shall not divulge a disciplinary report, letter of reprimand, or other disciplinary action to a third party, to a party who is not a part of the employer's organization, or to a party who is not a part of a labor organization representing the employee, without written notice..."); see also, Mich. Comp. Laws § 423.506.

[39] *See, e.g.*, Fla. Stat. § 741.313; Haw. Rev. Stat. § 378-71; 820 Ill. Comp. Stat. 180/20; Kan. Stat. Ann. § 44-1132; Wash. Rev. Code Ann. § 49.76.040.

[40] 20 U.S.C. §1232g; 34 C.F.R. Part 99.

or the student's family members; the address of the student or the student's family; a personal identifier of the student, such as a Social Security number, student ID number or biometric record; indirect identifiers such as a student's date or place of birth, or mother's maiden name; and other information that could reasonably identify a student.[41] Certain information published in student directories is exempt from the restrictions against disclosures of PII, provided the student (if over 18, or otherwise the student's guardian) is provided proper disclosure and an opportunity to opt out.

Amendments to FERPA in 2011 expanded permissible disclosures of PII for audits, evaluations and studies, so long as appropriate safeguards, including third party agreements, are in place.[42] The 2011 amendments also clarify that the FERPA privacy requirements may be enforced against state agencies and third party contractors that receive educational records, even though they do not receive direct DOE funding.

3 Types of Activities Subject to Privacy Protections

3.1 Online Behavior Generally

The growth of digital advertising globally, and in the U.S. in particular, has raised concerns by legislators, regulators and litigators related to targeted advertising and the collection of data concerning consumer behavior online and using mobile devices. There have been a number of "Do Not Track" legislative proposals at the federal and state levels, but with the exception of protections aimed at children, and an amendment to a California law effective January 1, 2014, none has been enacted.

The Federal Trade Commission (the "FTC") has taken recent positions, including in a Final Report released in March 2012, concerning online behavioral advertising targeted to consumers based on their identifiable search histories, web pages visited, online purchases made, and content viewed.[43] In 2011, the FTC announced consent orders settling enforcement actions against three companies, alleging that they engaged in deceptive practices in violation of the FTC Act due to the delivery of online behavioral advertising without having first obtained customer consent. One such action, against Google, resulted in a $22.5 million fine.[44]

[41] 34 C.F.R. § 99.3.

[42] 76 Fed. Reg. 75604–60.

[43] Protecting Consumer Privacy in an Era of Rapid Change: A Proposed Framework for Businesses and Policymakers, Mar. 2012, available at: http://www.ftc.gov/reports/protecting-consumer-privacy-era-rapid-change-recommendations-businesses-policymakers.

[44] *See* http://www.ftc.gov/enforcement/cases-and-proceedings/cases/2012/11/google-inc.

In addition, plaintiffs are claiming violations of a right to privacy, among other allegations, related to tracking online behavior and use of mobile devices. Typically, these class actions have alleged violations of the Electronic Communications Privacy Act ("ECPA") and the Computer Fraud and Abuse Act ("CFAA"), as well as various state laws. Collection of data concerning online behavior without consent is prohibited under the ECPA. So far, click-through privacy policies have been successful in defeating such claims so long as the policy discloses tracking and data collection practices.[45] The CFAA prohibits tracking and collecting information online behavior that results in losses of at least $5000, but claims based on CFAA have been successfully defended to date.[46] Class actions have also been filed relying on other statutes, including the Video Privacy Protection Act, which is discussed below.

The California Online Privacy Protection Act ("CalOPPA") requires online services that collect personally identifiable information (defined broadly) through the Internet about California consumers to conspicuously post a privacy policy satisfying specific content and format requirements.[47] As of January 1, 2014, an amendment to CalOPPA expanded content requirements to include disclosure of how the operator of the online service responds to "Do Not Track" signals or other mechanisms giving consumers the ability to choose whether to permit collection of online tracking information.[48] Additionally, online service operators must now also disclose whether parties other than the operator may collect personally identifiable information about an individual consumer's online activities over time and across different Web sites when the consumer uses the operator's site or service.[49]

As the appetite and technical capabilities for tracking online behavior increase, the risks that can result in insurance claims, arising from enforcement actions and plaintiffs' litigation, also continue to increase. Further, insurance companies may have direct exposures related to their own online data collection practices.

---

[45] *See e.g.*, *Mortensen v. Bresnan Communications LLC*, 1:10-cv-00013 (D. Montana) (Dec. 2010 Order, Dkt. 30 at p. 12, dismissing plaintiffs' class action allegations based on the federal ECPA on grounds that Bresnan's privacy disclosures disclosed its collection and tracking of user "browsing behavior" and concluding that by using "... Bresnan's Internet Service, ... [plaintiffs] gave or acquiesced their consent to such interception"); and *In re Facebook Privacy Litigation* (N. D. Cal.) (on May 12, 2011, dismissing the plaintiffs' ECPA claims with leave to amend); and *In re Facebook Privacy Litigation* (N.D. Cal. Nov. 22, 2011) (dismissing the plaintiffs' claims with prejudice on the ground, among other things, that no harm had been shown).

[46] *See e.g.*, *In LaCourt v. Specific Media, Inc.*, 2011 WL 1661532 (C.D. Cal. Apr. 28, 2011), the court held that plaintiffs failed to allege economic harm as required by the CFAA. Similarly, in *Bose v. Interclick; McDonald's USA, LLC; McDonald's Corporation; CBS Corporation; Mazda Motor of America, Inc. and Microsoft Corporation*, Case No. 1:10-cv-9183 (S.D.N.Y. Aug. 2011), the court dismissed with prejudice the plaintiff's claims of alleged violations of the CFAA for failure to allege harm. *See* Order, Dkt. 36 dated Aug. 17, 2011.

[47] Cal. Bus. & Prof. Code 22575-22579.

[48] *Id.*

[49] *Id.*

3.2 *Children's Online Behavior*

The online and mobile collection and use of personal information concerning children under the age of 13 years is regulated by the Children's Online Privacy Protection Act of 1998 ("COPPA"), and the rules promulgated by the FTC thereunder.[50] Effective July 1, 2013, a new FTC rule expressed a change of course by recognizing that COPPA is aimed at protecting children from inappropriate contact without parental knowledge, rather than preventing advertising to children.[51] Under the new rule, collection, use and disclosure of personal information of children under age 13 requires notice to parents and verifiable consent. Such information must also be kept secure, and operators are prohibited from conditioning participation and activities (such as games) on the collection of information that is not reasonably necessary for participation in the activity. For this purpose, the definition of personal information was expanded to include most persistent identifiers, geo location information, photographs and videos of children. While insurance is not marketed to children, the marketing activities of insureds may create exposures under policy provisions described in Sect. 8 below.

3.3 *Marketing Contacts*

Whether the interaction is online or at bricks and mortar locations, retailers, financial and other service providers (including insurers), and all other business enterprises must have policies in place to address the collection and use of marketing contacts, and must remain vigilant in tracking legal, regulatory and case law developments in this area. The collection of seemingly innocuous, even publicly available data, can be subject to restrictions and requirements that apply to marketing contacts.

In California, for example, the Song-Beverly Credit Card Act[52] prohibits businesses from requesting and recording "personal identification information" during a credit card transaction. While personal identification information is defined in the statute to include the individual's address, the California Supreme Court held in 2011 that ZIP code constitutes an individual's address for this purpose.[53] The decision noted the legislative intent to restrict the ability of retailers to collect

---

[50] 15 U.S.C. §§6501-6506; 16 C.F.R. Part 312.

[51] 16 C.F.R. Part 312; 78 Fed. Reg. 3972, January 17, 2013.

[52] Cal. Civ. Code §1747.08(b).

[53] *Pineda v. Williams Sonoma Stores, Inc.*, 51 Cal. 4th 524 (Ca. 2011).; also available at http://www.courtinfo.ca.gov/opinions/documents/S178241.PDF. *See* Edwards Wildman Palmer LLP Client Advisory, *California Supreme Court's ZIP Code Decision Exposes Retailers to New Litigation Hazard, Statutory Fines,* Apr. 2011, http://www.edwardswildman.com/files/upload/CA_Sup_Ct_ZIP.pdf.

information unnecessary to the transaction itself to restrict the retailer from marketing to the customer, or selling marketing lists to others. Given that search tools can find a person's address with name and ZIP code, the court construed the statute to cover ZIP code as well as a person's full address.[54]

Under a statute different from the California Song-Beverly Credit Card Act, the Supreme Judicial Court of Massachusetts reached a similar result, prohibiting retailers from collecting ZIP codes from customers at the time of credit card transactions to safeguard customer privacy against unwanted marketing activities.[55]

Also in California, the "Shine the Light Law"[56] requires businesses to disclose to customers upon request how their information has been shared with third parties. Alternatively, the business can permit the customer to opt out of third party sharing.

It is widely expected that through new statutes in various states, and through case law developments interpreting existing statutes, simple marketing contacts will increasingly be subjected to privacy requirements. These requirements will both limit the collection and use, and mandate the confidentiality and security, of such information.

3.4 *Video Viewing History*

The Video Privacy Protection Act (the "VPPA") is a federal statute that was enacted to protect customers' video viewing history, following attempts to embarrass a nominee to the U.S. Supreme Court based on his selection of movie rentals. Since then, the reach of the VPPA's privacy provisions has been extended by courts in various class actions to include online video viewing history.[57]

3.5 *Background Checking and Other Employment Issues*

Under the Fair Credit Reporting Act ("FCRA"), consumer credit reports can be used (with applicant or employee consent) for employment matters, including

---

[54] Several other states have statutes restricting retailers' right to collect contact information of customers, some of which are also the subject of litigation, although most are not yet subject to the interpretation imposed by the California Supreme Court. *See, e.g.*, Minn. Stat. Ann. § 325 F.982; N.J. Stat. §56:11-17.

[55] *Tyler v. Michaels Stores, Inc.*, No. SJC-11145, 2013 Mass. LEXIS 40 (Mar. 11, 2013). *See* Edwards Wildman Palmer LLP Client Advisory, *Massachusetts Supreme Judicial Court Expands Consumer Zip Code Privacy Protection in Tyler v. Michaels Stores*, Mar. 2013, http://digilaw.edwardswildman.com/?entry=4652.

[56] Cal. Civ. Code §1798.83.

[57] *In re Hulu*, No. 3:11-cv-03764- LB at 7-9 (N.D. Cal. Aug. 10, 2012).

hiring, promotion and retention.[58] Non-compliant use of these reports in the employment context can, however, result in exposure to employers. In January 2013, Kmart Corporation, a large retailer, settled claims that it violated FCRA by using credit reports in employment decisions without complying with required disclosures to the consumers (*i.e.*, employees), including disclosures concerning the consumer right to correct inaccuracies.[59] The claim covered 65,000 consumers, and was resolved (as to the alleged FCRA violations) with a $3 million settlement.

In addition, employers' use or alleged use of social media in hiring, firing and other employment matters has exposed employers to claimed violations of labor and employment laws, and privacy rights.[60] And, as noted in Sect. 2(b) above, several states have recently restricted access by employers and educational institutions to the social media accounts of employees, students and applicants.[61]

4 Prevention of Identity Theft and the "Red Flags" Rule

The Fair and Accurate Credit Transactions Act of 2003 ("FACTA")[62] is federal legislation directed at protecting consumers against identity theft as well as enhancing the accuracy of consumer report information. Under FACTA, for example, merchants are prohibited from displaying more than five digits of a credit card number on a receipt, and consumers are permitted to obtain a free copy of their credit report every 12 months from each nationwide credit reporting agency.

The FTC and the federal agencies that regulate the activities of financial institutions, including the Board of Governors of the Federal Reserve System, the Office of the Comptroller of the Currency, the Federal Deposit Insurance Corporation and the National Credit Union Administration, as well as the Securities and Exchange Commission and the Commodities Futures Trading Commission, have promulgated regulations to implement the identity theft provisions of FACTA. These regulations are commonly and collectively referred to as the "Red Flags Rule."[63] The Red Flags Rule furthers the purpose of FACTA by requiring covered entities to develop and implement a written Identity Theft Prevention Program designed to detect warning signs (or "red flags") that could indicate identity theft, and to respond in ways that would prevent or mitigate these instances.

---

[58] FCRA (15 U.S.C. §1681, et seq.) regulates "Credit Reporting Agencies" and imposes certain restrictions and notice requirements on the production and use of consumer reports.

[59] *See* http://www.searsfcraclassaction.com/.

[60] *See, e.g.*, Design Technology Group, LLC, 359 NLRB No. 96 (Apr. 19, 2013).

[61] For more information, see Employer Access to Social Media Usernames and Passwords, National Conference of State Legislatures, at http://www.ncsl.org/research/telecommunications-and-information-technology/employer-access-to-social-media-passwords-2013.aspx.

[62] Pub. Law 108 59, codified at 15 U.S.C. § 1681 et seq.

[63] 16 C.F.R. § 681.

For purposes of the Red Flags Rule, covered entities are financial institutions and creditors that maintain covered accounts as those terms are defined in the rule. Initially, the term "creditor" was very broadly defined to potentially include insurance companies, as well as lawyers, accountants and healthcare provider, which are not normally thought of among more traditional participants in the credit industry. The Red Flag Program Clarification Act of 2010, however, amended the definition of creditor to exclude those who advance funds for expenses incidental to a service provided by the person advancing funds. This change reduced the scope of the definition to cover more traditional creditors. The definition of "covered accounts" remains broadly defined to include (1) a consumer (rather than business) account offered or maintained by a financial institution or creditor that involves or permits multiple payments or transactions, and (2) any other account offered or maintained by a financial institution or creditor that presents a reasonably foreseeable risk of identity theft.

5 SEC Disclosures and Reporting

For public companies, the U.S. Securities and Exchange Commission (the "SEC") has a number of requirements related to the privacy and security of consumer data. Pursuant to the GLBA, which is discussed above, the SEC promulgated Regulation S-P, which requires financial institutions subject to SEC jurisdiction, including investment advisers, broker-dealers and investment companies, to provide privacy notices to consumers before disclosing nonpublic personal information to unaffiliated third parties.

In addition, the SEC issued guidance in 2011 to clarify that federal securities law may impose an obligation on registrants to disclose cybersecurity risks and cyber incidents.[64] Under this guidance, companies with publicly issued securities in the U.S. need to assess their exposures to cyber risk (*i.e.*, risks to a company's systems and data), and the procedures and resources devoted to addressing these risks, and disclose cyber risks and incidents that can have a material effect on the companies' operations or financial condition. If material, the availability of cyber insurance must also be disclosed.

6 Record Retention and Disposal

Some states impose specific requirements for retention and secure disposal of records containing customer information, regardless of the nature of the industry of the party holding the records. Under record disposal requirements in

[64] SEC CF Disclosure Guidance: Topic No. 2, Cybersecurity.

Massachusetts and New York, for example, records with Personal Information must be redacted, burned, pulverized, shredded or destroyed in some other way that will render the data unreadable. In Massachusetts, if third parties are contracted to dispose of such records, they must implement policies and procedures that prohibit unauthorized access to or use of Personal Information during collection, transport and disposal. Both states impose fines for noncompliance.[65]

Companies that dispose of records containing Personal Information also need to consider whether they are subject to disposal requirements imposed by federal law. The Fair and Accurate Credit Transactions Act of 2003, for example, requires businesses and individuals that use consumer reports, such as lenders, insurance companies, employers, landlords, car dealers, and debt collectors, to properly dispose of those consumer reports.[66]

7 Data Breach Notification Requirements

In the event of a data breach involving the theft, loss or other compromise of security of Personal Information, state laws and regulations in most U.S. states mandate notice of the breach to affected individuals, and some states also require reporting to regulatory agencies and state attorneys general.[67] Vast numbers of individuals may be involved in a single breach, and large breaches frequently affect residents of many jurisdictions. Compliance with these notification requirements generates significant costs to the breached entity, which may be recoverable, or partially recoverable through insurance, as described below in Sect. 8. The costs are usually related to the investigation of the incident, including forensic investigations; legal analysis of the findings under the applicable notification requirements; preparation and delivery of notice to affected individuals and governmental agencies; call center services to handle expected calls from consumers in response to the notification; and credit monitoring and other remediation services that may be offered to assist affected individuals.

Fifty-one U.S. jurisdictions, including 47 states, the District of Columbia, Guam, Puerto Rico and the U.S. Virgin Islands, have enacted data breach notification laws.[68] These laws define the types of incidents that constitute a breach, and specify the steps that a company must take in response to a breach that affects its residents.

---

[65] Mass. Gen. Law ch. 93I § 2; N.Y. Gen. Bus. Law § 399-h.

[66] 15 U.S.C. § 1681w(a)(1); *see also* 69 Fed. Reg. 68690–01 (Nov. 24, 2004), codified at 16 C.F.R. § 682.

[67] Data breaches requiring notification pursuant to these requirements can include a wide array of incidents, including hacks into company databases and systems; losses and thefts of devices and equipment ranging from cell phones to laptops, desktops, and other equipment; and inadvertent transmissions of data by email and otherwise.

[68] As of June 2015, the states that do not have such notification laws are Alabama, New Mexico and South Dakota.

Although the data breach notification laws of each of the 51 jurisdictions are similar, they contain significant variations. Even the determination of whether an event constitutes a breach that triggers the notification requirements may lead to different conclusions under different statutes. The clearest example of potential discrepancies is that only a small number of U.S. states include information in paper form in their definition of data that would trigger breach notification requirements.

Once it is determined that a breach or potential breach of data security may have occurred, the affected company must carefully review the requirements of each applicable jurisdiction to determine its obligations in that particular jurisdiction. The various laws purport to apply based on the residence of the individual whose data was compromised, and are not limited by the company's place(s) of business. Even most "local" businesses often find that they collect data from multiple jurisdictions.

In addition to these requirements, certain state regulators have issued requirements mandating notification of data breaches to the regulatory authority, when the breach involves a company licensed by the regulator. For example, licensees of the Connecticut Insurance Department (such as insurance companies, producers and third-party administrators) must report data breaches to the Connecticut Insurance Department.[69] These requirements have definitions of a reportable incident that often differ from the statutory data breach notification requirements, requiring additional levels of analysis and response in the event of an incident.

Under the federal Health Information Technology for Economic and Clinical Health Act (the "HITECH Act"), HHS promulgated the Health Breach Notification Rule[70] requiring notification to affected individuals and to the Office of Civil Rights of HHS in the event of a breach of the security of PHI. The Federal Trade Commission adopted a similar rule that applies to foreign and domestic vendors of personal health records, and their related entities and third-party service providers that maintain health information of U.S. citizens or residents.[71] The FTC rule does not apply to entities covered by the HHS rule.

In the event of a data breach, an initial and major task is to identify which jurisdictions' requirements apply. Entities often find themselves subject to the different, sometimes conflicting, requirements of multiple jurisdictions. A single data breach incident may have only one location at which the entity's data security was breached. Nevertheless, the individuals affected by the breach may reside in many different jurisdictions that impose data breach notification requirements. For example, if a laptop stolen from an office in California contains the Personal Information of residents of Maine, Massachusetts, New Hampshire and Vermont, and other countries, then the data breach laws of all those states and countries, as well as California, may be triggered. When a breach of a database or loss of computerized records involves information of individuals residing in different

[69] *See, e.g.*, Connecticut Insurance Department Bulletin IC-25, August 18, 2010.

[70] 45 C.F.R. Parts 160 and 164.

[71] 16 C.F.R. Part 318.

locations, the notification requirements of all U.S. states and other jurisdictions with such requirements are potentially triggered. In addition, entities experiencing a breach of medical or health information must consider applicability of both federal and state notification requirements, and the interplay between such requirements.

In recent years, the U.S. Congress has repeatedly considered enacting a federal breach notification requirement that would streamline and simplify the current myriad of state requirements that apply to data breaches generally.[72] The cost associated with the current statutory and regulatory landscape is very high, as companies that have suffered a breach must often conduct legal analysis under multiple state laws and regulations that differ from each other, and prepare notices to satisfy varying content requirements.

8 Insurance of Privacy and Data Protection Risks

Insurance markets operating in the U.S. and the rest of the world offering insurance products to U.S. insureds have developed specialized products addressing the various risks related to the privacy and security of consumer data. These policies and endorsements, and risks are often described colloquially as "cyber" policies and risks. Technically, "cyber" would be a subset of the relevant policies and risks, but not an accurate description of the entirety as they address privacy and data security. For example, it would be inaccurate to describe an exposure related to improper collection of consumer information as "cyber," even where the collection occurs on-line, and the policy that is purchased to cover such risks may include, but would necessarily extend beyond "cyber." Therefore, while the term "cyber" is commonly (albeit inaccurately) used to described all privacy and data security exposures and products, it is not used here for this purpose.

Perhaps the simplest segment of the market related to privacy and data security is targeted to address the needs of consumers. Consumers can purchase personal lines credit insurance and other coverage to protect against the harm that may result from identity theft and fraudulent transactions. Companies can also purchase commercial lines coverage to address their potential exposures where the data of their customers or employees, or others is lost, stolen or misused. These specialized products are in addition to more traditional business and property insurance products that can also be implicated in privacy and data security incidents.

In addition to specialized privacy and data security policies, which are further discussed below, other, more traditional types of policies are often implicated (with varying degrees of success) in privacy and data security incidents. These traditional policies include, with respect to first party losses by the breached entity(*i.e.*, direct losses of the insured), (1) property policies, which may cover property damage and

[72] As discussed above, there is currently a federal notification requirement in the healthcare industry under HIPAA.

business interruption losses; (2) fidelity and commercial crime; and (3) kidnap and ransom/extortion. Third party claims against a breached entity are, at times, submitted under (1) commercial general liability ("CGL") policies; (2) professional liability and other errors and omissions policies; and (3) directors and officers ("D&O") liability policies. Insurance professionals are now highly sophisticated on product development, sales, and claims, and their offerings continue to develop. This sophistication has resulted in refinement of wordings to cover intended privacy and data security risks under specialized policies and riders, and to exclude such risks from more traditional policies, such as property insurance, that may not have been intended to be implicated in the event of a breach of data privacy or security.

Traditional lines of insurance such as those enumerated above typically exclude or limit coverage of losses of electronic data and other records that are not tangible property. Nevertheless, in connection with data breaches, claims for business interruption have been made under property policies, for example. These claims have generally failed absent some physical damage to or loss of use of computer equipment or other facilities resulting from the breach. Some traditional property policies have, however, been augmented by endorsements or other manuscript language to provide some coverage for breach response costs, loss or corruption of electronic data, business interruption, or other damages suffered in a breach incident.

Many breaches of privacy or security of consumer information reportedly involve theft or other criminal activity. Therefore, fidelity and crime insurance may be implicated in these events, although these policies may also provide exclusions or limits related to electronic data and third party theft.

CGL policies, both Coverage A[73] and Coverage B[74] have been the basis for claims in data breaches. Due to the typical wordings and exclusions, Coverage A claims have not appeared to be successful to date. The inapplicability of Coverage B to losses arising out of privacy and data security incidents has been subject to challenges. Results of these claims in connection with data breaches have varied based on types of information exposed, the applicable laws of the relevant jurisdiction, and the specific wordings of the policies and exclusions. Insurers have modified policy wordings and added exclusions to further support the position that such policies do not apply to claims arising from breaches of data security and from collection and distribution of consumer information.

---

[73] Based on policy forms published by the Insurance Service Organization ("ISO"), Coverage A of a CGL policy typically provides coverage for sums the insured is legally obligated to pay to others as damages because of bodily injury or property damage, typically triggered by an accidental occurrence.

[74] Based on ISO policy forms, Coverage B of a CGL policy typically provides coverage for sums the insured is legally obligated to pay to others as damages because of "personal and advertising injury." In the past, enumerated offenses typically included "publication" in violation of a right to privacy, subject to various exclusions. In 2014, ISO is issuing endorsements deleting that prong of coverage and adding additional exclusions to further support the inapplicability of CGL policies to data breach claims.

A violation or breach of privacy or security by a person or business engaged in a profession or other service industry may result in a claim by the client of that person or business under a professional liability or errors and omissions ("E&O") policy. The threshold question for these claims is whether the violation or breach occurred within the scope of the service provided by the insured. While exclusions for electronic data are common, some may provide an exception to the exclusion for services that are incidental to the covered services, therefore triggering a duty to defend claims that arguably fit the exception. Moreover, some insurers offer breach response and other coverage by endorsement.

As breaches of privacy and data security have been reported to result in declines in the stock price of companies with publicly traded securities, claims have also been brought under D&O coverage. These claims have, for example, alleged (1) misstatements about the company's privacy and data security protections; (2) the failure of management and the board of directors to require and fund adequate levels of compliance or reasonable levels of security; or (3) the inadequacy of the company's breach response.

Increasingly in recent years, criminals have turned to cyber extortion. Typically, the malfeasant takes control of a computer system or database, and threatens to destroy the systems or data, or to publicize the data or the event itself, unless the victim makes a financial payment. Some policies have been specifically designed to address these threats. Kidnap and ransom coverage may extend to extortion, and these policies may also be implicated, depending on their terms, definitions and exclusions.[75]

To address the growing need for coverage of losses related to privacy and data security incidents, the insurance markets have developed specially designed wordings, both as specific policies, and as endorsements to more traditional policies. These specialized products can cover any combination of a variety of risks related to privacy and data security of consumer information, including the following:

1. first party breach response costs incurred by the breached entity;
2. business interruption from cyber attacks and other incidental business losses;
3. claims of wrongful collection, use or disclosure of data;
4. damages of third parties from data breaches; and
5. losses from cyber extortion.

In offering or purchasing these coverages, particular attention must be paid to definitions. For example, some of these policies (or endorsements) only cover electronic data, while others extend to data in any format, including paper. Other important terms of these policies may limit coverage to first party losses (*i.e.*, losses of the insured itself), or extend to damages to third parties. Some may cover only breaches of the insured's own computer systems, and may exclude or limit exposure for breaches of a vendor of the insured that compromise the privacy or security of

[75] As further described below, specialized cyber policies may also specifically include coverage for cyber extortion.

the insured's data. In connection with the direct costs related to the notification of affected individuals and government agencies, some policies limit coverage to notifications that are legally required. Experience with the various and varying U.S. laws requiring breach notification has shown that many companies experiencing a data breach opt to provide notifications that arguably may not be legally required. Another feature of these policies that merits particular attention is sublimits, which may provide for specific limits on amounts that may be indemnified for forensics, legal, mailing and printing, or other categories of expenses and damages. Issuers and purchasers of insurance should also focus on exclusions from coverage, for fines and penalties and the determination of whether payments such as contractually assess amounts are covered or excluded as fines and penalties.

The potential threats and exposures to companies that collect consumer data in the U.S. are persistent and evolving. In response to these threats and exposures, the global and U.S. insurance markets offer a variety of solutions, which also continue to develop and evolve.

Acknowledgment The author acknowledges with appreciation the contributions to this chapter made by his colleagues in the Privacy & Cybersecurity Group at Locke Lord LLP, particularly Karen L. Booth.

Reference

Romanosky S, Hoffman D, Acquisti A (2014) Empirical analysis of data breach litigation. J Empir Leg Stud 11(1):74–104

Part IV
Dispute Settlement and Litigation

Online Dispute Resolution and Insurance

Alkistis Christofilou

Contents

Abstract Online Dispute Resolution ("ODR") has been generated by the inherent need to swiftly and efficiently resolve the thousands of disputes arising in electronic commerce. This chapter focuses on presenting the main features of ODR; its relevance to existing alternative dispute resolution methods and practices; the role that technology can play to increase confidence to cross-border commerce;

The author gratefully thanks Smaragda Rigakou and Viktoria Chatzara for their invaluable contribution to this chapter.

A. Christofilou (✉)
Rokas Law Firm, Athens, Greece
e-mail: a.christofilou@rokas.com

P. Marano et al. (eds.), *The "Dematerialized" Insurance*,
DOI 10.1007/978-3-319-28410-1_12

and how these characteristics may be applied to the benefit of relaxing the ever increasing volume of disputes in the insurance market. The requirements for the design and implementation of a just process will be mentioned based on the works of international organizations such as UNCITRAL, OECD and ICC. Within the limited framework of the chapter, the regulatory tools instituted in the European Union are discussed in the context of the insurance regulatory framework and certain practical examples so far implemented, as to the extent they are likely to introduce ODR as a practical tool which shall be established as an alternative dispute resolution tool within the EU single market for insurance.

1 ODR and Insurance

Online Dispute Resolution (ODR) is a branch of dispute resolution which uses technology to facilitate or assist its function. It is often seen as being the online equivalent of alternative dispute resolution ("ADR"), including mainly negotiation, automated negotiation, mediation and arbitration.

To examine how ODR can be integrated in the insurance business and in the claims management process, it is essential that the basic functions and legal issues connected with ODR are presented. This chapter first provides a high level overview of ODR and its various mechanisms, of the principal legal issues related to its operation, and of the existing efforts of international organizations to regulate it. Furthermore, some representative ODR systems are described. It then focuses on the ADR/ODR package recently introduced in the European Union and its eligibility for the resolution of insurance disputes. Finally, it attempts to assess whether insurance can benefit from ODR processes.

2 Introduction and History of ODR

The exponential rise of the internet and of electronic commerce inevitably resulted in the creation of a considerable number of disputes between transacting parties. These conflicts are characterized by certain uniform features, which diversify them from the usual conflicts of the real world. Such features include the distance between the contracting parties, which may often be in different countries, or even continents; communications take place not concurrently, but in an asynchronous manner and often off working hours; there is a massive number of transactions, usually with low value and mostly generated in business-to-consumer "B2C" transactions; there are uniform trading practices. These trends are visible also in business-to-business ("B2B") transactions.

It is therefore difficult and perhaps practically unattainable, to resolve such disputes by recourse to traditional means, i.e. by going to court. To ask but few of the questions involved: Which one is the competent court? Where is it? Does the claimant have to physically attend the proceedings? What rules apply? Which is the applicable law? How will the claimant be represented? When will the outcome be available? How will it be enforced? And, last but not least, what is the cost? Is it reasonable, in relation to the value of the dispute? Similar issues apply with regard to regulatory or administrative agencies entrusted with the resolution of complaints.

As there seem to be no encouraging answers to these questions, we come across the phenomenon of millions of transactions, where in essence the fundamental right of recourse to the person's natural judge is excluded. The global legal order is not yet organised to tackle cyberspace conflict in an efficient manner. Not only are the legal issues undefined, but also the practical and financial complications are considerable. Should a consumer in Italy, who purchased a garment from a website situated in the USA, have to travel to the USA and employ a lawyer there, to litigate a claim for the garment being defective, the cost and the effort would be entirely disproportionate. Certainly it would also be so to litigate for a similar off-line dispute at national level; however a cross-continent dispute will be incomparably more costly and cumbersome. The several existing ADR options also show similar weaknesses while, additionally, their existence does not in itself safeguard satisfaction of the fundamental right of recourse to the proper court which is embedded in a number of constitutions, and generally of the right to a fair trial which is unequivocal in human rights conventions.

Transactional reality has imposed the emergence of a variety of systems for the resolution of disputes online. ODR was born from the synergy between alternative dispute resolution (ADR) and information and communication technology (ICT), as a method for resolving disputes arising online, for which traditional means of dispute resolution are inefficient or unavailable.[1]

Today, there is little doubt that there is an ongoing and growing need for ODR. E-commerce depends on users not only being able to conduct transactions, but also willing and trusting to do so. The new challenge is finding tools that can deliver trust, convenience, and expertise for many different kinds of conflicts.[2] It is being increasingly recognized that ODR has value in two ways, by resolving disputes and also by being part of an institution's trust building effort. Therefore, ODR can be seen as an asset to the e-merchant, rather than a peripheral feature of its system.[3]

In parallel to such systems, academic and theoretical activity has been developing. Although the Internet was invented in 1969, only in 1996 did the first articles about ODR appear in a law review.[4] Since its emergence in the 1990s ODR has intrigued researchers and professionals in a number of disciplines, ranging from law, communications, conflict theory, ADR theory and dispute resolution systems

[1] Rule (2002), p. 37.

[2] Katsh and Rifkin (2001), p. 73.

[3] Katsh (2012a), pp. 21–33.

[4] Katsh (1996), p. 953; Lide (1996), p. 193.

design, to game theory, mathematics and computer science.[5] However as it is still evolving, the ODR phenomenon has not yet developed its independent and distinctive theoretical base. It is maintained by ODR believers that not only will it develop to provide an efficient tool for resolving cyberspace conflicts, but it can profoundly influence the way in which dispute resolution is seen and implemented on- and offline.

3 What is ODR?

3.1 The Notion of ODR

ODR is a broad term that encompasses many forms of alternative dispute resolution ("ADR") which incorporate the use of the Internet, websites, email communications, streaming media and other information technology, as part of the dispute resolution process.[6]

There is no uniform definition of ODR; it has been described as the process that brings parties together online to participate in a dialogue about resolving their dispute[7]; or as "a co-existing universe interacting with traditional forms of dispute resolution".[8]

ODR's distinctive feature and quality is that by applying flexibility, innovative techniques and online technologies to the process, ODR can develop and refine the traditional ADR means of resolving disputes.[9]

3.2 Technology: The "Fourth Party" to the Dispute

ODR is critically characterized by the technological platform on which it develops. The importance of technology is recognized by its frequent naming as the "Fourth Party" on the setting of the dispute resolution procedure, alongside the two disputants and the neutral third party which assists in the process, while in automated ODR systems it may even substitute such neutral party.[10]

---

[5] For the features of the various ADR systems versus court proceedings, as well as for interdisciplinary issues regarding contact theory and communication theory in the ODR context see Wing and Rainey (2012), p. 41 ff.

[6] American Bar Association Task Force on E-Commerce and ADR (2002).

[7] See http://cyber.law.harvard.edu/olds/ecommerce/disputestext.html, point VI.A.

[8] Katsh (2012b), p. 14.

[9] CEN Workshop (2009), p. 10.

[10] The term "Fourth Party", established by E. Katsh and J. Rifkin, is described in Katsh and Rifkin (2001).

The technological input is described by analysts to take the following forms: When a negotiation is modeled, a computer can act as an intelligent agent using optimization algorithms that seek the best solution. A computer generated package can encourage the process, resolve impasses, and improve negotiated agreements—all without reducing the control of the process by the negotiating parties. Optimization algorithms utilize detailed and highly accurate information from all parties. With anything other than the very simplest of cases, this optimization is beyond the capabilities of any assisted human.[11]

The interception of law and technology is evident in the decision support systems that work as a supplement to the human knowledge management skills with computer-based means for managing knowledge. They accept, store, use, receive and present knowledge essential for the decisions to be taken.[12] These systems may be further divided in decision support tools and decision making tools. The former improve the decision makers' performance, whilst the latter automate the process, leaving minimal role for the user.

The limit between intervention and facilitation, and complete reliance on technology, is one of ODR's stakes. Operators of high-end automated systems are aware of the risks entailed when the human factor is fully absent during the system operation.

3.3 ODR Characteristics

The main qualities of ODR are that it is available independently of geographical location and time; it almost excludes direct interpersonal communication; it is cheap and efficient.

ODR is also seen as the implementation of ADR in the virtual world. Other than tackling online disputes, ODR may provide the platform to resolve disputes arising from off-line transactions generated in the real world and not in cyberspace. Designers of assisted negotiation systems maintain the view that in its more elaborate form it may even serve to facilitate and achieve the resolution of sophisticated multi-party disputes, or conflicts between countries and nations.

ODR departs from the traditional communication techniques inherent in the available dispute resolution systems: there is no face to face (F2F) communication, which prevents the passing of interpersonal and non-verbal messages and hues; this can be perceived both as an advantage and a disadvantage. In principle, communication is only in writing and it is often restricted by the path of the platform design: the system may be so simplified as to apply a multiple choice tool. The building of trust must rely on factors other than those used in mediation, where the mediator employs practices which will reduce conflict, promote interpersonal

[11] Thiessen et al. (2012), p. 345.

[12] Lodder and Zeleznikow (2012), pp. 73–94.

communication and focus on the object of the dispute rather than on the subjective circumstances of the parties. Still ADR and ODR mechanisms do share some common features, such as lower cost, greater speed, more flexibility in outcomes, less adversarial strategies, more informal sequences, privacy and solution oriented methods instead of blame-oriented techniques.[13] The ODR environment does not resemble to that of a court: in a court process the obligatory procedural rules alienate the disputants; communication between them is highly adversarial; it is formalized, distanced and conducted via third parties, which are the court and counsel; evaluation is usually based on the mental disposition of the person to his/her act, as it relies on the diagnosis of intention or negligence, and thus entails the component of blame.[14]

In ODR the true identity of the disputant may remain concealed throughout the procedure. Further to its impersonal character, ODR can place a party in a discriminated position if it is not fluent or experienced in the use of computers and the internet, irrespective whether such party could and has completed an electronic transaction. Confidentiality may be jeopardized given the inherent risk to privacy that is present in internet communications. However ODR enthusiasts argue that the claim for privacy has already been diluted in a large part of web communications, and this is predominant in the social media. What is pivotal in the evolution of ODR, it will have to adapt and encompass the new behavioural patterns that apply to internet users.

As in all automated systems, also in ODR the human monitoring and regular intervention is crucial to ensure the proper functioning of the system and, more importantly, to avoid errors in the choices the system makes. As intelligent as it may be, the system will still lack the qualities to make choices based on critical judgment and to make correlations based on inherent information other than that loaded on its data pool. The requirement for a just outcome enhances the need to avoid incorrect choices. There must therefore be at least technical and legal monitoring, also able to trace and preclude manipulative tactics and fraud.

There are a number of ODR forms and systems currently available, which range from a fully digitalized and impersonal procedure where the parties are guided and led to (possible) resolution by the system's functions, to a mixture between ODR and ADR in which the human interaction is augmented and may entail the exchange of documents or even extend to communication between the parties and their counsel in writing or by tele- or videoconference.

---

[13] See in this relevance among others Goodman (2003), pp. 1–16.

[14] Reference to the different and cognitively still unexplored human communication patterns over the internet, including over social media platforms, and on how these may be used by contact and communication theories, is made by Wing and Rainey (2012), p. 46 ff., with further references to writers and theory. A number of relevant articles are available in Mediate.com: www.mediate.com.

4 Insurance and Online Settlement

4.1 ODR and Insurance

The insurance industry is by its very nature one of the premier customers to the dispute resolution system. Claims administration and settlement cost are two major cost centers to an insurance undertaking. For insurers, the prolongation of the time a claim remains pending increases cost in all respects, both in terms of soft cost and of the actual compensation sum the insurer will finally be asked to pay, default and judgment interest being added up to the actual compensation sum. There are thousands of workplaces engaged in supporting the claims management and resolution process. It cannot be disputed, that each case has particular individual characteristics and deserves meticulous attention. On the other hand, whether internally or outsourced, it is common ground that improving efficiency in the claims resolution system would significantly reduce the industry costs to the benefit of company profits and of consumer savings on insurance cost, thereby releasing valuable human and other resources to engage in the improvement of the overall insurance product.

Furthermore, the insurance industry is reported to be the largest user of automated dispute resolution mechanisms.[15]

4.2 Fully Automated Systems

ODR providers for insurance disputes have emerged in the late 1990s. Historically, *Cybersettle*,[16] which is a completely automated system, paved the way in the US insurance dispute resolution market with its blind-bidding system which it patented and enhanced with a call center to address questions.[17]

The *Cybersettle* technology helps adjusters and lawyers to accelerate the settlement of insurance claims, allowing them to confidentially match offers and demands, and is now being used by major international insurance carriers to reduce claims backlog. Its "double blind-bidding" method is an advanced negotiation tool based on game theory, used[18] in disputes where two parties are involved. During the procedure, each party is invited to make offers or bids, which are kept hidden from the other party. If the divergence between the opposite offers is within a specific range, then the system automatically declares a settlement at the midpoint of the

[15] Rule (2002), p. 142.

[16] See a summary description of Cybersettle and other fully automated mechanisms in Sect. 4 of this chapter.

[17] Rule (2002), p. 143.

[18] Thiessen et al. (2012), p. 343.

two offers.[19] The double blind bidding process keeps the choices of the parties undisclosed to each other; however they can see what the stake is at each time. In this way the parties can quickly and confidentially decide what they are willing to accept. *Cybersettle* has been successfully applied to address a variety of claims and financial negotiations, including property damage, bodily injury and subrogation. It was followed by a number of competitors. Owing to the leading role of technology in the process, the procedure is not adversarial and personal; the resolution does not rely on the judgment of a person, but is reached by the automated system through the choices the parties make at each stage of the process.

A variation of the blind bidding process, where the human third party is dislocated by software-based decision making, is the so-called "visual blind bidding" method, which is used by the ODR platform *SmartSettle*. By contrast to the "double blind bidding" model, "visual blind bidding"[20] can also serve to resolve disputes involving more than two parties. The system has a different sequence in the process of revealing information to the other party. Once all parties agree to negotiate, they exchange open but anonymous, optimistic proposals setting out the bargaining ranges, whereas what each party is willing to accept remains hidden. The system declares the end of a negotiating session when all parties have accepted one or more proposals and a specific algorithm defines which one of the accepted proposals shall be determined as the final agreement in a way that rewards the first party which moved into the zone of agreement. This is employed as an incentive to the parties to compromise and accept a fair outcome faster.[21]

On the example of the automated systems a number of lessons could be learned. It became evident, that the penetration of ODR in insurance, like in other markets, heavily depends on the actors' mentality and readiness to engage in such a way to resolve disputes. Active publicity and awareness campaigns along with heavy investment in improving the system technically can forward this requirement. However if an ODR system is created, financed and monitored by insurers, it is susceptible to provoke mistrust by consumers and their counsel. In the discussed example, *Cybersettle* which was primarily financed by insurers, addressed this issue by establishing alliances, for example it engaged in cooperation with the largest plaintiffs' association in North America.

Furthermore, it became evident that while fully automated ODR systems are reliable, they cannot sufficiently cover the market needs. Fully automated systems are more suitable for example when the dispute has already been resolved as to the apportionment of liability, and negotiation has proceeded to the phase of determining the quantum of payment.[22] In contrast, the combination of automated tools with

---

[19] As described in detail in CEN Workshop (2009), p. 15. The model has widely expanded in the USA where it is used by insurers, claims adjusters and lawyers to agree on the quantum of compensation, without prejudicing the parties' right to go to court.

[20] Goodman (2003).

[21] Thiessen et al. (2012), p. 352.

[22] Goodman (2003).

traditional mediation mechanisms can improve efficiency by providing significant technical assistance, without challenging the benefits to settlement produced by human interaction. In the example of the blind bidding tools, where the system can bring together the opponents' settlement expectations by way of matching rounds of possible settlement sum ranges, this can succeed primarily with claims where the range of settlement expectations of the involved parties is not too far apart. It is also more likely to occur in cases of B2B claims. In these disputes both parties are knowledgeable and experienced, aware of the market settlement trends and able to recognise standard patterns in the disputed cases, while at the same time they tend to operate rationally rather than subjectively in seeking the resolution of the conflict. Technology can further provide significant assistance in the management of the claims files for insurance companies, claims adjusters and lawyers, especially where large numbers of claims are involved.

However, human interaction seems to be inevitably required if other dispute resolution needs must be addressed. There is a variety of available alternatives, shortly mentioned below.

4.3 Systems with Human Interaction

Not all ODR systems use the available technology to completely substitute the human neutral third party. There is another range of models, which combine factors from ADR processes and vary from mediation to med-arb and arbitration. The software in these systems is used to provide the parties and the human neutral third party with a certain procedure and/or to offer them specific advice for the evaluation of the case. It may even be reduced to simply assist the parties to the dispute, including the mediator or the arbitrator, to exchange documents, communicate their positions and opinions asynchronously and without having to meet face-to-face[23] and generally to apply e-technology in the process. Depending on how essential the actual involvement of the system is in the resolution of the dispute, ODR systems in which technology does not fully dislocate the human third party may range from consensual to adjudicative, as would online arbitration systems where the case is managed electronically.

There are ODR systems where parties actively communicate with each other and equally bargain with the assistance of technological means to reach a settlement. In such systems the dispute resolution process resembles the negotiation procedure, which is why such systems are often referred to as "assisted negotiation". In e-commerce, negotiation is the most widespread and efficient extra-judicial means of conflict resolution between consumers and businesses.[24] ODR platforms using the assisted negotiation method have been successful in targeting large

[23] Rabinovich-Erny and Katsh (2012), p. 53.

[24] Vilalta (2012), pp. 128–129.

numbers of similar disputes with highly automated ODR models, which provide parties with predefined fields where they can gradually and successively qualify their claim, recognize patterns from comparable disputes and match them with proposed resolutions.[25] Operating systems used in other areas of commerce or services may be used as paradigms to draw useful conclusions for insurance.

The example of a system that is mostly referenced as using the assisted negotiation method is *SquareTrade,* which was operated by eBay via a third party. *SquareTrade* and its successor system which is now monitored in cooperation with PayPal, the payment system used by eBay, seems to be recognized in bibliography as the most successful ODR application so far, as it is reported to have resolved over 60 million disputes which accounts for almost 80 % of the processed disputes. The system offers two levels of dispute resolution[26]: assisted negotiation and mediation. The process starts when an eBay buyer or seller files a complaint by filling out a web-based standard complaint form. According to the form, the type of dispute is identified and the claimant is presented with a list of solutions, from which the claimant selects the ones he agrees to. The other party is informed of the claim and the system process by e-mail and is asked whether it wishes to participate. If the response is positive, the respondent submits the response, selecting the resolutions it agrees to. During this initial stage, the parties try to reach an agreement by communicating with each other through the system's automated "Direct Negotiation" facility.[27] Should both parties agree to the same solution, the dispute is considered resolved.

If no agreement is achieved, the parties enter a second stage set within a negotiation environment where a web interface monitors the procedure by, for example, limiting the free text space, encouraging the proposition of agreements, setting deadlines and even controlling expressions in the dialogue. The software is used at this stage to monitor and channel the communications between the parties into a constructive negotiation. The process used in this second stage could be defined as "mediated negotiation" as the technological tools which are used perform actions that would be associated with a traditional mediator's role.[28]

If no agreement is reached, the parties can request the intervention of an individual (human) mediator for a nominal fee. The mediator will not act as a judge or arbitrator, but will seek to facilitate a positive discussion between the parties and will only make a settlement proposal if the parties so request. The proposal is not binding on the parties.[29]

A critical factor to the success is the additional component the system includes, which makes the resolutions enforceable in practice. PayPal will retain the funds

---

[25] CEN Workshop (2009), p. 15.

[26] Calliess (2006), p. 652 ff., available at: http://www.germanlawjournal.com/pdfs/Vol07No08/PDF_Vol_07_No_08_647-660_Articles Calliess.pdf.

[27] Goodman (2003) including a further detailed description of the system.

[28] The system's description is taken from Calliess (2006), p. 653.

[29] Goodman (2003).

paid by the purchaser and will not settle the transaction by paying the vendor before the lapse of an agreed time period in which the purchaser may raise its objections.

Another reported important feature of the system's software is its capacity to trace uniformities in the various disputes it handles. By systematically processing such uniform trends, eBay has improved its transaction platform and the guidance it provides to participants in the course of the transaction. In this way it has succeeded in avoiding a number of the frictions which lead to disputes and has thus developed a dispute-prevention function. These features have made the system more trustworthy and have added value to the transaction platform.[30]

4.4 Mediation, Med-Arb, Arbitration

There are a number of approaches to mediation, mostly tending to the mediator not imposing the decision on the parties, but leading the way to them to come to an agreement by downsizing the subjective elements of the dispute and focusing on the objective matter of the dispute. By contrast in arbitration, the neutral third party delivers a decision which is final and binding on both parties. Both systems can avail of ODR's electronic facilities to a variable extent. The arbitration agreement or the rules each ODR provider sets out determine the process, the evidence procedures, the issuance of the award, its enforceability and whether it can be appealed. There is a variety of arbitration rules concerning the evolution of the procedure; however in terms of system design, e-arbitration and e-assisted arbitration still follows the adversarial model.

Several arbitration-modeled ODR tools may be of use to the insurance industry to derive useful tools or concepts applicable for the better e-resolution of insurance disputes. A commonly referred ODR system which successfully functions as

[30] A different dispute resolution system is the one applied by Wikipedia. It is a complicated, multifaceted system which makes available a number of ADR options regarding the content of the postings. Wikipedia has developed its software to recognize certain patterns that provoke dispute, to detect cases where the content is edited by violation of the editing rules, and to delete it before being noticed by the readers; see Wikipedia: Dispute Resolution, available at: http://en.wikipedia.org/wiki/Wikipedia:Dispute_resolution; Rabinovich-Einy and Katsh (2012), p. 54.

arbitration is the Uniform Domain Name Dispute Resolution Policy (UDRP),[31] created by the Internet Corporation for Assigned Names and Numbers (ICANN).[32]

There is a variety of other examples which have applied or still apply in areas of dispute designated by large numbers and a high degree of homogeneity, to be found in a number of sectors of the market or of public administration.[33]

5 ODR Penetration in Europe

While in North America ODR seems to be developing, by contrast in Europe it has not flourished, albeit there has been considerable mobility at the time that followed the initial expansion of the internet. Privately driven initiatives did not prosper for a number of reasons, including competition by patented applications (such as *Cybersettle's*), or the fierce opposition by lawyers[34] or, importantly, the lack of an apprehensive culture in Europe by contrast to North America. A limited number of schemes have been introduced, to include among others RisolviOnline,[35]

[31] *Internet Corporation for Assigned Names and Numbers*, "Uniform Domain Name Dispute Resolution Policy", available at: http://www.icann.org/en/help/dndr/udrp.

[32] UDRP is used to resolve disputes arising between trademark owners and those who have registered a domain name in bad faith with the aim to profit from the reputation of a trademark by reselling the domain name for profit. According to UDRP and the Rules regulating the procedure, the complaint, the response and any other kind of communication between the opposing parties, as well as the documents attached to the complaint and/or response, shall be made exclusively in writing and electronically. As described in detail in the UDRP webpage and the relevant Rules populated by ICANN, the Administrative Panel, of which the members are chosen by the parties, can issue a decision requiring from the competent authority to cancel, transfer or make any other changes to a domain name. ICANN with the UDRP has achieved to develop an effective, transparent global ODR procedure based on contractual adherence that provides trademark owners the possibility to efficiently fight cybersquatting. The UDRP providers are reported to have dealt with over 30,000 domain name disputes. Their success derives from two aspects: First, the UDRP deals only with abusive registrations made in bad faith to take advantage of the reputation of existing trademarks. Secondly, it has incorporated a self-enforcement mechanism, which transfers and cancels domain names without the need for judicial involvement.

[33] To mention but a few, in the area of family disputes there is Family_Winner and AssetDivider in the US, which helps apportion the family fortune in the event of divorce. Negoisst has been developed in Germany to address multi-party complicated disputes. Canada has implemented a sports dispute resolution facility, the Sports Dispute Resolution Center of Canada (http://www.crdsc-sdrcc.ca), while the USA public administration is quite engaged in the process of implanting ODR to resolve administrative disputes between the state and citizens. For example, the National Archives and Records Administration (NARA) created the Office of Government Information Services (OGIS) to assist in the resolution of disputes over the Freedom of Information Act (FOIA).

[34] Whether ODR will signal the end of lawyers has been a matter of reflection for Suesskind (2008).

[35] RisolviOnline is a service of the Chamber of Arbitration of Milan (Italy), available at http://www.risolvionline.com.

Mediateur du Net[36] and the Internet Ombudsman.[37] In the European Union[38] the ODR expansion seems to be driven centrally through regulation rather than through market evolution. The European institutions have established an ODR platform with direct relevance to the financial services sector, FIN-NET. Furthermore, in 2013 the Consumer ADR Directive and the ODR Regulation were introduced, which are presented in the next sections.

5.1 *FIN-NET*

One of the fundamental goals of the European Union is the creation of a single market, where the free movement of goods and services will be ensured,[39] while a high level of consumer protection is safeguarded.[40] Within the framework of resolving disputes arising from the cross border provision of financial services, FIN-NET was established. FIN-NET is a financial dispute resolution network of national out-of-court complaint schemes in the European Economic Area countries, including the European Union Member States plus Iceland, Liechtenstein and Norway, which are responsible for handling out-of-court cross border disputes between consumers and financial services providers, i.e. banks, insurance companies, investment firms and others. This network was launched by the European Commission in 2001.[41]

FIN-NET has three specific objectives[42]: to provide consumers with easy and informed access to out-of-court redress in cross-border disputes; to ensure efficient exchange of information between European schemes so that the consumer's cross-border complaints can be handled as quickly, efficiently and professionally as

[36] Mediateur du Net is part of the *Forum des droits sur l'internet*, a non-profit organisation which counts with over 70 members, public organisations, associations and private companies; available at http://www.foruminternet.org/particuliers/mediation/.

[37] The Internet Ombudsman is offered by a neutral and independent organisation located in Vienna which receives funds from the Austrian Ministry of Social Affairs, Labour and Consumer Protection and the Chamber of Labour, available at http://www.ombudsmann.at. For a comparison of these providers see Gabarro (2009).

[38] A historical background of the ODR evolution in the EU is provided by Poblet and Ross (2012), p. 465 ff. There are a number of institutional initiatives, publicly funded research projects and private initiatives which have deployed over the last two decades in Europe. Also see Hodges (2013).

[39] Treaty for the Functioning of the European Union (TFEU) Article 26(2).

[40] Preamble of Regulation No 524/2013 of the European Parliament and of the Council on online dispute resolution for consumer disputes (Regulation on Consumer ODR), point 1, available at: http://eur-lex.europa.eu/LexUriServ/LexUriServ.do?uri=OJ:L:2013:165:0001:0012:EN:PDF; article 169 TFEU.

[41] See FIN-NET home page at http://ec.europa.eu/internal_market/fin-net/index_en.htm.

[42] FIN-NET Settling Cross Border Financial Disputes out of Court: Consumer Guide http://ec.europa.eu/internal_market/fin-net/docs/guide/consumer-guide_en.pdf.

possible; and to ensure that out-of-court dispute settlement schemes from different EEA countries apply a common set of minimum guarantees.

FIN-NET members will put the consumer in touch with the relevant out-of-court complaint scheme and provide the necessary information about it. The national ADR scheme will try to resolve the dispute according to its rules and taking into account the Commission Recommendation 98/257/EC.[43]

The members of FIN-NET are institutional or institution-related bodies, e.g. banking or consumer ombudsmen, dispute resolution bodies within service providers associations,[44] and not private entrepreneurial schemes which provide ADR/ODR as a business. In this sense FIN-NET may examine whether a particular entity shall qualify as ADR provider under the ADR Directive. Although it was set up over a decade ago, and there has been a constant increase in the number of disputes the FIN-NET members have handled per annum, the absolute number of disputes handled is still low. According to the FIN-NET Activity Report 2012, published in September 2013,[45] FIN-NET members handled 2.727 cross-border cases in 2012, of which 919 concerned the insurance sector, 1.325 the banking sector, 318 investments and 165 other cases, demonstrating in this way a significant increase since 2007, when they had handled a total number of 1.041 cross-border cases; notably the multitude thereof have been resolved.

The Report mentions a number of examples of cross-border disputes, which were successfully closed by recourse to the FIN-NET members. In one example, a British citizen was a named beneficiary in a French life insurance policy which refused to grant payment because the second named beneficiary had delayed to send the documentation required. The French Insurance Mediator, to which the matter was referred, intervened and payment was granted. Another case involved a resident of Poland, who had insured his boat with a German insurance company. The latter refused cover alleging the risk had occurred owing to the policyholder's gross negligence. The policyholder complained to the Polish Insurance Ombudsman who referred the matter to his German counterpart. As a result of the intervention of the two Ombudsmen, the matter was closed amicably. In another matter, a French hospital was held by the court liable for medical malpractice which caused the death of an Italian child. The French professional liability insurer of the hospital did not agree on the quantum of compensation with the child's parents, who referred the case to the French Insurance Mediator. With the Mediator's intervention the case was closed by settlement. In another case involving the UK Financial Ombudsman Scheme and the Financial Services Ombudsman's Bureau in Ireland, the Irish insurer conformed to the Irish Ombudsman's finding, that the UK resident—insured did not lose her bag because she had left it unattended, as the insurer alleged. As a

---

[43] Commission Recommendation 98/257/EC on principles applicable to bodies responsible for out-of-court settlement of consumer disputes.

[44] Such as the German Savings Banks Association and the Danish Complaint Board of Danish Securities and Brokering Companies.

[45] Available at: http://ec.europa.eu/internal_market/fin-net/docs/activity/2012_en.pdf.

result, the insurer had to pay the insurance indemnity or appeal the case to the High Court in Ireland. Another matter affected an Icelandic citizen who had purchased a personal accident and health insurance through an Icelandic broker from a UK insurance firm. When she was diagnosed with Parkinson's disease shortly after the purchase, the insurer declined cover alleging the policyholder had failed to inform them of a pre-existing disease known to her. The policyholder brought her claim to the Icelandic Insurance Complaints Committee, which ruled in her favour, however as the ruling was not binding on the insurer, the case ended up in court. These examples show that the FIN-NET members may take competence for various kinds of consumer insurance disputes, while the results are more efficient when the FIN-NET competent members cooperate to resolve the case.

While stakeholders seem to agree that FIN-NET represents an appropriate mechanism to solve cross border consumer financial disputes, it still has not achieved the intended response by consumers. This is attributed mainly to the lack of public awareness, low funding, and language barriers,[46] coupled by the low consumer confidence to purchasing financial services cross-border.[47]

5.2 *The Consumer ADR/ODR Package*

In the summer of 2013 the European Parliament and the Council[48] issued Directive 2013/11/EU on alternative dispute resolution for consumer disputes (Directive on Consumer ADR[49]) and Regulation 524/2013 on online dispute resolution for consumer disputes (Regulation on Consumer ODR[50]). These two legislative texts take into consideration the series of common principles, standards and best practices for ODR systems and providers issued by international organizations and constitute a set of rules which is legally binding on Member States and on individuals and legal persons in the EU.[51] They are intended to promote internal trade and to endorse less costly and more trustworthy mechanisms for the out-of-

[46] The FIN-NET website is available in only three languages.

[47] Evaluation of FIN-NET for the European Commission, http://ec.europa.eu/internal_market/fin-net/docs/evaluation_en.pdf. The evaluation contains recommendations for maintaining and improving the current structure, and enhancing consumer and stakeholders' awareness to the network.

[48] The legal basis is Articles 26, 169 and 114 TFEU.

[49] Directive 2013/11/EU of the European Parliament and of the Council of 21 May 2013 on alternative dispute resolution for consumer disputes and amending Regulation (EC) No 2006/2004 and Directive 2009/22/EC http://eur-lex.europa.eu/Result.do?T1=V1&T2=2013&T3=11&RechType=RECH_naturel&Submit=Search.

[50] Regulation No 524/2013 of the European Parliament and of the Council on online dispute resolution for consumer disputes http://eur-lex.europa.eu/LexUriServ/LexUriServ.do?uri=OJ:L:2013:165:0001:0012:EN:PDF.

[51] European Commission (2011).

court resolution of disputes.[52] It was estimated that if EU consumers could rely on well-functioning and transparent ADR for their disputes they could save around EUR 22.5 billion a year, corresponding to 0.19 % of EU GDP.[53] Pursuant to the European Commission, there are over 750 ADR schemes in the EU today. They work differently and have different names, e.g. arbitration, mediation, ombudsmen, complaints boards, etc..[54]

The new system is part of the "Single Market Act" package. It intends to provide simple, fast and low-cost out-of-court settlement procedures offered by qualified entities, designed to resolve disputes between consumers and traders arising from the sales of goods and services.[55] To facilitate the process, an ODR platform will be set up and maintained by the European Commission. The project intends to serve as a lever to boost growth, strengthen confidence and add value to the internal market and in particular to its digital dimension.[56]

EU Member States are required to enforce the legislation and administrative provisions necessary to comply with the ADR Directive by 9 July 2015 at the latest. Most of the provisions of the ODR Regulation will take effect on 9 January 2016 and will be directly binding on Member States.[57]

5.3 The Directive on Consumer ADR

The Directive applies to domestic and cross-border disputes concerning complaints of a consumer resident in the EU against a trader established in the EU.

The notion of consumer is defined in a limited way, to include any natural person who is acting for purposes which are outside his trade, business, craft or

---

[52] Morek (2011).

[53] Morek (2013) and Hornle (2012).

[54] In some countries, the existing ADR schemes cover only specific consumer disputes e.g. for financial services, energy supply, transport. In a few others, ADR covers all consumer disputes; and some offer the entire process online. ADR schemes can be established by public authorities, industry or in cooperation between the public sector, industry and consumer organisations. Funding may be private, public or a combination of both. In most EU countries, ADR is national rather than decentralised at regional or local level. Procedures are based on the parties' willingness to engage in the process. Most schemes are free for consumers or below €50, and are settled within 90 days on average. ADR decisions may be taken collegially e.g. by boards or by individuals—a mediator or ombudsman. The nature of these decisions ranges from non-binding recommendations, to decisions binding on the trader only or on both parties, and agreement of the parties; see further at http://ec.europa.eu/consumers/solving_consumer_disputes/non-judicial_redress/adr-odr/index_en.htm.

[55] Council of the European Union (2013).

[56] Benyekhlef and Vermeys (2013).

[57] Their enactment will be without prejudice to Directive 2008/52/EC of the European Parliament and of the Council on certain aspects of mediation in civil and commercial matters, available at: http://eur-lex.europa.eu/LexUriServ/LexUriServ.do?uri=OJ:L:2008:136:0003:0008:EN:PDF.

profession.[58] B2C complaints, such as claims for payment, and C2C conflicts are excluded.

The scheme is setting common minimum quality principles by asking Member States to ensure that approved entities providing ADR are impartial, transparent and efficient.

The Directive builds on earlier EU sector-specific legislation intending to re-regulate sensitive market sectors to the benefit of the internal market, such as post and telecommunications, or energy, and requires the formation of out-of-court dispute resolution mechanisms. The entities thus formed, and any other operating ADR providers, will now have to adapt to the updated requirements.[59] The existing out-of-court dispute resolution providers in the EU may apply to be qualified under the requirements of the Directive, for which they will have to comply with knowledge, independence, impartiality, transparency and efficiency requirements. The ADR facilities must be available and easily accessible online and offline to the disputants, irrespective of their location. The Directive at the same time does not include in its provisions a draft set of specific procedural rules applicable to ADR providers, apparently deeming that procedural issues are better left to each individual ADR scheme to determine.[60] Consumers will have access to the facilities free of charge or for a nominal fee. The parties will not have to retain a lawyer or a legal advisor, although the procedure will not deprive them of the right to do so at any stage.[61] Measures should be made available to ensure that the disputants are treated in an equal and fair way,[62] while the claims will not be time-barred owing to the operation of the ADR process.[63] The procedure must be completed within 90 days from receipt of the complaint.

Traders who commit to using ADR entities and the ODR platform must post the relevant details and links on their websites or in their Terms and Conditions of trade.

The use of ADR entities or the ODR platform will require the agreement of both the consumer and the trader; however the commitment of the consumer to submit to the ADR procedure is not binding on him if made before the conflict arose.[64] Moreover, the resolution which ends the ADR procedure will be binding on the parties only if they had been informed of its binding nature in advance and had

[58] ADR Directive, Article 4.1.(a). Recital 17 to the Preamble expands the application of the Directive notion to dual purpose contracts partly affecting the person's trade, provided the trade purpose is not the predominant one, available at: http://eur-lex.europa.eu/LexUriServ/LexUriServ.do?uri=OJ:L:2013:165:0063:0079:EN:PDF.

[59] Hornle (2012).

[60] Hornle (2012).

[61] ADR Directive, Article 8 (b).

[62] ADR Directive, Article 9.

[63] ADR Directive, Article 12.

[64] ADR Directive, Preamble Rec. 43.

specifically accepted it.[65] With regard to the outcome of the ADR procedure it is argued in theory that a greater degree of transparency is needed, by way of access to previous decisions or at least summaries, in order for participants to know what to expect, which would in turn lead to a higher settlement rate at an early stage in the procedure. Such early settlement will eventually ensure the financial viability of the ADR/ODR system.[66]

The ADR entities will be required to publish information regarding problems they have identified, which are either significant or occur repeatedly and cause conflict on a recurring basis. They will also be required to submit their recommendations to minimise these problems[67] and to cooperate with the other ADR providers and the national consumer protection authorities to optimise the system and develop best practices.

The harmonisation time limit lapsing on 9 July 2015, some Member States have enacted legislation,[68] or have taken preparatory steps.[69] It is interesting to note the example of the Greek law, which renders the settlement decision enforceable once any of the parties, registers it with the First Instance Court.

[65] ADR Directive, Article 10.2.

[66] Hornle (2012).

[67] ADR Directive, Preamble Rec. 30.

[68] In Greece, the Directive has been transposed into the Greek law by means of the Common Ministerial Decision (CMD) 70330οικ/09.07.2015 of the Ministers for Economy, Infrastructure, Marine and Tourism and for Justice, Transparency and Human Rights (Gov.Gazette B' 1421/ 09.07.2015). The provisions of the CMD set minimum requirements concerning expertise, independence and fairness for the ADR providers and for the natural persons active in the ADR schemes, such as obligation to have the necessary knowledge and skills with respect to ADR procedures, to be occupied for a term of sufficient duration to ensure their independence, not to be subject to orders by any of the parties of a dispute or their representatives. It is also provided that they shall comply with certain publicity requirements (including, indicatively, that they shall publish on their websites any contact details, the fact that they are registered in the Special Registry of ADR providers, the categories of disputes they may handle, the languages in which a dispute may be submitted and in which the ADR procedure takes place, etc.) and fulfill specific efficiency and fairness requirements. Furthermore, in the event a consumer submits a complaint to an ADR provider, the time period for the lapse of the consumer's claim against the trader is interrupted for the whole time of the ADR procedure, whereas the participation in an ADR procedure does not preclude the right of the parties to pursue their claims by judicial means and any of the parties is entitled to exit the procedure at any time. To be registered in the Special Registry, an ADR provider shall submit a series of information including its structure and funding, the people responsible for dispute resolution, their fees, the duration of their occupation, etc., its procedural rules, the average time required for the resolution of a dispute, the language(s) in which a complaint may be submitted and in which the procedure may be held, et al.

[69] See in this relevance Cortes (2015).

5.4 The Regulation on Consumer ODR

Under the ODR Regulation, the EU Commission should by 9 January 2016 design, establish, operate and maintain a free, interactive website through which parties can initiate ADR in relation to C2B and B2C[70] disputes concerning online domestic or cross-border transactions.[71] The platform was launched on 16 February 2016. Consumers or traders will be able to initiate the process by submitting to the platform an electronic complaint form and attaching relevant documents.[72] The ODR platform will inform the respondent of the complaint and of the need to agree on an ADR provider within a set time; it will provide information on the available qualified ADR providers in the jurisdiction, which are included in the Commission's consolidated list, and on their fees, if any. Once the parties agree on a specific ADR provider, the platform will electronically transmit to it the complete received complaint and supporting documents. The designated ADR entity will seek to resolve the dispute, optionally by using the free electronic option which the ODR platform will be offering. The physical presence of the parties or of their representatives will not be required, unless this is required by the ADR provider's procedural rules and both parties agree to it.[73]

To assist the Commission in the preparation of implementation guidelines, following the adoption of the ADR/ODR legislation, an Expert Group on Alternative Dispute Resolution of informal and temporary nature was set up at the Directorate-General for Justice and Consumers.[74] In July 2015 the Commission populated an implementing Regulation[75] to lay down the modalities for the electronic complaint form, the exercise of the functions of the ODR platform and the cooperation between the ODR contact points.

With respect to the identification of the competent ADR entity, the Commission Implementing Regulation provides that the ODR platform shall display to the respondent party an indicative list of ADR entities (where no ADR entity is defined in the electronic complaint form), based on the geographical address of the parties to the dispute and the sector the dispute relates to.[76] Moreover, the ODR platform

---

[70] Traders may only initiate proceedings against consumers if the national law so allows and in respect with disputes where the relevant ADR procedures are offered by providers qualified under the ADR Directive.

[71] ODR Regulation, Article 5.1; the Regulation excludes offline transactions, unlike the ADR Directive.

[72] ODR Regulation, Article 8.

[73] ODR Regulation, Article 10 (b).

[74] Expert Group on Alternative Dispute Resolution (E02879), http://ec.europa.eu/transparency/regexpert/index.cfm?do=groupDetail.groupDetail&groupID=2879&NewSearch=1&NewSearch=1.

[75] Commission Implementing Regulation (EU) 2015/1051 of 1 July 2015 *on the modalities for the exercise of the functions of the online dispute resolution platform, on the modalities of the electronic complaint form and on the modalities of the cooperation between contact points*; http://eur-lex.europa.eu/legal-content/EN/TXT/HTML/?uri=CELEX:32015R1051&from=EN, OJ L 171, 2.7.2015, pp. 1–4. The Regulation entered into force on 11.08.2015.

[76] Article 4 par. 1 of the Commission Implementing Regulation.

shall provide a search tool to help the parties identify the ADR entity competent to deal with their dispute among the ADR entities registered in the ODR platform.[77]

The ODR platform must be user-friendly, designed for all.[78] It will ensure privacy by design. It will translate the complaint into the right language for the respondent party and the ADR entity, among all official EU languages.[79] It will provide information on the available ADR solutions and their parameters, and statistical data concerning the outcome of the disputes it has hosted; on the relevant qualified providers and the ODR contact points. The Commission shall populate and make accessible the ODR platform through its websites which provide information to citizens and businesses.[80]

To support the operation of the system, each Member State shall designate one ODR contact point, which will be responsible to assist on issues that may arise from the functioning of the ODR platform, to facilitate communication between the disputants and the ADR entity, to assist with the submission of the complaint and the supplementary documents, to provide general information on consumer rights, etc.[81] The ODR contact points will cooperate to ensure the better development of the facility as a practical and reliable dispute resolution mechanism, and permit the formation of best practices. The Commission Implementing Regulation (EU) 2015/1051 specifically states in its Article 9 that the national ODR contact points shall provide support to the resolution to the best of their ability. In the example of the Greek CMD transposing the new ADR Directive, it is the Consumer Ombudsman—European Consumer Center of Greece that has been appointed as the national ODR contact point.[82] In the UK, in establishing an ODR contact point to help consumers with cross-border disputes submitted via the Commission's ODR platform, the preference was expressed to cover obligations under the ODR Regulation but to not extend the ODR requirements beyond these. The ODR Platform contact point must host at least two ODR advisors to assist and help with documentation in cross border disputes. The ODR Regulation allows the Government to decide whether the ODR contact point handles the following: disputes relating to a domestic complaint involving a UK consumer or business; and disputes initiated by business (potentially allowing complaints made by a business against a consumer) to be submitted to an ADR provider via the ODR platform. The Government expressed the view, that requiring the ODR contact point to extend to assisting consumers with disputes about domestic, as well as cross-border online purchases would dramatically increase its workload and risk duplicating the activity of the proposed helpdesk. Several responses to the public consultation launched in this respect supported this view. On the contrary, the view was supported that the contact point should have the flexibility to handle domestic complaints as it sees fit, because it

[77] Article 4 par. 2 of the Commission Implementing Regulation.

[78] The "design for all" focus ensures accessibility by all users, including vulnerable ones.

[79] ODR Regulation, Article 5.4.

[80] ADR Directive, Article 5 (3).

[81] ODR Regulation, Article 7.

[82] Article 5 point (β) of the CMD 70330οικ/2015.

is not always clear to an online consumer whether a purchase is cross-border or domestic.[83]

Personal data regarding a dispute shall be stored only for the time necessary to achieve the purposes for which they have been collected.[84] Personal data shall be automatically deleted from the electronic database after six months from the date the ODR platform was notified that the case was concluded.[85]

5.5 *Prospects of the Scheme with Regard to Insurance*

The ADR Directive combined with the ODR platform is the first *de lege lata* tool to become available over a considerable geographical and transactional area such as the EU. Its implementation is intended to facilitate trade and boost e-commerce in the single market, thereby guaranteeing the fundamental requirements for a fair process and for an effective remedy.

The ODR Regulation was welcomed by commentators as a step in the right direction. The fact that it will be available to consumers and ADR providers at no cost is already of significant value and so is the language tool which will facilitate communication by providing translations. It is early to assess how the platform will operate, as its final design has not yet been seen and tested.[86] This has raised discussion as it is a crucial factor for its eligibility and success in resolving disputes. The first response of the market participants with respect to the technical testing of

[83] See [UK] Government response to the consultation on implementing the Alternative Dispute Resolution Directive and the Online Dispute Resolution Regulation, at https://www.gov.uk/government/uploads/system/uploads/attachment_data/file/377522/bis-14-1122-alternative-dispute-resolution-for-consumers.pdf.

[84] See in this context Hornle (2012), referring that, should complaints data stored by the ODR platform lead to identifying an individual, these will be personal data; this should be seriously considered when designing the electronic database where such data shall be stored, as well as when defining when such data shall be accessible by other entities (i.e. ODR contact points, the Commission, the competent ADR entity, etc.), to ensure compliance with data protection legislation, also taking into account that the European Charter of Human Rights has elevated data protection to a human right (Article 8.1).

[85] With respect to information collected by the ODR platform, the Commission Implementing Regulation provides that the ADR entities, to which a complaint has been transmitted by the ODR platform and which have agreed to deal the dispute, shall, without delay and upon receipt of the complete complaint file, transmit to the ODR platform the date of receipt of the complete complaint file, which starts the 90-calendar day period referred to in the ADR Directive, and the subject matter of the dispute. Upon the conclusion of a dispute, the ADR entities shall transmit to the ODR platform the date of conclusion of the ADR procedure and its result.

[86] Benyekhlef and Vermeys (2013).

the Platform was positive.[87] Another expressed concern is that the completion of out-of-court dispute resolution online will be further hindered by the limited distribution of digital signature and the limited use of certified electronic mail.[88]

As drafted, the Regulation provides a platform for communication between complainants and potential ADR providers, rather than an operating electronic tool which will lead the parties to the actual resolution of the dispute through the use of an automated or semi-automated process. It does not seem to be hosting the possibility of direct communications between the parties, which is recognized as an important initial step often able to lead to the resolution of the conflict without further need of recourse to a mediating third party. Furthermore it is not described as containing a guidance tool which would provide benchmarks to the parties to facilitate resolution by guiding them by way of statistics or other information.[89] These factors are of critical importance for the resolution of insurance disputes and for the future eligibility of the platform.

In the European Union, legislation insists on the insurers providing complaints handling policies and mechanisms, and these are subject to regulatory supervision. The "Solvency II" Directive 2009/138/EC provides in the case of non-life insurance, a duty for the insurance undertaking to "*inform the policyholder of the arrangements for handling complaints of policyholders concerning contracts including, where appropriate, the existence of a complaints body, without prejudice to the right of the policyholder to take legal proceedings*".[90] A respective duty is provided in the case of life insurance as well. EIOPA, the EU insurance regulator, has issued implementing Guidelines to insurance undertakings, which however do

[87] Pursuant to Article 6 of the ODR Regulation, the Commission had to test the technical functionality and the user-friendliness of the ODR platform and of the complaint form in cooperation with experts in ODR from the Member States and consumer and trader representatives. This testing took place on the 25th and the 27th November 2014 with the presence of 120 participants (ADR/ODR experts appointed by Member States, consumer representatives, trader representatives including SMEs, and the European Disability Forum). According to the Commission's presentation to the Internal Market and Consumer Protection (IMCO) Committee of the European Parliament on 3rd March 2015, available at http://www.europarl.europa.eu/meetdocs/2014_2019/documents/imco/dv/odr_ppt_/odr_ppt_en.pdf, about 70 % of the participants provided an overall positive feedback for the ODR Platform, noting that it is easy to use and navigate, the information provided is clear and easy to understand and the complaint form is easy to submit. It was also suggested for further improvements that the next steps and the history of the case is made clearer, the exchange of messages is improved, the dashboards for ADR entities and ODR contact points are improved and the quality of translation is optimized.

[88] Grasso (2015).

[89] See in this relevance Cortes and Lodder (2014), pp. 21–22.

[90] Article 138(1) of Directive 2009/138/EC of the European Parliament and of the Council of 25 November 2009 on the taking up and pursuit of the business of Insurance and Reinsurance (Solvency II), OJ L 335, 7.12.2009, p. 1, which will take effect on 01.01.2016.

not make reference to any ODR mechanisms.[91] In the context of legal protection insurance, the Solvency II Directive in article 203 provides that Member States shall provide for the availability of arbitration mechanisms. Notably the industry has not reacted negatively to the initiative, as for example RIAD, the International Association of Legal Protection Insurance, during the public consultation period for the ADR/ODR mechanism has taken a positive stance with regard to legal protection insurers covering mediation costs.[92] Furthermore, the Principles of European Insurance Contract Law (PEICL) in Article 1:302[93] state that their application does not preclude access to out-of-court complaint and redress mechanisms otherwise available to the policyholder, insured or beneficiary.

Although the ADR Directive shall apply to disputes which arise either on- or off-line in domestic or cross border transactions, the ODR platform will only accept complaints arising from on-line transactions. At the current state of e-insurance penetration, this immediately excludes the large bulk of insurance complaints and claims. However this divide may be decreasing in view of the constant growth of insurance over the internet. Furthermore, the ODR platform will only host C2B complaints, while no B2B disputes will be admitted. This leaves out disputes between insurance undertakings, which are by nature more prone to be resolved swiftly on line owing to the expertise of the interested parties and the lack of the personal element in the dispute. Such claims are often handled by claims administrators and other professional service providers, who through the frequent use of the platform would be able to develop useful expertise and engage more actively in using the tool. On the other hand, while online marketplaces such as insurance aggregators selling insurance covers will have to post a relevant link on their website,[94] they may avail of the escape clause provided under the ADR Directive and, subject to regulatory restrictions,[95] refuse to participate in the dispute resolution process initiated by a consumer who filed a complaint. In this respect, easy as it may be for traders in general to invoke the escape clause, this will prove difficult for insurers, as they are subject to supervision and control including their response to complaints of policyholders or other insurance indemnity beneficiaries. The lack of efficient response may result in the imposition of penalties by the supervisory authority.

[91] European Insurance and Occupational Pensions Authority (EIOPA) Guidelines on complaints handling by insurance intermediaries of 03.12.2013, available at https://eiopa.europa.eu/publications/eiopa-guidelines/guidelines-on-complaints-handling-by-insurance-intermediaries/index.html.

[92] RIAD communication 5610333409-62 of March 2011.

[93] *Project Group "Restatement of European Insurance Contract Law"*, Draft Common Frame of Reference, Chapter III, Section IX, Insurance Contract, 1 August 2009, Article 1:302 (see bibliography for recent detailed reference).

[94] The new Directive (EU) 2016/97 on insurance distribution ("IDD") provides in Article 19.b.iii that insurance intermediaries shall inform their customers on the out-of-court redress procedures for any disputes between them.

[95] See EIOPA Guidelines on complaints handling by insurance intermediaries of 03.12.2013, fn 77 above.

It is further suggested that it would be useful if the system would provide for an additional feature in its design, which would allow the activation of artificial intelligence and statistical tools to identify and systematize findings of recurring conflict generators to exploit its potential to also serve as a conflict-prevention mechanism.[96] For the insurance market this would be a very useful element, taking into account the already existing bulk of precedent and the uniform characteristics of large groups of disputes.

The outcome of the process shall be enforceable subject to national law. In this regard, the Mediation Directive 2008/52/EC is a positive background, by providing that the agreement reached as a result of the mediation can be made enforceable if the parties so intend and if they follow a specific procedure as national law provides.[97] Notably Article 15 IDD provides that Member States shall ensure the setting up of procedures allowing customers and other interested parties, especially consumer associations, to register complaints about insurance and reinsurance intermediaries and undertakings, without however the outcome being binding, while the prescription of the claim will be suspended.[98] To promote the penetration of ADR/ODR in the insurance sector, ADR providers specialized in insurance disputes must emerge.

In assessing the possibilities of success of the ODR, the lessons learned from the FIN-NET example should be considered. Thus the mechanism should be more actively marketed and expanded in the EU Member States, and should be endorsed by insurers and intermediaries unions, as well as by consumer associations. The ADR schemes available should all become its members. Insurers should consider including mediation in the policies as an agreed step before court. Finally, the interaction with FIN-NET should be promoted.[99]

6 Justice Requirements

Any ODR system which will prevail or will be provided in the industry to facilitate out-of-court online dispute resolution, will have to meet the essential justice requirement, which is one of the fundamental human rights and claims a fair process and a fair outcome for any dispute resolution procedure.[100] Within the course of the international

---

[96] See relevant argumentation Hodges and Creutzfeldt (2013).

[97] Mediation Directive 2008/92/EC, Article 6.

[98] The Court of Justice of the European Union held in its decision of 18 March 2010 in Joined Cases C-317/08, C-318/08, C-319/08 and C-320/08, Rosalba Alassini, etc., that the right of access to justice is not breached if the agreement does not deny access to courts after an unsuccessful mediation procedure.

[99] See BIPAR Response to the European Commission's Consultation on the use of ADR as a means to resolve disputes related to commercial transactions and practices in the Eu, April 2011, p. 3. BIPAR is the European Federation of Insurance Intermediaries.

[100] Article 6, para. 1 of the European Convention for the Protection of Human Rights reads as follows: "In the determination of his civil rights and obligations …., everyone is entitled to a fair and public hearing within a reasonable time by an independent and impartial tribunal established by law. Judgment shall be pronounced publicly…".

dialogue regarding the setting of rules and standards on the virtual world of the internet, a number of international organizations and fora have engaged in exploring the needs and tools to safeguard justice requirements in online dispute resolution.

In a chronological order, a first reference to information technologies in the field of ADR methods was made by the Organization for Economic Co-operation and Development (OECD) in 1999.[101] Following this, the International Chamber of Commerce (ICC) expressed its opinion regarding ODR in 2003 and suggested best practice guidelines.[102] Within the same year the Global Business Dialogue on Electronic Commerce (GBDe)[103] in cooperation with Consumers International issued its *"Alternative Dispute Guidelines"*[104] with reference to ODR systems. A proposal regarding the creation of a region-wide cooperative scheme for ODR was made within the framework of the Seventh Inter-American Specialized Conference on Private International Law (February 2010) of the Organization of American States (OAS).[105] A significant number of papers, such as draft generic procedural rules[106] for a global ODR system or private enforcement mechanisms,[107] have been issued by the ODR Working Group III formed since July 2010 in the United Nations Commission on International Trade Law (UNCITRAL).

These international organizations initiatives share certain commonly accepted principles and standards. Next to availability, optional character, transparency, speed, low cost and efficiency, the basic requirements include the following:

(a). The e-merchant should provide a first-step internal mechanism to tackle with the dispute when it first arises, to address customer complaints in a fair, effective, transparent and timely manner, without undue cost or burden to the customer. Should such internal mechanism not lead to customer satisfaction, the customer should be notified of the availability and the features of a certain ODR system.

(b). ODR systems are optional and do not impede the consumer's access to justice.

(c). ODR providers must be transparent and make publicly available and easily accessible all the necessary information for the contracting parties to decide

[101] Recommendation of the OECD Council concerning Guidelines for Consumer Protection in the context of Electronic Commerce, 1999, pp. 7–8, http://www.oecd.org/internet/consumer/34023235.pdf. OECD issued these Guidelines in an attempt to attribute a global perspective to consumer protection and deal with the *"inherently international nature of the digital networks and computer technologies that comprise the electronic marketplace"*.

[102] International Chamber of Commerce (2003), p. 2.

[103] The Global Business Dialogue on e-Society (GBDe) is a worldwide, CEO-led, business initiative, established in January 1999 to assist the development of a global policy framework for the emerging online economy acting on a self-regulation basis, http://www.gbd-e.org/.

[104] Global Business Dialogue on Electronic Commerce (2003), p. 54 ff.

[105] Organization of American States (2010).

[106] United Nations Commission on International Trade Law-Working Group III (Online dispute resolution) (2013).

[107] See the paper "Online dispute resolution for cross-border electronic commerce transactions: overview of private enforcement mechanisms", United Nations Commission on International Trade Law-Working Group III (Online dispute resolution) (2013).

whether they wish to submit their dispute, including the types of dispute they address, all information regarding the procedure (preliminary requirements, online or offline as well procedure, etc.), and the dispute resolution officers' qualifications, roles and powers.

(d). Fairness of process requires that the procedure is easily accessible; it affects the language problem in international transactions; its impartiality is ensured by the use of specific tools and methods; parties are given fair opportunity to present their side of the facts and their arguments and to be represented or assisted by a third party.

(e). The difficulty to determine and apply the proper national law requires that decision to be made in equity and/or on the basis of codes of conduct.

(f). Confidentiality, Privacy and Data Protection: an ODR provider should abide by data protection rules, maintain a high level of security and authentication, conduct risk assessments and prepare a business continuity plan for unforeseen adverse circumstances and make available the relevant information.

(g). The outcome should be enforceable by way of enforcement mechanisms applied by each ODR provider.

7 The Example of Benoam

Benoam is an online arbitration system established in Israel in 2002 to resolve subrogation claims between insurance companies over property damages incurred in car accidents with no bodily injury.[108] As the system is a successful token of online dispute resolution of claims between insurance companies, it can serve as a useful example to draw ideas and understand how and insurance-focused ODR system could work.

It is reported that almost all of the insurance companies operating in the Israeli market have signed on to the system and keep being committed to referring all such claims exclusively to it.[109] The system emerged as a substitute for litigation in overloaded courts for a large number of low value disputes, and was intended to operate entirely online with some limited availability for face-to-face sessions, while a fully documented file would be available to the parties. Benoam is reported to have developed to a success with high levels of satisfaction by participants. Its primary success component is considered to be that its founders identified the specific needs of the particular environment and designed it as a tailor-made tool to cater for those needs. Over the years of its operation it has succeeded to remain connected to the evolving needs of its users and to create efficient tools addressing them.[110]

The system is reported to have proved valuable in a number of further important respects. Because of the centralized, accessible and effective tool it provided for addressing the claims, the insurance companies were able to improve their

[108] See Rabinovich-Einy and Tsur (2010a), pp. 529, 542; Rabinovich-Einy and Tzur (2010b), p. 8; Rabinovich-Einy and Katsh (2012a), pp. 151–199.

[109] *See immediately preceding citations.*

[110] Rabinovich-Einy (2006), pp. 253–293.

effectiveness more generally in terms of preserving and accessing data, handling complaints internally instead of relying on external legal services, and restructuring complaint handling within the agencies from a geographically based arrangement to a centralized one.[111] In addition, the intensive, online communication among the agencies through the system has produced more informal dialogue, which has benefited the agencies and has improved work relations among them.[112] Unlike usual arbitration systems, Benoam has built up a corpus of precedents which arbitrators conform with when addressing homogeneous circumstances.[113]

---

[111] Rabinovich-Einy (2008), p. 18.

[112] Rabinovich-Einy (2008), p. 18.

[113] The system's unique advantages are described in detail by Rabinovich-Einy and Katsh (2012), pp. 184–185, with further references to bibliography: "In terms of fairness and trust-building, the system has adopted an array of measures which together served to enhance consistency and equality in arbitrator rulings. For one, the detailed arbitration rules to which all users agreed when registering for the process, were a means for structuring the process *ex ante* to ensure fairness. Furthermore, the availability of an internal appeals mechanism before another arbitrator or a panel of arbitrators proved an effective *ex post* mechanism for strengthening fairness, albeit at some cost to the efficiency of the process.

Nevertheless, by setting time limits on the appeals mechanism and by proceeding with the execution of awards, the cost associated with appeals has been contained.

Another important means for ensuring fairness was the adoption of a form of *res judicata* and the emergence of "precedents" within the system. From the very beginning, *Benoam* adopted a practice of releasing "landmark decisions" to its site without identifying the parties to the claim. Over time, as more and more cases were being decided by *Benoam* while the courts handled fewer of these cases, new questions emerged requiring a clear and consistent rule so as to prevent a feeling of arbitrariness and the incentive to forum shop among arbitrators. Similarly, arbitrators adopted a practice of subjecting themselves to prior decisions by other arbitrators where the rules of *res judicata* applied, even when they disagreed with the outcome itself. Often, their reasoning would explain that they felt compelled to follow the previous ruling in the name of consistency and fairness.

To ensure the success of such developments, all communications and arbitration rulings were documented on the *Benoam* database and each insurance company had a copy of all proceedings to which it was a party. This is very different from the typical ADR process where proceedings are kept private, with very little data being documented. While arbitration proceedings are less sensitive to documentation than mediation, it is still true that in most arbitration contexts there is no extensive database kept. Claims are usually handled on an individual ad-hoc basis and there is rarely an attempt to address claims in a consistent and systematic manner as is done in the court setting. (There are course other exceptions such as the Uniform Domain-Name Dispute-Resolution Policy (UDRP) system established by the Internet Corporation for Assigned Names and Numbers (ICANN) for the resolution of domain name disputes. . . .) With broad documentation online came a change in the understanding of privacy, allowing for the release of certain rulings into the public domain (albeit in anonymous form) and the voluntary disclosure of previous rulings by some of the parties in their own proceedings in subsequent case.

Finally, these fairness-enhancing features have been strengthened by the fact that the users of the system are repeat players of similar power who typically alternate between the plaintiff and defendant positions. This has contributed to a level playing field both in the initial design stages of the system and in fellow users acting as *de facto* monitors of the system. This state of affairs is complemented by the employment of professional arbitrators (retired judges, attorneys, appraisers, traffic examiners, and CPAs) familiar with the field. . . . The same technology that required thorough planning of the dispute resolution process has also made data and documentation an automatic by-product and the analysis of information an inexpensive and instructive endeavor."

The Benoam system is set up so that data can be transferred automatically from the insurance companies' internal databases onto the Benoam forms; as a result efficiency and accuracy are enhanced and there is better communications and data management. The data transfer also assists enforcement: the arbitration decisions flow directly from Benoam to the Israeli Insurance Association, for the rulings to be executed under its auspices. The rulings are enforced on a fixed day of the month, regardless whether an appeal has been filed or not.[114]

Benoam is reported to have achieved the transfer of the bulk of the property damage claims from car accidents between insurance companies to its online dispute resolution system. "Beyond the effective and satisfactory resolution of individual disputes, the online system has led to the refinement of the rules governing such claims, thereby enhancing clarity and preventing similar problems from recurring".[115]

8 Summary and Conclusions

Transactions over the internet inevitably result in a number of disputes. As recourse to courts and traditional ADR facilities was difficult, disproportionately costly and inefficient, the cyberworld developed a number of functions and tools to resolve such disputes online. The tools and facilities which artificial intelligence can provide have been evolving and seem to be able not only to resolve a large number of conflicts, but also to identify the patterns which cause such conflicts and to develop and systematise methods preventing them from arising in the first place. Electronic tools are also capable of identifying similarities and discrepancies in the manner in which disputes with similar characteristics have been resolved, and in this way to establish a more streamlined treatment of conflicts with similar characteristics, with results which better satisfy the justice requirement. The focus shifts from locality, time, face-to-face communication and adversarial positioning, to swiftness, cost-effectiveness, efficiency, reduced formality, predictability and pragmatic enforcement.

The insurance industry has been pioneering in developing and employing such systems in the United States. ODR systems take a variety of forms, ranging from fully automated tools such as blind bidding based on game theory, to simple technological platforms providing technical aid which facilitates the operation of traditional ADR mechanisms and helps them work more efficiently. Automated systems where the procedure is software-driven are principally targeted to a large volume of low-value disputes with high homogeneity, which is prone to certain insurance disputes; the more complicated the dispute, the more necessary the input of expert human factor in the process.

[114] Rabinovich-Einy and Katsh (2012), p. 184.

[115] Rabinovich-Einy and Katsh (2012b), p. 55.

While in North America ODR seems to be developing, by contrast in Europe it has not flourished. Private initiatives did not prosper for a number of reasons including the lack of an apprehensive culture. In the European Union the ODR expansion seems to be driven centrally through regulation rather than through market evolution. To resolve disputes emanating from cross-border trade in financial products, FIN-NET was introduced; however its penetration is not considerable. In 2013 the Consumer ADR Directive and the ODR Regulation were introduced, which are set to become effective in the Member States by 9 July 2015 and 9 January 2016, respectively. The ADR Directive lays down the minimum requirements for ADR providers and for the ADR operations in domestic and cross-border disputes initiated by consumers against traders in the EU. The ODR Regulation requires the Commission to deploy a user-friendly ODR platform available to all at no cost, providing a case management tool which can be used by certified ADR providers.

Insurance is an ideal field where the beneficial effects of ODR can be applied, especially in high volume low cost consumer disputes. Without undermining the uniqueness of each case, consumer complaints and claims follow homogeneous and to a certain extent standardized patterns which often lead to resolutions with a number of uniform features. The monitoring of resolutions with similar patterns assists in the building of a reliable corpus of precedent which could both facilitate resolution and case management in the future and develop a level playing field for complainants and respondents. Whether the EU ADR/ODR initiative will be eligible for the resolution of insurance disputes will depend on a number of factors including the final design of the system, the degree to which public awareness will be promoted, whether it will expand to also encompass disputes emanating from off-line transactions. As long as effective ways are established to build-up an apprehensive mentality to ODR, and if inherent weaknesses are addressed, such as ways to tackle fraud in the system, ODR may prove a valuable tool to the more efficient functioning of the insurance market.

ODR is being supported and shaped by a corpus of theory and soft law that has been developing with the participation of academics and professionals and the engagement of international organisations, such as UNCITRAL, OECD and ICC, which lay down the principles and requirements for the design and functioning of ODR platforms to conform with the principles of fairness and proper procedure.

References

Benyekhlef K, Vermeys N (2013) The European regulation on consumer online dispute resolution – where are we now? Available at: http://www.slaw.ca/2013/07/23/the-european-regulation-on-consumer-online-dispute-resolution-where-are-we-now/

Calliess GP (2006) Online dispute resolution: consumer redress in a global market place. German Law J 07(08):647 ff

CEN Workshop (2009) Standardisation of online dispute resolution tools. CWA 16023, November

Cortes P (2015) The impact of EU law in the ADR landscape in Italy, Spain and the UK: time for change or missed opportunity? ERA Forum 16(2):125–147, http://link.springer.com/article/10.1007%2Fs12027-015-0388-x

Cortes P, Lodder AR (2014) Consumer dispute resolution goes online: reflections on the evolution of European law for out-of-court redress, pp 21–22. Available at http://papers.ssrn.com/sol3/papers.cfm?abstract_id=2414098

Council of the European Union (2013) Press Release 8671/13 of 22 April 2013, http://europa.eu/rapid/press-release_PRES-13-162_en.htm

Duca LD, Rule C, Loebl Z (2012) Facilitating expansion of cross-border e-commerce-developing a global online dispute resolution system (Lessons derived from existing ODR systems-work of the United Nations Commission on International Trade Law). Penn State law legal studies research paper no 25-2011

American Bar Association Task Force on E-Commerce and ADR (2002) Addressing disputes in electronic commerce. Final report and recommendations. http://www.americanbar.org/content/dam/aba/migrated/dispute/documents/FinalReport102802.authcheckdam.pdf

Global Business Dialogue on Electronic Commerce (2003) New York recommendations- Alternative dispute resolution guidelines- agreement reached between consumers international and the global business dialogue on electronic commerce, November 2003, 5th GBDe Summit, New York City (2003) < EN PDF 1,921 KB>, at http://www.gbd-e.org/publications.html

European Commission (2011) Alternative dispute resolution and online dispute resolution for eu consumers: questions and answers, 29 November 2011, MEMO/11/840, available at: http://europa.eu/rapid/press-release_MEMO-11-840_en.htm

European Commission (2015) The online dispute resolution (ODR) platform, presentation to IMCO, 3 March 2015, http://www.europarl.europa.eu/meetdocs/2014_2019/documents/imco/dv/odr_ppt_/odr_ppt_en.pdf

Gabarro S (2009) Mediation for B2C disputes: results of a study of three European ODR providers. http://idt.uab.es/files/unpub/2.pdf

Goodman JW (2003) The pros and cons of online dispute resolution: an assessment of cyber-mediation websites. Duke Law Tech Rev 2:1–16, Available at: http://scholarship.law.duke.edu/cgi/viewcontent.cgi?article=1073&context=dltr

Grasso G (2015) The online dispute resolution (ODR) in the European Union, 5 June 2015. Available at http://www.uianet.org/en/content/grasso-giorgio-online-dispute-resolution-odr-europ

Heiss H, Lakhan M (eds) (2011) Principles of European insurance contract law: a model optional instrument: with a postscript in honour of Fritz Reichert-Facilides, on behalf of the Project Group: Restatement of European Insurance Contract Law, Sellier European Law Publishers

Hodges C (2013) Making consumer ADR work. In: CDR conference, September, Oxford

Hodges C, Creutzfeldt N (2013) Implementing the EU consumer ADR directive, www.fijs.org

Hornle J (2012) Encouraging online dispute resolution in the EU and beyond- keeping costs low or standards high? Available at: http://www.odr.info/files/julia.pdf

International Chamber of Commerce (2003) ICC best practices for online dispute resolution (ODR) for B2C and C2C transactions, http://www.it-retten.dk/bog/bilag/23/ICC%20Best%20Practices%20for%20Online%20Dispute%20Resolution.pdf

Katsh E (1996) Dispute resolution in cyberspace. Conn Law Rev 28:953

Katsh E (2012a) ODR: a look at history. In: Katsh E, Rainey D, Abdel Wahab MS (eds) ODR theory and practice. Eleven International Publishing, The Hague

Katsh D (2012b) Introduction. In: Katsh D, Rainey MS, Wahab A (eds) ODR theory and practice. Eleven International Publishing, The Hague

Katsh E, Rifkin J (2001) Online dispute resolution: resolving disputes in cyberspace. Jossey-Bass, San Francisco

Kaufmann-Kohler G, Schultz T (2004) Online dispute resolution: challenges for contemporary justice. Kluwer Law International, The Hague

Lide EC (1996) ADR and cyberspace: the role of alternative dispute resolution in online commerce, intellectual property and defamation. Ohio St J Disput Resolut 12:193

Lodder AR, Zeleznikow J (2012) Artificial intelligence and online dispute resolution. In: Katsh E, Rainey MS, Wahab A (eds) ODR theory and practice. Eleven International Publishing, The Hague

Mediate.com, www.Mediate.com

Morek R (2011) ADR and ODR for EU consumers: proposals for new directive and regulation. Available at: http://kluwermediationblog.com/2011/12/09/adr-and-odr-for-eu-consumers-proposals-for-new-directive-and-regulation/

Morek R (2013) New legislation on ADR and ODR for consumer disputes adopted in the European Parliament. Available at http://kluwermediationblog.com/2013/04/09/new-legislation-on-adr-and-odr-for-consumer-disputes-adopted-in-the-european-parliament/

National Centre for Technology and Dispute Resolution (NCTDR) (2015) www.odr.info

Organization for Economic Co-operation and Development (1999) Recommendation of the OECD council concerning guidelines for consumer protection in the context of electronic commerce, http://www.oecd.org/internet/consumer/34023235.pdf

Organization of American States (2010) Draft United States proposal, draft [Model Law/Cooperative Framework] for electronic resolution of cross-border e-commerce dispute, 19 February 2010, http://www.oas.org/dil/esp/CIDIP-VII_doc_trabajo_gt_proteccion_consumidor_anexo_A__Borrador_Ley_Marco_Cooperativo_Modelo_Solucion_Electro.pdf

Poblet M, Ross G (2012) ODR in Europe. In: Katsh E, Rainey MS, Wahab A (eds) ODR theory and practice. Eleven International Publishing, The Hague

Rabinovich-Einy O (2004) Balancing the scales: the Ford - Firestone case, the internet and the future dispute resolution landscape. Yale J Law Technol 6(1): Article 1

Rabinovich-Einy O (2006) Technology's impact: the quest for a new paradigm for accountability in mediation. Harv Neg Law Rev 11:253–293

Rabinovich-Einy O (2008) Reflecting on ODR: the Israeli example, 2008 with further reference to Tsur, Roee Adv. Presentation, 2007

Rabinovich-Einy O, Katsh E (2012a) Technology and the future of dispute systems design. Harv Neg Law Rev 17:151–199

Rabinovich-Einy O, Katsh E (2012b) Lessons from online dispute resolution for dispute systems design. In: Katsh E, Rainey MS, Wahab A (eds) ODR theory and practice. Eleven International Publishing, The Hague

Rabinovich-Einy O, Tsur R (2010a) The case for greater formality in ADR: drawing on the lessons of Benoam's Private Arbitration System. Vermont Law Rev 34

Rabinovich-Einy O, Tzur R (2010b) Unclogging the collision course: the evolution of Benoam, an online private court. ACResolution

Rule C (2002) Online dispute resolution for businesses, B2B, e-commerce, consumer, employment, insurance, and other commercial conflicts. Jossey-Bass, San Francisco

Schultz T (2002) Online dispute resolution: an overview and selected issues. United Nations Economic Commission for Europe, Forum on Online Dispute Resolution, 6–7 June 2002

Suesskind R (2008) The end of lawyers? Rethinking the nature of legal services. Oxford University Press

The Sports Dispute Resolution Center of Canada, http://www.crdsc-sdrcc.ca

Thiessen E, Miniato P, Hiebert B (2012) ODR and e negotiation. In: Katsh E, Rainey MS, Wahab A (eds) ODR theory and practice. Eleven International Publishing, The Hague

United Nations Commission on International Trade Law (2010) Annotated provisional agenda, A/CN.9/WG.III/WP.104, 26 August 2010, http://daccess-dds-ny.un.org/doc/UNDOC/LTD/V10/559/93/PDF/V1055993.pdf?OpenElement

United Nations Commission on International Trade Law (2010) Note supporting possible future work on online dispute resolution in cross border electronic commerce transactions, A/CN.9/710, 26 May 2010, http://www.cisg.law.pace.edu/cisg/ODR/Institute_ODR_paper.pdf

United Nations Commission on International Trade Law- Working Group III (Online dispute resolution) (2013) 28th session, online dispute resolution for cross border electronic commerce transactions: draft procedural rules (A/CN.9/WG.III/WP.123), 9 September 2013, http://daccess-dds-ny.un.org/doc/UNDOC/LTD/V13/862/79/PDF/V1386279.pdf?OpenElement

United Nations Commission on International Trade Law- Working Group III (Online dispute resolution) (2013) 28th session, online dispute resolution for cross border electronic commerce transactions: overview of private enforcement mechanisms (A/CN.9/WG.III/WP.124), 13 September 2013, http://daccess-dds-ny.un.org/doc/UNDOC/LTD/V13/863/44/PDF/V1386344.pdf?OpenElement

Ury WB, Brett JM, Goldberg SB (1988) Getting disputes resolved: designing systems to cut the cost of conflict. Jossey-Bass, San Francisco

Vilalta E (2012) ODR in E-commerce. In: Katsh E, Rainey MS, Wahab A (eds) ODR theory and practice. Eleven International Publishing, The Hague

Wing L, Rainey D (2012) Online dispute resolution and the development of theory. In: Katsh E, Rainey MS, Wahab A (eds) ODR theory and practice. Eleven International Publishing, The Hague

Zeleznikow J (2002) Risk, negotiation and argumentation - a decision support system based approach. Law Probab Risk 1:37

Private International Law and On-Line Insurance Contracts

Katarzyna Malinowska

Contents

Abstract This chapter presents relations between the insurance contract concluded online and private international law, including the role of private international law in online insurance. The considerations concerning this issue are because of the fact that online insurance has no borders and is a transnational service. In consequence, there arises a necessity to analyze the need of protecting policyholders and consider effective methods of introducing such a protection. Private international law rules are considered to be among such methods. No doubts PIL is gaining importance along with the increase of the cross-border transactions, which in turn, are on the

Katarzyna Malinowska PhD, Partner at BMSP Legal Advisor (Warsaw), Lecturer of University of Leon Koźmiński in Warsaw, member of Research Council at Polish Chapter of AIDA.

K. Malinowska (✉)
BMSP Legal Advisors, Warsaw, Poland
e-mail: katarzyna.malinowska@bmsp.com.pl

P. Marano et al. (eds.), *The "Dematerialized" Insurance*,
DOI 10.1007/978-3-319-28410-1_13

increase with the vital help of the internet. What is the most important, it concerns not only B2B (as it used to be), but increasingly involves participation of the consumers. The purpose of the analysis is to show whether the PIL rules are effective rules. The chapter also presents other methods of protecting the parties to the transnational insurance contract and tries to show tendencies in modern jurisdictions worldwide. The issues considered in the chapter are viewed mostly from a European perspective, but as they go far beyond safe European legal reality, the international perspective of online contracting are also presented, especially with the aim of showing tendencies in online contracting in a global perspective.

1 Introduction: General Remarks

The chapter presents the relationship between online insurance contracts and modern private international law. Therefore, Sec. 2 is devoted to the presentation of online insurance contracts from an international perspective. To this end, an analysis of online insurance *versus* other type of online contracts will be carried out, to be subsequently followed by an analysis of the cross-border nature of the on-line insurance. The main problems appearing in the situations of insurance distributed transnationally with the help of internet will also be considered. Section 3 of the chapter deals with the specifics of the private international law *versus* contracting on-line, with special attention paid to the online insurance contracts. In this respect, a well-known problem shall be presented, i.e. whether the private international law is the right instrument to support entering into online cross-border insurance contracts, or whether some common substantive regulations distinctive for the internet should be adopted as a safeguard of the cross-border insurance.

It has been known for a long time already that on-line transactions are increasingly frequent world-wide,[1] in recent years gaining significant prevalence over contracting in the traditional way. This leads to a profound change in the manner modern business is conducted. No matter whether we call it an evolution or a revolution, using the internet for buying and selling goods and providing services poses several challenges for legislators and issues related to private international law are among those challenges. The significance of PIL consists in ensuring a legal safety of transactions, as concerns the legal effects of the contract, including validity thereof, as well as rights and obligations of the parties, which may be

[1] The recent statistics say about US$12.4 trillion of the value of the electronic transactions B2B and US$ 1.2 trillion in B2C and the prognostic that until 2017 e-commerce transactions will amount to approximately 5 % of all inter-company transactions and retail sales (WTO brochure), p. 3, Le Comite du Commerce electronique du Conseil canadien des responsables de la reglamentation d'assurance (2012), p. 3 Though, the EU claims that comparing to the efforts made in this respect, the total value of e-commerce is relatively low, as it amounts only to 4 % of total European trade; Commission Staff Working Document Online services, including e-commerce, in the Single Market, Brussels, 11.1.2012, SEC (2011) 1641 final.

substantially different depending on which legal system is governing the contract.[2] The role of private international law rules is increasing along with the growing globalization[3] involving an increasing number of electronic transactions, which are said to be "born global".[4] The necessity of applying PIL rules seems to be inevitable, as transnational character of contracts is an unavoidable consequence of concluding them with the help of the internet. The problem may look even more serious if we consider the fact that an increasing number of online contracts are concluded with the participation of consumers, who, having access to the internet, started to participate in cross-border commerce, at a wider scale than before.[5] These concerns regard almost all kind of contracts,[6] including insurance as one of the most sophisticated contracts nowadays.

No doubt that the internet, described as intangible, interactive and international[7] affects insurance, although since the beginning of its expansion, it has been stressed that "compared to the tangible products and even other forms of services, including financial services, on-line contracting in insurance face more problems".[8] Such problems could be overcome neither by the technical aspects of contracting online, nor by the conviction that insurance as an information product presents a natural potential in e-commerce and can easily become subject to digitalization.[9] The difficulties seem to result from several factors, the most important of which is that the "insurance products" are subject to less systematic standardization (as it may concern the other financial services), tend to be more complex, are taken out infrequently, and, further, they face regulatory impediments.[10] It has also been said that the insurance products differ in their suitability for marketing on the internet from other services, mostly in terms of the advice required, as well as the risk of information deficit on the side of the clients.[11]

The problems of private international law in the context of contracting on-line in cross-border insurance had not been initially noticed, although the postulate of minimizing legal uncertainty has become one of the first important postulates with

[2] Verbiest and Le Borne (2002).

[3] Opertii Badan (2007), p. 6.

[4] COM (97) 157; see also 59 recitals of ECD on "global nature of electronic communication". See also H. Kaviar et, A. Ahmadi (2010), p. 693, as well as Law Commission (2001), s.1.

[5] SEC (2011) 1640 final; see also Polanski (2006), p. 1.

[6] Natural exceptions will concern contracts concerning real estates and such other types of contracts that are related to the requirement of special form, eg. participation of the notary, etc.

[7] Haddadi Selma, 2001, p. 2.

[8] OECD (1998), p. 25.

[9] Falch (1998), p. 10.

[10] Baur et al. (2001), p. 16.

[11] The fewer parameters required for constructing the insurance product, the more chances for its successful distribution via the internet, see: Falch (1998), p. 10. Also Aljifri et al. (2003), pp. 13–138—where it is underlined that overcoming the trust barrier is crucial for any kind of online transactions, stating that the information security in e-commerce is one of the hottest topics;

respect to the electronic commerce.[12] Nowadays, while the basic issues of e-signature and electronic payment have been more or less settled and regulated,[13] the primary importance is being gained by material aspects of electronic contractual relations. These, as will be presented in the analysis below, cannot be nowadays considered solely from domestic legal systems and require a global approach, both with respect to the choice of law problems and substantive law of contracts. Such a tendency in electronic commerce is common for various types of contracts, although legislative works on some of them, for example sales contract, are quite advanced at the international level and some of them still face legal impediments throughout the world.[14]

The development of on-line technologies is still perceived as bringing both threats and advantages.[15] On the one hand, it is obvious that concluding international contracts with help thereof has become easier (and in some jurisdictions such development made cross-border contracts possible at all, by making the place of concluding the contract virtual), on the other hand, the need to protect the weaker party became not only a more imperative, but an immanent part of online contracting. This change in tendency results from the fact that for a long time, the international potential of e-commerce has been used chiefly in B2B transactions, where the need of protection of the parties is minimal. As now the goal for B2C online contracts is to become more frequent, the protective rules must follow them. PIL seems to be the most obvious type of such rules. However, is it also the most effective?

The present chapter will not encompass the issues related to the Rome I Regulation, the related issues shall be considered in the chapter of Anna Tarasiuk "European Private Law (Regulation Rome I) and On-line Insurance Contracts", with a reference made when needed.

2 Online Insurance Contracts in International Legal Perspective

This section of the chapter presents the modern notion of the online contract from a legal perspective, from the European law, as well as, to the extent possible, on international legal documents and other legal cultures.[16] The result of this analysis

[12] OECD (1998), p. 31 and 39.

[13] Among the others, in the US, The E-SIGN Act of 2000; in the EU European Directive 1999/93/EC; and in Australia—Electronic Transactions Act 1999.

[14] Such as the impediments imposed on commercial insurance in Shariah law.

[15] Comite du Commerce electronique du Conseil canadien des responsables de la reglementation d'assurance (2012), p.3.

[16] The author refers to the "documents", as not all the sources used in this chapter have a binding force, being sometimes just a frame of reference or soft law instruments.

will then serve as a basis for explaining the specifics of online insurance contracts. Such an approach seems to be necessary as insurance is usually one of the types of contracts regulated in the national civil law legislations and in spite of being distinctive, constitutes a part of the traditional civil law of contracts. Also, it cannot be ignored that insurance is one of the financial services, so an analysis is needed whether there exist a possibility of formulating conclusions common for various types of contracts concerning financial services. Besides, it seems plausible that problematic issues within the scope of electronic commerce should not be dealt with on a sector-by-sector basis, as it would entail a risk of adopting inconsistent resolutions of identical issues. A comprehensive, integrated approach should be used across various sectors.[17] Looking for a uniform definition of the online contract applicable to all kinds of contracts, including online insurance contracts seems to respond to that postulate. This is the goal of this section of the chapter.

2.1 *Online Contracts: Notion and Specifics*

2.1.1 Outline

This point will be devoted to the notion and specificity of online contracts, with a focus on differences between "traditional" contracts and online contracts. It may be noticed that several similar notions are in common use with respect to the same issue, i.e. electronic contracts, online contracts, internet contracts, web contracts, etc. Nonetheless, only the electronic contract seems to have source in legislation. Therefore, it seems reasonable to start the analysis of the definition of online contract by explaining what the "electronic contract" means. When doing so, we should remember that the notion of electronic contract is not purely a legal issue, as it is related to "e-commerce", being an economic phenomenon of an extremely broad meaning. Therefore, the legal analysis should also consider the economic purposes which electronic contracts are meant to serve and should aim at resolving such issues that enable or facilitate functioning of e-commerce.

Analysis of the notion of electronic contract, should consider several aspects, including not only civil law theory, but also technical aspects of computer and internet technology. Although an extensive regulatory activity may be observed in Europe[18] and at the global level in this respect, no consistent definition of electronic

[17] Boss (2011), p. 303.

[18] COM (2010) 2020 final; COM (2010) 245 final; SWD (2013) 153 final., the proposal for a Regulation "on electronic identification and trusted services for electronic transactions in the internal market" adopted by the EC on 04.06.2012, see http://eurlex.europa.eu/LexUriServ/LexUriServ.do?uri=COM:2012:0238:FIN:EN:PDF. Chapter VI, Final Provisions, Article 41 "repeals Directive 1999/93 and provides for the smooth transition of the existing electronic signature infrastructure to the new requirements of the Regulation".

contract may be found.[19] The explanations available in official documents concern only broadly understood e-commerce and are repeated in a similar manner in European and international documents.[20] Although the e-commerce legislation remains fragmented, which is also considered to be a cause for the absence of the uniform definition of electronic contract, as various legal instruments aim at different interests to be satisfied or protected.[21] It is not easy to find such definition in other jurisdictions. It may be attributed to the fact that first legislation attempts in western legislations, such as the United States, European Union Member States started only in the twenty-first century. These are the effect of many years of research and comparative works, but in emerging markets like China, India, Arabic countries, the ideas included in the recent legislations seem to be from the European, American or international concepts.

Thus, instead of one simple definition, there are several explanations what electronic contract may be. We may find them in statutory and academic documents. Analysing most of them, we may come to the conclusion that even from the civil law point of view, electronic contract is a broad notion. It encompasses both contracts that are concluded and performed via electronic means,[22] using the internet (e.g. downloading information via website), as well as such contracts which are only concluded online, but performed *off-line*, where the use of electronic means is not necessary or not feasible (e.g. physical delivery of tangible products bought on-line).[23] All this leads to the conviction that the main factors distinguishing the electronic contract from other types of contracts are (1) the conclusion of contract by use of electronic means used by both parties to the contract, as well as (2) lack of simultaneous presence of the parties. Thus, electronic

[19] It includes Directive 1999/93/EC on a Community Framework for electronic signatures, consumers' protection directives—mentioned in point 11 of preamble to ECD; see also Riefa (2009), p. 7. See however the proposal for a Regulation "on electronic identification and trusted services for electronic transactions in the internal market" adopted by the EC on 04.06.2012, see http://eurlex.europa.eu/LexUriServ/LexUriServ.do?uri=COM:2012:0238:FIN:EN:PDF. Chapter VI, Final Provisions, Article 41 "repeals Directive 1999/93 and provides for the smooth transition of the existing electronic signature infrastructure to the new requirements of the Regulation".

[20] Although it should be admitted that general definitions of e-commerce are quite consistent. The example of which may be given from WTO report, defining e-commerce as: "la vente ou l'achat de marchandises ou de services effectues sur des reseaux informatiques au moyen de methods specifiquement concues pour la reception ou la passation de commandes".

[21] Riefa (2009), pp. 7–8.

[22] See Judgment of 23.3.2010—joined cases C-236/08 to C-238/08, where, "by electronic means" is defined as meaning that "Service is sent initially and received at its destination by means of electronic equipment for the processing... and storage of data, and entirely transmitted, conveyed and received by wire, by radio, by optical means or by other electromagnetic means".

[23] Graham and Smith (ed) (2007), point 10-047, after Riefa (2009), p. 12; COM (97) 157, point 7; Riefa (2009), p. 11; the question has also been raised whether the contract, by conclusion of which the machines play a decisive role and no human is present, can still be called contracts, or new classification should be found.

contract will by nature be a distance contract[24] (the feature being important also for applying specific consumer protection). For such a broad definition it is indifferent whether such contract is performed online or offline[25] and the notion of electronic contracts includes both, cases when (1) agreement is concluded online and performed offline, as well as (2) cases when it is concluded and performed online. The contracting phase seems to be decisive for perceiving the contract as electronic or not.

The other division of electronic contracts that may be found, is the distinction between the direct and indirect electronic contracts, with the first category consisting of the contractual subject being intangible and stored electronically as software, etc., while the second, indirect electronic contracts are concluded online but performed in a traditional way (for example an electronically ordered book, delivered by post). A hint as to the definition of electronic contract may also be found in the ICT report concerning the OECD Model Survey, where the internet and electronic transactions are defined, the latter ones being broader and including the sale of goods and services via computer networks, also via e-mail, which is excluded from the definition of internet transactions. Both types include the performance of the contract online or offline.[26] Again, we see that the major aspect of electronic contracts is related to the method of concluding the contract.

In the doctrine, it has also been suggested that the notion of online contract is narrower than electronic contract, as the word "online" means concluding contract while having full access to the internet,[27] contrary to the contracts concluded electronically, but offline, when parties exchange the contractual documents stored electronically but without access to the internet at the moment of concluding thereof.

Although this chapter does not focus on general concepts of concluding contracts, it may be worth mentioning that according to some opinions, the traditional concept of offer and acceptance as the manner of concluding an electronic contract is questioned and it is considered rather as a kind of a complex process involving multiplied territories and entities, external to the contractual relation to which the traditional notions are not sufficient.[28] This leads to the more general question, whether using internet technology entails only the problem of recognizing a new, electronic form or it has a broader impact on contract law.[29] As it was mentioned,

---

[24] See Directive 2011/83 (which repealed Directive 1997/7 (DSD).

[25] Popiołek (2007), p. 11.

[26] OECD (2006).

[27] Gołaczyński (2007).

[28] Savirimuthu (2005), pp. 109–114.

[29] **Judgment of the Court (Grand Chamber) of 23 March 2010, joint cases C-236/08 to C-238/08, where the scope of the Article 14 of the ECD was considered and resulting thereof scope of liability of entities involved in rendering services of information society; it was stated there, that "*Article 14 of Directive 2000/31/EC of the European Parliament and of the Council of 8 June 2000 on certain legal aspects of information society services, in particular electronic commerce, in the Internal Market ("Directive on electronic commerce") must be interpreted as***

the legal provisions concerning e-commerce do not decide, whether "electronic" means just a form of concluding the contract equivalent to written form (when the offer and acceptance concept could be sustained) or reinventing general concepts of concluding contracts is required for making them applicable also to electronic contracts (or creating separate rules only for contracting online).[30] Legal documents, such as ECD or Uncitral Model Law seem to avoid answering that question, merely saying that concluding a contract online cannot be the reason of treating the contract void.

2.1.2 The European Union

When considering hard law rules of electronic contracts, such a definition can only be derived from the European directives concerning "information society", such as ECD, DSD (as replaced by 2011/83/EU Directive) and from some of the reports of the European Commission. They refer to "online services" as "services provided at a distance, electronically, at the request of the person who is the recipient of the services, in return for payment". E-commerce, having broad meaning, encompasses

meaning that the rule laid down therein applies to an internet referencing service provider in the case where that service provider has not played an active role of such a kind as to give it knowledge of, or control over, the data stored. If it has not played such a role, that service provider cannot be held liable for the data which it has stored at the request of an advertiser, unless, having obtained knowledge of the unlawful nature of those data or of that advertiser's activities, it failed to act expeditiously to remove or to disable access to the data concerned". Same standpoint was presented in case C-324/09 where, ECJ (Grand chamber) stated that "Article 14(1) of Directive 2000/31/EC of the European Parliament and of the Council of 8 June 2000 on certain legal aspects of information society services, in particular electronic commerce, in the Internal Market ("Directive on electronic commerce") must be interpreted as applying to the operator of an online marketplace where that operator has not played an active role allowing it to have knowledge or control of the data stored. The operator plays such a role when it provides assistance which entails, in particular, optimizing the presentation of the offers for sale in question or promoting them. Where the operator of the online marketplace has not played an active role within the meaning of the preceding paragraph and the service provided falls, as a consequence, within the scope of Article 14(1) of Directive 2000/31, the operator none the less cannot, in a case which may result in an order to pay damages, rely on the exemption from liability provided for in that provision if it was aware of facts or circumstances on the basis of which a diligent economic operator should have realized that the offers for sale in question were unlawful and, in the event of it being so aware, failed to act expeditiously in accordance with Article 14(1)(b) of Directive 2000/31."

[30] Interesting analyses of concluding insurance online were presented with respect to the Belgian law, but of universal value. The author warns against multiplying legal requirements as regards concluding insurance online, as they could potentially increase the insecurity of the consumers instead of reducing it, Jacquemin (2010), pp. 249–255. The author is of the view that, at least the conclusion of the insurance contracts is a kind of a process, although he does not relate it to using the internet, p. 251; see also Boss (2011), p. 307. It is stressed that nowadays it is not sufficient to merely remove the barriers for concluding contracts online and it is high time for the law to make them fully operational from the legal point of view. p. 308.

sale of goods and services, but also social networks, distance learning, etc. The basic criterion of e-commerce is the way of performing the activity, i.e. at distance, electronically, via the internet.[31] ECD does not define electronic contracts. Nevertheless, it devotes the whole Part 3 thereof to the issues of "agreements concluded by electronic means",[32] excluding the contracts concluded exclusively by exchange of electronic mail,[33] however. Such an approach may also suggest that the main focus is on the method, by which the contract is concluded and that it suffices that a contract is concluded online for it to be referred to as an electronic contract. ECD guarantees freedom to provide services online, including online insurance, on the European market and although it is binding only on European insurers, there is no doubt that its long-term goal is to facilitate synchronicity with other parts of the world and their legal solutions in respect to electronic commerce. ECD introduces the obligation of equal treatment of electronic contract as compared with the traditional contract (equivalence principle), forbidding qualifying them void for the mere reason of being concluded via electronic means of communication.[34] It is clear then that such approach neither interferes with the legal concepts of concluding civil contracts, nor with the form of concluding the contract, but imposes on the national legislators the obligation of introducing such regulatory framework that satisfies the above-mentioned requirements. The intended equality of online contracts should be maintained not only at the stage of contract formation, but also in course of its performance.[35] This specific requirement results in the disputes handled by the ECJ, which settled already several cases in this respect.[36]

As regards the implementation of the ECD in Member States laws, it should be stressed that although most of the Member States implemented the provisions of

---

[31] The same criteria adopted in WT/COMTD/W 193, p. 7.

[32] ECD regulated the electronic commerce as a part of the services of information society (recital no 17), which are defined as all kind of transactions consisting of sale/purchase of goods or services conducted over computer network by methods specifically designed for the purpose of receiving or placing orders, although the goods or services are ordered electronically, the payment and the ultimate delivery of goods or services do not have to be conducted online, see for example: Muñoz-López (2009), p. 167. An important hint with respect to the electronic contract notion is explanation of the expression "by electronic means" which is to "mean that a service is sent initially and received at its destination using electronic equipment for the processing (including digital compression) and storage of data, and that it is entirely transmitted, conveyed and received by wire, by radio, by optical means or by other electromagnetic means. The service must be conveyed from its point of departure to its point of arrival by means of electronic (processing and storage) equipment and by telecommunications means"; SEC (2011) 1641 final.

[33] Article 10 (4) and Article 11(3).

[34] Fras (2008), pp. 183–184. This view is supported by several judgments that prohibit the Member States from restricting the freedom to provide information society services from another Member States, see for example cases C-509/09 and C-161/10.

[35] Such an obligation results from Article 9 of the ECD, see also Law Commission (2001), p. 18.

[36] For example: *Scarlet vs SABAM*: C-70/10 (24 November 2011).

ECD in due time,[37] this has not led to introducing more precise definitions of electronic contract into the domestic laws. Most of them focus on introducing the information requirements related to the conclusion of the contracts by electronic means.[38] This view is supported by the analysis of the legislations of some of the Members States. One of them is Germany, where to implement Art. 10, 11 of the Directive, the German legislator inserted Section 312 g (former Section 312 e) into the German Civil Code.[39] The rule introduces special duties for the entrepreneur concerning the conclusion of contracts by electronic means. There is no definition of electronic contract again and the offer and acceptance concept is interpreted from Art. 130 BGB to the needs of electronic contract (also 133, 154 and 157 BGB). Although, it should be mentioned that BGB introduces a new distinguished "electronic form" requiring the secured electronic signature.[40] At the same time, BGB limits the possibility of using the electronic form to some types of transactions (suretyships, Art. 766 BGB).[41] On the other hand, a strong conviction is presented that "in general the traditional rules on issuing and receipt of a declaration of intent and on the formation of contract still are applicable, with a few modifications that notably concern the binding effect of a presentation of goods or services in the Internet".[42]

Similar situation may be found in France, where the implementation of the ECD took place in Loi n° 2004-575 du 21 juin 2004 pour la confiance dans l'économie numérique, where Article 26 introduces a kind of exception to the Civil Code rules

[37] Belgium: Loi du 11 mars 2003 sur certains aspects juridiques des services de la sociétè de l'information visés à l'article 77 de la Constitution. MB Ed. 2 du 17/03/2003 p. 12960 (C-2003/11126); Spain: Ley 34/2002 de 11de julio, de servicios de la sociedad de la informacion y de comercio electronico BOE n° 166 du 12/07/2002 p. 25388; France: Loi n° 575 du 21/6/2004 pour la confiance dans l'économie numérique; Ordonnance n° 2005-674 du 16/6/2005 relative à l'accomplissement de certaines formalités contractuelles par voie électronique.

[38] Although there were several problems regarding the scope of application of the ECD, which ended in preliminary rulings of the ECJ, the example of which is Google France Sarl, Google Inc v Luis Vuitton Malletier SA and others (2010) in which the court stated that "an internet referencing service constitutes an information society services consisting in the storage of information supplied by the adverstiser"; or case L'Oreal v eBay (2011), where it was stated that "an online marketplace was an information society service".

[39] "Umsetzung der Artikel 10 und 11 der RL: § 312 e Bürgerliches Gesetzbuch Umsetzung von Artikel 18 der RL: §§ 2 und 3 Unterlassungsklagengesetz"; Gesetz über rechtliche Rahmenbedingungen für den Elektronischen Geschäftsverkehr (Elektronischer Geschäftsverkehr-Gesetz (EGG)) Bundesgesetzblatt, Jahrgang 2001, Teil I Nr. 70 vom 20/12/2001, Seite 3721 See also Makris and Spiros (2004), pp. 161–168.

[40] Section 126a BGB defines "electronic form": (1) If electronic form is to replace the written form prescribed by law, the issuer of the declaration must add his name to it and provide the electronic document with a qualified electronic signature in accordance with the Electronic Signature Act [Signaturgesetz]. (2) In the case of a contract, the parties must each provide a counterpart with an electronic signature as described in subsection (1).

[41] Armbrüster (2013).

[42] Armbrüster (2013).

of the form requirement,[43] which in consequences led to the amendment of the Civil Code with respect to the contracting online and introduced, similarly as in Germany, the "electronic form" (l'écrit sous forme électronique doit répondre à des exigences équivalentes).[44] Similarly, the Dutch Civil Code provides for a specific provisions concerning agreements formed by electronic means, which confirm the equivalence of the contracts entered into by electronic means with the written contracts (Article 6:227a), upon some authenticity conditions. Additionally, it is worth noting that subsequent articles concerning electronic commerce, use in a clear way, the expression of "electronic contract". The approach of the UK law has been well described in the works of the Law Commission, reviewing the law "to ensure that it is up to date and that it reflects both existing and anticipated developments in trading practices", in electronic commerce, considering that the first legislation to facilitate electronic commerce in the UK was already enacted in 2000 as the Electronic Communication Act.[45] The main issues discussed with reference to the Article 9 of the ECD concerned the legal requirements for writing and a signature and it was stated that e-mails and website trading satisfy basically the requirements of the above (only electronic data interchange not). It is related to the fact that English law imposes few form requirements as regards the contract formation.[46]

It is also worth mentioning that the EU conducts periodical researches on progress in implementation of ECD rules, both with respect to the formal introducing the laws into the domestic legal systems of Member States, as well with respect to the development of e-commerce practices.[47] In response to the last research, many suggestions were made for more coherence in the *acquis*, especially in terms of data protection, insurance market mediation, private international law, and consumer protection.

---

[43] Dans les conditions prévues à l'article 38 de la Constitution, le Gouvernement est autorisé à procéder par ordonnance à l'adaptation des dispositions législatives subordonnant la conclusion, la validité ou les effets de certains contrats à des formalités autres que celles mentionnées à l'article 1108-1 du code civil, en vue de permettre l'accomplissement de celles-ci par voie électronique.

[44] Amendments were made to Le chapitre VII du titre III du livre III du Code Civil.

[45] The purpose of ECA was to build confidence in electronic commerce and the technology underlying it by providing a statutory approval scheme for cryptology providers, confirming the legal recognition of electronic signature, as well as providing mechanism for removing any legal obstacles to the use of electronic communication and storage and for enabling appropriate conditions to be imposed; the Law Commission (2001), pp. 1–2. Thereafter there were issued Electronic Commerce Regulations 2002 and DTI Guidance on the Regulations; see also: http://www.out-law.com.

[46] The Law Commission (2001), p. 17.

[47] Summary of the results of the Public Consultation on the future of electronic commerce in the Internal Market and the implementation of the Directive on electronic commerce (2000/31/EC).

2.1.3 North America

Despite its imperfection, the EU legal environment seems to be the most developed than that in the rest of the world,[48] including USA, where there are no special regulations concerning distance selling, including distance selling of insurance.[49] In the USA, the most important legal instrument concerning the electronic contract was designed to be the Uniform Computer Information Transaction Act (UCITA), which was, however, adopted by only two states.[50] It provided rules regarding the formation, governance, and basic terms of an electronic contract, according to which traditional contract principles and remedies also apply to electronic contracts. Electronic contracts were defined by UCITA as any kind of contract formed in the course of e-commerce by the interaction of two or more individuals using electronic means, such as e-mail, the interaction of an individual with an electronic agent, such as a computer program, or the interaction of at least two electronic agents that are programmed to recognize the existence of a contract.[51] In view of the failure to adopt uniform law on electronic contracts, the National Conference of Commissioners on Uniform State Laws proposed a legal framework for the use of electronic signatures and records in government or business transactions under the name of The Uniform Electronic Transactions Act (UETA) and Electronic Signatures in Global and National Commerce Act (e-sign) 2000.[52] It made electronic records and signatures as legal as paper and manually signed signatures.[53] The strong opposition to adopt uniform law on electronic contracts in USA may be surprising, when considering the first views of US academics with respect to the need of creating distinctive legal system for regulating electronic commerce. The recent trend does not however support this theory so strongly and seems to convince that the internet has not changed the basic rules of contract law and on-line communication is only a matter of forming the contract. Thus the main problem relating to the electronic contracts is related to the digital or electronic signature.[54] Following the above approach, the electronic contract, is a contract created wholly or in part through communications over computer networks. A cyber-contract can be created entirely by the exchange of e-mails where an offer and an acceptance are evident or they can be made by a combination of electronic communications, paper

---

[48] Even the European countries which are non-members of the EU, although developed, have no distinctive legislation on distance selling (including electronic sale); see for example Switzerland, Federation Romande des Consommateurs (2013).

[49] Comite du Commerce electronique du Conseil canadien des responsables de la reglamentation d'assurance (2012), pp. 3 and 12.

[50] See also Zhang (2007).

[51] http://UCITA.online.org.

[52] Geist, p. 15.

[53] Pauli (2007), p. 7.

[54] In 2000 the use of electronic signatures in commerce became sanctioned by the federal government with the passage of the "Electronic Signatures in Global and National Commerce Act", (15 USC§701).

documents, faxes and oral discussions[55] This definition, as results from the above analysis, is however not a legal definition, but one developed by the doctrine. It is clear again that it concentrates on the formation stage of the contract.

With respect to Canada, it is worth mentioning that in September 1999, "Conference pour l'harmonisation des lois au Canada" adopted a uniform law on electronic commerce (LUCE) from the Uncitral Model Law of 1996.[56] The above law constituted a basis for regulations binding now in all the Canadian provinces concerning electronic commerce. Additionally, in 2001 the concept of harmonized law for online sale was approved by the federal government of Canada.[57] It is worth noting that Canada, being a country of a developed legislation level, used the Uncitral document to make it a part of its legal system. This positive example is not the only example on the global level.

2.1.4 Asia

As regards other jurisdictions, special attention should be given to the Chinese Contract Law enacted in 1999. It has been based on Unidroit principles and expressly provides for a possibility of concluding electronic contracts, liaising them with the form of the contract.[58] Even if there is no definition of electronic contract, the law says that "[t]he parties may conclude a contract in written, oral or other forms,"[59] stating in Art. 11 that the written form includes a written contractual agreement, letters and electronic data (including telegram, telex, fax, electronic data interchange (EDI) and electronic mail). Apart from that, the new Contract Law explicitly refers to contracts concluded by electronic means in Articles 16.2, 26.2 and 34.2 with respect to the time of arrival of an offer and acceptance, and to the place of formation of the contract.[60] Additionally, the Law of Electronic Signature was adopted in 2004 saying that "electronic data messages that are able to demonstrate the contents tangibly and that may be retrieved and accessed at any time shall be deemed as complying with the written format required by laws and regulations", as well as, that "Electronic data messages shall not be rejected for use as evidence solely on the grounds that they have been created, transmitted, received or stored by electronic, optical, magnetic or similar means".[61]

The issues related to electronic contracts are also addressed in other Asian jurisdictions, for example India. The main law regarding contracts in that country is The Indian Contract Act, 1872. However, it proved to be insufficient for the

[55] Foster (1997–2000).

[56] Geist, p. 16.

[57] Comite du Commerce electronique du Conseil canadien des responsables de la reglementation d'assurance (2012), pp. 12–13.

[58] Zhang (2007), p. 211.

[59] Yuqing et H. Danhan (2000), p. 432; Kornet (2010), pp. 16–17.

[60] Z. Yuqing et H. Danhan (2000), p. 437.

[61] Junhua et al. (2012), pp. 633–634.

regulation of modern contracts, in particular electronic contracts and was "supplemented" by the act enacted in 2000 to support possibility of contracting electronically. It is the Information Technology Act and it attempts to solve some of the issues with respect to the formation and authentication of electronic contracts in the Indian law. Electronic contracts are usually defined as contracts modeled, specified, executed and deployed by a software system, but it is also stressed that "e-contracts are conceptually very similar to traditional (paper based) commercial contracts".[62]

2.1.5 Arabic Countries

The main problem with Arabic countries with respect to the contract law is that it is codified to a very narrow degree, as the parties often submit their relations to the Sharia law, causing the same problems for such contracts to be recognized internationally.[63] Saudi Arabia may be given as an example of an Arabic-Islamic legal system, where contract law has never been codified, evolving "from the directions and stipulations of Islamic law as they were received and defined by the jurists and religious intellectuals". The Arab countries however, participating actively in international commerce, do not abstain from the changes in contracts law. Therefore, for example Saudi Arabia created a legal framework regulating electronic contracts, Electronics Transaction Law of 2007, based on UNCITRAL.[64]

2.1.6 International Works on E-Commerce Law

As can be noticed, the new regulations enacted recently by countries not belonging to the Western civil law tradition which address the issues of electronic commerce, tend to base on the internationally adopted soft law instruments, such as Unidroit and Uncitral, the latter being particularly important with respect to the electronic contracts. The effect of the works performed within the United Nations, as well as other international organizations undertaking law-making initiative within their limits,[65] cannot be overestimated in this respect. The interest in e-commerce became an area of focus "because of its transborder nature and its potential for all

[62] Nagpal (2008), pp. 72–73.

[63] *Shamil Bank of Bahrain v Beximco Pharmaceuticals Ltd and others (2004)*. This issue became a part of widely discussed problem in course of drafting Rome I Regulation, i.e. whether the parties may refer also to non-state law, for example Shariah law or Jewish rules; Modern Law for Global Commerce.

[64] Moreover, in 2007, Saudi Arabia became a signatory to the Convention on the Use of Electronic Communication in International Contracts (Convention on e-contacting) albeit not yet in force.

[65] The most important, apart from Uncitral and Unidroit being the Hague Conference of the Private International Law, as well as American CIDIP (Inter-American Specialized Conference on Private International Law), OHADA (Organization for the Harmonization of Business Law in Africa; Opertti Badan (2007), p. 8.

countries in the areas of economic growth, trade and improved social conditions." Therefore, also such organizations as OECD[66] focus on building "trust for users and consumers", as well as "establish ground rules for the digital marketplace; enhance the information infrastructure for e-commerce; and maximize benefits of e-commerce".[67]

The main goal that was set with respect to the e-commerce on global level is to achieve certainty that e-commerce transactions constitute a legally effective substitute of traditional methods of contracting. Having this in mind, a concept of "electronic equivalence" has been adopted. Specific measures to ensure enforceability of electronic contracts on international level took in 1996 a form of the Model Law on Electronic Commerce. The document was elaborated with the intention to "facilitate the use of modern means of communication and storage of information, such as electronic data interchange (EDI), electronic mail and telecopy". The basic assumption made concerning the "establishment of a functional equivalent for paper-based concepts such as "writing", "signature" and "original"". This concept has been expressed in Article 5, which "provides that information or documents will not be denied legal effect or enforceability solely because they are in electronic format",[68] Specific provisions of Model Law, such as Article 8,[69] 11 and 12 provide for validity of electronic online contracts.[70] The above-mentioned document also does not define the electronic contract, but with regard to the issue of offer and acceptance, indicates clearly that the phase of concluding the contract, gives it the attribute of being electronic or not. An important role of that kind of documents is shown in their adoption by the countries belonging to different legal cultures, different economic systems, causing the adopted solutions to be increasingly universal, finally becoming parts of the hard law rules in the ratifying countries.[71] This seems to be the right approach to the problems resulting from the global cross-border electronic commerce, as solutions to global problems should be worked out globally.[72] E-commerce issues are also considered within the scope of the United Nations Convention on Contracts for the International Sale of Goods (CISG) adopted in 1980. Although it does not regulate

[66] See for example the "OECD Action Plan for Electronic Commerce" endorsed in 1998.

[67] M. Geist, p. 4.

[68] M. Geist, p. 14.

[69] It states that "*electronic documents will satisfy the requirements for "original" documents if there is a reliable assurance as to the integrity of the information and that the information is capable of being displayed to the person to whom it is to be presented*". See M. Geist, p. 14.

[70] According to Article 11, an offer and the acceptance of an offer may be expressed by means of data messages. Where a data message is used in the formation of a contract, that contract shall not be denied validity or enforceability on the sole ground that a data message was used for that purpose; Article 12 provides that "*as between the originator and the addressee of a data message, a declaration of will or other statement shall not be denied legal effect, validity or enforceability solely on the grounds that it is in the form of a data message*".

[71] See Opertti Badan (2007), p. 12.

[72] See extensive explanation van Loon (2007), p. 20 et subsq.

expressly e-commerce,[73] it is argued that the general rules concerning written form is sufficient to include electronic contracts.

2.1.7 Conclusions

To summarize this section, it should be concluded that the notion of the online contracts is commonly used alternatively with the notion of electronic contract for defining the same phenomenon. The majority of national laws, in particular, those including the European Union law, as well as the laws of its Member States, liaise the electronic contract with the formation of the contract stage. Such a concept has been based on ECD, which uses the expression of "the contract concluded by electronic means". However, when analyzed in detail, it becomes clear that the notion of "electronic" is broader and may encompass all stages of the contract life, while online contract addresses only the stage of concluding the contract. In result, online contracts will always be a kind of electronic contract (but not vice versa). Having in mind the above, for the purposes of this chapter, the notion of online contract will be replaceable by the notion of electronic contract, or, when suitable for explaining the general idea, "e-commerce" notion. The same shall apply to insurance (respectively, electronic insurance contract, or e-insurance).

The above-mentioned analysis did not develop the problem concerning the civil law theory of contracting online, which consists of the idea that offer and acceptance as decisive moments for forming the contractual relation lost their value and contracting online began to be a kind of a complex process deprived of the privity, where more elements, entities and devices take a part. These issues, although cannot be ignored, as they change the long-lasting concepts of basic meaning for the western civil laws, are not decisive (in the opinion of the author) for the purposes of this chapter.

As can be seen from various laws adopted worldwide, both in the form of a soft or hard law instruments, the similar, functional concept has been adopted. It does not assume in a decisive way what is the concept of contracting electronically, but focus on ensuring the equal treatment of the electronic contracts with those concluded traditional way. It can be observed in Europe, America and Asia, where main principles of Model Law or Unidroit were addressed.[74] Such an approach, apart from satisfying various ideas, seems also to be quite pragmatic.

[73] As to the written form, the UNIDROIT Principles give a general definition of "writing" in Article 1.10 which covers "any mode of communication that preserves a record of the information contained therein and is capable of being reproduced in tangible form."

[74] M. Geist, pp. 15–16.

2.2 *Notion and Specifics of Online Insurance*

2.2.1 Outline

This section of the chapter explains the notion of online insurance, as well as to find an answer whether online insurance notion also focus on its conclusion stage or encompasses the performance of insurance contract. To this end, first of all, European regulatory framework will be analyzed, and then, some of those jurisdictions where distinctive legal framework on insurance contract exists.

Elaborating the definition of online insurance has been recently subject to many attempts. Among various definitions, some are more of legal nature, while others more of technical or economic nature. Technically, online insurance is defined often as production and distribution of insurance services with the use of information technologies, or, in a narrower sense it is related to providing insurance coverage while the insurance contract is negotiated, offered and concluded online. This definition includes also the delivery of the insurance policy and the payment of insurance premium.[75] From the legal point of view however, the same with the general notion for the online contract, it should be noted that no distinctive legal definition of online insurance may be found.

2.2.2 Forming Online Insurance

Let us turn now to the analysis of the particular stages of insurance contract concluded online. Are there any distinctive features of online insurance? First, we may notice that electronic means may be applied almost at each contractual stage of insurance, at least from a technical point of view. The more important however is a legal qualification thereof. At the stage of concluding insurance contract, all the documents, such as insurance application form, insurance policy and other documents may be issued online (loaded from the insurer's website, etc.) from a technical point of view. The other issue may relate to the pre-contractual obligations such as delivery of documents and information to the policyholder and proof, that they were properly performed online. Although the problem of electronic signature may appear in this situation, where domestic laws require that the insurance documents be signed by the parties (such problem has been broadly discussed in USA), according to various jurisdictions, especially those based on Uncitral model law (as Chinese), as well as European ECD, using electronic means of communication, cannot lead to the insurance contract being void, thus in consequence, the performance of the pre-contractual duties online should be deemed to be legally effective.[76] The above does not however limit the possibility

---

[75] Banan (2009), p. 117.

[76] Although, it should be mentioned that the scope of application of ECD to insurance was subject to a discussion, MARKT/2522/02-FR Rev. 1, p. 10. But see for example the Law Commission

of imposing some requirements on the electronic contracts (such as e-signature, etc).

Again, exactly as with respect to all other contracts, the aforementioned regulations do not provide for the specific requirements, setting only the purpose that should be achieved. Although the frames of this chapter do not allow for an extensive analysis of the concepts of the conclusion of an insurance contract, it may be stated that most of the domestic jurisdictions approach the issue by encompassing the conclusion of online contracts by party autonomy as to the form of contract. Consequently, "the electronic means of concluding the contracts" are treated as an equivalent of the written form (see for example Chinese law); however, additional requirements may be imposed, such as electronic signature on the insurance policy.[77]

2.2.3 Performing Insurance Contract Online

The performance stage of an insurance contract may also be supported by electronic means, i.e. providing the required information to the policyholder by the insurer,[78] including payment of the premium by the policyholder. It may concern also the contract (policy) administration and losses adjustment.[79] However, what distinguishes online insurance from other types of online contracts is that in its substantial part, the insurance contract cannot be performed on-line.[80] The main insurer's performance, i.e., taking over the risk by the insurer has purely intangible nature

(2001), p. 31 et subsq, where the Law Commissioners stated that even basing on the Marine Insurance Act, there it is possible to recognize the insurance policies issued online as written documents in traditional meaning.

[77] See for example Dutch Civil Code, which in the Article 7:932 requires authenticated electronic signature on the insurance policy, quite opposite for example to the Polish Civil Code, Art. 809, where the issuance of the insurance policy does not require any particular form, thus also for online insurance no particular form (such as electronic signature) is required.

[78] This issue, as an obligation of the service providers, including insurance is a subject to a special attention of the regulators; see for ex ample case C-298/07 ("*Article 5(1)(c) of Directive 2000/31/ EC of the European Parliament and of the Council of 8 June 2000 on certain legal aspects of information society services, in particular electronic commerce, in the internal market ("Directive on electronic commerce") must be interpreted as meaning that a service provider is required to supply to recipients of the service, before the conclusion of a contract with them, in addition to its electronic mail address, other information which allows the service provider to be contacted rapidly and communicated with in a direct and effective manner. That information does not necessarily have to be a telephone number. That information may be in the form of an electronic enquiry template through which the recipients of the service can contact the service provider* via *the internet, to whom the service provider replies by electronic mail except in situations where a recipient of the service, who, after contacting the service provider electronically, finds himself without access to the electronic network, requests the latter to provide access to another, non-electronic, means of communication")*.

[79] Baur (2001), p. 18.

[80] Fras (2008), p. 186.

until the moment, the event insured occurs. After the event insured occurs, the type of the insurance will be decisive for stating whether the contract may be performed by use of electronic means or not. In case of damages insurance, payment of compensation as an amount of money may be effected via internet. However in assistance insurance (group 18) or legal protection insurance (group 17) or any other type of insurance where the insurer's obligation is not payment but undertaking some actions, the performance, as a principle, will be offline.[81]

2.2.4 Insurance as "Information Product"

The qualification of insurance as a kind of financial service by the DFD Directive[82] does not either make any distinction between traditional insurance and online insurance, or any distinction between electronic insurance from other types of financial services.[83] It is the nature of a service that determines the way it is distributed. Although we usually talk about selling or buying insurance (policy), it is obvious that from a legal point of view, there is no product in the common meaning, even if the insurance policy takes a form of a document.[84] Thus insurance product in the legal sense can be rather described as terms and conditions of the insurance coverage, i.e. the wording of the insurance contract.[85] Such product is created by concluding the insurance contract. This is why the insurance is called also "an information product", which until the occurrence of the event insured remains only in the sphere of information and easily may be performed with the help of modern information technologies.[86]

2.2.5 Insurance as an Electronic Financial Service

The question which needs to be analyzed separately is the possibility of deriving or setting common rules for insurance and other types of financial services concluded online. When analyzing the opinions on the development of e-finance it is almost always stressed that "e-finance is not new" as some forms of distant communication

[81] Reference is made to the Annex to the First Council Directive 73/239/EEC of 24 July 1973 on the coordination of laws, regulations and administrative provisions relating to the taking-up and pursuit of the business of direct insurance other than life assurance, as well as to the DIRECTIVE 2009/138/EC Of The European Parliament And Of The Council of 25 November 2009 on the taking-up and pursuit of the business of Insurance and Reinsurance (Solvency II).

[82] 2002/65/EC.

[83] MARKT/2522/02-FR Rev. 1, p. 2.

[84] Also, as a principle, it cannot be re-sold or transferred to third persons because of the obstacles resulting from the concept of "insurable interests" that should exist on the side of the policyholder.

[85] Dreher (1991).

[86] Banan (2009), p. 119.

were used since 1918 and in Nasdaq systems since 1971.[87] What makes the difference nowadays is the widening access of the consumers to the electronic trading, which "vastly changed the opportunities for the use of electronic payment systems, the operations of financial services and financial markets".[88] It has also been said that "e-finance would seem one of the most promising areas of e-commerce as financial services are information-intensive and often require no physical delivery".[89]

Electronic finance (e-finance) is defined as "the provision of financial services and markets using electronic communication and computation".[90] This includes also insurance, being qualified as one of the types of the financial services. The impact of the internet is underlined in many areas in financial services, beginning from banking activities (facilitating credit and loans process), securities companies and of course also insurance companies. As regards banking services, especially in loans, the role on internet is mostly connected with the accessibility of data bases allowing the assessment the borrower's credibility. But besides that, the internet as a distribution channel for depositary services is increasingly noticed. When comparing insurance to the banking sector, it is stressed that "in contrast to bank depositors, policyholders generally interact with their insurer only at time of sale and when filing a claim. Also in contrast to banking services, insurance policies tend to be quite heterogeneous and consumers tend not to be well informed about the products, making automation of the sales process difficult. Difference in regulation may also play role."[91]

There are numerous common issues for all types of financial services with respect to the electronic trading. This mainly concerns transparency of the information (as it is stressed, IT technology "helps to solve asymmetric information problem") and security of the transactions in terms of payment and data privacy.[92] Another issue characteristic for all kinds of financial services seems to be "disintermediation" as a result of using the internet technology in the distribution process. In this respect it is raised that "e-finance technologies reduce asymmetric information because they lower the costs of communication, computation and data processing, thus allowing buyers and sellers of financial assets to have more equal access to information".[93] Having this in mind, we may find that in terms of concluding transactions within the scope of e-finance, dominant majority of issues are pretty similar and require common approach. In all of them, the key point is to ensure validity, enforceability and security of the transactions. This however may

[87] Allen et al. (2001), p. 34.

[88] Allen et al. (2001), p. 34.

[89] Sato and Hawkins (2001), p. 1.

[90] Allen et al. (2001), p. 1.

[91] Allen et al. (2001), p. 8.

[92] Nieto (2001), pp. 92–95.

[93] Allen et al. (2001), p. 11.

end the similarities between insurance and the other e-finance.[94] The legal assessment of the issues related to the private international law can show in fact many differences resulting from the distinctive nature of particular financial services. The insurance, as the author believes, requires special legal treatment by the jurisdiction and choice of law rules (analysis of this issue will be developed in Sec. 3 below).

2.2.6 Conclusions

To sum up this section of the analysis, it should be stressed again that while the internet may be used for different stages of rendering insurance services as described above, such application of electronic means can only be of a supportive nature. Thus, online insurance, for the purposes of this chapter, is meant to be an insurance contract concluded online, regardless of the manner in which the insurance contract was subsequently performed. Also, as no specific regulations can be distinguished worldwide with respect to concluding insurance online (with the reservation that in some jurisdictions online insurance policy requires electronic signature), it seems that the legal solutions adopted to contracting online in general should apply to insurance and other financial services. This concerns mainly the acknowledgement of the "electronic form" as being the basis for valid contract of insurance. No special rules are necessary to insurance in front of other types of financial services. The most impact is put on information requirement, and this aspect is uniform for all the financial services.

2.3 Cross-Border Online Insurance

2.3.1 Outline

This section regards an international character of insurance and interrelations between the cross-border features of insurance and contracting online. Having in mind the title of this chapter, it is obvious that the issue of PIL application may come into question only in cross-border transaction. Therefore it is necessary to devote separate part of the chapter for presentation of the basic issues related thereto. While the main subject of considerations hereof is online insurance contract, it may be first worth stopping for a while to mention the general nature of insurance regardless of the form of its distribution. Can a cross-border character be attributed to insurance in general and if so, in which circumstances and to what extent? Answer to this question may affect the considerations presented in Sec. 3 below.

[94] Hughes and Middlebrook (2013), p. 264.

2.3.2 Universality of Insurance *versus* Regulatory Impediments

Nowadays, there are rather no doubts that insurance being an intangible service, not a product in the basic meaning, quite naturally may be used as transnational instrument. Such a feature of insurance is not an invention of the European Union that introduced extensive legislation in this respect, but a result of the lengthy history of insurance, beginning even 4000 years B.C., when it covered caravans in the Middle East or sea perils, when ship covered by insurance was crossing several sea borders, transporting cargos or citizens of different countries. In consequence, it can be noted that the insurance, even considering the particularities of national legal systems of the EU Member States, is governed by more or less the same principles.[95] Even if they differ from one state to another in some details, it is clear that the legal essence of the insurance coverage, expressed in the utmost good faith rule (*ubberrimea fides*), the compensation rule in property & casualty insurance, no liability for willful acts, as well as party autonomy principle remains the same. These common features cause that offering insurance coverage internationally or locally will mean pretty the same. That standpoint remains the same even in case these principles prove sometimes to be insufficient, where the high level of the legal protection of the policyholder comes in question, or where the religious reasons impose limits on concluding the insurance.[96] Such approach must in consequence lead to the statement that insurance is by nature a cross-border service, whether it is distributed in a traditional way or on-line.

If then by nature, insurance is a transnational service, its distribution by the internet makes this feature even more dominant. However, on the other hand, it is a source of some additional risks, being faced now on a worldwide scale. It cannot be ignored that direct selling of cross-border insurance requires that the attention is turned both to the cultural differences that might impact the success in distribution of insurance, as well as to the regulatory framework of the "target" countries. It is the regulatory framework that is perceived as the main factor contributing to the success or decline of cross-border insurance as it decides on the "product" content. It is also obvious, as the internet has no borders, that this framework must be considered not only with respect to European territory but also to the entire world. This is related to several factors, such as (1) a highly probable conflict of laws that may arise in cross-border transactions, (2) lack of private law integration in the EU and worldwide, as well as (3) the need of consumers protection being increasingly dominant. Although insurance contract seems to be cross-border by nature, it is also the fact that in terms of regulatory framework, it is a feature of developed jurisdictions, the example of which may be the EU and its process of integration, where at first only free movement of capital was enabled and the freedom of cross-border

---

[95] Malinowska (2008).

[96] The best example of the first approach is the EU extensive legislation on consumer and policyholder protection, the latter are Arabic countries, where commercial insurance is forbidden under Shariah law. Malinowska (2008), p. 302 et subsq.

services was the last of the steps leading to the internal market. Emerging insurance markets often prohibit or, at least, strictly limit cross-border insurance, the example of which may be China and India, where the foreign insurance is possible only if not concluded on their territory.[97] Online insurance seem to perfectly suit the needs of overcoming such obstacles, although needs special attention from the regulatory point of view.

2.3.3 "Cross-Border" Notion

Let us now explain the notion of cross-border insurance. The necessary element of cross-border insurance is its international character in such a meaning that insurance contract is related with more than one legal system. It is then opposite to the notion of domestic insurance, where all the significant features of insurance are related to one legal system. To state that insurance has a cross-border nature, it seems necessary to find that at least one of the *essentialia negotii* elements of the insurance contract is foreign and may be governed by another legal system. The foreign factor may be attributed for example to the location of the risk covered by insurance or the parties to the insurance contract (argument *rationae personae).*[98] It seems that it also concerns the situation where insurance contract is concluded by an insurer and policyholder of the same nationality, but for the benefit of a foreign insured. The most popular distinction of cross-border insurance is however related to the parties to the insurance contract. We may say then that it consists of rendering insurance services by a insurer with the seat in one state (home country), other than the state where the insurance claim is to be satisfied or where a policyholder has his habitual residence (host country).

Cross-border insurance may take different forms. There are many theories of how cross-border insurance can be distinguished, or divided. One of them distinguishes "pure cross-border insurance trade" (insurance contracts result from solicitations by an insurer domiciled in another country and it may occur also by electronic means, as well as traditionally through brokers; usually it concerns large risks), "own-initiative cross-border insurance trade" (when the insured initiated the contact with the insurer; also more often for corporate risks), and finally, consumption-abroad cross-border insurance trade (when an insured temporarily residing abroad enters into an insurance contract with a local insurer).[99]

Cross border insurance faces a few kinds of problems, the most important of which are the rules of law affecting the subject and scope of insurance coverage, as well as parties' rights and obligations, differing from state to state in spite of even the common cultural basis of insurance (as it is in Europe). As it pointed out above, the aforementioned issues decide in fact what the content of the insurance product

[97] Kessedijan (2000), p. 11, 130.

[98] Gołaczyński (2007), Popiołek (2007), p. 11 est subsq.

[99] Skipper (2006), p.2.

is. In consequence, the lack of common rules for insurance contracts worldwide, even in the form of soft law instruments, entails the necessity of handling the problem of cross-border insurance by measures resulting from the choice of law and jurisdiction rules. It is frequently raised that the issue of the "product content" would be easily resolved by adopting a uniform law of insurance contract, at least for cross-border transactions.

Such an idea results from the observations made in Europe, where freedom to provide insurance services removed many obstacles and direct legal impediments to conclude insurance with a foreign element, both with respect to large and mass risk insurance, but had no direct effect on increasing the number of cross-border transactions in insurance, including online insurance. To the contrary, it is underlined by the European Commission, that still much work is ahead in this sector, as the level of cross-border trade in insurance remains very low.[100] It is argued that the cross-border character of insurance constitutes itself a major risk, which entails a necessity to protect a weaker party to insurance contract in a particular way and that differences in contract law make it currently impossible to offer uniform insurance products across the EU. That generates additional costs for insurers (transferred then as premium to policyholders) and legal uncertainty in cross-border trade in insurance products.[101] It increasingly becomes vulnerable as from the moment when licensing regime has been freed throughout Europe. Constant progress in technical possibilities of concluding insurance contract online makes handling those issues crucial because of the fact that policyholders concluding insurance online may not even sometimes notice whether the insurance is domestic or cross-border and what the consequences thereof are.

2.3.4 Cross-Border Electronic Finance

Notion of cross-border e-finance brings basically the same values as in insurance. The analysis of the academic and practitioners texts on cross-border e-finance at various stages of its development shows the same threatens as nowadays. Although it has been said even that the e-finance cross-border are so easy and cheap comparing to traditional methods, as we can talk on "death of the distance",[102] still it is not the physical distance that raises most of the doubts. The main problems related to the cross-border services concern the trust deficit at the foreign market, as well as lack of familiarity of local market conditions and unwillingness of being subject to dispute settlements rules and consumer protection requirements of foreign jurisdictions.[103]

[100] It is said that "only 0.6 % of all motor insurance premiums and 2.8 % of property insurance premiums are offered to customers across EU borders".

[101] Banan (2009), p. 130.

[102] Sato and Hawkins (2001), p. 7.

[103] Sato and Hawkins (2001), p. 7.

What is known for insurance, it is also the truth for other e-finance. It has been stressed that "*while e-finance has been growing rapidly the last decades, this grow has not encompassed the cross-border trading*" *and that* "*the advantages of e-trading in finance has no power to overcome the constraints*". One of the most important disadvantage of acting online in a number of jurisdictions, is "*a multiplication of the compliance costs incurred vis-à-vis tax and other authorities*", as well as "*and perhaps most importantly, differences in financial regulation and other legal complications*"[104] Additionally, it has been noticed that the major problems hampering insurance to make radical progress in online sale that are common with other online finance is the vulnerability "*to uncertainties about the enforcement of contracts*".[105] In view of the importance of the values protected by insurance, this problem cannot be underestimated.

From the marketing point of view, it has even been said that "*the Internet channel could arguably be less attractive in insurance than in many other financial services, since transactions between individual insurers and their clients are comparatively rare. As for tailoring products on the Internet, the complexity of some insurance products increases the consumer's need for specific advice*". Also, it cannot be ignored, that in insurance it is "*difficult to standardize claims settlements, as this involves a large amount of investigation and decision making. Moreover, injured parties do in some cases (depending on jurisdictions) have a right to claim directly from the insurer of the party at fault*".[106]

2.3.5 Conclusions

As a summary of section 2 of this chapter, devoted to the analysis of the legal meaning of the electronic contract in general and insurance in particular, it may be stated that, the substantial importance of contracting online is focused on the conclusion stage of the contract and the same conclusion may be drawn as to the insurance contract. In this respect, there are no substantial differences between insurance and other types of contracts, in particular there are no such differences between insurance and other e-finance contracts. The modern jurisdictions do not provide for special legal treatment of electronic contracts, perceiving an electronic contract only in terms of the manner and form of concluding contracts. At the same time, the electronic form of concluding a contract is fully acknowledged nowadays and protection thereof is afforded by law.

The other issue being the subject of this section was the cross-border character of online insurance. As it was presented, online manner of concluding insurance contracts strengthens their transnational character. The major legal impediments observed currently with respect to cross-border insurance in practice concern the

[104] Sato and Hawkins (2001), p. 14.

[105] Christiansen (2001), p. 44.

[106] Christiansen (2001), pp. 48–49.

legal content of the insurance products, i.e. the rules of law being applicable to cross-border insurance together with the lack of harmonization of insurance substantive law. It may also be said that the universal principles of insurance were in practice dominated by highly protective rules or by strict religious norms.

From the market point of view, the standpoint according to which e-finance will develop must be shared. The evolution will, most probably, follow the progress in new technologies.[107] Such a trend will encompass also insurance, although the complexity of the products content in comparison with the other financial services makes this sector particularly vulnerable.

The above outline serves as a basis of the considerations presented in Sec. 3 of the chapter, treating private international law rules concerning online insurance and their impact on cross-border online transactions in insurance.

3 International Private Law Rules for Online Insurance Contracts

Section 3 of the chapter is devoted to the problems related to the private international law in the context of online insurance. As it was presented in Sec. 2, electronic transactions give much more opportunities for international relations than there are in "traditional" contracts and in consequence, the frequency of applying the private international law rules increases substantially. Hence, it is not just contracting online that is a source of problems nowadays, but mainly legal consequences of cross-border online contracting. That issue is more important because the online contract may "cross the border" involuntarily, by the parties surfing the internet. That is why the private international law rules are the necessary element for analyzing online cross-border transactions. This section also aims at finding an answer whether PIL rules are a sufficient tool for resolving problems related to cross-border online contracts, with the special attention paid to online insurance.

At first, the general concepts of PIL will be presented with respect to contracting online, and secondly, to what extent those general rules are applicable to insurance and what are the distinctive features of insurance that need a separate approach. The analysis in this respect has been conducted by considering the worldwide concepts worked out with respect to the choice of law rules, which, as the author believes are universal concepts, in spite of some differences between particular legal systems.[108]

[107] Business Navigator on E-finance for SMEs Exporters in Developing Countries. Geneva: ITC, 2005. vii, 70 p. Doc. No. BAS-05-47.E, p. 8.

[108] Such an assumption does not stand in contradiction with the ideas raising the necessity of creating independent system of conflict of laws rules solely for the internal market, which, to some extent was effected through adoption of the Rome I Regulation, see: Grundmann (2004), pp. 5–6 et subsq.

3.1 Private International Law and Online Contracts

3.1.1 Outline: Notion of "PIL"

The notion of private international law differs between the national legal systems.[109] Therefore, it is important to clarify the scope used for the purposes of this text. According to the most common approach, PIL includes (1) rules on choice of law deciding which country's substantive law is proper (applicable) to regulate the rights and obligations of the parties to the contract,[110] (2) rules on jurisdiction deciding which country's court have jurisdiction to consider the dispute of the parties to the contract, and (3) rules on recognition and enforcement of the decision in a foreign state.

What is also a true for Europe, PIL is said to be "*neither substantive nor procedural law but represent a third category of rules*".[111] But what is important and worth underlying is that PIL "*is domestic in its foundation, international in its focus. The regulation of conflicts problems is decentralized in the sense that every state has its own rules. But uniformity is a goal, and the way toward it leads first to bilateral choice-of-law rules and finally to unification by treaty*".[112]

It is true that the above approach is more characteristic for European perspective of PIL, while US system seems to perceive PIL rather like a "*body of conventions, model laws, national laws, legal guides, and other documents and instruments that regulate private relationships across national borders. Private international law has a dualistic character, balancing international consensus with domestic recognition and implementation, as well as balancing sovereign actions with those of the private sector. United States domestic law's nearest equivalent to private international law would be interstate "conflict of laws" or "choice of laws.*"[113]

One of the main tasks of PIL for contracts is to ensure legal stability of the contractual relations if there should appear an international (cross-border) element and the parties either have not chosen the law applicable to govern the relations, or such choice was not possible. PIL should therefore ensure predictability of the legal regime to be applied. It is stressed quite often also that PIL rules constitute a reflection of "*state interests weighted against the party autonomy*"[114] and in this respect express the state public policy, albeit the sensitive approach as to the regulation this context of contractual relations resembles rather private law rules.

---

[109] Green Paper (2003), p. 8, Sec. 1.2.

[110] It should just be mentioned that the notion of "proper" law is characteristic for common law systems, while "applicable" law for civil law traditions; nevertheless, they mean the same and can be explained as "law which governs the contract and the parties' obligations under it; it is the law which determines (normally) its validity and legality, its construction and effect, and the conditions of its discharge": see Clarke (1997), p. 16.

[111] Michaels (2008), p. 1616.

[112] Michaels (2008), p. 1616.

[113] Ford (2013), p. 1.

[114] Spamann (2001).

The scope of PIL rules to be imposed by the European legislator, meets its limits in the EC Treaty, Art. 65 which allows the regulation of the choice of law within such a scope as is necessary for the proper functioning of the internal market.[115] It is worth noting that this authority of the EU was set only after adoption of the Amsterdam Treaty. Although the first attempts to regulate this area in a complex way appeared in the form of Rome Convention, but of course did not consider the e-commerce being at its advent those days. E-commerce was however subject to a legislator discussion during the process of adopting Brussels I Regulation.[116] The principles of e-commerce set down in ECD also abstained from regulating the choice of law or jurisdiction matters.[117]

PIL gains specific importance in online transactions with participation of the consumers and its role will be on the increase along with the progress of the internet technology. As has been noticed by some authors, "*given the increasing ways the consumers can be targeted by foreign business today using technology such as websites, an increasing proportions of consumers will expect protection from a choice of law rules as they enter into electronic contracts with businesses*".[118]

The issues which are subject to a consideration below concern twofold problems that may appear by contracting online. First, whether the "traditional" private international rules are to be applied at all, and secondly how should they be applied. It must be remembered that PIL does not constitute a separate body of law, but rather is a kind of a network of state laws within the above mentioned scope. The considerations mentioned below will keep in mind 1 and 2 meaning of PIL, although the main focus will be put on the issues concerning the law applicable to electronic contracts.

The issues relating to PIL in terms of regulating online insurance services have been noticed as a source of potential risks only recently. As has been noticed already, at the beginning of the e-commerce, the major task was focused rather on ensuring safe methods of payment, as well as authentication and data encryption. Hence, the issue of PIL was noticed, it was not considered as a problem.[119] Some

---

115 Michaels (2008), p. 1622.

116 It concerned in particular the Article 13: see Gilles (2008), p. 89.

117 Gilles (2008), p. 87. See also cases c-509/09 and C-161/10, where the European Court of Justices stated clearly that *Article 3 of Directive 2000/31/EC of the European Parliament and of the Council of 8 June 2000 on certain legal aspects of information society services, in particular electronic commerce, in the Internal Market ("Directive on electronic commerce"), must be interpreted as not requiring transposition in the form of a specific conflict-of-laws rule. Nevertheless, in relation to the coordinated field, Member States must ensure that, subject to the derogations authorised in accordance with the conditions set out in Article 3(4) of Directive 2000/31, the provider of an electronic commerce service is not made subject to stricter requirements than those provided for by the substantive law applicable in the Member State in which that service provider is established.* Available at: http://conflictoflaws.net/2011/ecj-rules-in-e-date-advertising-and-martinez/.

118 Gilles (2008), p. 149.

119 The environment of online distribution was reported as "inconsistent regulatory approaches, cultural and psychological differences, the lack of online business models, as well as assurances

opinions were also expressed that the practical importance of PIL in online transactions, especially with participation of consumers, is not substantial, as there is a small number of disputes in these kinds of contractual relations, mostly because of the fact that the value of the transaction is usually low.[120] This view however in insurance cannot be supported, even in mass insurance, as the value of the insurance contract is not measured by the amount of the premium due from the policyholder, but by the value of the risk, being often related to the human life and health or substantial private assets. Finally, one of the conclusions which was drawn, directed the attention to the absence of consistent regulatory PIL approach across international jurisdictions being a factor creating barriers to electronic commerce.[121] It was suggested that a model law for commercial practices should be drafted at an international level, so it could serve as a common framework.[122]

3.1.2 "Extraterritoriality" of Online Contracts

The main feature of online contracts, having the consequences in PIL and introducing at the same time some complications, is their "extraterritorial" character,[123] meaning that the electronic impulse, being the medium of the statement of will of the parties to the contract, can be transferred worldwide, regardless of the fact where the parties are situated at the moment of exchanging their wills. The difficulty related to online contracts results from the fact that most of the conflict of laws rules are based on territorial factors and online relations are located solely in the electronic network liaising the electronic devices of its users. Additionally, the inconsistency of PIL rules on a global level leads to an uncertainty, which law governs the contract, as two different PIL acts may lead to opposite conclusions.[124] This network has no borders or simple tangible relations with the countries where the users are located. The electronic impulse, being the medium carrying the statement of will—the only required legal source of contracts concluded *solo consensu* (such as insurance), can run around the whole world until it reaches the addressee. The fact, however, that the contract takes place on the internet, at least during the stage of its conclusion, does not eliminate the need of legal assessment of the parties' rights and obligations resulting from that fact. The space, where the exchange of wills is effected, is international by nature, but an important question

about services provided and security of payments are issues that must be addressed" OECD (1998), p. 31.

[120] See Tang (2010), p. 9.

[121] OECD (1998), p. 31.

[122] OECD (1998), p. 39; Gabriel (2007), p. 224 et subsequent.

[123] The focus on that aspect was put from the beginning; see for ex ample case ALA v Pataki, where the court stated that "the internet is wholly insensitive to geographic distinctions. In almost every case, users of Internet neither know nor care about the physical location of the Internet resources they access". Geist, p. 19.

[124] Polański (2006).

is, what the legal importance of the medium (electronic impulse), being extraterritorial, is? Does it decide on the international (cross-border) status of the online contract, and consequently on the necessity of applying choice of law rules? The majority of views (shared also by the Author) expressed in this respect seem to give a negative answer and try to attribute the decisive character to the legal environment of the parties, i.e. the place of domicile or seat of the parties, or place where the agreement is to have legal effect.[125]

No doubt that online contracts, exactly as any other contract need to exist in a legal space, even if they are virtually concluded and performed. It should be stressed that no contract can exist in a legal vacuum and if it is to have a legal effect, a reference should be made to a system of law, which will be able to assess, in the first place, validity thereof, and secondly, the rights and obligations of the parties so as to give legal protection and enforceability of the performance or compensation for non-performance.[126] Thus, the main role of the PIL rules is to establish the law applicable and jurisdiction to the contract, which would give answer to the above-mentioned questions, by attributing proper meaning to the statement of will.[127] The modern theories bind sometimes the autonomy of parties' will with the possibility to derive the validity of contract from the *lex contractus* without the necessity to attributing it to any particular legal system. Although such a view seems to be also very attractive for applying it to online contracts, a strong opposition has been addressed to such a view, with a justification that "a contract needs to draw its binding force from a specific legal system extraneous to the contract itself" and "*pacta sunt servanda is not such a system per se...*".[128]

A kind of contradiction between traditional PIL rules and electronic contracts was raised at the inception of the academic works on that topic. The main source of such contradiction was "found" in the alleged traditional approach and concepts included in the private international law rules, which were said not to be suitable for online transactions because of the territoriality of PIL rules and "extraterritoriality" of the cyberspace where the e-commerce takes place.[129] It has been underlined that electronic space undermines traditional relations between physical territory and legal consequences of actions taken within the scope of such territory, mostly *"by destroying the link between the geographical location and power of local government over such location, as well as the effects of online behavior of individuals.*

[125] Popiołek (2007), p. 13.

[126] See inter alia Clarke (1997), p. 15.

[127] Maniruzzaman (1999), p. 145 and Lord Diplock [1983] 3 WRL 241, 245.

[128] Maniruzzaman (1999), p. 148; Lord Mcnair (1957), p. 7.

[129] This approach led also to denying the possibility to make a choice of law which is not a legal system of a particular country, such as for example Sharia law regulating other aspects of life and behavior, if not a law of an Islamic country applying Sharia law was indicated; although it was also admitted that it is possible to refer in arbitration proceedings to lex mercatoria, general principles of fair trading, etc. Chuah (2004), pp. 125–127; Chuah (2010), pp. 191–204. It has been underlined that the Rome I regulation expressly allows the parties to choose not only a law of a state, but also a non-state body law or an international convention (recital no. 13).

According to these views, attributing the activity on the internet to a law binding within territorial boundaries would mean that such an activity is a subject simultaneously to the laws of all countries"[130] by which the electronic impulse is transferred and possibly where the electronic equipment is located, as well as where the participants of the electronic data exchange have their residence.

3.1.3 Lex Electronica

The result of the studies made in this respect was the idea of the necessity of creating a distinctive system of law for online transactions.[131] According to the authors of that concept, it is no longer possible to treat the internet only as a medium that facilitates the exchange of information sent from one legal system to another, as it leads to unsatisfactory results in terms of the legal situation of the parties. Therefore, cyberspace should be treated as a distinctive place and border of laws should lie between virtual and non-virtual space and not between physical borders of states, citizens of which participate in e-commerce. According to this view, the most vulnerable issue would appear to be solved, i.e. the place of concluding the on-line contract or performing thereof.[132]

The aforementioned idea, represented by the American law school, was at first opposed by the European approach which presented the view that, although the internet is a kind of challenge for the old systems, it is sufficient to adjust existing private law rules to the new circumstances. In terms of PIL, the need of adjustment would focus mainly on the area of the "connecting factors", without the necessity of creating completely new and specific system, applicable solely to online contracts.[133] It results also from the main idea adopted in the EU, which aimed at achieving the same level of protection for both offline and online transaction,[134] associated with the theory that the medium used for concluding (and eventually performing) a contract should not have decisive influence on the parties' rights and obligations.[135] Against creating *lex electronica* spoke also a conviction that universal values expressed in modern law do not exclude variety of social relations, including electronic contracts.[136]

[130] D.R. Johnson et D. Post (1996), pp. 1370–1374.

[131] Tang (2010) p. 4.

[132] D.R. Johnson et D. Post (1996), p. 1378.

[133] The reasons for questioning of traditional private international law suitability to online transactions derive from practical issues, i.e. The difficulty for the courts to associate the "cyberspace's nature" with the traditional PIL rules. Muñoz-López (2009), pp. 163–190.

[134] The same idea towards consumers was expressed by OECD in OECD Recommendation DSTI/CP(98) 4 (2001).

[135] H. Kaviar, et A. Ahmadi (2010), p. 694.

[136] Goldsmith (1998), p. 1190, 1234.

Nevertheless, the extensive studies with respect to the possibility of creating supranational system of law based on *lex mercatoria* have been made,[137] leading however to the conclusion that instead of creating a new one, the existing rules need to be adjusted.[138] Although, it cannot be denied that a kind of custom law has already been created with respect to electronic contracts, and value thereof is the bigger, the more countries accepted and applied it. A good example of it is the UNCITRAL model electronic contract law. The basic principles adopted therein, like autonomy of will, *pacta sunt servanda, rebus sic stantibus*, etc. may also lead to the conclusion that electronic contracts do not require separate, new rules but can be easily governed by "traditional" concepts of law subject to necessary modifications.[139] That was also the approach of Regulations adopted by EU, mainly the Brussels and Rome I Regulations,[140] encompassing all kind of relations, whether they are virtual or not, supported by the ECD, DFD and DSD.[141]

A particular attention should be given to ECD rules in this respect. No doubts, it can serve as a hint as to the concept adopted by the EU (not judging whether it is a justified concept or not). Preamble (point 23) and Article 1 (4) of the directive says clearly that it abstains from introducing the distinctive rules for conflicts of law. Then, the Article 3 (1) ensures that the services provided by a service provider established in any of the Member States will not be subject to any restrictions with respect to the freedom to provide information society services.[142] This, from the author's view suggests the intention to integrate e-commerce with the general rules of running business on the internal market. Although it is not possible to avoid disputes or at least discussions on this field, they seem to focus on the necessity of special adjustments "traditional" PIL rules to the e-commerce specifics rather than creating separate ones. The way, the ECJ considers particular cases on that point

---

[137] Polański (2006).

[138] Gołaczyński (2007).

[139] Gołaczyński (2007).

[140] Council Regulation (EC) No 44/2001 of 22 December 2000, on jurisdiction and the recognition and enforcement of judgments in civil and commercial matters OJ L 12, 16.1.2001; Regulation (EC) No 593/2008 of the European Parliament and of the Council of 17 June 2008 on the law applicable to contractual obligations (Rome I) OJ L 177 of 4.7.2008.

[141] Giuliano-Lagarde Report, OJ (1980) Article 1; Garcimatin Alferez (2008), p. 64.; please note however that DSD has been repelled by the Directive 2011/83/EU on consumer rights, amending Council Directive 93/13/EEC and Directive 1999/44/EC of the European Parliament and of the Council and repealing Council Directive 85/577/EEC and Directive 97/7/EC of the European Parliament and of the Council.

[142] C-509/09 *"On the one hand, the country-of-origin principle may have a corrective effect on a substantive law level. The substantive law outcome under the law declared to be applicable pursuant to the conflict-of-laws rules of the State in which the court seized is situated is, in individual cases, altered in its content, where appropriate, and reduced to the less stringent requirements of the law of the country of origin. According to this interpretation, the country-of-origin principle does not affect the national conflict-of-laws rules of the State in which the court seized is situated and applies—in the same way as the fundamental freedoms set out in the EC Treaty—only in the context of an individual cost/benefit comparison at a national law level*".

clearly indicate supporting the idea of integrating the online services with well established rules of "traditional" market rather than creating distinctive ones. It should also be made clear that the more universal becomes such a concept, the bigger are chances for a successful development of e-commerce.[143]

It seems that a major possible problem in enforcing the universal approach to the PIL rules on worldwide scale is also the need of politics. As it was found by the doctrine *"in the field of private law, previous efforts to present the conflict of laws as 'neutral' have been unsuccessful, while governmental interests analysis, which might seem more appropriate in the field of conflicts of public law, carries the double stigma of discrimination or lex forism. But it may be that, however divergent regulatory policies might be, a shared need born of participation in the world market creates sufficient common ground between state economic laws for a global approach to be sustainable. (. . .) Taking the lead from shifts already taking place within the European Union itself, the price to pay for European legal doctrine would be to accept the conflict of laws as a tool of political economy"*.[144]

3.1.4 PIL in Electronic Finance

PIL in electronic financial services, including insurance are nowadays subject to a specific legal situation. Taking European legal system as an example, we may see that different approach is being effected with respect to the regulatory framework and to the contractual relations. Within the first dimension, the principle of home country control (with some exception resulting from the "general good") governs the provision of the financial services in Europe.[145] The same principle results from ECD, which proposes the rule of "country of origin".[146] At the same time, most of the contractual relations, in particular in B2C, are governed by the host country law, being applicable to the contracts concluded with the "habitual residents" of that country. It should be bore in mind that although all the financial services are regulated within the scope of the same regime (as in DFD), it does not mean that such a common approach is possible also in the field of PIL rules.

Having in mind the specifics of particular types of financial services, we may notice that the answer should be negative. Comparing banking, insurance and securities instruments, each of them need to address different values and apply different criteria for choosing the necessary limits of the parties' autonomy, as well

---

[143] Although ECD expressly states in Art. 4 that it should not be the case. It can also mean that the issues of law applicable to the online contracts exceed the scope of applying the country of origin rule. See for example Fallon and Meussen (2002), p. 474. There are some opinions, that only issues listed in ECD, Art. 3 are excluded from the scope of application of the country of origin rule, Szpunar (2014), p. 179; Szpunar (2005), p. 109, Hellner (2004), p. 201.

[144] Muir Watt (2002).

[145] Corcoran and Hart (2001), pp. 19–33. See also Muir Watt (2002).

[146] It should however be stressed that the scope of application of the "country of origin" rules raises doubts in the doctrine as to the fact whether it should be treated as a PIL rule.

as adopting the idea of connecting factors suitable for given type of service. Comparing them only in exemplary way (and not exhausting the subject), we may see that the banking services are subject to the highest standardization, while insurance nature requires to address the idea of the "risk" as a subject matter of the contract, in the rules affecting the conflict of laws. As regards the securities, we may not ignore the complexity of chains related to the holding of securities involving not only the law of obligations but also issues concerning the legal title to the security.[147] Each of the above financial services may bring different effects on third parties; in other words, has different social impact, which should be reflected in adopting different rules for the choice of law.[148] That fact was noticed by the European legislator, giving the effect in separate rules for insurance under Rome I Regulation.

3.1.5 Conclusions

The differences between contracting traditional way and electronic contracts cannot be ignored. In spite of the efforts by contract traditionalists to limit the need of electronic commerce only to the form of the contract and manner of exchanging statements of will between the parties, the question as to the similarities and differences between electronic and traditional contracts remains still open.[149] The answer seems to be crucial for the scope of application of PIL. In case the traditional approach is the correct one, it is true that the mere adjustments and modifications of standard PIL rules should be sufficient to answer the needs of electronic commerce. However, in case of the approach on distinctive electronic contract system of law wins, PIL rules known so far may appear to be neither sufficient nor suitable for regulating cross-border electronic contracts. It should also be stressed with respect to e-finance that while it was possible to adopt a common approach to the general issues concerning various financial services distributed online, PIL specifics requires to consider them separately (such as for example insurance *versus* securities).

[147] That is why, most of the problems concerning securities are analyzed separately. This is because the substantial fragmentation of law in the field of securities and differences in basic concepts of models of securities holding chain around the world. In securities law, the problems arise more with respect to the holding titles while in insurance it concerns the obligations of the parties and terms of coverage. Nevertheless, same as in insurance, it is stressed frequently with respect to the securities law, that the global convergence of the rules governing this sector of financial services should be agreed as soon as possible. See also, Gilles (2008), pp. 27–28, European Parliament (2009) IPA/ECON/NT/2011-09, Securities markets with a coherent legal framework, available at: http://www.Europarl.europe.eu/studies, p. 32.

[148] Although, even in such types of services that have minor third party effect, the full party autonomy seems to be impossible, see Muir Watt (2002), p. 95.

[149] See for example A. Ath. Gkoutzinis (2006), pp. 289–309.

3.2 *Role and Character of PIL Rules in Insurance*

3.2.1 Outline

This section of the chapter is devoted to the analysis of the role of private international law rules in insurance cross-border contracts concluded online. The analysis is made from the issues considered in point 1 above with the focus on the particularities of insurance. The aim of the analysis is to find out, to what extent, the "traditional" PIL rules may be applicable to insurance and what the main concerns in this respect are, if any.

3.2.2 Protective Insurance Law and PIL

As said above, the main role of PIL rules is to put the parties in a position not worse than in a domestic transaction, and with respect to electronic commerce, also to put them in a situation comparable to that of the traditional contracts. Although such view has particular importance in general B2C relations, it can also be applied to the insurance industry, and as it seems, in a broader scope. The EU law is a good example, as it presents the most sophisticated level of protecting the policyholder guaranteed by the legal regulation, while in the US it is mainly subject to a judicial decision. It may be related to the fact that insurance is a licensed activity and protection of a weaker party is not limited to consumer protection rules. The need of such protection may also result from the fact that the insurance contract privity rule is weaker than in other types of contracts in such a meaning that performance thereof and its wording may affect the legal situation of third parties, other than only the parties to the contract. It should be remembered that apart from the policyholder, there may appear also the insured (in insurance for the account of a third party), as well as beneficiaries (in life insurance) and the injured parties (in liability insurance), who may have claim against the insurer. In consequence, insurance contract regulation should consider the need of protecting the interests of the whole circle of entities potentially involved in the insurance relationship. It should be somehow considered when insurance contract is or may be subject to several systems of law, both in terms of substantive law, as well as *forum*.

The common feature of the European PIL regulations is that insurance contract is distinguished from other types of contracts and it has been given a special kind of regulation. It may result from the fact that distinction (from a protective point of view) is made not just between B2C and B2B contracts, but additionally, between large risk insurance and the other ("mass" risk) insurance. The rules regarding insurance of "mass" risks protect the policyholders as a weaker party, and grant a special protection. It results from the standpoint that substantive law rules of foreign laws (in particular outside Europe) may not ensure sufficient level of protection to policyholders. Therefore, the optimal way is that policyholder is protected by his own substantive law, even if discrepancies are not substantial, but still may lead to the loss of insurance coverage in unexpected situations.[150] The PIL rules for jurisdiction provide even a broader protection, which encompasses all types of insurance and policyholders, including large risks.[151]

Having in mind the global character of online insurance contract, one may wish PIL laws around the world to adopt similar concepts. The level of regulation of private international law rules globally is, however, not coherent and does not provide for equal level of protection in various kinds of civil contracts. The differences between the EU and USA are clearly obvious, even if at the moment, they represent more or less similar concept of federalism in the legal dimension. While the USA conflict of laws principles assume that the courts is empowered to decide on their discretion what law should be applicable to a contract (including the assessment whether the law chosen by the parties is a proper one),[152] the European Union adopted a more precise and predictable solution, précising the possibilities of the parties to chose the law applicable to the contract subject to some limitation of the parties' autonomy in this respect in the provisions of Rome I.[153]

The above situation also concerns insurance. First, private international law rules are codified only in civil systems of law, including Europe, where Rome I was adopted in 2009 replacing the domestic legislations in the EU Member States. The other example may be China, which enacted basic laws concerning private law, based on civil law tradition. The other systems given as an example herein above (point I of this Chapter), such as India and USA have not adopted uniform statutes on private international law. The issues of applicable law are there still a subject to the court decisions with the possibility of reaching different solutions in similar circumstances, as well as subject to international conventions implemented on an

[150] It concerns mostly differences between alpine and maritime tradition in insurance contract rules, which provide for example in different consequences of breach of warranties, etc.

[151] See Brussels Regulation Article 9.

[152] It is expressed in the notion of "personal jurisdiction, meant by the competence of the court to determine a case against a particular category of persons and it is required to determine whether given person may be subject to the competence of the court in which the suit is filed—see *Jay Kesan:* although the above doctrine has been subject to an evolution' reflecting changes of a more mobile society". "In order for a court to exercise jurisdiction there must be a statutory or common law source of jurisdiction, which does not surpass the limitations imposed by constitutional due process". Such statutory sources are usually "long arms" statutes enabling the courts to decide in case with a foreign element. During last decades, the American courts act based on several factors, among which may be distinguished such as "minimum contacts" (known also in insurance from case McGee v International Life Ins. Co, where the jurisdiction was acknowledged over an insurer concluding only one insurance contract in a given state, but still was confirmed as sufficient to apply the factor of "minimum contact" with the law of that state), "reasonable anticipation", "purposefully directed activities", "effect" cases, etc. The latter one having its source in the Restatement II, Sec. 37, Rosenblatt (2001). See Gilles.

[153] As it was also mentioned by R. Michaels, "*In the United States, choice of law largely concerns interstate conflicts between legal systems whose common laws are structurally quite similar but often differ significantly in their policies; choice of law in Europe deals with legal orders that differ more in doctrine and system than in their Policies*", The New European Choice of Law Revolution, Tulane Law Review, vol. 82, No. 5, May 2008., p. 1611.

irregular basis.[154] It is worth adding that even in those countries where PIL takes a form of an act, insurance contracts are usually not a distinguished type of contract for the purposes of specifying the law applicable.[155] Another solution has been adopted in Norway, where there are no codified PIL rules on general level. This results from the fact that the flexibility of choice of law rules is recognized as a higher value than the certainty. However, in some aspects, where the need of certainty was acknowledged as more important, specific provisions were adopted. Among them, the Act on Choice of Law in Insurance may be mentioned from European insurance II generation directives.[156]

In the consequence of a variety of solutions adopted globally, it seems important that the rules adopted on European level are as much universal as possible. The latest legislation seems to follow this idea and for example, the Rome I Regulation shall apply universally, regardless of the fact where the insurance risk is located. It suits best the needs of "extraterritorial" online insurance. This is also true that the more universal European rules are, the more influence they will have on global regulations. In this respect an international cooperation is necessary so that the European model of protective rules concerning the choice of law could work properly, as the major risk does not come from contracts concluded in Europe, where the substantive protective measures, being harmonized, ensure the comparable level of protection in insurance (and consumer) transactions,[157] but from insurers located outside the EU. No doubt, that the EU legislation should not ignore the legislations achievements of Unidroit and Uncitral, having in mind that new laws in emerging economies are based thereon.

3.2.3 Conclusions

This section of the chapter aims to show that the cross-border insurance contract concluded online needs special treatment under PIL rules, as it serves the satisfaction of the vital interests not only of the contracting parties, but also other persons or entities that may be involved. This aim is not satisfied on a global level, as only the

[154] As regards the USA, some reference may be made to Restatement II, where conflict of laws has been regulated in Section 187–188. Main international conventions signed by USA are listed at the site of US Department of State: http://www.state.gov/s/l/commercial/index.htm.; see also E.A. O'Hara et L. Ribstein (2009).

[155] Example of such approach is Switzerland, where insurance contracts are subject to general rules on contracts law included in Chapter 9, Articles 112–126 in Private International Law Act dated 18 December 1987; available on: https://www.bj.admin.ch//bj/en/home/themen/wirtschaft/internationales_privatrecht.html; same in China, where the Law of the Republic of China on the Laws Applicable to Foreign—Related Civil Relations was adopted on 28 October 2010 and regulates the law applicable for obligations in Chapter 6, Articles 41–47; see: The Chinese Journal of Comparative Law (2013) Vol. 1, No 1, pp. 185–193.

[156] Choice of Law in Insurance Act no 88/357 and 90/619; see Cordero Moss (2010).

[157] Tang (2010), p. 23.

EU regulations (Rome I) (and Norway), distinguish insurance contracts, providing for special rules in this respect. This may lead to undesired results, i.e. contradictory court verdicts on the same case in different countries.

3.3 Autonomy of Parties' Will in PIL Insurance Rules

3.3.1 Outline

This point shall be devoted to the consideration of the role the autonomy of the parties' will may have in modern insurance contracts, with the special focus on online cross border contracts, where the PIL rules come into question. Although this subject deserves an extensive analysis, the frames and purpose of this chapter allow only to signalize the main points thereof.

The autonomy of will, being the basis of modern contractual relations, is also reflected in PIL rules, namely in the freedom of choosing the law applicable to the contract, or the court competent to resolve the dispute.[158] The autonomy of will is considered to be one of the fundamental principles of the private international law and constitutes a part of the freedom of contract.[159] It is expressed as such in many international conventions, considered to be also one of the fundamental personal rights.[160] With respect to PIL, freedom of law choice means first of all a conscious choice of the parties to make the contract governed by specific legal system. This concept is a basis for modern rules adopted on the state of international level, although with some limitation, like it is in case of Rome I Regulation and Brussels Regulation. From the point of view of the "legal technique", it is the basic "connecting factor" (see more detailed analysis in the next point), specifying which law is applicable to the given contract. It is worth noting that all other connecting factors are meant to be in fact the "recreation" of the parties' will. Its value cannot be overestimated.

---

[158] Green Paper 2003, p. 10, Sec. 1.4.; see also Zhang (2007), p. 6; Muir-Watt (2002); Ivanova (2010), p. 13; Kuipers (2010), p. 1506.

[159] It is said to be derived from the individualistic and laisser-faire philosophy of the nineteenth century, although it is also strongly opposed by the legal positivists, saying that contracts derive their binding force from the law and from the wishes of its parties; Maniruzzaman (1999), p. 163. Nevertheless, it is present in the most recent laws concerning the contract law of international dimension, such as the international convention in contract law (Article 19 of CISG) (United Nations Convention on Contracts for the International Sale of Goods), as well as in the Principles of European Contract Law, which clearly says that Parties are free to enter into contract and to determine its contents, subject to the requirement of good faith and fair dealing, and the mandatory rules established by these Principles (Art. 1:102). See: University of Oslo (2012), pp. 5–6.

[160] The most important is Universal Declaration of Human Rights proclaimed on 10 December 1948; Similarly, the Basel Resolution of 1994 recognized the freedom of parties to choose the law applicable to the contract; The other may also be mentioned such as UN convention of 1980 concerning the international sale of goods (CISG).

3.3.2 Parties' Disparity and Autonomy of Will

The basic dilemma with respect to the autonomy of will in PIL appears along with the disparity arising between the contracting parties.[161] The situation in consumer contracts can be given as one example, insurance contracts as the other. The dilemma is then between affording the protection to the weaker party or providing the freedom to conduct online business on the other.[162] The reason why online contracts are subject to the particular interest of the legislator is that concluding online contracts deprive the parties of the certainty as to the rights and obligations under the contract, which results from the fact that they can differ from one legal system to another. Having said that, it becomes clear why PIL rules are so crucial to online insurance contracts in view of differing levels of protection afforded to the policyholders worldwide in spite of the universal features of insurance. The question which appears here, is whether PIL rules are sufficient to ensure certainty in online insurance relations.

The parties' autonomy, although being fundamental, does not remain unrestricted.[163] One of the limitations is introduced by the rules of choice of law.[164] The extent of the parties' autonomy in PIL in online transactions has been subject to many discussions in Europe during the process of converting the Rome Convention into Rome I Regulation. It was stated then that the parties' autonomy is "incompetent" in B2C transactions. A particular concern in this respect was addressed to the unlimited possibilities of the internet access by consumers and necessity to adjust the PIL rules to the extraterritorial character of online relations. In effect, the parties' autonomy principle in B2C transactions was split by introducing the criterion of "directed activity" on the internet and more concessions towards the full party autonomy were given in the case where consumers actively initiate concluding online contracts.[165] This idea has been modified in insurance, by introducing a distinction between large risks and all other risks, so called "mass risks".[166] The latter division does not correlate strictly with B2B and B2C

---

[161] Many, but for example, Merrett (2009), p. 55.

[162] van der Hof (2003), p. 166.

[163] One of the major restrictions is obviously based on the necessity of protecting the weaker party, such as policyholder, consumer, and employee, Lazic (2010), p. 102. See also Sambugaro (2008), p. I-127 and Gilles (2008), p. 144.

[164] See in detail: Muir-Watt (2002); Zhang. (2007).

[165] Tang (2010), p. 8; See: Art. 6 (1) of Rome I Regulations and Art. 15 (1) c of the Brussels I Regulation. See also the cases explaining the idea of "directed activity": Joined cases C-585/08 and C-144/09, *Peter Pammer* v *Reederei Karl Schlüter GmbH & Co. KG* and *Hotel Alpenhof GesmbH* v *Oliver Heller*, judgment of 07.12.2010; SEC (2011) 1641 final. See also Gilles (2008), p. 112 and the analysis of the "directed activity" as a connecting factor. See also a verdict analyzing the "directed activity" as a basis for jurisdiction: C-218/12 *Lokman Emrek v Vlad Sabranovic*.

[166] Contracting on-line with respect to large risks often has an additional aspect. Business clients use the internet for independent placing of large risks in such a way that a kind of risks auctions are organized, on which the insuring parties select the most suitable offer. No doubt, such *modus*

distinction. The result of the above is that an insurance policyholder may be subject to double protection regime, i.e. concerning B2C and distinctive one concerning insurance depending on the status and circumstances. It should be stressed that the distinction made in Rome I for insurance contracts, does not eliminate totally the application of the general rules, in particular the consumer protection regime.

3.3.3 Conclusions

As can be seen from this short presentation, modern role of parties' autonomy, although still perceived theoretically as the main principle, has became restricted in an extensive way, so that one may doubt whether it can keep such its character, or, quite opposite, the parties autonomy is granted now by the legislator. This can be observed specially in insurance, where two level restriction may apply. So far, it was the only feasible remedy agreed at European level to provide the protection for policyholders participating nowadays actively in online cross-border transactions, while globally even such solution has not been reachable.

3.4 Connecting Factors (Contacts) in Online Insurance Contracts

3.4.1 Outline

Below, the idea of "connecting factors" in online insurance will be presented, although, the more detailed analysis of that topic with respect to the European regulations has been included in Chapter of Anna Tarasiuk and her considerations on the Rome I Regulation.

As mentioned in point 3 above, the idea of the party autonomy is supported in PIL by the circumstances defined in the law, that "tie" the given legal issue (for example the validity of a contract) before the court to a particular legal system.[167] These circumstances are known under the name of "connecting factors" (or "contacts"[168]). Traditional private international law developed a whole structure of connecting factors, which are used in a case where no choice of law has been made by the parties or the choice is limited or excluded for certain types of contracts or subjects of contracts (for example relating to immovable property). The question which is worth considering, is what is the value of the traditional connecting factors for online transactions in general and also specifically for online insurance

---

operandi can be qualified as on-line insurance with all the aspects characteristic for cross-border insurance in case the prerequisites are met for that; see Baur (2009), p. 19.

[167] Cox et al. (2006), p. 207.

[168] Clarke (1997), p. 30.

contracts. Are there any other factors that could be or are already in use with respect to online insurance? The analysis, presented below, of the most common connecting factors aims at finding an answer.

The connecting factors in the traditional meaning are of objective nature, as opposed to the choice of law made by the parties, which is also considered as one of the connecting factors, but of the subjective character.[169] When considering the modern approach to the character of connecting factors, it should be stressed, however, that in the cases where more protection of parties is needed, the more objective connecting factors should be used. This is the specifics of consumer contracts, as well as insurance contracts, because of the necessity of the policy-holder protection.[170] Such an approach results from the conviction, that "*choice of connecting factors must not betray the underlying policies of the relevant legal category. It also explains why conflict rules vary across the board*".[171]

3.4.2 Concept of Connecting Factors

The concept of connecting factors is from "*closest connection" principle*, which should tie a contract to a particular legal system.[172] In such a sense, particular connecting factors are just the reflection of the closest connection rule, put in a statutory form. The idea of the closest connection (in other words, most significant relationship approach)[173] seems to be dominant in most of the jurisdictions and results from the statutes (as in China, Switzerland, European Union—Rome I),[174] as well as from court verdicts (as in USA) and international conventions (for example the Hague Convention on the Law Applicable to Contracts for the International Sale of Goods of 22 December 1986[175]). The idea of the closest connection

[169] Gołaczyński (2007).

[170] Fuchs (2009), p. 16.

[171] Muir Watt (2002).

[172] The modern doctrine underline the importance of new legislation initiatives aiming at unification of the connecting factors, Szpunar (2014), p. 210; Boelke-Woelke (2010).

[173] US Restatement II, par. 187–188; see also: Gabor (1988), pp. 541–542. The factor of the most significant relation replaced the other historical formulations, such as *lex loci*, and others, however is not the only one applied by the courts in US; "*several other approaches to choice of law have also been posited and accepted by some courts*". Sometimes they are however just a "simplified version of the most significant relationship", for example *center of gravity* connection. It has also been stressed that "currently U.S. states and the U.S. itself take a variety of approaches; none of the above approaches have been universally accepted"; B. Rosenblatt; see also Muir Watt (2002).

[174] See Article 117 of the Swiss Private International Law Act, Article 41 of the Chinese Law on the Laws Applicable to Foreign-Related Civil Relations; Hui (2009), pp. 3–4. Muñoz-López (2009), p. 174; Gilles (2008).

[175] According to Article 14 of the Hague Convention, "If a party has more than one place of business, the relevant place of business is that which has the closest relationship to the contract and its performance, having regard to the circumstances known to or contemplated by the parties at any time before or at the conclusion of the contract"; this rule is applied in the lack of choice by the

is also related to the notion of the "*characteristic performance*" *presumption*, in such a way that the closest connection between the given system of law and the contract is established by reference to the presumption of characteristic performance.[176] It is defined as "performance for which the payment is due (...) which usually constitutes the centre of gravity and the socio-economic function of the contractual transmission".[177] In modern PIL statutes, there is a proliferation of a provision according to which the contract (in the lack of choice) is governed by the law of the state, where the party obliged to effect characteristic performance, has its seat or domicile. This concept seems to have a great value for the online contracts, where all other connecting factors used traditionally, such as the place of concluding the contract,[178] place of performing the contract, etc. may have only temporal or accidental connection with the contract, while the seat or domicile of the party to the contract seems to suit the needs of online cross-border transactions, ensuring stability in finding the law applicable.[179] Such approach may differ, however, from country to country, while in some civil law jurisdictions, this factor has no significance.[180]

3.4.3 Connecting Factors in Online Contracts

As it was mentioned before, there are doubts raised in the doctrine with respect to the suitability of PIL traditional rules for online contracts, as habitually they were "designed for a material—order[181]". Thus, they seek a geographic connection with the contract, which is alleged to be decisive when determining the law applicable and the jurisdiction of a competent court. Even if when we look at the essence of all these doubts, it becomes clear that most of them relate not to the general idea expressed in PIL but to the specific connecting factors, such as the place of

parties (Article 7), when place of business is considered; See the text of the Hague Convention at: http://www.hcch.net/upload/conventions/txt31en.pdf.

[176] See for example, Shuhong et al. (2009), pp. 423–439.

[177] Giuliano-Lagarde report (1980), p. 20.

[178] There are still some jurisdictions, such as India, China, as well as in some states of USA, where it is possible to offer insurance by a foreign insurer not being licensed locally, only if the insurance contract has not been "transacted" at place; Krishnan (2013).

[179] It should be stressed that the connecting factors concerning the place of concluding the contract and place of its performance were considered to have little importance a long time ago. As an example may serve the opinions of American academics at the time of adopting the Second Restatement, see: www.kentlaw.edu/perritt/conflicts/rest187.htm and www.kentlaw.edu/perritt/conflicts/rest188.htm, see also Gołaczyński (2007).

[180] The Supreme Court in Netherlands stated that "the place of business of the party who is to effect the characteristic performance has no real significance as a connecting factor", Hoge Raad, 25 September 1992, 1992 NJ No 750, reported by Stuycken (1996) LMCLQ 18, 20: after Clarke (1997), p. 43.

[181] Muñoz-López (2009), p. 167; also Sirinelli (1998), p. 14.

concluding the contract and place of performance of the contract.[182] Analyzing this issue in view of the conclusions made in point I. 2 above as to the main features of contracting online, it may be said that online insurance would face similar problems as other online contracts in terms of factors relating to the "place of concluding the contract". However, it would be easier to resolve problems of the "place of performance" factor, as the performance of an insurance contract takes place as a rule offline. "Characteristic performance" in insurance constitutes the performance of the insurer, which is the promise to cover the negative consequences of the event insured.[183]

The above remarks are of some importance in these systems of law where there are no specific regulation concerning connecting factors in electronic contracts.[184] In Europe, however, it is a mere speculation, as a separate system of connecting factors was developed for insurance and, in addition, the Rome I was aimed (by power of the Article 5 of the Regulation) to answer the needs of electronic commerce in general, by adopting specific connecting factors also in this respect. Thus, while the USA approach is still inconsistent,[185] the EU legislation covers also the electronic commerce both with respect to the choice of law, including *forum*.

The most natural and basic connecting factor is still the law chosen by the parties (choice of law rule), as an express of the autonomy of will. This principle is recognized by most of the jurisdictions nowadays.[186] The question arises however, whether the choice of law rule may also be applied to the electronic contracts to the same extent as in traditional contract. In this respect, it should be noticed, that the choice of law, being made at the stage of concluding the contract, shows again that for the purposes of PIL the most important feature of the electronic contracts is the conclusion stage, while the performance is of secondary importance. Having this in mind as a rule, it seems that a choice of law may be applied to the electronic contracts with no legal difference from the traditional contracts. However, another question in this respect concerns the manner, in which the parties can make this choice, and whether it is only a technical issue (as an example of major concerns in

[182] Gilles (2008), p. 54; Świerczyński (2014), p. 212; Tang et al. (2012).

[183] It should be, however, considered that the "place of performance" of the contract was never a dominant connecting factors for example in the UK and the "place of concluding of contract" which simply lost its significance, see Clarke (1997), p. 31. However such an approach may be presented in such a flexible way mostly in common law countries, while in civil tradition legal systems it would rather need changes in the law.

[184] For example, in Article 41 of Chinese PIL it is stated that in the lack of parties choice, the law of the habitual residence of the party whose performance of obligation is most characteristic of the contract or the law that is most closely connected with the contract shall be applied. As compared with the American UCITA provisions, which (Sec. 190), provide for the connecting factor referring to the place of location of the service provider (licensor) at time of contracting, or the place where a copy or tangible medium was to be delivered to the consumer.

[185] There are certain cases, setting a tendency in considering the cases by the courts with respect to the internet disputes, such as "Zippo test", or Calder v Jones case, setting the "effects doctrine", Geist, p. 22.

[186] Giuliano-Lagarde Report (1980), pp. 15–16.

this respect may serve *click-wrap and clip-shrink contracts*)[187] or should be a subject of a special attention of the legislator (supporting the information need on the side of the consumer or replacing his self-awareness). There are however views that attribute the change in the basic elements of offer and acceptance to the internet technology.[188]

While discussing the connecting factors in online contracts on international level, two main concepts were considered, i.e. the "country of origin" or "country of destination", gaining a support accordingly the business groups or consumers.[189] In this respect, the differences between USA and European approach appeared quite clearly, as US business groups support basically the "country of origin" approach while in Europe, more consumer oriented, the "country of destination" has been gaining prevalence. A similar (but of a bit different effects) idea is derived from "targeting" concept, which would allow the entrepreneurs to "*confine their online activities (and thus their legal risks) to a limited number of jurisdictions, while ensuring that consumers retain the right to apply their local consumer protection laws to e-commerce*".[190]

3.4.4 Connecting Factors in Insurance

Having in mind the criteria used nowadays by the insurance legislations worldwide (although mostly in Europe), the most important factor, deciding on the cross-border character of the insurance is *location of the risk,* where the "risk" is understood as a subject of the insurance coverage.[191] According to the "closest connection principle" it is deemed that the insurance contract shows the closest connection with the state where the risk is located.[192] In this respect, location of the risk may have two consequences. First, it may be decisive for stating whether the insurance is of cross-border character or not and in result, whether the choice of law rules are to be applied. The second consequence may be crucial for deciding which law is applicable to the insurance contract. The *location of the risk* and other factors derived from the Rome I Regulation is analyzed in detail in chapter of Anna Tarasiuk.

---

[187] Exhaustive explanation of click-wrap contracts for this purpose presents Gilles (2008), p. 56, as well as set of principles set by the American Bar Association with respect to the validity of the wrap contracts: http://apps.americanbar.org/buslaw/newsletter/0064/materials/pp2.pdf. Gokhan (2012).

[188] It seems, however, that this issue does not change the principle and is rather a matter of proof and insurance online contracts will benefit in this respect from the strict rules of information duties imposed on the insurer, which must be fulfilled also in case of online contracting.

[189] Geist, p. 20.

[190] Geist, pp. 19–20; see however Gilles (2008), p. 113, where the "target-based test was considered in view of the Article 15 of the Brussels I Regulation and the necessity of an amendment was raised.

[191] Kowalewski (2005), p. 11.

[192] Schnyder (1994), p. 54.

The place of the occurrence of the event insured does not appear as a connecting factor for determining the law applicable, but can be decisive for the jurisdiction (*forum*). According to the Brussels Regulation, the specific jurisdiction rules have been provided for insurance matters. Apart from the connecting factor concerning the domiciliation of the parties, the factor of the "place where the harmful event occurred" has been distinguished (Art. 10 with respect to the liability insurance and insurance of real estates). Although the nature of such a "place" is not a virtual one and must be situated outside "cyberspace", it was already said above that performance of the insurance contract always is effected outside such a virtual space. Of course, this is a kind of a simplistic statement, as because of the variety of insurance risks, some of them may happen also in cyberspace (cyber risks) or in the territory beyond any state's border (outer space), although the nature of the insurance coverage causes insurance contracts, even those concluded online, to be always only "indirect" electronic contracts within the meaning used by the EU documents. Having the above in mind, the place where the harmful even occurs may also be applied to the online insurance without the necessity of adjusting this connecting factor.

Habitual residence notion as a connecting factor is increasingly becoming popular in international law.[193] The connecting factor related to the habitual residence of the policyholder (insured) caused a serious discussion with respect to the method of interpreting the connecting factors, i.e. whether the dynamic or rather static interpretation should be approached,[194] which found its end in the ECJ. Although the case in question concerned solely tax issues, it may be asked whether it means that the law applicable may change along with the change of the habitual residence of the policyholder, from one state to another (in accordance with the Rome I, it is the place of commitment).[195] The connecting factor related to the place

[193] The Hague Convention (1961), Regulation 2201/2003/WE, Chinese Act on private international law (2010), etc., although the attention has been drawn to the fact that legal acts rarely include the definition of the habitual residence. Such a definition has been provided in the Swiss Law (1987), according to which "une persone physique (...) a sa résidence habituelle dans l'Etat dans lequel elle vit pendant une certaine durée, même si cette durée est de prime abord limitée".

[194] The matter resolved by the European Court of Justice concerned the possibility of imposing taxes on the insurance policy in situation where the habitual residence of the policyholder changed after concluding the insurance contract (where such taxes may be applied only by the member state of the commitment). According to the static interpretation, member state of the commitment is being specified on one occasion when the contract is concluded (thus, only the member state where the policyholder had habitual residence at the moment of concluding the insurance contract may impose taxes in this respect). On the other hand, the dynamic interpretation was supported, according to which, the member state of the commitment may change in case the habitual residence changes (from one premium payment to the next) Opinion of Advocate General Kokkott (2012), point 30–32.

[195] Finally, the court verdict followed the dynamic interpretation in terms of taxes, however, stating in the justification that the issue of the law applicable to the contract should be treated independently of taxes, stating that it is possible to interpret the provisions concerning "state of commitment" to the effect that the applicable law does not change when the policyholder transfers his habitual residence, as the law applicable is not to affect the fiscal arrangements; Judgment of

of residence is also used in the Brussels Regulation, where it takes notion of "domicile" with respect to both insurers and policyholders, both corporate and natural persons. It is claimed that "habitual residence" factor satisfies the needs of both online and offline contracts with respect to the protection of consumers[196] and it is difficult to oppose.

Significance of the server location. The question whether the location of the server is of any importance in the context of choice of law has been often subject to academic considerations.[197]Although ECD seems to close the discussion. Although it is expressly stated in point 23 of the Preamble and Article 1(4) that ECD does not provide any rules within the scope of private international law, neither changes the existing ones, it also says clearly that the location of the server cannot interfere with the jurisdiction matters, in particular, it does not mean the place of the establishment of the entrepreneur providing services online (point 19 of the preamble). Similarly, the location of the website or rather the place of making it available to the public (see below), cannot be a connecting factor or decisive for determining the law applicable, as it is of no importance for the negotiation, conclusion or performance stage of the contract. The "nationality" of the website, cannot also be perceived as having the closest connection with the contract. In this situation, also the place of concluding an online contract does not have substantive connection with the server location.[198] The same may be said with respect to the insurance online contracts.

Significance of website being accessible. That issue became a subject to some disputes resolved by ECJ (for example C-509/09), where provisions of the ECD were interpreted in the context of conflict of laws rules. According to the prevailing opinion, the place where the website is accessible is of secondary importance[199] and, further, it cannot lead to a situation where the provider of an electronic commerce service is made subject to stricter requirements than those provided for by the substantive law applicable in the member state in which the service provider is established.[200]

---

the court of (first chamber) of 21 February 2013, case C-243/11 RVS Levensverzekeringen NV v Belgische Staat.

[196] Gilles (2008), p. 150. Nonetheless, according to the Rome I, the requirement of "directed activity"—i.e. specific invitation or advertising is particularly important for application of the "friendly" to consumer rules of choice of law; see also Green Paper, p. 31.

[197] See for example Gilles (2008), p. 115.

[198] Fawcett et al. (2005), p. 1235.

[199] See however the dispute between France and Yahoo!, concerning the auctions of Nazi memorabilia being available at the website directed to US clients but also accessible from France, which was forbidden in France but allowed in US, see. Geist, pp. 22–23.

[200] Article 3 of Directive 2000/31/EC of the European Parliament and of the Council of 8 June 2000 on certain legal aspects of information society services, in particular electronic commerce, in the Internal Market ("Directive on electronic commerce"), must be interpreted as not requiring transposition in the form of a specific conflict-of-laws rule. Nevertheless, in relation to the coordinated field, Member States must ensure that, subject to the derogations authorised in accordance with the conditions set out in Article 3(4) of Directive 2000/31, the provider of an

Insurance connecting factors in USA—a note; It is difficult to speak up for all the states of the USA, as each of them may adopt a separate set of rules with respect to the choice of law. The difficulty consists also in the substantive competence afforded to the American courts with respect to the applicable law of insurance and reinsurance. Nevertheless, it is worth mentioning that, the concept of the "most significant relationship" plays vital role. To assess, the law of which state has the most significant connection with the insurance contract, the court applies, as it is in Europe the connecting factors ("contacts"). Additionally, the "state interests" in having its law applied, are subject to an assessment in some cases. An important hint (but only of an indicative nature) what can decide on the most significant relationship contains Restatement II, which in Section 193 states that "*with regard to "fire, surety and casualty" policies, the "location of the insured risk will be given greater weight than any other single contact in determining the state of the applicable law.*"[201]

Most of the States law does not contain detailed rules which regulate the protection of the consumer or the policyholder under large insurance contracts, although the court in applying the most significant relationship test *tends to prefer the application of a law which will favour the insured (for example the law of the state of the insured, in case the location of the risk factor does not prevail). Additionally it is raised that the law of the principal location of the risk has no application where the risks were "nationwide or global" in scope. Further, where a policy covered risks in multiple states "the insured's domicile" should be regarded "as a proxy for the principal location of the risk"*.[202]

3.4.5 Conclusions

The analysis of the connecting factors made in this section was aimed at proving that contracting online is not in contradiction with the main connecting factors used by PIL on European and also on a global level and in consequence, there is no necessity to create distinctive PIL rules for online contracts. The modern connecting factors, shifting the importance from the territory where the contract has been concluded or performed, to the territory where parties habitually reside, seem to suit the needs of both, traditional contracting and e-commerce. Additionally, in Europe, as well as in US Restatement II, the distinguished factor of *risk*

---

electronic commerce service is not made subject to stricter requirements than those provided for by the substantive law applicable in the Member State in which that service provider is established.

[201] An interesting example of deciding on the location of the risk factor is the case *Zurich Insurance Company v Shearson Lehman Hutton Inc*. There was a dispute as to whether the location of the risk was at the bank's head office in New York, or Texas where judgment had been entered. But the court considered that even if the place of the risk had been Texas, the interest of the state of New York in having its law applied would have outweighed the place of the risk: R. Cox QC (2013).

[202] *Certain Underwriters at Lloyd's, London v Foster Wheeler Corp,* R. Cox QC (2013).

location in insurance seems to be a good reflection of traditional concept of the *closest connection principle*. This connecting factor is of such a universal value and may suit even the new concepts of contract formation in e-commerce. All the above shows that simple adjustments are sufficient to address the needs of e-commerce and in this way they correlate with the long lasting PIL concepts and traditions.

4 PIL *versus* Integration of the Substantive Laws

4.1 Outline

As already noticed, the questions whether PIL is suitable for efficient regulating of the global e-commerce based on exclusivity are recently quite frequent. An extensive analysis and broad discussion on the deficiencies of PIL in this respect are observed on an international level[203] with a simultaneous indication, that instead of PIL, an integration of substantive law should be seriously considered for online cross-border transactions. This section of the chapter focuses on presenting shortly the outcome of these discussions in relation to online cross-border insurance.

4.2 Divergence of Contract Law

The problem of integrating the substantive law in insurance has been subject to many discussions and disputes so far. It does not however touch solely insurance, but all kinds of cross-border transactions worldwide. The best picture in this respect is given by statistics, according to which, most of electronic contracts are concluded in B2B transactions and not with the consumer participation. This is attributed to the fact that US and European law regulating B2B electronic contracts is more integrated within the scope of soft law instruments such as the Vienna Convention on the International Sale of Goods and the UNIDROIT Principles of International Commercial Contracts and such instruments may also be applicable to electronic transactions, while no such integration exists with respect to the consumer e-commerce.[204] This shows that the main obstacle to increasing the number of online contracts is the legal divergence of the rules concerning electronic commerce. Even only with respect to the EU, increasingly frequent are the opinions that a minimal and fragmented harmonization and complex legislation create altogether obstacles for cross-border services, including online contracts.[205] This issue has been addressed in the EU report on insurance contract law, where the differences

[203] Gabriel (2007), p. 224 et subsequent.

[204] Kaufmann Winn et Haubold (2002), p. 23.

[205] Riefa (2009), p. 21.

between national laws at the stage of concluding the insurance contracts have been raised. In particular, it has been stressed that "understanding the differences in disclosure requirements in different markets and adapting the products tends to result in added costs which are ultimately born by policyholders" and that "those differences also preclude online contracting through the use of a single interactive website". Similar problems result from the differences as regards the form of contract requirements.[206] This issue seems to be even more problematic on a global level, as on the one hand, the online transactions cannot be technologically restricted, and on the other, the laws are far from being in line with this process.

4.3 PIL as Integration Tool

Is private international law a sufficient tool to answer that? It is hard to state that on a global level. It is caused by the fact that PIL rules are subject to integration only with respect to some kinds of contracts, and a limited number of countries have signed the international treaties in this respect.[207] Generally, each country has its own PIL rules (statutory or based on case law), that decide which law is applicable and what court is competent to resolve the dispute. That leads often to an uncomfortable situation where a judge must apply a law of a foreign country, sometimes from completely different legal tradition. Additionally, in case of mandatory rules, two legal systems may apply at the same time. In Europe, where the unification of the PIL rules has been achieved in took a form of the regulation (Rome I), the above-mentioned impediments have not been removed. This is because, mostly, to the strict choice of law rules adopted in Rome I with respect to the consumer cross-border transactions, including insurance. In consequence, the most of the cross-border transactions concern B2B trade, where the parties can enjoy free choice of law, although even in B2B contracts, the necessity to consider a foreign system of law constitutes an impediment and being a disadvantage to one of the parties, can increase substantially the costs of transaction.[208]

The same concerns insurance where in most of contracts, apart from large risks insurance, the law governing contract is imposed on the parties. Further, the

[206] European Union (2014), pp. 37–38. The attention has been drawn to the requirement of the existence of a signed written document as a condition for the validity of the insurance contract in some Member States, while in others, there is a simple obligation of the insurer to provide contractual documents in written form after the conclusion of the contract. No doubt, that "the requirement of a signed written document, unless interpreted such as to include electronic communication, impedes online contracting".

[207] Nonetheless, it cannot be denied that the efforts to unify the PIL rules on a global level have been made since XIX century and behind them, there stood an idea that only unified PIL rules may ensure the uniformity of court verdicts around the world with respect to the law applicable. Jayme (1995).

[208] Riefa (2009), p. 3.; Wagner (2007), p. 42; Wallis (2006), p. 191.

concepts of insurance coverage, together with the main parties' obligations differ much even only throughout Europe. It goes without saying that the two main insurance cultures in Europe, so called *alpine and marine* insurance cultures tend to interpret the parties' obligations in a totally different way. What may be the reason of an easy exclusion of insurer's liability in the UK, will not be recognized as such in Belgium or Poland, where strict protective rules, supported by restrictive interpretation of the courts are present.[209] This may be the cause of false underwriting provisions (reserves) being made for claims by a British insurer selling insurance in Poland and in consequence of limiting the offer available online. This is not what the creators of internal market concept aimed at.

Therefore, it seems that PIL rules, even if very sophisticated, unified and ensuring high level of protection to consumer, are not a sufficient tool for the development of cross-border online insurance market. It may lead to a conclusion that PIL may solely constitute the first step, or a temporary solution on the path leading to full integration of the contract law (or private law in general)[210] as the optimal solution for cross-border online contracts. This is particularly important for online cross-border contracts and at the same time hardest to achieve.[211]

4.4 *Integration of Substantive Rules*

4.4.1 Europe

Is then the substantive law an answer to that? Nowadays we may observe around the world a few different types of processes aiming at an integration of the contract law. First one takes place in Europe and it is an intended process, encompassing also insurance industry, where the idea of unifying the contract law, at least with respect to distance (including online) contracts is now strongly supported.[212] It arises from the fact that the cross-border trade is still perceived as insufficient (and that has not changed much during the last years),[213] in spite of enacting advanced regulations

[209] Belgium act on insurance contracts is known as one of the most restrictive to insurers and most protective to policyholders.

[210] COM (2002) 654 final.

[211] This statement seems to have significant importance in the situation, where (as in insurance sector) the choice of law by the parties is strictly limited, see Grundman (2013), pp. 237–238. Although it may seem that choice of law rules can be a substitute to the harmonized rules of substantive law, it is not so with respect to the branches of industry where the protection of one of the parties is particularly important, as it is in insurance.

[212] COM (2011) 635 final.

[213] To See first of all the report of Experts Group, which aims at finding the justification and possible solutions on cross-border insurance problems; as it was pointed out, the practical result of the substantive law divergence are "the costs generated by the required adjustments to foreign mandatory contract laws (...). This factor may prevent insurers from using their freedom to provide services to enter foreign insurance markets (...). At the same time, it may prevent

within the area of public law, which enable an effective use of the freedom of establishment and freedom of services, and, further, introducing extensive pro-consumer legislation, also in terms of PIL. The main reason still seems to be the differences in substantive law of contracts between the Member States. With respect to online cross-border contracts, even the legislation specially designated for that is not helpful, as ECD cannot be recognized as a substantive law for online contracting in any aspects, being the only the instrument enabling online contracts to be validly concluded throughout Europe and in all other aspects it is "contract law neutral".[214]

It is pointed out in Giuliano-Lagarde report that "*harmonization of substantive law does not always contrive to keep pace with the dismantling of economic frontiers. The problem of the law to be applied will therefore continue to arise as long as substantive law is not unified. The number of cases in which the question of applicable law must be resolved increases with the growth of private relationships across frontiers*".[215] It seems therefore that not just harmonization of certain aspects of contract law (mostly of protective pro-consumer nature as until now), but a unification of contract law within the scope of cross-border would be an optimal solution, as it helps to minimize the "information and cognitive load for users to compare different rules".[216] But is it feasible?

The concept which is now under serious consideration of the EU, is a kind of a second regime contract law within the national system of law of Member States, existing alongside the pre-existing provisions of the domestic contract laws. Such a regime, to be adopted in the form of the regulation could be identical for all Member States, although it will be applied on a voluntary basis, upon express consent of the parties to the cross-border contract.[217] Introducing such a second contract regime is not aimed at substituting the PIL rules, including the choice of law. The choice of the European contract law regime will follow the choice of the law of a particular member state (where the choice is possible), but at the same time more choice possibilities will be in B2C relations. It may be stated then that PIL is a kind of basis for applying the European contract law regime, as it proved to be insufficient (together with the directives regulating private law issues) as an instru-

customers from shopping for foreign products, making insurance markets inaccessible to "active" foreign customers. For example, insurers offering their services online usually reject applications from abroad. While a number of factors may be the reason for this behavior, becoming submitted foreign mandatory contract law and foreign jurisdiction may be an important one"; European Union (2014), p. 27; Verbiest and Le Borne (2002).

[214] Kaufmann Winn et Haubold (2002); Schneider (2001), pp. 344–345.

[215] Giuliano-Lagarde Report (1980), p. 4.

[216] Low (2013), pp. 379–380. It is underlined by the author that the reduction of the necessity of choice may bring, as some studies have shown, positive results in terms of attracting consumers to certain product of services.

[217] Giuliano-Lagarde Report (1980), p. 8.

ment enabling effective functioning of the internal EU market.[218] It should be stressed once again that the whole concept of a second regime of contract law which is going to start with European Sales Law[219] and will continue with other types of contracts, most expectedly also with insurance contract, is designed directly and expressly for cross-border contracts, the major part of which are contracts concluded on a distance basis, including those concluded online. Therefore, there is no doubt that the modern laws not only are adjusted to the digital contracts, but are created with the aim of serving them. It should not however be perceived as a reflection of the American law concepts of creating a separate law regime for electronic commerce, but as a result of the fact that digital contracts are so strongly related to the cross-border trade (and globalization) and constitute an important part of contracting nowadays in general.

The evolution from PIL rules as a method of strengthening the cross-border trade, up to the concept of contract law integration can be seen very clearly, as illustrated by the example of insurance, which was subject to legal integration in the EU as one of the first branches. That process began in 1970s of the twentieth century, parallel to that of banking services. The European Union recognized then that insurance services can easily cross the borders of the Member States, if only basic freedoms are applied, the first of them being the freedom of capital movement, followed by the freedom to provide services. With the adoption of the second generation of the insurance directives, the internal market with free cross-border services was theoretically created, but, as already mentioned, that has not lead to the growth in transnational insurance turnover. The research made by the EU in this respect has shown that the main problem lies not in the internal market organization, as it was released by the single license rule, but in differences in substantive law on insurance contracts and differences in the implementation of the insurance directives. An answer to this problem was found by applying one of the two solutions: (1) regulation of the conflict of laws issues in a way protecting the policyholder, or (2) unification of the provisions of the insurance contract on the EU level. While the latter proved to be impossible at that stage of the European integration (draft of relevant directive drafted in 1979 was finally withdrawn in 1993) because of the lack of political will to interfere in the national systems of the insurance private law, the first one resolved the problem in quite a superfluous way. In result, the legal aspects of the conflict of laws in insurance force insurers to adopt terms and conditions of insurance coverage to the systems of the law of each member state where the insurance is distributed.

---

[218] Proposal to European Sales Law regulation says that the Regulation "will apply exclusively to cross-border transactions. That is why it must be examined from the point of view of private international law and related rules of conflict of laws already in force within the European Union, particularly to the Rome I Regulation (...)" A. Sixto, Sanchez-Lorenzo (2013), pp. 191–217.

[219] Proposal for a Regulation of the European Parliament and of the Council on a Common European Sales Law, COM (2011) 635 final see also Sanchez-Lorenzo (2013), pp. 191–217. Grundmann (2013), pp. 225–242.

The supplementary actions, such as the harmonization of particular consumer rights cannot substitute the second solution, whereas such a harmonization usually has a minimal character, leading sometimes to even more discrepancies in internal legal systems of the EU Member States and causing a lack of legal certainty. This was the reason for adopting the Code of the EU online rights as a kind of guidelines summarizing the existing rights of the digital consumer aiming at the increase of the confidence of the "digital consumer".[220] Such negative consequences of the partial harmonization also resulted in the idea of unifying the insurance contract law becoming increasingly vivid. Works on *Restatement of Principles of European Insurance Contract Law* are ongoing, performed by academic circles and will probably soon be presented as an official EU document for an optional application, being in line with a general tendency in unifying the European private law by means of soft instruments.[221]

In considering the advance stage of works on legislation concerning some of the contracts, such as sale or insurance contracts, respecting their online, cross-border nature, it seems that the way forward in respect of integrating the contract law in Europe has been decided, although some doubts are still being raised from time to time. The basic reason for that is the number of national legislations that will have to be removed if, for example a European Civil Code is to be adopted.[222] On the other hand, it is also observed that the consumers (but also other types of contractors) suffer from a kind of overload of information necessary to acknowledge before entering into a cross-border contract,[223] resulting from the complex structure of the protective rules deriving from various statutory sources, the best example of which may be the legislation of the EU within the scope of consumer protection.

As described above, the European process of legal integration is the effect of many years of attempts to create fully operational internal market. The evolution of the methods applied, starting from a minimal harmonization of particular contractual aspects, including the choice of law rules, through full harmonization, and finally reaching the consent to unify at least some of the contract laws, shows clearly that PIL rules cannot ensure undisturbed cross-border trade, if not accompanied by substantive uniform rules of contract. Applying them to online contracts makes it almost impossible. Insurance is one of the best examples. It must also be said that the optional instruments on contract law, although being a positive step forward, remain still in PIL concepts, so they must be perceived as a half way to the full contract law integration.

---

[220] Code is a part of the initiative of the Digital Agenda for Europe, Gema (2013), p. 9.

[221] Fuchs (2008), pp. 50–51; see also for the reasons of harmonizing substantive law: Clarke (1997), p. 43; Clarke and Heiss (2006); Heiss (2007).

[222] Wallis (2006).

[223] Low (2013), pp. 379–380. It is underlined by the author that the reduction of the necessity of choice may bring, as some studies have shown, positive results in terms of attracting consumers to a certain product of services.

4.4.2 Outside Europe: Note

The other evolution in this respect which we can observe in various part of the world is visible, in particular, in emerging market countries. This seems to be a natural process, and consists of adopting new laws being in line with the worldwide trends and even copied from the international conventions or other documents that regulate choice of law principles, but also basic contract law rules, including concluding online contracts. The most spectacular examples of such approach were mentioned in point I.2. herein, and concern the recent laws adopted in China, India, Saudi Arabia, etc, following the patterns, such as Uncitral, Unidroit, including European directives.

5 Conclusions

Summarizing the considerations of this section, it aims to present the consequences of basing the international e-commerce solely on PIL rules, avoiding the interference in substantive contract laws. In the author's opinion it has been clear for some time, that PIL has a limited power to support the cross-border online transactions. The conclusion is that, although PIL introduces (to some extent) the legal certainty in cross-border transactions, it does not eliminate the disadvantages related to the necessity of applying unknown rules of law by one party to the contract. In result, the integration of the substantive contract law is more important in online cross-border contracts than in "traditional" ones, as an online contract very easily, sometimes even invisibly for the parties, crosses the borders of legal systems. This statement is of a general nature, regardless the fact whether the party obliged to apply foreign system is a consumer or a powerful holding.

6 Final Remarks: The Modern Role of PIL in Online Insurance Contracts

A few distinctive conclusions may be drawn from the above-mentioned analysis of the online insurance contracts with respect to the private international law.

1. Insurance contract is one of the traditional civil law contracts, and its nature and main principles have not been changed by being concluded online. To the contrary, the traditional cross-border nature of insurance became just more dominant in the view of the possibilities given by the internet technology. In result, the online insurance contract is subject to the same problems that are faced by other types of civil law contracts, without significant differences (such as different connecting factors applied in PIL for insurance). That conclusion concerns also the discussion appearing now in the doctrine as to the need of

reforming the substantive contract law to adjust it to the needs and character of the omnipresent electronic communication. It concerns mostly the stage of concluding the contract (main feature of online insurance) and the doubts as to the possibility of applying traditional concepts of offer and acceptance.

2. On the other hand, the opposing part of the doctrine standing against the simple adjustment of the traditional contract law to the electronic contracts, perceives a rise of a fundamental change challenging the contract law, leading to the necessity of creating new principles, but also by appearing completely new types of contracts that cannot stay within the frames of existing contract rules.[224] Indeed, most of the active growth of modern e-commerce lies in the areas dominated by the new types of contracts, and they require also new approach and possibly, new regulations.[225] Such doubts cannot be just overruled.
3. The online insurance, although one of the financial services, deserves separate legal consideration and regulation, especially with respect to the choice of law rules. The reason for such an approach results from the fact that the main content of the "insurance product" consists not only of the risk coverage (similar in its financial dimension to other types of financial services) but also on the specific of the parties' obligations, the performance of which may significantly affect the outcome of the risk transfer depending on the law applicable to the contract.
4. The need of reforming the existing rules of contract law, as well as the private international law, results from the constant advances in technology.[226] No doubt, that modern contract law should ensure the interoperability of the technology and contract rules. These conclusions apply fully to insurance, with the reservation however, that on the EU level, the provisions of the insurance contract are subject to constant legislation works, both as hard law, as well as soft law, is concerned. These legislations attempts, although still in their drafting stage *(PEICL)*, consider the needs of the electronic commerce, abolishing the main impediments of concluding the insurance online. The hard law rules, included in ECD, DSD, DFD, etc, although highly fragmented, ensure at least the validity of the online insurance. No doubts however that e-commerce, also in insurance, should be embraced from the legal point of view as an integral part of the business and therefore regulated in such a way that guarantee to the policyholders same legal protection as achievable in the non-digitalized relations.
5. Having in mind the failed path of ensuring the growth in the European cross border insurance services by implementing a uniform choice of law rules, it seems that the practical role of PIL is limited. As was shown in the statistics, it has no power to strengthen the cross-border online contracts. Such a statement concerns mostly B2C transactions, as well as insurance of mass risks. In B2B

[224] Nimmer† (2007), pp. 21–22.

[225] Nimmer† (2007), pp. 21–22.

[226] Kaufmann Winn, et Haubold (2002), p. 23.

relations, it cannot be denied that application of PIL choice of law rule, sustains (strengthens) the parties' disparity, putting one of them in more advantageous position in relation to the other. Therefore, it may be said that both, harmonized insurance contract law provisions together with private international rules can act together and be complimentary to each other in protecting the parties to the insurance contract. On the European level, such situation of coexistence of PIL together with harmonized substantive law rules seems to be unavoidable, as the idea of the second regime increasingly becomes popular. It is highly probable that PEICL will soon become the second regime of insurance contract law to be chosen based on PIL rules. Although it is only a half way, no doubt that it is a milestone in a good direction.

6. The European approach however is not sufficient for ensuring stability of online transactions, as internet network does not stop at European borders. The online contracts being by nature transnational brought the increasing necessity of approaching worldwide legal systems in those aspects that can be related to the conclusion and performance of online contracts. This remark concerns to the same extent online insurance, which is a service easily digitized and distributed by electronic means from the technical point of view, but the cross-border potential of which has not been so far sufficiently used because of the lack of access to the necessary information comparable to the level ensured by the insurance brokers. As explained, the essence of an "insurance product" consists of specific wording of insurance terms and conditions. It causes the potential success of the cross-border online insurance to depend substantially on the level of the legal and informational certainty. This in consequence requires an existence of integrated substantive laws on insurance, as well as uniform PIL principles. Neither of the above, functioning separately will allow to achieve the above goal.
7. No doubt that PIL, even considering its deficiencies in creating effective, secured basis for equal online transactions, plays a great role in the global e-commerce. It is inherently related to the globalization and cross-border transactions, thus the postulate that any legislator contributes to the global convergence becomes vital, although it may still seem as a wishful thinking. Because of the easy access to the internet on a global level, cross-border commerce became increasingly available for consumers. This causes the role of PIL in its protective dimension substantially to increase together with the need of working out its uniform principles worldwide.[227]
8. As shown by the examples given herein above, the process of approaching laws of different countries already began some time ago and clearly finds its reflection also in the PIL rules by adopting model contract patterns, worked out by international organizations, as soft law. Although, the general rules worked out by Uncitral, CISG and Unidroit cannot fully apply to insurance, being not enough specific for the sophisticated nature of insurance contracts, a separate

[227] See Basedow (1997) and Muir-Watt (2002).

documents for insurance might follow the success of uniform rules for sales contracts or others. A scenario of creating a uniform global law (possibly as soft optional instrument) on electronic contracts with PIL rules serving as a security for any differences between legal systems then becomes more likely. It might be then the first step towards supranational law for electronic contract, encompassing also insurance at a later stage.

References

Aljifri HA, Pons A, Collins D (2003) Global e-commerce: a framework for understanding and overcoming the trust barrier. Inf Manag Comput Secur 11(2/3):13–138

Armbrüster C (2013) Recent developments in European e-commerce law, with case studies

Banan MR (2009) How is e-insurance in developing countries ? Georgian Electron Sci J Comput Sci. Telecommun 5(22):116–137

Baur E, Birkamaier U, Rutsmann M (2001) The economic importance of insurance in Central and Eastern Europe and the impact of globalization and e-business, Economic Commission for Europe, Committee for trade, industry and enterprise development, 13-15.06.2001, http://www.unece.org/fileadmin/DAM/trade/ctied/ctied5/trade0115e.pdf. Accessed 5 Feb 2016

Basedow J (1997) Souveraineté territoriale et globalisation des marchés. Recueuil des cours de l'Académie 264:9–177

Boss AH (2011) Becoming operational: electronic registries and transfer of rights. In: Modern Law for Global Commerce (eds) UN Proceedings of the Congress of the United Nations Commission on International Trade Law held on the Occasion of the Fortieth Session of the Commission Vienna, 9–12 July 2007, p 303

Christiansen H (2001) Electronic finance: economics and institutional factors, Financial Affairs Division Occasional Paper, No. 2

Chuah J (2004) Private international law – choice of law- Islamic law, Shamil Bank of Bahrain EC v Beximco and others [2004] EWCA Civ 19, English Court of Appeal. J Int Marit Law 10 (2):125–127. Available also at http://www.wmin.ac.uk/westminsterresearch. Accessed 5 Feb 2016

Chuah JCT (2010) Impact of Islamic law on commercial sale contracts – a private international law dimensions in Europe. Eur J Commercial Contract Law 4:191–204

Clarke MA (1997) The law of insurance contracts. LLP, p 43

Clarke M, Heiss H (2006) Towards a European insurance contract law? Recent developments in Brussels J Bus Law 600

Corcoran AM, Hart TL (2001) The Regulation of Cross-Border Financial Services in the EU Internal Market: A Primer for Third Countries, p 19–33, http://papers.ssrn.com/abstract=274849. Accessed 5 Feb 2016

Cordero Moss G (2010) Recent private international law codifications. National Report for Norway. In: International Academy of Comparative Law, 18th International Congress of Comparative Law, Washington, July 25 to August 1, 2010, Topic II.B. Private International Law

Cox R, Merrett L, Smith M, (ed.), Clarke MA (2006) Private international law on reinsurance and insurance. Informa Law, p 254

Cox QC R (2013) Choice of law: New York and English approaches to insurance and reinsurance contracts. In: Research handbook on international insurance law and regulation. Available at: http://www.raymondcoxqc.com/wp-content/uploads/2013/01/Choice-of-Law-New-York-and-English-Approaches-to-Insurance-and-Reinsurance-Contracts.pdf. Accessed 5 Feb 2016

Dreher M (1991) Die Versicherungen als Rechtprodukt. die Privatversicherung und ihre rechtliche Gestaltung. Mohr Siebeck

Falch M (1998) Electronic distribution and cross-border trade in insurance services. Electron Mark 8(4): 10, 1998
Fawcett J, Harris J, Bridge M (2005) International sale of goods in the conflict of laws, Oxford Private International Law Series. Oxford University Press, Oxford, p 1235
Federation Romande des Consommateurs (2013) Commerce en ligne: loi Suisse versus reglamentation europeenne 4.01.2013, www.frc.ch/articles/loi-suisse-versus-reglamentation-europeenne. Accessed 5 Feb 2016
Ford D (2013), Private International Law, electronic Resource Guide https://www.asil.org/sites/default/files/ERG_PRIVATE_INT.pdf. Accessed 5 Feb 2016
Foster J. S., Esq. (1997-2000) Electronic Contracts and Digital Signatures. Available at: http://www.corbinball.com/articles_legal/index.cfm?fuseaction=cor_ArticleView&artid=506&sectionCode=art_legal. Accessed 5 Feb 2016
Fras M (2008) Reżim prawny umowy ubezpieczenia zawieranej drogą elektroniczną - zagadnienia materialnoprawne i kolizyjne. In: Pazda M, Popiołek W, Rott-Pietrzyk E (eds) Europeizacja prawa prywatnego. Wolters Kluwer, T. 1., pp 180–202
Fuchs B (2009) Normy kolizyjne dla umów ubezpieczenia w prawie wspólnotowym i w prawie polskim – zagadnienia wybrane, Rejent 1/2009
Fuchs D (2008) Właściwość sądu i właściwość prawa w europejskich ubezpieczeniach gospodarczych Prawo Asekuracyjne 2:50–51
Gabor FA (1988) Stepchild of the New Lex Mercatoria: private international law from the United States perspective. Northwestern J Int Law Bus 8(3):541–542
Gabriel HD (2007) Choice of law, contract terms and uniform law in practice. In: Modern Law for Global Commerce Proceedings of the Congress of the United Nations Commission on International Trade Law held on the Occasion of the Fortieth Session of the Commission, Vienna, 9–12 July 2007, p 224 et subsquent https://www.uncitral.org/pdf/english/congress/09-83930_Ebook.pdf. Accessed 5 Feb 2016
Geist M, A guide to global e-commerce law, p 15. https://www.itu.int/ITU-T/special.../Attach04.doc. Accessed 5 Feb 2016
Gema T (2013), Harmonization of European contract law. Slowly but surely. LESIJ 1(No. XX):9
Goldsmith J (1998) Against cyberanarchy. Univ Chi Law Rev 65(4):1240
Gołaczyński J (2007) Umowy elektroniczne w prawie prywatnym międzynarodowym. Kluwer
Garcimatin Alferez FJ (2008) The Rome I regulation: much a do about nothing ? The European Legal Forum (E) 2:64
Gkoutzinis A (2006) Internet banking and the law in Europe. Regulation, financial integration and electronic commerce. Cambridge University Press, Cambridge, pp 289–309
Graham JH, Smith (2007) (ed) Internet law and regulation, 4th edn. point 10-047
Giuliano M, Lagarde P (1980) O J (1980), Report on the Convention on the Law Applicable to Contractual Obligations, C 282/1
Grundmann S (2013) Costs and benefits of an optional European sales law (CESL). Common Mark Law Rev 50:225–242, Kluwer
Grundmann S (2004) Internal market conflicts of laws from traditional conflict of laws to an integrated two level order, Les Conflits De Lois Et Le Système Juridique Communautaire. In Fuchs A, Muir Watt H, Pataut E, Dalloz (eds) pp 5–6 et subsq
Haddadi Selma M (2001) Paiement en ligne: securite juridique et securite technique. Universite de Nice Sophia Antipolis, Nice
Heiss H (2007) Insurance and Europe. In: Hendrikse, Rinkes (eds) Principles of European insurance contract law. Uitgeverij Paris, Zutphen, pp 85–102, also published on SSRN at http://papers.ssrn.com/sol3/papers.cfm?abstract_id=1122244, pp 41–59
van der Hof S (2003) European conflict rules concerning international online consumer contracts. Inf Commun Tech Law 12(2):166
Hughes SJ, Middlebrook ST (2013) Virtual uncertainty: developments in the law of electronic payments and financial services, Research Paper Number 283 The Business Lawyer, vol. 69, p 264

Hui W (2009) A review of China's Private International Law during the 30-year period of reform and opening –up, Asian Law institute, Working Paper Series No. 002, pp 3–4
Jacquemin H (2010) Conclusion et prevue du contrat d'assurance dans l'environment numerique, Forum de l'assurance, n 100, Janvier 2010, pp 249–255
Johnson DR, Post D (1996) Law and border – the rise of law in cyberspace. Stanford Law Rev 48 (5):1370–1374
Kaufmann Winn J, Haubold J (2002) Electronic promise: contract law reform and e-commerce in a comparative perspective, http://www.law.washington.edu/Directory/docs/Winn/Electronic_Promises_Revised.pdf; L. Rev. 567. Accessed 5 Feb 2016
Kaviar H, Ahmadi A (2010) Judicial jurisdiction solution for electronic consumer contracts in European Union. World Acad Sci Eng Technol 42:706
Kesan J (1991) Personal jurisdiction in cyberspace. http://www.cyberspacelaw.org/kesan/kesan1.html. Accessed 1 Jul 2015
Kornet N (2010) Contracting in China: comparative observations on freedom of contract, contract formation, battle of forms and standard form contracts. Electron J Comp Law 14.1:16–17, http://www.ejcl.org. Accessed 5 Feb 2016
Kowalewski E (2005) Ubezpieczenia transgraniczne – aspekty prawne, Forum Dyskusyjne, Zeszyt 5, KNUIFE, p 11
Krishnan S (2013) The difficulties of cross-border insurance, insurance insight of 29.01.2013, http://www.insuranceinsight.com/insurance-insight/opinion/2239300/opinion-the-. . .19.09.2013
Le comite du commerce electronique du conseil Canadien des responsables de la reglamentation d'assurance (2012) Le commerce electronique des produits d'assurance, Janvier 2012, www.ccir-ccrra.org
Le commerce electronique, La documentation francaise. www.ladocumentationfrancaise.fr/dossiers/internet-monde/. Accessed 5 Feb 2016
Low G (2013) A psychology of choice of laws. Eur Bus Law Rev 24:380
van Loon H (2007) Process and value of uniform commercial law, Round Table in: Modern Law for Global Commerce Proceedings of the Congress of the United Nations Commission on International Trade Law held on the Occasion of the Fortieth Session of the Commission, Vienna, 9–12 July 2007, p 224 et subsquent https://www.uncitral.org/pdf/english/congress/09-83930_Ebook.pdf. Accessed 5 Feb 2016
Makris S (2004) Implementation of the directive on electronic commerce into Greek law and consumers protection in the area of electronic commerce, comparison with German law. Eur Leg Forum (E) 3:161–168, IPR Verlag GmbH München
Malinowska K (2008) Umowa ubezpieczenia w Europie bez granic. Branta
Maniruzzaman AFM (1999) Choice of law in international contracts – some fundamental conflicts of law issues. J Int Arbitr 16(4):145
Mcnair (1957) The general principles of law recognized by civilized nations. BYBIL 1: 7
Michaels R (2008) The new European choice of law revolution. Tulane Law Rev 82(5):1611
Muñoz-López JE (2009) Internet conflict of laws: a space of opportunities for ODR. International Law, Revista Colombiana de Derecho Internacional 14:163–190
Merrett L (2009) Choice of law in insurance contracts under the Rome I Regulation. J Priv Int Law 5:60–63
Nimmer RT (2007) The legal landscape of e-commerce: redefining contract law in an information era. J Contract Law 23:21–22
Muir Watt H (2002) Choice of law in integrated and interconnected markets: a matter of political economy. Electron J Comp Law 7.3, (September 2003), http://www.ejcl.org/ejcl/73/art73-4.html. Accessed 5 Feb 2016
Muir Watt H (2002) Party autonomy in international contracts: from the makings of a myth to the requirements of global governance. Available at: http://www.columbia.edu/cu/alliance/Papers/Article_Horatia-Muir-Watt.pdf. Accessed 5 Feb 2016
OECD (1998) Dismantling the barriers to global electronic commerce, Turku, (Finland): 19-21 November 1997 – Conference Report", OECD Digital Economy Papers, No 38, OECD Publishing. Http://dx.doi.org/10.1787/236647320075

OECD, Direction Des Affaires Financieres, Fiscales Et Des Entreprises Directorate For Financial, Fiscal, And Enterprise Affairs, p 44. *paris-europlace.net/files/news059121.pdf*, Accessed 5 Feb 2016

OECD (2006) ICT Use by Businesses: Revised OECD Model Survey, January 2006, DSTI/ICCP/IIS(2005)2 FINAL. Available at: http://www.oecd.org/sti/sci-tech/35867672.pdf. Accessed 5 Feb 2016

O'Hara EA, Ribstein L (2009) Conflict of laws and choice of law, Law& Economic Research Paper Series, Paper No LE09-30.Illinois Law & Economics Research Paper No. LE09-030; Vanderbilt Law and Economics Research Paper No. 09-34, forthcoming Elgar's Encyclopedia of Law and Economics. Available at: http://ssrn.com/abstract=1499311

Opertii Badan D (2007) Modern Law for Global Commerce, Process and value of uniform commercial law. Keynote address in: Modern Law for Global Commerce Proceedings of the Congress of the United Nations Commission on International Trade Law held on the Occasion of the Fortieth Session of the Commission, Vienna, 9–12 July 2007, p 220 et subsquent, https://www.uncitral.org/pdf/english/congress/09-83930_Ebook.pdf. Accessed 5 Feb 2016

Pauli K (2007) Electronic signature and secure forms in the insurance industry: taking the P&C Pen to the Web, p 7. Available at: http://towergroup.com. Accessed 5 Feb 2016

Polanski P (2006) Towards a supranational internet law. J Int Commercial Law and Technol 1(1):1

Popiołek W (2007) Prawo właściwe dla umownych zobowiązań elektronicznych w konwencji rzymskiej i projekcie rozporządzenia Rzym I, Kolizyjne aspekty zobowiązań elektronicznych, Materiały z konferencji, p 11

Poullet Y (2007) Electronic contracts and contract law principles. In: Liber Amicorum Guido Alpa: private law beyond the national systems. British institute of international and comparative law, London, pp 759–772, 14p

Riefa C (2009) The reform of electronic consumer contracts in Europe: towards an effective legal framework. Lex Electronica 14(2)

Rosenblatt B (2001) Principles of jurisdiction, http://cyber.law.harvard.edu/property/domain/Betsy.html. Accessed 5 Feb 2016

Sambugaro G (2008) What "law" to choose for international contracts ? Eur Leg Forum (3): I-127

Sanchez-Lorenzo SA (2013) Common European sales law and private international law: some critical remarks. J Priv Int Law 9(2):191–217

Savirimuthu J (2005) Online contract formation: taking technological infrastructure seriously. UOLTJ 2:109–114

Schnyder A (1994) Partie autonomie. In Reichert F (eds) Failides. Tubingen, p 54

Schneider C (2001) Zur Umsetzung der E-commerce-Richtlinie im Regierungsentwurf zur Schuldrechtsmodernisierung, Kommunikation & Recht 2001. 27 Eur., pp 344–345

Shuhong Y, Yonping X, Wang B (2009) The closest connection doctrine in the conflict of laws in China. Chin J Int Law 8(2):423–439

Skipper HD (2006) Foreign insurers in emerging markets, Issues and Concerns, IIF Occasional Paper, No 1 International Insurance Foundation 1997, p 2

Sirinelli P (1998) Le village virtuel et la creation normative. In: Boele-Woelki K, Kessedijan C (eds) Which court decides ? Which law applies?, vol. 14. Kluwer International, The Hague/Boston

Spamann H (2001) Choice of Law in a Federal System and an Internal Market, Jean Monnet Working Paper 8/01, The Jean Monnet Center for International and Regional Economic Law & Justice. Available at: http://www.jeanmonnetprogram.org/archive/papers/01/012601.html. Accessed 5 Feb 2016

Tang Z (2010) Private international law in consumer contracts - a European perspective. J Priv Int Law, electronic copy available at: http://ssrn.com/abstract=2090954

Tang J, Wenxueb J, Yang S (2012) The deficiency of e-commerce contract and some propose to perfect. In: 2012 International Conference on Future Energy, Environment, and Materials, pp 633–634. Available online at www.sciencedirect.com

Gokhan A (2012) Party autonomy, choice of law and wrap contracts. Masteroppgave, University of Oslo, pp 5–6 https://www.duo.uio.no/handle/10852/34430?show=full. Accessed 5 Feb 2016

Verbiest T, Le Borne M (2002) L'offre de produits d'assurance sur Internet: le point juridique, www. droit-technologie.org/actuality-526
Wallis D (2006) European Contract Law – The Way Forward: Political Context, Parliament's Preoccupation and Process, & ERA Forum 8
WTO brochure, E-commerce in developing countries, opportunities and challenges for small and medium-sized enterprises, www.wto.org, p 1. Accessed 5 Feb 2016
WTO, Comite du commerce et du developpement, Commerce electronique, developpement et petites et moyennes entreprises, WT/COMTD/193
Yuqing Z, Huang D (2000) The new contract law in the people's Republic of China and the UNIDROIT principles of international commercial contracts: a brief comparison, Rev. Dr. Unif. 2000-3
Zhang M (2007) Contractual Choice of Law in Contracts of Adhesion and Party Autonomy, Legal Studies Research Paper Series, Research Paper No. 2007-25, 41 Akron L. Rev, p 6. Available at: http://ssrn.com/abstract=1017841. Accessed 5 Feb 2016

Cases

Lord Diplock (1983) 3 WRL 241, 245
Scarlet vs SABAM: C-70/10 (24 November 2011)
Joined cases C-585/08 and C-144/09, Peter Pammer v Reederei Karl Schlüter GmbH & Co. KG and Hotel Alpenhof GesmbH v Oliver Heller, judgment of 07.12.2010. Available at: http://eurlex.europa.eu/LexUriServ/LexUriServ.do?uri=CELEX:62008J0585:EN:NOT

European Private Law (Regulation Rome I) and On-Line Insurance Contracts

Anna Tarasiuk

Contents

Anna Tarasiuk: Phd candidate, Counsel at Hogan Lovells (Warszawa) LLP Oddział w Polsce (anna.tarasiuk@hoganlovells.com), member of the Executive Secretariat of the Polish Chapter of AIDA.

A. Tarasiuk (✉)
Counsel Hogan Lovells, Warsaw, Poland
e-mail: tarasiuk@oirpwarszawa.pl; anna.tarasiuk@hoganlovells.com

P. Marano et al. (eds.), *The "Dematerialized" Insurance*,
DOI 10.1007/978-3-319-28410-1_14

Abstract This chapter focuses on the EU private law regulations in relation to on-line insurance contracts. As an introduction, it includes a description of the legislative background of Rome I to illustrate the history and the complexity of legislation of insurance matters in private international law. It also tackles the issue of protection of the weaker party to the contractual relationship as a useful background related to both—a contract concluded at a distance and an insurance contract itself. Special attention is paid to practical issues regarding on-line insurance contracts. This chapter also discusses the applicability of the provisions of Rome I to this type of contracts. Furthermore, particular factors determining the applicable law for on-line insurance contracts are analysed. These are classified according to two main criteria: the type of the contract and the location of a risk. This was made to capture the essence of the conflict rules governing on-line insurance contracts in the EU private law.

1 Introduction

The number of cross-border insurance transactions has recently grown in Europe. Although "e-commerce is still limited to less than 4 % of total European trade"[1], the entire European insurance industry tends to expand—according to the statistics of 2012, it is the largest in the world (33 %), followed by North America (30 %), and Asia (29 %).[2] The value of life gross written premiums in Europe has significantly changed—from EUR 75,244 million in 2005 in Germany to 90,355 million in 2010.[3] Poland has also noted a huge rise in life written premiums from the level of EUR 3,779 million in 2005, up to EUR 7,729 million in 2011.[4] The United Kingdom remains the largest European insurance market where the life gross written premium reached EUR 149,576 million in 2011.[5]

As early as 1970s the European common market countries recognised that insurance services can easily cross the borders of the Member States if only basic freedoms are applied.[6] As a result of the legislative changes over the years, as well

[1] Commission Staff Working Document Online services, including e-commerce, in the Single Market, Brussels, 11.1.2012, SEC(2011) 1641 final, p. 4.

[2] http://www.insuranceeurope.eu/uploads/Modules/Publications/final-key-facts-2013.pdf, p.7 (date of entry: 01.07.2014).

[3] http://www.en.gdv.de/wp-content/uploads/2013/12/Statistical-Yearbook-German-Insurance-2013.pdf, p. 16 (date of entry: 24.07.2015).

[4] Statistics N 49: "The European Life Insurance Market in 2012", March 2014; Table I.1.1.—Total direct life premium income; http://www.insuranceeurope.eu/statistics-n°49-european-life-insurance-market-2012-dataset (date of entry: 08.03.2016).

[5] *Ibidem.*

[6] Malinowska and Świątkowski (2013), p. 36.

as market demands, the aggregate growth in life insurance premium income obtained by distance selling became significant. As an illustration, in 2011, the market share of the life insurance premiums obtained by distance selling in individual contracts reached 10.4 % in the UK, while this figure was at the level of 3.2 % in France, and 1.3 % in Belgium.[7] The numbers definitely show that the cross-border insurance contracts concluded at a distance become increasingly popular. It is even said that insurance should be qualified, by its nature, as a transnational service.[8]

The Internet plays a significant role in insurance services, and in many other contracts as well. E-commerce is inherently cross-border trade,[9] and the Internet can bring together nationals of various countries interested in entering into insurance relationships. Thanks to its accessibility, the Internet seems to be a perfect source for customers seeking insurance coverage on their own.[10] It does not only facilitate the selection of offers directly from insurance companies websites, but can also be a useful tool enabling the clients to compare various insurance offers (e.g. on dedicated portals focused on comparing insurance offers subject to given criteria). The Internet may also be a convenient and financially efficient form of cross-border distribution of insurance in other countries, without the necessity to establish a complex insurance distribution network. It seems clear that in the case of some lines of insurance, concluding insurance contracts on-line is "*increasingly becoming the norm*".[11] However, in the case of more complicated insurance products (including life insurance), there are still certain issues that need to be solved by the market, should the insurers wish to develop this kind of distribution channel (including the willingness of a potential client to talk to a "*human being*"[12]). There is no doubt that other challenge for insurers relate to coping with various legal regulations, in particular imposing the necessity to follow additional legal obligations in the case of selling insurance on-line. By and large, such obligations require that a specific approach be taken by insurance companies and special attention be paid both in respect of legal and operational aspects. Regardless of possible difficulties, the on-line distribution channel becomes increasingly popular. The same applies to other forms of distance selling, including, for instance, telesales (call centres). Undoubtedly, E-commerce is a very promising distribution channel enabling the insurance companies to benefit from new

[7] Statistics N°47: "The European Life Insurance Market in 2011", 05 Feb 2013—Statistical publication—http://www.insuranceeurope.eu/facts-figures/statistical-publications/life (date of entry 24.07.2015).

[8] Malinowska and Świątkowski (2013), p. 34.

[9] Fras (2008), p. 182.

[10] A. Arora: E-Insurance: Analysis of the Impact and Implications of Ecommerce on the Insurance Industry (http://citeseerx.ist.psu.edu/viewdoc/download?doi=10.1.1.132.173&rep=rep1&type=pdf (date of entry: 01.07.2014).

[11] N. Golia: Is E-Commerce Right for Insurance? (available at http://www.insurancetech.com/business-intelligence/is-e-commerce-right-for-insurance/240155645 (date of entry:01.07.2014).

[12] *Ibidem.*

technologies.[13] However, "*the effective creation of a transnational online services market is feasible mainly due to the increase in consumer confidence in this form of offering services and goods*"[14] which aim serves the proper regulation that would ensure this safety and confidence on the side of the consumer.

Although the EU undoubtedly aims at a free movement of goods and services, it is quite difficult to keep the local legislations at a similar level of trade safety and obligations of market participants. The complexity of the regulations increases, for example, in terms of the consumer's matters or law applicability to insurance contracts. Therefore, the issue of legislation of European on-line insurance contracts may seem quite complicated.[15] In fact, although it is rather structurally composite, the legal regulations governing cross-border contractual insurance matters create a logical structure, based on the several pillars reflecting the most important regulatory matters.

One of the pillars, having a great impact on the whole contractual regulation of insurance business, is the issue of applicable law. Previous experience shows that the constantly growing cross-border contract transaction market made this area of law extremely important. When a contractual relationship involves parties, property, or events located in more than one jurisdiction, and the substantive laws of those jurisdictions differ, the question as to which substantive laws govern the rights and the obligations of such parties, becomes essential. The trade barriers between jurisdictions have been removed and the choice of law tends to have a great impact on transactions and litigations planning.[16] As a result, actions have been taken to regulate this area e.g. under the Rome Convention on the Law Applicable to Contractual Obligations of 1980[17] (the "**Rome Convention**") which had an important impact on insurance contractual relationships and on other contracts.

Currently, the conflict of law rules in terms of contractual relationships in the EU are covered by Rome I[18] ("**Rome I**") which, after 17 December 2009 has been applied to international insurance contracts in Europe.[19] Its complexity derives from the fact that it is a reflection of different legal traditions represented in the EU.[20]

---

[13] Meshkat et al. (2012) pp. 640–647.

[14] Malinowska (2014), pp. 42–43.

[15] Fras (2008), p. 183.

[16] O'Hara and Ribstein (2009), p. 2.

[17] Regulation (EC) No 593/2008 of the European Parliament and of the Council of 17 June 2008 on the law applicable to contractual obligations (Rome I) Official Journal L 177, 04/07/2008 P. 0006–0016.

[18] Regulation (EC) No 593/2008 of the European Parliament and of the Council of 17 June 2008 on the law applicable to contractual obligations ("Rome I") (OJ L 17, 04.07.2008, pp. 6–16).

[19] Pilich (2012), p. 198.

[20] Cox and Smith (2006), p. 5.

Rome I is the EU law of general application. As it is a regulation, according to Article 288 of the Treaty on the Functioning of the European Union[21] (ex-Article 249 Treaty establishing the European Community) is "*fully binding and directly applicable in all Member States*".[22] As a result, Rome I took effect "*automatically and simultaneously in all Member States as there [was] no need for it to be transposed or implemented by national legislation*".[23]

Rome I determines the law that applies to both cases within the EU and outside the EU. It may apply to the contractual relationships concluded and/or executed in a non-EU Member State also between the non-EU entities that came to a Member State to participate in litigation.[24] It should be remembered, however, that the scope of the application of Rome I covers only such insurance contracts that relate to a "conflict" between at least two different legal systems. In other words, there must be a real connection with the law of more than one EU Member State according to the objective or subjective criteria.[25]

Consumer issues arising in the case of contracts concluded by way of electronic means had no impact on the final content of the Rome I in terms of the insurance contracts.[26] "*The point has either been overlooked altogether or it has been decided that, rather than add an extra layer of complexity (...), the problem of the applicable law to online contracts should be left to the courts to apply the general choice of law rules in contract.*"[27] Therefore, because of the lack of specific regulations governing on-line insurance contracts, the general provisions of Rome I applicable to international insurance contracts also apply to on-line insurance contracts.

Additionally, according to Rome I, insurance contracts and consumer contracts are expressly separated by two different articles of that legal act.[28] Those two articles cannot be applied at the same time to one insurance contract as Rome I draws a direct line of separation between those two types of contracts. Obviously, the reason regarding the need for some extra level of protection towards consumers

---

[21] Consolidated versions of the Treaty on European Union and the Treaty on the Functioning of the European Union—Consolidated version of the Treaty on the Functioning of the European Union—Protocols—Annexes—Declarations annexed to the Final Act of the Intergovernmental Conference which adopted the Treaty of Lisbon, signed on 13 December 2007—Tables of equivalences, (OJ C 326, 26.10.2012, pp. 1–390).

[22] Garcimartin Alferez (2008), p. I-61.

[23] *Ibidem*, p. I-61.

[24] Garcimartin Alferez (2008), p. I-61–I-62. The author also refers to other literature on the problem of the legal basis for giving the instrument a universal character: Bonomi (2003), p. 53 *et seq.*, p. 59; Garcimartín (2007), p. 78; Heiss (2006), p. 750 *et seq.*, p. 751; Lagarde (2006), p. 331 *et seq.*, p. 332; Lein (2005), p. 391 *et seq.*, p. 393 with further references; Groupe européen de droit international privé (GEDIP) (2003), p. 9; Max-Planck Institute for Comparative and International Private Law (2004), p. 1 *et seq.*, p. 11.

[25] Pilich, (2012) p. 199.

[26] Popiołek (2007), p. 23.

[27] Seatzu (2003), p. 252.

[28] Please see Articles 6 and 7 of Rome I.

in the insurance relationship envisaged under Rome I may be a general rule presented in the judgment of the European Court of Justice of 4 December 1986 (Case 205/84), according to which: "*the insurance sector is a particularly sensitive area from the point of view of the protection of the consumer both as a policy-holder and as an insured person*".[29] Still, the division between the protection in insurance and consumer contracts has led to a more complex and restrictive regime, rather than a simpler one.[30]

Considering the above, it should be noted that the European rules on private international law comprise a number of certain contracts—mainly those perceived to involve individuals—that tend to be marked out for special treatment. The special treatment that is applied in such cases is not a reflection of different legal approaches of the EU Member States, but one public policy. What is of crucial importance is defining the appropriate question or issue, as this will determine what kind of rules should be applied to certain contracts, for instance in the case of insurance and reinsurance.[31] The purpose of this chapter is to demonstrate the specific nature of insurance contracts, which is crucial from the point of view of separating the regulation of the insurance contract under Rome I.

2 Legislative Background of Rome I

2.1 Unification of Laws

The idea of Rome I was to unify a variety of legal sources regarding the conflict of laws in one document. The first source regarding the conflict of law rules of insurance contracts appeared in 1967 as a proposal for the negotiation of a unified conflicts code.[32] As a rule, it referred to the law of place of residence of the policyholder, excluding the admissibility of the choice of law. That principle was altered by regulations regarding compulsory insurance—in this case the obligation to apply the mandatory provisions of law of the EU Member State imposing the obligation of insurance applied. Unlimited choice of law was approved only to the contracts of insurance of goods in transit.[33] Projects starting from 1974 became a greater compromise.[34] The legislative process accelerated after the judgment of the

[29] Judgment of the European Court of Justice of 4 December 1986. Commission of the European Communities v Federal Republic of Germany, Case 205/84, European Court reports 1986, p. 03755.

[30] James (2007), p. 257.

[31] Cox and Smith (2006), pp. 4–5.

[32] R. Wulf-Henning: EEC Treaty Article Fifty-nine and its implications for conflicts law in the field of insurance contracts, p. 130, Duke Journal of Comparative & International Law, Vol. 2:129, (available at http://scholarship.law.duke.edu/cgi/viewcontent.cgi?article=1309&context=djcil) (date of entry: 24.07.2015).

[33] Kropka (2010), p. 22.

[34] *Ibidem.*

European Court of Justice in the already cited case 205/84.[35] In its reasoning, the European Court of Justice allowed for a wide scope of compromise on the Community regulation regarding insurance and indicated that "*in certain fields insurance has become a mass phenomenon*". *Contracts are concluded by such enormous numbers of policyholders that the protection of the interests of insured persons and injured third parties affects virtually the whole population.*[36]

Considering the above and constituting a compromise, the conflict of law rules were included in the second and third generation of the directives. The most important provisions regarding the law applicable to insurance contracts were included in Articles 7 and 8 of Second Council Directive 88/357/EEC[37] ("**Directive 88/357/EEC**") and Article 4 of the Council Directive 90/619/EEC,[38] replaced later by Article 32 of Directive 2002/83/EC.[39] The Rome Convention and the various directives on insurance were intended to be instruments that would introduce harmony in the EU legal systems.[40] However, despite many EU directives and regulations on insurance, the substantive laws on insurance matters still considerably differed within the EU. Because of the complex references, there were cases where it was difficult to apply the insurance directives or the Rome Convention. Needless to say, in those cases the rules regulating the conflict of law at the national level had to be applied. As there was some room left for various interpretations of the rules regulating the conflict of law, these rules have not been applied throughout the Member States in the same way.[41]

After 6 years and many rounds of consultations, as well as political debates,[42] the Rome Convention has been reviewed and "*finally converted into a Community*

[35] http://eur-lex.europa.eu/LexUriServ/LexUriServ.do?uri=CELEX:61984CJ0205:EN:PDF (date of entry: 01.07.2014).

[36] *Ibidem*, Paragraph 30 and 31.

[37] Second Council Directive of 22 June 1988 on the coordination of laws, regulations and administrative provisions relating to direct insurance other than life assurance and laying down provisions to facilitate the effective exercise of freedom to provide services and amending Directive 73/239/EEC (88/357/EEC) (OJ L 172, 4.7.1988, p. 1–2).

[38] Council Directive 90/619/EEC of 8 November 1990 on the coordination of laws, regulations and administrative provisions relating to direct life assurance, laying down provisions to facilitate the effective exercise of freedom to provide services and amending Directive 79/267/EEC (OJ L 330, 29.11.1990, p. 50–61).

[39] Directive 2002/83/EC of the European Parliament and of the Council of 5 November 2002 concerning life assurance (OJ L 345, 19.12.2002, p. 1–51).

[40] Cox and Smith (2006), p. 208.

[41] Kramer (2008), p. 23.

[42] See, e.g., Commission Green Paper on the Conversion of the Rome Convention of 1980 on the Law Applicable to Contractual Obligations into a Community Instrument and its Modernization, COM (2002) 654 final (Jan. 14, 2003). The European Commission maintains an extensive list of replies to this Green Paper. For comments on this Green Paper, see, for example, Max Planck Inst. for Foreign Priv. and Priv. Int'l Law, Comments on the European Commission's Green Paper on the Conversion of the Rome Convention of 1980 on the Law Applicable to Contractual Obligations into a Community Instrument and Its Modernization, 68 RABELS ZEITSCHRIFT 1 (2004);

instrument: the Rome I Regulation".[43] Although being quite a new legislation tool, it was mainly based on the Rome Convention, which it replaced. It is also said that it had maintained "*the pre-existing patchwork*".[44]

It should be noted that Rome I applies to all the EU Member States, except for Denmark. At first, it did not apply to the United Kingdom either, which originally opted-out, but then decided to join the applicability of Rome I.[45] Rome I comprises 29 Articles, only one of which[46] directly concerns the law applicable to insurance contracts.

2.2 *Protection of a Weaker Party to the Contractual Relationship*

The analysis of the EU legislation indicates that the idea of protecting the weaker party by the rules on the conflict of laws is widely reflected in the EU regulations. For instance, Recital 23 of the Preamble to Rome I states: "*as regards contracts concluded with parties regarded as being weaker, those parties should be protected by conflict-of-law rules that are more favourable to their interests than the general rules*". Specific rules being the exclusions to the general rules stipulated in Rome I (in the Article 3 and Article 4), can be found for example in Article 6 (for a consumer) and in Article 7 (for a policyholder).[47]

The policyholder often acts as the weaker party to the insurance contract in most of the EU Member States, including Poland. The insurer that is able to provide insurance cover under certain conditions, which it considers and proposes (including the insurance cover and the amount of premium), seems to be in a better factual (and, consequently, legal) position than the policyholder that usually (in consumer contractual relationships) can only consent to the proposed conditions or decide not

---

Von Ulrich Magnus & Peter Mankowski, The Green Paper on a Future Rome I Regulation-on the Road to a Renewed European Private International Law of Contracts, 103 ZEITSCHRIFT FÜR VERGLEICHENDE RECHTSWISSENSCHAFT 131 (2004). See also Commission Proposal for a Regulation on the Law Applicable to Contractual Obligations (Rome I), COM (2005) 650 final (Dec. 15, 2005) [hereinafter Proposal]. On this Proposal, see, for example, Max Planck Inst. for Foreign Priv. and Priv. Int'l Law, Comments on the European Commission's Proposal for a Regulation of the European Parliament and the Council on the Law Applicable to Contractual Obligations (Rome I), 71 RABELS ZEITSCHRIFT 225 (2007) [hereinafter Max Planck Inst. 2007]; see also Lein (2005).

[43] Vernooij (2009), p. 71.

[44] Kuipers (2011), p. 118.

[45] Commission Decision of 22 December 2008 on the request from the United Kingdom to accept Regulation (EC) No 593/2008 of the European Parliament and the Council on the law applicable to contractual obligations (Rome I) (OJ L 10.15.1.2009, p.22).

[46] Article 7 of Rome I.

[47] Fuchs and Jagielska, p. 33.

to. In some jurisdictions,[48] the policyholder does not have to be a consumer to be treated as a weaker party to the contract. The general idea is that the policyholder contracts with the more powerful entity. Rome I provides for a special treatment of the party to the insurance contract being the policyholder. The aim of such protection by the rules of conflict of laws is not only to provide a substantial level of protection within the applicable laws, but also to protect the weaker party against the costs and lack of information resulting from the application of foreign law.[49]

According to Article 7 of Rome I, under the condition stipulated therein, the parties to the insurance contract have, as a rule, the possibility of choosing the applicable law. Therefore the policyholder can choose the law which is more convenient or favourable for him/her. This guarantees that the policyholder stays more secured in a more familiar legal background. This may be especially important for those policyholders who change their place of residence or travel around different EU Member States.

3 Applicability of the Rome I Regulation to On-Line Insurance Contracts

3.1 Relation to Provisions Regulating the Insurance Contract

Insurance contracts were not supposed to be included in the Rome I from the start. It is said that "*insurance has made a late arrival on the scene*".[50] Formulating the choice-of-law rules for insurance contracts posed a number of difficult questions and, no surprise, this area proved to be controversial during the drafting of the Rome I regulation. It should be noted that the choice of a foreign law may have widest practical implications on the insurance contract—"*for instance, where an English insurer is asked to underwrite a transport risk under German law, it ought to be aware that German law prohibits clauses of promissory warranties exempting the insurer from its obligation to pay insurance money without negligence on the part of the policyholder even in transport insurance, which is a large risk.*"[51]

---

[48] Please see the Polish Civil Code, as an example.

[49] Fuchs and Jagielska, p. 33.

[50] James (2007), p. 257.

[51] Final Report of the Commission Expert Group on European Insurance Contract Law, p. 27, http://ec.europa.eu/justice/contract/files/expert_groups/insurance/final_report.pdf (date of entry: 01.07.2014).

Accordingly, while drafting Rome I, it was agreed that certain key directives regarding the choice-of-law rules should be considered. It is worth repeating at least three of them after L. Merrett[52]:

1) There is always a tension between party autonomy (ie favouring full freedom of choice for the parties) and the need to protect the weaker party in a transaction. This tension might require different rules to be applied in different contexts or to different sorts of contracts (eg consumer contracts).
2) In some areas, and insurance is a good example, different countries might have mandatory or overriding rules which govern certain aspects of the contract regardless of the law which would otherwise apply. It is a difficult question as to what effect should be given to such mandatory rules.
3) The choice-of-law rules must be seen against the general background of the common market and the need to promote cross-border trade; an aim that is still far from being achieved in the insurance market.[53]

When discussing the applicability of Rome I to the insurance contracts, it should be underlined, that Rome I does not provide for its own definition of an insurance contract. Although national regulations of the EU Member States very often provide for such definitions, the interpretation of the notion "insurance contract" should not be solely made based on them, but the applicable EU legislation should be taken into account as well.

By the same token, as regards on-line insurance contracts, these have not been, so far, defined by any of the legal instruments of the EU even in spite of the fact that e-commerce is subject to extensive regulation.[54] With respect to electronic forms of concluding a contract in a general aspect, the EU legislation requires that it is treated in the same manner as other forms of conclusion of contracts. In other words, the legal systems of the Member States should not, *inter alia*, recognise agreements as null and void only because they are concluded with the use of electronic means.[55] This rule has been implemented in the EU Member States.[56] As an example, Polish regulations do not make validity of the insurance contract conditional on any special form in which it should be concluded—there are no restrictions as regards electronic form. Article 809 of the Polish Civil Code merely reserves the written form for documentary purposes.[57]

Further analysis of notion of the "insurance contract" may be then, useful. It seems that there are at least two theories of understanding the insurance contracts:

---

52 Merrett (2009), pp. 55–56.

53 Merrett (2009) also refers to: Clarke and Heiss (2006), noting that "hardly any cross-border services are provided by insurers".

54 Malinowska and Świątkowski (2013), p. 32.

55 Fras (2008), p. 184.

56 Please see Directive 2000/31/EC of the European Parliament and of the Council of 8 June 2000 on certain legal aspects of information society services, in particular electronic commerce, in the Internal Market ('Directive on electronic commerce'), (OJ L 128, 17.07.2000, pp. 1–16).

57 The written form of a statement may also be required by other Polish legal provisions, but not the Civil Code or the direct insurance regulations.

the theory of cash benefit, according to which the performance of the insurer is the payment of a sum of money in the case of occurrence of an insurance event, and the theory of risk, defining the performance of the insurer as being the "provision of insurance protection". Under Directive 2011/83/EU,[58] insurance should be qualified as a kind of financial service. One may say that it is therefore closer to the theory of cash benefit where policyholders prepaid (by way of premiums) for cash benefits which they receive under certain conditions. Having regard merely to this theory, the insurance may resemble a deposit or an investment,[59] but obviously, it is not such an instrument at all—it has been excluded from the scope of the II Markets in Financial Instruments Directive (2014/65/EU) (Article 2)[60] and included in the same standards for insurance contracts under separate regulation as stated in a proposal for a revision of the Insurance Mediation Directive.[61] One may also say that the essence of assistance insurance is focused on the concept of providing the insured with access to certain goods or services. Therefore, in this type of insurance, the benefit does not necessarily take the form of compensation or the form of cash benefit.[62]

It is clear in the legal doctrine that the insurance risk itself is the most important feature of an insurance contract.[63] Accordingly, two main factors should be regarded as determining the applicable law for the on-line insurance contract under Rome I: the kind of the risk protected (type of the insurance contract) and the location of such risk. As previously indicated, the EU regulations do not provide for a direct definition of the "insurance contract", therefore, the work on the "Restatement of European Insurance Contract Law" should be mentioned as giving guidance for such definition on a non-legislative level. The "Principles of European Insurance Contract Law (PEICL)" project is part of a wider program set up several years ago to create a Common Frame of Reference for European general contract law.[64] According to Article 1:201 (1) of the PEICL, the term "insurance contract" means a contract under which one party, the insurer, promises another party, the

[58] Directive 2011/83/EU of the European Parliament and of the Council of 25 October 2011 on consumer rights, amending Council Directive 93/13/EEC and Directive 1999/44/EC of the European Parliament and of the Council and repealing Council Directive 85/577/EEC and Directive 97/7/EC of the European Parliament and of the Council (OJ L 304, 22.11.2011, p. 64–88).

[59] Fein (2006), pp. 16–7.

[60] Directive 2014/65/EU of the European Parliament and of the Council of 15 May 2015 on markets in financial instruments and amending Directive 2002/92/EC and Directive 2011/61/EU (OJ L 173, 12.6.2014, p. 349–496).

[61] Proposal for a Directive of the European Parliament and of the Council on insurance mediation, http://ec.europa.eu/internal_market/insurance/docs/consumers/mediation/20120703-directive_en.pdf (date of entry: 01.07.2014).

[62] Raczyński, p. 179.

[63] E. Kowalewski: Ubezpieczenia transgraniczne—aspekty prawne, available at: http://www.gu.com.pl/index.php?option=com_content&view=article&id=11800&catid=121&Itemid=144 (date of entry: 27.07.2015); Kropka (2010), p. 35.

[64] http://www.out-law.com/page-8948 (date of entry: 01.07.2014).

policyholder, a cover against a specified risk in exchange for a premium. It seems that the abovementioned characteristic is a sum of ideas about the concept of the insurance contract as it refers both to the theory of cash benefit and the theory of risk. For comparison purposes and to determine similarities, Article 805 § 1 of the Polish Civil Code[65] provides for the following definition of the insurance contract: "*by a contract of insurance the insurer, within the scope of activity of its enterprise, shall assume the obligation to effect the specified performance in the case of the occurrence of the accident envisaged in the contract, and the policyholder shall assume the obligation to pay the premium*". In Latvia, the insurance contract is defined under Article 1(5) of "The Insurance Contract Law".[66] Under this provision, an insurance contract is an agreement between an insurer and a policyholder according to which the policyholder undertakes to pay an insurance premium in the manner, time and amount specified by the insurance contract, as well as to meet other obligations under the contract, and the insurer undertakes to pay the insurance benefit to the person stated in the contract on the occurrence of an insured event in compliance with the insurance contract.[67] Definitions seem to be similar which means there seems to be a common ground for the definition of the insurance contract in the EU, which is similar to the one proposed by the PEICL.

Additionally, in terms of insurance contracts under Rome I, the PEICL may be found useful not only in respect of the area of definitions. Under the rule of choice of law established under Rome I, which will be discussed further herein, the choice of the "General Principles of Contract Law" as a law regime applicable to govern the contractual obligations has not been excluded.[68] This also applies to the PEICL. If these are to apply, the non-binding rules shall become the law applicable, and replace the relevant local provisions if the parties decide to do so. As a result, these principles would represent the 28th insurance contract law regime in the EU.[69]

3.2 Relation to the Provisions Regulating Sale at a Distance and Contracts Concluded by Way of Electronic Means

As previously indicated, under Rome I, the consumer contracts and insurance contracts are separated by regulation of different articles, and none regulation of

[65] The Act dated 23 April 1964 the Civil Code (L.J. unified text of 2014 item 121, as amended).

[66] Latvijas Vēstnesis No. 188/189 on 30 June 1998. (The official Gazette of the Government of Latvia); https://www.vestnesis.lv/op/2016/48.1.

[67] http://unpan1.un.org/intradoc/groups/public/documents/UNTC/UNPAN018394.pdf (date of entry: 30.11.2013).

[68] Heiss (2006), p. 16.

[69] Basedow (2004), pp. 108–109; Loacker (2009), p. 296; Basedow (2008), p. 115; Lakhan and Heiss (2010), p. 10.

Rome I does make any distinction between traditional insurance and on-line insurance. The representatives of the legal doctrine suggested, however, that there is a "*necessity of creating a distinctive system of law for online transactions.*[70] *According to the authors of that concept, it is no longer possible to treat the Internet only as a medium that facilitates the exchange of information sent from one legal system to another, as it leads to unsatisfactory results in terms of the legal situation of the parties.*"[71] This standpoint has been challenged by saying that the existing private law regulations can be sufficiently adapted to the new times. It has been also said that general and comprehensive values that have been adopted in the current regulations should not be treated as excluding the electronic means of concluding the contracts. As a result, there is no need to create peculiar regulations for the Internet transactions in insurance. That was also the approach adopted by the Rome I regulation.[72]

4 Factors Determining the Applicable Law for On-Line Insurance Contracts

Rome I provides for many factors determining the applicable law for insurance contracts, including on-line insurance. Firstly, pursuant to Articles 28 and 29 of Rome I, the effect of the Rome I regulation is limited to the contracts concluded after 17 December 2009. To all insurance contracts that had been concluded before this date, the previous conflict rules of the Rome Convention and insurance directives would apply.[73] Therefore, the first factor determining the applicable law for an on-line insurance contract is the moment in which the contract has been concluded. Secondly, the limitations of Rome I itself are to be mentioned. Article 1(2)(j) excludes, from the scope of the regulation, insurance contracts arising out of the operations carried out by organisations other than undertakings referred to in Article 2 of Directive 2002/83/EC of the European Parliament and of the Council of 5 November 2002 concerning life assurance[74] ("**Directive 2002/83/EC**") the object of which is to provide benefits for employed or self-employed individuals belonging to an undertaking or group of undertakings, or to a trade or group of trades, in the event of death or survival or of discontinuance or curtailment of activity, or of sickness related to work or accidents at work. The latter limitation can cause complex issues in some jurisdictions to be addressed. For example, some

[70] Tang (2010), p. 225, as cited by Malinowska and Świątkowski (2013) p. 35.

[71] Malinowska and Świątkowski (2013), p. 35.

[72] Malinowska and Świątkowski (2013), p. 36.

[73] Kramer (2008), p. 33.

[74] OJ L 345, 19.12.2002, p. 1. Directive as last amended by Directive 2008/19/EC (OJ L 76, 19.3.2008, p. 44).

authors believe that this provision applies to contracts concluded by individuals subject to the Polish social insurance scheme within the open pension funds (OFE),[75] but there are also opposing voices in the legal doctrine.[76] Further, not all insurance contracts are covered by the special rule of Article 7 of Rome I, as some are still regulated by the general provisions of Rome I (e.g. other than large risks when they are located outside the territory of the EU Member States), which will be discussed further.

4.1 Types of Contracts

The law applicable in a given situation also depends on the type of the insurance contract. In this respect, one can distinguish different rules determining the applicable law for the following categories of contracts: large risks and mass risks, life or non-life insurance, reinsurance and compulsory insurance.

As mentioned before, Article 7 of Rome I does not apply to all insurance contracts and in the cases of those exceptions, the general rules of Rome I will apply. For instance, pursuant to Recital 33 of Rome I, Article 7 does not apply to the risks other than large risks (mass risks) when they are located outside the territory of the EU Member States. Also, Article 7(1) of Rome I provides that it does not apply to reinsurance contracts.

To limit the analysis to the main rules arising out of Article 7 of Rome I for the purposes of this section, it is useful to distinguish three pillars, constituting the basis on which the article has been constructed. The first pillar is the choice of law allowed by the regulation in the context of a given type of risk or, in other words, the type of the contract. It is common for all the provisions of Rome I to have the choice of law as the starting point—it is a fundamental and preferred concept governing contractual relationships.[77] It was deliberately aimed for Rome I to be governed primarily by the principle of party autonomy.[78] The second pillar seems to be the law of the habitual residence, while the third one is the law of the country where the risk is located. Whether the connecting factor of the habitual residence or the location of risk applies, or not, also depends on the type of risk. An exception to this system is made for the contracts regarding compulsory insurance.[79]

---

[75] Kropka (2010), p. 92.

[76] Pilich (2012), p. 201.

[77] N. Rozehnalova, J. Valdhans: A Few Observations on Choice of Law (January 29, 2010). Czech Yearbook of International Law, available at: http://ssrn.com/abstract=1752116 (date of entry 17.06.2014).

[78] Bisping (2013).

[79] Kramer (2008), p. 37.

4.1.1 Large Risks

As to the category of large risks, the applicable law is regulated in Article 7(2) of Rome I, in connection with Article 3 of Rome I. It does not include any definition of a large risk, but refers in this respect to Article 5(d) of the First Non-Life Directive 73/239/EEC[80] ("**Directive 73/239/EEC**") (as amended). The definition of large risks comprises three rules. All of them exclude life insurance, which means that every life insurance contract should be treated as a mass insurance contract.[81] Pursuant to the discussed Article 5(d) of the Directive 73/239/EEC, large risks generally include transport (such as aircraft, ships or rail) and other risks where the policyholder carries on a business over a certain capacity.[82] According to Article 7(2) of Rome I, the parties to an insurance contract, in the case of a large risk, retain the freedom to choose the applicable law. In the case where the parties have not chosen the applicable law, the insurance contract related to the large risk will be governed by the law of the place of the habitual residence of the insurer. This rule also applies to the situations where the choice of law was partial, with respect to the scope within which no choice of law was made.[83] However, if it is clear from all the circumstances of the case that the contract is manifestly more closely connected with another country the law of that country will apply. It should be noted that the aforementioned rules are in conformity with Article 4 of Rome I, where the law of the of the country where the party required to effect the characteristic performance of the contract has his habitual residence, i.e. the insurer, is designated as the applicable law, unless the law of another country is manifestly more closely connected. Therefore, this rule brings large-risk insurance contracts in line with the rule applicable to other (commercial) contracts.

It should also be underlined that, pursuant to Article 3 of Rome I, the choice of law must either be expressly made or clearly demonstrated by the terms of the contract or the circumstances of the case.[84] The said Article, however, also provides for an important restriction that regards the application of the compusory

[80] First Council Directive of 24 July 1973 on the coordination of laws, regulations and administrative provisions relating to the taking-up and pursuit of the business of direct insurance other than life assurance (73/239/EEC) (OJ L 228, 16.8.1973, p. 3–19), as amended by Second Council Directive 88/357/EEC of 22 June 1988 on the coordination of laws, regulations and administrative provisions relating to direct insurance other than life assurance and laying down provisions to facilitate the effective exercise of freedom to provide services and amending Directive 73/239/EEC (OJ L 172, 04.07.1988, p. 1–14). Please note that Directive 88/357/EEC and Directive 73/239/EEC were repealed with the effect from 1 January 2016 by the Directive 2009/138/EC of the European Parliament and of the Council of 25 November 2009 on the taking-up and pursuit of the business of Insurance and Reinsurance (Solvency II) (OJ L 335, 17.12.2009 p. 0001–0155). However, in accordance with Article 310 of the Solvency II, references to the repealed Directives shall be construed as references to the Solvency II.

[81] Kropka (2010), p. 129.

[82] Currently, definition of large risks is included in Article 13 point 27 of Directive 2009/138/EC of the European Parliament and of the Council of 25 November 2009 on the taking-up and pursuit of the business of Insurance and Reinsurance (Solvency II) (OJ L 335, 17.12.2009, pp. 1–155).

[83] Kropka (2010), p. 145.

[84] Popiołek (2007). p. 23.

provisions. The choice of law of a different country than the country where the elements of the contract are located, will not prejudice the application of any compulsory provisions in the law of that country. Similarly, according to Article 3 (4) of Rome I in case all other elements relevant to the situation at the time of the choice are located in one ore more EU Member States, the parties' choice of applicable law other than that of a Member State shall not prejudice the application of provisions of the Community law, where appropriate as implemented in the Member State of the forum, which cannot be derogated from by agreement.

4.1.2 Mass Risks Within the EU

Article 7 of Rome I differentiates between the contracts where the policyholder is deemed to be in need for special protection and other contracts. Therefore, the provision distinguishes between the contracts on mass risks on the one side and the contracts on large risks.[85] Article 7(3) of Rome I lists, under letters a-e, the only possibilities of the choice of law in the case of mass risks and such choice is much more limited than in respect of large risks. Basically, the parties can choose either the law of any Member State where the risk is located at the time the contract is concluded, or the law of the country where the policyholder has its habitual residence (letters a-b). For each contract falling under Article 7(3) of Rome I, it can be determined that the risk is undoubtedly located in the EU Member States.[86] Furthermore, pursuant to Article 7(3) of Rome I, in the case of commercial or professional insurance covering risks located in two or more Member States, the parties can choose the law of any of them, or the law of the policyholder's habitual residence (letter e). However, in the aforementioned three cases, if the EU Member States grant greater freedom of choice of the law applicable to the insurance contract, the parties may take advantage of that freedom. For insurance contracts covering risks limited to events occurring in an EU Member State other than the Member State in which the risk is located, the choice is restricted to the law of that Member State (letter d).

If no choice of law is made in the case of mass risks insurance, the insurance contract will be governed by the law of the EU Member State in which the risk is located at the time the insurance contract was concluded. To non-life insurance contracts, Article[87] 13 (13) of the Directive 2009/138/EC of the European Parliament and of the Council of 25 November 2009 on the taking-up and pursuit of the business of Insurance and Reinsurance ("**Solvency II**")[88] will apply. In most cases, the risk will be located in the Member State in which the policyholder has its habitual residence, but in the cases of a building and buildings and their contents

[85] Gruber (2009), p. 111.

[86] Kropka (2010), p. 156.

[87] Previously regulated by 2(d) of the Directive 88/357/EEC.

[88] Directive 2009/138/EC of the European Parliament and of the Council of 25 November 2009 on the taking-up and pursuit of the business of Insurance and Reinsurance (Solvency II) (OJ L 335, 17.12.2009, pp. 1–155).

insurance Solvency II provides that it will be the place where the property is located and, for motor insurance, the EU Member State in which the vehicle is registered. In case of policies of duration of fourt months or less covering travel or holiday risks, it will be the Member State where the policy was taken out.

4.1.3 Life Insurance

For life insurance contracts, Article 7(3) (c) of Rome I provides for that the only choice that can be made is the law of the EU Member State whose national is a given policyholder. The choice of law cannot be, therefore, affected by the nationality or residence status of the insured, beneficiary or other person that is involved in the insurance relationship. Again, if no choice of law is made, the contract should be governed by the law of the EU Member State in which the risk is located at the time of concluding the contract. In the case of life insurance, the risk is located in the place where the policyholders have their habitual residence[89] (Directive 2002/83/EC, Article 1(1) (g)).[90] From the Rome I principles, it seems unacceptable to apply Article 7(3) (c) of Rome I to those cases where the policyholder is a national of a third country—not being a Member State.[91] Similarly, the legal doctrine indicates that it is difficult to determine the choice of law of the home country of the policyholders with respect to the British citizens, especially, when a British citizen has no habitual residence in the United Kingdom.[92] The problem was that in the case of British citizens the admissibility of choice of their home country law may refer to three different results: the English law, the Scottish law and the law of the Northern Ireland.[93] Article 7(3) (c) of Rome I does not provide for the answer how to act in a situation of multiple nationality of the EU Member States.

Additionally, interesting consequences of mandatory national regulations in terms of life insurance that may also be considered from the point of view of Rome I may be observed in other jurisprudences, such as Austrian or German. Under these two legal regimes the exclusion clauses in life insurance, according to which the insurer is exempted from liability in the case of a suicide committed by a person at risk is absolutely restricted. *"In Germany, the insurer has to pay out insurance money in any event if the person at risk commits suicide more than 3 years after the contract was concluded (Section 161(1) sentence 1 German*

[89] It should be noted that the notion of habitual residence and its possible changes caused interpretation problems; please see Case C-243/11: Judgment of the Court (First Chamber) of 21 February 2013 (request for a preliminary ruling from the Rechtbank van eerste aanleg te Brussel (Belgium))—RVS Levensverzekeringen NV v Belgische Staat (OJ C 114 of 20.4.2013, p. 10.

[90] Currently: Article 13 (14) of Directive 2009/138/EC of the European Parliament and of the Council of 25 November 2009 on the taking-up and pursuit of the business of Insurance and Reinsurance (Solvency II) (OJ L 335 of 17.12.2009, pp. 1–155).

[91] Garcimartin Alferez (2008), pp. I-74–I-75.

[92] Dicey et al., pp. 1736–1737.

[93] *Ibidem*, p. 1737.

Insurance Contract Act). Within the first 3 years of the contract term the insurer will only have to pay out insurance money if the person at risk committed suicide in a state of mental incapacity (Section 161(1) sentence 2 German Insurance Contract Act)".[94] There are differences in applying of the latter rule in case of Austria. According to Section 169 of the Austrian Insurance Contract Act, this rule applies regardless of the time when suicide has been committed.[95] *"Furthermore, Section 153 of the German Insurance Contract Act grants policyholders of life insurance contracts a right to participate in profits (including hidden reserves) earned by the insurer. Such profits must be calculated and distributed in the manner prescribed by Section 153 of the German Insurance Contract Act. While the right to participate in profits may be excluded as a whole, any modification or exclusion of such right is prohibited under Section 153(1) of the German Insurance Contract Act"*.[96]

4.1.4 Reinsurance

Reinsurance contracts have been directly excluded from the scope of application of Article 7(1) of Rome I.[97] It is said that this solution, which has already been implemented under the Rome Convention almost with the same wording, comes out of many interconnections of reinsurance in Europe with the common law system. There is no doubt that there is a fundamental difference between contracts of insurance and contracts of reinsurance.[98] Moreover, there are reinsurance customs and standards that are considered as internationally recognised, independent sources of law. [99]

According to legal doctrine, reinsurance agreements are designed to allow an insurer to spread the risk and also to expand its capacity by accepting risks that would otherwise be beyond its financial resources.[100] As in that case the parties to the contract have equal status, the restrictions related to the possible choice of law are not as much needed. As a result, the common law approach that was the closest to the specificity and practicality of reinsurance contracts that developed over the years on the European market was adopted,[101] and, according to Article 3 of Rome I, the parties may choose the applicable law. The rules for ascertaining the

[94] The final report of the Commission Expert Group on a European Insurance Contract Law adopted on 24 January 2014: http://ec.europa.eu/justice/contract/files/expert_groups/insurance/final_report.pdf, p. 30 (date of entry: 01.07.2014).

[95] *Ibidem.*

[96] *Ibidem*, p. 30.

[97] Pilich (2012), p. 205.

[98] Cox and Smith (2006), p. 208; Please also see Raim and Langford (2008), pp. 40-5–40-8.

[99] Graber et al. (2012), p. 285.

[100] Merkin (2009), p. 69.

[101] *Ibidem*, p. 70.

applicable law in the absence of any express or clearly demonstrated choice are those stated in Article 4 of Rome I. The prevailing positions in the legal doctrine are that the rule relevant to reinsurance is in Article 4(1) (b) "*a contract for the provision of services shall be governed by the law of the country where the service provider has his habitual residence*".[102] However, other standpoints indicate that as "*Article 4(1) makes no special mention of reinsurance contracts, the applicable law is determined by Article 4(2).*" [103] Therefore, in such cases, the reinsurance contract according to Article 4(2) of Rome *I "shall be governed by the law of the country where the party required to effect the characteristic performance of the contract has his habitual residence.*" and that would open discussion to the understanding of "the characteristic performance of the reinsurance contract". However, according to some representatives of the German legal doctrine, *"the reinsurance contract is a service contract in the meaning of 4(1) (b) or that the reinsurer's performance is characteristic for the contract in the meaning of Article 4(2) of the Rome I Regulation, thus leading to the reinsurer's law"*. [104]

The "habitual residence" of a company is defined in Article 19 of Rome I as being its place of central administration.[105] Under Article 19(2) of Rome I, *"where the contract is concluded in the course of the operations of a branch, agency or any other establishment, or if, under the contract, performance is the responsibility of such a branch, agency or establishment, the place where the branch, agency or any other establishment is located shall be treated as the place of habitual residence"*. Therefore, in the case of a branch of foreign reinsurer established in one of the EU Member States, the location of the branch would be decisive. Additionally, under Article 19(3) of Rome I, *"for the purposes of determining the habitual residence, the relevant point in time shall be the time of the conclusion of the contract"*.

The rule of habitual residence may be impacted by Article 4(3) of Rome I, which allows the court to apply the law of a country to which the contract is "*manifestly more closely connected*". The use of the word "manifestly" indicates an increased role of the presumption. Furthermore, Article 4(4) of Rome I states that if the applicable law cannot be determined under the said presumption the contract is governed by the law of the country with which it is most closely connected. Here yet, some authors of the German legal doctrine indicate that *"the reinsurance contract is more or most closely connected to the original risk, making the respective governing law applicable under Article 4(3) or (4) of the Rome I Regulation"*.[106]

[102] *Ibidem*, p. 74.

[103] Gruber (2009), p. 114.

[104] Sieg and Schaloske (2012), p. 145.

[105] Merkin (2009), p. 74.

[106] Sieg and Schaloske (2012), p. 145.

4.1.5 Compulsory Insurance

Private international law issues of compulsory insurance are regulated in Article 7 (4) of Rome I and provides for some some additional rules according to which the contract must comply with the requirements of the EU Member State imposing the obligation to insure. First rule indicates that the insurance contract shall not satisfy the obligation to take out insurance unless it complies with the specifict provisions relating to that insurance laid down by the Member State that imposes the obligation (Article 7 (4) (a) first sentence). The actual character of the referral to the country imposing the obligation to take out insurance was subject of discussions in the legal doctrine. Some authors presented view that this regulation does not seem to be a source of conflict rule or that these rules "*are based on the mechanism of overriding mandatory provisions*".[107] Irrespective of the above, it seems that there should be elements that provide for further indication of the interpretation of the connection between the Member State that imposes the obligation to take insurance and the Member State that contains ther respective provisions.[108] Article 7 (4) (a) further indicates that in case of contradiction between the law of that state and the law where the risk is located, the law of the EU Member State imposing the obligation to insure will prevail. In connection with the above an interesting issue can arise in case the obligation to take out insurance in relation to the same risk is imposed by more than one EU Member State. Some authors suggest that in case "*the risk is situated in one and the same Member State, then the concurrence and contradiction between two or more laws should lead to the application of the lex fori in order to determine which of these laws should prevail.*"[109] Article 7 (4) (b) provides for a third important rule that empowers the the Member States to lay down that the insurance contract shall be goverened by the law of the Member State that imposes the obligation to take out insurance. This obviously again excludes the choice of law by the parties to the insurance contract if such an obligation was imposed by the relevant Member State. An express provision as an illustration of such is German Article 46c (2) of the EGBGB.[110] In other words "*If the contract fulfils a German obligation to insure, German law is to apply exclusively.*"[111]

[107] Pilich (2006), p. 214 and extensive literature that this author provides.

[108] Please see Pilich (2006), p. 216, that proposes that "the law imposing the obligation must be objectively connected with the given contract" and provides further analysis.

[109] Pilich (2006), p. 216 that cites Seatzu (2003), pp. 210–211.

[110] Introductory Act to the Civil Code promulgated on 21 September 1994, Federal Law Gazette [Bundesgesetzblatt] I p. 2494, last amended by Article 17 of the Act of 20 November 2015, Federal Law Gazette I p. 2010; http://www.gesetze-im-internet.de/englisch_bgbeg/englisch_bgbeg.html#p0181 (date of entry: 28.07.2015).

[111] Dr. Jens Gal/Prof. Dr. Manfred Wandt, Response to the Questionnaire on Mandatory Insurance, AIDA German Chapter, www.aida.org.uk/docs/Germany.doc (date of entry: 01.07.2014).

4.1.6 Contracts with Policyholders That Are Considered Consumers Under National Legislation

The last issue relating to the question of the type of a contract refers to the issue of consumer protection, which has already been briefly addressed. At this point, however, the matter will be considered from a different perspective. Although it has been previously mentioned that the provisions which generally apply to insurance contracts (but not those envisaged for consumer contracts) are relevant for establishing the law applicable to the specific case of on-line insurance contracts, one may argue that consumer protection provisions may, in some cases, also apply. Those potentially applicable consumer protection provisions should not be taken from Rome I, but from relevant national legislation.

It should be noted that Article 9(1) of Rome I provides for a special legal institution of overriding mandatory provisions. Such provisions are defined as provisions the importance of which is regarded as crucial by the relevant EU Member States for safeguarding their public interests, such as its political, social or economic organisation, to such an extent that they are applicable to any situation falling within their scope, irrespective of the law otherwise applicable to the contract under Rome I. "*That means that these are rules so important to protect specific interests of a country that must be applied even if the different rules of another law should be applicable in that situation.*"[112] In other words, overriding mandatory provisions supersede the objectively determined applicable law.[113] The overriding mandatory provisions are closely connected with the European Court of Justice decision in Arblade (C-369/96)[114] and they should be analysed in accordance with EU freedoms expressly provided for in the Treaties.[115] Using this institution, a court can apply the overriding mandatory provisions of the forum (Article 9(2)) and may give effect to the overriding mandatory provisions of other EU Member States if those provisions render the performance of the contract illegal (Article 9(3)). However, the above does not provide a clear answer to the question on whether a national court can decide on the direct applicability of the national legal provisions if such provisions provide the policyholders with special consumer treatment under the insurance contract.

[112] S. Travnickova, Limitations of choice of law—mandatory rules and internationally mandatory rules, Acta Universitatis Brunensis Iuridica No. 337, 2009, p. 3 (available at http://www.law.muni.cz/sborniky/dp08/files/pdf/mezinaro/travnickova.pdf (date of entry: 27.07.2015).

[113] Bisping (2013), see also: van Bochove (2014) p. 147, http://www.erasmuslawreview.nl/files/ELR_2014_03_005.pdf (date of entry: 26.07.2015), Simona Travnickova, Limitations of choice of law—mandatory rules and international mandatory rules, http://www.law.muni.cz/sborniky/dp08/files/pdf/mezinaro/travnickova.pdf (date of entry: 25.07.2015).

[114] Judgement of the European Court of Justice dated 23 November 1999—Criminal proceedings against Jean-Claude Arblade and Arblade & Fils SARL (C-369/96) and Bernard Leloup, Serge Leloup and Sofrage SARL (C-376/96), ECLI:EU:C:1999:575; Cox and Smith (2006), p. 254.

[115] Cox and Smith (2006), p. 255.

The institution of overriding mandatory provisions is rather complex and it is difficult to establish which provisions are to be deemed as overriding mandatory provisions. In particular, *"German courts have shown great restraint in declaring provisions overriding and have decided that provisions, which mainly protect private interests, are not of an overriding mandatory character. (...) French and English courts, in turn, have been less restrained."*[116]

The question whether the mere objective of the consumer protection may confer certain legal regulation as in the case of overriding mandatory provisions remains unresolved. On the one hand, as indicated above, European courts are reluctant to use this tool, but, on the other, one should consider the arguments related to the protection of the values accepted by the legal systems of the EU Member States. It is worth mentioning that in England the Consumer Credit Act 1974[117] and the Unfair Contract Terms Act 1977[118] are generally considered overriding. From this, it may be claimed as probable that the protection of consumers should take effect as the overriding mandatory provisions.[119]

Some authors indicate that to understand what law is to be applied to an insurance contract, one should also consider a possible application of overriding mandatory provisions.[120] There are also opinions stating that, "*unless the definition of overriding mandatory rules in Article 9 (1) significantly narrows when such rules can be applied, the fact that the policy may be subject to mandatory rules in each Member State will remain a significant discentive to cross border trade*" consequently, "*whilst the private international law rules may well be an improvement, the only real solution may well remain the harmonisation of mandatory insurance rules*".[121]

4.2 Location of a Risk

Additional factor determining the applicable law for an insurance contract, including on-line insurance contracts, must be the location of the risk. Also, in the case of on-line insurance contracts, in particular, legal doctrine emphasizes that main

[116] Bisping (2013).

[117] Bisping (2013) provides with the case of OFT vs. Lloyds 2008 1 AC 316, but states that this is misconceived. Further reading: Ch. Bisping: Avoid the Statutist Trap. The International Scope of the Consumer Credit Act 1974, 2012 8 JPIL 1. See also: English vs. Donnelly 1958 SC 494, a Scottish decision, which is also relied on in England as precedent for the proposition that consumer credit law is of an overriding mandatory nature.

[118] Bisping (2013) provides with a supporting opinion of Dicey et al. (2006). For a critique see Mann (1978), p. 661.

[119] Stone (2010), p. 343.

[120] Merrett (2009), p. 63.

[121] *Ibidem*, p. 67.

attention should be given to the location of a risk.[122] It is somehow related to the condition of the type of the contract as described above, but there are still a few issues that should be described separately. First of all, contrary to the previously applicable legal regime governing the applicable law for the insurance contract, Rome I covers the risks situated both within, and outside, the EU. It also regulates contracts covering risks located within the EU territory, concluded by the insurers that are not established in the EU.[123] As regards the issues of geographical nature, it should also be mentioned that the regulation of Rome I has, in principle, a universal territorial application, in that Article 2 provides that any law specified by Rome I will be applied, irrespective of whether it is the law of an EU Member State. However, as previously mentioned, Rome I is not applied in every EU Member State—Denmark does not take part in that regulation.

It seems that the most discussed problem regarding the insurance regulation under Rome I concerns exactly the location of the risk, namely, the case of direct insurance of mass risks situated in any third (non-EU) state. One of the advantages of the Commission's initial proposal on Rome I was that it removed the distinction between the risks located inside and outside the EU. Rome I itself also removes this distinction but to a more limited extent. The special rules set out in Article 7 apply to all contracts of insurance relating to large risks, wherever the risk is located. As a result, in large risks cases it will no longer be necessary to consider where the risk is located. But for risks not qualified as large risks the distinction remains. The question whether the risk is located within or outside the EU determines whether the special rules set out in Article 7 of Rome I, or the general rules, apply[124] as the particular group of non-large risks located outside the EU is entirely excluded from the scope of Article 7. This continued distinction is considered in legal doctrine as the main weakness of Rome I.[125] Contracts of non-large risks situated outside the EU will be subject to the normal choice-of-law rules set out in the body of the Rome I, particularly Article 3 and Article 4. But importantly, such contracts will also be subject to the consumer provisions in Article 6. If an insurance contract is concluded by a person acting outside their trade or profession and the other requirements of Article 6 are satisfied, they will therefore be subject to special, more restrictive rules for consumer contracts. But this compromise does not exclude doubts. *"The combined application of Articles 3, 4 and 6 is not transparent and is complex."*[126] The legal doctrine perceives the exclusion of Article 7 as *"an obvious inconsistency because it potentially deprives a large number of policyholders of the protection guaranteed by the commented rule of law."*[127] Therefore, *"it is to be hoped that when the Commission carries out its review of*

[122] Kowalewski (2005), p. 26; Fras (2008), p. 195.

[123] Kramer (2008), p. 33.

[124] Merrett (2009), p. 53–54.

[125] *Ibidem*, p. 62.

[126] *Ibidem*, p. 59.

[127] Pilich (2012), p. 205, please also see cited Heiss (2008) pp. 279–280.

the law applicable to insurance contracts under the Review Clause of Article 27 *that it will be possible to formulate rules capable of applying to all insurance contracts, regardless of where the risk is situated.*"[128]

The location of a risk is a particularly complicated issue in the case of on-line insurance contracts. It is because of the fact that on-line contracts are concluded without simultaneous physical presence of the parties,[129] and the communication leading to the conclusion of the contract and the actual conclusion of the contract "are located" on the Internet, i.e. in the electronic space (cyberspace). Cyberspace raises important and challenging new legal issues relating to electronic communications.[130] While a classic conflict of law rules usually refers to the indication of the relevant territory—it is difficult to refer to such territory in case of contracts concluded through electronic communication. These are actually "located" in the network connecting electronic devices, which "*has neither borders nor simple links to the areas of the countries in which participants of these relations are located and the consequences resulting there from take place.*"[131] As a result, an "*electronic impulse, being the medium carrying the statement of will, the only required legal source of contracts concluded solo consensu (such as insurance), can run through the whole world until it reaches the addressee.*"[132]Secondly, there is no doubt that a server containing electronic information can be placed in various locations around the world.

If, therefore, the Internet is "*extraterritorial*",[133] the electronic contracts should be regarded as located in an "*electronic network liaising the electronic devices of its users.*"[134] If the network does not have borders and there are no territories to refer to, the decisive relevance cannot simply refer to the territory of conclusion of the contract, because it is difficult or even impossible to establish the appropriate one. Therefore, it seems reasonable to indicate that other factors should be used as decisive in terms of the application of the conflict of law rules, such as "*legal environment of the parties (domicile, seat, etc.) or the place where legal or factual effect of the on-line contract arises*".[135]

Regardless of the above, it should also be noted that nature of "the location of the Internet" was the source of many other questions such as to whether a website can

---

[128] Merrett (2009), p. 66.

[129] Fras (2008), p. 193; and Prawo właściwe dla umownych zobowiązań elektronicznych w konwencji rzymskiej i projekcie rozporządzenia Rzym I: Kolizyjne aspekty zobowiązań elektronicznych, Materiały z konferencji. WoltersKluwer Polska 2007, p. 11.

[130] Hardy (1994), p. 994.

[131] Popiołek (2007), p. 10.

[132] Malinowska and Świątkowski (2013), pp. 34–35.

[133] Stosio, p. 274; and Malinowska and Świątkowski (2013), p. 34.

[134] Malinowska and Świątkowski (2013), p. 35.

[135] K. Malinowska: Transnational e-insurance, conflict of laws and IPG http://www.ipg-online.org/news/item/8 (date of entry: 9.03.2016).

be treated a branch office or an establishment[136] and therefore linked to a certain "territory". Fortunately, there is quite a clear consensus in this respect.[137]

5 Experience of Non-EU Member States

Eventually, it may be observed that in the countries not being the EU Member States, not bound by the regulations of Rome I, the accepted solutions within the scope of private international law are very similar to those included under Rome I. In the case of Norway, private international law within contracts remains mainly non-codified. This seems to be a result of the approach that the flexibility of choice of law rules should be recognized as a higher value than the certainty. However, in some aspects, where the need of certainty was acknowledged as more important, specific provisions were adopted, such as the Act on Choice of Law in Insurance.[138] But even before the adoption of the aforementioned, the solutions used in Norwegian judicature in a particular case of insurance contracts to a wide extent, mirrored the ideas currently found in Rome I. Still, Norwegian law seemed to be treated in a favourable, preferable manner when choosing the law applicable.[139]

It should also be noted that many of the solutions adopted in Rome I (life insurance, location of the risk) were modelled on the Swiss legislation.[140] Hence, it seems that the unification of laws and its consequences have a wider effect, which is not limited only to EU Member States. Although it is inevitable that many differences between the relevant EU and non-EU legal systems will exist, some of the non-EU regulatory solutions may be helpful while applying Rome I. For example, the legal doctrine is quite clear in a statement that at least Swiss insurance law may be useful in the process of applying the Rome I regulation. Swiss codification of private international law is generally recognized as the most developed and detailed in the world.[141] A few points seem noteworthy for the purposes of this chapter in the case of the law applicable for insurance contracts with an international element under Swiss private insurance law: IPR-Gesetz.[142] For

---

[136] Summary of discussions, Electronic Commerce and International Jurisdiction, Ottawa, 28 February—1 March 2000, p. 9.

[137] Directive 2000/31/EC of the European Parliament and of the Council of 8 June 2000 on certain legal aspects of information society services, in particular electronic commerce, in the Internal Market ('Directive on electronic commerce') (OJ L 128, 17.07.2000, p. 1–16).

[138] Act of 27 November 1992 no. 111 on Choice of Law in Relation to Insurance; http://www.finanstilsynet.no/en/Insurance-and-pensions/Insurance–pensions/Topic/Activity-of-EEA-insurance-companies-in-Norway/.

[139] Recent private international law codifications, folk.uio.no/giudittm/IACL_10_PIL_Norway.pdf.

[140] Fras (2010).

[141] Martinek and Poczobut (2003), s. 741–742.

[142] Bundesgesetz uber Internationale Privatrecht (IPRG) (1988), s. 5–60.

example, Article 116 of the IPR-Gesetz expresses a fundamental principle that contracts are subject to the law chosen by the parties. Swiss law provides for an unlimited choice of law and, it does not require the existence of any connection between the contract and the law chosen.[143] However, as mentioned before, while describing the law applicable for on-line insurance contracts under Rome I, this applies to the law protecting the policyholders in general, with no reference to its distance consumer character. Quite the opposite, Swiss law does recognize the consumer character of the insurance contract. In each case, under the provisions of Swiss law, given the massive nature of insurance contracts, the fact whether a given contract is of a consumer nature or not, must be determined at the first instance. Once the contract has been determined as being of consumer nature, according to Article 120 of the IPR-Gesetz, the provisions provide for a permanent link and the choice of law is precluded.[144] Only when the insurance contract is not of consumer nature, the applicable law should be determined by means of traditional rules of conflict. The choice of law should be made by the parties and only when the parties do not make the relevant choice, the applicable law is determined according to Article 117 point 1 of the IPR-Gesetz, i.e. based on the principle of the closest connection.[145]

6 Conclusions

The current legal regime for the applicable law in terms of insurance, including on-line insurance contracts is mostly from a single provision of Article 7 of Rome I. However, Article 7, because of its complexity, creates many regimes of the choice of law, including: full choice (i.e. large risks), limited (mass risks within the EU) and very much restricted (i.e. compulsory insurance). In view of the above, it may happen that one insurance contract may assume multiple "*personalities*".[146]

Notwithstanding the above, as it was presented in the chapter, the key factors determining the applicable law for on-line insurance contract are the types of a contract i.e. the type of the risk insured and the location of the risk. This should lead to the conclusion that the most important item in Rome I within the scope of the insurance contracts is the "risk" itself. It is recognized as "*a factor which allows the use of the norms of a particular legal system to insurance relationship*".[147]

From the historical point of view, it seems that the idea of unification of the private international law of the insurance contracts under the Rome I regulation has been expected for a long time. There is no doubt that, Rome I constitutes, "*together*

[143] Fingerhuth (1989), p. 4 and 10.

[144] Amstutz et al. (1996), p. 843; Nebel (1996), p. 1225.

[145] Fras (2010).

[146] Malinowska and Świątkowski (2013), p. 39.

[147] Fras (2010); Kowalewski (1999), pp. 38–39.

with the Rome II regulation, a big step forward on the way to building a Code of European Private International Law. In this sense it has to be welcomed".[148] However, one may claim that the results of application of Rome I may not be so praiseworthy.[149] Some of the representatives of legal doctrine are of the opinion that the manner of implementation of Rome I leaves considerable uncertainty. As already mentioned, Article 27 of Rome I raises the question whether there is a need for a reform or whether the existing rules should keep their *status quo*. There are critical voices related to the new rules under Rome I. One may also state that the implementation of Rome I was "*another recent failure of the European law-giver*".[150] Many scholars have especially criticized the complexity of the rules by comparing them to a "*maze*"[151] or a "*jungle*".[152] However, there are also voices supporting the regulations introduced by Rome I, claiming that the insurance provisions in Rome I follow the existing EU law on the topic, which—although complex—do not seem to have caused difficulty in practice.[153]

Additional perspective may be provided on creating a report required by the review clause contained in Article 27 of Rome I. The said clause was another basis for claiming that the Community legislator was not absolutely satisfied with its work,[154] especially that the insurance contracts are explicitly mentioned in the said article.[155] The review clause obliges the Commission to submit, to the European Parliament, the Council and the European Economic and Social Committee, the report on the application of the regulation and possibly, if appropriate, proposals of amendments. The report will include the study on the law applicable to insurance contracts and the assessment of the impact of the provisions to be introduced, if any, as well as the evaluation on the application of Article 6 of Rome I, in particular as regards the coherence of Community law in the field of consumer protection. However, although the obligation had been imposed, no review has been published yet.

Regardless of the possible criticism, it should be stated that under current EU regulations, the party autonomy has been and will remain a fundamental principle in European private international law in matters of contractual obligations.[156] It is also vital for the provisions regarding insurance contracts under Rome I. It is noteworthy that legal doctrine supporting the idea of adapting current international

[148] Garcimartin Alferez (2008), p. I–79.

[149] *Ibidem.*

[150] Heiss (2008), p. 261; also very critical Fricke (2008), p. 443.

[151] Gruber (2009), p. 110, citing: Kramer (2008), p. 23, 41.

[152] Gruber (2009), p. 110, citing: Mankowski (2008), p.133, 144.

[153] James (2008), p. 118.

[154] Garcimartin Alferez (2008), p. I-61.

[155] Lando and Nielsen (2008), p. 1687, 1710 (pointing out that no impact assessment had been carried out).

[156] Heiss (2009), p. 1, with reference to: Lagarde and Tenenbaum (2008), p. 727 and 735; Solomon (2008), p. 1709, p. 1722; Mankowski (2009), p. 2, 3.

provisions to the needs of electronic commerce[157] stands for the maximum use of the freedom of contract.[158] This means that the characteristics of on-line contracts and the characteristics of insurance contracts are currently included under Rome I. It seems, however, that the issue of the manner of concluding the contract was not under consideration while drafting Rome I because it does not provide for specific provisions in this respect.

The review of the EU private law regulations in relation to the on-line insurance contracts may provide for numerous findings. The first one, which seems to be the most vital, is that the complexity of the regulation is inevitable. This has been proven by the historical experience of the legislation and it seems that it does not limit the European insurance industry in its further development and extension. Nonetheless, bearing in mind that the insurance business depends on both the contractual relationships and the customer relations, we need to constantly look forward to the solutions that would simplify the insurance regulations, including the rules of the choice of law. This seems to be particularly important in the world in which on-line contracts tend to be concluded more frequently, not only because it allows us to save time but also that it is designed to be simple and user-friendly. This, however, should also be done in the spirit of protecting the weaker party to the contractual relationship, being a value strongly appreciated in the European Union. It must also be noted that the European legislation regarding on-line insurance contracts must reconcile different, often conflicting interests, and serve various customers with respect to many different and complicated contractual relationships.

There is no doubt that the structure of the regulation regarding on-line insurance contracts and the conflict of laws is a complicated net of factors and interdependencies. It should be stated, however, that it is logical and justified in respect of its purpose. Therefore, despite its complexity it should not be treated as an important obstacle to entering into cross-border insurance relationships in Europe. Rather, it should further encourage the application of on-line means of communication and assure adequate security under EU legislation.

References

Amstutz M, Vogt NP, Wang M (1996) In: Honsell H, Vogt NP, Schnyder AK (hrsg.) (eds) Kommentar zum schweizerischen Privatrecht. Internationales Privatrecht, Basel und Frankfurt am Main, p 843

Arora A (2003) E-insurance: analysis of the impact and implications of ecommerce on the insurance industry. http://citeseerx.ist.psu.edu/viewdoc/download?doi=10.1.1.132.173&rep=rep1&type=pdf (date of entry: 01.07.2014)

[157] Summary of discussions, Electronic Commerce and International Jurisdiction, Ottawa, 28 February ro 1 March 2000, p. 11.

[158] *Ibidem*, p. 5.

Basedow J (2004) Der Versicherungsbinnenmarkt und ein optionales europäisches Vertragsgesetz. In:Wandt M (ed) Kontinuität und Wandel des Versicherungsrechts. Festschrift für Egon Lorenz zum 70. Geburtstag. VVW, Karlsruhe, pp 108–109
Basedow J (2008) The optional application of the principles of European insurance contract law. In: Fuchs A (ed) European contract law—ERA forum special issue 2008 (ERA Forum scripta iuris europaei), vol 9. Springer, Heidelberg, p 115
Bisping C (2013) The common European sales law, consumer protection and overriding mandatory provisions in private international law. Int Comp Law Q 62(2):463, Westlaw
Bonomi A (2003) Conversion of the Rome convention into an EC instrument. YPIL 53–59
Bundesgesetz uber Internationale Privatrecht (IPRG) Bundesblatt 1988 I:5–60
Clarke M, Heiss H (2006) Towards a European insurance contract law? Recent developments in Brussels. J Bus Law 600
Cox R, Smith M (2006) Private International law of reinsurance and insurance. Informa, London, pp 4–5, 208, 254, 255
Dicey A, Morris JHC, Collins L (eds) (2006a) The conflict of laws, 14th edn. Sweet & Maxwell, London, pp 1–058
Dicey A, Morris JHC, Collins L (2006b) The conflict of laws. Sweet & Maxwell, London, pp 1736–1737
Fein ML (2006) Banking and financial services, vol I, Lslf edition. Aspen Publishers
Fingerhuth F (1989) Anknüpfung des Versicherungsvertrages im schweizerischen IPR-Gesetz—Eine Standortbestimmung. Zeitschrift für vergleichende Rechtswissenschaft 88: 4, 10
Fras M (2008) Reżim prawny umowy ubezpieczenia zawieranej drogą elektroniczną—zagadnienia materialnoprawne i kolizyjne. In: Pazdan M (ed) Europeizacja prawa prywatnego, vol 1. Warsaw, pp 182–184, 193, 195
Fras M (2010) Umowa ubezpieczenia w szwajcarskim prawie prywatnym międzynarodowym—Rozprawy Ubezpieczeniowe nr 9(2/2010)
Fricke M (2008) Das Internationale Privatrecht der Versicherungsverträge nach Inkrafttreten der Rom-I-Verordnung. VersR, p 443
Fuchs B, Jagielska M, Kolizyjnoprawna ochrona strony słabszej stosunku ubezpieczenia. p 33
Garcimartin Alferez FJ (2008) The Rome I Regulation: much ado about nothing? Eur Leg Forum (E) 2:I-61, I-62, I-74, I-75, I-79
Garcimartín F (2007) The Rome II Regulation: on the way towards a european private international law code. EuLF I: 77–78
Golia N, Is e-commerce right for insurance? http://www.insurancetech.com/business-intelligence/is-e-commerce-right-for-insurance/240155645 (date of entry:01.07.2014).
Graber CK, Lang C, Kunszt Z (Prager Dreifuss Ltd) (2012) Insurance & reinsurance—Switzerland, European Lawyer Reference. Nigel Brook Clyde & Co LLP—Sweet & Maxwell, p 285
Groupe européen de droit international privé (GEDIP) (2003) Réponse au Livre vert de la Commission sur la transformation de la Convention de Rome en instrument communautaire ainsi que sur la modernisation, p 9. Available at www.gedip-egpil.eu
Gruber UP (2009) Insurance contracts. In: Ferrari F, Leible S (eds) Rome I Regulation: the law applicable to contractual obligations in Europe. Sellier European Law, p 111, 114
Hardy T (1994) The proper legal regime for 'Cyberspace'. College of William & Mary Law School, William & Mary Law School Scholarship Repository. Faculty Publications. Paper 656, p 994
Heiss H (2006) Die Vergemeinschaftung des internationalen Vertragsrechts durch Rom I und ihre Auswirkungen auf das österreichische internationale Privatrecht. JBL 750–751
Heiss H (2006) Towards a European insurance contract law: restatement – common frame of reference – optional instrument? http://www.aidahungary.org/wp-content/uploads/2014/02/AIDA2006_11_24_Helmut_Heiss_eloadas.pdf (date of entry 09.03.2016), p 16
Heiss H (2008) Insurance contracts in Rome I: another recent failure of the European legislature. In: Yearbook for private international law, vol. 10. p 261

Heiss H (2009) Party autonomy. In: Ferrari F, Leible S (eds) Rome I Regulation: the law applicable to contractual obligations in Europe. p 1
Heiss H (2006) Towards a European insurance contract law: restatement – common frame of reference – optional instrument? http://www.aidahungary.org/wp-content/uploads/2014/02/AIDA2006_11_24_Helmut_Heiss_eloadas.pdf (date of entry 09.03.2016), p 16
James S (2007) Rome I—the uncertainty remains. p 257
James S (2008) Rome I: shall we dance: shall we dance? Law Financ Mark Rev 2:118
Kowalewski E (1999) Ryzyko w działalności człowieka i możliwości jego ograniczenia. In: Sangowski (red.) T (ed) Ubezpieczenia gospodarcze. Warszawa, s 38–39
Kowalewski E (2005) Problematyka kolizyjnego prawa ubezpieczeniowego. Państwo i Prawo 2:26
Kowalewski E, Ubezpieczenia transgraniczne—aspekty prawne. Available at: http://www.gu.com.pl/index.php?option=com_content&view=article&id=11800&catid=121&Itemid=144 (date of entry: 27.07.2015)
Kramer X (2008) The New European conflict of law rules on insurance contracts in Rome I: a complex compromise. ICFAI Univ J Insur Law 23, 33, 37, 41
Kropka M (2010) Kolizyjnoprawna regulacja umowy ubezpieczenia w Rozporządzeniu Rzym I. Katowice, p 22, 35, 92, 129, 145, 156
Kuipers JJ (2011) EU law and private international law: the interrelationship in contractual obligations. Martinus Nijhoff Publishers, Leiden, p 118
Lagarde P (2006) Remarques sur la proposition de règlement de la Commission européenne sur la loi applicable aux obligations contractuelles (Rome I). Rev crit DIP 331–332
Lagarde P, Tenenbaum A (2008) De la Convention de Rome au règlement Rome I. Revue critique de droit international privé, pp 727, 735
Lakhan M, Heiss H (2010) An optional instrument for European insurance contract law. Merkourios - Eur Contract Law 27(71):10
Lando O, Nielsen PA (2008) The Rome I Regulation. Common Mark Law Rev 45:1687, 1710
Lein E (2005) Proposal for a regulation on the law applicable to contractual obligations (Rome I) COM (2005) 650 Final, 15.12.2005. YPIL 391–393
Loacker LD (2009) Insurance soft law? Versicherungsrecht, p 296
Malinowska K, Świątkowski P (2013) Cross-border electronic insurance and modern dispute resolution in the European Union. Prawo Asekuracyjne 4: 32, 34–37
Malinowska K (2014) Consumer protection in e-insurance in European Union law. Insur Rev (Wiadomości Ubezpieczeniowe) 4:42–43
Mankowski P (2008): Die Rom I-Verordnung—Änderungen im europäischen IPR für Schuldverträge. Internationales Handelrecht 133, 144
Mankowski P (2009) Die Rom I-Verordnung. Zeitschrift für Europarecht 2, 3
Mann FA (1978) Unfair Contract Terms Act 1977 and the conflict of laws. Int Comp Law Q 27:661
Martinek M, Poczobut J (2003) Doświadczenie Niemiec i Szwajcarii w kodyfikacji prawa prywatnego międzynarodowego. Kwartalnik Prawa Prywatnego 4:741–742
Max-Planck Institute for Comparative and International Private Law (2004) Comments on the European Commission's Green Paper on the conversion of the Rome Convention of 1980 on the law applicable to contractual obligations into a community instrument and its modernization. RabelsZ 68:1–11
Merkin R (2009) The Rome I Regulation and reinsurance. p 69, 70, 74
Merrett L (2009) Choice of law in insurance contracts under the Rome I Regulation. J Priv Int Law 5:53–56, 59, 62, 63, 66, 67
Meshkat L, Farkhondehnia F, Bagheri Z, Alihoseini O, Sanayeimatak S, Esmaeili M, Mostafalo M, Ebadati H, Masaratbakhsh M (2012) Electronic insurance and its application in e-commerce. Interdiscip J Contem Res Bus 4(8):640–647
Nebel R (1996) In: Honsell H, Vogt NP, Schnyder AK (hrsg.) (eds) Kommentar zum schweizerischen Privatrecht. Internationales Privatrecht, Basel und Frankfurt am Main, p 1225

O'Hara EA, Ribstein LE (2009) Conflict of laws and choice of law. Vanderbilt University Law School and University of Illinois College of Law, p 2

Pilich M (2012) Law applicable to insurance contracts in the light of the Rome I Regulation. Studia Iuridica 54:198, 199, 201, 205, 206, 209, 214, 216

Popiołek W (2007) Prawo właściwe dla umownych zobowiązań elektronicznych w konwencji rzymskiej i projekcie rozporządzenia Rzym I. In Kolizyjne aspekty zobowiązań elektronicznych : materiały z konferencji. Wolters Kluwer Polska—OFICYNA, Warsaw, p 23

Raczyński A, Świadczenie ubezpieczyciela w ubezpieczeniu assistance. In: Gnela B, Szaraniec M (ed) Kierunki rozwoju ubezpieczeń gospodarczych w Polsce. Wybrane zagadnienia prawne, p 179

Raim DM, Langford JL (2008) Understanding reinsurance. In: Martinez LP, Mayerson MS (eds) New Appleman insurance law practice guide. LexisNexis, pp 40-5–40-8

Seatzu F (2003) Insurance in private international law: a European perspective. Bloomsbury Publishing, London, p 252

Seatzu F (2003) Insurance in private international law, a European perspective. Hart Publishing, Oxford

Sieg O, Schaloske H (Noerr LLP) (2012) Insurance & reinsurance—Germany, European lawyer reference. Nigel Brook Clyde & Co LLP—Sweet & Maxwell, p 145

Solomon (2008) The private international law of contracts in Europe: advances and retreats. Tulane Law Rev 82:1709, 1722

Stone P (2010) EU Private international law, 2nd edn. Edward Elgar Publishing, Cheltenham, p 343

Stosio A (2002) Umowy zawierane przez Internet. p 274

Tang ZS (2010) Private international law in consumer contracts – a European perspective. J Priv Int Law 6(1):225

Travnickova S (2009) Limitations of choice of law—mandatory rules and internationally mandatory rules, Acta Universitatis Brunensis Iuridica No. 337, p 3. http://www.law.muni.cz/sborniky/dp08/files/pdf/mezinaro/travnickova.pdf (date of entry: 27.07.2015)

van Bochove LM (2014) Overriding mandatory rules as a vehicle for weaker party protection in European private international law. Erasmus Law Rev 7(3):147

Vernooij NV (2009) Rome I: an update on the law applicable to contractual obligations in Europe. Columbia J Eur Law On-line 71

Wulf-Henning R, EEC Treaty Article 59Fifty-nine and its implications for conflicts law in the field of insurance contracts. Duke J Compar Int Law 2(129):145130. http://scholarship.law.duke.edu/cgi/viewcontent.cgi?article=1309&context=djcil (date of entry: 24.07.2015)

Erratum to: The "Dematerialized" Insurance

Pierpaolo Marano, Ioannis Rokas, and Peter Kochenburger

P. Marano et al. (eds.), *The "Dematerialized" Insurance*,
DOI 10.1007/978-3-319-28410-1

DOI 10.1007/978-3-319-28410-1_15

The original version of the book contained an error which have been corrected. The correction is given below:

Preface was not included in the original version of the book

The updated online version of this book can be found at

DOI 10.1007/978-3-319-28410-1

The updated online version of the original book can be found at
http://dx.doi.org/10.1007/978-3-319-28410-1

P. Marano et al. (eds.), *The "Dematerialized" Insurance*,
DOI 10.1007/978-3-319-28410-1_15

Index

P. Marano et al. (eds.), *The "Dematerialized" Insurance*,
DOI 10.1007/978-3-319-28410-1

Printed by Printforce, the Netherlands